Transforming U.S. Workforce Development Policies for the 21st Century

Transforming U.S. Workforce Development Policies for the 21st Century

Carl Van Horn
Tammy Edwards
Todd Greene
Editors

2015

W.E. Upjohn Institute for Employment Research
Kalamazoo, Michigan

Library of Congress Cataloging-in-Publication Data

Transforming U.S. workforce development policies for the 21st century / Carl Van Horn, Tammy Edwards, and Todd Greene, editors.
  ISBN 978-0-69240-536-9 (pbk. : alk. paper)

2015940596

The facts presented in this study and the observations and viewpoints expressed are the sole responsibility of the authors. They do not necessarily represent positions of the Federal Reserve Bank of Atlanta, the Federal Reserve Bank of Kansas City, or Rutgers University.

Cover design by Peter Hamilton and Odie Swanegan.
Index prepared by Diane Worden.
Printed in the United States of America.
Printed on recycled paper.

Contents

Acknowledgments

The publication of *Transforming U.S. Workforce Development Policies for the 21st Century* is the culmination of nearly two years of brainstorming, planning, writing, reviewing, and editing by many individuals. We are grateful for this chance to acknowledge those who were instrumental in bringing the vision for this book to life.

First and foremost, we wish to acknowledge the nearly 70 authors who contributed chapters and case studies for this volume. We thank them for their contributions, insights, patience, and cooperation throughout this entire process. Their work here has the potential to transform our nation's workforce development and educational policies and strategies.

We owe special thanks to Stuart Andreason, community and economic development adviser at the Federal Reserve Bank of Atlanta; Robin Ratliff, assistant vice president and public information officer at the Federal Reserve Bank of Atlanta; and Steven Shepelwich, senior community development adviser at the Federal Reserve Bank of Kansas City, all of whom reviewed drafts of this book and provided invaluable advice.

We are grateful to several staff from the Federal Reserve Bank of Atlanta: graphic designers Peter Hamilton and Odie Swanegan, who produced the cover design; Kyan Bishop, outreach director; Chevelle Wilson, business analyst; and Karen Leone de Nie, assistant vice president, community and economic development. We also thank Heidi Kaplan, senior community affairs analyst for the Board of Governors of the Federal Reserve Board.

Kathy Krepcio, executive director of the Heldrich Center, and Maria Heidkamp, senior researcher at the Heldrich Center, worked closely with us over the past two years, suggesting potential authors, reviewing chapter and case study proposals, and reviewing and providing feedback on both draft and final manuscripts. Robb C. Sewell, senior writer/editor, worked with the editors, authors, and the W.E. Upjohn Institute for Employment Research on the submission, review, and production of manuscripts, and on marketing the book. Communications assistant Christine Jenter worked with authors to provide them with feedback on their draft chapters. A number of Heldrich Center researchers reviewed chapters, including Jennifer Cleary, William Mabe, Michelle Van Noy, and Charyl Yarbrough.

Finally, we are indebted to the staff at the Upjohn Institute. Special thanks to Randall Eberts, president; Kevin Hollenbeck, vice president, senior economist, and director of publications; Richard Wyrwa, manager of publications and marketing; and Allison Hewitt Colosky, editor. Quite simply, this book would not be possible had it not been for their contributions.

Foreword

Our country's workforce development policies and programs were largely developed more than 30 years ago and are insufficient to address the needs of our modern economy. While disruption in traditional occupations (and the skill sets needed for those occupations) has increased over the last few decades, overall workforce development funding has diminished and is not likely to increase.

More comprehensive restructuring and truly innovative approaches are needed to meet the human capital demands of employers. More and better information is also needed to inform job seekers about an increasing range of private and public options from which they can obtain the skills and credentials to be successful. It is in response to these and other trends that *Transforming U.S. Workforce Development Policies for the 21st Century* was developed. The book provides thoughtful perspectives on how workforce development efforts, often based on approaches from decades ago, might be rethought to better respond to these trends.

Transforming U.S. Workforce Development Policies for the 21st Century is the result of a partnership between the John J. Heldrich Center for Workforce Development at Rutgers University and the Federal Reserve Banks of Atlanta and Kansas City. While the Heldrich Center has a longstanding reputation for advancing promising policies and practices, and the Fed has also undertaken extensive research and analysis of labor markets, workforce development is a relatively new area for the Federal Reserve—one in which we are now actively engaged.

The Federal Reserve has a dual mandate of promoting price stability and maximum employment. Our concern about optimally functioning labor markets is consistent with the latter half of the mandate. While the overall weakened economy following the Great Recession suggests that cyclical challenges are a key driver of unemployment rates, Federal Reserve leaders have identified some structural issues as contributing to slack in labor markets (Yellen 2014). For example, as part of our regular information-gathering processes, we have often heard industry leaders state that open positions remain unfilled despite elevated unemployment levels. While we and our Federal Reserve System colleagues have suggested that monetary policy will not fully address labor market weaknesses, several of us have spoken about the important role of workforce development in improving labor market outcomes (Lacker 2013; Lockhart 2014).

To deepen our understanding about labor market dynamics in low- and moderate-income communities, Federal Reserve Banks convened 32 meetings around the country in 2011, bringing together a variety of stakeholders, including economic developers, school officials and academics, business leaders, and government representatives.[1] While each meeting had a different focus, one consistent theme identified in nearly every meeting was the need for improved, responsive, and more coordinated workforce development efforts. In the intervening years since these initial meetings, the Federal Reserve's community development function has been particularly invested in improving workforce development policies and practices by leveraging the Fed's data and research capabilities along with our ability to convene diverse stakeholders.

Transforming U.S. Workforce Development Policies for the 21st Century is an excellent example of how the Federal Reserve, in partnership with a strong collaborator in the Heldrich Center, is bringing thoughtful ideas about how workforce development efforts might be reshaped to respond to our modern and dynamic economy.[2] Every state, region, and locality faces workforce development challenges and possesses diverse assets and resources that call for customized solutions. It will be critical for efforts to be more nimble, more responsive to employers, and more closely aligned among the various components of the workforce development process.

The chapter and case study authors in this book are well-positioned to address these issues, and we thank them for their contributions. The policy and practice perspectives presented are not an endorsement or roadmap from the Federal Reserve, but are intended to spur innovative thinking that results in context-specific solutions.

–Esther George and Dennis Lockhart

Esther L. George is president and chief executive officer of the Federal Reserve Bank of Kansas City and a member of the Federal Open Market Committee, which sets U.S. monetary policy.

She has more than 30 years of experience at the Kansas City Fed, primarily focused on regulatory oversight of nearly 200 state-chartered banks and 1,000 bank and financial holding companies in seven states. She was directly involved in the banking supervision and discount window lending activities during the banking crisis of the 1980s and post-9/11.

During the most recent financial crisis, she served as the acting director of the Federal Reserve's Division of Banking Supervision and Regulation in Washington, D.C. She hosts the Federal Reserve Bank of Kansas City's annual Economic Policy Symposium in Jackson Hole, Wyoming, which is attended by central bankers from around the world.

She is a native of Missouri.

Dennis P. Lockhart is president and chief executive officer of the Federal Reserve Bank of Atlanta and is also a member of the Federal Open Market Committee.

He took office in March 2007 and is responsible for all the Bank's activities, including monetary policy, bank supervision and regulation, and payment services. Before joining the Fed, he served on the faculty of Georgetown University's School of Foreign Service and was an adjunct professor at Johns Hopkins University's School of Advanced International Studies.

Previous leadership positions include serving as chairman of the Small Enterprise Assistance Funds and as managing partner at the private equity firm Zephyr Management LP. He also worked for 13 years at Heller Financial, where he served as president of Heller International Group, which had activities in commercial finance and investment in Europe, Latin America, and Asia. In 2000, he served as chairman of the advisory committee of the U.S. Export-Import Bank. In the 1970s and 1980s, he held various positions, both international and domestic, with Citicorp/Citibank (now Citigroup).

He is a native of California.

Notes

1. See http://www.federalreserve.gov/communitydev/appendix-b-list-of-forums-and-forum-summary-notes.htm (accessed March 19, 2015).
2. A conference considering many of these topics was also held in October 2014. See https://www.frbatlanta.org/news/conferences/2014/141015-workforce-development.aspx (accessed March 19, 2015).

References

Lacker, Jeffrey M. 2013. "Starting Early in Workforce Development." Paper presented at the Charlotte Branch Conference Center, Charlotte, NC, November 5. http://www.richmondfed.org/press_room/speeches/president_jeff_lacker/2013/lacker_speech_20131105.cfm (accessed March 19, 2015).

Lockhart, Dennis. 2014. "Strategic Workforce Development: Training for Employability." Paper presented at "Transforming Workforce Development Policies and Practices for the 21st Century," held on October 16 at the John J. Heldrich Center for Workforce Development, Rutgers University, New Brunswick, NJ. https://www.frbatlanta.org/news/speeches/2014/141016-lockhart (accessed March 19, 2015).

Yellen, Janet L. 2014. "Labor Market Dynamics and Monetary Policy." Paper presented at the Federal Reserve Bank of Kansas City Economic Symposium, held on August 22 in Jackson Hole, WY. http://www.federalreserve.gov/newsevents/speech/yellen20140822a.htm (accessed March 19, 2015).

1
Introduction

Carl Van Horn
Todd Greene
Tammy Edwards

Workers and employers in the United States face new realities and uncertainties that current public policies and programs were not designed to address. The Great Recession and other disruptive forces have altered the environment that workers, job seekers, businesses, educational institutions, and government all face. These forces include globalization, labor market volatility, pervasive and rapid technological changes, shifting demographics, and resource constraints. Workforce development and educational policies must be transformed during an era of scarce resources, new technologies, increased personal responsibility for career navigation and management, shifting skill requirements, and changes in the nature of employment.

This volume includes a wide range of chapters and case studies that examine the state of the labor market and potentially transformative workforce development and education strategies and policies designed to improve opportunities for job seekers, students, and workers, especially those encountering the greatest difficulties in the labor market. Ideally, these strategies and policies would meet the needs of employers and society for a highly skilled, well-educated, competitive, and productive workforce. They also would deliver effective and efficient solutions that can be adopted by federal, state, or local/regional governments, as well as by educational institutions, businesses, and nonprofit organizations.

Several chapters and case studies focus exclusively on addressing the difficulties experienced by the long-term unemployed, those with limited formal education, older and youth workers, minorities, and individuals with disabilities. The authors examine the funding and performance of unemployment insurance, postsecondary educa-

2   Van Horn, Greene, and Edwards

tion, reemployment programs, Workforce Investment Boards, the labor exchange system, and the potential impact of the Workforce Innovation and Opportunity Act of 2014. The authors describe evidence-based strategies and policies from states, communities, and private firms that offer some potential for meeting the fundamental needs of job seekers and employers. The chapters and case studies were selected after an independent review by the editors and their colleagues at the Federal Reserve Banks of Atlanta and Kansas City and the John J. Heldrich Center for Workforce Development at Rutgers University.

THE IMPACT OF THE GREAT RECESSION

As a result of the Great Recession and fundamental transformations in the U.S. economy, millions of Americans are either unemployed or fear they will no longer be able to retain their jobs. Nearly six years after the official end of the recession, American workers are encountering volatility and uncertainty in the labor market. Job growth has been consistent but inadequate to provide enough jobs for everyone who wants one. Wages have increased but have not kept up with the pace of inflation, and labor force participation rates are at their lowest levels in three decades.[1] Long-term unemployment rates remain at unprecedented levels.

In many ways, the U.S. economic recovery has been impressive. Although about 8.7 million jobs were lost between the start of the recession in December 2007 through early 2010, in the past 57 months, jobs added to the U.S. economy have totaled nearly 10.9 million. During 2014 alone, employment increased by 2.65 million, matching the rate of annual job growth during the economic boom of the late 1990s (Furman 2014). The unemployment rate declined from 8.2 percent in March 2012 to 5.5 percent in February 2015. The unemployment rate for the short-term unemployed—those out of work six months or less—returned to prerecession levels.

Other labor market indicators, however, face ongoing headwinds. While the unemployment rate has declined for the past four years, job growth has been insufficient to absorb the additional workers who joined the labor force and the millions who are either unemployed or working part time but seeking full-time jobs. The economy is still several million jobs short of what it would need to return to levels of full employment at the beginning of the twenty-first century. In fact, " . . . at the current rate it will take until early 2019 for the economy to accommodate new entrants into the work force and get back to where it was before the recession," according to the Brookings Institution (Schwartz 2014). Moreover, the negative effects of the Great Recession did not fall evenly across workers in the United States. Unemployment rates remain high for teenagers (17.1 percent), those without a high school diploma (8.4 percent), blacks (10.4 percent), and Hispanics (6.6 percent) (U.S. Bureau of Labor Statistics 2015a).

Lower unemployment rates were achieved, in part, because hundreds of thousands of workers left the labor force altogether. For example, the number of workers classified as "discouraged"—individuals who have given up looking because they do not believe jobs are available—was 732,000 in February 2015 and remains above prerecession levels. In addition, nearly 7 million people are working part time but would prefer full-time jobs (U.S. Bureau of Labor Statistics 2015a). And, in one of the most troublesome indicators of the labor market's recovery, more than one in six men in the prime working ages of 25 to 54—over 10 million workers—are either unemployed or no longer looking for work (Wessel 2014).

Another harsh legacy of the Great Recession is the persistent problem of the long-term unemployed—workers who remain jobless for more than six months (Federal Reserve Board of Governors 2013). More than five years into the recovery, there are still 2.7 million long-term unemployed workers, almost a third (31.1 percent) of all unemployed job seekers (U.S. Bureau of Labor Statistics 2015a). The percentage of long-term unemployed workers has declined from 46 percent in 2010, but it still exceeds the 26 percent level experienced in 1982, the worst previous recession. Unemployment rates in 29 states are at or near postrecession levels, but long-term unemployment remains above prerecession levels in 41 states (U.S. Bureau of Labor Statistics 2015b).

In summary, the Great Recession was an economic crisis of a magnitude not experienced since the Great Depression more than 70 years ago. The Heldrich Center for Workforce Development conducted a national Work Trends survey in early 2013 and found that nearly one-quarter (23 percent) of respondents reported being laid off from either a full-time or part-time job during the recession and the early years of the recovery (Szeltner, Van Horn, and Zukin 2013). Just over one in three laid-off workers found a new job within six months; 16 percent got another job in two months or less. Yet, one-third of respondents said they spent more than seven months seeking a new job, and 1 in 10 searched unsuccessfully for more than two years. Even more troubling, 22 percent of Americans who were laid off in the past four years have yet to find new work. An analysis by Krueger, Cramer, and Cho (2014), using data from the U.S. Census Bureau, found even deeper problems: "Only 11 percent of those who were long-term unemployed in a given month returned to steady full-time employment a year later."

Laid-off workers who obtained a new job generally settled for less pay in their new positions. Among those workers who did find a job, nearly three-quarters were employed full time, one-fifth were employed part time, and the remainder reported self-employment (full time and part time) or military service (Szeltner, Van Horn, and Zukin 2013). Nearly half (48 percent) said their current job was a step down from the one they had before the recession. A majority (54 percent) reported lower pay in their new job compared to the job they had before being laid off. One-quarter said their job was a step up and higher-paying than their last position. Among those reporting lower pay in their new job, one-third said their pay was cut by more than 30 percent compared to the job they had at the start of the recession, another third said their pay dropped by 11 percent to 20 percent, and the remaining third experienced a cut of less than 10 percent.

LONG-TERM STRUCTURAL CHANGES

Well before the Great Recession rocked the American economy, during the height of the 1990s boom, millions of job seekers were already experiencing the harsh shocks of a rapidly churning labor market. Even before the collapse of the stock market and housing prices, the volatile twenty-first century economy was transforming work as seismic changes in technology and finance crumbled small and giant corporations and upended entire industries. Before the Great Recession, workers at all educational and skill levels experienced job losses through downsizing, mergers, and acquisitions and were forced to search for new opportunities.

Early in the the twenty-first century, labor market realities are fundamentally different than they were in the mid-twentieth century. Thirty years ago, most jobs were stable, or even permanent; now most jobs are temporary or contingent. Workers in the mid-twentieth century most likely could remain with a firm and ride the seniority escalator to better jobs and higher pay. Today's workers no longer have that expectation.

In just a few decades, a fairly stable economy rapidly changed. Advances in technology and industry made it much harder for labor market specialists, let alone average workers, to predict the direction of the labor market. Imagine high school seniors or first-year college students choosing among dozens of fields of study expected to prepare them for a career that will take them deep into the twenty-first century. It is no surprise that many are perplexed when making these choices. No matter which path these young people pursue, it is clear that obtaining a high school or postsecondary credential is only one step on the path of what is likely to be a lifetime of continuing education.

Expectations about retirement are also fundamentally different than they were a few decades ago. Late in the twentieth century, most workers assumed they would retire by age 65, if not earlier. Today, many Americans do not believe they will ever be able to afford to quit working. Many in the baby boom generation are either unable or unwilling to leave the workforce because they do not have enough savings. Fewer retired workers can look forward to guaranteed pension benefits from their employers. Often these benefits have been replaced with "defined contribution plans" that offer no guarantees and depend on contributions to and investment earnings from the employee's account (Van Horn 2013).

CHALLENGES FOR WORKFORCE AND EDUCATION POLICY AND PROGRAMS

U.S. citizens and political, business, and educational leaders are confronted by fundamental new challenges in a global, competitive, technology-driven environment where economies, entire industries, and companies are transformed with lightning speed. How does the United States, through its laws and institutions, build a productive and competitive workforce and restore the promise of upward mobility? The broad forces shaping the U.S. labor market were not created by the Great Recession, but they have been coursing through the labor market for the past 20 years. This new economic landscape, while still evolving, has already created an uncomfortable "new normal" for American workers. The immense disruptions caused by globalization and technological advancements mean that larger numbers of workers can no longer expect permanent jobs and careers. Moreover, many large employers view temporary contract or contingent work as preferable human resources strategies. As a result, employer-based investments in workers' education and training are declining, placing more responsibility for developing human capital on the individual worker.

There is an urgent need to address the long-simmering crisis in the American workforce that has become less equitable and tougher on those without advanced education. Addressing this altered economic landscape requires fundamentally new workforce development policies. The core challenge is how to educate, train, and retrain people so that they can achieve their full potential and offer employers valued skills. The nation must move forward with large-scale transformations of our workforce and education policies to improve the prospects for workers and the economy in this globalized, technology-driven economy. The new realities of work in the twenty-first century will continue to rapidly evolve. Workers and policymakers must adapt or suffer further wrenching economic adjustments.

CHAPTERS AND CASE STUDIES

This volume brings together the contributions from leading scholars and practitioners that describe significant policy and program reforms to address the current major workforce challenges. The volume is divided into four parts.

Part 1, "Transforming the U.S. Workforce Development System," examines the strengths and limitations of U.S. workforce policies for workers, with special attention to the needs of the long-term unemployed, those with limited formal education, individuals with disabilities, older workers, minority adults, and youth. The chapters in this section describe and analyze the funding and performance of the public labor exchange, unemployment insurance, postsecondary education, reemployment programs, and Workforce Investment Boards.

Part 2, "Redesigning Workforce Development Strategies," offers ideas to help educators and workforce programs better serve employers and job seekers, tasks that will require several fundamental changes in policy and practice. Authors cover such topics as improving labor market and career information and intelligence, reforming unemployment insurance, restructuring postsecondary education financial assistance programs, delivering online training and education courses, improving credentialing, developing performance reporting, and integrating employers into the development and delivery of education and skills training.

Part 3, "Building Evidence-Based Policy and Practice," includes chapters and case studies that examine how systematic data collection and analysis and evaluations are being used to improve state and local workforce programs. These authors demonstrate that such approaches can be effective in transforming policies to better serve job seekers, students, and employers.

Part 4, "Targeted Strategies," includes chapters and case studies on effective policies and programs for meeting the needs of American workers and employers. Authors highlight evidence-based practices from states and communities and describe why these approaches offer potential for helping both job seekers and employers. The authors consider how these practices could become more widely available throughout the United States.

CONCLUSION

The chapters and case studies in this volume are compelling and offer stimulating new approaches to local, regional, state, and national policies and programs. The impressive array of authors individually and collectively present perspectives intended to provoke serious and ongoing discussions about what is needed to support a robust and effective workforce development system.

To this end, the Federal Reserve Banks of Atlanta and Kansas City, along with the John J. Heldrich Center for Workforce Development, are committed to furthering these discussions, advancing new policy approaches, and highlighting best practices. While space limitations precluded many relevant case studies from appearing in this volume, the Federal Reserve Bank of Atlanta will produce two companion pieces that will explore many promising practices and models of workforce development and job training. The first of these publications will identify and examine effective models for workforce development intermediaries; the second will explore examples of career-based training for secondary students, incumbent workers, and hard-to-serve populations. These cases will help promote stronger alignment between the workforce development community and outside stakeholders, and will suggest powerful approaches to training.

Note

1. According to the Bureau of Labor Statistics, after increasing in the 1970s, 1980s, and 1990s, the labor force participation rate reached and maintained an all-time high of 67.1 percent during 1997–2000. Since then, the labor force participation rate has been falling and is currently 63.7 percent, the lowest the rate has been since the early 1980s (see Toossi [2013]).

References

Federal Reserve Board of Governors. 2013. *A Perspective from Main Street: Long-Term Unemployment and Workforce Development.* Washington, DC: Federal Reserve Board of Governors. http://www.federalreserve.gov/communitydev/long-term-unemployment-and-workforce-development.htm (accessed March 13, 2015).

Furman, Jason. 2014. *The Employment Situation in November.* Washington, DC: Council of Economic Advisers. http://www.whitehouse.gov/blog/2014/12/05/employment-situation-november (accessed March 13, 2015).

Krueger, Alan B., Judd Cramer, and David Cho. 2014. "Are the Long-Term

Unemployed on the Margins of the Labor Market?" Presented at the Brookings Panel on Economic Activity, held in Washington, DC, March 20–21.

Schwartz, Nelson D. 2014. "Hiring Rises, but Number of Jobless Stays High." *New York Times*, April 4, B:7.

Szeltner, Mark, Carl Van Horn, and Cliff Zukin. 2013. *Diminished Lives and Futures: A Portrait of America in the Great-Recession Era.* New Brunswick, NJ: Heldrich Center for Workforce Development, Rutgers University.

Toossi, Mitra. 2013. "Labor Force Projections to 2022: The Labor Force Participation Rate Continues to Fall." *Monthly Labor Review*, December. http://www.bls.gov/opub/mlr/2013/article/labor-force-projections-to-2022-the-labor-force-participation-rate-continues-to-fall.htm (accessed March 13, 2015).

U.S. Bureau of Labor Statistics. 2015a. *The Employment Situation, February 2015.* Washington, DC: U.S. Bureau of Labor Statistics. http://www.bls.gov/news.release/empsit.nr0.htm (accessed March 13, 2015).

———. 2015b. *Current Unemployment Rates for States and Historical Highs/Lows.* Washington, DC: U.S. Bureau of Labor Statistics. http://www.bls.gov/web/laus/lauhsthl.htm (accessed March 13, 2015).

Van Horn, Carl E. 2013. *Working Scared (or Not At All): The Lost Decade, Great Recession, and Restoring the Shattered American Dream.* Lanham, MD: Rowman & Littlefield.

Wessel, David. 2014. *America Isn't Working: More than One in Six Men between 25 and 54 Is without a Job.* Washington, DC: Brookings Institution. http://www.brookings,edu/blogs/up-front/posts/2014/02/06 (accessed March 13, 2015).

Part 1

Transforming the U.S. Workforce Development System

2

Reimagining Workforce Policy in the United States

Larry Good
Ed Strong
Corporation for a Skilled Workforce

CHANGING LABOR MARKETS IN AN ERA OF PERPETUAL VOLATILITY

Workforce policies and investments need to be reimagined, because labor markets are changing in fundamental ways. We need to develop policies, funding, and service models that align with challenges posed by labor markets in the twenty-first century—an era characterized by perpetual volatility. This chapter offers some ideas about potential new models that would better align workforce investments with needs within an economy in transformation.

Disruptive forces are everywhere; whole industries are being transformed by innovation and changes in technology at a pace that continues to accelerate. The result is increased uncertainty and turbulence in the scale and nature of employment in many industries, and often dramatic shifts in skill requirements and how occupations are defined.

Labor market dynamics are evolving in response to these powerful forces, and the following new patterns are emerging:

- **Employment is taking on increasingly varied forms.** Fewer people are working in full-time, long-term engagement with a single employer. Alternative models are emerging and growing in use, including limited-term, project-based employment; people piecing together multiple part-time jobs; and microentrepreneurship. A Kelly Services report (Drobocky 2012) finds that 44 percent of U.S. workers define themselves as "free agents," defined as workers who consult; perform temporary, freelance, or contract work; or have their own businesses. For some, operating as a "free agent" is a preference, providing them flexibility and freedom in how they work. For others, it is a necessity. Part-time work for economic reasons (not by choice), as in previous economic downturns, has increased to about 20 percent of the working population, most of whom are prime-aged workers, 25–54, with limited education (Valletta and Bengali 2013).

- **Workers increasingly can be located anywhere and do their work at any time.** In an era of high-speed broadband and cloud computing, workers don't always have to be located at a specific employer site to do their work, changing long-held assumptions about the geographic location of work.

- **Increased labor market volatility is resulting in unprecedented long-term unemployment and underemployment.** As Van Horn (2013) compellingly describes in *Working Scared (or Not at All)*, record numbers of experienced workers are unable to find new jobs for a year or more, while a substantial number of young adults are either unemployed or underemployed. Although some of this can be attributed to unusually slow job growth during a recovery, this pattern reflects what is likely to be a continuing change in U.S. labor market dynamics.

- **Workers' employment success depends increasingly on attaining a postsecondary credential and continuing to learn throughout their careers.** In aggregate, those with a bachelor's degree do far better in both employment and income than those without a degree. And recent research finds that certain associate degrees, certificates, and industry certifications provide similar labor market advantage. The Georgetown Center on Education and the Workforce projects that by 2020, 65 percent of all U.S. jobs will require education and training beyond high school. Today, 44 percent of workers have attained degrees and/or market valued certificates (Carnevale, Rose, and Hanson 2012). An important related trend is the accelerated pace at which specific knowledge and skills become obsolete and the expectation that workers must continue to refresh and add onto their capabilities across their work lives to remain employable. A team of Deloitte researchers posits that the skills college graduates acquire while in school have an expected shelf life of five years (Eggers, Hagel, and Sanderson 2012).

- **Technology is increasingly being used to aid and even drive hiring decisions.** Games are now being tested that use "big data" to select the best candidates for jobs (Peck 2013). Employers invest heavily in technology aimed at ensuring they hire workers who will be a good fit with their needs. On the other side of the coin, few job seekers have similar sophisticated aids to help them in presenting themselves so that they maximize their potential to be hired. How do job seekers "learn the game" and get on a level playing field with employers?

These examples illustrate the reality that twenty-first century labor markets operate very differently than they did in the relatively recent past, reflecting the global transition to a knowledge-centered economy. Public workforce policy, funding models, and operating approaches were built for the prior economy.

Krepcio and Martin (2012) identify five major trends within the twenty-first century economy impacting the workforce system: 1) a slow growth economy and a jobless recovery, 2) changing labor markets and employment relations, 3) advances in information and communication technology, 4) demographic changes, and 5) reduced funding for the system.

Congress's adoption of bipartisan, bicameral agreement on successor legislation for the Workforce Investment Act (WIA) occurred in July 2014, after more than a decade of failing to do so. The new Workforce Innovation and Opportunity Act (WIOA) adopts many widely sought-after changes and appears to be a substantial improvement over WIA. The authors applaud in particular elevating credential attainment to a performance standard on par with current employment outcomes and the requirements for systemic adoption of industry sector partnerships and career pathways approaches. The new law emphasizes interconnecting educational attainment and employment results, focusing on helping workers gain not only initial reemployment but also knowledge and skills that help them advance into better jobs over time. However, while passage of this important legislation offers short-term improvements, it does not reduce or remove the need to fundamentally rethink U.S. workforce development policy to align it with radically different labor market realities, and the level of investment covered by the new legislation is minuscule compared to the overall need and other forms of investment in education and training. We should think more broadly than the dedicated funds for workforce investment. The ideas expressed in this chapter offer a starting point for how the United States could reimagine our approach to workforce development policy and funding on a broader scale.

DOES WORKFORCE INVESTMENT MATTER?

Why do we care so much about investing in workforce development? Because the stakes are so high within increasingly harsh labor markets. Consider several indicators. The demand for labor in general is far below the supply of job seekers and is expected to be so nationally for several years to come. Yet paradoxically, there are jobs going unfilled because there is a lack of people with the skills employers are looking for to fill those jobs. There were approximately 3.4 million workers unemployed for 27 weeks or more as of May 2014 (Bureau of Labor Statistics 2014). Long-term unemployment has remained at unprecedented high levels, even as the short-term unemployment rate has returned to prerecession levels. The long-term unemployed represent 34.6 percent of the total unemployed. Labor force participation rates are lower than seen in more than three decades, having dropped from 66 percent in March 2004 to 62.8 percent in May 2014 (Bureau of Labor Statistics 2014). Wages have remained stagnant for the past decade (Shierholz and Mishel 2013), constricting consumer spending and lowering standards of living for many families.

Millions of current or potential U.S. workers live at high risk of prolonged unemployment, erratic income, and poverty. Those at risk include people without a degree or other market-valued postsecondary credential, workers whose skills are either obsolete or no longer valuable to employers, the 25 percent of American adults with gaps in literacy and numeracy, older workers (who are disproportionately more likely to face long-term unemployment), young people who are disconnected from both school and work, and young people who have achieved a credential but struggle to enter career path employment.

Certainly, skills gaps are not the only causes of long-term unemployment, but they are a factor that can and should be addressed.

Without a workforce development public policy and investment strategy, the United States faces the prospect of an increasingly two-tier economy in which some prosper and others are left with little hope for self-sufficiency. The societal costs of inaction are enormous, in terms of both increased demand on social supports and the missed opportunity for productive work by millions who will be either unemployed or underemployed.

Belfield, Levin, and Rosen (2012) calculate the total lifetime fiscal and social costs of the 6.7 million "opportunity youth"—those between 16 and 24 who are attached neither to school nor work. Their finding: each opportunity youth who does not successfully engage in education and employment represents a total societal cost of nearly $1 million—a risk of $6.3 trillion across the whole cohort.

Investing in developing our workforce must be a national priority. How to do it and how to fund it are the subjects of the bulk of this chapter. We begin in the next section by considering the shape of current U.S. workforce strategies.

THE "SYSTEM" TODAY: A PATCHWORK QUILT OF PROGRAMS

We do not believe there is a real workforce development "system" in the United States. Our national workforce investments are essentially a series of separate domestic policy programs, each designed to serve a specific need or target group. We have programs for trade-impacted workers, veterans, those interested in specific career fields, older workers, youth, Native Americans, those on welfare, those in public housing, those in blighted areas, and those with low basic skills. Each program has its own rules and its own outcome measures, political constituency, and advocacy groups.

The limits of the current patchwork of investments have been recounted through multiple reports and study panels. The U.S. Government Accountability Office (2011) has issued numerous reports across more than three decades describing the large number of separate job training programs, program overlaps, and the need for greater coordination among them. We highlight three disconnects below:

1) Integrating resources is hard. Those trying to "move the needle" on important challenges today—whether at a national, state, or local level—must attempt to weave multiple programs housed in many different agencies to achieve aligned work. As challenging as this may be, it is important for both employers and job seekers to have access to aggregated and coordinated resources without having to visit multiple agencies and follow the rules of multiple funding streams. Many examples of valiant efforts to integrate resources from multiple programs to impact a large-scale issue can be found. But the aligning work is difficult, is time consuming, is not directly funded by any of the programs, and typically is not fully successful.

2) Outdated metrics. The Office of Management and Budget has led an important effort to bring some cohesion to federal workforce programs by creating a common set of measures that apply to multiple federal funding streams that provide a degree of consistency on outcomes and by establishing definitions for how to measure them (U.S. Department of Labor 2005). However, as we will explore further in this chapter, we question whether the measures contained in current programs are the right ones. Current measures drive the system toward a focus on short-term employment outcomes and not skills development and credential attainment, increasingly essential to long-term economic success.

3) Underinvestment. A third key limitation in current workforce policy is underinvestment in some areas of crucial need. A glaring example: public funding for basic skills development by adult learners. Solid literacy and numeracy are essential to obtaining a job from which the holder can build career pathways that result in good jobs. Numerous studies have concluded that 25 percent of working-age adults in the United States function with low basic skills today (National Commission on Adult Literacy 2008). The proportion of the workforce with low basic

skills exceeds 50 percent in communities with concentrations of poverty. An estimated 40 million adults need to improve their basic skills to succeed (New America Foundation 2014).

Roughly $2 billion is spent annually on basic skills improvement, with approximately two-thirds of that coming from states and one-third from WIA (U.S. Department of Education 2014). That might sound like a lot of money, until the scale of need is added to the equation. That total amounts to roughly $20 per person with low basic skills, which is clearly insufficient to achieve meaningful impact in removing one of the major barriers to economic self-sufficiency. While each individual's literacy needs are different, in 2008 the average cost of serving an adult in a literacy program was $1,000 (Sum and McLaughlin 2008).

The following three examples of disconnects are a subset of a far longer list of challenges inherent in current public policy regarding workforce development. In thinking about how to address them, we propose moving away from thinking in terms of "workforce development programs" as the needed approach. We believe attempting to solve workforce issues through programs is fundamentally flawed (Power and Urban-Lurain 1989).

1) Programs are structured in isolation. Each program typically defines its own target population, permissible services, metrics, rules, and administrative requirements. And while enabling legislation for a given program may cross-reference others, it is nearly impossible to make a suite of programs fully consistent.

2) Programs result in fragmented service delivery. Federally funded workforce programs come from multiple congressional committees, are housed in several departments, and flow to different agencies at the state and local levels—inevitably with different program years, reporting requirements, and widely varying eligibility. Organizations managing workforce development services live with the constant challenge of weaving the resources across multiple programs into coherent service delivery. Success tends to be a result of local relationships and skill at doing "workarounds" to overcome the conflicts and gaps.

3) Programs tend to calcify. Once the effort to create a program succeeds, the resulting apparatus tends to be left in place for many years. Although initially a program may align well with a specific labor market need, as time goes on the program tends to be locked in place while needs are changing dramatically. A federal program model carries with it a multiyear life cycle from conception to conclusion/replacement—far too slow for perpetually volatile conditions. WIA is a telling example of the slow pace of change. The original WIA legislation was enacted in 1998 and now, more than 15 years later, has finally been updated and reauthorized. And even now, no longitudinal evaluation of WIA has been completed that would inform future legislation. And, in reality, programs rarely end. Instead, as new needs become urgent, typically new programs are created to meet those needs.

THE DIMENSIONS OF TWENTY-FIRST CENTURY WORKFORCE POLICY

The United States needs both a different workforce policy framework and a new approach to executing that policy in order to be responsive to challenges posed by harshly changing labor market conditions. Twenty-first century workforce policy needs to embrace at least three major dimensions: lifelong learning, career navigation, and employment/reemployment. We see three "givens" that should become the norm as each of those dimensions is tackled:

1) Unprecedented integration of work and learning. The old paradigm of going to school first and then embarking on a career has been increasingly obsolete for some time now. In twenty-first century labor markets, the new norm is interweaving work and learning, starting in K–12, continuing through initial post-secondary learning, and then on through the continuing acquisition of new knowledge and skills throughout a career. Work and learning must happen simultaneously, not sequentially, allowing for learning to have experiential context and for work to be improved by learning.

2) Systemic collaboration among employers and educators. Many current "promising practices" in workforce policy, including sector strategies, career pathways development, community college reinvention, and earn-and-learn initiatives, contain experiments in crafting robust and agile collaborations that can change rapidly as demands shift among employers and educators and that are far deeper than traditional advisory committee models. These collaborations are full-scale partnerships with shared vision, shared costs, and shared responsibilities. This is far different from what is generally in place today. We need that in-depth partnership approach to become the norm, and not stay merely a promising practice.

3) Turning competencies into a unifying currency. Knowledge economy labor markets focus on competencies—what a worker knows and can do. Competencies can become a unifying language in labor markets, spanning the many credentials in use—degrees, certificates, industry certifications, licenses, badges, and more. This approach would allow employers to ascertain what job applicants know and can do, and individuals to understand what knowledge, skills, and capabilities they need to add to their portfolios to be qualified for specific careers.

We explore those three dimensions, and then consider financial models, metrics, and governance approaches for twenty-first century workforce policy.

LIFELONG LEARNING

The most critical dimension of twenty-first century workforce policy must be to ensure that lifelong learning is widely available, affordable, and results in workers' regularly acquiring new and enhanced skills that increase their employability.

As noted earlier, workers with at least a bachelor's degree fare much better in employment and income, as do those with market-valued associate's degrees, certificates, and/or industry certifications. The greater success of workers with postsecondary credentials reflects increased employer demand for higher-level skills. In both the United States and other industrialized countries, the proportion of jobs requiring high-skill workers is increasing substantially (Manyika et al. 2012). Surveys indicate that employers in fields such as advanced manufacturing cite skills shortages as reasons for why they cannot expand or improve productivity (Morrison et al. 2011). Admittedly, other researchers asking different questions find that although the skills gap is overstated, it still exists, and it could be filled through reasonable training efforts (Osterman and Weaver 2014). The pressure for increasing H-1B visas for skilled immigrant labor remains intense.

Obviously, not all jobs require high skills. While the United States continues to have millions of jobs that do not require postsecondary educational attainment, the pattern is clear: the preponderance of good-paying jobs require a degree or other postsecondary credential.

The United States needs a substantial increase in the level of educational attainment by young people entering the labor market. Certainly demand at any given time is impacted by the cyclical nature of our economy, but the trajectory is upward for educational attainment to keep the United States competitive globally, and we need our primary pipeline to focus on increased educational attainment. But, equally important, workers must continue to update their knowledge and skills, as well as acquire new ones throughout their work lives. Workforce policy needs to support both young people and current workers in acquiring needed skills and associated credentials.

Workforce policy must also focus on tearing down the basic skills divide. An estimated 40 million adults in the United States lack the fundamental literacy and numeracy skills to function in today's society (U.S. Department of Education 2003). The United States has no meaningful strategy today to impact that huge number.

This does not mean that policy should be encouraging "quick fix" training that typically has little lasting impact—a lesson learned from job training programs of the past. Nor should policy encourage long-term training that lacks connection to employer demand. Rather, policy should focus on encouraging workers to engage in education that enhances their capabilities and results in credentials that are valued by employers.

How should twenty-first century workforce policy address these needs for increased and continuing educational attainment?

- **Build out public-private skill development partnerships to scale.** We should draw from the innovative experimentation going on in employing industry sector partnerships, career pathways development, and industry-education partnerships, and greatly expand and improve the resulting approaches. These informal partnerships found in communities across the nation can be both expanded and replicated to the point where viable partnerships are functioning in key industries in every labor market. These approaches are built on common principles but operationally take on varying flavors depending on the context of the industry and community involved. Further, the costs of entry are modest. If industry and education leaders see challenges they want to collaboratively tackle, the only upfront cost is typically for someone to facilitate their work. These characteristics make this approach easy to replicate. The continuing challenge in doing so is to identify a sufficiently compelling problem to jointly tackle and/or a clear line of sight to the return on the time and resources invested through the partnership work to convince employers to join the partnerships.

- **Craft public-private shared funding of learning.** We should use public funding to incent coinvestment in learning, resulting in a balance of costs among government, the employer/industry involved, and the learner. One example of a coinvestment approach is the Michigan Advanced Technician Training Program, where community colleges and manufacturing employers combine efforts to increase the pipeline of skilled entrants to technical careers (Michigan Economic Development Corporation 2014). State community college support is combined with employer paid tuition and student expenses, as well as paid employment/work-based learning experience in between classroom semesters. Similar manufacturing-education joint learner development models are being tried in several other states.

- **Create a large-scale, multiyear campaign to dramatically improve basic skills among working age adults.** We propose forming a national collaborative campaign in which the federal government, foundations, and business jointly fund campaigns in states and regions to substantively remove the basic skills gaps as a barrier to entry and advancement for workers. This would require a substantial investment, likely totaling at least $1 billion over several years. It would need a very strong national public-private leadership team to succeed. At a state and regional level, this work could be adapted to regional context and led by any number of coalitions at varying geographic levels. We envision this as a time-limited effort (perhaps 10 years) with highly visible metrics, funding tied to results, and use of evidence-based approaches now being undertaken in some locales. Making this sort of investment would represent a game changer for millions of Americans who today have little chance of realizing self-sustaining employment.

- **Restore public investment in postsecondary education and tie the increase to improving results.** In most states across the nation, state support for colleges and universities fell during the Great Recession and remains far below what it needs to be today (*Chronicle of Higher Education* 2014). Making that investment a greater priority within state budgets is essential. At the same time, the movement to increase expectations about results, such as student credential attainment, should also be expanded.

- **Provide learners with "stackable" credit for all learning.** At many community colleges today, more than 50 percent of the education undertaken by students doesn't provide them with credits. Workforce policy needs to ensure learning results in units of credit that reflect competencies attained, regardless of where and how that learning takes place.

CAREER NAVIGATION

Another key dimension of twenty-first century labor markets is that they're incredibly difficult to navigate. As industries and occupations rapidly and continually change, it has become enormously challenging for learners to understand their career/employment choices and the educational requirements associated with those options.

Current public policy and service delivery doesn't provide much help. Every relevant system—K–12 schools, higher education, and workforce agencies—has reduced its support for counselors and advisors as a result of cost pressures and institutional priorities. Additionally, many of those charged with career advising at those institutions are themselves disconnected from the labor market in terms of knowledge, skills, and relationships and are therefore ill-equipped to advise someone on career pathways and job seeking. In a system that measures outcomes with largely supply-side measures, that is always going to be the norm, and as we build new systems we need to design metrics that reinforce the need for close connections to the labor market and employers.

At the same time, despite an explosion of e-tools, the marketplace lacks reliable self-navigation supports. In too many places, the only people obtaining competent advising on career navigation questions are those buying it from career coaches, typically higher-income job changers.

The costs of inadequate career navigation supports include lengthened job searches and prolonged unemployment/underemployment, as well as false starts in education direction that lengthen the path to credential attainment and use up finite financial aid resources.

U.S. workforce policy can improve the availability of high-quality career navigational supports by emphasizing a combination of high-touch and high-tech approaches.

- **Create a cadre of career navigation advisors.** We should replace the current reality of individual schools and workforce centers—each attempting to provide support with inadequate funding and varied staff skills—with a new model. We propose catalyzing the creation of a new profession of highly skilled career navigation advisors. These advisors would be well versed in current career pathway options spanning multiple industries, and would be skilled at helping individuals understand their options and strategies to attain educational and employment success. Incubation for this approach could come from a combination of public and philanthropic leadership. For example, the Obama administration convened a task force around the substantial challenge of impacting young people disconnected from school and work that articulated the need and urgency of action that were then followed by multiple foundations' combining efforts

to fund catalytic work to advance needed change. Similar support could spur development of national, state, and/or regional
approaches to building the cadre we envision. Ongoing funding
for such a cadre in a community could come from joint support
from K–12 and postsecondary schools, workforce development
agencies, industry sector partnerships, and others sharing interest. Access could involve a sliding scale of individual payments
based on income. Employers could support access to a career
navigation advisor for their workers, as part of either a retention
strategy or a mobility strategy.

- **Accelerate development of e-tools that support career navigation.** Early stage experiments can be found in the creation of
reliable online self-navigation tools. The Institute of Electrical
and Electronic Engineers has published a single industry-focused career navigation tool.[1] Membership is required for full
access, but the essentials of how an online career navigator for
professionals in the electrical and electronics field can be seen
on the referenced Web site. However, our experience tells us
that career navigation tools typically offer fragments of needed information and fail to maximize the potential aggregation
needed. Tools are needed that can be used to do robust, user-
customized information searches that span choices regarding
career pathways, education, financial aid, jobs, and credentials.
Those tools should employ decision-support technologies, such
as predictive analytics, that add power to the results and also
include customer feedback and access to outcomes data. Our
observation is that software and platform developers are eager
to create the tools; U.S. workforce policy needs support to accelerate the development of robust, reliable career navigation
tools. That support could include leading in the articulation of
customer needs requirements, in establishing database business rules that expedite integration of data sets with appropriate privacy protections, and in organizing key stakeholders to
provide input to developers. Government (federal and state
in particular) and foundations can provide important leadership
in both developing the case for a new model for career navigation and facilitating the basic standards that should be observed
in establishing such portals, including expectations of connectiv-

ity among providers. We freely admit that there is much to be developed in this arena before it is a functioning system, but the need is there, and we challenge policymakers to find the right space to make this a reality. Organizations such as LinkedIn are already doing this with a focus on professionals. We need a system that can serve all levels of workers and employers.

We see these two approaches working in tandem. Users will have widely varying preferences for the amount of "high touch" they want and need. With proper periodic guidance, users will be able to seek out and aggregate large amounts of data to inform their choices throughout their careers.

EMPLOYMENT/REEMPLOYMENT: RETHINKING ONE-STOP CAREER CENTERS

Labor exchange has been a core function of workforce policy for the past 80 years. Basic job matching, such as that done through the Employment Service, has been supplemented with an array of targeted programs providing more intensive supports to workers dislocated by plant closings and other large-scale employment disruptions. Combining those two approaches was a core premise behind the Workforce Investment Act of 1998—bringing services together under one roof rather than having to visit multiple locations to get the combined services they needed.

The vehicle for this service integration was the creation of One-Stop Career Centers (now known as American Job Centers). The centers were designed around job search and presumed most users needed only a well-designed resource room to succeed, with smaller cohorts needing staff support and retraining, usually short term.

It was a good approach for the time. In many cases, the centers became a substantial upgrade from the resources previously available to job seekers. And even today, many thousands of Americans use them each year as part of their job searches. The question for twenty-first century workforce policy is whether the American Job Center model as now conceived still works. Our take is that the premise and metrics for centers need to be modified substantially.

A key function of One-Stop Career Centers has been job matching. States (or consortia thereof) run their own data systems into which employers can list available jobs and match their registered clients with the jobs. The federal government tried to create a national job bank and link all the state systems together, but it wisely abandoned that in favor of relying on the many emerging private job matching database services. But states have, for the most part, continued to maintain their own job matching systems, and many measure themselves against a penetration rate of what percentage of jobs are listed by employers with their job matching systems. Unfortunately, we find this to be a flawed approach with too much effort going to enlisting employers for the simple purpose of posting their jobs. We believe that workforce development should leave this business to others.

The rapid growth of privately developed and managed online job and talent matching vehicles challenges the value of continuing public investment in this function. The tools are diverse and are emerging and changing frequently. As a set, they offer multiple options for workers to engage in job search and employers to find good candidates for openings.

From a job seeker standpoint, a key is whether a sufficient number of quality job bank sites/tools are free or low cost to use. Thus far, the answer to that question appears to be yes. If the market changes over time in terms of user pricing, public investments could subsidize use of these tools far less expensively than running a publicly supported set of data systems.

The core programs operated through the centers have emphasized short-term placement results as the central metric. While we discuss metrics later in this chapter, it is important to note here the adverse impact that job matching measures have on the system. By personal observation, the authors have seen cases where a local One-Stop system is fixated on getting listings of jobs, registering participants in their systems, and then essentially waiting until the participants find a job on their own. A lot of energy goes into contacting registrants to see what progress they have made and whether they got a job—energy that could have gone to advising and skills development. But reaching immediate placement goals drives activity toward the numbers count and not a deeper service model. We need to change the mindset on what is delivered and how (Strong 2012).

- **American Job Centers should become hubs for career navigation and supporting workers in obtaining market-valued credentials.** Rather than focusing on job matching, centers should be adapted to become a home for the cadre of career navigators proposed above, with highly skilled staff providing users with customized help to assess their career pathway choices, identify financial aid to support their learning, and understand the market value of the array of possible degrees and certifications that can be attained. Centers should be focused on whether customers get the information they need to make good career planning choices, and on ensuring that those customers can get supports they need while engaged in education and employment transition, not on whether the center can "take credit" for someone finding a job. Metrics are discussed at the meta-level later in this chapter. Those metrics will need to be parsed out so that the functions within the new system support the larger measures and that each component has its own set of measures that build to the larger goals.

- **States should get out of the business of operating job boards/ talent banks.** The market for such e-boards is vast, and the investment required for states to operate their own does not make sense. Rather, American Job Centers, high schools, colleges, libraries, and other public agencies should offer those seeking learning and employment good information about how to effectively take advantage of the various opportunities to access job information that fits the individual and where that person is on her/his pathway. We do believe that those entering a pathway at a very low skills level will need and should receive "high touch" support from career navigators to help them navigate their options.

- **Reemployment support needs to focus on credential attainment.** An overriding lesson from the large-scale dislocations of the past 30 years is that many workers who are laid off will need to acquire new and/or enhanced skills to make a successful transition to a new job with a career path opportunity. That means that metrics for reemployment efforts need to center on credential attainment and funding strategies on providing financial support for the learning required to attain needed credentials. This work should be grounded on an assessment of the competencies already possessed by the transitioning worker, and then identifying the shortest paths to credentials that will be valued in the labor market. Reemployment should then be measured in terms of the employment results achieved by the worker after obtaining a needed credential, including the connection of that credential to the new job.

Reconceiving the One-Stop Centers as hubs for obtaining help in career navigation requires rethinking where centers are located and the scale at which they operate. A navigation-centered model may argue for increasing the number of sites housed at community colleges and universities, for example, as well as others that are integrated with community-based efforts that focus on increasing postsecondary attainment. It is fair to question whether the large One-Stop sites that were put into place in many communities in the past make economic sense in a business model that may include having career navigators doing substantial work at other community locations to reach customers effectively.

RECONCEIVED METRICS

The old adage that you get what you measure rings true in workforce development. The traditional metrics for employment-related adult programs are entered employment, retention, and average earnings. The exact computation of these are too complex to delve into here, and it has no value in this discussion except to note that the employment measurement starts at the time a participant exits from a program (i.e., is no longer receiving any services). The other measures follow from that point of exit but are extended in time to assess postprogram status. These measures assume that program participation is a one-time event that ends when employment is obtained and therefore discourages strategies that involve postemployment services. Programs want to have the best possible outcomes on these measures since, at least under WIA, there have been incentives for achieving specified benchmarks and possible sanctions if they are missed over time.

The measures for youth, a much smaller part of the total workforce investment package, are actually closer to what we think the adult measures should be. They include placement in employment or education, attainment of a degree or certificate, and literacy and numeracy gains. While not at all perfect, these measures at least target some of the skills development issues that are important for adults as well, and they can be milestones to achieving family-sustaining jobs, the ultimate objective.

But none of the measures are adequately aligned with the changes necessary in workforce policy overall. If we are focusing on lifelong learning, recognizing diversity and varying needs, career pathways, and attainment of labor market–relevant credentials, we need to examine new ways of measuring individual progress that can be aggregated to show overall gains in the nation's competitiveness. Any measure must be tested to ensure we are getting the return on investment we need and that the measures do not produce unintended consequences. That last point is easier said than done.

In order to shift to a workforce investment strategy that moves away from public programs as the organizing vehicle, metrics must align with investments that are done through financial aid, tax policy, and educational supports. We should frame metrics in terms of goals that are simple, understandable by the general public, and contributing to the common good. Multiple examples of that can be found in the educational attainment goals set by a number of states. Two such examples:

1) Governor Bill Haslam of Tennessee has an initiative called Drive to 55—55 percent of the adult population will have a postsecondary degree or certificate by the year 2025 (State of Tennessee 2013). This is a straightforward goal and can be measured over time. Tennessee's education policy decisions are made in support of that goal. Interim progress can be measured, and there is public awareness of the relevance of the goal to Tennessee's economic prosperity.

2) Governor Martin O'Malley of Maryland in 2010 launched a statewide campaign called Skills2Compete—Maryland set a goal to increase the number of Marylanders with the postsecondary skills needed to fill the burgeoning middle jobs that are growing rapidly in the state (State of Maryland 2014). Again, this is a goal that is easy to understand and easy to track.

We need to look at those kinds of broad macro-metrics for our workforce development investments. The investments will not be in programs but will be in people—millions of people, not just the comparatively small numbers historically enrolled in workforce programs. So our measures need to embrace the broad policy goals with which investments need to align. These policy goals will be far reaching and impact all systems related to developing a skilled workforce. For example, Pell Grants may need to be reexamined to ensure they are supporting the broad goals suggested in this chapter.

Some examples would be to reduce the number of adults who have basic skills deficiencies, increase the number of adults who fill middle skill jobs, increase earnings of workers (measured over time) who follow career pathways, and increase the wages of low-income workers. The measures might be applied at the national, state, and local (regional) levels without regard to programs. Baselines could be established and targets set per year or over multiple years. Reports on the nation's, the state's, and the region's workforce health might be required and widely publicized by relevant bodies at each level just named. Who might those bodies be? That is another question to raise here but one to which we likely will not produce an answer. But we do point to examples where data collection and analysis are not housed in one agency. The Florida Pre K–20 Education Data Warehouse is a possible model to examine since it separates implementation from measurement.

There are multiple problems this nation faces. Each one could and often does have its own campaign highlighting to the public where we are, what we need to do, and how we are doing. It is happening with such diverse issues as childhood obesity and smart phone use while driving. A critical element is getting crowd support behind an effort and steering all relevant resources toward a common goal. Collective Impact (Kania and Kramer 2011) is emerging as one means of gathering momentum to address a pressing public issue that is bigger than one body can address. We mention this in the section on measures because metrics are one piece of a larger endeavor to change behaviors and create better paths for people. A good example is Lumina Foundation's Goal 2025, which aims to have 60 percent of the adult population in the United States attain a postsecondary degree or credential that will give them competitive standing in the labor market. Lumina dedicates its funding to reform institutions, engage employers, advance state and federal policy, change higher education business models, and take other needed steps to create a social movement to achieve the Goal 2025. Tracking progress will play a critical role in that process; indeed, Lumina issues a report annually about the progress toward the goal in every state and county in the nation. During the first five years of an 18-year campaign, the percentage of adults aged 25–64 with at least an associate's degree has increased yearly, with the annual rate of change increasing as well. The pace will need to continue to accelerate to reach the 60 percent by 2025 goal. Lumina has set 10 interim measures with goals to be achieved by 2016 that they believe will significantly contribute to achieving the ultimate 2025 goal (Lumina Foundation 2014). We expect the same type of process for the overall reform of investments in workforce policy.

Metrics will drive outcomes but they are not enough alone. They must be combined with a whole new way of doing business and whole new financing models.

FINANCING MODELS

We propose a number of workforce strategies that require substantial funding, most notably investments in lifelong learning, including a campaign to reduce greatly the basic skills gaps that block too many Americans from viable career pathways and employment. How can we fund these strategies?

First, we presume that the cost of greatly expanding adult learning will not be funded solely or primarily by the federal government. The federal budget balancing requirements and pressures experienced in recent years show no evidence of being resolved any time soon.

At the same time, it may be difficult to persuade states and communities accustomed to thinking about workforce development as a federally funded function that they should now absorb a substantial part of the cost of needed services. However, the return in measureable economic prosperity should be a compelling selling point. Similarly, employers facing increasingly shorter innovation cycles and less long-term employment may logically question the basis for their increasing expenditures for skill development. And individuals/families already experiencing record levels of student loan debt acquired in the course of going to college after high school will have limited capability of paying for adult learning themselves.

The reality that every stakeholder will be able to offer reasonable resistance to becoming the primary funder of lifelong learning argues that the only models that can work are ones that spread that risk across all of them. Shared funding options for adult learning include the following:

- **Accounts.** The creation of the 401(k) 30-plus years ago contributed to moving retirement funding from being primarily an employer responsibility to being an individual one with (in some cases) employer contributions. More recently, health savings accounts have been used as a vehicle to help families manage their spending in that arena. Within workforce development, both individual development accounts and Individual Training Accounts have been used at limited scale. Accounts offer some consistent attributes: customer control, portability, and an emphasis on saving for future events. Funding could be put into accounts from all stakeholders; many of these systems operate with matching provisions and tax benefits to encourage individual contributions. Such an approach has been introduced in the proposed Lifelong Learning Accounts Act, which would set up employee- and employer-sponsored savings accounts targeted at educational advancement. While not enacted federally, Washington State has been a leader in championing these accounts and has enacted state legislation putting them in place in the state.

- **Tax credits.** The largest antipoverty investment in the nation is the Earned Income Tax Credit, which has enjoyed bipartisan support for many years. It provides low-income workers with a refundable tax credit that grows with their incomes until reaching a phase-out level. The effect has been to encourage low-income people to leave welfare for work and to provide them with needed support until they reach self-sustaining income levels. This approach has proven to be fundable and supportable at a large scale. Smaller-scale tax credits have been used to support postsecondary learning, currently including the American Opportunity Credit and the Lifetime Learning Credit. A choice for workforce policy is to substantially expand the use of tax credits as a federal funding strategy. Following the model of the Earned Income Tax Credit, which is a part of every financial literacy course for low-income families, the benefits are clear and can be substantial. For a working family, EITC can be the difference between living in poverty or not. Large-scale take-up of a workforce tax credit would require a similar kind of awareness campaign and clear articulation of the value to both the individual and society of the credit.

- **Pell Grants for adult learners.** This tool has been effective in supporting low/moderate-income students in obtaining postsecondary education. However, Pell Grants were designed to help full-time traditional students, and they work less well with adult learners who often are attending part time. Current policy work being done by several groups is raising the idea of developing an adult worker-centered Pell approach to complement the grants aimed at traditional students. The College Board (2013) released a report that outlines two separate tracks for Pell Grants, one for transitioning young students and another for adult learners. That report is the basis for a legislative campaign that the Study Group, which authored the report, is spearheading. This approach offers another way to target financial aid to adult learners who would otherwise struggle to afford needed education.

- **Public-private collaboratives.** As noted earlier, intriguing experiments are under way in which work and learn models are being employed to accelerate and contextualize education. In some of these models, employers are paying the learner wages during the time spent on the job as well as providing tuition support for the courses taken. Various combinations can be imagined of the balance of employer support, public support, and individual funding that would be possible in different industry/occupational training situations.

If a combination of these approaches is used to finance the ongoing expanded learning that is central to twenty-first century workforce policy, a short-term variant will be needed to achieve the scale of results necessary to strengthen basic skills. The enormous literacy and numeracy challenges found among adult workers require a large investment spanning a few years that can greatly reduce the number of working-age adults with basic skills gaps. If that can be accomplished, a much smaller scale of ongoing support for remediation of basic skills gaps would be required and could be incorporated into the models described above.

It is likely that the large-scale basic skills improvement campaign will require a combination of public investment (federal, state, and local), business support, and philanthropic support. Solving this challenge is central to the readiness of U.S. workers; the costs of not responding are large in terms of the income and social supports that will be required if large-scale improvement is not achieved.

Beyond financial strategies to support adult learning, the workforce policy approach requires ongoing support for three other key functions:

1) Intermediaries. Industry sector partnerships and similar collaboratives require support from staff with the capacity to do skilled facilitation and provide expert research and analytic capability for the partnership. Our experience suggests that this work requires at least partial public funding, potentially with match requirements from the collaboratives themselves.

2) Career navigators. The cadre of expert navigators described earlier could be supported through a combination of funding from K–12 school districts and colleges, workforce support through reframed American Job Centers, and sliding-scale client fees.

3) Reframed American Job Centers. If the next generation of centers is charged with becoming strong education- and career-advising resources, ongoing funding will include contributing to support for the cadre of career navigators. Centers will also need staff who are adept at helping customers understand their options for financing learning, and for obtaining the support services they require to successfully navigate transitions. This work requires public funding for important, ongoing infrastructure; it could and should be funded directly, and the Job Centers should shift from being a collection of agencies to unified operations with clear, bounded missions.

Some of the costs discussed can be covered by repurposing existing federal workforce program funding, particularly by moving away from a program model and by explicitly getting out of some functions, such as running job boards and talent banks. But this reframing represents a great time to move from a dominantly federally funded model to a shared federal/state/local approach to public funding, as can be found in many other areas of public policy. A model of a shared funding approach exists today in the Unemployment Insurance system. This funding model could be repurposed to support career changes beyond interim benefits. There have been modest modifications to this tightly bound system, such as those that support job sharing and allow benefit receipt while engaging in training, but it is time to think more broadly about how these funds could be used to support retraining and career navigation in a way that helps mitigate the need for income support. Already, 16 states levy an additional tax in conjunction with unemployment taxation to support worker education and training (U.S. Department of Labor 2012). This base provides a solid starting point for rethinking and interconnecting unemployment reduction and retraining.

While current laws share authority and responsibility at all three levels of government, the reality is that if the federal dollars are the primary source of funding, most attention gets placed on meeting the federal measures and reacting to federal regulatory requirements. Shifting to a shared funding model would improve the ownership and balance among the three levels of government of workforce investments and strategies.

Finally, we offer thoughts on three other considerations for future workforce policy: 1) the role of workforce boards, 2) community colleges and workforce development, and 3) supporting entrepreneurship as part of workforce development.

DO WE NEED WORKFORCE BOARDS?

Local/regional workforce boards made up of business, education, labor, community organizations, and government have been a key part of workforce structure in the United States for the past 35 years. As we think about the foci for workforce investment suggested above, are these boards still relevant?

We submit that they can be very relevant, but with a modified mission. Today, the central business most workforce boards are in is the management of federal grants—operating One-Stop Centers, procuring providers, monitoring expenditure of federal funds, and reporting on associated performance measures.

If we shift the funding of adult learning into some combination of the models suggested earlier, the crucial work these boards could do moves away from grant management and more to what some leading boards do today:

- **Community convening and leadership.** Workforce boards can, and in some cases do, act as catalytic agents to bring community stakeholders together to identify and tackle important workforce issues in their labor markets.

- **Broker and organize multiple resources.** Rather than dominantly focusing on managing a few federal grants, workforce boards could become resource brokers, skilled at organizing a mix of relevant public funds (federal, state, and local), industry funds, and foundation support for key initiatives.

- **Community workforce metrics.** In moving the focus from program measures to scalable impact metrics, workforce boards could become leaders in their regions in tracking and assessing progress being made at a community/regional level.

The geography of workforce boards now is predominantly based on political boundaries rather than labor markets. To increase their effectiveness and impact in terms of the strategic leadership work needed, they should have a regional labor market focus, which we believe will allow much closer ties to economic development.

COMMUNITY COLLEGES AND WORKFORCE DEVELOPMENT

In recent years, growing national attention has been paid to community colleges as the chief provider of workforce training. On the surface, this is a logical step toward investing in longer-term, labor market–relevant training. Nearly $2 billion is being invested in creating new models within community colleges to be employer driven, and focused on labor market–relevant training and credential attainment (U.S. Department of Labor 2014). These are wise investments in an infrastructure that needs major overhaul. Success rates for completing courses of study at community colleges or transferring to four-year schools has been a subject of concern and debate. No matter how you slice it, completion rates are well below what the general public would expect. At best, the completion rate is 40 percent (Juszkiewicz 2014).

Regardless of the rates, community colleges play multiple roles in their service areas. They are the stepping stone to transfer to four-year schools. They are the providers of credentials and degrees that improve labor market competitiveness for adult learners. They are the place a person goes to upgrade one skill or to take a course for simple personal enrichment. These are certainly many roles to play. In their workforce preparation role, which has received much attention from President Obama, community colleges are being looked to as the prime workforce development providers, especially for adult learners who need to upgrade their portfolios to compete for middle-skills jobs.

There is interest in strengthening community colleges' connections with employers, particularly through sector strategies, making course offerings and curriculum employer driven. These are not traditional modes of operating for community colleges, but there is movement in the right direction through grants to make this vital connection. We see great potential for community colleges to play major roles in developing our workforce, particularly our adult learners, but a long path remains to be traveled before they can completely fulfill that potential. We encourage continued attention on this segment of the workforce development system as we know it today. Community colleges, in general, already have strong workforce arms that are primarily aimed at incumbent worker training. In technical fields, community colleges have in place good internship models, and many are well integrated with employers. Comparatively, their costs are low and they can focus on labor market–relevant, stackable credentials. In our opinion, more movement is needed in order to fit the schedules of adult learners and to integrate work and learning, but the potential is there. We should be building on this valuable resource.

WORKFORCE DEVELOPMENT AND ENTREPRENEURSHIP

The unprecedented sluggishness in hiring during the current recovery raises a challenge to the past century's assumptions about jobs, which centered on workers being full-time employees of an organization as the dominant/desired model. Current forecasts suggest that employment as traditionally defined won't return to prerecession levels for years to come, and that the result will continue to be an imbalance in which too many workers seek too few jobs.

We're beginning to see hints of an alternative framework in which a substantial percentage of people build a pieced-together income strategy, either because they can't find a full-time job, or because they prefer the control and flexibility of self-packaging. In addition, community development strategy in many places centers on encouraging people to become entrepreneurs—not necessarily in the large-scale, venture capital sense but rather in a "create your own job in your own neighborhood" sense.

Entrepreneurship can and should become a stronger workforce investment strategy. This is a teachable skill that has received slight attention in our workforce world, and has been discouraged by performance metrics centered on placement in an existing job. Entrepreneurship as a strategy is important in an economy in which whole occupations are being destroyed, as new, never before thought of occupations are being created. If nurtured properly, entrepreneurs create those niches and can be employers beyond one-person shops. We need entrepreneurship as part of our workforce arsenal.

Note

1. See www.ieee.org/education_careers for a preview of the career navigation tool (accessed November 26, 2014).

References

Belfield, Clive R., Henry M. Levin, and Rachel Rosen. 2012. *The Economic Value of Opportunity Youth*. Washington, DC: Corporation for National and Community Service.

Bureau of Labor Statistics. 2014. "Employment Situation Summary." Washington, DC: Bureau of Labor Statistics. http://www.bls.gov/news.release/empsit.nr0.htm (accessed April 21, 2014).

Carnevale, Anthony, Stephen J. Rose, and Andrew R. Hanson. 2012. *Certificates: Gateway to Gainful Employment and College Degrees*. Washington, DC: Georgetown Center on Education and the Economy.

Chronicle of Higher Education. 2014. "25 Years of Declining State Support for Public Colleges." *Chronicle of Higher Education*, March 3. http://chronicle.com/article/25-Years-of-Declining-State/144973/ (accessed July 14, 2014).

College Board. 2013. *Rethinking Pell Grants*. New York: College Board. https://www.collegeboard.org/releases/2013/new-rethinking-pell-grants-report-explores-ways-meet-needs-younger-and-older-students (accessed July 14, 2014).

Drobocky, Kristin. *Free Agency Is Here*. Troy, MI: Kelly Services. http://www.kellyocg.com/uploadedFiles/Content/Knowledge/Ebooks/Free Agency is Here - A Finance Perspective.pdf (accessed July 14, 2014).

Eggers, William D., John Hagel, and Owen Sanderson. 2012. "Mind the (Skills) Gap." *Harvard Business Review Blog Network*, September 21. http://blogs.hbr.org/2012/09/mind-the-skills-gap/ (accessed July 14, 2014).

Government Accountability Office. 2011. *Multiple Employment and Training Programs: Providing Information on Colocating Services and Consolidating Administrative Structures Could Promote Efficiencies*. GAO-11-92. Washington, DC: Government Accountability Office.

Juszkiewicz, Jolanta. 2014. *Recent National Community College Enrollment and Award Completion Data*. Washington, DC: American Association of Community Colleges.

Kania, John, and Mark Kramer. 2011. "Collective Impact." *Stanford Social Innovation Review* 65(Winter): 3641.

Krepcio, Kathy, and Michelle Martin. 2012. *The State of the U.S. Workforce System: A Time for Incremental Realignment or Serious Reform?* New Brunswick, NJ: John J. Heldrich Center for Workforce Development, Rutgers University.

Lumina Foundation. 2014. *Closing the Gaps in College Attainment: A Stronger Nation through Higher Education*. Indianapolis, IN: Lumina Foundation. http://www.luminafoundation.org/publications/StrongerNation2014-infogra.pdf (accessed July 14, 2014).

Manyika, James, Susan Lund, Byron Auguste, and Sreenivas Ramaswa-my. 2012. "Help Wanted: The Future of Work in Advanced Economies." McKinsey Global Institute discussion paper. Various locations: McKinsey Global Institute. http://www.mckinsey.com/insights/employment_and_growth/future of_work_in_advanced economies/ (accessed April 24, 2014).

Michigan Economic Development Corporation. 2014. "Michigan Manufac-turing Advanced Technician Training." Lansing, MI: Michigan Economic Development Corporation. http://www.mitalent.org/mat2/ (accessed May 16, 2014).

Morrison, Tom, Bob Maciejewski, Craig Giffi, Emily Stover DeRocco, Jennifer McNelly, and Gardner Carrick. 2011. *Boiling Point? The Skills Gap in Manufacturing.* New York and Washington, DC: Deloitte and the Manufacturing Institute.

National Commission on Adult Literacy. 2008. *Reach Higher: Overcoming Crisis in the U.S. Workforce.* New York: National Commission on Adult Literacy.

New America Foundation. 2014. "Adult Education: Title II of the Workforce Investment Act." Washington, DC: New America Foundation. http://febp .newamerica.net/background-analysis/adult-education-wia-titleii/print (accessed July 14, 2014).

Osterman, Paul, and Andrew Weaver. 2014. "Why Claims of Skills Shortages in Manufacturing Are Overblown." Issue Brief No. 376. Washington, DC: Economic Policy Institute.

Peck, Don. 2013. "They're Watching You at Work." *The Atlantic* online, December. http://www.theatlantic.com/magazine/archive/2013/12/theyre-watching -you-at-work/354681/ (accessed September 9, 2014).

Power, Philip H., and Jan Urban-Lurain. 1989. *Creating a Human Investment System.* Report to the governor. Lansing, MI: Michigan Job Training Coor-dinating Council.

Shierholz, Heidi, and Lawrence Mishel. 2013. *A Decade of Flat Wages.* Wash-ington, DC: Economic Policy Institute.

State of Maryland. 2014. "Skills2Compete Maryland." Annapolis, MD: State of Maryland. http://www.skills.maryland.gov/ (accessed April 23, 2014).

State of Tennessee. 2013. "Haslam Shifts 'Drive to 55' Initiative into High Gear." Nashville, TN: State of Tennessee. http://news.tn.gov/node/11295 (accessed April 23, 2014).

Strong, Ed. 2012. *One-Stop Centers Must Be Reinvented to Meet Today's Labor Market Realities.* Ann Arbor, MI: Corporation for a Skilled Work-force. http://skilledwork.org/publications/one-stop-career-centers-must-be -reinvented-to-meet-todays-labor-market-realities/ (accessed July 15, 2014).

Sum, Andrew, and Joseph McLaughlin. 2008. *CLM Brief 3: Estimates of the Nominal Annual Budgetary Costs of Delivering Adult Basic Education Services to 20 Million Adults in 2020.* Washington, DC: National Commission on Adult Literacy.

U.S. Department of Education. 2003. "National Assessment of Adult Literacy." Washington, DC: U.S. Department of Education. http://nces.ed.gov/NAAL/ (accessed July 14, 2014).

———. 2014. "Adult Education—Basic Grants to States." Washington, DC: U.S. Department of Education. http://www2.ed.gov/programs/adultedbasic/index.html (accessed April 21, 2014).

U.S. Department of Labor, Employment and Training Administration. 2005. "Common Measures at a Glance." Washington, DC: U.S. Department of Labor.   http://wdr.doleta.gov/directives/attach/TEGL17-05_AttachA.pdf (accessed April 8, 2014).

———. 2012. "UI Law Comparisons." Washington, DC: U.S. Department of Labor. http://workforcesecurity.doleta.gov/unemploy/pdf/uilawcompar/2012/financing.pdf (accessed July 14, 2014).

———. 2014. "Trade Adjustment Assistance Community College Career Training Grants." Washington, DC: U.S. Department of Labor. http://www.doleta.gov/taaccct/ (accessed April 21, 2014).

Valletta, Rob, and Leila Bengali. 2013. "What's Behind the Increase in Part-Time Work?" FRBSF Economic Letter, August 26. San Francisco: Federal Reserve Board of San Francisco.

Van Horn, Carl E. 2013. *Working Scared (Or Not At All).* Lanham, MD: Rowman and Littlefield.

3
Reemploying Unemployment Insurance Claimants

A Good Government Investment

Richard A. Hobbie
Rutgers University

Yvette J. Chocolaad
National Association of State Workforce Agencies

This chapter discusses a strategy to reemploy unemployment insurance (UI) claimants with dedicated and cost-effective eligibility assessments and job search assistance. Although evidence supporting this strategy began accumulating in the late 1980s, resources to implement it have not been fully or consistently allocated by the federal government. With "universal services" emphasized in the Workforce Investment Act (WIA) of 1998, resources were spread thinly, and opportunities to improve the efficiency of the UI system were missed. Here we review some of the challenges that have led the U.S. Department of Labor (USDOL) to propose this strategy, the evidence on cost-effectiveness, the new USDOL "Reemployment Vision," and recommendations for improving federal policy in this area.

The phrase *good government investment* has a dual meaning. First, evidence shows the strategy is a good government investment because it can have a high government benefit-cost ratio, and substantial net government benefits in the form of budget savings if provided to many UI beneficiaries. Also, UI claimants benefit from reduced unemployment duration, increased employment, and perhaps increased earnings, and employers benefit from filling job vacancies more quickly and ultimately from lower unemployment taxes. Second, it is a *good-government* investment because it can help lower benefit overpayments, thereby improving the integrity of state programs. Assessing eligibility and assisting UI beneficiary job search more closely can reduce major causes of overpayments, such as lack of job search documentation and the failure of some beneficiaries to report their return to work in a timely fashion.

In general, we recommend the following five improvements:

1) Promote and expand the "Reemployment Vision," which was developed by a workgroup of federal, state, and local government and nonprofit organization officials convened by USDOL

2) More than quadruple the administration's proposed investment in eligibility assessments and reemployment services for UI claimants to $800 million per year

3) Develop and apply new performance measures to encourage rapid reemployment of UI claimants

4) Research effective job search strategies

5) Increase grants to states for UI administration so they can provide more effective UI eligibility assessments

A PROPOSED STRATEGY FROM THE U.S. DEPARTMENT OF LABOR

In the USDOL fiscal year (FY) 2015 budget justification to Congress, the administration proposed to "build on the success" of existing efforts and establish an ". . . enhanced, integrated, and expanded Reemployment and Eligibility Assessments (REA) and Reemployment Services (RES) program in all states" (USDOL 2014). Based on a promising model and evidence in Nevada, the proposal would require about 1.3 million UI claimants estimated to be in the top quarter of those most likely to exhaust their UI benefits and an estimated 63,000 ex-service member claimants to participate in REA and RES. The integrated REA and RES would be "in-person interviews to review eligibility for UI benefits; provisions of labor market and career information to claimants to inform their career choices; support for the development of reemployment and work search plan(s); orientation to services available through 'American Job Centers,' also called local One-Stop Career

Centers; and provision of staff-assisted reemployment services, including skills assessments, career counseling, job matching and referrals, job search assistance workshops, and referrals to training as appropriate" (USDOL 2014).

The program names Reemployment and Eligibility Assessments and Reemployment Services are confusing but derive from federal law. Table 3.1 summarizes the main elements of each approach. Eligibility assessments should be conducted in normal UI administration, but this aspect has atrophied over the years as a result of cuts in funding of employment services and UI administration. Assessments of reemployment prospects, usually performed by One-Stop Centers, are the precursors to helping UI claimants find employment in a cost-effective manner. Reemployment services, such as job search workshops or job matching, also are administered by One-Stop Centers. They help UI claimants improve their search for work, an unfamiliar and daunting task for many dislocated workers. Reemployment services also help employers find qualified workers through job matching, a struggle for many employers who say they cannot find qualified workers at the wages they offer.

Although USDOL officials were aware of the accumulated positive evidence on the effectiveness of reemployment services for UI claimants, their budget justification cited only specific recent research results on an integrated REA/RES approach in Nevada that found

- claimants were significantly less likely to exhaust their benefits;
- claimants had significantly shorter UI durations and lower total benefits paid (1.82 fewer weeks and $536 lower total benefit outlays)[1];
- claimants were more successful in returning to work sooner in jobs with higher wages and retaining their jobs; and
- $2.60 of savings were produced for every $1.00 of cost (USDOL 2014).

In FY 2014, the federal government appropriated a total of about $80 million for REA in most states. The administration's FY 2015 proposal would nearly double that to about $158 million for the integrated REA/RES approach in all states. Mandatory funding would be provided based on the projected number of targeted UI beneficiaries, at a cost of

Table 3.1 Comparison of Reemployment and Eligibility Assessments (REA) and Reemployment Services (RES)

Characteristic	REA 2010 grant requirements	RES requirements[a]
Participant selection	REAs target claimants based on a range of factors including benefit week, location, likelihood to exhaust, and others.	RES target claimants based on likelihood of exhaustion and benefit duration.
Participation	• Identified claimants are required to participate fully in all REA components. • Claimants must report to the One-Stop Career Center in person for staff-assisted services.	States determine participation requirements for RES; some made participation mandatory while others did not.
Activities and services	Required activities for REA claimants: participate in initial and continuing UI eligibility assessments; participate in individual labor market information sessions; participate in an orientation to One-Stop Career Center; register with the state's job bank.	Allowable activities for RES claimants: job search and placement services; counseling; testing; occupational and labor market information; assessment; referrals to employers, training, and other services.
Plan development	Reemployment plan must be developed and include work search activities, appropriate workshops, or approved training.	Recommends reemployment plans for RES claimants who would benefit from additional RES and or referrals to WIA, particularly those who are not a viable candidate for job opportunities in the region.

[a]Under the American Recovery and Reinvestment Act.
SOURCE: Barnow and Hobbie (2013).

$150 per beneficiary, and state UI programs would be required to coop-erate with state employment service agencies to implement the inte-grated approach.[2] USDOL estimates its proposal would yield gross out-lay savings to the federal unemployment trust fund in FY 2015 of about $420 million, for a net savings of about $262 million in the first year.[3]

CHALLENGES TO REEMPLOYING UI CLAIMANTS

The strategy of emphasizing reemployment, and not just UI bene-fits, has a long history, but a plethora of system challenges has impeded its effective implementation. We have identified eight such challenges.

1)   Slow and insufficient response to structural economic change.

The UI and employment service systems were slow to respond to a proportionate rise in permanent layoffs since the early 1980s (Groshen 2011) and the secular rise in long-term unemployment that was exac-erbated by the Great Recession of 2007–2009. The federal government provided insufficient resources to reemploy the long-term unemployed after the early 1990s. Instead, it emphasized temporary benefit exten-sions, typified by added spending in response to the Great Recession of over $200 billion on emergency unemployment compensation for the long-term unemployed, and only an additional $250 million on reem-ployment services aimed at UI beneficiaries and $148 million for other labor exchange services under the Wagner-Peyser Act (Barnow and Hobbie 2013).

Under the Social Security Act of 1935 and the Federal Unemploy-ment Tax Act of 1939, the federal-state UI system was designed to pro-vide temporary and partial wage replacement to covered and eligible workers. All states established federally approved UI programs under these laws. State unemployment taxes finance the regular benefits, up to 26 weeks in most states, and all state unemployment tax revenue is deposited in the respective state accounts of the federal unemployment trust fund. States earn interest on their balances and regularly withdraw trust funds to pay state benefits. Federal grants to states for administra-tion are authorized, and the Secretary of Labor is charged with provid-ing enough funds to states for "proper and efficient administration" of state UI programs. In addition, in response to recessions, the federal government usually covers the cost of emergency benefit extensions, beyond the state benefits and permanent federal-state extended benefits (up to 13 or 20 additional weeks of benefits, depending on state unemployment rates), out of general revenues.

State law and administration are supposed to ensure UI claimants have sufficient earnings in a base year to be "monetarily eligible" for unemployment benefits and that they meet certain "nonmonetary" qualification requirements, such as being able to work, available for work, and actively seeking work. State UI and employment service administrators are supposed to assure that claimants "certify" their ability to work, their availability for work, and their active work search, and to refer them for job search assistance provided by the state employment service or training provided by One-Stop Career Centers. State employment services are supposed to help these workers find new employment.

The system seemed to work well for temporary unemployment, but concerns about "structural unemployment," the mismatch between the demand for labor and the supply of labor, grew beginning in the 1950s. It was thought that advancing production technologies and other economic changes were displacing workers, and that workers were remaining unemployed longer than expected.

It was not until the 1990s that the UI program was partly refocused on permanent layoffs and reemployment services for the long-term unemployed. In 1993, the federal government enacted the Emergency Unemployment Compensation Amendments, which, in part, provided for the establishment of ". . . a program encouraging the adoption and implementation of a system of profiling new claimants for regular unemployment compensation to identify which claimants are most likely to exhaust such benefits and who may be in need of reemployment assistance services to make a successful transition to new employment."

The new policy was a response to the decline after the early 1980s in the proportion of temporarily laid-off unemployed workers during recessions (Groshen 2011), and new evidence showing that if the system could identify UI claimants who were likely to exhaust UI benefits and provide reemployment assistance early, they would return to work earlier than otherwise. Subsequently, profiling aimed at reducing long-term unemployment was implemented in states, but added funding for reemployment services was not allocated from other employment and training programs as promised (Wandner 2010).

2)   Inconsistent policy.

In 1997, the USDOL wrote an Employment Service Program Letter (USDOL 1997) to encourage states to improve reemployment services to profiled and referred UI claimants. In part, it said to

- provide job search assistance to UI claimants early;
- tailor services to the UI claimants' reemployment needs; and
- provide more and better reemployment services, such as job search workshops, including employers, labor market information, job clubs, regular reassessment of UI claimants' plans, job-loss, financial and health insurance counseling, automated service plans, and collaboration with other service providers.

Many states and localities adopted such approaches, but resources were spread thinly, with an emphasis on universal services under WIA. Meanwhile, in the early 2000s federal reemployment policy swung away from RES to REA as policymakers took a more skeptical view of the effectiveness of RES. While this occurred, the National Association of State Workforce Agencies (NASWA) sent a letter to USDOL, urging the federal government to take a balanced approach of REA and RES (NASWA 2004). But the message went unheeded until February 2009, when the federal government enacted the American Recovery and Reinvestment Act (ARRA) of 2009, which provided one-time funds of $250 million for RES.

3)   Decentralization of the workforce development system.

Decentralization of the workforce development system led to greater emphasis on serving all customers and to relatively less emphasis on reemploying UI claimants. The workforce development system became more of a federal-state-local partnership as it evolved under the Manpower Development and Training Act of 1962, the Comprehensive Employment and Training Act of 1973, the Job Training Partnership Act of 1982, WIA, and now the Workforce Innovation and Opportunity Act of 2014 (WIOA). WIA, which was enacted when the economy was at near full employment, emphasized "universal services." With limited resources in the system, there also might have been a tendency to focus on customers not receiving UI benefits or those most in need as the system was flooded with workers seeking help, particularly in the aftermath of the Great Recession.

WIA created local One-Stop Career Centers in which the employment service and the UI program are required partners. Local Workforce Investment Boards govern the One-Stop Centers, but the employment service and UI program are state programs. Local officials do not have the incentive that state officials have for saving state UI benefit outlays. This is one reason why the administration's FY 2015 proposal requires state UI programs to cooperate with state employment service programs, but the cooperation needs to be mutual and might not be as forthcoming from One-Stop Centers with other priorities determined locally.

4) Reduced funding for Wagner-Peyser Act labor exchange services.

Since the mid-1980s, real (adjusted for inflation) federal grants to states for Wagner-Peyser Act labor exchange services, a primary source of federal funding for job search assistance for the unemployed, were cut by about half (see Figure 3.1). Even accounting for additional funding

Figure 3.1 Funding for Employment Service State Allotments (nominal and constant 2009 dollars)

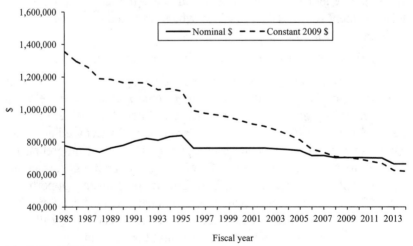

SOURCE: USDOL.

under ARRA, a recent study estimates average per participant spending on labor exchange services fell from \$55 before the recession to \$38 during the early stages of the recovery (Eberts and Wandner 2013). This made it difficult for states to provide job search assistance for all workers in general and UI claimants in particular (Wandner 2010). Localities might have picked up some of this loss by spending more WIA funds on labor exchange services instead of training. The federal government partially worked around this problem with limited funding for RES grants in FYs 2001–2005 of about \$35 million per year (see Table 3.2 for REA/RES funding). However, the federal government ceased such funding in FY 2006, until a large one-time appropriation of \$250 million in FY 2009 was provided under the ARRA (Barnow and Hobbie 2013), and temporary, mandatory funding was provided for long-term EUC claimants under the Middle Class Tax Relief and Job Creation Act. But, no more funds were appropriated for RES for regular UI claimants after ARRA.

Table 3.2 Funding for Reemployment Services and Reemployment and Eligibility Assessments

Fiscal year	RES funding (\$)	Number of states[a]	REA funding (\$)	Number of states
2001	35,000,000	53		
2002	35,000,000	53		
2003	34,773,000	53		
2004	34,576,000	53		
2005	34,290,000	53	17,794,479	21
2006			10,601,852	19
2007			16,056,832	19
2008			15,757,313	19
2009	247,500,000[b]	53	39,280,972	34
2010			53,382,216	34
2011			48,734,731	38
2012			75,563,770	43
2013			64,259,656	41

[a]States include Washington, D.C., Puerto Rico, and Virgin Islands.
[b]RES fiscal year 2009 is American Recovery and Reinvestment Act funding.
SOURCE: USDOL.

5)   Elimination of America's Job Bank.

In 2006, the federal government defunded America's Job Bank (AJB), which was a nationwide system containing about half of the state job banks, which had job vacancy listings. This eliminated the ability of the participating states to access job vacancies in the other participating states. The conclusion to kill the AJB stemmed from a belief that a burgeoning commercial Internet job bank market provided extensive job vacancy listings and, therefore, there was no need for a nationwide public job bank. However, this ignored critical roles government can play in verifying legitimate employers advertising job vacancies, ensuring the job vacancies are in fact open, eliminating duplicate job vacancy listings often found on commercial Internet job sites, and protecting the health and safety of job seekers from dangerous or criminal job vacancy listings on the Internet.

The elimination of AJB was, however, a temporary setback. States reacted by creating the National Labor Exchange (NLx) through the efforts of NASWA and an alliance with DirectEmployers Association, whose more than 700 members are Fortune 1,000 companies. Today the NLx has over 1.5 million unique and current domestic job vacancy listings with verified employers that are updated daily, which is about 50 percent more than existed in the AJB at its peak. Also, unlike the AJB, all states, the District of Columbia, Guam, and Puerto Rico participate in the NLx.

6)   Disconnection of UI claimants from reemployment services.

While the need for connecting UI claimants to job opportunities seemed to be growing, and evidence was mounting that providing job search assistance early in claims was cost-effective, new remote claims-taking technologies were implemented that substantially disconnected claimants from in-person job search assistance. Previously, claimants had to apply for UI in local offices where they might also seek job search assistance. USDOL initiated revolutionizing claims taking with the targeted funding of telephone call center technology in the mid-1990s, and that was quickly overtaken by Internet claims-taking technology. Soon nearly all initial and continued claims were being taken remotely.

7) Disproportionate emphasis on timely payment of benefits.

In the early 1970s, the federal government placed paramount importance on the prompt payment of unemployment benefits. The U.S. Supreme Court, on April 26, 1971, issued the *California Department of Human Resources Development v. Java* decision, which struck down a provision of California law that said, "If an appeal is taken from a determination awarding benefits, the benefits in issue are not to be paid until the appeal has been decided." The court found the Social Security Act conditioned federal grants for state administration of UI on the state providing methods of administration that ". . . are found by the Secretary of Labor to be reasonably calculated to insure full payment of unemployment compensation when due." Further, the court said Congress intended "when due" to mean ". . . at the earliest stage of unemployment that such payments were administratively feasible after giving both the worker and the employer an opportunity to be heard" (USDOL 1971).

In 1993, the federal government enacted the Government Performance and Results Act (GPRA). Late in the 1990s, USDOL responded with implementation of a new system, Unemployment Insurance Performance Measurement System, which reinforced the emphasis the *Java* decision placed on timely payment of benefits. The system had 10 core measures that emphasized timeliness and quality of administration but excluded reemployment. It was not until late 2006 that the department began reporting on a new core measure focusing on reemployment of claimants, the entered employment rate, which is defined as the percent of individuals receiving a first payment of UI in a quarter who were reemployed in the subsequent quarter.

Today, the three primary measures under the GPRA are 1) percent of intrastate payments made timely, 2) percent of recoverable overpayments that have been detected, and 3) entered employment rate. Some states believe they have struggled to meet federal standards set for these measures because they do not receive enough administrative funds from the federal government and have not been able to upgrade their 1970s or 1980s vintage computer benefit systems. Also, UI directors have complained about the reemployment performance measure because employment services and One-Stop Career Centers have responsibility for reemployment, not UI programs.

8)   Reduced funding for base UI administration.

Since the mid-1990s, the base funding (adjusted for inflation and a fixed base workload) for federal grants to states for UI administration has declined to levels lower than those in the mid-1980s, at about $1.7 billion today (see Figure 3.2).[4] Adoption of remote claims taking, such as over the telephone or the Internet, that might have increased efficiency could explain some of the decline in funding for the base, but the drop has made it difficult for states to administer their programs in general, which might also have affected their abilities to assess adequately the continued eligibility and reemployment prospects of claimants.

Meanwhile, the federal government has worked around the decline in base UI administrative funding with temporary supplemental funding through appropriations for REAs and supplemental budget request grants for information technology modernization. These "workarounds" have produced a limited and unpredictable stream of federal funding in lieu of more consistent and predictable annual base funding. Beginning in 2005, the federal government provided about $18 million in grants for REAs, which funded services that should have been funded with the base federal grants if there had been more funding for UI and

Figure 3.2   Appropriations for State UI Administration per 2.0 Million Average Weekly Insured Unemployment (adjusted into constant 2009 dollars)

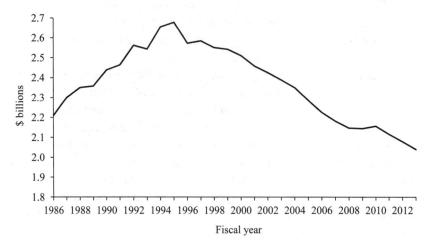

SOURCE: USDOL.

employment services (see Table 3.2). These special grants have been provided each year since and have grown to $80 million in FY 2014, but the supplemental budget requests in particular are likely to shrink as unemployment declines.[5]

Some states have tried to compensate for federal underfunding of base grants for state UI administration by supplementing federal grants with state funds. In FY 1994, for example, some states provided state supplements to federal base grants of about $50 million in total. Such aggregate supplements quadrupled to about $222 million in 41 states in FY 2013. However, not all states have been able to provide supplemental funds, and states disagree with USDOL that the federal grants alone are sufficient for proper and efficient administration of the program.

THE EVIDENCE

The research evidence to support mandating and funding both REA and RES for UI claimants has grown compelling in the past 25 years, beginning with the results of a New Jersey demonstration project reported in 1989, and ending with highly positive evaluations of Nevada's integrated REA/RES program released in 2012 and 2013.[6] Collectively, the evidence demonstrates that engaging claimants in REA and RES early in their unemployment spells, as a condition of continued eligibility for benefits,

- reduces the percent of claimants receiving UI and accelerates the return to work almost immediately;
- may enhance job search skills, depending on the design and delivery of the RES;
- reduces UI program spending by cutting the average number of weeks of UI benefit receipt;
- is low-cost and cost-effective, even during economic downturns, suggesting government can fund REA and RES from savings in UI benefit payments; and
- seems to help address the problem of long-term unemployment, as it reduces the percent of claimants who remain on UI for a long time and who exhaust benefits.[7]

The evidence rests primarily on the findings of rigorous random assignment evaluations. Promising features include

- early intervention,
- the provision of REA and a comprehensive package of RES,
- integrated service delivery,
- mandatory participation and enforcement of participation requirements, and
- engagement of as many UI claimants as funding permits.

2009 Nevada REA/RES Initiative

The 2009 demonstration in Nevada of an integrated REA/RES program was cited by the administration as a basis for its FY 2015 proposal. The Nevada evidence came out of a USDOL review of the impact of its federal REA initiative, which it conducted during the Great Recession, when benefit extensions were available in response to the high unemployment rates. The review focused on REA initiatives in Nevada, Florida, Idaho, and Illinois. In Florida, Illinois, and Idaho, new UI claimants in the treatment group were required to participate in an REA interview (and received some limited RES during the REA interview) but were referred for most services to different staff in "operationally independent" employment and training programs.[8] In Nevada, claimants in the treatment group were required to participate in both REA and RES, and the eligibility monitoring and services were provided "seamlessly by the same staff member." In three of the four states—Nevada, Florida, and Idaho—the study measured reductions in duration of regular UI receipt ranging from a little less than 0.5 to 1.8 weeks, and for regular UI and extended benefits combined ranging from 1.1 to 3.0 weeks. Reductions in regular UI benefit payments ranged from $97 to $526 (Poe-Yamagata et al. 2011).[9]

Nevada's program had the largest impacts, with reductions in regular UI benefit duration of 1.8 weeks, and in benefits of $526.[10] It also demonstrated an impressive benefit-cost ratio of 2.6 (counting reductions in regular UI benefits only; it was 4.0 when counting both regular and extended benefits).[11] The Nevada program reduced the percent of claimants exhausting benefits by 10.4 percentage points, or 15 percent, providing support that the strategy would reduce long-term unemployment among UI claimants.

Poe-Yamagata et al. (2011) concluded that Nevada's integration of REA and RES was a likely cause of the greater program effects. With this integration, Nevada provided "additional services, and with greater consistency, than other states." Nevada spent an average of $201 per treatment group member on the REA ($53) and RES ($148). It should be noted this calculation is an underestimate of the cost per participant because it is an average that includes treatment group members who did not participate in REA and/or RES (because, for example, they found employment or exited the UI program before participating), as well as those who did.[12]

A subsequent, independent, and yet-to-be-published analysis of the Nevada program results by one of the original authors looked at UI exit patterns to determine what "underlying program mechanisms" contributed to the program's effectiveness (Michaelides 2013).[13] Did most of the effects occur early when notice of the REA/RES requirements raised the cost of staying on UI for some claimants and, perhaps, encouraged other claimants to focus more quickly on their job search efforts? Or, did most of the effects occur after claimants participated in the RES, suggesting the RES were "effective in enhancing the job search abilities of recipients, particularly of those with limited job search experience, thus helping them to get reemployed?" The author finds that the larger proportion of the impacts occurred after claimants appeared for the initial REA/RES meeting, and concludes that ". . . the personalized services offered by the Nevada REA/RES program were themselves effective in enhancing job search efforts of recipients and in helping them to exit UI earlier than they would have in the absence of those services." Thus, while the Nevada study shows independent effects from REA and RES, an integrated approach that includes REA and comprehensive RES likely yields the biggest impacts (Michaelides et al. 2012, Michaelides 2013).

Evidence from Earlier Studies

Earlier evidence on the effectiveness of REA and RES steadily accumulated through demonstrations conducted from the mid-1980s by USDOL, individual states, or both.[14] In the demonstrations, UI claimants were required to participate early in their UI claims, but timing and strategies differed. While some of the studies targeted specific categories of UI claimants, such as those most likely to exhaust benefits, others were not restricted substantially. However, most often claimants with employer recall dates or some claimants belonging to unions were exempt from targeting, which also was consistent with state law and practice.

The demonstrations varied in their emphasis between UI eligibility and work search monitoring on the one hand and reemployment services on the other, but the distinctions between the two approaches were not always substantial. First, mandatory job search assistance, or RES, naturally facilitates greater oversight of UI eligibility (Wandner 2010).[15] Second, if the RES that claimants are required to participate in are minimal or not of high quality, if the RES do not differ much from what claimants could and would have accessed on their own, or if few claimants actually receive the RES (e.g., due to weak enforcement of participation mandates), most effects (on UI exit rates) of RES will stem from the inconveniences and encouragements for work search that are associated with mandatory participation requirements, rather than from enhanced job search skills of claimants. In fact, in the earlier demonstrations in which UI exit rates were examined, unlike the Nevada demonstration of 2009, the majority of impacts on UI exit rates occurred before or concurrently with the RES interventions. This suggested to some that the RES, while effective at deterring UI receipt, were not helpful in enhancing the effectiveness of UI claimants' job search skills, which some researchers have surmised is at least partly due to the minimal RES provided in many of the demonstrations (Michaelides 2013; Wandner 2010).

Two of the earlier studies, in Maryland and Washington, demonstrated the importance to the integrity of the UI program of intensive monitoring of UI claimant eligibility through the continued claims process. These studies found that UI eligibility monitoring on its own is highly cost-effective to government and important for reducing UI duration.

The Maryland UI Work Search Demonstration conducted in 1994 found UI benefit receipt fell nearly one week for those required to make more employer contacts, or who were told their employer contacts would be verified, while benefit receipt rose nearly a half week in cases where the requirement to document employer contacts was eliminated (Benus 1997). The earlier Washington Alternative Work Search Experiment, conducted in 1986 and 1987, found eliminating the requirement to report employer contacts and attend an eligibility review increased UI duration an average of two to three weeks (Johnson 1991).

Collectively, these earlier studies also demonstrated that *early* and *mandatory* engagement of UI claimants in the job search activities of the workforce system is a cost-effective strategy that reduces UI duration and accelerates reemployment.[16] (See Appendix 3A for summaries of the evidence.) Across most of the studies, reductions in UI duration ranged from nearly a half week to four weeks, with typical impacts toward the lower half of that range. Many of the studies measured impacts for the first year only, so long-run returns on investments may be higher than the short-term findings suggest.

Overall, these one-year impacts, plus the generally low costs of the services, resulted in high government benefit-cost ratios in most of the sites, even just from the perspective of the workforce system (comparing reductions in UI benefit payments to the costs of the services, and not accounting for potential increases in tax revenues or broader social benefits).

THE U.S. DEPARTMENT OF LABOR REEMPLOYMENT VISION

Regional Summit on Reemployment

From March to June of 2009, USDOL held regional forums on reemployment of UI claimants to provide "timely and regionally-customized technical assistance to the system" (USDOL 2009). This effort was a follow-up to a national January 2009 "Reemployment Works!" Summit held in Baltimore, Maryland, which "identified key reemployment principles and areas of focus."[17] General findings from the summit indicated that the system needed to collect, analyze, and provide workforce information to job seekers, employers, economic developers, educators, and other interested parties and groups; invest in information technology and tools; assess job seeker skills; and have flexibility in service delivery. The report on the summit said the following:

- Many states increased their use of profiling (i.e., identifying specific target groups, such as those most likely to exhaust benefits) and were trying to match job openings with claimants' skills, knowledge, abilities, experience, and interests.
- Some state UI programs increased collaboration with One-Stop Career Center staff through cross-training.
- Some states tried to integrate labor market information more into career counseling.
- Some states reduced duplicate data collection and shared more data.
- Some state rapid response teams introduced workers to the workforce system earlier.
- Some states used data mining to link job seekers to employers not engaged in the workforce system.
- Some states used social media for outreach, job vacancy referrals and other services.
- Many states increased availability of online tools for skills assessments, resume writing, and interviewing.

After ARRA funds were spent by the end of 2011, however, service levels for targeted reemployment services for UI claimants (and training) resumed their downward trend (Wandner 2013).

The National Reemployment Vision

The National Reemployment Vision was developed by a group of federal, state, local government, and nonprofit organizations called the "National UI Connectivity Workgroup" (USDOL 2010). The workgroup included state UI and workforce agency staff, local Workforce Investment Board and One-Stop Career Center staff, and NASWA staff to work with USDOL national and regional staff members. The Vision emphasizes the *UI claimant is foremost a job seeker*. It has four main elements, which are being developed and demonstrated in selected states in a joint effort by USDOL and NASWA:

1) An Integrated Workforce Registration tool to allow job seeker information to be collected once for all programs, thereby avoiding duplicate data entry and streamlining the process for customers and program staff. This also includes a Workforce Integrated Profile Page for each job seeker that provides personalized, real-time information on job openings, services, training and other activities, messages, and UI claims functions.

2) Real-time triage of services aims to provide the job seeker and staff with personalized and continuously updated job vacancy listings, skills assessments, career information, and labor market information to guide job searching.

3) Job matching and assessment of skills transferability involve continuously connecting job seekers' knowledge, skills, abilities, experiences, and interests with job vacancy listings. It also involves assessing whether job seekers could transfer their employment characteristics to other occupations and whether some skills training might assist such transfers.

4) Social networking involves use of such applications as email, Facebook, Twitter, and LinkedIn to facilitate continuous communications of job seekers with the workforce system, employers and other job seekers through, for example, virtual job clubs and job search communities.

Two efforts are ongoing to demonstrate and spread the elements. First, New York and Mississippi are participating in the UI/Workforce Connectivity Pilot project. Mississippi has implemented the Integrated Workforce Registration and Workforce Integrated Profile Page in six One-Stop Career Centers, and New York will implement it in late 2014 in selected counties. Second, New Jersey joined this effort as the third pilot state in mid-2014.

Idaho and Minnesota also are involved in developing other elements of the Vision. Social media contributions include such examples as online job clubs and job coaching, virtual career fair software, live chats, talent communities, training in the use of social media, and communities of practice for workforce practitioners. Six additional states (California, Illinois, Kansas, Kentucky, Iowa, and Georgia) have joined this effort and are receiving technical assistance from the original four states and the NASWA Information Technology Support Center.

RECOMMENDATIONS FOR IMPROVEMENT

Promote and Expand the USDOL Reemployment Vision

The technologies needed to connect UI claimants to the workforce system are necessary, albeit not sufficient, for reorienting the UI system in a cost-effective way toward reemployment. In a period of constrained budgets, with high levels of long-term unemployment and heightened expectations for high-quality self-service options, it is important that federal and state partners continue to advance the Reemployment Vision and the information technologies currently being piloted. This is an ongoing process with a high level of interest and commitment by many states and the Office of Unemployment Insurance at USDOL, but progress will depend on a continued focus, as well as funding for future information technology investments by federal and state governments, and sufficient administrative (including technical staff) capacity in the states.

Given the decentralized nature of the workforce system, states also should seek ways to assist and encourage localities to make reemployment of UI beneficiaries a high priority, even though beneficiaries have temporary income support that other job seekers might not have. The improved job matching and other technological tools piloted in the Reemployment Vision should help that effort.

Quadruple the Administration's FY 2015 Funding Proposal

The administration's FY 2015 proposal is for a REA/RES program of about $158 million that would help 1.3 million UI claimants at a per beneficiary cost of $150. Instead of serving only the top one-fourth of claimants most likely to exhaust their UI benefits, we suggest serving all claimants profiled. Assuming constant returns to scale and the benefit/cost ratios implicit in the administration's estimates, a program four times the size of its proposal would have a gross cost of $632 million, gross savings of $1.68 billion, and a net savings of $1.048 billion. It would serve over 5 million UI claimants. In addition, we suggest increasing the amount provided per claimant based on the Nevada evidence to at least $200. That would raise the gross cost to $800 million or more.

Congress presents a gauntlet of divided Committee jurisdictions for this proposal. The tax writing committees, the House Committee on Ways and Means, and the Senate Committee on Finance have jurisdiction over UI taxes and mandatory spending on benefits; the workforce committees, the House Committee on Education, and the Workforce and the Senate Committee on Health, Education, Labor and Pensions have jurisdiction over the Workforce Innovation and Opportunity Act and the Wagner-Peyser Act; and the Committees on Appropriations have jurisdiction over discretionary spending.

There also is strong political resistance to additional mandatory federal spending, even if it leads to net saving for the federal budget, a decline in UI benefit outlays, a reduction in the federal budget deficit in the near term, and perhaps an eventual decline in state UI taxes to finance benefits. The congressional budget process does not recognize the attendant savings. Instead, it demands offsetting tax increases and/or spending cuts elsewhere in mandatory spending under its pay-as-you-go requirements. Without recognition of the short-run savings potential, it will be very hard for Congress to enact such a program. For mandatory spending, either formal recognition of the savings as offsets, equivalent offsets, or a waiver of the pay-as-you-go requirements would be needed. On the discretionary side, additional spending for REA/RES would have to fit under the discretionary budget caps, which would require cuts in other discretionary spending to avoid breaching the caps.

Apply New Performance Measures for Reemployment of UI Beneficiaries

State UI directors have complained about the reemployment performance measure for the UI program. They say the program should not be evaluated on the basis of reemployment because they have no control over the reemployment of UI beneficiaries. They say reemployment is the responsibility of One-Stop Career Centers in general and the Wagner-Peyser Act employment services function in particular. The administration should not only require state UI programs to coordinate with employment service programs on reemployment programs, but it also should devise an entered employment measure for UI beneficiaries to place the onus of reemployment on the entities providing reemployment assessments and service—One-Stop Centers or Wagner-Peyser Act employment service programs.

The state of Texas saw improvement in UI claimant reemployment performance after adopting such an approach to performance measurement. The state devised a "rapid reemployment" measure, the percent of UI claimants reemployed within 10 weeks, that was included in contracts with local workforce boards. The state data show that adoption of the measure, coupled with other policies and the use of technology, seemed to result in significant improvements in the system's focus on UI claimant reemployment. The rapid reemployment rate, which was 40 percent when the measure was adopted in 2003, was significantly higher (between 42 and 55 percent) during the Great Recession and the period since (Miller 2013).

Conduct Research on Effectiveness of Alternative Job Search Strategies

While the research evidence shows that REA and RES are cost-effective approaches to accelerating UI claimant reemployment and addressing long-term unemployment, the variation in research results and in state approaches to RES suggests a need to evaluate the effectiveness of various job search strategies included in state RES efforts. Why, for example, did Nevada's 2009 reemployment demonstration seem to show greater effects of RES on the success of job search efforts than earlier studies that evaluated UI claimant exit rates (and mainly found RES deterred UI receipt)?

Evidence on the effectiveness of job search assistance for a different target population, welfare recipients, also has accumulated. This began with job search assistance studies in Louisville in the early 1980s that were the "most independent and robust" to that point and led to further studies and the widespread adoption of job search assistance as a strategy for state welfare reform efforts (Gueron and Rolston 2013, p. 83; Greenberg, Deitch, and Hamilton 2009, pp. 23–28). To learn more, the Office of Planning, Research, and Evaluation at the U.S. Department of Health and Human Services is currently undertaking a multiyear effort designed to learn more about the "effectiveness of various job search methods and the components of (job search assistance) programs" for the population served by the Temporary Assistance Needy Families program (Klerman et al. 2012, p. 1).

Ideally, a similar effort focused on UI claimants would shed light on the value of various job search assistance (RES) strategies for different groups of UI claimant job seekers. This information is needed even more if the system continues to operate with highly constrained budgets.

Increase State UI Administration Funding

Part of the reason there is a need for added funding for UI eligibility assessments is that the federal government has been underfunding state grants for employment services and UI administration. If the federal government appropriated sufficient funds for state administration of UI—say, about $200 million more per year—there might be no need to fund UI eligibility assessments separately because these could be part of normal UI program administration, if only states had enough administrative funding each year to execute them fully and properly.

This option faces the same political challenges as REA/RES and even more difficult budgetary challenges. The grants to states for UI administration category are defined as discretionary spending as opposed to the mandatory spending for UI benefits and the proposed REA/RES program funding. Discretionary funding is subject to budget caps on spending by functional category. Any additional spending on state UI administration or employment services could not be offset by taxes or mandatory spending cuts, but rather would have to be within the discretionary spending caps as allocated to the respective Labor, Health and Human Services, and Education and Related Agencies Subcommittees in the Appropriations Committees of the United States House of Representatives and Senate (Collender 1993).

None of these recommendations are easy to enact or implement. However, each of them could help to improve the efficiency and the integrity of the UI system, and could cut government costs and, ultimately, employer unemployment taxes.

Notes

The authors thank our colleagues Jim Van Erden, for acquiring and displaying some of the data in the text, and Josie Link, for research assistance. We also thank Rick McHugh, an attorney with the National Employment Law Project, who reviewed an earlier draft and gave us some valuable suggestions. The authors' recommendations are their own and do not reflect the policy positions of the National Association of State Workforce Agencies.

1. These impact data are from a U.S. Department of Labor follow-up study (Michaelides 2013) that extended an original analysis (Poe-Yamagata et al. 2011) "using updated data on UI receipt and wages." The follow-up study made only slight changes to the impact estimates of the original study.
2. This is in contrast to the usual "discretionary spending," under which an aggregate amount would be appropriated for services and then allotted among the states. The mandatory funding is modeled after a recent, temporary REA/RES program that provided $85 per beneficiary. It was added to the Emergency Unemployment Compensation (EUC) program under the Middle Class Tax Relief and Job Creation Act of 2012 (P.L. 112-96).
3. The Congressional Budget Office (CBO) has not developed estimates on this proposal. Such estimates would be developed if the House Committee on Ways and Means were preparing to mark up a bill including such a program or if the CBO were producing a report on such reemployment programs.
4. The average weekly number of insured unemployed is a measure of workload that is calculated by dividing the total number of continued weeks of UI claimed by 52 weeks.
5. Supplemental budget requests are likely to decline because their source of funding, the difference between the projected funding that is needed and the actual funding for realized workload in the fiscal year, will shrink. This tends to happen as unemployment falls and projections overshoot actual costs.
6. REA and RES are terms that derive from recent federal statutes; they are used here regarding initiatives of earlier periods, even though the terms did not apply then. Loosely, REA includes assessing and enforcing UI eligibility and work search requirements, and RES includes job search assistance services (see Table 3.1). Several researchers and research organizations have catalogued and synthesized this evidence, including Wandner (2010) and Balducci, Eberts, and O'Leary (2004).
7. Benefit-to-cost ratios presented here are from the perspective of the workforce system (taking into account reductions in regular UI benefit payments) and not the government at large (also taking into account increases in tax revenue from boosted earnings). They ranged from about 1:1 to 4:1, with most estimates in the bottom half of that range. These high returns reflect the relatively low cost of services and relatively large reductions in UI benefit payments.
8. The federal REA grant program requires states to exclude claimants who seek

work only through their union hiring hall and claimants with a definite return-to-work date. Illinois targeted claimants with high-demand skills. All states limited REA to claimants who had received at least the first UI benefit payment and were able to work and available for work.

9. There was no impact in Illinois. The Illinois results are not conclusive because the REA program suffered from inconsistent implementation, and the evaluation was based on a small sample. Illinois restricted the program to claimants with high-demand skills. The Emergency Unemployment Compensation program was in effect during this period.

10. Based on the strong impacts in Nevada, USDOL conducted a follow-up study (Michaelides et al. 2012) that extended the Nevada analysis "using updated data on UI receipt and wages." The results of the original study held up, with only slight changes in the impact estimates (for example, the average reduction in regular UI benefit duration was 1.8 weeks, and the reduction in regular UI payments was $536).

11. A USDOL (2011) report included the following statement: ". . . cost information in the study, except for Nevada, does not include the cost of providing reemployment services or training. These costs could not be evaluated because they were not tracked for either the control or treatment groups. Nevada differs from the other states in this respect because the State, on its own initiative, decided to track the information to ensure an understanding of both the overall savings and to better understand how REAs assist claimants."

12. Email from Eileen Poe-Yamagata, of IMPAQ International, to Yvette Chocolaad, NASWA, June 22, 2014.

13. This study has been submitted to a labor economics journal.

14. The impetuses for these studies were changing labor market conditions (with proportionately more permanent layoffs during recessions that triggered concerns about structural unemployment, as outlined in the previous section) and federal budget constraints that required greater evidence-based justification for additional program investments (Wandner 2010).

15. For example, in the New Jersey demonstration, among other activities, claimants were notified by letter of a requirement to participate, to attend an orientation, and to make periodic contact to discuss job search activities. These activities are common to many UI eligibility monitoring initiatives, such as the REA initiatives of the current era.

16. Also, while earnings outcomes have not been the primary focus of the studies, collectively the studies show no or small and positive impacts on earnings and/or wages.

17. See the USDOL workforce3one.org Web site link: https://reemploymentworks. workforce3one.org/ws/reemploymentworks/pages/summit.aspx?pparams= (accessed November 7, 2014).

Appendix 3A

Summary of Evidence on the Effectiveness of Job Search Assistance for Unemployment Insurance Claimants (1989–2006)

Table 3A.1

• Strengthening Connections between UI and One-Stop Delivery Systems (2004). A USDOL-funded demonstration in Wisconsin tested the combination of enhanced UI eligibility oversight with either of two intensities of job search assistance for claimants screened in through the Worker Profiling and Reemployment Services initiative. Profiled claimants less-prepared for job search or with few transferable skills were required to participate in comprehensive job search assistance, while those with better job search skills or more transferable skills were given minimal assistance. Overall, comparing treatment and control groups, the program reduced average UI duration by 0.6 of a week and UI benefits by $147. For those in the first treatment group (intensive services), average UI duration fell nearly a week and benefits by $233 (Almandsmith, Adams, and Bos 2006).

• Evaluation of WPRS Systems (1996–1997). This six-state demonstration found that an intervention of minimal, mandatory job search assistance targeted on individuals screened as most likely to exhaust UI benefits reduced UI duration in five of the six states, from one day to one week. In the five states, UI benefits were reduced an average of from $21 to $140. The following was one conclusion from the study:

> "Our customer satisfaction survey found that customers highly valued more extensive services, and those who received such services found [them] much more helpful than other claimants . . . [S]tates in which [the intervention] reduced UI receipt were also states with large impacts on claimants' receipt of services. Improving [services], therefore, is likely to both increase customer satisfaction and result in greater UI savings" (Dickinson, Decker, and Kreutzer 2002, pp. 77–78).

• Job Search Assistance Demonstration (1995–1996). A demonstration in Washington, D.C., and Florida, targeted on those with the highest probabilities of exhausting benefits, tested two different job search assistance interventions and found that they reduced average UI duration by nearly a half week (Florida) and one week (D.C.), and UI exhaustion rates by 4 percent (Florida) and 8 percent (D.C.). Note that in Florida, participation requirements were not strongly enforced. The authors recommended that

> "If states want to expand services received by claimants . . . states should make particular services mandatory for all claimants referred to [the intervention], or at least encourage local offices to be aggressive in using individual service plans to set and enforce service requirements." (Decker et al. 2000, p. xxvi)

(continued)

Table 3A.1

• Worker Profiling and Reemployment Services in Kentucky (1994–1996). A demonstration in Kentucky to gauge the effects of targeting RES on those most likely to exhaust benefits required that profiled UI claimants attend an in-person orientation. The claimants were referred to a minimal package of job search assistance services. The program reduced UI duration an average of over two weeks and UI benefits by $143, and appears to have been highly cost-effective (no formal analysis was done, but the reported cost of the intervention was $22 per recipient, on average) (Black et al. 2003).

• Maryland UI Work Search Demonstration (1994). This demonstration that did not involve targeting was focused on examining the cost-effectiveness of various work search policies. It found that new UI claimants required to participate in a time-intensive job search assistance workshop received UI for an average of a half week less than claimants in a control group, and received an average of $75 less in UI benefit payments (Benus 1997).

• Reemploy Minnesota (1988–1990). A state-funded demonstration in Minnesota provided personalized and intensive job search assistance modeled after the New Jersey demonstration (see below). It targeted all UI claimants except those on short-term layoff, with union membership, or enrolled in training. The job search assistance intervention reduced UI duration an average of four weeks, with a benefit-cost ratio of 2.0 from the perspective of the workforce system (Greenberg and Shroder 2004).

• Nevada Claimant Employment Program (1988–1989). A demonstration in Nevada that was not restricted to permanently separated workers or those most likely to exhaust UI tested the idea that intensive services are cost-effective and emphasized "adequate time to deal with claimants." It found that intensive, staff-assisted job search assistance reduced UI duration an average of two weeks, more than paying for itself with a benefit-cost ratio of over 2.0 considering reductions in UI benefit payments (Hanna and Turney 1990).

• New Jersey UI Reemployment Demonstration (1986–1987). This demonstration tested identifying displaced workers early in their UI claims and providing RES to speed reemployment. UI claimants over 25 who had been with their previous employer three or more years (but not on short-term layoff or with union membership) were required to participate in job search assistance composed of comprehensive, personalized services. The intervention reduced UI duration by an average of a half week, and the UI benefit exhaustion rate by 6.7 percent. Benefit payments declined an average of $87. The intervention paid for itself when taking into account reductions in UI benefit payments. Subgroup findings suggested the intervention had the

> " . . . greatest impact on workers who had readily marketable skills and experience . . . the demonstration might have had an even greater impact on UI receipt if the eligibility requirements had been set whereby a wider range of claimants were enrolled, including those whose reemployment prospects were relatively good" (USDOL 1989, 1990, 1996).

NOTE: See also Balducci, Eberts, and O'Leary (2004); Greenberg and Shroder (2004); and Wandner (2010).

References

Almandsmith, Sherry, Lorena Ortiz Adams, and Han Bos. 2006. *Evaluation of the Strengthening the Connections between Unemployment Insurance and the One-Stop Delivery Systems Demonstration Project in Wisconsin, Final Report*. Oakland, CA: Berkeley Policy Associates.

Balducci, David E., Randall W. Eberts, and Christopher J. O'Leary. 2004. *Labor Exchange Policy in the United States*. Kalamazoo, MI: W.E. Upjohn Institute for Employment Research.

Barnow, Burt S., and Richard A. Hobbie. 2013. *The American Recovery and Reinvestment Act: The Role of Workforce Programs*. Kalamazoo, MI: W.E. Upjohn Institute for Employment Research.

Benus, Jacob. 1997. *Evaluation of the Maryland Unemployment Insurance Work Search Demonstration*. Prepared for the Maryland Department of Labor, Licensing and Regulation (DLLR). Bethesda, MD: Abt Associates. http://www.oui.doleta.gov/dmstree/op/op98/op_02-98.pdf (accessed July 3, 2014).

Black, Dan A., Jeffrey A. Smith, Mark C. Berger, and Brett J. Noel. 2003. "Is the Threat of Reemployment Services More Effective than the Services Themselves? Evidence from Random Assignment in the UI System." Washington, DC: U.S. Department of Labor. http://www-personal.umich.edu/~econjeff/Papers/AER012703.pdf (accessed April 21, 2014).

California Department of Human Resources v. Java 402 U.S. 121 (1971).

Collender, Stanley. 1993. *The Guide to the Federal Budget: Fiscal 1994*. Washington, DC: Urban Institute.

Decker, Paul T., Robert B. Olsen, Lance Freeman, and Daniel H. Klepinger. 2000. *Assisting Unemployment Insurance Claimants: The Long-Term Impacts of the Job Search Assistance Demonstration*. Report prepared for U.S. Department of Labor, Unemployment Insurance Service. Washington, DC: Mathematica Policy Research. http://wdr.doleta.gov/owsdrr/00-2/00-02.pdf (accessed April 21, 2014).

Dickinson, Katherine, Paul Decker, and Suzanne Kreutzer. 2002. "Evaluation of WPRS Systems." In *Targeting Employment Services*, Randall W. Eberts, Christopher J. O'Leary, and Stephen A. Wandner, eds. Kalamazoo, MI: W.E. Upjohn Institute for Employment Research, pp. 61–90.

Eberts, Randall W., and Stephen A. Wandner, 2013. "Data Analysis of the Implementation of the Recovery Act Workforce Development and Unemployment Insurance Provisions." Kalamazoo, MI: W.E. Upjohn Institute for Employment Research.

Greenberg, David, and Mark Shroder. 2004. *The Digest of Social Experiments*. 3d ed. Washington, DC: Urban Institute.

Greenberg, David H., Victoria Deitch, and Gayle Hamilton. 2009. "Welfare-to-Work Program Benefits and Costs: A Synthesis of Research." Oakland, CA, and New York: MDRC.

Groshen, Erica L. 2011. "Temporary Layoffs during the Great Recession." *Liberty Street Economics* (blog), April 6. Federal Reserve Bank of New York. http://libertystreeteconomics.newyorkfed.org/2011/04/temporary-layoffs -during-the-great-recession.html#.U7WpEfldVuM (accessed November 6, 2014).

Gueron, Judith M., and Howard Rolston. 2013. *Fighting for Reliable Evidence.* New York: Russell Sage.

Hanna, James, and Zina Turney. 1990. "The Economic Impact of the Nevada Claimant Employment Program." UI Occasional Paper 90-4. Washington, DC: U.S. Department of Labor, Employment and Training Administration.

Johnson, Terry R. 1991. "Evaluation of the Impacts of the Washington Alternative Work Search Experiment." UI Occasional Paper 91-4. Washington, DC: U.S. Department of Labor, Employment and Training Administration. http://workforcesecurity.doleta.gov/dmstree/op/op91/op_04-91.pdf (accessed November 6, 2014).

Klerman, Jacob, Robin Koralck, Ashley Miller, and Katherine Wen. 2012. *Job Search Assistance Programs—A Review of the Literature.* OPRE Report No. 2012-39. Washington, DC: U.S. Department of Health and Human Services. http://www.acf.hhs.gov/sites/default/files/opre/job_search.pdf (accessed July 3, 2014).

Michaelides, Marios. 2013. "Are Reemployment Services Effective in Periods of High Unemployment? Experimental Evidence from the Great Recession." Unpublished paper.

Michaelides, Marios, Eileen Poe-Yamagata, Jacob Benus, and Dharmendra Tirumalasetti. 2012. *Impact of the Reemployment and Eligibility Assessment (REA) Initiative in Nevada.* Columbia, MD: IMPAQ International.

Miller, Reagan. 2013. "Focus on Back to Work: How Claimant Reemployment Helped Transform Texas Workforce Solutions." NASWA webinar presentation. http://naswa.org/assets/utilities/serve.cfm?1=1&gid=4d22d992-da2a -4c04-9483-5bf432be580d&PATH=&SAVE=0&IS_CLICKTHROUGH =0&dsp_meta=0 (accessed November 7, 2014).

National Association of State Workforce Agencies (NASWA). 2004. "NASWA Letter to USDOL Re: Taking Balanced Approach to REA and RES." Letter to Honorable Emily Stover DeRocco from NASWA President Catherine B. Leapheart. Washington, DC: NASWA.

Poe-Yamagata, Eileen, Jacob Benus, Nicholas Bill, Hugh Carrington, Marios Michaelides, and Ted Shen. 2011. *Impact of the Reemployment and Eligibility Assessment (REA) Initiative.* Columbia, MD: IMPAQ International.

U.S. Department of Labor (USDOL). 1971. *The Java Decision.* UI Occasional Paper 11-26. Washington, DC: U.S. Department of Labor, Manpower Administration. http://ows.doleta.gov/dmstree/uipl/uipl_pre75/uipl_1126 .htm (accessed July 7, 2014).

———. 1989. *New Jersey Unemployment Insurance Reemployment Demonstration Project.* UI Occasional Paper 89-3. Washington, DC: U.S. Department of Labor, Employment and Training Administration. http://work forcesecurity.doleta.gov/dmstree/op/op89/op_03-89.pdf (accessed April 21, 2014).

———. 1990. "UI Research Exchange." UI Occasional Paper 90-4. Washington, DC: U.S. Department of Labor, Employment and Training Administration. http://workforcesecurity.doleta.gov/dmstree/op/op90/op_04-90.pdf (accessed April 21, 2014).

———. 1996. "The New Jersey Unemployment Insurance Reemployment Demonstration Project: Six-Year Follow-Up and Summary Report Revised Edition." UI Occasional Paper 96-2. Washington, DC: U.S. Department of Labor, Employment and Training Administration. http://workforcesecurity .doleta.gov/dmstree/op/op96/op_02-96.pdf (accessed December 4, 2014).

———. 1997. "Employment Service Program Letter No. 01-98." Washington, DC: U.S. Department of Labor, Employment and Training Administration. http://workforcesecurity.doleta.gov/dmstree/espl/es98/espl_01-98 .htm (accessed December 4, 2014).

———. 2009. *Regional Recovery and Reemployment Forums: Final report.* Prepared by TATC Consulting. Bethesda, MD: TATC Consulting. http:// www.doleta.gov/Regional_Forums_Final_Report_062609.pdf (accessed July 3, 2014).

———. 2010. *A National Call for Innovation: Rethinking Reemployment Services for UI Claimants—A Report of the Unemployment Insurance and Workforce System Connectivity Group.* Washington, DC: U.S. Department of Labor. http://naswa.org/assets/utilities/serve.cfm?path=/sections/pdf/2010/ UI_Connectivity_Baseline_Final_Report_20101018.pdf (accessed December 4, 2014).

———. 2011. *Report to Congress on FY 2009 Appropriation for Reemployment and Eligibility Assessments.* Washington, DC: USDOL.

———. 2014. "FY 2015 Congressional Budget Justification: Employment and Training Administration." Washington, DC: U.S. Department of Labor, Employment and Training Administration.

Wandner, Stephen. 2010. *Solving the Reemployment Puzzle: From Research to Policy.* Kalamazoo, MI: W.E. Upjohn Institute for Employment Research.

———. 2013. "The Public Workforce System's Response to Declining Funding after the Great Recession." Working Paper No. 5. Washington, DC: Urban Institute.

4

Learn and Earn

Connecting Education to
Careers in the 21st Century

Anthony P. Carnevale
Andrew R. Hanson
Georgetown University Center on Education and the Workforce

By 2020, 65 percent of job openings will require at least some postsecondary education and training (Carnevale and Smith 2013). However, not all higher education is created equal: the costs, risks, and returns on postsecondary education and training programs are highly variable. For today's high school graduates, and an increasing share of middle-aged adults, decisions about whether to enroll in college, which institution to attend, and which program of study to pursue will have critical economic consequences.

As things now stand, however, they are making those decisions in an information vacuum. The U.S. postsecondary education system is a kaleidoscope of institutions and interests, and educational policies vary from state to state. Most importantly, there is no unified data system that connects postsecondary fields of study and degrees with actual labor market demands. Such a system would enable students to better understand how their training is likely to fit into the real-world job market, and it would also motivate institutions to be more accountable for shaping their programs to fit their students' needs.

The good news is that the data and technology needed to create such a system already exist, and the costs of integrating them into a unified whole are relatively low. The federal government is the logical place to house the exchange: given the frequency with which people, especially new college graduates, move across state lines, it would be difficult for any given state to track its labor market outcomes. Only one major barrier remains—a 2008 federal ban on the creation of a student unit record system. Currently, the federal government collects data at the institution level, rather than the student level, which prevents users of the data from answering questions about what students learned while enrolled, as well as what happens to them in the labor market after they graduate, and how outcomes vary for students with different demographic characteristics. Proponents of the ban, largely from the higher education sector, cite privacy concerns, but colleges and universities are already legally required to send student-level data to the Department of Defense and Internal Revenue Service, and already voluntarily send data on more than 140 million students to the private National Student Clearinghouse (McCann and Laitinen 2014).

The Great Recession left millions of college graduates looking for jobs, and since then the media, students, and parents have devoted increasing attention to the value proposition of postsecondary education. The need for more transparency in the higher education sector has become apparent, and politicians have stepped in. In 2013, Senators Ron Wyden (D-OR) and Marco Rubio (R-FL) introduced the Student Right to Know Before You Go Act, which would repeal the federal ban on a student unit record system and require postsecondary institutions to report labor market outcomes of their graduates. McCann and Laitinen (2014) detail the political barriers obstructing the repeal of the ban, but there is broad bipartisan support.

But connecting the dots in the data we already have is only the beginning. As the time it takes for young people to gain traction in the labor market has lengthened, we need to find ways to simplify and accelerate the transition from education to careers. This includes strengthening career education, tying the funding of postsecondary education and training programs with cost and labor market demand, strengthening connections among institutions with education and employment missions, and scaling up competency-based education initiatives. This chapter will outline the new realities of the U.S. labor market and explore ways in which a learning-labor exchange could help students and institutions adapt to those new realities.

WHAT WE KNOW ABOUT THE LINK BETWEEN
EDUCATION AND THE LABOR MARKET

- *On average, more education pays.* Over a lifetime, college graduates earn $2.3 million on average, compared to $1.3 million for high
  school graduates (Carnevale, Rose, and Cheah 2011). This earnings
  gap appears to be widening: the wage premium workers receive from
  a college education—the difference in earnings between high school
  and college graduates—increased from 40 percent in 1970 to 84 percent in 2010.

- *Majors and fields of study have an even larger influence on earnings than degree level.* Within and across degree levels, people have
  vastly different earnings:

  - College graduates who majored in the highest-paying fields earn
    up to three times as much as those who majored in the lowest-
    paying fields (Carnevale, Strohl, and Melton 2011), making the
    difference in earnings between the most- and least-paid college
    graduate greater than the difference between the average college
    and high school graduates.

  - A bachelor's degree in petroleum engineering translates into a
    median annual wage of $120,000, compared with $29,000 a year
    for a bachelor's degree in counseling psychology. And while
    degrees from prestigious institutions do confer advantages, a
    teacher with a bachelor's degree from Harvard still typically
    makes less than an engineer with an associate's degree from a
    community college.

  - The choice of majors also affects college graduates' chances of
    landing a job in the first place. The unemployment rate of recent
    college graduates for information systems, for instance, was
    nearly 14.7 percent, compared to 4.8 percent for graduates who
    majored in nursing (Carnevale and Cheah 2013).

  - The importance of field of study is so powerful that workers
    with less education in one field frequently earn higher wages
    than those with more education in another. Overall, 30 percent
    of workers with an associate's degree earn more than the median

worker with a bachelor's degree (Carnevale, Rose, and Cheah 2011), and one-quarter of male certificate holders earn more than the median male bachelor's degree holder (Carnevale, Rose, and Hanson 2012).

- *Occupations also play a strong role in determining wage and employment outcomes.* Workers with less education can out-earn those with more education if they gain access to high-paying occupations. For example, an engineering technician with an associate's degree typically earns more than a high school guidance counselor with a master's degree.

- *Within occupations, degree level still matters in determining earnings.* Among engineers, for example, an associate's degree holder earns $65,000 annually, a bachelor's degree holder earns $85,000, and a graduate degree holder earns $103,000.[1]

THE SHORTAGE OF SKILLED WORKERS AND THE NEED FOR A MORE EFFICIENT EDUCATION AND TRAINING SYSTEM

Despite the high average economic returns to higher education, the supply of skilled workers in the United States has not kept pace with employer demand (Carnevale and Rose 2011). Since 1983, the demand for college-educated workers has grown by an average rate of 3 percent each year, while the supply has only grown by 2 percent. As the demand for postsecondary education and training has increased, high school graduates have been left behind. Between 1970 and 2010, high school–educated men's wages declined by 41 percent (Jacobs 2013a), as young men have lost access to middle-wage, blue-collar jobs in the manufacturing industry and have been forced to shift into lower-paying food, personal service, sales, and office support occupations (Carnevale, Hanson, and Gulish 2013). In short, the failure of the U.S. human capital development system to adequately develop in-demand skills in its workforce has created a paradox: a large number of highly skilled job vacancies at a time when millions of Americans are looking for work (Jacobs 2013b).

Among high school students, college-age young adults, and older adults, the United States lags substantially behind its peers in literacy, numeracy, and problem solving in technology-rich environments (OECD 2013). U.S. teenagers and high school graduates have weaker basic skills than their international peers, especially in math, where 25 percent score below the baseline level, compared to 10 percent in Finland and Korea (Kuczera and Field 2013). What's more, they don't seem to be catching up: between 1994 and 2004, there was no growth in U.S. teenagers' literacy skills (Desjardins and Warnke 2012). Baby boomers rank average in numeracy skills relative to their international peers, and American teenagers and college-age adults rank dead last in numeracy (OECD 2013).

In terms of postsecondary attainment, the United States is actually losing ground to its international peers. The baby boom generation ranked first in bachelor's degree attainment and third in postsecondary attainment internationally, but today's generation of young adults ranks 12th in bachelor's degree attainment and 11th in postsecondary attainment overall.[2] The largest room for growth is in career-focused associate's degree programs, where the United States ranks 17th internationally, at 10 percent. By comparison, 25 percent of young adults in Canada earn a career-focused associate's degree.

Under current projections, the United States will need 11 million more workers with postsecondary credentials between 2014 and 2020 to satisfy the labor market's demand for college-educated workers.[3] The recession of 2007–2009 led to the decline of low-skill construction and manufacturing jobs, replaced by jobs in health care, biotech, nanotech, clean energy, and advanced manufacturing jobs, most of which require at least an associate's degree (Soares and Steigleder 2012). This increased the level of skills mismatch in the labor market, as former construction and manufacturing workers scrambled to retrain and move into different careers (Şahin et al. 2012).

Closing the gap between the supply and demand for skilled workers will pay off in higher wages for workers (due to higher skill levels and productivity). Higher-paid workers will mean more tax revenue for federal, state, and local governments and less dependency on government programs; more productive workers will boost employer profits and lead to higher economic growth, which benefits everybody. Education contributed one-third of the U.S. economy's productivity gains between 1950 and 2000 (Carnevale and Rose 2011). Adding an extra year of schooling for all Americans by 2025 would increase gross domestic product (GDP) growth by between $500 billion and $1 trillion, providing an additional $150 billion in state, local, and federal taxes.[4]

How can we close the gap between the lagging supply of skilled workers and the growing demand? High school graduates enroll in postsecondary programs at a high rate (70 percent); the problem is that not enough of them actually finish. There are now 75 million Americans in their prime working years (aged 25–54) who do not have a postsecondary credential. Nearly 37 million have some college credit, and roughly 15 million have at least two years of college credit. Increasing the production of the U.S. education and training system by 11 million workers with postsecondary credentials is a feasible task, but it will require increasing college completion rates as well as developing high-quality adult education and workforce development programs to educate and retrain prime-age workers forced to change careers due to changing labor market dynamics, as workers shift from blue-collar jobs to high-skill service jobs.

The United States comprises three primary sectors charged with education and training missions: 1) K–12 schools, 2) postsecondary education and training institutions, and 3) employers. Altogether, they account for roughly $1.6 trillion of spending on human capital development: $610 billion on K–12 general education, $483 billion on postsecondary education, and $528 billion on employer-based training ($164 billion on formal training and $364 billion on informal, on-the-job training).[5]

A lot of those dollars are spent ineffectively. Workforce development programs in this nation, particularly services funded under the Workforce Investment Act (WIA), are too focused on getting unemployed and displaced workers into jobs instead of engaging them in a long-term skill development strategy, though the evidence demonstrates that this is a less effective strategy (Jacobs 2013a). Unlike its international peers, the United States does not invest in active labor market policies, such as job training. We rank 28th—second to last—in federal expenditures on workforce training among developed countries, spending only 0.1 percent of our GDP compared to the 0.7 percent average, and 1 percent in Germany and Denmark (Jacobs 2013a). The U.S.

workforce development system should operate as part of an ongoing education and training system for workers, not merely as a massive job placement service.

In other developed countries, workforce development institutions largely operate separately from institutions primarily focused on general, academic education. In the United States, however, this is not the case—postsecondary programs with academic education and workforce missions are located at the same institutions. In fact, the majority of postsecondary programs of study are career focused: 57 percent of postsecondary degrees and awards are in fields primarily focused on preparing students and trainees for the labor market.[6]

However, improving education and training will require increased public spending, which makes it politically unfeasible for at least the near future. More to the point, what we spend now is spent ineffectively. Ours is one of the least productive education and training systems among developed nations, as measured by the postsecondary attainment rate relative to spending on education and training as a share of GDP (Carnevale, Hanson, and Gulish 2013). Put more simply, we rank 11th in postsecondary attainment despite spending more than anybody else. Most of that spending has been at the federal level: between 2000 and 2010, total federal aid to postsecondary education more than doubled, to $169 billion. At the same time, state expenditures per pupil at postsecondary institutions declined because of budget constraints and growing enrollment reflecting increased demand for postsecondary education and training (U.S. Department of Education 2012).

Proposals to reform education and training in the United States should focus, then, on enhancing the productivity and efficiency of its education and training system. Technological innovations have shown some promise to improve pedagogy and learning, but the best way to enhance productivity is to align education and training programs with the competencies the labor market demands. As it is, many students are making poor choices about what to study, and many postsecondary education and training institutions are funneling students into postsecondary programs of study that do not lead to gainful employment. Jacobson and LaLonde (2013) find, for example, that only one-quarter of Florida community college students complete a degree or certificate with a moderate or high return. Carnevale, Rose, and Hanson (2012) find that half of postsecondary certificates do not meet that standard (even though certificates do pay off, on average).[7] Additionally, among women who either dropped out of college before earning a credential or earned an associate's degree, 52 percent work in jobs that only require a high school diploma.[8]

The public should prioritize funding education and training programs that have labor market value. Promoting our citizens' autonomy as individuals—their ability to access a broad array of cultural goods and fully participate in a democracy—is an important goal, but it cannot be met until individuals can meet their basic needs. The inescapable reality is that work is central in American society. Those unequipped with the knowledge and skills necessary to get, and keep, good jobs are denied full social inclusion and tend to drop out of the mainstream culture, polity, and economy. In the worst cases, they are drawn into alternative cultures, political movements, and economic activities that pose a threat to mainstream American life.

Moreover, if public money is not spent funding education and training programs that promote access to high-paying careers, it is a missed opportunity to move low-income Americans and other disadvantaged social groups into the middle class. It is also a missed opportunity to increase the skills and productivity of the workforce, which would lead to broader growth and economic prosperity for all Americans.

FOUR IDEAS FOR REFORMING EDUCATION AND TRAINING IN THE TWENTY-FIRST CENTURY

Promote Transparency in the Outcomes of Education and Training Programs by Building a Learning-Labor Exchange

The most cost-effective way to ensure education and training programs are effectively preparing students and trainees for the labor market is to ensure that students, educators, practitioners, and policymakers are making informed decisions that are in line with their goals. Because the costs, risks, and returns to postsecondary programs of study are so highly variable, we need more quality, coherence, and transparency in cost and outcomes.

The current major source of data about postsecondary institutions, the Integrated Postsecondary Education Data System (IPEDS), is plagued with problems. It was designed for a postsecondary education system that mostly comprised 18-year-old high school graduates who enrolled full time at a four-year college or university and graduated from the same institution within three to five years. This means that IPEDS does not include data on half of students enrolled at two-year colleges, outcomes for students who take longer than the typical completion time, the academic preparedness of students, or students who have not graduated but are still enrolled. The federal government cannot even analyze the effectiveness of Pell Grants, the largest federal investment in higher education.[9]

However, addressing the problems with IPEDS still leaves another major problem with the current mechanisms for evaluating postsecondary programs of study: the lack of transparency about the labor market outcomes of students and trainees who enroll in and complete postsecondary education and training programs. Building a learning-labor exchange will allow us to assess the extent to which particular education and training programs result in tangible employment outcomes. Such an exchange could be used to track outcomes from early childhood education through high school, postsecondary education, and the workforce. Already, we have earnings data in state unemployment insurance (UI) databases that can be linked to transcript record data using individuals' Social Security numbers. The Department of Labor's Wage Record Interchange System facilitates the sharing of wage data across states. In addition, there is the Department of Education's State Longitudinal Data Systems (SLDS) grant program, which funds state-based programs that integrate education data in P-20 data warehouses that link student records between pre-K and college into a single system. Of the 25 states that have received grants under the SLDS program so far, Florida, Utah, and Texas have developed advanced data systems that in turn link this education data to workforce and public assistance data (Eyster, Anderson, and Durham 2013). For example, California's community college system has used these data to develop a "salary surfer" Web tool, which allows students and career counselors to determine their likely salaries and probability of finding a job for given occupations and industries.[10] Pennsylvania has developed a similar tool called

"Career Coach." However, these tools have not been established for a long enough time frame for researchers to assess their effectiveness.

Building a learning and labor exchange would require minimal up-front costs, but those costs would generate long-run savings because of the reduced regulatory burden on education and training institutions and the decreased need for the assorted surveys and disconnected data they use now. Vollman and Carnevale (2009) estimate that the start-up costs would be roughly $60 million for the most comprehensive learning and labor exchange, along with $14 million in ongoing costs, a small fraction of a percent of the $295 billion of public spending on postsecondary education and training each year (Snyder and Dillow 2013).

A learning-labor exchange would also minimize the need for aggressive federal oversight or costly state regulations, such as the roughly 850,000 hours that institutions spend annually to comply with the reporting requirements for IPEDS (Laitinen 2014). However, the information system that would most effectively increase the efficiency of our education and training system is a student unit record system, which would collect data directly from and about students, as opposed to aggregated data from institutions; this practice is currently prohibited by law.[11] Congress should repeal this prohibition in the pending reauthorization of the Higher Education Act. A student unit record system would provide unique student identifiers through Social Security numbers that could be connected to from states' unemployment insurance records, which contain data on wages, occupations, and employers. The two information "feedstocks"—transcript records and wage records—needed to build a learning and labor exchange have already been developed, they just need to be connected. Repealing the student unit record ban, along with passage of the Student Right to Know Before You Go Act, which has received bipartisan support, would create the foundation for a learning-labor exchange that would fundamentally restructure our education and training system for the twenty-first century.

Another approach would be to create online learning exchanges, in which job-search engines would match job openings and career pathways to specific courses being offered by traditional postsecondary institutions and online degree programs. These learning exchanges would promote healthy market competition among postsecondary institutions, which in turn would minimize the need for aggressive federal oversight or expensive state regulation. In other words, greater transparency would lead to more informed consumers and policymakers, which would encourage consumers to vote with their feet and institutions to focus on the labor market value of their programs instead of prestige.

The Department of Education is the ideal institution to administer the learning-labor exchange. First, centralizing the data would create economies of scale and cost efficiencies to replace our current system, in which each state runs its own exchange. It would also allow students, families, and policymakers to compare the efficacy of programs of study and institutions across various states. And it is a natural role for the federal government to play, given its substantial investments in postsecondary institutions.

But a learning-labor exchange alone will not ensure success at promoting the alignment between education and careers. The next step is to ensure that the high-quality information gets into the hands of those it would benefit, via user-friendly tools and information campaigns. Report cards, similar to the Department of Education's "College Scorecard," should be published at the program level, and should include such information as expected earnings, the job placement rate, the probability of completion based on students' characteristics (academic background, work experience, interests, financial resources, and family constraints), program cost, loan default rate, and median loan amount.[12] Because career counselors within institutions may not provide objective guidance about the effectiveness of programs of study at their institutions (Kuczera and Field 2013), we need public information tools and initiatives.

Develop Outcome Standards for Education and Training Programs to Ensure the Public Is Getting the Most Bang for Its Buck

Transparency itself won't be enough to move individuals and institutions toward programs with demonstrable labor market value; there should also be outcome standards in order to receive public funds. Given the size of its investment, the public has not done enough to hold institutions accountable for how public dollars are spent and whether education and training programs are effective. This is due to the public's limited access to information, as well as to the fact that workforce development programs and postsecondary programs have a variety of definitions for what constitutes successful program outcomes.

Taken together, this lack of transparency and outcome standards means that ineffective public and private training programs continue to attract trainees and public funds that could be used more effectively. The Obama administration's proposed Gainful Employment regulations provide a framework for establishing a minimum outcome standard for the receipt of public funds. The regulations are designed to evaluate the effectiveness of certificate programs at Title IV institutions and all education and training programs at for-profit colleges (except liberal arts bachelor's degree programs). In total, the regulations will apply to more than 55,000 programs at 5,600 postsecondary institutions (U.S. Department of Education 2011).

Employability is an appropriate metric for all postsecondary programs; students ought to know their probability of finding a job and comparative earnings level after completing a postsecondary program of study. At the same time, gainful employment regulations should only be used to regulate postsecondary programs of study that promise employment and earnings as a direct effect. Programs focused on academic education, by contrast, can use weighted metrics that also include assessments of learning.[13]

The core metrics that could be used as outcome standards are earnings, job placement in field, student loan debt default rate, and debt-to-earnings ratio. These metrics are better alternatives than completion, cost, and learning metrics alone. For example, completion itself is a poor indicator of success. If an enrollee completes a program and can't find a job, or ends up working in a job with lower wages than when she started, why should completion be viewed as a success? Why should a trainee who acquires valuable skills and drops out of a training program to work in a high-wage job be counted as a failure? Moreover, maximizing completion rates can be counterproductive if they simply encourage institutions to shift enrollments to less-challenging programs or to serve the most-advantaged students. Nursing programs are more difficult to complete than cosmetology programs, but some completions are more valuable than others; nursing graduates are more employable and more highly paid than cosmetology graduates. Gainful employment metrics can also improve cost metrics by evaluating program costs relative to earnings returns. Nursing programs also cost more than cosmetology programs, but the earnings returns are much higher for nursing.

Similarly, postsecondary education and training accreditors should utilize these metrics in their accreditation standards. At some accrediting bodies, these initiatives are already under way. For example, the Accrediting Council for Independent Colleges and Schools, a major national career-related education accrediting body, requires accredited education and training institutions to report graduates' job placement rate in their field of study. Institutions must maintain a job placement rate of 60 percent or higher in order to remain accredited. While the majority of postsecondary education and training institutions are subject to academically focused accreditation standards, they should be updated to align with twenty-first century demands by incorporating labor market metrics.

Simplify and Accelerate the Transition between Education and Careers

Compared to other developed countries, the transition from high school to postsecondary education and training in the United States is lengthy and complex. For example, high school graduates can spend 10 years or more navigating the postsecondary system before entering the labor market, while apprenticeships in European countries generally enroll students in their late teens, allowing them to earn while learning and achieve competencies in their target careers by their early twenties. The United States is moving in the opposite direction: here, the age at which young adults gain traction in the labor market actually increased from 26 in 1980 to 30 in 2012 (Carnevale, Hanson, and Gulish 2013). There are two major logjams: between high school and postsecondary education, and between postsecondary education and career.

One reason for the first difficulty is that high school curricula are largely focused on purely abstract, academic content, so students are required to enroll in a postsecondary program of study in order to gain exposure to career preparation and guidance.[14] In part because students are not exposed to career options in high school, they do not make strategic decisions about their careers until much later in life. In some cases, the first career guidance young adults encounter is at One-Stop Career Centers (financed by the Department of Labor through WIA) after they become unemployed.

Strengthening career and technical education

To accelerate the transition between high school and postsecondary education, school districts, and state and local governments should develop and strengthen career and technical education programs. Career and technical education represents an opportunity to build an academically rigorous middle pathway that strikes a balance between abstract academic content and learning by doing. Research has already shown that this kind of career and technical education engages students, improves their math and reading skills (Stone et al. 2006), and prevents young men in particular from dropping out of high school. Countries that offer strong career and technical education pathways have more success at transitioning young people into the labor market than those with a uniform pathway, as in the United States.

Such high school career and technical education programs should bridge either directly into the labor market or into a career-focused postsecondary program of study, as well as allow for lifelong learning and upward career and educational mobility. To ensure the curriculum will be rigorous, matched to labor market demand, and confer a credential with labor market value, curriculum developers should use industry-recognized standards to plan courses of study. To ensure that these courses are relevant to specific labor market demands, they should cooperate with local employers, Workforce Investment Boards, community colleges, and regional economic developers. At the same time, career and technical education curricula must maintain their academic rigor. The demise of vocational education in the 1970s was due to its lack of rigor, which effectively shut out students from pursuing further education.

These programs must be state-led, since the main federal program that supports career and technical education, the Perkins Act, provides only roughly $1 billion of the $20 billion spent nationally on high school career and technical education programs.[15] Federal funding can incentivize states to spend money effectively, but for the most part, states must scale up these programs themselves. Texas, for example, has especially scaled up career and technical education programs and enrolled more than 1 million students with greater than 90 percent of students meeting postsecondary performance standards for technical skills (Association for Career and Technical Education 2014).

High schools should also partner with local employers to expose students to a professional work environment by providing students with work-based learning opportunities such as internships, co-ops, and apprenticeships. Work-based learning also encourages students to think strategically about career decisions and, in many cases, earn wages to pay for further education and training along their chosen career ladders.

Alongside career and technical education, dual enrollment initiatives can accelerate young adults' entrance into the labor market. There is broad support for these initiatives; the problem lies in how the funding is allocated. The Office of Career, Technical, and Adult Education (formerly the Office of Vocational and Adult Education) provided a framework for articulation agreements for dual enrollment initiatives through revisions to the Perkins Act. The revisions would "require all consortia applying for state subgrants to establish or adopt secondary-postsecondary articulation agreements for each funded career and technical education program. State leaders would be expected to create statewide articulation agreements and encouraged to support policies that maximize the award of college credit to students who complete registered apprenticeship programs and industry-based training" (U.S. Department of Education 2012). Not only will dual enrollment accelerate the transition of young adults into careers, it will also give them access to a wider variety of courses than high schools alone can provide.

Creating stronger links between education and training institutions

The second logjam is the transition between postsecondary education and career. Unlike high school curricula, many postsecondary education and training programs focus on career preparation but remain plagued by the lack of alignment between their programs and the demands of the labor market.

Promoting transparency and developing outcome standards will promote this alignment, but reforms within institutions and at the state level are also needed to address problems at the micro level. There are administrative roadblocks, too—namely, funding mechanisms and decentralization, which create silos of disconnected institutions and programs that have similar goals but that cannot leverage the efficiencies that result from specialization and economies of scale. The critical next steps are to break down the barriers between education, job training, workforce development, and regional economic development.

Community colleges. Community colleges are the critical link at the center of the U.S. education and training system. Today, there is no single place where individuals can coordinate all their career development activities, locate all the education and training resources available to them, and find real-time information about local, regional, and national labor markets. Similarly, public support programs, such as Unemployment Insurance, do not provide beneficiaries with immediate information or resources about job search or retraining. Community colleges are the ideal institutions to integrate these services and resources, as most Americans are geographically proximate to a community college, and community colleges' missions are more focused on workforce development than other postsecondary institutions.[16]

The best community colleges have formed a web of relationships with high schools, four-year colleges and universities, regional employers, local Workforce Investment Boards, One-Stop Career Centers, and regional economic planners (Holzer 2011). The Pathways in Technology Early College High School has partnered with IBM and City University of New York to create a smooth transition between high school and high-demand jobs in information technology occupations. In an era of rapidly growing costs of postsecondary education and training, community colleges have effectively controlled costs. The average tuition for a student at a community college in 2013–2014 was $3,300, compared to $8,900 at public four-year colleges and $30,100 at four-year nonprofit colleges (College Board 2013).[17] Community colleges are the only postsecondary institutions that actually lowered their cost per full-time equivalent student between 1999 and 2009 (Desrochers and Wellman 2011).[18] They are, in short, ideally positioned to play a central role in order for the United States to tackle its projected supply shortfall of skilled workers.

However, community colleges currently face a supply shortfall of their own: money. They are unable to satisfy the demand for programs of study with high labor market returns due to the structure of funding mechanisms for postsecondary education and training, as well as recent budget constraints that have not kept pace with their growing enrollment.

Unbundling postsecondary education funding. In some cases, students do not enroll in programs of study with high labor market demand because they lack the academic skills necessary to succeed. Nearly 80 percent of enrollees in adult basic education and adult secondary education programs perform below the 9th grade level, and 40 percent perform below the 6th grade level (Rutschow and Crary-Ross 2014). But even after controlling for academic ability, students enroll in high-demand programs of study at relatively low rates (Holzer and Nightengale 2009).[19] This gap arises because in the current system, community colleges are funded based on enrollment, not on program costs or the labor market value of the program offered. This discourages them from expanding high-cost programs that have high labor market value, such as nursing and allied health programs; the long wait lists for admission into high-cost, in-demand programs tends to divert students into academic or liberal arts programs that can be provided at a relatively low cost. The result has been a shortage of career-oriented programs of study that prepare students for in-demand careers. In a market that operates efficiently, supply expands to meet demand. Enrollment-based funding prevents this from happening.

The solution to this supply problem is to unbundle and repackage the pricing mechanisms in postsecondary education. Institutions should charge higher tuition for programs of study that cost more to provide. This will give institutions an incentive to expand costly programs that have substantial labor market value. The impact of that higher tuition on students would be mitigated or offset completely in two ways: by financial incentives for students who complete their studies, and by replacing the current system of funding on the basis of enrollment alone with funding mechanisms that offer financial incentives to institutions that can show a high completion rate in courses with high labor market value.

Restructuring funding, though, will not address the problems posed by decentralization. A uniquely American phenomenon, decentralization has many benefits. By providing institutions with flexibility and autonomy, it encourages creativity and innovation. Because it brings a diverse mix of students into institutions via a variety of paths, it fosters an intellectually rich and creative environment. At the same time, decentralization creates confusion: because this diverse mix of young adults are not given clear guidance about what comes next, many get lost, change their minds, or find the educational system difficult to navigate. The result is increased costs and a longer route between school and career. Because the students who need the most help navigating this complex path frequently come from disadvantaged backgrounds, this confusion also exacerbates racial and class inequalities.

However, the solution is not necessarily to consolidate programs or institutions. There are 47 federal programs with workforce development elements, administered by nine federal agencies (Government Accountability Office 2011). That sounds inefficient, but many of those programs have specialized knowledge developed to serve specific groups. Consolidation might achieve minor administrative efficiencies at the cost of overall *effectiveness*.

Enhancing workforce development programs by leveraging partnerships. The most cost-effective form of workforce development training is high-intensity programs focused on developing skills and competencies, as opposed to short-term programs focused on job placement and labor force attachment (Jacobs 2013b). The problem is that workforce development programs lack the money to do this. Public spending on active labor market policies has been declining since the 1980s (Jacobs 2013a). In 1980, 34 percent of human capital investments by the federal government was spent on job training and employment services; by 2010, it was 9 percent. WIA, which provides job training for unemployed workers through the Title I Adults and Dislocated Workers Program, is currently funded at $3–$4 billion. If it were funded at the same level as the Comprehensive Employment and Training Act in 1979, it would receive $25–$30 billion.[20] Moreover, WIA, which was passed with broad bipartisan support, has not been reauthorized in the 10 years since it was first up for reauthorization in 2003.[21]

Given the lack of resources or political will to scale up workforce development programs to effectively target skill building, the next best alternative is to let these programs focus on what they can do well, while building stronger connections to other institutions in the education and training system, such as high schools, community colleges, and regional economic development agencies. The outcomes of every workforce development program, and every postsecondary program of study, should be evaluated by using common labor market metrics in the learning-labor exchange and by developing an outcome standard on which to base funding.

"Career pathways" is a model that connects the decentralized patchwork of education and training programs and institutions into a straightforward track toward in-demand careers. Washington State, California, Illinois, Minnesota, and Wisconsin have all piloted career pathways programs, as have national and regional initiatives led by the Joyce Foundation. Centered at community colleges, career pathways have been widely embraced as the most effective structure for promoting access and completion of postsecondary programs of study without stifling upward career mobility. The Department of Labor's Employment and Training Administration; the Department of Education, Office of Career, Technical, and Adult Education; and the Health and Human Services' Administration of Children and Families have all united to embrace the career pathways model. A career pathway is "a series of connected education and training programs and support services that enable individuals to secure employment within a specific industry or occupational sector, and to advance over time to successively higher levels of education and employment in that sector. Each step on a career pathway is designed explicitly to prepare the participant for the next level of employment and education" (U.S. Department of Education 2012). Career pathways combine adult basic education and career training on the path to a postsecondary credential with labor market value, while forgoing excessive remediation. They also use stackable credentials, which allow students to earn marketable certificates and certifications on their way to more ambitious degrees and career goals. Career pathways programs also accelerate program completion by teaching general education and career education simultaneously.

This approach will alleviate the disadvantages of decentralization. In this system, each education and training institution has a clear role to play, but partnerships leverage local knowledge and skills to create synergies and promote specialization. Community colleges can partner with school districts on dual enrollment initiatives and basic adult education services; employers and regional Workforce Investment Boards work together to plan program offerings and provide high-quality internships, apprenticeships, and work-study opportunities. Meanwhile, One-Stop Career Centers offer job placement services.

Enhance the Productivity of Postsecondary Education Programs by Shifting from the Seat Time–Based Credit Hour to Competency-Based Education

Currently, most postsecondary programs of study are focused on seat time and the credit hour. This means that students who learn quickly spend extra hours in the classroom, while those who need extra time end up earning a low grade or failing the course and having to take it over.[22] By recognizing only accredited course work presented in class, the credit hour system also discourages individuals from learning outside the classroom. It is based on a twentieth century model, in which education took place in the lecture hall. Yet we live in a time when new technologies, such as sophisticated assessment software, have encouraged modulated learning, where students advance at their own pace, and educators are facilitators and mentors, not lecturers. The credit hour system's monopoly on postsecondary learning prolongs the time it takes for individuals to acquire competencies with labor market value and muddles the value of postsecondary credentials. Consequently, industry-based certifications—which are based strictly on assessments of actual competency—have risen to prominence over the past decade.

In contrast, competency-based education uses prior learning assessments, which include standardized tests and portfolios of work, to understand the skills individuals have acquired outside of formal education programs. The University of Wisconsin has, for example, developed the UW Flexible Option, which encompasses a series of self-paced, competency-based degree and certificate programs that allows students to demonstrate mastery of competencies through prior course work, military training, or on-the-job training.[23] Competency-based education is often, though not always, focused on career preparation. For example, Brandman University, a private nonprofit postsecondary institution focused on working adults, has utilized the Department of Labor's Occupational Information Network (O*NET) to map occupational competencies onto its curricula.

This is not a new idea: prior learning assessments have been used for years by the American Council for Education to provide veterans with credit for what they learned in the military, and by the College Board, which uses advanced placement examinations as a way for high school students to earn college credits.

By making the skills workers develop in postsecondary programs more transparent, competency-based education will also benefit students by making the process of matching job seekers and employers more efficient.

Competency-based education and prior learning assessments have broad support from the American public (Lumina Foundation and Gallup 2013), but because the federal financial aid system is largely based on the credit hour, they face large institutional barriers. Even so, there are signs of change. More than 20 institutions across the United States are using competency-based education in some form—notably, Western Governors University.

CONCLUSION

The U.S. postsecondary education system is a kaleidoscope of institutions and interests, educational policies vary from state to state, and there is no unified data system connecting postsecondary fields of study and degrees with actual labor market demands. In order to improve opportunities for job seekers, meet the needs of employers, and improve the effectiveness of workforces, we need to reengineer postsecondary education by devising better ways of linking courses of study to career pathways. This will enable students to better understand how their training is likely to fit into the real-world job market, and it will motivate institutions to be more accountable for shaping their programs to fit their students' needs. For this to happen, however, we must first tackle the job of integrating the patchwork quilt of information systems that now exist among various states, agencies, and institutions into a comprehensive set of data that connects postsecondary programs with career pathways.

In a world where postsecondary education is more important than ever but less and less affordable, maintaining equal access to the American dream will be increasingly dependent on efficiency. Forging better connections between the needs of the labor market and postsecondary education will not only serve the needs of employers but will also hold colleges more accountable for providing degrees of value to their students. It will also give low-income students better strategies and clearer pathways for getting a college degree that will help them pursue a meaningful career—and a small piece of the American dream.

Notes

1. Georgetown University Center on Education and the Workforce analysis of the U.S. Census Bureau's March Current Population Survey, 2013. Reported annual earnings are from 2012.
2. Georgetown University Center on Education and the Workforce analysis of data from OECD (2013). See http://www.oecd.org/edu/eag2013%20(eng)--FINAL%2020%20June%202013.pdf (accessed April 23, 2014). See Table A1.3a. Percentage of the population that has attained tertiary education by type of program and age group (2011). The age groups are 55–64 for the baby boom generation and 25–34 for young adults. Postsecondary attainment refers to "Total tertiary attainment" category and bachelor's degree attainment refers to the "Tertiary-type A and advanced research programs."
3. Georgetown University Center on Education and the Workforce estimate based on the supply-demand methodology in Carnevale and Smith (2013).
4. Georgetown University Center on Education and the Workforce estimate based on methodology in Carnevale and Rose (2011). This model predicts economic growth as a function of workers' average educational attainment as measured by years of schooling, under a primary assumption of human capital theory that schooling enhances individuals' skills and productivity.
5 Georgetown University Center on Education and the Workforce analysis of data from the American Society of Training and Development.
6. Georgetown University Center on Education and the Workforce analysis of data from U.S. Department of Education (Snyder and Dillow 2013, Tables 320–322).
7. Carnevale, Rose, and Hanson (2012) define "substantial labor market value" as providing at least a 20 percent wage premium over a high school education.
8. Based on a Georgetown University Center on Education and the Workforce analysis of data from the Current Population Survey, March supplement, 2010–2012. The analysis defines jobs requiring some college or an associate's degree as working in an occupation where the share of workers in that occupation with at least some college is greater than the share of the labor force with at least some college. However, if the median annual earnings for the occupation are closer to the median earnings for workers with some college or an associate's degree than to the median earnings for high school–educated workers and at least 10 percent higher than the median annual earnings for high school–educated workers, then the worker is classified as appropriately qualified for the occupation.
9. Georgetown University Center on Education and the Workforce analysis of data from the 2012 National Postsecondary Student Aid Study panel using the National Center for Education Statistics' PowerStats.
10. http://salarysurfer.cccco.edu/SalarySurfer.aspx (accessed April 23, 2014).

11. McCann and Laitinen (2014) describe in detail how the student unit record system ban came about.
12. As Ruder and Van Noy (2013) note, earnings information should include the full distribution, not only the median.
13. Lumina Foundation's Degree Qualifications Profile provides a comprehensive and ambitious model for including both the quantitative and qualitative dimensions to learning that can, in theory, break down the tensions between specific and general learning; occupational and academic learning; and the tensions in the economic, cultural, and civic roles of postsecondary education. Their approach mixes both educators' and employers' perspectives in a consensus-building process. This bottom-up approach is most attractive because it relies more on faculty consensus and expertise as well as the ground-level perspectives of other stakeholders rather than top-down and more narrow measurement models like gainful employment.
14. Adoption of the Common Core represents a continued emphasis on curricula primarily focused on abstract, academic content.
15. Based on the assumption in Klein (2001) that the Perkins program accounts for 5 percent of national spending on secondary career and technical education programs.
16. However, career preparation is one of the central missions of four-year colleges and universities as well. For example, the majority of four-year college undergraduates are enrolled in career-focused majors (Carnevale, Strohl, and Melton 2011). There is also an opportunity for these institutions to incorporate labor market services into their institutional structures.
17. See Table 1A, Tuition and Fees column in College Board (2013). Prices are rounded to the nearest 100 for readability.
18. See Figure A2 in the appendix in Desrochers and Wellman (2011).
19. Holzer and Nightengale (2009) find this trend is especially strong among low-income students.
20. The Comprehensive Employment and Training Act was the federal program job training bill that provided unemployed workers with public service jobs. It was signed into law in 1973 during the Nixon administration until the Job Training Partnership Act (JPTA) replaced it in 1982 during the Reagan administration. WIA then replaced the JPTA in 1998 during the Clinton administration.
21. The Workforce Investment Act H.R.1385 received 91 votes in the Senate and 343 votes in the House of Representatives.
22. The exceptions to this are industry-based certifications, which are test-based and typically do not require individuals to complete a program of study to receive a certification.
23. http://flex.wisconsin.edu (accessed April 23, 2013).

References

Association for Career and Technical Education. 2014. "Texas Fact Sheet." Alexandria, VA: Association for Career and Technical Education. https://www.acteonline.org/TexasStateFactSheet2014 (accessed August 22, 2014).

Carnevale, Anthony P., and Ban Cheah. 2013. *Hard Times 2013: College Majors, Unemployment and Earnings.* Washington, DC: Georgetown University Center on Education and the Workforce. http://cew.georgetown.edu/unemployment2013 (accessed April 23, 2012).

Carnevale, Anthony P., Andrew R. Hanson, and Artem Gulish. 2013. "Failure to Launch: Structural Shift and the New Lost Generation." Washington, DC: Georgetown University Center on Education and the Workforce. http://cew.georgetown.edu/failuretolaunch (accessed April 23, 2012).

Carnevale, Anthony P., and Stephen J. Rose. 2011. "The Undereducated American." Washington, DC: Georgetown University Center on Education and the Workforce. http://cew.georgetown.edu/undereducated (accessed April 23, 2012).

Carnevale, Anthony P., Stephen J. Rose, and Ban Cheah. 2011. "The College Payoff: Education, Occupations, and Lifetime Earnings." Washington, DC: Georgetown University Center on Education and the Workforce. http://cew.georgetown.edu/collegepayoff (accessed April 23, 2012).

Carnevale, Anthony P., Stephen J. Rose, and Andrew R. Hanson. 2012. "Certificates: Gateway to Gainful Employment and College Degrees." Washington, DC: Georgetown University Center on Education and the Workforce. http://cew.georgetown.edu/certificates (accessed April 23, 2012).

Carnevale, Anthony P., and Nicole Smith. 2013. "Recovery: Job Growth and Education Requirements through 2020." Washington, DC: Georgetown University Center on Education and the Workforce. http://cew.georgetown.edu/recovery2020 (accessed April 23, 2012).

Carnevale, Anthony P., Jeff Strohl, and Michelle Melton. 2011. "What's It Worth? The Economic Value of College Majors." Washington, DC: Georgetown University Center on Education and the Workforce. http://cew.georgetown.edu/whatsitworth (accessed April 23, 2012).

College Board. 2013. *Trends in College Pricing, 2013.* New York: College Board. https://trends.collegeboard.org/sites/default/files/college-pricing-2013-full-report-140108.pdf (accessed April 23, 2012).

Desjardins, Richard, and Arne Jonas Warnke. 2012. "Ageing and Skills: A Review and Analysis of Skill Gain and Skill Loss over the Lifespan and over Time." OECD Education Working Papers 72. Paris: OECD.

Desrochers, Donna M., and Jane V. Wellman. 2011. *Trends in College Spend-*

ing, 1999–2009. Delta Cost Project. Washington, DC: U.S. Department of Education.

Eyster, Lauren, Theresa Anderson, and Christin Durham. 2013. "Innovations and Future Directions for Workforce Development in the Post-Recession Era." Working Paper No. 7. Washington, DC: Urban Institute.

Government Accountability Office. 2011. *Multiple Employment and Training Programs: Providing Information on Colocating Services and Consolidating Administrative Structures Could Promote Efficiencies.* Washington, DC: Government Accountability Office. http://www.gao.gov/new.items/d1192.pdf (accessed April 23, 2012).

Holzer, Harry J. 2011. "Raising Job Quality and Skills for American Workers: Creating More-Effective Education and Workforce Development Systems in the States." Washington, DC: Urban Institute. http://www.brookings.edu/~/media/research/files/papers/2011/11/workforce-holzer/11_workforce_holzer_paper.pdf (accessed April 8, 2015).

Holzer, Harry J., and Demetra S. Nightingale. 2009. *Strong Students, Strong Workers Models for Student Success through Workforce Development and Community College Partnerships.* Washington, DC: Center for American Progress. http://www.americanprogress.org/issues/2009/12/pdf/strongstudents.pdf (accessed April 23, 2012).

Jacobs, Elisabeth. 2013a. *Creating a Virtuous Circle: Workforce Development Policy as a Tool for Improving the Prospects of America's Unemployed Workers.* Washington, DC: Brookings Institution. http://www.brookings.edu/research/papers/2013/12/04-reforming-workforce-development-us-human-capital-policies (accessed April 23, 2014).

———. 2013b. *Principles for Reforming Workforce Development and Human Capital Policies in the United States.* Washington, DC: Brookings Institution. http://www.brookings.edu/research/papers/2013/02/13-workforce-development-jacobs (accessed April 23, 2014).

Jacobson, Louis S., and Robert J. LaLonde. 2013. *Using Data to Improve the Performance of Workforce Training.* Washington, DC. Brookings Institution, The Hamilton Project, http://www.hamiltonproject.org/files/downloads_and_links/THP_JacobsonLaLonde_Brief2.pdf (accessed April 23, 2014).

Klein, Steven. 2001. *Financing Vocational Education: A State Policymaker's Guide.* Berkeley, CA: MPR Associates.

Kuczera, Malgorzata, and Simon Field. 2013. *A Skills beyond School Review of the United States.* OECD Reviews of Vocational Education and Training. Paris: OECD Publishing. http://dx.doi.org/10.1787/9789264202153-en (accessed April 23, 2014).

Laitinen, Amy. 2014. "The Omnibus Bill and a Data Tradeoff We Don't Need

to Make." *Ed Central* (blog), January 16, New America. http://www.ed
central.org/omnibus-bill-better-data-burden-tradeoff-really-make/#sthash
.ekTosdDc.dpuf (accessed January 13, 2015).

Lumina Foundation and Gallup. 2013. *America's Call for Higher Education Redesign: The 2012 Lumina Foundation Study of the American Public's Opinion on Higher Education.* Indianapolis, IN and Washington,
DC: Lumina Foundation and Gallup. http://www.luminafoundation.org/
publications/Americas_Call_for_Higher_Education_Redesign.pdf
(accessed April 23, 2014).

McCann, Clare, and Amy Laitinen. 2014. *College Blackout: How the Higher
Education Lobby Fought to Keep Students in the Dark.* Washington, DC:
New America Foundation. http://newamerica.net/sites/newamerica.net/

Organisation for Economic Co-operation and Development (OECD). 2013.
OECD Skills Outlook 2013: First Results from the Survey of Adult Skills.
Paris: OECD. http://dx.doi.org/10.1787/9789264204256-en (accessed April
23, 2014).

Ruder, Alex, and Michelle Van Noy. 2013. "Using Administrative Data to
Improve Major Choices for College Students." New Brunswick, NJ: Heldrich Center for Workforce Development at Rutgers University. http://
www.heldrich.rutgers.edu/sites/default/files/products/uploads/variation-
Presentation.pdf (accessed April 23, 2014).

Rutschow, Elizabeth Zachry, and Shane Crary-Ross. 2014. *Beyond the GED:
Promising Models for Moving High School Dropouts to College.* New York
and Oakland, CA: MDRC. http://www.mdrc.org/sites/default/files/Beyond
theGEDFR0.pdf (accessed April 23, 2014).

Şahin, Ayşegül, Joseph Song, Giorgio Topa, and Giovanni L. Violante. 2012.
Mismatch Unemployment. New York: Federal Reserve Bank of New York.
http://www.newyorkfed.org/research/economists/sahin/USmismatch.pdf
(accessed April 23, 2014).

Snyder, Thomas D., and Sally A. Dillow. 2013. *Digest of Education Statistics
2012.* Washington, DC: U.S. Department of Education. Institute of Education Sciences, National Center for Education Statistics (accessed April 23,
2014).

Soares, Louis, and Stephen Steigleder. 2012. *Building a Technically Skilled
Workforce: Partnerships between Community Colleges and Industries Are
the Key.* Washington, DC: Center for American Progress (accessed April
23, 2014).

Stone, James R., Corinne Alfeld, Donna Pearson, Morgan V. Lewis, and
Susan Jensen. 2006. *Building Academic Skills in Context: Testing the Value
of Enhanced Math Learning in CTE.* Columbus, OH: National Dissemination Center for Career and Technical Education. http://www.aypf.org/

forumbriefs/2007/Resources/MathLearningFinalStudy.pdf (accessed April 23, 2014).

U.S. Department of Education. 2011. *Committee on Measures of Student Success: A Report to Secretary of Education Arne Duncan.* Washington, DC: U.S. Department of Education. http://www2.ed.gov/about/bdscomm/list/acmss.html (accessed April 23, 2014).

U.S. Department of Education, Office of Vocational and Adult Education. 2012. *Investing in America's Future: A Blueprint for Transforming Career and Technical Education.* Washington, DC: U.S. Department of Education. https://www2.ed.gov/about/offices/list/ovae/pi/cte/transforming-career-technical-education.pdf (accessed April 23, 2014).

Vollman, James, and Anthony P. Carnevale. 2009. *National Broadband Plan: Broadband Access for All Americans: Facilitating an Efficient and Effective Labor Market.* Washington, DC: Georgetown University. http://apps.fcc.gov/ecfs/document/view?id=7020351160 (accessed April 23, 2014).

5

The U.S. Approach to Higher Education and Workforce Development

Separate Parts in Search of a Whole

Harry J. Holzer

Georgetown University and American Institute for Research

In the United States today, roughly three-fourths of all high school graduates enroll in and attend a college or university. Many hope to attain skills and credentials that will enable them to find high-paying jobs as soon as they finish college and enter the labor force.

Unfortunately, large percentages of these students (especially at our public two-year institutions) drop out without earning any college credential. Even among those who do obtain a credential, they receive virtually no counseling or other information about the job market while they are there and frequently earn degrees with only modest labor market value. In the meantime, public funding for our workforce development system has been shrinking for decades, with fewer people obtaining job training over time, while our workforce institutions remain relatively separate from those of higher education.

How did the United States arrive at such a juncture? What are the strengths and weaknesses of our systems of higher education and workforce development? What would constitute the most effective reforms that we could introduce in both realms through policy? This chapter seeks to answer these questions.

THE SEPARATE SPHERES OF HIGHER EDUCATION AND JOB TRAINING

During most of the twentieth century, higher education and job training were viewed as quite separate activities with very different roles to play in the U.S. economy. Enrollment in colleges and universities expanded dramatically after World War II, with student tuition levels subsidized at least partly by the federal GI Bill, but also by states as they built their own higher education systems. Local public two-year colleges have often been seen as stepping-stones to four-year schools, though they also prepared students for a number of occupations. The public and private four-year colleges (which now number well over 2,000) have provided liberal arts degrees as well as more focused preparation for a range of occupations (such as accountants, teachers, and engineers). Among those majoring in liberal arts fields, many have gone on to obtain graduate degrees in a range of professions, while others found work directly after college in fields that didn't require specific occupational preparation.

In contrast, until the 1960s most job training was relatively short-term and occurred in the workplace, where newly hired or promoted workers would receive both formal and informal preparation for the jobs they were beginning, and where the costs of such training were split between employers and workers (Mincer 1974). This was true in both white-collar and blue-collar jobs and in a wide range of industries, such as manufacturing and service sectors. Somewhat longer-term training was also provided in some cases, such as apprenticeship programs in construction.

Federally funded job training began with the Manpower Development and Training Act of 1962, as a response to concerns over regional pockets of structural unemployment. But these efforts shifted their focus to the disadvantaged rather than the displaced and expanded quite dramatically in the late 1960s and 1970s, beginning with the War on Poverty and subsequent passage of the Comprehensive Employment and Training Act (CETA) in the early 1970s (Holzer 2013). Job training under CETA was provided in classroom settings as well as on the job. In the late 1970s, CETA funded considerable amounts of public service employment for the poor, along with job training. Funding for CETA reached its peak (adjusted for inflation) in 1980 at the end of the Carter administration.[1]

CHANGES AFTER 1980: THE JOB TRAINING PARTNERSHIP ACT AND BEYOND

During the 1980s and 1990s, CETA evolved first into the Job Training Partnership Act (JTPA) and then the Workforce Investment Act (WIA). In 2014, WIA became the Workforce Innovation Opportunity Act (WIOA). With each new legislative iteration, more authority devolved to local workforce groups (known as Workforce Investment Boards) that represented local stakeholders, including business, labor, and education agencies. Over time, the presence of local businesses on the Workforce Investment Boards grew, with the goal of steering training dollars toward growing industry sectors with greater demand for skills.

WIA created funding for some 3,000 new One-Stop Career Centers (now called American Job Centers) around the country, at which a new range of workforce services have been provided. These have included *core* services, which is essentially modest staff assistance with job search, and *intensive* services, in which job seekers receive aptitude testing and career counseling. Individuals can only receive training once they have first received core and intensive services. In addition, greater choice has been provided for those obtaining training, with funding ultimately provided through vouchers (known as Individual Training Accounts [ITAs]). Individuals receiving such vouchers can shop among local training providers, about whom information is provided at the One-Stop Centers across the nation.

Funding for these activities is provided through separate funding streams for adults, dislocated workers, and youth. A range of other programs and services, including the Job Corps for youth, are also funded through the various titles of WIOA (Besharov and Cottingham 2011).[2]

But funding through this legislation has diminished fairly consistently over the past three decades, even while some new funds for workforce services have appeared in other (small) federal programs and agencies.[3] Public service employment has disappeared completely from this legislation, while the numbers of workers receiving training (especially among the disadvantaged) has declined steadily over time (Holzer 2009). For those receiving ITAs, training is mostly modest and very short term.[4] By most measures, federal expenditures on workforce services relative to the size of our economy and labor force are very modest, in comparison with most other industrial countries.[5]

Why has federal workforce funding, especially for job training, diminished so much over time? Partly this has occurred because of growing doubts about the cost-effectiveness of these services. A large body of evaluation research on federal job training programs has developed in this time period, and results have been decidedly mixed, though usually more positive than the critics allege. Publicly provided training for disadvantaged adults under JTPA and WIA have generally appeared to be cost-effective, even if its impacts are not terribly large (on average) and sometimes they fade over time.[6]

But perhaps another reason for the decline in funding is that job training, in its traditional form, has become viewed as a weak substitute for higher education as preparation for the job market. After declining in the 1970s (because of a temporary glut of college-educated workers who pursued higher education to avoid the draft for the Vietnam War), the economic value of college degrees rose substantially, beginning in the 1980s. By the year 2000, the ratio of earnings for four-year college graduates to high school graduates had roughly doubled, relative to where it stood in 1980.[7]

Greater numbers of good-paying jobs now require either two- or four-year college degrees (Autor 2010). These jobs are especially prevalent in the growing service sectors of the economy, particularly in fields such as health care, education, and finance; jobs for non–college graduates in these fields also expanded dramatically, though they paid much lower wages (Carnevale, Smith, and Strohl 2010). Compensation for jobs requiring more than a bachelor's degree (BA) have grown even more dramatically over time, and even in the years since 2000 when average compensation for those with only a BA has stagnated (Mishel 2010).

At the same time, the numbers of good-paying production and clerical jobs for those without higher education have diminished, as their wages and benefits declined or they were eliminated due to the growing power of new technologies and globalization. Institutional changes, such as declining unionism and declining relative values of statutory minimum wages, reinforced the changes generated by these market forces (Autor, Katz, and Kearney 2008; Card and Dinardo 2007). Though some fields—notably construction—continued to provide such opportunities (at least until the Great Recession began), those in manufacturing, mining, and many other traditional sectors have declined dramatically in number (Autor 2010).

Under these circumstances, students have been flocking to two- and four-year colleges. Though enrollments declined initially during the 1980s, they eventually rose quite substantially. Unfortunately, the numbers of new college graduates did not rise as rapidly as the numbers of new enrollees, as completion rates fell. Most economists believe that the supply of new college graduates has failed to keep pace with the growing demand for these skills in the economy, and therefore the premium paid to college graduates has stayed very high (Goldin and Katz 2008).

For disadvantaged workers, college is now viewed as the best route to higher-paying jobs, rather than more traditional job training. A range of programs in two-year colleges, including certificate programs as well as those for associate's (AA) degrees, provide options for advancement for those whose academic skills are perhaps not strong enough for four-year colleges and universities. Though the official price tags on higher education have risen quite dramatically over time, so did a number of forms of financial assistance, including Pell Grants, whose maximum values and numbers rose sharply after 2000. Indeed, federal expenditures on Pell Grants now total about $36 billion per year—and it now constitutes the largest source of public funding for workforce development in the United States today—since up to half of Pell Grant recipients are also older and independent students, who are often seeking shorter-term vocational training rather than BA (or even AA) degrees (College Board 2013).

The importance of college education as preparation for the job market has grown for one additional reason: the lack of high-quality career and technical education (CTE) options for students in high school. Traditionally, vocational education in high schools provided some direct training for non-college-bound students. But, beginning in the 1960s, such education faced criticisms over the "tracking" of low-income and minority students away from college, and over its low quality more broadly. Efforts to generate other "school-to-work" pathways were attempted in the 1990s under the School to Work Opportunities Act (Neumark 2007) but fizzled afterward due to weaknesses in that legislation (with a modest amount of federal money spread very thinly over almost all public school districts in the nation), ideological opposition (from conservatives who claimed that the program amounted to federal bureaucrats planning the future lives of children), and indifference from the program's primary constituents (such as the business community).

While the quality of CTE students and curricula appears to have improved since 2000, as the federal Perkins Act has encouraged state and local reforms, enrollments remain limited. Most students and their families continue to see CTE as a less preferred substitute for college rather than as a source of potential preparation for college (as well as careers); in reality, too many such programs at the high school level remain substitutes for "college prep" rather than complements or alternative pathways to getting there. And U.S. employers continue to view (perhaps correctly) high school graduates who have no specific technical training or work experience as bringing little skill and value to their workplaces, while those in Germany and other EU countries where high-quality CTE is more widely available and more heavily utilized are viewed much more positively by their employers (Hoffmann 2011; Symonds, Schwartz, and Ferguson 2011).

THE STRENGTHS AND LIMITATIONS OF HIGHER EDUCATION AS WORKFORCE PREPARATION

With its high enrollment rates, higher education in the United States offers a very wide range of both youth and adults an opportunity to earn credentials that should prepare them for well-compensated jobs. A very diverse set of institutions—public and private, two- and four-year, for-profits and nonprofits—gives students an enormous range of options from which to choose. For those completing a degree, the average economic returns on their investments remain very strong, even though the costs of the investments have risen substantially over time. And, as noted earlier, many sources of aid are provided to students so they often don't have to pay the "sticker price" as advertised (Dynarski and

Scott-Clayton 2013). In response to these incentives, the rates of college graduation have finally risen in the United States, especially during the Great Recession of the past six or seven years.

But major problems remain. As noted earlier, completion rates among enrollees remain quite low. In particular, completion rates among minorities and low-income students at four-year colleges lag dramatically behind those of whites and/or middle- and upper-income students (Holzer and Dunlop 2013). For those at two-year colleges, fewer such gaps exist, but overall completion rates are very low. A number of sources of the completion gap have been identified by researchers, including the weak academic preparation of so many students (combined with very ineffective remediation programs), poor information regarding their college options (and underenrollment by strong low-income students in the higher-quality schools whose graduation rates are substantially higher), the pressures of providing income for their families among older students or those who became parents at early ages, and the rising cost of higher education (Bound, Lovenheim, and Turner 2010; Haskins, Holzer, and Lerman 2009).

On the last issue, state appropriations for public colleges and universities have not been rising sufficiently in recent years to keep tuition there from rising as well (Baum, Kurose, and McPherson 2013). This is especially problematic for families with limited financial assets (whose housing values no longer provide additional wealth to pay for college, as they did during the housing boom years [Lovenheim 2011]). As a result, many students pile up substantial debt while in college. For those who do not complete their degree programs, or whose labor market earnings will be limited even when completing the degree (due to the continuing weakness of the U.S. job market for young workers at all education levels), paying off this debt can be quite burdensome.

This raises another issue: in addition to low completion rates and a weak job market, some college students also face limited job market success because they experience such a paucity of workforce development services. Many students who effectively received no exposure to labor market information or career guidance in high schools also get very little in college. Most colleges themselves provide little in the way of career counseling (or even academic counseling, in some cases), and little information on national, state, or local labor markets is available to students there. Thus, most have fairly little information on the fields of study that will prepare them for work in economic sectors where employment is growing and demand will be strong, or those that offer relatively better compensation for a particular degree level. While one could obtain such information (and personal counseling about the kind of education needed and one's aptitude for it) in a One-Stop (or Jobs Center) office, very few students receive such services (Jacobson and Mokher 2009); and the capacity of these offices would likely not be sufficient to handle a much larger inflow if more students were interested (Heaney 2011).

In many cases, students do not necessarily enroll in fields that are well-compensated. Of course, there are many determinants of these choices, including the relative strengths of their preparation for and interest in math and science relative to other fields. In the private liberal arts colleges, students are explicitly choosing fields of study for their academic interests and broad intellectual preparation rather than their ultimate rates of market compensation, and this is true to a lesser extent at public institutions as well. This strategy is particularly well-suited for those intending to pursue a postgraduate degree, who will obtain more career-specific skills later on, though not for those who hope for more immediate employment-related skills and jobs.

Still, for those seeking strong employment opportunities immediately after graduation, more guidance could be quite helpful. Thus, in a market where the variance in returns to college degrees across fields is extremely high, the choices made are not necessarily financially optimal, and many students choose fields that are not particularly well-compensated (Jacobson and Mokher 2009). Furthermore, most students get too little job search information to help them connect with employers when they finish, and institutional linkages between colleges and employers remain quite weak, so students' abilities to find the best-paying jobs for which they have prepared are also limited.

Even students' completion rates might be impaired in many cases by the lack of clear perceived links between their classroom schooling and the needs of employers, since motivation and understanding are often enhanced when academic schooling is provided *contextually* rather than abstractly. Models of work-based learning provide this context automatically, and this might contribute to their higher success rates in many cases, as we note below. Additionally, the contrast between the structure and guidance provided to students in proprietary occupational colleges, as opposed to unstructured community colleges, might well contribute to the higher rates of graduation and employment rates afterward at the former relative to the latter, as has been noted by a number of analysts (Davis and Cho 2013; Rosenbaum 2001; Scott-Clayton 2011).

WHAT WOULD IMPROVE EDUCATION AND WORKFORCE OUTCOMES AMONG U.S. STUDENTS?

Based on the discussion above, I believe that we could improve both the education and workforce outcomes of workers in the United States, especially the disadvantaged, by undertaking the following:

- an expansion of high-quality CTE and work-based learning,
- an expansion of sectoral training models involving employers and community colleges,
- reforms in financial aid and remedial education that would improve college completion rates as well as workforce outcomes, and
- other efforts to better integrate higher education and workforce services and make both more responsive to the U.S. economy.

In each case, efforts to maintain quality and at least some focus on the disadvantaged are important, while avoiding the creation of windfalls for the business community.

Expanding High-Quality CTE and Work-Based Learning

As the European experience noted earlier suggests, a more effective and higher-quality system of CTE in high school might raise the earnings of those who do not enroll in college and improve high school graduation rates. Indeed, empirical evidence suggests that CTE has had such effects in the last few decades (U.S. Department of Education 2004). In the best such systems, though, CTE would no longer be seen as a substitute for college and would enroll those preparing for college as well. Contextualizing academic learning might improve academic performance among those who learn better when material is presented in applied manners rather than purely abstractly; and, since large fractions of students bound for college are interested in career preparation rather than liberal arts, such a CTE curriculum might improve the college performance of these students as well.

Recent evidence suggests that the quality of curriculum has already improved for CTE students, with many more taking math and science courses in high school than in earlier decades. Changes in the Perkins Act, through which the federal government provides some modest financing of state and local CTE programs, have also generated pathways from high school CTE to "career clusters and related pathways" in every state (Holzer, Linn, and Monthey 2013).

Still, a range of potential improvements in CTE would further the goal of creating high-quality CTE systems in secondary schools around the nation. These improvements (Holzer, Linn, and Monthey 2013) would include

- high-level academic material, including advanced placement work for the highest performers;
- a curriculum that teaches occupational and general employability skills as well as academics;
- work-based or project-based applied learning across a range of traditional academic disciplines;
- engagement with employers and industry associations, to make sure curricula are relevant to the needs of growing industry sectors;
- supports for disadvantaged students who might struggle with more rigorous curricula;
- faculty and staff development to support the skills of teachers and counselors in these areas; and
- assessment tools to measure student skills in these areas and allow for accountability.

A number of academic models around the nation have incorporated these characteristics and achieved some scale. For instance, High Schools That Work is a model that has been implemented at dozens of high schools in several (mostly southern) states, which generates high achievement scores, graduation rates, and college attendance through its CTE curricula. Linked Learning is a model that has been implemented districtwide in some California school districts, providing high-quality CTE instruction to all students.

While no rigorous evaluation evidence exists for these two models, such evidence does show that Career Academies—a model of industry-focused instruction within broader high schools that has been implemented in several thousand high schools across the nation—can generate very large improvements in earnings for students, especially at-risk males, for many years beyond graduation without any loss of academic performance (Kemple 2008). Newer versions of the Career Academies are trying to improve the college preparatory curricula in these models; and rigorous evaluation of newer teaching models (Castellano et al. 2012) show that math and science instruction at high levels can be integrated into CTE curricula.

More broadly, CTE and work-based learning need not be limited to secondary schools in the United States. A range of "career pathway" models that begin in community colleges and combine classroom instruction and academic credential attainment with paid work experience are also being developed around the nation (Choitz 2014; Fein et al. 2013) to generate occupational training for a range of postsecondary students, including the disadvantaged.

Other forms of work-based learning show promise as well. For instance, apprenticeships focus primarily on occupational learning through paid work experience on the job. Many new forms of apprenticeship now combine such learning with community college curricula that generate AA degrees. In this way, students can obtain real work experience—which young people have had great difficulty attaining in recent years, especially since the beginning of the Great Recession—with the attainment of valuable postsecondary credentials. Paid internships and various forms of incumbent worker training could be encouraged as well (Hollenbeck 2008).[8]

Evaluation evidence suggests high returns over time to workers who participate in apprenticeship programs (Lerman 2010). Worker persistence in these programs is high, even among the disadvantaged, since paid work experience is very appealing to this group. Wisconsin, Georgia, and South Carolina have taken major steps to expand such programs, at only modest public cost (Holzer and Lerman 2014).

Sectoral Models

In sectoral training models, training providers target key industries with high-demand growth and good-paying jobs (especially for those without BAs) while preparing individuals for work in these industries. Intermediaries generate partnerships between these providers (who increasingly are community colleges) and employers in these industries. The intermediaries treat both the employers and the trainees as stakeholders, and they must gain the confidence of the former by sending them well-skilled workers. But the workers themselves are also highly motivated, as they know the training prepares them for existing jobs that they can clearly see at the end of the training period.

Rigorous evaluation evidence shows that, at their best, sectoral models can generate very large impacts on worker earnings among both adults and youth (Maguire et al. 2010; Roder and Elliott 2011). These models generally do not serve those with weak basic skills or other characteristics of the "hard-to-employ." Questions also remain about their long-term impacts, especially if and when workers change jobs or their industries restructure, and whether the strong results from a small number of sites in those evaluations can be replicated and scaled.

Still, the evidence to date has been strong enough that many states are trying to scale up these models by building partnerships between local industries, community colleges, and workforce boards for high-demand sectors (National Governors Association 2013). Indeed, these states now see sectoral training as the basis of their workforce and economic development programs, but whereas many such partnerships are being developed, we have very little evidence on numbers of participants or completion rates in these efforts.

Reforming Counseling, Financial Aid, and Developmental Programs for College

Given the very low completion rates among low-income or minority students in both two- and four-year colleges, are there reforms in practices in these sectors that might improve these rates as well as subsequent labor market success for these individuals? Undoubtedly, greater availability of high-quality early childhood programs and reforms in elementary and high school systems would improve the academic preparation and therefore the success rates of those attending college; however, assuming that this will not happen quickly or fully, what else can we do for college enrollees to improve rates of success?

One possibility is in the area of financial aid. Despite our growing expenditures in this area, rigorous evidence that Pell Grants actually raise higher educational attainment (as opposed to enrollment) is quite thin (Long 2013). To address this issue, a recent report from the College Board (2013) suggests a range of reforms in the Pell Program, both for younger students and those who are older (e.g., 25 and older) who are primarily part-time students in more vocational tracks. The reforms are based on evidence that such aid is more accessible when it is simplified and more transparent, but also that having clear academic performance standards and supports can improve completion rates (Dynarski and Scott-Clayton 2013). It also reflects the recent evidence that providing information about college quality to college applicants can raise the tendency of low-income but high-performing students, who now overwhelmingly apply to very local colleges, to instead apply to and attend more highly ranked schools, where completion rates are much higher (Hoxby and Turner 2013).

Accordingly, the College Board report (2013) calls for more simplified and transparent income eligibility requirements, where students would be easily able to determine their own eligibility; clearer academic performance standards, which would provide stronger incentives for students to perform well and therefore to graduate; and individually tailored guidance and support systems, with somewhat different services provided for dependent and independent students, and including mandatory career counseling for the latter (see also Baum and Scott-Clayton [2013]).

Another area where reforms are clearly in order is in developmental (or remedial) education. Large factions of students, especially at community colleges, now enroll and begin to attend without having the necessary academic preparation to do college-level work, and they are often assigned to (noncredit) developmental classes at the outset. But, to date, most evidence suggests that such classes rarely have positive effects on academic outcomes of students, and sometimes have negative ones (Clotfelter et al. 2013). Many colleges, even at the two-year level, require that students pass Algebra 1 before taking for-credit classes in many fields, even though it is not clear that such math skills are required for many majors.

We are beginning to find clear evidence of developmental education programs that have more positive effects on postsecondary education outcomes. This seems to occur when these programs are more accelerated, and more integrated into material for credit rather than being "stand-alone" (Bettinger, Boatman, and Long 2013). Integrating the remedial material directly into skills training or at least into the context of labor market information appears particularly helpful. Examples of successful acceleration include the Accelerated Study in Associated Programs approach at the City University of New York, while integration with labor market training or information can be found respectively in the Integrated Basic Education and Skills Training approach in the state of Washington or the GED Bridge Program at LaGuardia Community College in New York. Efforts to reform the placement methods that colleges use for remediation, and even their requirements for successful completion, are starting to be considered as well.

Integrating Higher Education and Workforce Services with Labor Markets

Though cooperation between local higher education agencies or institutions and workforce boards has been rising over time, the two sets of agencies remain fairly "siloed" in most locations around the country. The extent to which both are really responsive to the labor demand needs of the local economy is largely limited.

The limited effects of the labor market on higher education in particular reflects a problem of too little labor market *information* among students and too few *incentives* to be responsive to that market among institutions. Given the paucity of career counseling and information for students, it is not surprising that students pay so little attention to labor market trends when marking their choices of major (Long, Goldhaber, and Huntington-Klein 2014). With administrative education and labor market data as well as real-time job vacancy data becoming more available over time, our ability to remedy this problem seems to be growing. Though the colocation of Job Centers and college campuses appears to be growing (with as many as one-fourth of all centers now located on college campuses), the majority of U.S. students still appear to have little access to (or take too little advantage of) such services.

Many public institutions of higher education also have little incentive to be responsive to these forces. State subsidies for higher education in both two- and four-year colleges usually reflect student "seat time" and are rarely tied to either academic or subsequent labor market success. In addition, instructor and equipment costs in high-demand sectors (such as health technology or advanced manufacturing) are often high, further diminishing the financial incentives or abilities of colleges to expand instructional capacity in these areas. As a result, anecdotes abound of students flocking to colleges at the trough of the recession and seeking to take courses in health care and health technology, only to find these classes oversubscribed and thus unavailable to them on a timely basis.

Of course, this is not to say that there is no role for liberal arts majors at public institutions, especially at the flagship four-year schools. But incentives to be at least somewhat more responsive, especially at institutions where many or most students are seeking vocational certifications, could be made by tying state education subsidies at least partly to average credit attainment and program completion rates.[9] Where this is being done—and at least half of the states are beginning to move in this direction—care must be taken not to generate unintended consequences at schools, which might now have an incentive either to "cream-skim" with higher admissions requirements or to lower graduation requirements in high-demand fields. But some attempts to improve these incentives, especially in the labor market, seem to be in order.[10]

CONCLUSION: GETTING FROM HERE TO THERE

I have argued in this chapter that our public system of workforce services and training has diminished over time and has largely been replaced by rising enrollments in higher education (with Pell Grant financing for low-income students). But education completion and the subsequent earnings of students are both limited for a variety of reasons, at least some of which reflect the separation of higher education from workforce services and an underdevelopment of course work and curricula that are relevant to the job market. Thus, the separation of higher education and workforce services from each other and from the labor market is at least partly responsible for the weak outcomes we observe in both.

How might this situation be remedied? States need to take the lead in encouraging more development of their higher-quality CTE systems in secondary schools, work-based learning models, career pathways, and sectoral initiatives involving partnerships between business, workforce boards, and community colleges. These partnerships are, in fact, growing across the nation (National Governors Association 2013), though more needs to be done to encourage broad participation in them. The states should implement performance standards for their subsidies to publicly funded higher education institutions, both two- and four-year; these performance incentives should be based on the subsequent earnings of students in the labor market as well as academic performance and program completion (with incentives being roughly split between these two sets of outcomes). The provision of labor market information about job opportunities and career counseling more broadly should be made more readily available on college campuses. States should also consider technical assistance and financial incentives for employers implementing apprenticeship programs or other forms of incumbent worker training (Holzer and Lerman 2014).

To monitor both the scale and the quality of these developments, states should make better use of their administrative higher education and earnings data, as Zinn and Van Kluenen (2014) propose. They should actively monitor the outcomes associated with any such programs created above, and do at least modest evaluations of their impacts on educational attainment and earnings, especially among the disadvantaged.[11]

The federal government can do more to encourage this process in two ways. First, the U.S. Departments of Education and Labor have developed a wide range of competitive grants programs in recent years to encourage the kinds of partnerships described above and greater responsiveness of higher education to workforce needs and the labor market. These grant programs have included the Workforce Incentives for Regional Economic Development grants of the more recent Bush Administration; and the Trade Adjustment Assistance Community College and Career grants, Workforce Innovation grants, and Career Connect grants of the Obama administration. But many of these grants have themselves led to small-scale and fragmented programming, rather than state-level innovation and systems development.

Accordingly, a program that targets states and encourages large-scale implementation of the approaches described above should be used, perhaps modeled after the Race to the Top grants from the Department of Education that had such large impacts on state-level programs in the K–12 years. Holzer (2011) describes what such a program would look like and how it would be administered.

Furthermore, the federal government should use its upcoming authorizations of several major federal programs, such as the Higher Education Act, the Perkins Act, and WIA to encourage these trends as well. For instance, the Pell Grants authorized under the Higher Education Act could be reformed along the lines suggested above, Perkins could be made more of a competitive grant to encourage state-level development of high-quality CTE and work-based learning (as both the recent Bush and Obama administrations have proposed), and workforce programs could do more to encourage sector partnership and career pathway development while improving performance measurement (as the recently enacted Workforce Innovation and Opportunity Act of 2014, with widespread support in both houses of Congress, would encourage).

It is also important to mention some important caveats to these ideas. As noted earlier, any efforts along these lines should be carefully monitored to encourage not only high-quality education and workforce programs (in terms of impacts on outcomes), but to maintain at least some focus on the disadvantaged while avoiding large windfalls for employers. Doing so while maintaining employer interest is a difficult balancing act; swinging too far in one direction (toward the needs of the disadvantaged) or the other (kowtowing to employers) should be carefully avoided. Careful monitoring of student and worker outcomes in these efforts, and rigorous evaluations of any programs implemented, are needed to achieve and maintain this balance.

Furthermore, the tension between general and specific skill development needs to be acknowledged. The evaluation evidence suggests that sector- or occupation-specific programs generate some of the strongest outcomes for disadvantaged youth and adults. But, over the long term, some general (or portable) skill development is very important, especially since many workers will change employers and even sectors over time. Furthermore, sectors that today show strong employment growth might show much less tomorrow, in a dynamic labor market where technology and globalization can cause rapid shifts in the locus of labor demand. The more general the skill development, however, the more reluctant employers will be to pay for it (Becker 1996), and this must be taken into account as well by program developers and administrators.

Finally, sectoral programs and others centered around community colleges will likely not be successful with the hardest-to-serve students—in other words, those reading well below the 9th- or 10th-grade level, or those with very poor work experience or physical or emotional disabilities. While our knowledge of what serves to boost employment of these groups is much more limited, our workforce policies should not forget them. Accordingly, experimentation with and evaluation of efforts to meet their needs should proceed as well.

Notes

1. Expenditures under CETA in 1980 were approximately $17 billion (Holzer 2009), or roughly $40 billion in today's dollars.
2. Title I includes the three funding streams above and the Job Corps, as well as other smaller programs; Title II funds Adult Basic Education; Title III encompasses the former Wagner-Peyser Act funding for One-Stop Offices; and Title IV contains miscellaneous expenditures.
3. Funding for WIOA currently totals about $5 billion, which is down nearly 90 percent in real terms from its peak in 1980. But the U.S. Government Accountability Office (2011) reports total funding in 2010 of about $18 billion for workforce services in 47 different federal programs, the largest of which are the various streams of WIA plus Temporary Assistance for Needy Families (TANF) and state vocational rehabilitation programs.
4. The average value of an ITA today is just a bit over $2,000, according to Andersson et al. (2013).
5. The funding listed in the U.S. Government Accountability Office report constitutes just 0.1 percent of GDP and might rise to 0.2 percent if Pell Grant funding of vocational education is included. According to O'Leary, Straits, and Wandner (2004), this total lags behind expenditures by most countries in Europe on such services.
6. See Andersson et al. (2013) and Heinrich et al. (2011) for evidence on WIA and summaries of evaluations of JTPA.
7. The ratio of BA to high school earnings increased from roughly 0.35 in 1979 to 0.70 in 2000.

8. Hollenbeck (2008) describes state investments in incumbent worker training before the onset of the Great Recession, though some states have cut back on these expenditures since that time.
9. See the National Conference of State Legislatures (2014).
10. Though most states now are focusing only on measures of average academic performance and completion of their students for determining subsidies to colleges, Holzer (2014) argues that labor market outcomes of students through the first five years after they leave, such as their average earnings or employment rates (especially among disadvantaged or minority students), should also be used. Colleges and universities would face stronger incentives to expand teaching capacity in areas of high labor demand, even though the costs of equipment and instructors in such fields might be higher.
11. States could, for instance, do evaluations using difference-in-difference analysis of employment outcomes of young or disadvantaged workers in different counties or metropolitan areas based on the timing of introduction and implementation of new programs or procedures.

References

Andersson, Fredrik, Julia I. Lane, Jeffrey Smith, Harry J. Holzer, and David Rosenblum. 2013. "Does Federally Funded Job Training Work? Nonexperimental Estimates of Training Impacts Using Longitudinal Data on Workers and Firms." NBER Working Paper No. 19446. Cambridge, MA: National Bureau of Economic Research.

Autor, David. 2010. "The Polarization of Job Opportunities in the U.S. Labor Market." Washington, DC: Center for American Progress.

Autor, David, Lawrence F. Katz, and Melissa S. Kearney. 2008. "Trends in U.S. Wage Inequality: Revising the Revisionists." *Review of Economics and Statistics* 90(2): 300–323.

Baum, Sandy, Charles Kurose, and Michael McPherson. 2013. "An Overview of American Higher Education." *The Future of Children* 23(1): 17–40.

Baum, Sandy, and Judith Scott-Clayton. 2013. "Redesigning the Pell Grant Program for the 21st Century." Washington, DC: The Hamilton Project, Brookings Institution.

Becker, Gary. 1996. *Human Capital*. Chicago: University of Chicago Press.

Besharov, Douglas J., and Phoebe H. Cottingham, eds. 2011. *The Workforce Investment Act: Implementation Experiences and Evaluation Findings.* Kalamazoo, MI: W.E. Upjohn Institute for Employment Research.

Bettinger, Eric, Angela Boatman, and Bridget Terry Long. 2013. "Student Supports: Developmental Education and Other Academic Programs." *The Future of Children* 23(1): 93–115.

124 Holzer

Bound, John, Michael Lovenheim, and Sarah Turner. 2010. "Why Have College Completion Rates Declined? An Analysis of Changing Student Preparation and Collegiate Resources." *American Economic Journal: Applied Economics* 2(3): 129–157.

Card, David, and Jonathan Dinardo. 2007. "The Impact of Technological Change on Low-Wage Workers: A Review." In *Working and Poor: How Economic and Policy Changes Are Affecting Low-Wage Workers*, Rebecca Blank, Sheldon Danziger, and Robert F. Schoeni, eds. New York: Russell Sage, pp. 113–140.

Carnevale, Anthony, Nicole Smith, and Jeff Strohl. 2010. *Help Wanted: Projections of Jobs and Education Requirements through 2018*. Washington, DC: Georgetown Center on Education and the Workforce.

Castellano, Marie, Kirsten Sundell, Laura T. Overman, and Oscar A. Aliaga. 2012. "Do CTE Programs of Study Improve Student Achievement? Preliminary Analyses from a Rigorous Longitudinal Study." *International Journal of Education Reform* 21(2): 98–118.

Choitz, Vickie. 2014. "Alliance for Quality Career Pathways Programs." Washington, DC: Center for Law and Social Policy.

Clotfelter, Charles, Helen Ladd, Clare Muschkin, and Jacob Vigdor. 2013. "Developmental Education in North Carolina Community Colleges." CALDER Postsecondary Working Paper. Washington, DC: American Institutes for Research.

College Board. 2013. *Rethinking Pell Grants*. Washington, DC: College Board.

Davis, Jenkins, and Sung-Woo Cho. 2013. "Get With the Program: Accelerating Community College Students' Entry into and Completion of Programs of Study." New York: Center for Community College Research, Columbia University.

Dynarski, Susan, and Judith Scott-Clayton. 2013. "Financial Aid Policy: Lessons from Research." *Future of Children* 23(1): 67–91.

Fein, David, Howard Rolston, David Judkins, and Karen N. Gardiner. 2013. "Learning What Works in Career Pathways Programming: The ISIS Evaluation." Unpublished paper. Bethesda, MD: Abt Associates.

Goldin, Claudia, and Lawrence Katz. 2008. *The Race between Education and Technology*. Cambridge, MA: Harvard University Press.

Haskins, Ron, Harry Holzer, and Robert Lerman. 2009. *Promoting Economic Mobility by Raising Postsecondary Education*. Washington, DC: Pew Research Centers.

Heaney, David. 2011. "One-Stop Management and the Private Sector." In *The Workforce Investment Act: Implementation Experiences and Evaluation Findings*, Douglas J. Besharov and Phoebe H. Cottingham, eds. Kalamazoo MI: W.E. Upjohn Institute for Employment Research, pp. 141–152.

Heinrich, Carolyn J., Peter R. Mueser, Kenneth R. Troske, Kyung-Seong Jeon, and Daver C. Kahvecioglu. 2011. "A Nonexperimental Evaluation of WIA Programs." In *The Workforce Investment Act: Implementation Experiences and Evaluation Findings*, Douglas J. Besharov and Phoebe H. Cottingham, eds. Kalamazoo MI: W.E. Upjohn Institute for Employment Research, pp. 371–406.

Hoffmann, Nancy. 2011. *Schooling in the Workplace*. Cambridge MA: Harvard Education Press.

Hollenbeck, Kevin. 2008. "Is There a Role for Public Support of Incumbent Worker Private Sector Training?" Upjohn Institute Working Paper No. 08–138. Kalamazoo MI: W.E. Upjohn Institute for Employment Research.

Holzer, Harry. 2009. "Workforce Development as an Antipoverty Strategy: What Do We Know? What Should We Do?" In *Changing Poverty, Changing Policies*, Maria Cancian and Sheldon Danziger, eds. New York: Russell Sage, pp. 301–329.

———. 2011. "Raising Job Quality and Skills for American Workers." Discussion Paper 2011-10. Washington, DC: The Hamilton Project, Brookings Institution.

———. 2013. "Workforce Development Policies in the U.S." In *Legacies of the War on Poverty*, Martha J. Bailey and Sheldon Danziger, eds. New York: Russell Sage, pp. 121–150.

———. 2014. "Improving Employment Outcomes for Disadvantaged Students." In *Policies to Address Poverty in America*, Melissa S. Kearney and Benjamin H. Harris, eds. Washington, DC: The Hamilton Project, Brookings Institution, pp. 87–95.

Holzer, Harry, and Erin Dunlop. 2013. "Just the Facts Ma'am: Postsecondary Education and Labor Market Outcomes in the U.S." CALDER Postsecondary Papers. Washington, DC: American Institutes for Research.

Holzer, Harry, and Robert Lerman. 2014. "Work-Based Learning to Expand Jobs and Occupational Qualifications for Youth." Washington, DC: Center on Budget and Policy Priorities.

Holzer, Harry, Dane Linn, and Wanda Monthey. 2013. *The Promise of High-Quality Career and Technical Education Programs in the U.S.* Washington, DC: College Board.

Hoxby, Caroline, and Susan Turner. 2013. "Informing Students about Their College Options: A Proposal for Broadening the Expanding College Opportunities Project." Washington, DC: The Hamilton Project, Brookings Institution.

Jacobson, Louis, and Christine Mokher. 2009. *Pathways to Boosting the Earnings of Low-Income Students by Increasing Their Educational Attainment*. New York: Hudson Institute.

Kemple, James. 2008. *Career Academies: Long-Term Impacts on Work, Education and Transitions to Adulthood.* New York: MDRC.

Lerman, Robert. 2010. "Expanding Apprenticeship: A Way to Enhance Skills and Careers." Washington, DC: Urban Institute.

Long, Bridget Terry. 2013. "Supporting Access to Higher Education." In *Legacies of the War on Poverty*, Martha J. Bailey and Sheldon Danziger, eds. New York: Russell Sage, pp. 93–120.

Long, Mark, Dan Goldhaber, and Nick Huntington-Klein. 2014. "Do Students' College Major Choices Respond to Changes in Wages?" CEDR Working Paper No. 2014-6. Seattle, WA: Center for Education, Data, and Research.

Lovenheim, Michael. 2011. "The Effect of Liquid Housing Wealth on College Enrollment." *Journal of Labor Economics* 29(4): 741–771.

Maguire, Sheila, Joshua Freely, Carol Clymer, Maureen Conway, and Deena Schwartz. 2010. *Tuning into Local Labor Markets.* Philadelphia: Private/Public Ventures.

Mincer, Jacob. 1974. *Schooling, Experience and Earnings.* New York: Columbia University Press.

Mishel, Lawrence. 2010. *Reasons for Skepticism about Structural Unemployment.* Washington, DC: Economic Policy Institute.

National Conference of State Legislatures. 2014. "Performance-Based Funding for Higher Education." Washington, DC: National Conference of State Legislatures. http://www.ncsl.org/research/education/performance-funding .aspx (accessed August 26, 2014).

National Governors Association. 2013. *State Sector Strategies Coming of Age.* Washington, DC: Center for Best Practices.

Neumark, David, ed. 2007. *Improving the School-to-Work Transition.* New York: Russell Sage.

O'Leary, Christopher, Robert A. Straits, and Stephen A. Wandner, eds. 2004. *Job Training Policy in the United States.* Kalamazoo, MI: W.E. Upjohn Institute for Employment Research.

Roder, Anne, and Mark Elliott. 2011. *A Promising Start: Year Up's Initial Impacts on Low-Income Young Adult Careers.* New York: Economic Mobility Corporation.

Rosenbaum, James. 2001. *Beyond College for All.* New York: Russell Sage.

Scott-Clayton, Judith. 2011. "The Shapeless River: Does a Lack of Structure Inhibit Students' Progress at Community Colleges?" New York: Center for Community College Research, Columbia University.

Symonds, William C., Robert B. Schwartz, and Ronald F. Ferguson. 2011. *Pathways to Prosperity: Meeting the Challenge of Preparing Young Americans for the 21st century.* Cambridge, MA: Pathways to Prosperity Project, Harvard Graduate School of Education.

U.S. Department of Education, Office of Vocational and Adult Education. 2004. *National Assessment of Vocational Education, Final Report*. Washington, DC: U.S. Department of Education.

U.S. Government Accountability Office. 2011. *Multiple Employment and Training Programs: Providing Information on Colocating Services and Consolidating Administrative Structures Could Promote Efficiencies*. Washington, DC: U.S. Government Printing Office.

Zinn, Rachel, and Andy Van Kluenen. 2014. "Making Workforce Data Work." Washington, DC: National Skills Coalition.

6
The Future of the Public Workforce System in a Time of Dwindling Resources

Stephen A. Wandner

Urban Institute and W.E. Upjohn Institute for Employment Research

This chapter looks into the future of the public workforce system by examining the system's long-term federal funding and program trends. The most important change in the public workforce environment over the past three decades has been a downward trend in federal funding for the basic workforce programs: the Wagner-Peyser Act Employment Service (ES) and federal training programs, including both the Job Training Partnership Act (JTPA) and Workforce Investment Act (WIA) programs. The effects of the decline in funding are much worse in real terms than in monetary terms because most workforce services are provided by workforce professionals whose pay generally increases yearly.

At the same time that funding has declined, the demand for public workforce services has increased. Two factors contribute to the rising demand for services. First, the percentage of U.S. workers permanently laid off has increased. Employers have been less likely to lay off employees temporarily, especially during recessionary times. As a result the temporary layoff rate has remained flat over recent business cycles (Groshen and Potter 2003). Thus, workers on temporary layoffs who generally do not need reemployment services have been replaced by workers on permanent layoffs who cannot expect to be called back to their former jobs. These dislocated workers must seek new jobs and perhaps new occupations. Most of them have been employed for many years and have no recent work search experience, so they need help finding their next jobs. Second, in recent years, permanently laid off workers who want to return to work have tended to remain unemployed for longer periods of time and need greater assistance than previous permanently separated workers.

The cuts in federal funding and the continuing high demand for public workforce services has led to a decline in per person expenditures for those seeking workforce services. This decline in per person expenditures has been evident for many years. The addition of one-time funding for workforce programs during the Great Recession of 2007–2009—authorized by the American Reemployment and Reinvestment Act (ARRA, or the Recovery Act) of 2009—provided only a brief respite from the continuing decline in per person expenditures.

State workforce agencies have had to adapt to a reduction in resources, and if the trends continue, they will have to respond to an even more difficult fiscal environment. One aspect of their response has been to shrink the basic programs' infrastructure. State workforce programs have sharply reduced the number of frontline workers who serve the public, as well as the number of local workforce offices providing services to the public. At the end of 2003 there were almost 3,600 such offices, but today there are just over 2,500—a decline of about 30 percent (U.S. Department of Labor 2014; Wandner 2013, p. 8).[1] The steady decline in program resources continued at the same time that administrative costs needed to support large numbers of local Workforce Investment Boards (LWIBs) remained high. More recently, state agencies have responded by reducing their administrative overhead, such as decreasing the number of LWIBs that oversee the local workforce programs and increasing the role of the governors and the states in workforce program administration.

State workforce agencies also have responded to funding cuts by changing both the way that they provide services and the mix and number of services that they provide. By far the most expensive service provided is job training. The amount of training offered has thus declined, with only 200,000–300,000 WIA Adults and Dislocated Workers receiving training each year—this is only 1–2 percent of workers seeking assistance from the public workforce system. Instead of training, job seekers receive less expensive employment services, often in the form of automated services in computer resource rooms with little staff assistance. Job seekers see fewer and fewer frontline workforce professionals and instead have to make their own way through the computer-based job-seeking process. Thus, there has been a gradual but profound change in the mix of services that job seekers receive, and, responding to a national survey, state workforce administrators say that they believe the change generally represents a degradation of the quality of services (Wandner 2013).

The outlook is for continued decline in resources and continued strong demand for employment services. As a result, we can expect that infrastructure will further deteriorate, and as a result, the quality and number of in-person services will also continue to decline.

This chapter relies on historical data about the public workforce programs and their funding. These data were assembled and organized in the Public Workforce System Dataset (PWSD) from U.S. Department of Labor (USDOL) reporting data (Eberts, Wandner, and Cai 2013). The chapter also makes use of responses to a survey of workforce administrators that was designed by the author and the staff of the National Association of State Workforce Agencies (NASWA). The survey, conducted by NASWA in late 2012, asked the administrators how their states had responded between 2010 and 2012 to the end of the one-time supplemental federal funding made available through the ARRA. Most states had exhausted this funding by the end of 2010 and were struggling with funding levels at or below the level preceding the onset of the Great Recession (Wandner 2013).

THE ENVIRONMENT

Declining Funding

Over the past 30 years, the funding (in current dollars) for workforce programs has declined or remained stagnant. However, the pattern of funding for the three major programs for adult workers has varied greatly. Funding for the Wagner-Peyser Act Employment Service programs has been in decline for nearly two decades, reaching a high of $839 million in 1995, and dropping to a low of $664 million in 2014. The JTPA/WIA Adult program has declined dramatically and steadily, from $1.89 billion in 1984 to just less than $800 million in recent years. By contrast, permanent worker displacement has been a persistent and growing labor force problem since the 1970s. As a result, the funding for the JTPA/WIA Dislocated Worker program increased steadily until it reached a peak of $1.27 billion in 2000, declining only slightly and remaining fairly steady at above $1.1 billion until 2010, but declining to $1.0 billion in 2014.

The Great Recession did not change the downward trend in workforce program funding—it simply added an overlay of a one-time supplemental increase in program funding from the Recovery Act that was obligated or expended quickly, starting in mid-2009 and largely exhausted by late 2010. Thus, by the end of 2010, states found that their total workforce resources in current dollars had declined to below pre-recession levels (see Table 6.1).

The reduction in federal funding meant that state workforce programs had to either supplement it or reduce the number of workers served, change the mix of services participants received, or alter the methods of providing services. Most states did not supplement funding; rather, the effect of the decline in federal funding fell most heavily on program participants, who now generally receive fewer one-on-one services and instead receive automated, group, or less intensive services. Overall, the federal funding cuts and the states' responses led to fewer clients receiving services and less intensive services for clients who did receive assistance. On net, expenditures per participant declined.

The Career and Technical Education and Adult Basic and Literacy Education (Adult Education) programs also serve individuals in need of training for work. They provide competitive grants, evaluation contracts, innovative programs, and other national activities. The Adult Education state grants assist adults without a high school diploma or the equivalent to become literate and obtain the knowledge and skills necessary for postsecondary education, employment, and economic self-sufficiency. Career and Technical Education programs enroll students at nearly 1,300 public high schools and 1,700 two-year colleges. They are organized by 16 career clusters and 79 career pathways, offering a broad range of career options.

These two programs provide limited overlap with WIA and Wagner-Peyser Act programs, and recently they have been funded at roughly the same level as those workforce programs. Since the mid-1980s, they have not suffered the same early and continuous funding reductions as have the Wagner-Peyser Act and JTPA/WIA Adult programs (see Table 6.1.) Rather, like the WIA Dislocated Worker program, they reached a peak later and have since not declined substantially. Career and Technical Education and Adult Education, however, can only supplement the

Table 6.1 Workforce Program Budgets, Program Years 1984–2014 ($000)

Year	Wagner-Peyser Act	WIA Adult	WIA Dislocated Workers	CTE state grants	Adult Education grants
1984	740,398	1,886,155	223,000	742,731	100,000
1985	777,398	1,886,151	222,500	842,148	101,963
1986	758,135	1,783,085	95,703	813,113	97,579
1987	755,200	1,840,000	200,00	881,967	112,881
1988	738,029	1,809,486	215,415	888,243	134,036
1989	763,752	1,787,772	227,018	918,404	162,210
1990	779,039	1,744,808	370,882	936,723	192,795
1991	805,107	1,778,484	421,589	1,008,488	240,777
1992	821,608	1,773,484	423,788	1,152,848	282,260
1993	810,960	1,015,021	413,637	1,173,727	299,808
1994	832,856	988,021	894,400	1,180,477	299,808
1995	838,912	996,813	982,840	1,107,847	273,843
1996	761,735	850,000	878,000	1,084,896	254,860
1997	761,735	895,000	1,034,400	1,136,195	349,828
1998	761,735	955,000	1,080,408	1,144,047	355,828
1999	761,735	954,000	1,124,408	1,150,147	385,000
2000	761,735	950,000	1,271,220	1,188,150	470,000
2001	796,736	950,000	1,162,032	1,237,500	560,500
2002	796,735	945,272	1,233,688	1,314,500	591,060
2003	791,557	894,577	1,150,149	1,325,826	587,217
2004	786,887	893,195	1,171,408	1,327,846	590,233
2005	780,591	889,498	1,184,784	1,326,107	585,233
2006	715,883	864,199	1,189,811	1,296,306	579,552
2007	715,883	826,105	1,112,046	1,296,306	579,563
2008	703,377	861,540	1,183,840	1,271,694	567,468
ARRA	396,000	495,000	1,237,500	0	0
2009	703,576	861,540	1,183,840	1,271,694	639,567
2010	703,576	861,540	1,182,120	1,271,694	639,567
2011	702,169	769,576	1,061,807	1,131,503	607,443
2012	700,842	770,811	1,008,151	1,130,857	606,295
2013	664,184	730,624	955,591	1,071,866	574,667
2014	664,184	766,080	1,001,598	1,125,000	577,700
2015	664,184	766,080	1,001,598	1,125,000	597,700

NOTE: Budget numbers are all in current, non-inflation-adjusted dollars.
SOURCE: Wagner-Peyser Act, WIA Adult, and Dislocated Worker Data include only formula funding and come from USDOL budget documents. WIA and Wagner-Peyser Act supplemental funding from the American Recovery and Reinvestment Act was a one-time increment that was available for two years and was largely expended in second half of 2009 and 2010. Adult Education and Career and Technical Education data come from the Department of Education historical data at https://www2.ed.gov/about/overview/budget/history/edhistory.pdf (accessed September 5, 2014) and from the Department of Education Budget Background and Summary for FY 2015 at http://www2.ed.gov/about/overview/budget/budget15/summary/15summary.pdf (accessed September 5, 2014).

training needs of some workers to a limited extent, and can do little to support the tens of millions of workers in need of staff-assisted employment and reemployment services.

The Pell Grant program provides financial aid to low-income undergraduate students to ensure access to postsecondary education. The program currently provides nearly $33 billion in aid to students, helping to make college available to nearly nine million students, providing maximum grants of $5,730 to full-time students. Most workers served by public workforce programs, however, attend training programs part time or for limited periods, and they are not enrolled in undergraduate degree-granting programs (D'Amico 2006).

Limited Supplemental State Funding

With the end of Recovery Act supplemental funding, the need for state supplementation of federal funding became acute in 2011 and 2012. Yet, despite the shortage of federal funds to serve the flow of unemployed workers to local workforce offices, states generally did not do any supplementation. Of the 45 state workforce agencies responding to the workforce agency survey, 29 (64 percent) provided no supplemental funding, even as overall federal funding declined. In the 16 states that did supplement federal funding, Wagner-Peyser Act programs were by far the most frequently supplemented programs, with 11 states supplementing these programs. Five states supplemented WIA programs.

The source of supplemental funding included state general revenue, Reed Act funds (funds required to be distributed to the states when there is an excess of funds in the Unemployment Trust Fund), UI Penalty and Interest funds, and state special funds. Such funding, however, was limited. In the case of Reed Act funds, few states had any remaining funds from a 2002 $8 billion Unemployment Trust fund distribution (Wandner 2013).

Continuing High Demand for Public Workforce Services

Demand for public workforce services has increased in recent years because greater numbers of workers have been permanently laid off and find it more difficult and time consuming to find their next jobs. Over the past three decades, worker dislocation has been a significant problem in the United States. By 1984, the problem had become widely recognized, and the Bureau of Labor Statistics (BLS) responded by initiating a biennial series of special dislocated worker surveys as supplements to the Current Population Survey in order to estimate the magnitude of the problem and to discern any trends in worker dislocation. These surveys have shown that each year during the 1980s approximately two million long-tenured workers were dislocated. While the numbers of dislocated workers increased during periods of recession, they remained high in all years, even those with relatively low unemployment. In the 1980s, worker dislocation was concentrated in the goods-producing sector of the economy, but there also was significant dislocation among workers in the service sector and white-collar workers (Congressional Budget Office 1993).

The nature of worker dislocation has changed since the 1980s, however, and the problem has become more pervasive. In the 1990s, the percentage of worker dislocation among service-sector and white-collar workers increased, narrowing the gap relative to goods-producing industries (Hipple 1999). While the rate of worker dislocation remained higher in manufacturing and construction than other industries, in 2002, the actual number of white-collar dislocated workers (1.194 million) was almost twice the number of dislocated blue-collar workers (0.646 million) and nearly 10 times the number of dislocated workers in service occupations. The number of long-tenured dislocated workers in 2002 was 2.0 million (Helwig 2004).

In the seven fiscal years between 2006 and 2012, the number of unemployed workers collecting a first payment from the UI program has ranged between 7.4 million and 14.4 million. In July 2013, USDOL projected the number to remain steady at over eight million over the next five years (USDOL 2013). At least half of these UI recipients, or approximately four million of them, are likely to be permanently separated from their jobs and likely will benefit from receiving reemployment services. In addition, reemployment services might be needed by workers who do not collect UI, including by reentrants into the labor force.

The total number of dislocated workers has followed a cyclical pattern. Thus, the numbers of dislocated workers grew sharply during the Great Recession. The total number of dislocated workers rose during the 2007–2009 BLS survey period to 15.4 million, up from 8.5 million during the 2005–2007 period (Bobeley 2011).

For over three decades, the permanent layoff rate has been much greater than the temporary layoff rate. In addition, the permanent layoff rate was, and continues to be, highly cyclical, increasing sharply in recessionary periods. On the other hand, the percentage of workers who were temporarily laid off was once also highly cyclical, spiking upward during recessions. After a period of time many workers were rehired, having collected UI during the business slowdown, but then were brought back as demand began to climb again. That pattern has been largely eliminated. In good times and bad, the temporary layoff rate is now steady and low.

With permanent layoffs becoming more important, more unemployed workers need assistance in returning to work. Studies have shown that dislocated workers experience substantial earnings loss when they return to work (Kletzer 1998). Based on the BLS survey data, it has been estimated that, between 1985 and 1995, dislocated workers experienced wage losses of 13 percent, comparing their wages before and after unemployment (Farber 1997). Losses relating to dislocation also take place with respect to employment: for the 2001–2003 BLS survey, 35 percent of job losers were still not employed at the survey date, and 13 percent of those who had lost full-time jobs were only employed part time (Farber 2005). Dislocated workers also experienced longer durations of unemployment before they returned to work.

The demands on the public workforce system can be expected to remain high in future years, with relatively high levels of unemployment and continuing long durations of unemployment. Since 2002, the total number of Wagner-Peyser Act participants has varied between 13.3 million in 2005 and the Great Recession high of 22.4 million in 2009. For the foreseeable future, absent a major recession, the number of workforce participants in need of staff-assisted services is likely to remain in the range of 15–20 million. Those participants will almost all be permanently separated unemployed workers. Most of them will be in need of staff-assisted services and job search assistance, but as can be seen from Table 6.2, fewer of them are receiving these services. The provision of staff-assisted services has declined from about three-quarters of all participants in the early 2000s to less than two-thirds in recent years. Similarly, job search assistance has declined over the

Table 6.2 Active Job Seekers Participating in Wagner-Peyser Act Programs, in Millions (and Percent), PYs 2002–2012

Program year	Total participants	Received staff-assisted services	Received job search activities	Referred to employment
2002	14.9	11.6 (78%)	8.2 (55%)	5.8 (39%)
2003	15.2	11.4 (75)	8.0 (53)	6.0 (39)
2004	14.2	10.5 (74)	7.2 (51)	5.6 (39)
2005	13.3	10.5 (79)	4.5 (34)	5.4 (41)
2006	14.7	9.4 (64)	4.4 (30)	4.7 (31)
2007	17.8	9.7 (54)	4.8 (27)	4.7 (26)
2008	19.7	11.9 (60)	5.8 (29)	4.8 (24)
2009	22.4	14.2 (63)	7.7 (34)	5.8 (26)
2010	21.8	13.4 (61)	6.2 (28)	5.2 (24)
2011	19.1	12.1 (63)	5.9 (31)	4.8 (25)
2012	18.4	12.0 (65)	6.1 (33)	3.9 (21)

SOURCE: USDOL, Employment Service ETA 9002 reports.

same period from provision to more than half of all participants to less than one-third. A decline in the percentage of participants referred to employment is also apparent, but that decline is, in part, due to higher levels of unemployment and fewer job openings per job seeker during and after the Great Recession. What Table 6.2 does not reveal, however, is that even those who are getting staff-assisted services are getting less help. Instead of receiving one-on-one assistance, they are likely to be searching for work on computers in local workforce office resource rooms, receiving occasional answers to questions that they have asked about using the automated services (Wandner 2012).

Declining Expenditures per Participant

The decline in expenditure per participant in the WIA and Employment Service programs is the net effect of the cuts in funding and the increase in the need for services. The reduction in per participant expenditures has been substantial and occurring for some time, although it was temporarily halted by the availability of the one-time ARRA funding. For example, Employment Service expenditures per participant in current dollars were approximately $60 in early 2006 but declined to approximately $35 in early 2009; ARRA supplementation raised ES expenditures per participant to above $40, but the expenditures dropped again to close to $30 by the beginning of 2011 (see Figure 6.1).

As shown in Figure 6.2, a similar reduction in per person expenditures also took place for WIA Dislocated Workers, where expenditures per person had been as high as $1,700 in early 2006 but fell to approximately $700 in early 2009. With ARRA funding, WIA Dislocated Worker per participant expenditures increased briefly to above $800 but declined to approximately $600 as ARRA funding was exhausted.

WIA Adults also experienced a sharp decline in per person expenditures from nearly $1,000 per participant in 2006 to approximately $350 before ARRA supplementation took effect (see Figure 6.3). The ARRA funding raised expenditures per participant to $400 in late 2009 but fell to approximately $325 by the beginning of 2011 (Eberts, Wandner, and Cai 2013).

Figure 6.1 Wagner-Peyser Act Employment Service (ES) Expenditures per Participant, with and without Recovery Act Funding

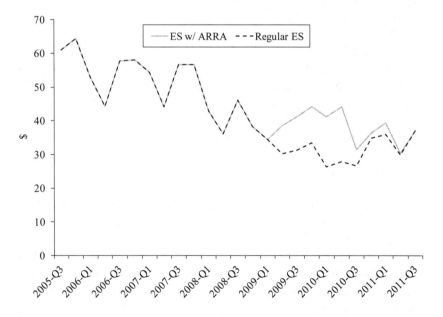

SOURCE: Eberts, Wandner, and Cai (2013).

Figure 6.2 WIA Dislocated Worker Expenditure per Participant, with and without Recovery Act Funding

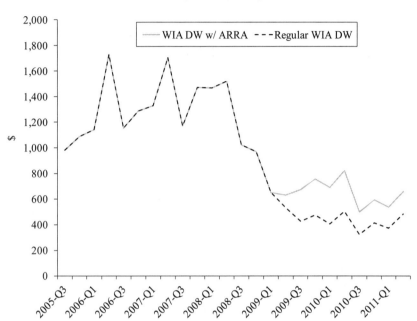

SOURCE: Eberts, Wandner, and Cai (2013).

For each of these three workforce programs, the effect of ARRA funds was limited and of short duration. Annual appropriations and expenditures for the three workforce programs were mostly flat before and after the Recovery Act funding period. For example, FY2009 funding for the three programs amounted to $3.09 billion compared with FY2011 funding of $3.00 billion, a reduction of 3 percent. Recovery Act funding provided additional resources for all three programs during a time of increased program participation, which was more than enough to raise expenditures per participant for the first year of Recovery Act funding. However, the Recovery Act funds remaining for the second year were not enough to offset the continued increase in the number of participants in each program, and expenditures per participant fell in the second year of the Recovery Act funding period. Despite increased total funding, the per participant funding for the three workforce programs

Figure 6.3 WIA Adult Expenditure per Participant, with and without Recovery Act Funding

SOURCE: Eberts, Wandner, and Cai (2013).

was lower (in current dollars) by the end of the Recovery Act period than it was before the recession. Recovery Act funds made up a small portion of this difference, but appropriations were not sufficiently long lasting to keep up with the increase in enrollments and allow a return of per participant expenditures to prerecession levels (Wandner and Eberts 2014).

Thus, with the exhaustion of the ARRA funding, state workforce agencies were faced with continuing high workloads for their workforce programs, but without the supplemental funding to serve the continuing increase in demand for services. In contrast, UI funding continued at recessionary levels as Congress repeatedly extended the Emergency Unemployment Compensation program. As a result, state workforce administrators had to decide how to manage their programs with reduced resources.

It is not likely that per participant expenditures will increase significantly in the future; rather, the downward trend will likely continue. The result will be increased pressure to reduce the public workforce infrastructure and employment service costs. There will be fewer LWIBs, fewer local workforce offices, and fewer frontline staff. Job seekers will receive less training and fewer staff-supported services. All remaining services will be highly automated.[2]

The remainder of this chapter examines how the WIA and Employment Service programs responded and adapted to reduced resources. Much of the information on responses is taken from the survey of workforce program administrators that asked how the administrators responded between July 2010 and June 2012.

RESPONSES OF STATE WORKFORCE AGENCIES TO DECLINING RESOURCES

Twenty years ago, the Clinton administration initiated a One-Stop Career Center initiative with the expectation that the state workforce system and its partners would provide extensive employment and training services throughout the nation. This plan depended on the assumption that federal workforce resources would expand. Federal funding did not increase, however, after the Republicans swept both houses of Congress in 1994, and the expected resources for the One-Stops never materialized.[3] In the ensuing 20 years, there has been a long downward trend in federal funding of the public workforce system and, more recently, a sudden sharp decline that occurred following the exhaustion of Recovery Act monies at the end of 2010. As a result, there have been two types of responses:

1) infrastructure changes: reductions in the number of LWIBS, the number of local workforce offices, the staffing of the local offices; and

2) changes in the nature of services provided to workers and employers.

INFRASTRUCTURE CHANGES

Operating the public workforce system is expensive, with over 500 LWIBs, over 2,500 local offices, and tens of thousands of workers (USDOL 2014; Wandner 2013). States have not been able to maintain the same infrastructure that they had maintained before federal funding was reduced. They have reacted by cutting the costs required to provide services to workers. These cuts consist of reducing administrative costs by reducing the number of LWIBs, reducing the cost of local office operations by reducing the number of local offices, and reducing the number of frontline workers providing services to workers and employers.

Local Workforce Investment Boards: Eliminating or Reducing Numbers

The administrative structure of the WIA program is twofold, consisting of state WIBs and LWIBs. State WIBs set broad workforce policy. They develop state workforce plans and develop and improve state workforce systems. Members of state WIBs include the governor, members of the state legislature, representatives of business and labor, local elected officials, organizations delivering services, and state agency representatives. The governor selects the chair of the state WIB. The state WIB can perform the LWIB function in a single WIB state.

LWIBs are designated by the governor. The LWIBs' functions include developing local workforce plans, selecting One-Stop operators and providers, identifying eligible training providers, developing budgets, and conducting administration and oversight. Its members must include representatives of business, educational institutions, community-based organizations, economic development agencies, and One-Stop partners. LWIBs are expensive to operate. As federal workforce funding declines, states are closing local workforce offices and reducing staff, the quantity of services provided, and the number of LWIBs that oversee the operation of local workforce offices. By late 2013, the number of LWIBs had declined to 565 for an average of only 10 per state. However, states have responded in different ways—most have tried to maintain LWIBs (and local offices) in local communities, keeping a considerable number of LWIBs in each state. For example, Massachusetts has 16, Illinois has 23, and California has 49. LWIBs are spread throughout these and many other states, and, in those states, the governance of the WIA system is indeed local (USDOL 2014).

Maintaining this local governance structure, however, has become increasingly untenable over time. Increasing numbers of states are substantially reducing the number of LWIBs or eliminating them altogether. Nine states have only a small number of LWIBs—five or fewer: Alabama (2), Hawaii (4), Kansas (5), Maine (4), Mississippi (4), Nebraska (3), Nevada (2), New Mexico (4), and Rhode Island (2). In general, these states have called upon a small number of LWIBs to administer fairly large areas of the states, foregoing local administration in many areas of the states (NAWB 2014).

A number of states have taken yet more drastic action (see Table 6.3). Nine states have given up on local WIA administration altogether and have become "single WIB" states where there are no LWIBs and program administration has been transferred to the state capital where it is conducted by the state WIB: Alaska, Delaware, Idaho, Montana, New Hampshire, North Dakota, South Dakota, Utah, and Wyoming. In these states, statewide administration of the WIA program is similar to that of the two other workforce programs—the Wagner-Peyser Act Employment Service and the Unemployment Insurance programs—giving the governor much greater control over the entire workforce system.

For example, on July 1, 2005, Idaho became a single WIB state. The main reason for this change was the state's desire to eliminate administrative costs so that it could maintain services to individuals after Idaho's WIA funding was reduced by 37 percent between 2002 and 2004. At the time, the Bush administration issued WIA planning guidelines requiring states to submit new WIA state plans for the program year starting

Table 6.3 States with Five or Fewer Local Workforce Investment Boards

Number of LWIBS	States and number of LWIBs
Five or fewer	Alabama (2) , Hawaii (4), Kansas (5), Maine (4), Mississippi (4), Nebraska (3), Nevada (2), New Mexico (4), Rhode Island (2)
None	Alaska, Delaware, Idaho, Montana, New Hampshire, North Dakota, South Dakota, Utah, Wyoming

on July 1, 2005; reduce administrative costs and overhead; and increase the number of individuals participating in training. In response, then Governor Kempthorne approved a WIA state plan to consolidate the six Idaho LWIBs into a single WIB, after getting a waiver from USDOL to make this change. The state estimated that consolidation allowed Idaho to save $1 million annually in administrative costs, which could be redirected to operate training services. Idaho estimated that without this change WIA would have served 400 fewer Idahoans. Under the new structure, the percentage of Idaho's WIA budget being spent on direct participant services increased from 36 percent to 50 percent.[4]

The pressure to reduce the number of LWIBs appears to be greatest in states with low population densities, small populations, and small geographic areas. The reduction is highly concentrated in the geographically large, sparsely populated states of the northern Rocky Mountain area. Nonetheless, the pressure to reduce the number of LWIBs is likely to continue and expand to other states if federally provided resources remain stagnant or continue to decline. The ratio of administrative to program costs has been increasing, and there are limits to how great it can get.

Reducing the number of LWIBs or eliminating them completely is also a policy choice that puts more decision-making authority in the hands of governors and other state officials. For example, the current Mississippi workforce system was launched by Governor Haley Barbour's 2004 decision to make workforce system changes that reduced the number of LWIBs from six to four and consolidated the workforce system—WIA and the ES—into a single statewide entity overseen by the Mississippi Department of Employment Security. The major goals of these changes were to reduce costs, increase program efficiency, and increase state control of workforce programs. This consolidation held Mississippi in good stead, allowing a rapid statewide response to Hurricane Katrina in 2005, but it also has been the basis for increasing WIA and ES program integration and the automation of the workforce system in the years since 2004.

The Mississippi WIA program is unusual. It is administered by the state Department of Employment Security. Local job center office managers are ES employees. The ES has been the primary service deliverer for WIA since the program started. Most local WIA contracts for service delivery are with the ES.

The Mississippi Department of Employment Security is the WIA state administrative body, and it exerts strong control over the system; it distributes WIA funds to the LWIBs. The LWIBs contract customer operations to the ES for the majority of local operations (except in northeastern Mississippi). The Department of Employment Security owns and manages the local offices and the equipment in them. While the LWIBs control the WIA funds and programs, they usually contract back to the Department of Employment Security to provide services.

Consolidation has been part of Mississippi's response to the decline in federal funding for WIA and ES programs. Equally as important has been a process to automate Mississippi's workforce and UI programs.[5]

Thus, the historical devolution of control of JTPA and WIA from state to local governments seems to be failing in the public workforce system. The starving of workforce programs has gradually made the local administration of these programs impractical. As time passes, these programs are likely to become increasingly state run, regardless of whether or not Congress reauthorizes a WIA-like program.

An illustration of the anomalies in LWIB policy is that Vermont with a population of over 600,000 has 12 LWIBs, whereas New Hampshire, its neighbor, with a population of 1.3 million, has none. The state WIB in New Hampshire oversees a program that has abandoned local control, whereas Vermont has very strong local control with one LWIB for every 52,000 people.

The number of single WIB states is likely to increase whether or not WIA is reauthorized.[6] For example, in Iowa in 2014, Senator Jack Hatch made one of the planks in his gubernatorial political platform that he would reduce the number of LWIBs. He argued that the current governor, Terry Branstad, was tied to the past and was not "modernizing" the workforce system to make the Iowa government more efficient and effective.[7]

Closing Local Workforce Offices: Reduced Access

Reducing the number of One-Stops can yield substantial cost savings. As a result, 42 percent of state workforce administrators reported reducing the number of One-Stops in their states in the two years after mid-2010. The number of One-Stops also declined during the mid-2000s, from approximately 3,600 in 2003 and 2004 to below 3,000 by the end of 2008 (see Table 6.4). The financial pressure on state workforce agencies was eased, however, toward the end of the Great Recession. Spurred by the additional 2009 ARRA funding, the decline in the number of One-Stops was arrested, and the number increased slightly in 2009 and 2010. With ARRA funding largely exhausted by September 2010, however, the decline resumed and reached 2,533 by the end of January 2014. Over 1,000 One-Stops closed between September 2003 and January 2014—a 29 percent decline in the number of One-Stops (see Table 6.4).

Most of the decline in the number of workforce local offices was in the smaller affiliate offices rather than in the larger comprehensive offices. Between December 2003 and January 2014, more than 800 affiliate offices (almost half) closed, while less than 250 comprehensive offices closed.

Under WIA, the comprehensive offices must be staffed by all partner programs, while the affiliate offices may have only one or a small number of partners in the office, most often the ES and at least one other workforce partner. Since affiliate offices are more likely to be located in

Table 6.4 Number of Local Public Workforce Offices in the United States, 2003–2013

Date	Comprehensive One-Stop Career Center	Affiliate One-Stop Career Center	Total
December 29, 2003	1,955	1,627	3,582
December 28, 2004	1,945	1,638	3,583
December 29, 2005	1,900	1,559	3,459
December 29, 2006	1,864	1,401	3,265
December 29, 2007	1,773	1,395	3,168
December 31, 2008	1,801	1,149	2,950
December 31, 2009	1,853	1,133	2,986
September 28, 2010	1,867	1,133	3,000
March 31, 2011	1,854	1,075	2,929
April 30, 2012	1,756	1,034	2,793
January 24, 2013	1,755	962	2,717
January 24, 2014	1,708	825	2,533
February 7, 2015	1,652	823	2,475

SOURCE: USDOL, Career OneStop Web site: www.servicelocator.org (accessed September 5, 2014).

rural areas, the availability of services in these nonurban areas declined substantially, although rural workers have been shown to need workforce services and to have difficulty getting these services at alternative locations. Rural workers generally have long trips to get to distant comprehensive workforce offices and are less likely to access One-Stops remotely than urban workers (Dunham et al. 2005).

Alternative Delivery Systems in Response to Declining Number of One-Stops

State workforce agencies tried to ameliorate the reduced access to local workforce offices by providing alternative methods of receiving workforce services. When workforce administrators were asked what alternative delivery systems they used to offset the decline in the numbers of One-Stops in their states, 80 percent reported that between July 1, 2010, and June 30, 2012, they implemented alternative service delivery approaches. The most frequently cited measure (14 states) was enhancing the capacity and accessibility of virtual services, generally through remote computer access without staff assistance. The other measures in order of the number of state responses were: providing services at libraries and other public facilities; using mobile One-Stop Career Centers; other; and increasing the number of satellite offices. Some of these alternatives, however, such as Internet virtual services, kiosks, and libraries depend on the ability of workers to engage in self-service job searches without trained staff-assisted service support. Others, such as mobile and satellite offices, provide limited and intermittent services. The loss of access to local offices thus has not been offset in all states, and when it has, it generally has been without in-person services or with limited access to in-person services.

To a limited extent, community-based and faith-based organizations can fill the gap created by declining public workforce offices. Operating as "job clubs," the best and biggest of these organizations can provide a wide range of services. However, even the largest of these organizations frequently meet only once or twice a month and provide evening services working cooperatively with public workforce agencies. Most of these organizations supplement rather than substitute for public workforce agencies with their job matching, assessment, counseling, labor market information, and referral to training services (Trutko et al. 2014).

Other Cost-Cutting Measures

State workforce agencies have used a wide array of methods to reduce costs. Over 70 percent of all responding states reported other types of cost cutting measures. By far the largest number of states (13 responses) reduced staffing, including through attrition, hiring freezes, and staff reassignments. Other methods of cost reduction mentioned by two or more states included travel restrictions (Idaho, Missouri, Washington, Wyoming), reductions in staff training or online training (Massachusetts, North Dakota, New York), increased use of online services and technology (New Jersey, Ohio, Virginia), reductions in overhead and centralizing of administration (Florida, Pennsylvania, Washington) reductions in services or service options (Colorado, North Carolina) and reducing materials for clients or putting them online (Oklahoma, Wyoming).

Reducing Local Office Staff

State workforce programs generally have found that they cannot maintain the staffing structure that they had built when there was more funding, particularly after the loss of temporary ARRA funding by the end of 2010. In the two years after ARRA funding terminated, more than 80 percent of states reported significant staff reductions in each of the major workforce programs, including the WIA Adult, WIA Youth, ES, and Reemployment Services programs.

Of the states that reported staff reductions, there were four staffing strategies described by states to deal with the end of ARRA funding:

1) overhiring permanent staff with ARRA funding and then retaining through attrition (Alabama);

2) increasing the number of Wagner-Peyser Act and Reemployment Services staff throughout the state by hiring temporary staff into permanent positions that opened because of attrition, eliminating intermittent staff (Indiana);

3) voluntary retirement (Massachusetts); and

4) attrition of permanent (Virginia) and part-time (New Jersey) staff.

In the future, it will be more difficult to reduce staff if real funding does not increase. State agencies were able to anticipate the end of ARRA funding, and many were able to avoid layoffs. In the future, states will find it more difficult to downsize without layoffs.

CHANGING AND REDUCING SERVICES PROVIDED

There have been two main changes in the provision of workforce services: 1) changing the mix of services from more expensive to cheaper services, e.g., to job search assistance and away from training; and 2) transitioning from staff-assisted to more automated services.

Changing Mix of Services

The trend in providing workforce services is to reduce expensive training services and increase the use of cheaper employment services. The basic reason why so few unemployed workers receive publicly provided training is that the public workforce system has been inadequately funded, with funding declining over the past few decades both in real and in nominal terms. Although supplemental ARRA funding eased the shortfall somewhat, it was not nearly sufficient to fully deal with the need for training services. Another explanation for the decline in training, however, is related to the misperception of what local workforce offices do.

Training Services

The total funding of WIA programs greatly overstates their ability to provide education and training funds to workers because WIA funds must be used to cover other things as well. WIA and Wagner-Peyser Act funds are frequently the sole support of the over 2,500 state workforce offices that provide public labor exchange and other reemployment services, as well as offer training referrals to workers all around the United States. The vast majority of funds from these two streams are used to provide reemployment services and to maintain local workforce offices. Without funding devoted to nontraining services, the state workforce offices would shut down, and the tens of millions of workers they serve each year would have nowhere to go for help in returning to work. That is part of the reason why, nationally, workforce programs expend only a small portion of their funds on training. A study for USDOL estimated that only between 18 and 27 percent of departmental workforce funds were expended on training in 2002 (Mikelson and Nightingale 2005). Of the $6.5 billion appropriated to "training programs" in that year, only between $1.1 and $1.7 billion was actually expended on training. The small percentage of WIA funding spent on training is not surprising since WIA is a universal access, one-stop program that must serve all workers who walk through the doors of the local workforce offices and for which most workers only need WIA Core and Intensive Services. Providing limited training also is not surprising given that workers participating in local workforce office programs go through a triage process before they are referred to training.

Looking at the public workforce system at the local level, similar results can be seen. One LWIB in Montgomery County, Maryland, is an example. In recent years, 13,000–14,000 individuals looked to the county service provider for help in finding jobs. Montgomery County, like most areas across the nation, faces a severe budget constraint. For example, if it were going to provide training vouchers in the modest amount of, say, $4,000 to half the individuals coming to their offices, the cost would be at least $25 million per year. Yet, the county's actual 2012 annual budget was less than $3 million, out of which its operating expenses had to be paid. Dividing the annual budget by the number of program participants yields only about $200 per visitor. Clearly, these local offices cannot afford to provide training to many individuals.

But the problem is much worse, because the Montgomery County workforce offices cannot turn individuals away. They have to serve everyone who walks through their doors. If they provided all individuals with comprehensive in-person job search assistance at a cost of, say, $300 per person, their cost would be nearly $4 million without providing any training. The cost of providing training and reemployment services means that most individuals will receive limited services, and many services will be self-service instead of in-person services. Reemployment services require, among other things, staff and telephones for in-person services and computers for self-service.

Montgomery County's planned $2.827 budget for July 2012 through June 2013 broke out as shown in Table 6.5.

The cost of providing basic employment services to 14,000 individuals consumes the lion's share of the annual budget. The major costs are employee salaries and benefits, as well as contractor costs, most of which are used to provide employment services. Computers and telephone service also are critical to providing reemployment services.

Since the great majority of expenditures are made to provide basic employment services and run the office, training in Montgomery County—and in other local workforce offices around the nation—has to be limited to what funds remain after paying for the basic expenses. Similar to the national average results seen above, available training funds were expected to be less than 20 percent of the total budget. Thus, the preponderant cost of running a local workforce office is providing services other than training, and the image of the WIA system as a pure training system is a myth. The local workforce office training "residual" could be much larger only if the WIA program were not starved for resources, but in reality, workforce funding is likely to decline rather than increase.

Limited funding for training under JTPA and WIA has meant that these programs supply only a small portion of the training received by American workers and a small portion of the funding for the training needed by unemployed workers. Historically, the JTPA and WIA programs have provided only modest amounts of training. In the years 1993–2012, between 142,000 and 291,000 JTPA/WIA Adults and Dislocated Workers received training, representing less than 3 percent of

**Table 6.5 Summary of Budget of Montgomery County, Maryland,
Workforce Offices, PY 2012 ($ millions)**

Cost category	Planned expenditures
Salaries and benefits	1.870
Contractors	0.223
Training	0.504
Computers	0.030
Telephone	0.026
Other	0.304

SOURCE: Workforce Solutions Group of Montgomery County.

those seeking help in finding jobs from the local workforce offices (see Table 6.6). Once the dislocated worker program was fully implemented in 1996, training for Adults and Dislocated Workers experienced a strong downward trend through 2008. While ARRA funding sharply increased training in 2009 and 2010, the downward trend resumed in 2011 with the exhaustion of ARRA funds. It can be expected that the decline in training participation will continue unless the public workforce budget increases. More likely, since the other costs of operating job centers and providing reemployment services also will continue to

Table 6.6 Number of Adults and Dislocated Workers Receiving Job Training, under JTPA and WIA, PYs 1993–2012

Year	Adults	Dislocated workers	Total
JTPA			
1993	126,100	80,800	206,900
1994	126,500	94,00	220,500
1995	118,400	130,500	248,900
1996	113,400	147,400	260,800
1997	110,800	143,700	254,500
1998	112,200	134,900	247,100
1999	83,100	110,000	193,200
WIA			
2001	75,963	66,192	142,155
2002	107,671	98,540	206,211
2003	102,950	102,415	205,365
2004	109,492	95,113	204,605
2005	105,457	83,699	189,156
2006	109,528	77,160	186,688
2007	109,676	66,662	176,338
2008	98,214	54,953	153,167
2009	129,914	84,969	214,883
2010	160,190	129,908	290,098
2011	133,640	120,452	254,092
2012	115,594	98,683	214,277

NOTE: No WIASRD data book was prepared for PY 2000.

SOURCE: WIA and JTPA program data from WIASRD and SPIR data books, various years. See www.doleta.gov/performance/results/pdf, various years, Tables II-11 and III-12 (accessed September 5, 2014).

increase, training levels will decline whether workforce program budgets remain static or decline. Thus, the current mix of services is unsustainable—cheaper employment services will displace more expensive training costs, and computerized employment services will replace in-person services.

The Department of Education CTE and Adult Education programs can supplement the training of some job seekers, but these programs also are small and cannot satisfy much of the unemployed workers' needs for training. By contrast, private businesses provide the bulk of training in the United States. It has been estimated that 85 percent of establishments with 50 or more employees and 70 percent of all establishments provide training to their employees each year. Estimates of workers receiving training is less exact, ranging between 26 and 65 percent (Lerman, McKernan, and Riegg 2004).

Reemployment Services

A number of experimental evaluations of reemployment services/job search assistance have shown its cost effectiveness, including experiments in the District of Columbia, Minnesota, Nevada, and New Jersey. Job search assistance has been shown to provide dislocated workers with the tools to find work more rapidly, thus reducing the duration of compensated unemployment. Other studies have shown that UI eligibility reviews also reduced the duration of compensated UI without providing job search assistance. While one study using Kentucky data concluded that the "threat" of job search assistance was more important than its provision, the small effect of the offer was found to be due to Kentucky's provision of very small amounts of job search assistance during the period analyzed (Wandner 2010, pp. 164–165). More recently, the Reemployment and Eligibility Assessment (REA) program has been implemented and evaluated. REAs provide both UI eligibility reviews and reemployment services. An experimental evaluation of the REA program demonstrated that both reemployment services and eligibility reviews reduce compensated UI durations (Benus et al. 2008).

Reviews of the use of job search assistance around the world have found it to be the single most effective public workforce intervention (Auer, Efendioglu, and Leschke 2005; Martin and Grubb 2001). Auer et al. reviewed evaluated programs among all International Labor Organization members around the world, while Martin and Grubb reviewed programs in the industrial nations that belong to the Organization for Economic Cooperation and Development. Both analyses compared the entire range of public workforce services offered by member countries and assessed their relative effectiveness.

The positive net benefits of a New Jersey experiment were particularly influential in the enactment of the Worker Profiling and Reemployment Services (WPRS) initiative in 1993, which required states to develop a targeting mechanism ("worker profiling") that identified dislocated workers most likely to exhaust their entitlement to UI benefits. These workers were to be provided with job search assistance ("reemployment services") to the extent that states were able to fund these services. When enacted, the program was an unfunded mandate since Congress did not appropriate any funds for reemployment services. Between 2001 and 2006, however, Congress provided limited funding as Reemployment Service Grants. Much greater funding ($250 million) was provided as Reemployment Services Grants by the ARRA in 2009, but these funds were exhausted by the end of 2010 (Eberts, Bartik, and Kline 2013).

Since the Great Recession, the WPRS system has continued to provide job search assistance services to dislocated workers in the form of orientations, assessments, counseling, placement services, job search workshops and referrals to training. The quantity of these services has declined sharply since 2010, with the loss of ARRA funds. Table 6.7 shows the decline in the WPRS system in the three years since 2010. The percentage of unemployed workers receiving UI benefits profiled and referred to services also has declined. Once referred workers report to receive services, there are few services to provide to them. This is true of all reemployment services, but it is particularly true of referrals to training. With limited training slots, WIA staff members have asked that fewer workers be referred (Wandner 2013).

Although WPRS has declined in the three years after 2010, it shows that as a system it can adapt to declining public workforce resources, serving fewer unemployed workers, but at the same time identifying those most likely to become long-term unemployed (and benefit from services) and referring those workers to reemployment services.

Table 6.7 Worker Profiling and Reemployment Services and Unemployment Insurance First Payment Data, 1994–2013

Year	First pays	Profiled	Referral	Reported	Orientation	Assessment	Counseling	Placement	Job search workshops	Training
1994	7,959,281	122,065	23,087	17,184	14,126	9,876	5,883	5,671	11,042	4,492
1995	8,035,229	4,061,731	456,533	453,005	283,508	246,655	140,301	267,281	213,512	74,292
1996	7,995,135	7,208,694	821,442	1,036,806	512,045	507,824	214,528	613,544	338,508	166,456
1997	7,325,093	6,985,048	745,870	990,041	474,891	455,914	194,818	630,760	336,959	160,741
1998	7,341,903	6,982,571	783,779	1,033,482	477,913	416,027	191,315	676,284	296,681	156,462
1999	6,967,840	6,483,514	803,401	990,737	447,032	403,195	198,571	668,496	253,451	141,398
2000	7,035,783	6,475,605	977,440	1,229,352	557,250	471,712	146,917	645,170	342,856	113,879
2001	9,868,193	8,952,312	1,154,743	1,499,364	666,610	531,020	129,136	506,172	452,439	120,093
2002	10,092,569	9,178,024	1,220,466	986,719	619,917	462,643	125,103	376,757	369,756	76,448
2003	9,935,108	8,238,485	1,147,448	919,450	595,564	423,977	114,142	378,180	400,245	70,295
2004	8,368,623	7,037,337	1,106,776	880,263	602,833	343,903	93,215	378,181	379,735	73,508
2005	7,917,301	6,441,561	1,128,710	845,789	607,905	350,443	109,697	376,342	355,843	77,915
2006	7,350,734	6,340,253	1,170,126	856,587	627,668	406,158	134,837	405,558	369,564	92,200
2007	7,652,634	6,586,553	1,230,093	911,055	644,797	425,711	149,101	437,744	390,454	100,780
2008	10,059,554	8,516,931	1,268,037	937,580	667,340	480,929	143,097	404,234	385,151	124,306
2009	14,172,822	12,252,030	1,906,088	1,400,553	1,075,837	658,200	214,673	537,908	557,746	199,230
2010	10,726,566	9,385,195	2,071,260	1,855,394	1,269,088	1,020,482	340,281	690,437	664,020	210,746
2011	9,474,531	9,276,794	1,834,026	1,848,467	1,118,276	757,079	302,995	871,116	576,356	157,767
2012	8,656,495	7,272,231	1,686,510	1,338,512	939,873	705,622	279,126	595,334	529,981	160,942
2013	7,879,212	5,525,609	1,252,607	945,306	657,377	521,184	203,353	459,570	399,456	71,425

SOURCES: USDOL ETA 5159 and ETA 9048 reports.

Fewer In-Person Services: Movement to Self-Service and Automated Services

Workforce administrators said that they adapted to the end of ARRA funding by increasing self-service and reducing in-person services. This trend is likely to continue in a workforce world of static or declining resources. Part of the system response consists of making use of alternative delivery systems and other cost-cutting measures, including introducing travel restrictions, reducing staff training or using online training, increasing the use of online services and technology, reducing overhead and support, centralizing administration, reducing services or service options; and reducing material for clients or putting them online.

An overwhelming majority of states (82 percent) reported increasing the automation of program administration and program services. Of these states, many reported that automation enabled them to serve more customers (70 percent) as well as improve quality for some customers (60 percent). But 30 percent reported that automation diluted service quality for some or all customers. Forty-three percent reported that automation reduced costs, and a quarter reported that it reduced the number of required staff. Many states (60 percent) reported resulting changes at the local or state level in the administration of workforce programs due to automation.

Automation of program services included UI claims takings, online UI Eligibility Reviews, job search and job matching (including providing information about job openings and job orders, career assessments, Reemployment Services orientation, providing labor market information, and operating virtual job fairs).

Automation of programs administration included staff training, program and financial reporting, case management, approved training provider processing and listing, and Individual Training Account invoicing. States reported that the most significant impacts of automation were enabling them to provide services to more customers (26 states) and to improve the quality of services (22 states).

Clearly, automation was implemented to reduce costs and to reduce staff with the hope that more customers could be served without degrading service quality to customers. Several states (Georgia, Hawaii, Maryland, South Dakota, Tennessee) pointed out that the move to automated self-service affects customers in different ways: technically savvy and more educated customers can do well with self-service, while other customers suffer a decline in the quality of services they receive, with some customers feeling alienated by the reduction in staff services. The less technically savvy and less educated workers tend to be older, minorities, and concentrated in rural areas and urban centers. Urban workers are likely to have greater skills and access to computers than rural workers (Dunham et al. 2005). Minorities are likely to have fewer skills and less access to computers.

The decline in in-person services has an adverse effect on the Unemployment Trust Fund that pays for unemployment benefits. Intense in-person job search assistance has been shown to speed the return to work of UI recipients. If reemployment services are not provided, workers stay on UI longer and the Unemployment Trust Fund is adversely affected.

Impact on the Quality of Customer Experience

Administrators were asked how the reduction in the number of local offices and other cost reduction measures affected the quality of the customer experience with workforce programs. Very few of the 45 responses indicate that cost reduction measures improved customer experiences. For the remainder, there was a split in responses between customer experience being either diminished or not significantly impacted. Examining the individual written descriptions of the impact on the customer experience, there is little to suggest any improvement for customers. One-on-one services were generally replaced with computer-delivered or group services. Intensive and training services generally diminished, and there were long waits until the local office staff members that remained were available to provide services. Exceptions were improved services from the opening of two new local offices in the District of Columbia and enhanced Reemployment Services activity in South Carolina. It is not likely an accident that these two jurisdictions were among the minority of states that were able to supplement funding for services.

LOOKING TO THE FUTURE

Impact on Workers and Employers

The anticipated future impact of declining funding for the public workforce system is generally negative. Job seekers and employers will receive less one-on-one assistance in finding jobs and finding workers to fill job openings. Because the remaining employment services will be highly automated, the effect of the change in service delivery will be uneven. The effect on the computer savvy—educated, younger, and prime-age workers—will be limited. These workers make greater use of automated methods in their daily lives and will have a greater ability to use automated, self-service tools.

On the other hand, less educated and older workers will have greater problems using automated tools. If they cannot receive in-person assistance, they may fall through the cracks, unable to make use of the complex job search tools that have become widespread.

All workers will find that there is a decline in the availability of WIA-funded training. The limited funding available for training will continue to be in short supply. Workers trying to build their job skills will have to find other sources of funding for training or do without training.

Job seekers will find that they have less access to the public workforce system. There will be fewer local workforce offices. Comprehensive offices will be maintained in major metropolitan areas, but the number of offices will continue to decline in small towns and rural areas, where the remaining access is concentrated in the smaller affiliated workforce offices. The decline in offices in rural areas and small towns will leave fewer alternatives for job seekers with less access to Internet services, particularly if distances to remaining local offices are great.

Changes Made by State Agencies

State workforce administrators have made changes in the operations of the public workforce system over the past two decades as public workforce funding declined. Between July 2010 and June 2012, the funding decline continued. Twenty-seven states said that they had made major changes at the state or local level in the administration of their workforce programs, such as merging or reengineering business processes. Eighteen said no such changes had been made. Of the current or recent changes in program administration, the greatest number of changes described by 14 states were reorganizations, reassignments, mergers, and consolidations (Alabama, Arizona, Colorado, Florida, Georgia, Idaho, Maryland, Massachusetts, North Carolina, Ohio, Oklahoma, South Carolina, Tennessee, Wyoming), while Arizona merged WIBs and Ohio consolidated local services. Mergers with commerce or economic development agencies occurred in four states (Florida, North Carolina, Oklahoma, and South Carolina); business reengineering occurred in seven (Colorado, Massachusetts, Minnesota, Missouri, Nevada, Texas, and Washington).

Looking to future potential changes, 20 state administrators indicated that they were considering program and administrative changes. These changes included consolidating WIBs to make single statewide WIBs, and changes, streamlining, and consolidation to deal with current and possible future funding reductions.

CONCLUSION

There is no reason to expect increased public workforce funding in the short run. If funds remain constant or decline further, the quantity of services provided must decline as the cost of services increase. Thus, unless there is a major policy change, the workforce system is likely to continue in the direction that it has been heading. The result will be continuing declines in funding per participant. Despite the end of the Great Recession in 2009, the need for public workforce services will continue to remain high. Unemployment is higher than after recent recessions, workers are generally permanently displaced, and they tend to remain unemployed for longer periods of time.

State workforce agencies have experienced a decline in funding after the Great Recession. Most states did not supplement federal funding, and even those states that did only replaced part of the lost funding.

The majority of state supplementary funding went to Wagner-Peyser Act employment services.

Funding declines resulted in a wide variety of reductions in workforce programs. Further, the mix of program services changed sharply, and less intensive services replaced more intensive services, with training and intensive services declining substantially. States, however, tried to maintain core, employment, and reemployment services.

In addition, the great majority of states reduced staffing levels. Most states reduced one-on-one staff-assisted services, replacing them with automated services as well as with group services.

State workforce agencies are likely to respond by continuing to reduce the number of LWIBs and local workforce offices. These offices will be staffed by few frontline workers. In response to the decline in staffing, workers and employers will receive fewer in-person services. Job seekers and employers will face more automated services. As workers of all ages become more proficient in using computers, more automated services will be accessed remotely from home computers or satellite offices (e.g., libraries). Finally, more low-cost employment services will be provided by the public workforce system instead of training. Remaining workforce training will increasingly be low-cost and provided remotely.

As public workforce resources have declined, so has the quantity of in-person reemployment services. Similarly, training has been limited. But these reemployment services have been carefully targeted, other than those limited resources made available through the WPRS system.

At least eight things can be done to help the public workforce system cope with the decline in program resources:

1) While limited, the public workforce services can be improved with better targeting to serve those workers most in need of reemployment services and by providing them with the kinds of services that will help them the most. One approach is expanded use of WPRS for dislocated workers. Targeting services also can be done more broadly for all workers in need of job seeking and training services. This type of targeting can be conducted in local workforce offices as demonstrated in Georgia with its use of a Frontline Decision Support System. Similar systems can be developed for national programs such as the Job Corps (Eberts, O'Leary, and Wandner 2002).

2) Targeting is particularly important for training services, since they are by far the most expensive services that workers receive. Research has shown that there are a small number of high earnings/high-return training options that benefit workers and are cost effective for the public workforce system. This training is concentrated in the sciences, math, health services, engineering, as well as in specialized blue-collar fields such as auto mechanics (Jacobson, LaLonde, and Sullivan 2002). To gain reasonable rates of return on training, the national- and state-level public workforce systems need to more carefully evaluate demand occupations, and training should be restricted to high-wage/high-return occupations.

3) There is a lack of balance between the funding of administrative services and the funding for employment services. Administrative costs have remained high while funding for services has declined. In response, administrative costs have been reduced somewhat in recent years by decreasing both the number of local offices providing services and the number of LWIBs, but most of the cost savings have come from closing local offices. While cost savings make more room to provide services, the decline in the number of local offices makes it more difficult for workers and employers to receive services, especially in less densely populated areas. In the future, the public workforce programs can better serve workers and employers if emphasis is placed on decreasing the number of LWIBs rather than decreasing local workforce offices.

4) The private sector is likely to assume a greater share of the burden of providing workforce services, expanding current practices that substitute private for public workforce services for both employers and workers. Large employers currently are improving their search for workers to fill job openings. One example is the development of the National Labor Exchange, operated by the National Association of Workforce Agencies and DirectEmployers, an employer association that helps its large-employer members find workers to fill job openings using data from participating employers and from the state workforce job banks. Skilled workers can make use of headhunters. However, smaller

employers and lower-wage workers are less able to make use of private workforce services. In the future, low-wage job seekers and small employers are likely to have difficulty finding alternative private methods to compensate for the decline in public workforce services as they search for work and search for employees, respectively.

5) Local workforce offices already are making use of alternative sources of funding beyond formula-funded grants. Among the nontraditional sources of funding are USDOL competitive grants, as the department commits a substantial funding to non-formula-funded activities. (However, only a small number of LWIBs receive competitive grants, so there will be more losers than winners.) Local offices also can compete to find funding from non-USDOL sources. Examples are providing employment services to nonemployment public organizations, such as prisons and jails, and contractually screening potential new employees for the private firms.

6) The public workforce system also can be made more effective by improving system performance measures. Unadjusted measures of performance do not measure the system's "value added." Rather, unadjusted measures give credit to or punish state and local workforce agencies for issues outside their control, including labor market conditions in the areas in which they provide services and the relative difficulty of serving certain demographic groups. There should be greater use of regression-adjusted performance measures that account for these labor market conditions and the demographics of the populations served (Eberts, Bartik, and Kline 2009). The rewards for state performance similarly should be regression adjusted since unadjusted measures have been shown not to reflect value-added measures of performance (Wandner and Wiseman 2011).

7) Some use of this approach has been implemented in the past, but a boost has come from the Workforce Innovation and Opportunity Act of 2014. Section 116 of the bill would require regression adjustment of state performance measures. This approach should improve the outcomes of the WIA programs if properly implemented. The approach also could be extended to the local level

to assess the performance of LWIBs as they provide workforce services to workers who vary with respect to their demographics and to adjust for differences in economic conditions among LWIBs in a state.

8) The public workforce system should continue to be rigorously evaluated, especially using experimental methods. While the Congress and state legislatures do not always respond positively to rigorous program evaluations, such evaluations have helped to initiate new programs and saved well-performing programs from the chopping block.

Notes

1. The number of American Job Centers in the United States is available daily from the U.S. Department of Labor's Service Locator at the CareerOneStop Web site. The number of American Job Centers declined from 3,582 on December 29, 2003, to 2,694 on August 11, 2013 (Wandner 2013, p. 8). On May 28, 2014, the Service Locator indicated that there were 2,513 American Job Centers in the United States.
2. Of the 45 state workforce administrators responding to a 2012 survey, 26 indicated that automation allowed them to serve more customers. Twenty-two responded that automation improved service to some or all customers, while 11 responded that automation diluted quality for some or all customers (Wandner 2013).
3. Author interview with Lawrence Katz, August 14, 2007.
4. E-mail to David Balducchi from Rogelio (Roy) Valdez, deputy director, Field Services and Workforce Division, Idaho Department of Labor, January 31, 2014.
5. Author interview with Dale Smith, executive director, chief operating officer, Mississippi Department of Employment Security, February 11, 2014.
6. However, the Workforce Innovation and Opportunity Act would fix local workforce areas for two years after enactment.
7. E-mail from Jack Hatch to David Balducchi (March 7, 2014) in response to March 7 e-mail from Balducchi to Hatch presenting the WIA single WIB analysis from this chapter.

References

Auer, Peter, Umit Efendioglu, and Janine Leschke. 2005. *Active Labour Market Policies around the World: Coping with the Consequences of Globalism*. Geneva: International Labour Office.

Benus, Jacob M., Etan Blass, Eileen Poe-Yamagata, and Ying Wang. 2008. *Reemployment and Eligibility Assessment (REA) Study: Final Report*. Employment and Training Administration Occasional Paper 2008-2. Washington DC: U.S. Department of Labor.

Bobeley, James M. 2011. "Characteristics of Displaced Workers 2007–2009: A Visual Essay." *Monthly Labor Review* 134(9): 3–15.

Congressional Budget Office. 1993. *Displaced Workers: Trends in the 1980s and Implications for the Future*. Washington, DC: Congressional Budget Office.

D'Amico, Ron. 2006. *What's Known about the Effects of Publicly-Funded Employment and Training Programs*. Social Policy Research Associates. ETA Occasional Paper 2006-10. Washington, DC: U.S. Department of Labor, Employment and Training Administration.

Dunham, Kate, Annelies Goger, Jennifer Henderson-Frakes, and Nichole Tucker. 2005. *Workforce Development in Rural Areas: Changes in Access, Service Delivery, and Partnerships*. ETA Occasional Paper 2005-07. Washington, DC: U.S. Department of Labor, Employment and Training Administration.

Eberts, Randall T., Timothy J. Bartik, and Ken Kline. 2009. "Estimating a Performance Standards Adjustment Model for Workforce Programs That Provides Timely Feedback and Uses Data from Only One State." Working Paper No. 09-144. Kalamazoo, MI: W.E. Upjohn Institute for Employment Research.

Eberts, Randall, Christopher O'Leary, and Stephen A. Wandner, eds. 2002. *Targeting Employment Services*. Kalamazoo, MI: W.E. Upjohn Institute for Employment Research.

Eberts, Randall, Stephen Wandner, and Jing Cai. 2013. "Data Analysis of the Implementation of the American Recovery and Reinvestment Act Workforce Development and Unemployment Insurance Provisions." In *The American Recovery and Reinvestment Act: The Role of Workforce Programs*, Richard A. Hobbie and Burt S. Barnow, eds. Kalamazoo, MI: W.E. Upjohn Institute for Employment Research, pp. 267–307.

Farber, Henry S. 1997. "The Changing Face of Job Loss in the United States, 1981–1995." Industrial Relations Section Working Paper No. 382. Princeton, NJ: Princeton University.

Farber, Henry S. 2005. "What Do We Know about Job Loss in the United States? Evidence from the Displaced Worker Survey, 1984–2004." Industrial Relations Section Working Paper No. 498. Princeton, NJ: Princeton University.

Groshen, Erica L., and Simon Potter. 2003. "Has Structural Change Contributed to the Jobless Recovery?" *Current Issues in Economics and Finance* 9(8):1–7.

Helwig, Ryan T. 2004. "Worker Displacement in 1999–2000. *Monthly Labor Review* 127(6): 54–68.

Hipple, Steven. 1999. "Worker Displacement in the Mid-1990s." *Monthly Labor Review* 122(7): 15–32.

Jacobson, Louis, Robert LaLonde, and Daniel Sullivan. 2002. "Measures of Program Performance and the Training Choices of Displaced Workers." In *Targeting Employment Services*, Randall W. Eberts, Christopher J. O'Leary, and Stephen A. Wandner, eds. Kalamazoo, MI: W.E. Upjohn Institute for Employment Research, pp. 187–214.

Katz, Lawrence. 2007. Interview of Lawrence Katz by Stephen A. Wandner (August 14).

Kletzer, Lori G. 1998. "Job Displacement." *Journal of Economic Perspectives* 12(1):115–136.

Lerman, Robert I., Signe-Marie McKernan, and Stephanie Riegg. 2004. "The Scope of Employer-Provided Training in the United States." In *Job Training Policy in the United States*, Christopher J. O'Leary, Robert A. Straits, and Stephen A. Wandner, eds. Kalamazoo, MI: W.E. Upjohn Institute for Employment Research, pp. 211–243.

Martin, John T., and David Grubb. 2001. "What Works and for Whom: A Review of OECD Countries' Experience with Active Labour Market Policies." *Swedish Economic Policy Review* 8(2): 9–56.

Mikelson, Kelly S., and Demetra Smith Nightingale. 2005. *Expenditures on Public and Private Job Skills Training in the United States*. Washington, DC: The Urban Institute.

National Association of Workforce Boards (NAWB). WIB Finder. Washington, DC: NAWB. http://www.workforceinvestmentworks.com/workforce_board_finder.asp (accessed January 31, 2014).

Smith, Dale. 2014. Interview of Dale Smith, Executive Director, Chief Operating Officer, Mississippi Department of Employment Security by Stephen A. Wandner (February 11).

Trutko, John, Carolyn O'Brien, Stephen A. Wandner, and Burt Barnow. 2014. *Formative Evaluation of Job Clubs Operated by Faith- and Community-Based Organizations: Findings from Site Visits and Options for Future Evaluation*. Report prepared for the Chief Evaluation Officer of the U.S.

Department of Labor, May. Washington, DC: U.S. Department of Labor. http://www.dol.gov/asp/evaluation/reports/Job_Clubs_Evaluation-Final_Report-May.pdf (accessed April 8, 2015).

U.S. Department of Labor (USDOL). 2013. *UI Outlook: FY 2014 Budget, Midsession Review.* Washington, DC: U.S. Department of Labor. www.workforcesecurity.doleta.gov/unemploy/pdf/MSR.pdf (accessed September 5, 2014).

———. 2014. "America's Service Locator: WIB Locator." Washington DC: U.S. Department of Labor. www.servicelocator.org/wibcontacts/default.asp?state=CA&Ist=10# (accessed May 28, 2014).

Wandner, Stephen A. 2010. *Solving the Reemployment Puzzle: From Research to Policy.* Kalamazoo, MI: W.E. Upjohn Institute for Employment Research.

Wandner, Stephen A. 2012. "The Response of the U.S. Public Workforce System to High Unemployment during the Great Recession." Unemployment and Recovery Project Working Paper 4. Washington, DC: Urban Institute, September. http://www.urban.org/UploadedPDF/412679-The-Response-of-the-US-Public-Workforce-System-to-High-Unemployment.pdf (accessed April 8, 2015).

———. 2013. "The Public Workforce System's Response to Declining Funding after the Great Recession." Unemployment and Recovery Project Working Paper No. 5. Washington, DC: Urban Institute. http://www.urban.org/publications/412866.html (accessed September 5, 2014).

Wandner, Stephen A., and Randall Eberts. 2014. "Public Workforce Programs during the Great Recession." *Monthly Labor Review* July: 1–18. http://www.bls.gov/opub/mlr/2014/article/public-workforce-programs-during-the-great-recession.htm (accessed September 19, 2014).

Wandner, Stephen A., and Michael Wiseman. 2011. "Financial Performance Incentives." In *The Workforce Investment Act: Implementation Experience and Evaluation Findings*, Douglas J. Besharov and Phoebe H. Cottingham, eds. Kalamazoo, MI: W.E. Upjohn Institute for Employment Research, pp. 277–312.

Part 2

Redesigning Workforce Development Strategies

7
Creating and Communicating Critical Information about Workforce Credentials

Stephen Crawford
Robert Sheets
George Washington University

The past decade has seen enormous growth in the number and variety of college degrees, educational certificates, industry certifications, occupational licenses, and badges that schools and certification bodies award, and which recipients present to employers as evidence of specific competencies. One result is increased uncertainty about the quality and value of labor market credentials and how they relate to each other. Employers wonder what holders of credentials really know and can do; students wonder about the value of a particular credential, compared to others, as they decide whether to invest time and money to obtain it. Regulators and student loan managers share these concerns, and all this uncertainty makes the labor market function much less efficiently than it would if there were greater transparency and trust.

This chapter argues that the solution to this problem is the voluntary standardization of the terms used to describe and endorse labor market credentials, combined with an open data registry for posting and accessing the resulting information. This standardization of terms would focus on the most important features of credentials—those that are essential for determining and comparing their quality, portability, and value in the labor market. It also argues that this solution can be achieved through a public-private collaborative and voluntary action.

In fact, an initiative along these lines is already well under way. Funded by a Lumina Foundation grant to George Washington University's Institute of Public Policy, in partnership with the American National Standards Institute (ANSI), this initiative involves more than four dozen major credentialing stakeholders, including the nation's leading business and higher education associations and the U.S. Departments of Commerce, Education, Labor, Defense, Energy, and Health and Human Services. It encompasses all labor market credentials, from college degrees and educational certificates to industry certifications and occupational licenses to such microcredentials as "badges." This initiative is engaging these stakeholders through an open and collaborative process established by ANSI that has been successful in promoting transparency, interoperability, and trust in other sectors, including health care and energy. This process is designed to explore the role of a national public-private collaborative.

The results so far have been impressive. For many of 18 or so credential "descriptors" (i.e., relevant features critical in determining quality, portability, and value), the initiative has not only developed definitions, it has laid out the standardization problem, explained the basic dimensions and related coding schema, and spelled out paths to implementation. It has also developed detailed plans for a "reference model" for cross-walking competency statements written by different communities of practice, an open metadata registry for posting and accessing comparable credentialing information, pilot projects for testing several registry applications, and a collaborative of stakeholders that will assess the lessons learned from the pilots and decide whether to try to take the system to scale and make it sustainable through an appropriate governance structure and business model.

STANDARDIZATION AS A PUBLIC POLICY TOOL

This chapter's argument exemplifies a promising but underdeveloped approach to public policy implementation in education and workforce development: the use of standards to create or improve markets to serve public purposes. Standards are agreed-upon definitions of the fundamental characteristics and interfaces of all types of entities in the marketplace, including products, services, processes, systems, organizations, and even people. The United States and other countries promote the development and implementation of national and global standards and conformity assessment systems to facilitate trade, improve the performance of industry, protect consumers, and increase competition (National Research Council 1995). Standards promote competition—and collaboration—by facilitating transparency and fostering "interoperability," thereby reducing information complexity and switching costs. Conformity assessment systems define the approaches for certifying that an entity conforms to the standards used to describe it in the marketplace, and they promote confidence and trust in the marketplace.

Unfortunately, standardization has received little attention in examinations of public policy tools. For example, Kamarck (2007) contrasts "government by market" to government by network (through contracts with private service providers) and government by traditional bureaucracy. Government by market, she argues, is the best option "when a policy consensus is reached that requires many hundreds of businesses or many thousands of people to change their behaviors" (p. 20). Most of Kamarck's examples, from bottle deposit laws to tradable pollution permits, involve financial incentives. She does not discuss the role of standards in creating markets that are transparent enough for incentives to work, much less the benefits standards can provide even without financial incentives. This can be seen clearly in how standardization has been used to promote comparability and improve quality in health care and improve environmental reporting and management.

Standards help create more effective markets by making products or services comparable enough that consumers can weigh their relative merits and determine the price-value trade-off. Such informed choice creates competition to deliver the qualities that consumers most value at prices they are willing to pay. If employers and students could make more informed choices about which credentials best meet their needs, they could obtain better results with lower transaction costs. Similarly, the economy would benefit from a more highly skilled workforce whose education and training were provided by more productive institutions.

The first section of this chapter examines the credentialing problem, offers a vision of an effective credentialing system, and explains the need for a broadly coordinated effort to realize that vision. The second section describes three complementary strategies for achieving the vision: 1) developing more standardized terminology for describing the market-relevant features of credentials; 2) developing similar standardized terminology for describing the quality assurance (QA) entities such as accreditation organizations that accredit, approve, or endorse these credentials; and 3) creating a public-private "registry" for making available essential and comparable information about credentials and QA entities. The third section describes the kinds of registry applications that employers, students, workers, and others are likely to value, and explains the role of a "credentialing collaborative" in this initiative, modeled on ANSI collaboratives that have been used to coordinate standardization initiatives in other sectors. A final section summarizes the argument and draws some conclusions.

THE CREDENTIALING PROBLEM

Labor market credentials are attestations to the completion of specific training or education programs by students or to the passing of career-related knowledge and skill tests by candidates. They include but are not limited to educational degrees, certificates, industry certifications, and occupational licenses. Employers rely on them to provide second- or third-party validation—by a reputable credentialing organization or third-party assessor—of a job applicant's possession of certain knowledge and skills. The public relies on them for assurance that certain workers—from welders and electricians to pilots and physicians—are qualified to practice a particular occupation or work role.

An Increasingly Chaotic Credentialing Marketplace

For a modern, knowledge-based economy to function efficiently, the meaning of various credentials must be clear. Employers need to know what kind and level of knowledge and skill the holder of credential A has, compared to the holder of credential B, and how much to trust the claims made. Students and workers who seek to improve their position in the labor market need to know what jobs various credentials will qualify them for, what bump in earnings capacity they are likely to experience, how often they may have to renew a particular credential, and whether it is a stepping stone to higher-level credentials.

Similarly, those who give or lend students and workers money to pursue new credentials, including taxpayers, need to know what various credentials mean and which education and training organizations to trust. Finally, credentialing organizations themselves, especially the good ones, have an interest in the ability of the market to recognize the distinctive features and value of the credentials they award.

In short, nearly all Americans have a stake in the nation's credentialing system, but unfortunately, the current system is not meeting their needs. Many employers express frustration at the difficulty of finding job candidates who possess the needed knowledge and skills, despite large numbers of people seeking work. Service veterans struggle to translate skills they learned in the military into civilian credentials and jobs. Young adults entering the labor market do not know what credentials will get them where they want to go and how best to obtain them. Individuals who need or wish to change careers find it difficult to translate skills and knowledge that may be of value in other occupations into credentials that will be recognized or college credits that will count toward a degree.

From the perspective of these "consumers" of credentials, the problem is the uncertainty about what different credentials signify. From the perspective of reformers, however, the problem is more systemic. It is the lack of transparency, trust, and portability in the nation's highly fragmented and complex credentialing "system." The result is unnecessarily high costs, wasted time, and inadequately informed decision making.

Skeptics may ask, if we've lived with this reality for so long, why bother trying to change it now? The answer is threefold. First, the problem has become more serious, as rapid growth in the number and variety of credentials, combined with the breakdown of traditional boundaries between different types of credentials (i.e., degrees, industry certifications), has intensified doubts about the quality and value of many credentials. Second, recent advances in information technology make it possible and practical, for the first time, to fix the problem. Finally, there is a new willingness among the key stakeholders to do the work required, due in part to their concerns about new competitors (e.g., for-profit, online, and competency-based providers) and growing pressure on governments to ensure the value of investments in postsecondary education.

Silos and communities of practice

Today's complex and fragmented credentialing "system" developed over many years, through the interplay of loosely connected education and training providers, personnel certification bodies, accreditation organizations and federal and state regulatory agencies and boards. One result has been the emergence of different "communities of practice," each using its own technical language and quality criteria that other communities find difficult to decipher. Further complicating matters, these communities are supported by highly specialized reporting and data systems, which, though designed to promote transparency within certain sectors, are difficult to integrate with systems designed for other communities. For example, higher education institutions participate in a community of practice that includes accreditation bodies and federal and state education agencies. This community has its own language and terminology for describing degrees and certificates, as well as its own quality criteria established through its accreditation systems and federal and state regulatory agencies. Similarly, industry and professional certification organizations participate in their own communities of practice—communities with different languages and quality criteria (i.e., standards) and different accreditation and regulatory bodies. More generally, education and training in the United States is highly decentralized and subject to limited oversight by the federal government and most state governments.

At the same time, there are overlaps among these communities, such as when college and university degrees are linked to certification or licensing systems—this is often the case in engineering and health care. These links are even used by the academic community as outcomes to demonstrate the quality of the education they provide. Such a segmented and complex system makes it very difficult for employers, students, workers, and government funders to compare and evaluate the major features and overall value of different credentials.

Growing number and variety of credentials

The credentialing marketplace is growing rapidly, as more employers require credentials beyond high school and more people pursue them. Increasingly, these credentials include educational certificates, industry certifications, and occupational licenses. A recent report

(Ewert and Kominski 2014) reveals that fully one-quarter of adults in the United States, many of whom have a degree as well, have one or more nondegree credentials, and that full-time workers with them have higher median earnings than those without.

The greatest growth has been in educational certificates, which now represent half of all community college credentials awarded. According to Georgetown University's Center on Education and the Workforce (Carnevale, Rose, and Hanson 2012), "Certificates have grown from 6 percent of postsecondary awards in 1989 to 22 percent today . . . [and] have superseded associate's and master's degrees as the second most common award in the American postsecondary education and career training system" (p. 3).

These new credentials have different and frequently changing names and claims regarding their quality and value. They vary as well in how they present their scopes of application, such as the types of employers and jobs that value them. They also vary in their claims regarding how they can be transferred, bundled, and stacked with other credentials, and whether and how they recognize prior learning. The lack of "stackability" of many credentials poses problems for students and employers. That's one reason employers in some industries (e.g., oil and gas, information technology) set rigorous standards for certifications, which has prompted several Texas community colleges to partner with them to create stackable credentials that allow students to reenter college seamlessly when they need more training (Garcia 2014). There has also been considerable growth in the numbers and types of industry and professional certifications offered in such major industries as health care, energy, information technology, and manufacturing. ANSI estimates that the number has climbed from 3,000 a few years ago to more than 4,000 now, with fewer than 10 percent of them accredited.[1]

Many of these certifications are sponsored or endorsed by long-standing industry and professional associations with strong employer engagement. Others, however, are the creations of independent assessment vendors with varying levels of industry involvement and recognition. In short, certifications vary widely in how to qualify for and attain them, and in their cost and market value.

Finally, there is the rapid expansion of "badges," MOOC (massive open online courses) certificates of mastery, and other "microcredentials" that can be aggregated into higher credentials. Badges are now offered by such credible schools and programs as the Kahn Academy, Carnegie Mellon, MITx, and edX. This movement resembles the growth in "competency-based" resumes and portfolios, with links to documentation and evidence of performance, and in the skill profiles now being used in professional networking sites (e.g., LinkedIn), which have become a major resource for employer recruitment and hiring.

New credentialing models and breakdowns in traditional boundaries

The credentialing market is also witnessing the emergence of new, hybrid credentialing models that combine various features of the traditional models. To be sure, there have always been relationships among different types of credentials, such as when professional certifications require certain educational credentials and are integrated into education degree and certificate programs. However, such combining has grown more complex and varied. Competency-based credentialing, involving direct and prior learning, is leading many colleges and universities to adopt characteristics normally associated with industry and professional certifications. Some institutions are "unbundling" assessment and credentialing from education and training, making them look even more like certification organizations.

In addition, many college programs, especially those moving to competency-based models, are now fully integrating industry and professional certifications into their degrees and certificates, and folding the costs of these certifications into tuition and fees. This integration is being reinforced by industry- and government-led initiatives to promote comprehensive education and career pathways. Some colleges are developing industry certifications in cooperation with national and regional industry partners and/or the federal government, and are seeking accreditation from industry accreditation organizations in addition to traditional higher education accreditation bodies.

On the other hand, some industry and professional certification programs do not share many of the features normally associated with certification systems, such as ongoing renewal requirements and due process procedures for "removing" a certification from an individual. At the same time, they are developing programs or partnering with others to offer online education and training services, much like educational degree and certificate programs. This growing trend is bringing down the traditional "arms-length" relationships between industry certification and education and training programs, and is now raising major questions about the third-party, independent status of industry certification organizations.

Finally, the badge movement and related efforts regarding competency-based portfolios and skill profiles on professional networking Web sites are sparking further innovation in credentialing. These developments challenge widely held assumptions about what credentials are and what differentiates them from each other and from other attestations of competencies now circulating in the marketplace. In short, there is growing heterogeneity within these communities but increasing overlap among them, adding to the complexity of the broader credentialing "system."

Crisis of Confidence

The rapid growth and change in the world of credentialing is shaking confidence in the quality and value of almost all credentials. Employers increasingly complain that college graduates lack the skills expected and needed. According to a recent poll (Gallup and Lumina Foundation 2014), 96 percent of chief academic officers think their institutions are equipping their graduates for the workforce, but only 11 percent of employers strongly agree. At the same time, high unemployment and debt among college graduates is causing students and families to question the value of many higher education credentials. All this is sparking spirited debates about whether and how colleges and universities should work with employers to better understand their needs and to better communicate the knowledge and skills they teach and the assessment practices they use.

In response, "accountability initiatives" have arisen that are pushing educational institutions to define and operationalize program outcomes, including student learning, credential attainment, and employment and earnings. Similarly, competency-based credentialing is raising questions about the competencies involved and the assessments and QAs used to create confidence in them. Reinforcing these questions are growing concerns about credit transfer, prior learning assessment, and the lack of recognition of competencies of posttraditional students with extensive work experience and training, including returning veterans. The proliferation of industry and professional certifications, including similar ones competing in the same industry, is raising related concerns in the certification community, where there is a growing awareness that certifications have varying levels of employer support and recognition.

Most efforts to address these problems have focused on one credentialing silo or issue. Now, however, several initiatives are building connections among credentialing reform efforts. They include the Lumina Foundation's Degree Qualifications Profile, Department of Labor initiatives around industry-based competency models and competency-based work profiling systems (using O*NET), state initiatives around career cluster frameworks and sector-based pathways, industry endorsement initiatives, and such global initiatives as Europass, which is promoting the standardization of credentialing documentation across Europe. Most of these show considerable promise in their chosen arenas and are starting to make connections to other related initiatives. Yet, their varying frameworks, technical terminologies, and quality criteria are not likely to yield the improvements needed in comparability and interoperability (e.g., mutual recognition, credit transfer) across different types and dimensions of credentials. Real progress requires a more comprehensive approach.

A decade or two ago, talk of a comprehensive approach would have been utopian. Three recent developments, however, suggest that the time has come to attempt it. First, the growing support for and practice of competency-based education has set the stage for a shift to credentials that describe the competencies achieved, preferably in comparable terms. Second, any attempt in the United States to create a more coherent credentialing marketplace stands to benefit from the wealth of experience acquired by other countries making similar efforts, most notably those in the European Union. Finally and most importantly, advances in Web technologies now make it reasonably cheap and easy to create more standardized terminology and a public-private registry for all kinds of credentials.

A comprehensive approach begins with a broad vision of an effective credentialing system and spells out ways to achieve it. Given the preceding analysis of the problem, we believe that the vision should be of a competency-based credentialing system characterized by high levels of transparency, quality, trust, and portability. Transparency would enable interested employers, whether individual firms or industry associations, to communicate clearly their competency requirements. Such communication would be via a standardized terminology that is also used by—or readily translated into—the terminology used by credentialing organizations. It also would enable reporting the distribution and concentration of employers providing this information. The quality and trustworthiness of credentials would be as high as needed, because credentialing organizations could be easily assessed on whether they address employer-defined competencies and whether the level of QA assures that credential holders have the competencies represented by the credentials.

Trust would be high because employers could clearly communicate the level of QA they require, using a standardized terminology for describing quality criteria that is also used by credentialing organizations and those who accredit and endorse them. This would allow students to use these quality criteria and accreditation and endorsement signals to choose pathways for attaining high-quality and trusted credentials. Finally, credentials would be more portable than today because employers everywhere would use more standardized terminology to define competency and credentialing requirements (including QA criteria), and credentialing organizations would do the same. This improved portability would allow students to build competency-based, stackable credentials from multiple credentialing organizations that are more flexible in meeting variable and changing employer requirements.

In summary, the fragmented and complex nature of labor market credentialing in the United States, with its distinct communities of practice using different technical languages and quality criteria, make it very difficult for stakeholders to compare and evaluate different credentials. The recent growth in the numbers and kinds of credentials is exacerbating this problem and producing a crisis of confidence in credential quality and value. The solution involves taking advantage of recent advances in information technology to create a credentialing system characterized by high levels of transparency, quality, trust, and portability.

Three Complementary Strategies for Solving the Credentialing Problem

Let us turn then to the nature of and requirements for transparency, trust, quality, and portability.

Transparency is present when labor market participants (such as students, workers, and employers) and stakeholders (such as funders and regulators) have access to complete, accurate, and "comparable" information on all the features of credentials that are important for determining quality and value. These features include how credentials can be attained and used, eligibility, costs, where they can be applied, and how different credentials relate to each other in terms of mutual recognition and transfer as well as pathways to other credentials and careers.

Quality has many meanings but in general can be defined as "fitness for intended use." Determining whether a credential is fit for its intended use requires information on intended application and how competencies were developed and validated with employers for this intended relevance and whether employers confirm or endorse their application. It also requires information on intended value, including labor market value (e.g., employment and earnings) and transfer value (e.g., credit transfer). Another widely cited dimension of quality is whether a product or service is provided "defect free." Applied to credentialing, this dimension refers to whether individual credential holders actually have the competencies described in their credentials within acceptable levels of variance. Ascertaining that requires information on the type of assessment used to determine competency and the degree of validity and reliability involved in awarding credentials. It also requires information on QA systems.

Trust is critical because it permits confidence that the information provided in the marketplace is complete, accurate, and up-to-date, and that there are systems in place to review and reaffirm this over time. Different types of credentials require different levels of confidence, depending on employer needs, government regulations, and the risk tolerance of market participants. Of course, providing higher levels of confidence usually means higher costs. In some cases, employers may settle for self-declaration by individuals; in others, they may demand evidence from credentialing organizations. In more critical cases, however, they may require some type of third-party review to ensure accurate and reliable information.

Portability is present when credentials are sufficiently "interoperable" to allow mutual recognition of competency attainment across various types of credentials, and are recognized across different industries and occupations as well as states and eventually countries. Interoperability is the necessary foundation for competency-based, stackable credentials from multiple credentialing organizations that are more flexible in meeting changing employer requirements.

Improving transparency, quality, trust, and portability requires robust data systems for publishing and accessing comparable information on key features of credentials. It also requires credentialing organizations and their accreditation and regulatory partners to voluntarily post these data to some kind of registry. Doing so need not be costly; indeed, today's technologies make it possible to automate the updating of posted information. Below we spell out the three strategies we recommend for realizing this vision of a credentialing system characterized by high levels of transparency, quality, trust, and portability.

Strategy 1: Developing More Standardized Language

The first strategy addresses the need for comparable information about all types of credentials related to quality and value. There are many different ways to provide comparable information, but they all require some type of standardized terminology involving common definitions and classification frameworks and typologies. Below is our first cut at defining the key features or "descriptors" of credentials and credentialing organizations for promoting transparency, portability, trust, and quality.

Transparency and portability: What do market participants need to know?

- Credential name, version, and type. The name(s) used to describe the credential in the marketplace, along with related classification names (e.g., CIP codes) used in reporting systems; the version of the credential that is being described; and the type of credential based on common definitions of credential types such as degree, certificate, certification, and license.

- Competency requirements. The competencies required to earn a credential, expressed in a formal and structured language that make any competency description easily comparable to competency descriptions expressed in other formal and structured languages. Further explanation is provided below.

- Type and scope of primary application. The intended type of application and the scope of the primary application, such as job roles (e.g., types of occupations), industry context (e.g., health care), and geographic area.

- Labor market value. The degree of employer recognition and support, and the expected career returns in terms of employment and earnings or other types of recipient valuation, such as recognition and status.

- Credential transfer value. How the credential relates to other credentials for transfer or recognition of competencies (e.g., eligibility, mutual recognition, credit transfer, advanced standing) and to meet the requirements of other credentials.

- Education and career pathway connections. How the credential fits with other credentials within education and career pathways.

- Eligibility requirements. What is needed to get the credential in terms of assessment, work experience, education (e.g., high school diploma, college degree), and other eligibility requirements?

- Education and training opportunities. The available education and training opportunities to prepare for assessments, gain necessary education requirements, and become credentialed.

- Credential holder profile. The number and characteristics of credentialed individuals and their geographic locations.

- Occupational regulation and licensing. The relationship to federal and state occupational and professional regulation and licensing requirements.

- Maintaining credentials. What is needed to maintain a credential's status in terms of continuing education or other requirements?

- Credential removal. Can the credential be revoked and if so, what is the process?

- Costs. The costs involved in meeting eligibility requirements and receiving and maintaining the credential.

Trust and quality: What assurances do market participants need?

- Competency development and validation. The process used to identify, develop, and validate competencies based on the scope of application.

- Assessment. How competencies are assessed and documented and what level of assurance (i.e., validity and reliability) is provided that people have the required competencies.

- Quality assurance. What systems do credentialing organizations have in place to assure that all requirements, including assessments, are met in awarding credentials; that the credential is providing the intended value (e.g., labor market value); that all information provided to the market (transparency) is accurate and reliable; and what third-party QA entity accredits, approves, or endorses their credentials?

- Authentication. What systems do credentialing organizations have in place to authenticate credential holders and communicate the current credentialing status of all credential holders to employers and other labor market participants, as well as to education and workforce development funders and regulators?

- Version management and control. How the system manages changes in all major features over time and keeps records on credentialing system versions (e.g., competency requirements, assessment systems, costs).

It will not be easy to develop a more standardized terminology for these key descriptors across all segments of the credentialing marketplace. The major segments already have long-established and specialized languages that may be difficult to integrate into a common overarching framework. Success will require the development of frameworks or reference models that enable different credentialing communities to crosswalk and translate different languages, allow for constant change and adaptations, and promote greater harmonization over time. It also will require standardized terminology that permits enough customization to meet the needs of specialized communities without losing comparability. Other challenges include how to operationalize many of these descriptors and establish a data infrastructure for sharing the resulting data. Finally, another challenge is how to provide the necessary market incentives for credentialing organizations to provide this comparable information.

Despite these challenges, developing a more standardized terminology is entirely possible. Moreover, it would provide the needed foundation for public and private initiatives to improve credentialing *quality* in the United States.

- Industry organizations could more clearly define the quality criteria they use to recognize and endorse credentialing systems, and could align and harmonize endorsed systems in their career and education pathway frameworks.

- Higher education degree frameworks such as the Degree Qualifications Profile (DQP) could use this terminology to improve the understanding of competency levels for each type of degree and to improve the capacity of institutions to develop clear and assessable competency statements—statements that are appropriate for their degree level and their connections to other types of credentials (e.g., industry certifications).

- Credentialing organizations could more easily benchmark themselves against other credentialing organizations, national standards, quality criteria established by industry organizations, and the quality criteria established by reform initiatives and leading qualification frameworks.

- Third-party higher education accreditation organizations and accreditation organizations for industry certifications could use the more standardized terminology to align and harmonize their QA systems.

- Government agencies could use the terminology to align and harmonize their own quality criteria with accreditation organizations and industry and reform initiatives. The new language could also provide a clearer and more consistent funding and regulatory environment.

- Federal and state government agencies could use this terminology to build better consumer and labor market information systems based on a registry.

Strategy 2: Aligning QA Systems

The second strategy addresses the need to align and harmonize accreditation systems and industry endorsement systems, as well as related credentialing reform initiatives attempting to improve QA in the credentialing marketplace. As in the first strategy for credentials, it focuses on using more standardized terminology to communicate clear and comparable quality criteria for all types of credentialing. It also addresses how these QA systems and related initiatives could leverage the proposed registry to improve "transparency" in the credentialing organizations they endorse, accredit, or otherwise approve.

Alignment and harmonization of quality criteria

As described above, the existing credentialing system involves a wide variety of accreditation, approval, and recognition organizations using a broad range of criteria to provide QA. Although there have been attempts at collaboration among these organizations, little progress has occurred.

In higher education, the national, regional, and specialized organizations that accredit institutions and programs express criteria for quality in very specialized languages and terminologies that their communicates of practice have developed over decades. Similarly, in the world of industry and professional certification, a wide variety of national and international accreditation organizations use their own quality criteria. There are points of connection between higher education and industry accreditation involving professional associations (e.g., engineering), but most organizations operate largely within their respective QA silos.

This situation is further complicated by the tendency of federal and state regulatory and licensing agencies to use still different criteria for assuring quality, and leading national and state industry associations to endorse credentials as "industry-recognized," using yet different criteria. In addition, state education agencies (e.g., Career and Technical Education offices) produce their own lists of recognized industry credentials, and federal, state, and local workforce development agencies designate approved providers of education and training.

Given the confusion in the credentialing marketplace described in the problem statement above, there is a clear need to align and harmonize the quality criteria used by these public and private QA organizations. There are many approaches to doing that. One is to use a common terminology to standardize the way these organizations classify and communicate their quality criteria, as well as the actions (e.g., status granted to a credentialing organization or specific credential) they take and what they are assuring when they accredit, approve, or endorse. This would provide greater transparency in comparing quality criteria without requiring adoption of the same criteria. It would allow stakeholders to compare and contrast the quality criteria among different accreditation organizations so they more fully understand what accreditation means for a credentialing system or organization. Such a change would respond to the recommendations of accreditation expert Paul Gaston (2014) for moving toward more consensus, alignment, and coordination of accreditation standards, protocols, actions (e.g., accreditation status), and vocabulary.

This also could serve as a useful first step toward further alignment and harmonization across higher education and industry accreditation, as well as industry and government recognition and endorsement systems. This increased transparency and identification of commonalities would lower costs for institutions and reduce the redundancy of QA processes that could lead to further collaboration among QA systems. There are many commonalities among various credentialing QA systems. For example, most QA bodies are moving toward the assessment of outcomes rather than on the many processes that lead to outcomes. Inclusion of these common components in a credentialing registry would increase the transparency and comparability of QA systems, which themselves would experience market and regulatory pressure to cooperate once the opportunity existed.

In sum, the second strategy would align endorsement, approval, and accreditation quality criteria; facilitate transparency and benchmarking; and engage QA systems in encouraging credentialing organizations to use the registry to meet transparency requirements. Success would require an unprecedented but entirely plausible coordination of all public and private organizations involved with QA in the credentialing marketplace, ranging from higher education and industry accreditation organizations to federal and state regulatory agencies to industry-led endorsement systems. The credentialing initiative described in the beginning of the chapter involves many of these bodies, and thanks to its partnership with ANSI, it is well situated to reach out to others.

Strategy 3: Creating a Public-Private Credentialing Registry

The third strategy addresses how, in practice, to provide more comparable and trustworthy information to the credentialing marketplace based on the standardized terminology and related frameworks described above. This plan reflects three assumptions. First, whatever the approach, it is vital to address the scale of the challenge—the growing number and variety of credentials and the sheer number of documents and data systems that must be accessed and integrated to provide comparable information on the proposed descriptors. Second, effectiveness requires building from existing procedures used by credentialing organizations to communicate information in the marketplace and related data infrastructures that support these efforts. Third, it is important not to impose additional reporting burdens on credentialing organizations and their accreditation and regulatory bodies, as well as other QA entities.

Finally, transparency requires guides and tools that can present comparable information in usable ways. A sound approach will promote the development of guides and tools for employers, students, and other stakeholders who may use this information to improve credentialing quality. This could involve using techniques like those employed in national and state "open data" initiatives in health care and transportation. These initiatives would provide applications developers with free access to a rich data infrastructure to create a wide variety of applications ("apps") for different types of stakeholders.

Harnessing the power of credentialing Web sites

Publicly accessible and searchable Web sites based on widely adopted Web technology standards are by far the most widely used "one-stop" mechanism for communication within the credentialing marketplace. These sites use content management systems to publish information from multiple sources, including both documents and databases. Most credentialing organizations already use their Web sites to publish information on some of the proposed "descriptors" for credentialing systems and provide linkages to internal or external supporting documents and databases. They also use their sites to address "transparency" requirements from federal and state regulatory agencies and accreditation organizations.

For example, most universities, four-year colleges, and community colleges use their Web sites to provide information on their different programs, including those programs' scopes of application, course requirements (which may involve student learning outcomes), and application and eligibility criteria as well as tuition, fees, and other costs. They also provide linkages to documents that contain more detailed information, including college catalogs and reports on institutional and program performance and accreditation status. Starting with credentialing Web sites addresses the problem of scale, because existing Web sites already contain more detailed information on more types of credentials than is currently available in any existing national or state reporting system.

These Web sites will soon be able to do much more. The World Wide Web Consortium (W3C) and related global and national standardization organizations are helping to promote Web technologies that move the Web from a "Web of documents" to a "Web of data," housed in distributed data systems throughout the world. Semantic Web technologies enable people to publish data on the Web in the form of structured documents and databases; build common terminology, vocabularies, and advanced ontologies; and develop query languages for accessing and using these data through applications. These Web technologies, plus advances in computational linguistics or natural language processing, provide the foundation for the Credentialing Registry discussed later in this chapter.

There are two major problems with using existing credentialing Web sites as the building blocks for a national public-private data infrastructure. First, these sites provide noncomparable information presented in widely varying formats and organizing structures. This information is also drawn from a variety of source documents and databases, some of which are managed by other organizations, such as data clearinghouses and state regulatory agencies. Second, they are not usually designed to regularly publish and share information with other data systems and maintain a regular updating schedule or manage version control with historical records of previous versions. However, these problems can be fixed with the following two solutions:

1) **Develop data standards for the common terminology.** Examples include standards developed through the Common Education Data Standards and the Postsecondary Education Standards Council as well as standards developed for human

resource information systems, such as work undertaken by the HR Open Standards Consortium. These data standards should address all types of data contained in both traditional data systems and structured documents (e.g., competency statements found in technical documents) consistent with Web standards and tools discussed earlier.

2) **Develop a public-private registry.** Establish an open public-private registry similar in design and function to the existing Learning Registry.[2] This registry could be based on a decentralized and open distribution network model that fully reflects the diversity and segmentation of the credentialing marketplace and the diversity of the communities organized around different types (e.g., degrees and certificates) and domains (e.g., industry pathways, state licensing, and regulation) of credentialing. The distribution network could involve network nodes within and across communities that could be used by both producers (i.e., credentialing organizations) and users (e.g., applications developers).

- **Share credentialing system data.** The registry could be used to publish, share, and access comparable data about all types of credentialing systems based on data standards for the common language using formal, comparable definitions, coding systems and dictionaries, and frameworks, taxonomies, and other types of schema. Credentialing systems would be able to publish (push) data about themselves and access (pull) comparable data about other systems. This could include the publishing and sharing of descriptor schema (e.g., coding schemes, taxonomies, classification frameworks) and crosswalks. It could include guides and tools for publishing, accessing, comparing, and analyzing credentialing system descriptions and schema.

- **Link to related registries and data systems.** Establish linkages with related registries such as the Learning Registry as well as with possible future registries for occupational descriptions or e-portfolios, especially registries that contain common or related data items such as competencies. Establish linkages to other data systems including national and state longitudinal data systems and clearinghouses.

- **Create an applications marketplace**. Support an open marketplace of Web-based applications. These applications would be designed to improve transparency for stakeholders, including employers, education, and training providers, and federal and state government funding and regulatory agencies. They could provide guidance on writing competency statements, provide more accessible and valid consumer and labor market information based on career pathway and education qualifications frameworks, develop more efficient clearinghouses for credit transfer and market value recognition, develop credentialing resource centers for compiling and sharing information on different types of credentials or those meeting specified quality criteria, and develop employer and industry endorsement systems or consumer rating systems for credentialing systems based on their credentialing transfer and labor market value.

This strategy will require the alignment and harmonization of current data standards initiatives, as well as the leveraging of Web technology standards that are critical in harnessing the potential power of credentialing Web sites and registries. These requirements are addressed below when discussing the role of a credentialing collaborative.

BUILDING AN OPEN APPLICATIONS MARKETPLACE

The ultimate value of a credentialing registry containing comparable data on credentials and QA entities will be determined by how it is actually used by employers, students, and workers, and by labor market intermediaries to improve the credentialing marketplace. This will require an open applications marketplace with application developers providing new Web tools and resources for all major stakeholders in the credentialing marketplace. Guided by an advisory committee representing these stakeholders, the initiative described here has identified several potential applications that could add value in the credentialing marketplace. The next phase of the initiative will refine and test several "apps," including the following three, on a beta-version of the credentialing registry.

1) **Credentialing guidance**—compiling directories or inventories of credentials that are based on the criteria (e.g., scope of application, market value) defined by industry groups, government agencies, and career and education guidance systems.

2) **Employer signaling and talent pipeline management**—providing tools for employers to use for communicating their competency and credentialing requirements, and working with education and training and credentialing partners to improve their talent pipeline performance.

3) **Credentialing transfer value**—providing tools to improve the transfer value of credentials based on competencies rather than more traditional currencies, such as credit hours through competency-based clearinghouse applications that can analyze a wide variety of credentials, such as degrees, certifications, badges, and prior learning assessments.

ROLE AND SCOPE OF A CREDENTIALING COLLABORATIVE

At the beginning of the chapter, we said that government by market could be achieved through the use of standards and financial incentives. But how do standards get developed and enforced? Informal de facto standards are based on widespread use or the dominance of one or more players that use or support them. Formal standards are developed through a process managed by recognized standards development groups under the coordination of national and global standards governance bodies. These can be voluntary and implemented based on their value and acceptance in the marketplace (and often promoted through government policies). Alternatively, they can be involuntary and enforced through laws, regulations, and other policy tools. We favor voluntary standards for defining credentials in the United States.

The development and implementation of voluntary credentialing standards requires a broad-based public-private partnership that brings together all the major stakeholders (public and private). The best way to do all this is through a credentialing collaborative similar in role and function to public-private collaboratives facilitated by ANSI.

Background: ANSI and the Global Standards Network

The United States and other countries promote national and global standards and conformity assessment systems for a wide variety of purposes, including facilitating global trade, improving industrial performance, increasing competition, and protecting consumers. ANSI facilitates the development of American National Standards by accrediting standards-developing organizations. It also accredits conformity assessment organizations to determine the fulfillment of standards requirements. ANSI also provides the bridge to global standards and conformity assessment initiatives and serves as the official liaison to such international bodies as the International Organization for Standardization and the International Accreditation Forum. This is an important connection, enabling the United States to address increasingly global credentialing challenges in cooperation with other countries.

Need for a Credentialing Collaborative

Quite separately from its accrediting work, ANSI frequently establishes "standards collaboratives" (formerly called panels) to explore the need for improvements in critical areas. It established a Healthcare Information Technology Panel to harmonize and integrate standards for sharing health care information for clinical and business applications. It has conducted similar collaboratives for energy efficiency, homeland security, nanotechnology, nuclear energy, biofuels, and electronic vehicles. In each case it staffed these as a neutral convener of all the major stakeholders. An ANSI-sponsored collaborative does not develop standards itself but rather works with stakeholders to harmonize existing ones, identifies any need for additional ones, and develops plans for their development by others.

The next phase of this credentialing transparency initiative will involve the formation of a similar standards panel on credentialing, with one minor and one more substantive difference. The minor one is that the collaborative will be convened and hosted by ANSI's affiliate, Workcred, rather than ANSI itself. The bigger difference is that the stakeholders in this collaborative will focus on evaluating the value produced and lessons learned from the next phase's testing of a beta-version of the registry and of the three "apps" mentioned above. Early in the process, working committees of stakeholders will establish the performance measures, metrics, and benchmarks. Later they will assess the test results against these benchmarks and determine whether and how to take the system to scale, including what kinds of governance and business models would make it sustainable.

CONCLUSION

This chapter began by showing how a complex and confusing credentialing system is hurting employers, students, workers, and the economy. It then presented three strategies for making the system more coherent and efficient. Together, these strategies emphasize the use of voluntary standardization to achieve transparency, consistency, and comparability in descriptions of all credentials and to align all quality criteria. They employ a distributed, Web-based data infrastructure—a registry—to enable cheap and easy access to meaningful and current credentialing information. The chapter also described an existing initiative that has engaged all the key stakeholders in a promising effort to implement these strategies. Future publications will report on its results.

Notes

1. Personal communication from Dr. Roy Swift, ANSI's Chief Workforce Development Officer, April 2014.
2. The Learning Registry is a new approach to capturing, connecting, and sharing data about learning resources available online established by the Departments of Education and Defense but supported by many other organizations, including the Library of Congress. For more information, see www.learningregistry.org.

References

Carnevale, Anthony, Stephen J. Rose, and Andrew Hanson. 2012. *Certificates: Gateway to Gainful Employment and College Degrees: Executive Summary*. Washington, DC: Georgetown University Center on Education and the Workforce.

Ewert, Stephanie, and Robert Kominski. 2014. *Measuring Alternative Educational Credentials: 2012*. Washington, DC: U.S. Department of Commerce, U.S. Census Bureau.

Gallup and Lumina Foundation. 2014. *What America Needs to Know about Higher Education Redesign: The 2013 Lumina Study of the American Public's Opinion on Higher Education and U.S. Business Leaders Poll on Higher Education*. Washington, DC, and Indianapolis, IN: Gallup and Lumina Foundation.

Garcia, Reynaldo. 2014. "Stackable Credentials: An Approach for Middle Jobs and Beyond." *Educause Review* Online, January 27.

Gaston, Paul, L. 2014. *Higher Education Accreditation: How It's Changing, Why It Must*. Sterling, VA: Stylus.

Kamarck, Elaine, C. 2007. *The End of Government . . . As We Know It: Making Public Policy Work*. Boulder, CO: Lynne Rienner Publishers.

National Research Council. 1995. *Standards, Conformity Assessment and Trade into the 21st Century*. Washington, DC: National Academy Press.

8
Moving Sectoral and Career Pathway Programs from Promise to Scale

Christopher T. King
Heath J. Prince
University of Texas

While the evidence is still emerging, it is clear from the handful of rigorous studies that have been conducted to date that sectoral and career pathway programs can be highly effective strategies for increasing the employability, employment, earnings, and other outcomes for job seekers. It is highly likely that such strategies lead to positive economic results for employers as well. They also yield lasting net benefits for taxpayers and society as a whole. The question then is how to sustain, replicate, and bring them to scale, which is the focus of this chapter.

It is important to note at the outset that, positive evidence notwithstanding, sustaining and scaling these strategies face a steep uphill battle, in no small part due to the legacy of decades emphasizing doing things "on the cheap." Whether from the 1990s welfare reform efforts that stressed "work-first" labor force attachment models or from the early "sequence-of-services" approach embedded in the Workforce Investment Act (WIA) of 1998, strategies stressing real investments in skills leading to jobs paying wages offering economic self-sufficiency simply were not part of the policy and program landscape.

THE RISE OF SECTORAL AND CAREER
PATHWAY STRATEGIES

Emergence

The family of strategies to help low-income, low-skilled individuals succeed in the labor market and to help employers meet their needs for workers with the right mix of skills began to emerge in the 1980s and 1990s. Initially, these sector-based strategies were designed to respond to the needs of key industry groups in various sectors by aggregating employer demand for common skills. It was assumed that this would introduce an efficiency and rationality missing from the existing workforce development system. While some of these programs focused on the low-skilled population, many more tended to help employers find and improve the skills of a more highly skilled and educated segment of the workforce.

Motivated by a need to improve workforce development programming, and acknowledging the reality that skills training would likely occur over the lifetime of the individual, advocates for career pathways strategies sought to create structured, sequential training and education opportunities that, over time, allow a worker to gain the skills needed to continue to advance in the labor market. With time, as it became clear that effectively meeting the skill needs of employers and the advancement needs of workers also required better structured program offerings from community colleges, sectoral strategies began to evolve into broader career pathway approaches involving provider institutions, especially community colleges, as well as employers. In some cases, this has meant the integration of career pathways into broader sector-based strategies. In others, however, it has meant the development of *occupational* career pathways almost completely free of any recognition of sectorwide needs.

Finally, given the desire to address the particular needs of job seekers pursuing sectoral and career pathway opportunities, many of whom had basic skills deficits that impeded their progress in for-credit as well as noncredit course sequences, so-called bridge programs—programs that aim to provide occupationally contextualized basic education in order to prepare participants to enter more formal postsecondary programs—

were developed. Some of these programs (e.g., Integrated Basic Education and Skills Training [I-BEST]) are now seen as national models for helping low-skilled adults contextually build basic *and* occupational skills at the same time in the pathways and sectors they are pursuing.

Sector Strategies, Career Pathways, and Their Integration

While many career pathways programs claim to be sector-based, this is rarely the case, and for good reason. Sector-based strategies emerged independently and prior to career pathways as a framework for organizing investment in skills training. Over a relatively short period of time, however, what began as an effort to define advancement paths for workers participating in sector programs became a distinct career pathways approach to training as the workforce development field began digesting the expanding literature on the relationship between income and postsecondary credentials. This shift in emphasis from aggregating employer demand for skills within a sector to one focused on postsecondary credentials marked the beginning of what are known now as career pathways models.

While the precise origins of this evolution toward a focus on postsecondary credentials are likely not identifiable, simple observation of the changes in the workforce development field between the mid-1990s and early 2010s suggests that some early successes with sector-based programs and the appeal of providing workers with a semblance of employment security through career pathways programs led to the growth in foundation and, ultimately, government support for programs that would not only provide skills training but also potentially lead to a credential that, unlike some occupationally specific skills, was transferable.

A key distinction between sectoral strategies and career pathways models is that the former tend to be driven by employers organized within a sector, while the latter may focus on the needs of particular sectors but do not necessarily rely on employers as critical "drivers" and are typically occupationally, rather than sector, focused; they may successfully train and place dozens of certified nursing assistants each year with little direct input from health care employers, relying on labor market analysis, want ads, job vacancy postings and other information. Effective career pathway efforts may be developed and operate mainly within community and technical colleges, but usually only with considerable input from employers in growth sectors.

Sector Strategies

An organizing principle of sector-based programs is the assumption that there are efficiencies to be gained from collectively addressing the common skills needs of similar employers within an industry sector. For example, paper manufacturers in Western Massachusetts can, in theory, identify skill needs common across their companies, work with a local training provider to create training curricula, and hire from a common pool of workers trained in the skills needed. This approach is seen as a departure from past practice in which multiple training providers, to degrees varying between "hardly at all" and "effectively," identified the skills in demand, created curricula they felt would meet this demand, and then competed among each other to have their trainees hired. Duplication of effort, inconsistency in training standards, and the occasional fly-by-night training providers all contributed to employers' suspicion of the "second chance system," not to mention the sometimes very poor services delivered to participants. Additionally, education and training institutions have little incentive to engage employers because their funding is based on enrollment in, and sometimes completion of, classes rather than on job placement.

Sector-based programs have expanded considerably since the first efforts emerged in the early 1980s. They have included the following, among others:

- The Bay State Skills Corporation was established in Boston in 1981 as an economic development tool that built education and industry partnerships to produce skilled workers for high-tech companies (initially) in Massachusetts.[1] It subsequently merged with the Industrial Service Program to become the Corporation for Business, Work and Learning, doing business as the Commonwealth Corporation. This may be one of the earliest examples of a concerted sectoral strategy in action. Commonwealth Corporation has continued to play a key role in fostering these strategies.

- San Antonio's Project QUEST was designed in 1990–1991 and enrolled its first participants in 1992.[2] Its numerous off-spring—Valley Initiative for Development and Advancement, or VIDA (Weslaco, TX, 1995), Capital IDEA (Austin, TX, 1998), Advanced Retraining & Redevelopment Initiatives in Border Areas, or ARRIBA (El Paso,TX, 1999) and several others—now span the South and Southwest, from Arkansas and Louisiana to Arizona and New Mexico. The Southwest Industrial Areas Foundation and its local interfaith affiliates develop and sponsor these projects. Project QUEST was explicitly designed to be driven by employers in key sectors of the economy (e.g., health care). These efforts provide intensive longer-term skills training, typically offer stipends to offset the costs of training and foregone earnings, and ensure broad-based community support (Campbell 1994; Deaton and McPherson 1991).

- The Wisconsin Regional Training Partnership (WRTP) was established in 1992 as part of an effort to "renew the industrial base of Milwaukee."[3] It relied on a model of preemployment training for job seekers, helping them to qualify for family-sustaining jobs in the industrial sector. With the creation of Wisconsin Works (W-2) by Governor Tommy Thompson, WRTP provided opportunities for former welfare recipients and other low-income central city residents to acquire the skills they needed to qualify for family-sustaining jobs. Since 2001, when the organization began expanding into the construction sector as part of a grant from the U.S. Department of Labor/Employment and Training Administration (USDOL/ETA), WRTP has been known as WRTP/BIG Step.

- The JOBS Initiative, which was launched by the Annie E. Casey Foundation, operated for eight years starting in 1995 in Denver, Milwaukee, New Orleans, Philadelphia, St. Louis, and Seattle.[4] It aimed to connect young inner-city residents to family-supporting jobs and to improve the way urban labor market systems worked for low-income, low-skilled workers. The Initiative emphasized finding jobs with career opportunities and promoting longer-term job retention for participants, stressed the importance of both employers and job seekers as customers, focused on outcomes to track performance, and used data to promote accountability.

- National Network of Sector Partners—funded by Ford, Mott, Annie E. Casey, and the William and Flora Hewlett Foundations—was formed in 1999 under the leadership of the late Cindy Marano and is an initiative of the Insight Center for Community Economic Development.[5] It is a nationwide membership organization (e.g., sector initiative leaders, researchers, employers, labor unions, funders) that promotes and supports sector initiatives.

- Washington State Skills Panels—regionally based, industry-driven partnerships of employers, public systems, and other stakeholders—began operating in 2000 and have expanded statewide in a number of key sectors, including the wine industry in the Walla Walla area in the southeastern part of the state.[6] They now appear firmly embedded in the state's approach to workforce and economic development.

- The Accelerating Adoption of State Sector Strategies Initiative, a joint effort of the National Governors Association, the Corporation for a Skilled Workforce, and the National Network of Sector Partners, was launched in 2006 with support from the Ford, Charles Stewart Mott, and Joyce Foundations.[7] The initiative sparked interest in and supported the adoption of sector strategies in a dozen or more states relying on three major mechanisms: a six-state Learning Network (Arkansas, Illinois, Massachusetts, Michigan, Pennsylvania, and Washington), a five-state Policy Academy (Georgia, Minnesota, North Carolina, Oklahoma, and Oregon), and a Knowledge Exchange open to all states (NGA Center for Best Practices, National Network of Sector Partners, and Corporation for a Skilled Workforce 2008).

With major support and leadership from the Annie E. Casey, Ford, and Rockefeller Foundations, sectoral strategy efforts began morphing into the "workforce intermediary" activity in 2003 and 2004 (see Giloth [2004]). This activity centers around the convening function of third parties, typically some sort of CBO, but occasionally labor/management partnerships, community colleges, Workforce Investment

Boards (WIBs), or employer associations, to mediate between groups of employers and training providers to meet skill demands. The National Fund for Workforce Solutions, which was launched in 2007, led to further expansion of sector strategies fostered by workforce intermediaries with a mix of Ford, Annie E. Casey, Hitachi, and Joyce Foundation support, as well as early funding from USDOL/ETA.

Key Sectoral Strategy Components

Sectoral strategies generally strive to improve the economic situation of workers through increased employment, wages, benefits, and earnings over time. They also seek to improve access to employees with the necessary skills, increase productivity, and boost regional competitiveness. As noted above, these strategies directly engage employers and associations of employers by industry sector to better understand and respond to their hiring and career advancement requirements.

Sectoral strategies tend to act as *integrators* (Glover and King 2010, p. 231). According to Conway et al. (2007), they

- target specific industries and/or clusters of occupations;
- intervene through credible organizations (often "workforce intermediaries");
- support workers competing for quality job opportunities as measured by wages, benefits, and advancement opportunities;
- address employer needs and competitiveness; and
- create lasting change in labor market systems helping workers and employers.

At their best, they also tend to complement cluster-based economic development in states and regions that are actively pursuing such strategies by articulating career pathways and career advancement opportunities, developing standardized industry training, establishing standards for job quality and working conditions, assisting with market coordination, brokering business networks, and helping to develop strategic plans (NGA Center for Best Practices 2002, p. 32).

Sector Partnership Features

As noted above, sector-based approaches typically include career pathways elements in that they aggregate employer demand for skill across a range of occupations, working to meet skill needs at multiple levels within a sector and to advance workers along a sector-based career path. The converse does not typically apply, however, in that while they may include the term *sector* in their title, most career pathways programs lack many of the defining features of sector partnerships, as well as the competencies needed to implement them.

The National Network of Sector Partners estimates that some 1,000 sector partnerships are operating across the country, and about half of the states and the District of Columbia are either exploring or implementing such strategies.[8] Such partnerships tend to span multiple industry sectors (83 percent) and have the features shown in Table 8.1.

A Career Pathways Typology

At present, there are essentially two types of career pathways operating. The first type is built around an articulated set of courses, or components of courses, that permit individuals to learn skills and gain postsecondary credentials related to a specific occupation. These pathways identify entry and exit points along the way, from which individuals can enter postsecondary course work, exit into the labor market with a marketable skill and certificate to vouch for it, and reenter at a later point, earning credits that "stack" toward the completion of a degree. This type of career pathway emphasizes advancement along a well-defined postsecondary and employment track.

A second type of career pathway relies much less on a continuing role for postsecondary education for advancing individual workers. Instead, this type identifies occupations that appear to have career pathways built in, and it focuses more on preparing individuals, often through postsecondary courses resulting in the earning of industry-recognized certificates. This type more closely resembles the work-first approach to workforce development, placing the onus on workers to take care of their own advancement.

Measurements of success differ between these two types. With the former, success is typically measured in terms of advancement through postsecondary course work and/or training, earning of certificates, placement in the labor market, earnings gains, and labor market retention. With the latter, metrics of success are typically limited to placement in a high-demand occupation, gains in earnings, and labor market retention.

Table 8.1 Sector Partnership Characteristics

Key features	Findings
Industry sectors	Sector-based programs operate in 22 different industry sectors, including health care (66 percent), manufacturing (57 percent), and construction (40 percent), which continue to be the three main industries targeted. More than a third of sector partner organizations operate in the energy and utilities sector, a growing trend.
Organizational types	Workforce Investment Boards (27 percent) and community-based organizations (22 percent) are the most common sectoral organizations, though many others (e.g., unions, community colleges) are in the mix as well.
Geographic scope	Sector partnerships are mainly city, county, or regional in scope (75 percent), while others are statewide or nationwide (22 percent combined).
Target populations	Individuals with low incomes and racial minorities make up large shares of participants served by sector partnerships, 50 percent and 46 percent, respectively. In addition, over one-fifth of participants are displaced/ dislocated workers, nonnative English speakers, and those with less than 12 years of education.
Common services	Almost all (93 percent) sector partnerships offer direct services to workers or job seekers. The most common service is job seeker training (e.g., soft skills and job readiness training), followed by incumbent worker training (technical or trade skills), career counseling and management, and placement services.
Extended duration	Most (85 percent) have partnered on sector initiatives for at least 3 years with a median time of 6.5 years.

SOURCE: Mangatt (2010).

Common Denominators in Career Pathways Programs

Career pathways programs are typically targeted to regional labor markets, sometimes focused on key employment sectors. They also combine education, training, and on-the-job learning.

Career pathways programs also aim to provide a framework for workforce development by integrating the various programs and resources of community colleges, workforce agencies, and social service providers in more structured sequences (Alssid, Goldberg, and Klerk 2002). According to Jenkins (2006, p. 6), the ideal types of pathways offer "a series of connected education and training programs and support services that enable individuals to secure employment within a specific industry or occupational sector, and to advance over time to successively higher levels of education and employment in that sector."

Depending on the target group, career pathways programs may offer three levels of training: basic skills training, entry-level training, and upgrade training and education. They often provide paid internships as well. Such efforts have included Shifting Gears, a high-profile effort launched in 2007 and supported by the Joyce Foundation and matching state funds in six states (Illinois, Indiana, Michigan, Minnesota, Ohio, and Wisconsin) as a "state policy-change initiative."[9] Shifting Gears innovations included "breaking longer diploma and degree programs into shorter certificate modules, prioritizing industry and occupational sectors that offer good jobs in career pathways, and offering classes at a wider variety of places, days, and times" (Strawn 2010, p. 2). At least two Shifting Gears states' efforts—Wisconsin Industry Partnerships and Illinois Career Clusters—stressed strong ties to sector and industry initiatives for their state adult education reforms.

Career pathways programs often feature what are referred to as bridge programs, or occupationally contextualized basic education programs, to bring low-income, low-skilled students' basic skills up to levels that allow them to make progress in for-credit courses and advance effectively to the point of obtaining certificates and/or degrees with proven value in the labor market (Jobs for the Future 2010; Strawn 2011). The need to create these bridges became clear as career pathway efforts began coming to grips with the basic skill deficiencies their participants arrived with and the obstacles these presented for their advancing in the programs on any reasonable timeline. In some instances, these became explicit "career pathways bridges" programs. Examples of these programs include the Breaking Through Initiative and Washington State's I-BEST. Sectoral strategies sometimes include such bridge programs as well, depending on the entry-level skills of the job seekers they serve.

THE EVIDENCE: DO THESE STRATEGIES WORK?

The evidence base for sectoral and career pathways programs and their expansion remains thin, but it is growing, and there is much more in the evaluation research pipeline.[10] Only a handful of highly rigorous impact evaluations have been carried out to date, though many more implementation studies have been conducted. Table 8.2 shows the more prominent impact evaluations that these programs have included.

Note that these evaluations mainly estimate the impact of the intent to treat; the Capital IDEA and I-BEST evaluations also estimate the impact of the treatment on the treated. The difference between the two estimation approaches can be substantial when a large share of those assigned to a particular treatment fail to receive it.

Effects on Program Participation

Most process studies report that sectoral and related programs tend to have high rates of participation in program services, as well as high program completion and credential rates, distinguishing them sharply from typical education and training programs that have served low-income, low-skilled populations in the United States in recent decades. It has been quite common for those assigned to different training strategies in major national evaluations—such as the Job Training Partnership Act Study in the late 1980s and early 1990s (Orr et al. 1996) and the National Evaluation of Welfare-to-Work Strategies (NEWWS) in the mid- to late 1990s (Hamilton 2002)—not to receive the treatment at all, while many of those assigned to the control group have in fact received similar services. Unfortunately, few of the more rigorous evaluations of sectoral or career pathway programs have tracked increased

Table 8.2 Rigorously Evaluated Sector-Based, Career Pathway, and Bridge Programs

Method	Description
Random assignment	Three sectoral training programs—Per Scholas (New York City), Jewish Vocational Service (Boston), and the Wisconsin Regional Training Partnership (Milwaukee)—conducted by Public/ Private Ventures and the Aspen Institute (Maguire et al. 2010).
Quasi-experimental evaluation and return-on-investment analysis	Capital IDEA, an Austin, Texas–based sectoral training program conducted by researchers at the Ray Marshall Center at the University of Texas at Austin's LBJ School of Public Affairs (Smith, King, and Schroeder 2012; Smith and Coffey (Chapter 31 in this volume).
Random assignment	Comprehensive Employment Training (CET) Replication initiative, a sectoral career pathway program for youth, conducted by MDRC (Miller et al. 2005).
Random assignment	Year Up, a multisite career pathway, sectoral, and bridge program for youth and young adults, conducted by Economic Mobility (Roder and Elliott 2011, 2014).
Quasi-experimental	Washington State's Integrated Basic Education and Skills Training bridge program conducted by researchers at the Community College Research Center at Columbia University (Zeidenberg, Cho, and Jenkins 2010).

participation, completion, or credential rates. Table 8.3 shows the statistically significant results from these studies.

Labor Market Impacts

Rigorous evaluations of sector-based and career pathway programs also estimated meaningful, statistically significant impacts on key labor market outcomes of interest for participants, and these impacts tended to be longer-lasting than those of typical workforce programs.

Table 8.3 Participation Effects from Sector-Based, Career Pathway, and Bridge Program Evaluations

Program	Participation effects
Per Scholas, Jewish Vocational Service-Boston, Wisconsin Regional Training Partnership (WRTP)	Participation in education and training services was fully 32 percentage points higher for participants in the three sectoral programs relative to controls.
Comprehensive Employment Training (CET)	Participating CET youth received 145 more hours of training and earned credentials at a rate 21 points above that for controls.
Year Up	Year Up participants were actually 13 points *less* likely to have attended college in the four years following random assignment than controls; adjusting for non-receipt of services (i.e., the effect of the treatment on the treated), participants were fully 20 points less likely to have attended college.
Integrated Basic Education and Skills Training (I-BEST)	I-BEST participants experienced a 17-point increase in service receipt, a 10-point increase in college credits earned, and a 7.5-point increase in occupational certifications earned three years after enrollment; however, there were no statistically significant effects on the number of associate's degrees earned.

SOURCE: King (2014).

Employment

With the exception of Year Up and I-BEST, participation in sector-based and career pathway programs was associated with statistically significant increases in employment extending from two to seven and a half years postprogram. Even in programs that did not boost overall employment rates (such as Year Up), program participation led to increased employment in the targeted sectors, typically in much better jobs than those held by control group members.

Earnings

Sectoral and related strategies generally produced significant increases in earnings for participants. Earnings impacts of 12–30 percent were found extending from two to seven and a half years after enrollment and stemmed from both increased duration and hours of work as well as higher wages. For example,

- WRTP participants earned 24 percent more than controls over the two-year study period, largely from both higher wages and working more hours; they were much more likely to work in jobs paying $11 and $13 per hour than controls. Participation in Jewish Vocational Services-Boston and Per Scholas was associated with similar results.

- Participation in Austin's Capital IDEA led to substantial earnings increases over nearly eight years post program and also increased participants' eligibility for Unemployment Insurance by 11–12 percentage points, allowing many of these low-income workers to become eligible for the first-tier safety net.

- Year Up participants' earnings exceeded those of controls by 32 percent three years after the program, largely as a result of trainees working in jobs that were full- rather than part-time (and paying higher wages—$2.51 per hour more).

Finally, one of the few studies to examine ROI estimated internal rates of return (IRR) of 9 percent for taxpayers and 39 percent for society over 10 years; the estimated IRRs were 17 percent for taxpayers and 43 percent for society over 20 years (Smith and King 2011). Returns for individual participants were even higher, at 73 percent and 74 percent for 10 and 20 years, respectively.

So, while the evidence is still emerging, these studies suggest that sectoral and career pathway programs can be highly effective strategies for increasing the employability, employment, earnings, and other outcomes of job seekers. While it is likely that these programs also benefit employers by improving worker productivity and enhancing their economic competitiveness and profitability, these are not impacts that have been estimated to date, either in simple outcomes studies or more rigorous evaluations. The findings also suggest that these strategies may yield lasting net benefits for taxpayers and society as a whole.

APPROACHES TO PROGRAM REPLICATION AND SCALING: A BRIEF REVIEW

Replicating effective program models, those supported by rigorous evidence, and taking them to something approaching scale with fidelity and a modicum of success have long been the concern of policymakers at the federal and state levels. Excellent examples of replication and scaling efforts in recent years include those around the Comprehensive Employment Training (CET) program in the 1990s, the push to expand workforce intermediaries across the nation led by the National Fund for Workforce Solutions since the mid-2000s through the use of funders' collaboratives, the initiative to replicate the I-BEST approach in the 2000s, the Southwest Industrial Areas Foundation (SWIAF) efforts to build a network of sectoral/career pathway programs since the 1990s, and the ongoing work of the Alliance for Quality Career Pathways to establish quality career pathway approaches in the states led by the Center for Law and Social Policy (CLASP), the National Governors Association (NGA) and others, to name some of the better known ones.

These and other efforts have employed differing models and approaches, have faced numerous challenges, and have been able to take advantage of opportunities along the way. Some have enjoyed more success than others. Examining these in the context of the literature on replication offers lessons that may be applicable to the replication and scaling of sectoral and career pathway models.

Replication and Scaling Models

Bradach (2003) describes five approaches to replication and scaling: 1) the franchise approach, 2) mandated replication, 3) staged replication, 4) concept replication, and 5) spontaneous replication. Franchising is typically utilized by a central or national office that is coordinating the expansion of a model with a highly standardized set of components, such as CET. Mandated replication is often directed by government, federal or state, which wants to expand a particularly effective service model, as may happen under the newly reauthorized Workforce Innovation Opportunities Act of 2014. Staged replication generally entails a three-staged approach starting with a pilot testing for concept viability, moving to a demonstration phase, and ultimately to full replication (e.g., the JOBS Initiative of the 1990s and the National Fund for Workforce Solutions [NFWS] starting in the mid-2000s).

Concept replication is focused more loosely on components and general principles guiding the model, rather than on specific components, e.g., I-BEST, NFWS, and AQCP. Finally, spontaneous replication is characterized as an approach that is more bottoms-up, responding to demands for information and assistance from partners who are potential collaborators on program expansion, such as SWIAF. This is one useful conception of these models. There may be others worth considering as well.

Big-Picture Challenges and Opportunities

Replication and scaling are fraught with challenges. To be sure, the biggest of these is simply the lack of adequate resources. In the face of reasonably convincing evidence that a "better mousetrap" exists, without resources program officials are unlikely to promote these strategies. Equally problematic, resources may well be present but may be tied to conducting business as usual, whether in terms of WIA's sequence of services that leave little funding for training, or the community college system's emphasis on enrollment in programs over labor market outcomes for career pathways participants.

Second, key components, activities, or services for effective models may simply not be permitted under particular programs or funding streams, or they may be difficult to support and implement across funding streams and platforms. For example, while more intensive, longer-term training is a component of sector-based and career pathway programs, Temporary Assistance for Needy Families and Supplemental Nutrition Assistance Program employment and training programs may not readily allow them, despite the presence of a large population in need.

Third, state or local policy orientations and priorities—for example, a continuing preference for work-first, labor force attachment approaches—may also inhibit expansion of these models, federal provisions notwithstanding. There is wide variation from state to state and WIB to WIB in the share of WIA expenditures on skills training (Barnow and King 2005; Mikelson and Nightingale 2004).

Finally, community and technical colleges exhibit a large range in terms of their priorities and focus as well. Some are eager partners in workforce training initiatives and have strong connections with employers and industry associations, while others are largely focused on performing the academic transfer function for four-year institutions of higher education. Expanding sectoral training and career pathways in such communities would be daunting.

There are also big-picture opportunities. First, the policymaking community and the wider public appear to be acutely aware of the skills challenges the United States now faces if it hopes to maintain its edge in global competition. They also seem to be highly supportive of and willing to fund evidence-based initiatives to address these concerns. Importantly, this support tends to cross the political aisle.

Second, there is probably strength in expanding using multiple replication models: any number of organizations and networks now appear to be strongly supportive of the expansion of sector-based and career pathway approaches in ways that seem to fit many, if not most, of the replication models.

Finally, career pathways approaches are tailor-made for the "completion agenda" promoted by the Obama administration and taken up by multiple governors, emphasizing the attainment of postsecondary credentials by 60 percent of the adult population by 2025. If it is to meet this goal, the completion agenda will not only need to focus on traditional students, but it will also need to include as an objective increasing the occupational skills and education of nontraditional students (i.e., working-age adults). Well-designed career pathways programs that include multiple postsecondary entry and exit points, award industry-recognized credentials, and work toward a postsecondary degree are highly complementary to the broader postsecondary goals set by the administration.

SPECIFIC CHALLENGES TO SUSTAINABILITY AND SCALE

Multiple challenges to expansion and sustainability exist for both career pathways and sector-based programs, not least of which is the current congressional stalemate that serves as the backdrop to these efforts. Congressional attitudes aside, career pathways and sector-based programs will need to clear several hurdles before replacing business-as-usual in the workforce development field. Descriptions of these hurdles follow.

Entropy

Career pathways programs have gained considerable traction in recent years, with specific programs and studies written into UDSOL requests for proposals, and multiple national and state initiatives supported by private foundations and state agencies. Despite this support, however, and despite (broad) guidelines put forward in federal requests for proposals, the approach has suffered from inconsistency in design, definition, and implementation, making it difficult to determine whether the approach is effective versus whether a particular career pathways program has succeeded in meeting its goals. This point is not lost on proponents. Career pathways advocates, such as CLASP, the Workforce Strategies Center, and Jobs for the Future, have attempted to create frameworks to assist in standardizing the approach with a common definition of terms, metrics, and outcomes to which career pathways programs should conform.

These frameworks each contain many of the same fundamental career pathways elements—some level of employer engagement, a recognition of the importance of postsecondary credentials, and the need for support services. However, they vary along several lines, including the key partners and their roles (are career pathways primarily part of the workforce development system or the postsecondary education system; are individuals or systems, whether workforce development or postsecondary education, primarily responsible for mapping out advancement opportunities?), and the importance placed on a clearly articulated set of outcome metrics. On this latter point, CLASP has developed beta versions of a framework as part of its Alliance for Quality Career Pathways (CLASP 2013b), in which it specifies a series of interim education and training and labor market outcomes, as well as a set of suggested criteria that can be used by developers to create and assess the performance of career pathways.

The absence of a clear and widely accepted definition of what constitutes a career pathway has contributed to a sort of entropy as the practice has expanded. Where definitions exist (e.g., USDOL's guidance memos), enforcement of the application of these definitions often falls short. One USDOL-supported career pathways program currently operating was funded thanks to a proposal that provided a state-of-the-art definition of a career pathways model. However, holding the several WIBs involved accountable for implementation of this approach, as opposed to the short-term training for which they have opted, has fallen largely to an intermediary with no real authority for mandating WIB compliance.

If career pathways and sector-based models are ever to replace the status quo, and if the evidence base for their effectiveness is to grow, some mechanism, such as restrictions on eligibility for applying for future innovation grants, for holding implementers accountable, will need to be put into place and routinely used. Absent this, WIBs, with some justification, will be tempted to use this funding to replace funding lost in prior years.

Funding Erosion

Federal, state, and local funding for workforce development programs has seen steady erosion over the past few decades, with ARRA investments in 2009 the exception that proves the rule (see Eberts and Wandner [2013]). With the exception of Pell Grants, federal funding for employment and training programs has remained essentially flat and, since 2000, has even seen modest declines from already poorly funded levels. Until very recently, state and local funding has fared little better than federal support for workforce development programs.

The erosion of funding for workforce development programs reflects a broader attitude among policymakers, one that sees human capital development as a cost to minimize rather than an investment that will produce positive returns. As the center of the policy discourse has shifted rightward over the past two decades, advocates for social safety net programs in general, and employment and training programs in particular, have lost ground to advocates for a leaner government, tax cuts, and, implicitly, a greater degree of self-reliance. Successfully portraying workforce development programs as second-chance programs has meant, among other things, that innovation in the field, such as career pathways and sector-based programs, often comes at the expense of current programs, rather than in addition to. "Robbing Peter to pay Paul" is a recipe for failure, and efforts to sustain the more effective programs will continue to suffer as a result.

Poaching

While an improvement on the status quo, sector-based programs are not without limitations. Where the ideal type of sector-based program described above has existed, it has had to guard against "poaching" among participating employers—that is, against the practice of employers hiring participants from training programs before they have actually completed the program.

This workforce development equivalent of the "tragedy of the commons" has undermined many promising sector-based programs, particularly in times of tight labor markets. Indeed, by virtue of the fact that these programs are designed to respond to critical education and skills shortages, career pathways and sector-based programs are often the victims of their own success. One career pathways program operating in a state currently experiencing a boom in its extraction industry has had to contend with employers hiring students long before they have completed their programs and, more important, earned the certificates that should serve them over the long term. Only after lengthy negotiations between the colleges and employers has this practice begun to turn around.

Lack of Substantial Support from Employers and Industries

On the other side of the poaching coin is the difficulty in remaining relevant to employers. Sector-based programs are effective only when there is significant employer engagement. As noted above, employer engagement can take many forms, including providing input on training curricula, donating machinery on which to train, providing subject matter experts to assist with instruction, funding worker training, hiring, or some combination of these.

However, gaining and maintaining employer engagement is subject to a number of factors, not least of which is demand for skills in the targeted industry. The tight labor markets of the late 1990s and early to mid-2000s made for relatively high levels of employer engagement and led to the creation of a number of particularly innovative workforce development programs (see, for example, Barnow and Hobbie [2013]). With the onset of the Great Recession in 2008 and the sharply increasing unemployment rates across the board, sector-based programs began to experience difficulties in maintaining employer interest. Larger numbers of skilled workers looking for employment, coupled with the contraction of the overall economy, led to a waning interest in sector-based programs among employers.

The cyclical nature of employer engagement has been, and will continue to be, a limiting factor in sector-based strategies' ability to significantly influence the larger workforce development system, unless the approach is systematically adopted as the organizing framework for public investment in workforce development. This position currently is held by postsecondary education-based career pathways approaches that place a greater emphasis on the awarding of marketable certificates and credentials than on organizing sector actors around the key characteristics of sector-based strategies noted above, namely, working directly with employers in a given sector to identify common skill needs, factoring the regional economy into the equation, and promoting worker advancement as a function of skill development within a specific sector. Career pathways programs right now are dominated by occupational-based rather than sector-based training, rarely taking the regional economy into consideration, and frequently operating with little, if any, direct employer input. Also, the focus on bringing the low-skilled into the labor market seemingly would no longer be of interest to employers who can be more selective and favor the already prepared applicant.

Cross-Platform Conflicts

Long considered one of several venues for skills training, including apprenticeships and on-the-job training, postsecondary institutions have become the venues of choice for workforce development practice in general and, more recently, sector-based programs and career pathways in particular. This move was supported by a growing literature on the merits of postsecondary credentials for labor market advancement, as well as the wider dissemination of innovative programming among some higher education institutions (e.g., the North Carolina Community College System, admittedly designed primarily for workforce development and, later, the Washington State Board for Community and Technical Colleges).

However, this move has been resisted by postsecondary institutions, especially by community college faculty, over concerns that the academic mission of the institutions is diminished by acting as training providers rather than as transfer institutions. Resistance also has come from WIBs over concerns that the ever-shrinking pot of employment and training funds is being increasingly repurposed to provide education and training services for participants in postsecondary education programs (namely, the repurposing of WIA training funds, the significant percentage of Workforce Investment Fund projects with postsecondary partners, and the designation of postsecondary institutions as the grantees in USDOL's Trade Adjustment Act Community College Career Training initiative).

In addition, the metrics by which a career pathways or sector-based program may measure success—such as completion of industry-recognized credentials, advancement in the labor market, or earnings gains—often work at cross-purposes with the metrics by which WIBs measure success—typically limited to placement, earnings gains, and retention. Where a WIB is funded to implement a career pathways program, effectively implementing the program must include some method for taking these more comprehensive metrics into account.

These tensions, while certainly still present, have become somewhat less visible as policies take root and the administration endorses a closer alignment between workforce development and postsecondary education. Notable exceptions to these tensions exist, however. Washington State's Skills Panels and Wisconsin's efforts under the Shifting Gears Initiative, for example, have successfully combined not only postsecondary credentials with workforce development system funding and support, but also, especially in Wisconsin, combined a genuine sector-based approach with a career pathways model. As noted above, Washington was able to achieve this through state policy that enabled the creation of a network of regional, sector-based collaboratives.

Wisconsin's success was built on several factors, including solid design and implementation, close coordination between principal actors in the state's Department of Workforce Development and the community and technical college system, a replication of this relationship at the regional level between WIBs and community colleges, seed funding from the Joyce Foundation, state funding, and executive-level buy-in. To be sure, there are other examples, but each likely has some of these elements in common.

Weak Adult Education Programming

The emergence of bridge programs and the implementation of con-textualized instruction in the I-BEST spinoffs are an acknowledgment of the difficulties in serving minimally literate, low-skilled individuals in programs that are ultimately designed to provide workers with liter-acy and skill levels sufficient to fill high-skilled, high-demand occupa-tions. Adult education has long been viewed a relative backwater in the realm of workforce policy and programming (see, for example, National Commission on Adult Literacy [2008]). Funding has been severely lim-ited and has largely flowed to state and local programs regardless of performance, while content and curriculum have received inadequate attention, all despite the critical role of basic skills in helping adults prepare for more advanced skills training.

Poor Participant Supports

Given that a large majority of sector and career pathways programs are funded by the second-chance public workforce development system, it stands to reason that these funds are targeted to serve a population that requires significant support to complete their programs. However, career pathways or sector programs rarely come funded at the levels needed to pay for most of the more basic support services, such as child care, transportation, or assistance with books and fees, let alone many of the other services that can contribute to program completion, such as tutoring, mentoring, or career counseling. Instead, funding comes with a small fraction of the support needed, with the expectation that existing or matching funds will be used to make up the difference.

Even when appropriately funded, implementing support services can be difficult. Integrating the provision of services into a postsecondary-based career pathways or sector-based program requires coordination between staff who understand the needs brought by the population being served and a postsecondary faculty who may object to the interruption to routine that the provision of these services can represent. Here again, the traditional mission of postsecondary education comes into conflict with the focus on workforce development that career pathways and sector-based programs represent. Changes to student orientation programs, additional flexibility in course scheduling due to work and transportation conflicts, limited funding available for counselors with the requisite skills for serving nontraditional student populations, and time required for faculty training in the need for these services each represent strains on the status quo and create friction points.

Work-First Policy "Hangover"

Despite the innovations that career pathways and sector-based programs represent, both are still burdened by a hangover of sorts from the previous era of work-first policies. These policies emphasized very short-term training and placement in employment over longer-term education and training programs that prepare individuals for employment in family-supporting occupations that also provide opportunities for advancement. The work-first mantra was: "Get a job; get a better job; get a career." Work-first is now widely discredited on numerous fronts, ranging from intensive, longitudinal research on labor market transitions showing that remaining in low-wage jobs and sectors typically leads to wage stagnation (e.g., Andersson, Holzer, and Lane 2005; Brown, Haltiwanger, and Lane 2006; Holzer et al. 2011), as well as longer-term evaluation results demonstrating that the near-term labor market impacts of labor force attachment tend to fade out, while skills investments persist over time (e.g., King 2004; King and Heinrich 2011).

KEY OPPORTUNITIES FOR GOING TO SCALE

The greatest opportunities for taking sectoral and career pathway models to scale are found in a number of different workforce and education arenas that are discussed below. All of them are likely to be aided to an extent as yet unknown by the newly enacted Workforce Innovation Opportunities Act, which passed both houses of Congress with near unanimity and was signed into law by President Obama on July 22, 2014. Further assistance may be forthcoming by way of Perkins and Higher Education Act reauthorizations if Congress can sustain its rare bipartisan comity on them.

National Networks and Initiatives

Over the past few decades, a number of national networks have grown up in support of sectoral and career pathway strategies. These seem to offer the best opportunities for scaling up such strategies over time in that they are committed to these strategies, have developed specialized expertise and lasting relationships with providers and employers in key sectors, and in some cases have created political and related community networks to sustain and support them. Some of the more noteworthy of these are discussed below.

National Fund for Workforce Solutions

The NFWS was launched in the mid-2000s by the Annie E. Casey, Ford, and Rockefeller Foundations to foster the use of workforce intermediaries and sectoral strategies led by funder collaboratives in communities across the country. USDOL, the Hitachi Foundation, and other funders joined the effort soon after, and, nearly a decade on, NFWS-supported projects are operating in more than 30 communities. NFWS sites offer another major opportunity for scaling up sectoral and career pathway strategies for many reasons, not least of which is that they have already established critical operating relationships among funders and providers and have also gained traction with employers and industry groups in these same communities.

The NFWS has engaged over 4,500 employers in 90 sector partnerships, serving nearly 55,000 individuals, to whom over 37,000 degrees and credentials were awarded between 2008 and 2013. More than 500 regional and local funders have contributed approximately $200 million in matching funds. The sector partnerships supported by the NFWS often include organized labor, WIBs, CBOs, and educational institutions, with some partnerships consisting solely of a labor-management partnership.

Labor/management partnerships

Several longstanding sector partnerships are labor/management partnerships. The American Federation of State, County and Municipal Employees (AFSCME) District 1199c's Training and Upgrading Fund in Philadelphia works with several area employers to train over 2,000 health care workers per year. Service Employees International Union Local 615's Voice and Future Fund works with a range of Boston firms and universities to create career ladders for custodial workers. WRTP has, since 1997, received funding from private foundations, state agencies, USDOL, and numerous others to work with unions and employers to, among myriad other investments, create registered building trade and manufacturing apprenticeship programs in the Milwaukee area.

Southwest Industrial Areas Foundation

As noted earlier, the SWIAF was one of the pioneer organizations in the sectoral arena, launching Project QUEST in the early 1990s and then seeding spinoff projects in communities all across the South and Southwest, including Capital IDEA in Austin and Houston, ARRIBA in El Paso, and VIDA in the Lower Rio Grande Valley, as well as efforts in Arizona, Arkansas, Iowa, and Louisiana. Each of these efforts has a somewhat different focus and base of operations tailored to the needs and priorities of the local Industrial Areas Foundation (IAF) affiliate organizations. They also have a critically important feature: political organization and clout emanating from the local community and the ability to mobilize strong support for their efforts from a wide base of governmental and philanthropic sources (see Glover et al. [2010]). IAF groups have also pushed state legislative initiatives that foster the spread of sectoral strategies as they have done in Texas with state funding. For example, House Bill 437, which was advocated by the Network of Texas IAF organizations, was signed into law by Texas Governor Rick Perry and was designed to fill high-demand, high-wage jobs in Texas.[11] House Bill 437 will move the successful Jobs and Education Training Program's Launchpad Fund to a new college home as the Texas Innovative Adult Career Education Grant Fund. The legislature also budgeted $5 million for the fund to invest in high-skill training over the next two years. This is a model that likely can be replicated in other states.

National Network of Sector Partners

As noted earlier, the National Network of Sector Partners (NNSP) has operated as a major support group for sectoral strategies since 1999. The fact that the NNSP operates with a mix of philanthropic funding plus member dues gives it staying power that some other efforts may lack. Member dues reflect a level of commitment to sectoral strategies that can be leveraged for other support over time. Additionally, NNSP partners are members of the sectoral strategies "choir," which reaches out to others with a credibility that is important for sustainability.

Alliance for Quality Career Pathways

The Alliance, a collaboration among the Center for Law and Social Policy, the Joyce Foundation, the Corporation for a Skilled Workforce, and others, also represents a real opportunity for sustaining and scaling effective workforce services built around career pathway strategies. The collaborators all are recognized leaders in this area and have chosen to focus on quality services and relationships, as well as metrics for measuring service provision and its outcomes and impacts over time.

State policy support

A number of states have provided continuing support for sectoral and career pathway strategies over time. Some of these are noted below. In addition, the overwhelming majority of states have training funds that have been created from UI tax diversions, or in some cases state general revenues; these may provide a mechanism for scaling these strategies as well.

Commonwealth Corporation

The Commonwealth Corporation in Massachusetts may well be the earliest of sectoral strategy initiatives, having gotten into the field in the early 1980s. As a quasi-public entity, it provides an excellent example of consistent bipartisan state support for sector strategies that could be replicated in other states.

Washington State skills panels

Washington embedded support for sectoral strategies in state policy starting in 1990 and has continued to foster sectorally based skills panels in regions across the state to the present.[12] Washington's skills panels encompass a wide variety of industry sectors, ranging from the wine industry in Walla Walla in the southwestern corner of the state to interactive media in Seattle to advanced manufacturing and clean energy in a multistate region. The second generation of its skills panels was launched as the High Skills, High Wages Fund in 2008.[13]

Texas initiatives

As noted above, Texas has supported sectoral and broader cluster-based strategies through a series of executive and legislative initiatives for over a decade, only in part due to the urging of the IAF and its affiliates. The Texas workforce system has emphasized training for jobs in growth occupations and industry sectors, at least since passage of state workforce reform legislation in mid-1995, but it has also continued such a focus with the governor's 2005 Texas Industry Cluster Initiative stressing support for economic and workforce development in Advanced Technologies and Manufacturing, Aerospace and Defense, Biotechnology and Life Sciences, Information and Computer Technology, Petroleum Refining and Chemical Products, and Energy. It is also noteworthy that the Texas Association of Workforce Boards recently put forth a set of recommendations supporting career pathways models for education and workforce development in the state (Texas Association of Workforce Boards 2014).

State training funds

State training funds are an as-yet underutilized source of support for sectoral and career pathway strategies, although greater attention has been focused on them in recent years (for example, see King and Smith [2007]). Whether funded from diverted UI taxes or state general revenues, such funds now operate in more than 40 states and often fund skills training in growth sectors via community and technical colleges in partnership with employers or industry groups. Political support for these funds appears to be robust and is particularly strong within the business community. Aligning these funds more closely with sectoral and career pathway strategies should be relatively easy as policy initiatives go.

The Workforce Innovation Opportunities Act of 2014 raises the profile and standing of sectoral and career pathway strategies considerably, but it remains to be seen whether USDOL will be able to go beyond mere encouragement to actually incentivize the adoption of such strategies by states and LWIBs as part of a more concerted national policy. To its credit, USDOL has contracted with several organizations to begin providing technical assistance to states and local boards to foster more widespread adoption of these strategies.[14]

Key provisions of the Workforce Innovation Opportunities Act regarding sectoral and career pathway strategies include the following:

- elimination of WIA's sequence of services, combining the formerly core and intensive services into a career services category, in which career pathways and sector-based training programs are encouraged;

- requirement of workforce boards to promote proven promising practices, including the establishment of industry or sector partnerships; and

- promotion of integrated or contextualized Adult Basic Education, English as a Second Language, and occupational training.

RECOMMENDATIONS AND CONCLUDING OBSERVATIONS

There is clearly a significant and growing body of solid practice in the sector-based and career pathways fields. Adages such as necessity being the mother of invention, or about the mind-concentrating effects of being hanged in a fortnight, certainly apply when it comes to innovation in the workforce development field over the past few decades. Faced with the need to educate, train, or "upskill" the workforce, whether so workers can advance or so employers can remain competitive (or, ideally, both), programmers and policymakers have developed an array of practices to address the demand for higher-order skills.

However, sector-based strategies and career pathways, while innovative and often effective, speak to the absence of a coherent, adequately supported national system for ensuring that workers receive the assistance needed to advance in the labor market, and employers are assured that they will have access to a workforce with the skills required to make them competitive.

And while valid arguments could once be made that national competitiveness depended on the education and skills of the workforce, it is difficult to square the tepid investments in workforce development over the past 20 years with the fact that, on average, U.S. economic growth has outpaced the OECD average since the first quarter of 2012, suggesting that the economy has found a way to return to competitiveness postrecession despite underinvestment in its human capital.

This may have been achieved by the shift, predicted by many, toward a smaller, more technically skilled and higher-educated workforce than was required in the past. Technological advances and the offshoring of lower-skilled manufacturing jobs may have translated into structural changes in the labor market not easily remedied by improvements, no matter how innovative, in workforce development programming.

Still, labor shortages in key sectors of the economy persist and, according to some industry leaders, will only get worse in the near future.[15] This suggests that, despite structural changes in the economy, scaling up effective sector-based and career pathways strategies will likely be necessary if the economy is to remain competitive. Few would argue that the country's current high school and postsecondary completion rates are adequate for either a competitive economy or the upward mobility of the workforce.[16]

Moreover, many would likely agree that, for too long, private foundations have carried a disproportionate burden for investing in innovation in workforce development. Bringing these strategies to scale will require a renewed commitment from federal and state government to raise revenue (i.e., reverse the tax cuts handed to the wealthy over the past 30 years) and invest it in programs designed to lift the poor out of poverty and equip them with the education and skills required to live a fulfilling and self-determined life. While politically unpopular, these steps are the minimum necessary to narrow the widening gap between the wealthy and the rest, and to give credibility to legislators' claims that the United States is a country in which prosperity is broadly shared.

In addition, and even less politically popular than either raising taxes or investing in the social safety net, there is the reversal of policies that have undercut organized labor's ability to represent workers. It should be noted that the education and training that career pathways provides have been an integral part of the apprenticeship system for many decades, and the employer engagement and aggregation of training needs typical of the better sector-based programs have been part and parcel of organized labor's relationship with industry. It should also be noted that those OECD countries that have consistently vied with the United States as most economically competitive, such as Germany, or are currently emerging out of the recession at a faster pace, such as Australia and Korea, rely heavily on good working relationships between labor and industry. Attempting to re-create and bring to scale strategies that have long been a part of a labor contract without organized labor will subject them to politically driven budgeting decisions, rather than decisions about what is best for workers and industry.

Rigorous evaluations have documented that career pathways and sector-based programs can be effective strategies for providing workers with the education and skills required to succeed in the labor market, and for providing employers with a workforce that can keep them competitive. Scaling up these practices is essential to creating the workforce development system of the twenty-first century, but this can be accomplished only if these practices are part of a more comprehensive commitment to workforce development that includes a significantly larger investment on the part of government and, ideally, representation of workers' interests by organized labor.

Notes

1. For more on the Commonwealth Corporation, see http://www.commcorp.org (accessed January 25, 2015).
2. Information about Project QUEST can be found at http://www.questsa.org (accessed January 25, 2015).
3. More information about WRTP/BIG Step is at http://www.wrtp.org (accessed January 25, 2015).
4. More information about and reports from the JOBS Initiative are provided at http://www.aecf.org/MajorInitiatives/CenterforFamilyEconomicSuccess/TheJobs Initiative.aspx (accessed January 25, 2015).
5. For more information about NNSP, see http://www.insightcced.org/communities/ nnsp.html (accessed January 25, 2015).

6. Washington State's Skills Panels are described more fully at http://www.wtb.wa .gov/IndustrySkillPanel.asp (accessed January 25, 2015).
7. See http://www.sectorstrategies.org/accelerating-state-adoption-sector-strategies (accessed January 23, 2015).
8. These data are based on a survey report published by the National Network of Sector Partners (Mangatt 2010).
9. Indiana participated only in the initial stages of the Shifting Gears Initiative.
10. This section draws, in part, on the extended discussion in King (2014).
11. For more information, see http://www.ntotx.org/home/nto-applauds-governor -perry-for-5-million-investment-in-jobs (accessed January 25, 2015).
12. See http://www.wtb.wa.gov/IndustrySkillPanel.asp (accessed January 25, 2015).
13. Much more information on the latest generation of skills panels can be found at http://www.wtb.wa.gov/HSHWStrategicFund.asp (accessed January 25, 2015).
14. Maher and Maher, a New Jersey–based human resources consulting firm, is working with Jobs for the Future, the Ray Marshall Center, and others on this effort.
15. Boeing Airlines Vice President of Human Resources, Alan May, announced at the annual National Fund for Workforce Solutions conference in Chicago on June 27, 2014, that approximately 50 percent of Boeing's workforce was within five years of retirement age.
16. For example, see OECD (2013) and Crellin, Kelly, and Prince (2012).

References

Alssid, Julian L., Melissa Goldberg, and Sarah M. Klerk. 2010. *Building a Higher Skilled Workforce: Results and Implications from the BridgeConnect National Survey.* Barrington, RI: Workforce Strategy Center.
Andersson, Frederick, Harry J. Holzer, and Julia I. Lane. 2005. *Moving Up or Moving On: Who Advances in the Low-Wage Labor Market?* New York: Russell Sage.
Barnow, Burt S., and Richard Hobbie, eds. 2013. *The American Recovery and Reinvestment Act: The Role of Workforce Programs.* Kalamazoo, MI: W.E. Upjohn Institute for Employment Research.
Barnow, Burt S., and Christopher T. King. 2005. *The Workforce Investment Act in Eight States.* Albany, NY: Nelson A. Rockefeller Institute of Government. http://doleta.gov/reports/searcheta/occ (accessed November 19, 2014).
Bradach, J. 2003. "Going to Scale: The Challenge of Replicating Social Programs." *Stanford Social Innovation Review* 1: 18–25.
Brown, Clair, John Haltiwanger, and Julia I. Lane. 2006. *Economic Turbulence: Is a Volatile Economy Good for America?* Chicago: University of Chicago Press.
Campbell, Brett. 1994. *Investing in People: The Story of Project QUEST.* San

Antonio, TX: Communities Organized for Public Service (COPS) and Metro Alliance. http://www.cpn.org/topics/work/quest1-2.html#ch1 (accessed December 12, 2013).

Center for Postsecondary and Economic Success at CLASP. 2013. "A Framework for Measuring Career Pathways Innovation: A Working Paper." Washington, DC: Center for Law and Social Policy.

Crellin, Matt, Patrick Kelley, and Heath J. Prince. 2012. "Increasing College Attainment in the United States: Variations in Returns to States and Their Residents." *Change: The Magazine of Higher Learning* 44(4): 35–41.

Deaton, Brian, and Robert McPherson. 1991. *Design of Project QUEST.* Austin, TX: Center for the Study of Human Resources, University of Texas at Austin.

Eberts, Randall W., and Stephen A. Wandner. 2013. "Data Analysis of the Implementation of the Recovery Act Workforce Development and Unemployment Insurance Provisions." In *The American Recovery and Reinvestment Act: The Role of Workforce Programs*, Burt S. Barnow and Richard A. Hobbie, eds. Kalamazoo, MI: W.E. Upjohn Institute for Employment Research, pp. 267–307.

Giloth, Robert P., ed. 2004. *Workforce Intermediaries for the Twenty-First Century.* Philadelphia: Temple University Press.

Glover, Robert W., and Christopher T. King. 2010. "The Promise of Sectoral Approaches to Workforce Development: Towards More Effective, Active Labor Market Policies in the United States." In *Human Resource Economics: Essays in Honor of Vernon M. Briggs, Jr.*, Charles J. Whalen, ed. Kalamazoo, MI: W.E. Upjohn Institute for Employment Research, pp. 215–251.

Glover, Robert W., Tara Carter Smith, Christopher T. King, and Rheagan Coffey. 2010. *CareerAdvance®: A Dual-Generation Antipoverty Strategy, An Implementation Study of the Initial Pilot Cohort July 2009 through June 2010.* Austin, TX: Ray Marshall Center for the Study of Human Resources, Lyndon B. Johnson School of Public Affairs, University of Texas at Austin.

Hamilton, Gayle. 2002. *Moving People from Welfare to Work: Lessons from the National Evaluation of Welfare-to-Work Strategies.* New York: MDRC.

Holzer, Harry J., Julia I. Lane, David B. Rosenblum, and Frederick Andersson. 2011. *Where Are All the Good Jobs Going? What National and Local Job Quality and Dynamics Mean for U.S. Workers.* New York: Russell Sage.

Jenkins, Davis. 2006. *CAREER PATHWAYS: Aligning Public Resources to Support Individual and Regional Economic Advancement in the Knowledge Economy.* Barrington, RI: Workforce Strategy Center.

Jobs for the Future. 2010. *The Breaking Through Practice Guide.* Boston: Jobs for the Future.

King, Christopher T. 2004. "The Effectiveness of Publicly Financed Training in the United States: Implications for WIA and Related Programs." In *Job Training Policy in the United States*, Christopher J. O'Leary, Robert A. Straits, and Stephen A. Wandner, eds. Kalamazoo, MI: W.E. Upjohn Institute for Employment Research, pp. 57–100.

———. 2014. "Sectoral Workforce and Related Strategies: What We Know … and What We Need to Know." In *Connecting People to Work: Workforce Intermediaries and Sector Strategies*, Maureen Conway and Robert P. Giloth, eds. New York: American Assembly Press, pp. 209–238.

King, Christopher T., and Carolyn Heinrich. 2011. "Does Workforce Development Work?" Paper presented to the APPAM Research Conference, held in Washington, DC, November 3–5.

King, Christopher T., and Tara Carter Smith. 2007. "State Unemployment Insurance-Supported Training Funds." In *Strategies for Financing Workforce Intermediaries: Working Papers*, Heath Prince, ed. Boston: Jobs for the Future/National Fund for Workforce Solutions, pp. 69–122.

Maguire, Sheila, Joshua Freely, Carol Clymer, Maureen Conway, and Deena Schwartz. 2010. *Tuning in to Local Labor Markets: Findings from the Sectoral Employment Impact Study*. Philadelphia: Public/Private Ventures.

Mangatt, Rivinder. 2010. "Sector Snapshop: A Profile of Sector Initiatives, 2010." Oakland, CA: National Network of Sector Partnerships, Insight Center for Community Economic Development.

Mikelson, Kelly S., and Demetra Smith Nightingale. 2004. *Estimating Public and Private Expenditures on Occupational Training in the United States*. Washington, DC: U.S. Department of Labor.

Miller, Cynthia, Johannes M. Bos, Kristin E. Porter, Fannie M. Tseng, and Yasuyo Abe. 2005. *The Challenge of Repeating Success in a Changing World: Final Report on the Center for Employment Training Replication Sites*. New York: MDRC.

National Commission on Adult Literacy. 2008. *Reach Higher: Overcoming Crisis in the U.S. Workforce*. New York: National Commission on Adult Literacy.

NGA Center for Best Practices, National Network of Sector Partners, and Corporation for a Skilled Workforce. 2008. *Accelerating State Adoption of Sector Strategies: An Eleven-State Project to Promote Regional Solutions to Worker and Employer Needs, Phase I Project Report*. Washington, DC: NGA Center for Best Practices, National Network of Sector Partners, and Corporation for a Skilled Workforce.

Organisation for Economic Co-operation and Development. 2013. *OECD Skills Outlook 2013: First Results from the Survey of Adult Skills*. Paris: OECD.

Orr, Larry L., Howard S. Bloom, Stephen H. Bell, Fred Doolittle, and Winston Lin. 1996. *Does Training for the Disadvantaged Work? Evidence from the National JTPA Study.* Washington, DC: Urban Institute Press.

Roder, Anne, and Mark Elliott. 2011. *A Promising Start: Year Up's Initial Impacts on Low-Income Young Adults' Careers.* New York: Economic Mobility Corporation.

———. 2014. *SUSTAINED GAINS: Year Up's Continued Impacts on Young Adults' Earnings.* New York: Economic Mobility Corporation. May.

Smith, Tara Carter, and Christopher T. King. 2011. *Exploratory Return-on-Investment Analysis of Local Workforce Investments.* Austin, TX: Ray Marshall Center for the Study of Human Resources, Lyndon B. Johnson School of Public Affairs, University of Texas at Austin.

Smith, Tara C., Christopher T. King, and Daniel G. Schroeder. 2012. *Local Investments in Workforce Development: 2012 Evaluation Update.* Austin, TX: Ray Marshall Center for the Study of Human Resources, Lyndon B. Johnson School of Public Affairs, University of Texas at Austin.

Strawn, Julie. 2010. *Shifting Gears: State Innovation to Advance Workers and the Economy in the Midwest.* Chicago: Joyce Foundation.

———. 2011. *Farther, Faster: Six Promising Programs Show How Career Pathways Bridges Help Basic Skills Students Earn Credentials That Matter.* Washington, DC: Center for Law and Social Policy, Center for Postsecondary and Economic Success.

Texas Association of Workforce Boards. 2014. *The Workforce in Texas: Aligning Education to Meet the Needs of Texas Employers.* Dallas: Texas Association of Workforce Boards.

Zeidenberg, Matthew, Sung-Woo Cho, and Davis Jenkins. 2010. "Washington State's Integrated Basic Education and Skills Training Program (I-BEST): New Evidence of Effectiveness." CCRC Working Paper No. 20. New York: Community College Research Center, Teachers College, Columbia University.

9
Employer Involvement in Workforce Programs

What Do We Know?

Burt S. Barnow
George Washington University

Shayne Spaulding
Urban Institute

Over the last several decades, policymakers and funders have increasingly expected local workforce systems and programs to make the engagement and involvement of employers a priority. In a field where the primary goal is to place people in jobs, one might think the engagement of the employers that will hire job-seeker customers would be a fundamental practice. However, the workforce system and workforce training programs have not always prioritized employer engagement, and workforce systems and organizations still struggle with how to effectively involve employers.

The main reason workforce organizations engage employers is to help program customers achieve success in the labor market by ensuring that job seekers possess the skills required by employers, and/or by helping them make the connections to available job opportunities through the relationships built with employers. While employers may use workforce organizations for reasons of corporate social responsibility, the most successful partnerships emerge because of the important functions that workforce organizations can serve for employers. They can help employers recruit and screen qualified applicants for available positions and provide training for potential applicants and incumbent workers. These activities can not only help employers with their human resources needs, they can also help them offset the cost of training and recruitment.

In this chapter, we explore the history of employer involvement in workforce programs in the United States, the different models of employer engagement, and what is known about the effectiveness of such efforts. We discuss why organizations and workforce systems struggle to engage employers, what can be learned from their experiences, and possible strategies for encouraging deeper connections with employers in order to improve outcomes for those who participate in workforce training programs.

WHAT DO WE MEAN BY EMPLOYER ENGAGEMENT?

Employers can play a variety of roles in the preparation of the workforce. Primarily, they provide training to the workers in their own firms or organizations either directly or through contracts with external training providers. Research has shown that the majority of employers provide training to their workers, whether through informal training, formal training, or tuition reimbursement (Lerman, McKernan, and Riegg 2004; Mikelson and Nightingale 2004). While the federal government currently does not collect data on employer investments in training, findings from several industry surveys indicate that employer investments in training dwarf public workforce system resources for job training, even in the context of projected increases under the new Workforce Innovation and Opportunity Act (WIOA), which authorizes about $3 billion for Adult, Youth, and Dislocated Worker programs for fiscal year 2016. One study estimates that employers spend between $46 and $54 billion annually on education and training (Mikelson and Nightingale 2004). When the costs of trainee wages and administrative costs are removed and only direct training costs are considered (trainer salaries, books, materials, etc.), the amount that employers spend on training is much lower: between $8 billion and $17 billion per year, but still much larger than the resources available for training through the workforce system. The Association for Talent Development (2013; formerly the American Society for Training and Development) estimates employer expenditures to be much higher—$164.2 billion in 2012.[1]

This chapter focuses on programs that are financed by government or philanthropies and aimed at serving the disadvantaged, as opposed to staff development and training efforts targeted at incumbent workers that are led and paid for by employers. We are interested in efforts by state and local workforce systems and training providers to involve employers in the management (through boards), design, and delivery of workforce programs, and in the hiring of program graduates and other entry-level workers who are served by workforce systems and programs. We are also interested in understanding the most robust forms of employer engagement where workforce organizations don't simply involve employers in training efforts, but treat them as clients, as is found in both customized and sectoral training.

While there are a variety of ways that workforce organizations engage employers, we do not review the evidence of all possible employer engagement strategies. Rather, we focus on some key examples of employer engagement to see what can be learned. For example, we do not discuss apprenticeship models, where apprentices participate in classroom-based and work-based learning programs that are designed through collaborations of employers and educational institutions. Nor do we examine the evidence for other strategies that involve other types of learning at the workplace (internships, externships, clinical experiences). We also do not explore the engagement of employers in community college programs, because evidence is limited; however, recent investments in building the capacity of community colleges to respond to employer needs may add to what we know about the effectiveness of employer engagement strategies. Finally, we do not explore the research on what is known about state-funded customized training programs.[2]

Employer Engagement in Federal Workforce Policy and Programs

The involvement of employers became more central to federal workforce policy with enactment of the Job Training Partnership Act (JTPA, 1982), which required majority participation of employers in local advisory committees called Private Industry Councils (PICs), as state and local governments were given increased discretion over the operation of federally funded workforce programs. While local advisory councils existed under the 1973 Comprehensive Employment and Training Act (CETA), the prior law governing workforce programs, they did not become part of federal policy until 1978, and even then they were perceived as weak by employers (Guttman 1983).[3] JTPA required that the majority of local councils consist of private industry representatives. Unlike CETA, in which local councils had very little power, PICs were described in the JTPA legislation as "equal partners" in the administration of local workforce programs (Guttman 1983). Despite JTPA calling for expanded involvement of employers, employer involvement was still largely limited, with the exception of efforts in a few local areas, and even those with strong linkages to employers did not demonstrate stronger performance (Bailey 1988).

WIA replaced JTPA and carved out a stronger role for employers in the workforce system by giving local boards, renamed Workforce Investment Boards (WIBs), the authority to *set* local policy. WIA was similar to JTPA in that it required majority representation from the business community, but the law for the first time recognized employers as customers of the workforce system. Despite success in some state and local areas in engaging employers in the local workforce system, evaluations have shown that employers still do not play a strong role in the administration of local workforce systems, as we discuss later in this chapter.

Most recently, the Workforce Innovation and Opportunity Act (WIOA) was signed into law in 2014, replacing WIA. The new statute leaves many of the core elements of WIA, aiming to organize multiple programs and funding streams under a single piece of legislation, but it includes an even stronger emphasis on employer involvement across these programs, including new employer engagement requirements in state and local plans, new performance metrics related to employer engagement, encouragement that states and local areas adopt sector- or industry-based strategies, higher allowable reimbursement rates for on-the-job training, and changes to employer contribution requirements for customized training programs. The extent to which the new law reflects a marked change in how the workforce system works with employers will be determined, in part, by the new regulations and how they are implemented. At the writing of this chapter, regulations related to WIOA were still being drafted with final rules slated to go into effect in 2016.

Under WIOA, WIBs and American Job Centers (formerly One-Stop Career Centers) remain at the center of service delivery, with a constellation of other public and private providers playing important roles at the local level. Public agencies involved in local service delivery include the Employment Service (sometimes referred to as the Job Service), which provides labor exchange services for job seekers, including individuals receiving Unemployment Insurance benefits; state and local agencies administering the Temporary Assistance for Needy Families (TANF) program, which provides poor families with children time-limited cash benefits, workforce preparation, and job placement; and local community college systems, which offer job training through both non-credit and for-credit programs.[4] Little is known about the involvement of employers in these programs. While the Employment Service has some involvement of employers in local oversight, federal TANF law does not emphasize employer involvement, and the level of employer engagement varies in community college programs. Where these actors are strong partners in the WIB or American Job Center delivery system, they may benefit from the employer engagement activities of WIBs.

Through the evolution of federal workforce policy, delivery of education and training services has increasingly devolved from the responsibility of government agencies to an array of local providers, including faith-based and community-based organizations, community colleges, for-profit colleges, and proprietary schools. While it remains to be seen how new employer engagement requirements under WIOA will affect the way these entities do business, in recent years the federal government, many local governments, and private foundations have sought to encourage employer engagement by grantees. For example, the U.S. Department of Labor (USDOL) has issued a number of competitive grant solicitations with an emphasis on "demand-driven" strategies, which refers to the practice of workforce organizations responding to issues of employer demand as opposed to job-seeker "supply." Other federal agencies have also placed an emphasis on employer involvement. For example, the U.S. Department of Health and Human Services requires consultations with employers as part of its Health Profession Opportunity Grants, which aim to improve opportunities for TANF recipients and other low-income individuals in accessing available jobs in the health care sector. Several foundation-funded demonstration projects and other large-scale, privately funded national initiatives have also sought to encourage workforce training providers and local systems to more effectively engage employers. Table 9.1 shows some examples of publicly and privately funded national efforts.

Table 9.1 Employer Engagement in National Initiatives

Initiative name	Funder	Grantees	Program description	Employer engagement description
High Growth Job Training Initiative (2001–2007)	USDOL	Wide range of organizations, including industry associations, community colleges, non-profit organizations, state workforce organizations, and other entities	Aimed at preparing workers for opportunities in selected sectors defined by high demand and emerging skills needs, influenced by technological change	Aimed at creating market-driven, strategic partnerships among private industry, education institutions, and the workforce investment system
Community-Based Job Training Grants (2005–2009)	USDOL	Community and technical colleges	Designed to support workforce training for high-growth/high-demand industries and capacity building for community and technical colleges	Required active engagement of employers in the project, participation in grant activities, including: Defining the program strategy and goals; identifying needed skills and competencies; designing training approaches and curricula; implementing the program; contributing financial support; and, where appropriate, hiring qualified training graduates
Workforce Innovation in Regional Economic Development (WIRED) grants (2006–2008)	USDOL	State governors overseeing regional partnerships	Regional effort to increase employment and advancement opportunities to a broad population of workers and create high-skill, high-wage jobs	Employer representation and effort to link economic development and workforce development activities

Trade Adjustment Assistance Community College Career Training Grants (2012–2015)	USDOL	Community colleges and other institutions of higher education	Provides funds to expand and improve ability to deliver education and career training programs that can be completed in two years or less and are in high demand.	Required engagement of employers, local industry associations, and/or national industry associations as partners.
Health Profession Opportunity Grants	HHS	States, local WIBs, institutions of higher education and Indian tribes and tribal organizations	Provides education and training to TANF recipients and other low-income individuals for occupations in the health care field that pay well and are expected to either experience labor shortages or be in high demand	Participants must earn employer- or industry-recognized certificates, based on consultations with employers
Casey Jobs Initiative	Annie E. Casey Foundation	Workforce intermediaries (see description in text)	Effort in six cities to connect inner-city young men and women to family-supporting jobs in the regional economy and to improve the way urban labor market systems work for low-income, low-skilled workers	Funded workforce intermediaries expected to treat employers as customers equal to job seekers
National Fund for Workforce Solutions	Multiple national and local funders	Local funding collaboratives	National funders support local communities to organize and sustain regional funding collaboratives that invest in worker skills and their key regional industries	Goal is to develop employer-driven workforce strategies to help low-wage workers and job seekers obtain career opportunities, while creating talent supply chains that close skills gaps and strengthen local economies

A third type of entity that has emerged in recent years is the "workforce intermediary" aimed at bridging the gap between employers that demand trained workers and the training organizations that "supply" them. Workforce intermediaries are defined less by organizational form—WIBs, labor unions, and nonprofit organizations can all be workforce intermediaries—than by a set of common characteristics. As described by Giloth (2004), workforce intermediaries convene local stakeholders for the purpose of creating advancement opportunities for low-wage workers. In addition, workforce intermediaries

- take a dual customer approach (workers and employers);
- go beyond job matching (supporting curriculum development, identifying appropriate training providers);
- act as integrators of workforce funding, programs, and information;
- are generators of ideas and innovations; and
- are not single-purpose or single-function organizations.

The idea is that it is difficult for training providers that are driven primarily by the mission to serve the disadvantaged to build relationships with the for-profit sector because they do not understand industry needs, do not speak the language of employers, and may not be positioned to respond to the breadth of employer needs with respect to training. Intermediaries who broker relationships with a variety of employers and providers in a local area may be able to identify the best organization to respond to a particular employer need and can help avoid the issue of single employers being approached by multiple training providers within the workforce system.

FORMS OF EMPLOYER ENGAGEMENT

Employer Engagement Strategies

Workforce organizations use a variety of strategies to engage employers for the purpose of improving job seeker outcomes. We divide these strategies into four categories to characterize the types of employer engagement: 1) program management and oversight, 2) program design, 3) delivery, and 4) hiring.

Program management and oversight

Employers can be engaged in the management of programs. Participation in oversight or advisory boards offers one opportunity to engage employers in the management of programs. While it is a requirement under both WIA and WIOA that employers make up the majority of state and local WIBs, training providers and intermediaries may also seek employer involvement on their oversight boards. Many vocationally focused community college departments, for example, require employer advisory boards. Employers can also participate in college or university-wide boards or councils, which are aimed at building a connection between the educational institution and the community.

Program design

Governing boards may fill general oversight functions, but they also can play a role in program design and development. Boards may give employers the opportunity to provide feedback on the types of programs that should be offered by an organization or in a local community, or feedback on the content of curricula used to train participants. Employers who are not board members can be engaged in the development of programs and curricula. The input that employers provide on the design of training programs can include information on the required technical and soft skills, the appropriate length of training, the credentials recognized by employers, and common challenges experienced by the employer with the current workforce in the targeted position. Employers can provide feedback on eligibility requirements, screening tools, curricula, assessment tools, textbooks, and other classroom materials. They can also provide advice about the value that work experience—through workplace simulations, internships, or clinical experiences—will play in the employability of program graduates. In programs that involve customized training for incumbent workers or on-the-job training, employers are more directly responsible for the oversight and development of training.

Program delivery

Employers can also be engaged in the delivery of training programs. Clymer (2003) noted that it is important to "make employers part of the woodwork" as the general approach to employer engagement. Involvement in the day-to-day operations of training programs can include the following:

- participating in decisions about who is accepted into the program;
- participating as instructors or guest presenters in training;
- hosting work experience opportunities (apprenticeships, internships, clinical experiences) at the work site;
- providing opportunities for mentorship, job shadowing, or other exposure to the workplace;
- helping students prepare for job search (resume review, mock interviews, etc.); and
- volunteering for the program in other ways.

The level of involvement by employers will likely reflect some combination of the employers' need for trained workers; their confidence in an organization's ability to give them what they need (including, perhaps, an advantage in competing for trained workers in a labor market for in-demand workers); and a sense of civic responsibility.

Hiring

Programs involve employers in hiring in a number of ways, including through the job development efforts of training organizations and through wage subsidy programs that aim to encourage employers to hire participants by offsetting all or a portion of a hired worker's wages. While there have been many attempts to get employer partners to contractually agree or commit to hire program graduates, these have not typically been successful because employers do not want to be legally bound to hire individuals who have not been screened for their qualifications and suitability for open positions. Depending on the length of a particular training, the employer's needs might change by the time an individual has completed the program. Furthermore, employers want the opportunity to consider other potential candidates so as to ensure they hire the most qualified and best-suited applicants for the job. Instead, if agreements are made, they often take the form of giving program graduates first priority in hiring decisions. Community benefit agreements are sometimes structured to require businesses locating in particular areas to hire from those communities, but the requirements are usually that a portion of hires comes from a particular community or organization (Gross 2008).

Workforce organizations seek to build relationships with employers in the management, design, and delivery of a program largely to help ensure that program graduates will meet job requirements and be hired by employers who hire workers with those skills. Workforce systems, training providers, and workforce intermediaries also seek to build relationships with employers to learn about available job opportunities and help program participants—who often lack the social and professional networks—get their "foot in the door." Relationships with employers are often built by staff members—called job developers, employment specialists, or account managers—or specialized units whose responsibility it is to broker relationships with employers and provide access to jobs. These staff can help employers manage some of the human resource functions of an employer by screening candidates for open positions. Wage subsidies can further offset some of the costs of hiring and training new workers, as is the case with on-the-job training (OJT).

Models of Employer Engagement

While many workforce organizations aim to incorporate one or more of these employer engagement practices into their programs, not all are employer-focused. Organizations vary in the degree to which they view employers as customers and the extent to which they are successful in involving them in programs. Pindus and Isbell (1996), in their review of employer involvement in workforce programs, distinguish employer-based training from employer-centered training. Employer-based training is characterized by employer involvement, whereas employer-centered training emphasizes working directly with firms and treating the firms as clients. Employer-centered training programs can be either customized for a single employer (customized training) or designed to meet the needs of a group of employers within an industry or that employ people in the same occupations (sectoral training).

Because these approaches represent the most robust forms of employer involvement, we describe them in more detail below.

Customized training

Workforce organizations may work with individual firms to provide customized training either for existing workers or to fill a set of open positions within a company or organization. Customized training can aim to provide job-specific skills for new workers or to help incumbent workers retain their jobs or advance. It also can focus on general skills, such as basic education or customer service. Under WIA, employers were required to pay for 50 percent of the costs of training tailored specifically to meet the needs of individual employers and to commit to hiring program graduates.[5] Under WIOA, states and localities are given more flexibility with respect to determining the amounts the employers have to pay, depending on such factors as the size of the employer, number of employees trained, and other factors to be determined by the state or local area. The law requires only that employers pay "a significant portion" of the training costs, while keeping in place the requirement that employers participating in WIOA-funded customized training commit to hire program graduates. In addition to the federal government, many states have implemented customized training programs as a strategy for meeting local employer needs and influencing business location decisions (Duscha and Graves 2006).

Sectoral training

Workforce organizations can also work with groups of employers to try to meet shared needs by operating sectoral programs.[6] Sector-based approaches offer the advantage of scale with more job opportunities being available for participants when working across multiple firms.

Conway et al. (2007) define sectoral strategies as a "systems approach" to workforce development that

- focuses on industry sectors or clusters of occupations;
- intervenes through a credible organization, or group of organizations;
- improves the employment-related skills of workers;
- meets the needs of employers; and

- creates changes in the labor market that sustain benefits to employers.

In several respects, sectoral strategies bear resemblance to the concept of workforce intermediaries, which organize local actors within workforce systems in order to advance low-wage workers.[7] While many sectoral strategies are focused on access to jobs for low-income populations, others simultaneously focus on improving job quality; for example, the Paraprofessional Healthcare Institute in the Bronx operates a training program, social purpose business, and policy center aimed at making improvements for the direct care workforce.

Many workforce organizations—whether they are community-based organizations, community colleges, proprietary schools, or other for-profit or nonprofit service providers—seek to engage employers without offering customized services or managing sectoral initiatives. However, they may play important roles in sector-based programs, offering job readiness, preparation for the General Educational Development (GED) test or other high school equivalency tests, programs to improve English language skills, vocational skills training leading to certificates or degrees, or support services for those enrolled in training. Any of these organizations may see a value in engaging employers in their programs and can play important roles in broader sectoral efforts.

THE EFFECTIVENESS OF EMPLOYER INVOLVEMENT

As we have seen, employer involvement in workforce investment programs can take many forms and can vary in the degree to which employers are the focus of training efforts and the strategies that are used to engage employers. In this section, we review the literature on what is known about the effects of employer involvement. We focus on some key examples of employer engagement that reflect the strategies and models of employer engagement described above. We provide an analysis of what is known about the involvement of employers in governance boards as an example of efforts to engage employers in the management of programs. To explore the evidence around the engagement of employers in the design and delivery of programs and employer-centered models, we look at two evaluations of sector-based programs. Finally, as an example of employer engagement in hiring, we examine what is known about OJT.

Employer Engagement through Workforce Investment Boards

As already discussed, WIA, like JTPA before it, required state and local boards to include employer representatives as a majority of the membership. Although states and local workforce investment areas complied with the rules, evaluations have shown that employers have typically not played a major role in administering the boards. There were two major evaluations of the implementation of WIA, and both concluded that employers generally do not play a major role in developing policies for local workforce boards. D'Amico et al. (2004, pp. 1–17) conclude, "Local workforce areas are embracing business engagement in principle, but in practice they are lagging in their ability to engage business seriously in strategic planning or serve them as customers with high-quality services." Similarly, Barnow and King (2005, p. 14) conclude, "It is difficult to measure business involvement in the workforce development system. The impression is that WIA has not yet achieved the strong employer role envisioned by the statute or promoted by the U.S. Department of Labor, although some states and areas have accomplished more in this respect than others." Barnow and King cite a number of explanations for the failure of boards to play a major role, including the overly large size of the boards, their lack of influence over workforce issues in their areas, the bureaucratic nature of the boards and the programs they administer, and employers' perceived lack of value added from their involvement. It may be that this perceived failure is one of the factors that led to a stronger focus on employer engagement under WIOA.

D'Amico et al. (2004) and Dunham, Salzman, and Koller (2004) develop lists of successful strategies to engage business in local workforce program planning activities, such as making sure that meetings are short and well organized, arranging for mutual appointments on partner organizations' boards, and developing sectoral initiatives where economic development and workforce development needs will overlap.

Quantitative evaluations of sectoral training programs

Sectoral training programs are currently highly regarded because they not only get substantial employer input for workforce investment programs, they also help regions and communities focus their activities on sectors of interest. In this section, we review findings from two quantitative evaluations of sectoral programs, the Sectoral Employment Impact Study and Capital IDEA.

The Sectoral Employment Impact Study.[8] Although sectoral programs have been popular for a number of years, the first evidence from a large-scale randomized controlled trial came from Maguire et al. (2010) with the release of the Sectoral Employment Impact Study. In this demonstration, three mature sectoral programs were selected by the researchers to implement their programs with randomly selected control groups so that the impact of the programs could be determined. The programs differed significantly in the characteristics of customers served, the industries covered, and the location of the sites.

- **The Wisconsin Regional Training Partnership (WRTP)** is an association of employers and unions, described as a workforce intermediary, that develops short-term training programs (typically two to eight weeks long) to meet the needs of specific employers. For the demonstration, their training programs in the construction, manufacturing, and health care sectors were included.

- **Jewish Vocational Service (JVS)-Boston** is a nonprofit organization. It operates one of Boston's American Job Centers for Workforce Investment Act customers and serves a range of disadvantaged customers, including refugees, immigrants, and welfare recipients. JVS-Boston's training programs in medical billing and accounting were included in the demonstration.

- **Per Scholas** is a New York City organization that combines vocational training with a program to recycle computers and distribute them to low-income individuals. Per Scholas's computer technician training program, which included training for repair and maintenance of computers, printers, and copiers, was included in the demonstration.

All three organizations were described as involving employers in the design of programs by providing input into program offerings or curricula. They also involved employers in the delivery of programs by offering opportunities for participants to gain work experience or asking employers to participate in program activities, such as mock interviews for participants and job fairs.

The participants served in the three programs were screened to make sure they met the programs' normal entry requirements, which included having reading and/or math levels at the 6th to 10th grade or higher. Participants were roughly evenly split between men and women (47 percent men), and most were African American (60 percent) or Latino (21 percent). A majority of the participants were over 24 (70 percent), and roughly one in five (22 percent) had been convicted of a felony. A majority of the participants had a high school diploma (53 percent) or a GED (22 percent), with 18 percent having more than a high school education and 7 percent having less. The participants had not been very successful in the labor market when they applied to the programs. About one-third (34 percent) were employed full or part time at entry, and only 10 percent worked full time for the 12 months prior to entry. Total earnings in the year prior to entry averaged $9,872.

The programs varied significantly in length and composition. The WRTP program was the shortest, with training lasting between two and eight weeks. Training at Per Scholas was for 15 weeks, and JVS-Boston programs lasted 20–22 weeks. In addition to vocational training, all three programs provided services to improve employability and supportive services. WRTP offered essential skills training, and Per Scholas offered life skills training; these components dealt with issues such as timeliness, attendance, dealing with child care, goal setting, and communication. JVS-Boston and Per Scholas both offered internship programs to give participants work experiences prior to obtaining an actual job.

The study used an experimental design to determine impacts on employment, earnings, and other outcomes of interest. A total of 1,296 individuals who applied to the programs and met the standards set by the programs were randomly assigned to treatment and control groups. Telephone follow-up interviews were conducted between the twenty-fourth and thirtieth month after the baseline survey. The follow-up survey had a 79 percent response rate, with 75 percent for the control group and 82 percent for the treatment group, yielding 1,014 individuals for the impact analysis.[9]

All three programs in the study were successful at increasing employment and earnings over the 24 months following the baseline survey. Impacts are presented for the entire 24-month follow-up period and for months 13–24. In Table 9.2, we present findings for months 13–24, as this period does not include the in-program period and thus is more likely to reflect gains from the program. For the three sites combined, there are positive, statistically significant gains in employment and earnings for participants. Control group earnings in months 13–24 after random assignment averaged $13,662, compared to $17,673 for the treatment group. The gain in earnings of $4,011 is much larger than is typically observed in evaluations of training programs. The gains result from both increased hours of work and an increase in the wage rate. During months 13–24, the treatment group worked 1,380 hours on average, compared to 1,130 for the control group, for a gain of 250 hours.

All three sites exhibited statistically significant earnings gains for the whole follow-up period, as well as for months 13–24, and the range for those months was fairly narrow. Hours worked also had a consis-

Table 9.2 Selected Impacts on Annual Earnings for the Sectoral Employment Impact Study for Months 13–24

Outcome	All sites	Wisconsin Regional Training Partnership	Jewish Vocational Service- Boston	Per Scholas
Total earnings, 24 months ($)	4,509***	6,255***	4,339**	3,827
Total earnings, months 13–24 ($)	4,011***	3,735***	4,237***	4,663***
Hours worked, 24 months	245***	241	298*	225
Hours worked, months 13–24	250***	191*	335***	249**
Sample size	985	335	313	337

NOTE: *p < 0.10, **p < 0.05, ***p < 0.01.
SOURCE: Maguire et al. (2010).

tently positive impact, but the site impacts ranged from 191 hours in WRTP to 335 in JVS-Boston for months 13–24. The researchers also estimated impacts for 10 subgroups, and although the magnitudes varied somewhat by subgroup, the earnings impacts for months 13–24 were all statistically significant. Subgroups analyzed include both sexes, youth (defined two ways), African Americans, formerly incarcerated individuals, individuals who had received welfare, foreign born, and Latinos.

The Sectoral Employment Impact Study (Maguire et al. 2010) provides the strongest evidence currently available that sectoral programs can have a large impact on employment and earnings. The study includes three diverse programs operating in different areas and used rigorous methods. The only aspect of the evaluation that is of concern is that it is not clear how much the strong outcomes stem from the sectoral nature of the programs rather than the fact the programs might simply be exceptional programs. The report does not provide much detail on the sectoral aspects of the programs, although at several points the report notes that the programs have strong ties to employers. Thus, the Sectoral Employment Impact Study shows that good sectoral programs can generate large earnings and employment impacts, but it does not provide a good guide to others for implementing a strong sectoral program.

Capital IDEA. Operated by Travis County, Texas, Capital IDEA is a long-term sectoral training program that offers occupational training and extensive support services to low-income residents of the county. It takes a sectoral approach and focuses on occupations with high demand, typically with starting wages of $16 per hour or higher in health care, information and electronic technologies, utilities, and skilled trades (Smith and King 2011). The program's major focus is nursing and allied health careers, with three-quarters of the participants training in these occupations. It was founded in 1998 by Austin Interfaith to help move Texans stuck in dead-end jobs to higher-paying skilled positions.[10] The Ray Marshall Center at the LBJ School has been evaluating the program since 2006.

The most recent evaluation of Capital IDEA covers 879 individuals who enrolled in Capital IDEA in 2003 and 2004 and were no longer in the program by 2008 (Smith, King, and Schroeder 2011). Outcome variables in the study are quarterly employment, quarterly earnings, qualifying for unemployment insurance benefits, and whether the person filed an unemployment insurance claim.[11] Program impacts were estimated using a quasi-experimental method using matching (Smith, King, and Schroeder 2011). The comparison group was drawn from individuals from two sources: those who registered to search for work in the state's Working Texas program and those who received "core" services under WIA. Thus, the counterfactual is not individuals who received no services but rather individuals who received low-intensity services. Matching was performed using weighted multivariate matching, where variables with greater preservice differences between the treatment and comparison groups received greater weight. Matching was done without replacement (i.e., each comparison group member could be included only once), and no calipers were applied to assure that matches were reasonably close.[12] Matching variables included age, race/ethnicity, time elapsed since first earnings, employment status at entry, average quarterly earnings over the four years prior to earnings, percent of time in a workforce development service in the year prior to program entry, prior enrollment in another workforce program (Project RIO), and whether the person was qualified for unemployment insurance at the time of entry. Exact matches were carried out on county of residence, year of program entry, and whether or not the person experienced a dip in earnings of 20 percent or more in the year of program entry.

Impact estimates for employment, earnings, and qualifying for unemployment insurance benefits (which is based on employment and earnings) were large compared to typical training program impact estimates and were statistically significant (see Table 9.3). Quarterly employment was 10.9 percentage points higher for Capital IDEA participants, average quarterly earnings increased by $1,223, and the proportion qualifying for unemployment insurance benefits increased

Table 9.3 Impact Estimates for Capital IDEA

Impact measure	Estimated impact
Quarterly employment (%)	10.9***
Average quarterly earnings ($)	1,223***
Qualified for unemployment insurance benefits (%)	10.8***

NOTE: ***p < 0.01.
SOURCE: Smith, King, and Schroeder (2011).

by 10.8 percentage points. Ray Marshall Center researchers also conducted a cost-benefit analysis for Capital IDEA. They found that for
participants, the annual rate of return was 73 percent for the first 10
years after enrollment and 74 percent annually for the first 20 years
after enrollment. For all of society, they estimated the annual rate of
return to be 39 percent for the first 10 years and 43 percent for the first
20 years.

Because the evaluation of Capital IDEA relied on a quasi-experimental design, it necessarily must make fairly strong assumptions.
The key issue in most matching-based evaluations is whether the treatment and comparison groups are matched on all relevant variables.
Although the researchers matched on a substantial number of variables
(at least 16), they did not eliminate matches where the match was not
close. Moreover, Capital IDEA is a highly selective program, and a
large number of applicants are rejected.[13] It is impossible to know if the
comparison group members would have been accepted to the program
had they applied. Thus, although the Capital IDEA program appears to
have a strong conceptual model and seems successful, we give the specific evaluation results less weight than the findings from the Sectoral
Employment Impact Study.

OJT in national training programs

Employer-based training through OJT has been an option in national
training programs since the 1960s. In OJT in federally sponsored training, employers hire eligible workers and are reimbursed for the costs of
formal and informal training for the new worker during the initial work
period. Under WIA, reimbursement was up to 50 percent of the salary
and could last for a maximum of six months. WIOA maintains language
allowing for reimbursement of up to 50 percent of wages but allows the
state or local areas to reimburse employers as much as 75 percent if the
training meets certain conditions elaborated in the law. Evaluations of
OJT programs typically find OJT to be at least as effective as classroom
training and other options. Unfortunately, none of the major evaluations are based on randomized controlled trials where OJT is randomly
assigned, so we provide evidence from evaluations of CETA and the
JTPA.[14]

The CETA program was the nation's major employment and training program from 1975 through 1983, when it was replaced by JTPA.

Although the CETA program operated over 40 years ago, OJT has not changed significantly since then. The most common approach to developing comparison groups, propensity score matching, had not yet been developed when the CETA evaluations were carried out, so impact estimates used matching on individual variables and regression analysis to estimate treatment impacts. The USDOL made the data gathered for evaluating the program widely available and supported several evaluations; some researchers obtained research support from other sources. As explained below, the more recent program, JTPA, did not estimate the impact of receiving OJT, so the CETA estimates are the most recent estimates of OJT impacts from a national impact study.

USDOL created the Continuous Longitudinal Manpower Survey (CLMS) to evaluate CETA. Each quarter beginning in 1975, a nationally representative sample of CETA participants was selected and interviewed, and Social Security earnings data for subsequent years was linked to the CETA data. A comparison group database was created by linking Social Security earnings data to data from the March Current Population Survey (CPS) sample. The USDOL evaluation contractor, Westat, then selected comparison groups by matching individuals in the CPS sample to the CETA database. USDOL later made the CLMS data available to other researchers, including several groups who responded to a request for proposals asking for alternative approaches for evaluating CETA. Barnow (1987) summarizes the findings from 11 studies by activity and demographic group. Table 9.4 lists the estimates of OJT impacts from the various studies. Although there are a few negative impact estimates for some specific demographic groups, they are never statistically significant. Most of the impact estimates are in the $500–$1,000 range, and most are statistically significant. In 2014 dollars, these are roughly equivalent to $1,800–$3,600 impacts.[15] OJT and public service employment most commonly had the largest impacts on earnings, with somewhat smaller impacts for classroom training, and impacts close to zero for work experience programs.

The National JTPA Study used random assignment in 16 local programs across the nation to evaluate the JTPA program, and the study is summarized in Bloom et al. (1997). The National JTPA Study researchers conducted random assignment after the local programs had decided whom they wished to serve and the appropriate service strategy for them. The researchers found that program officials identified applicants

Table 9.4 The Impact of CETA On-the-Job Training on Annual Earnings for Various Groups

	Overall	White women	White men	Minority women	Minority men	Women	Men
Westat (1981)	850*	550*	750*	1,200*	1,150*	—	—
Westat (1984) FY 76	531*	—	—	—	—	—	—
Westat (1984) FY 77	1,091*	—	—	—	—	—	—
Bassi (1983)	—	805-382*	—	1,368*-1,549*	2,053*-2,057*	—	—
Bassi et al. (1984) non-welfare disadvantaged adults	—	701*-724*	616*-756*	223-244	772*-812*	—	—
Bassi et al. (1984) welfare	—	190-318	995-1,231*	564-587	454-750	—	—
Bassi et al. (1984) youth	—	(127)-12	452-463	861*-877*	(260)-(58)	—	—
Bloom and McLaughlin (1982)	—	1,200*	(200)	800*	1,500*	700*-1,100*	300
Dickinson, Johnson, West (1984) adults	—	—	—	—	—	35	(363)
Dickinson, Johnson, West (1984) youth	—	—	—	—	—	996*	(348)
Geraci (1984)	—	—	—	—	—	882*	612*

NOTE: *p < 0.05. — = authors did not estimate impacts for that group.
SOURCE: Barnow (1987).

who were relatively job ready and suitable for either OJT or job search assistance (JSA) if no OJT slots could be identified. Thus, individuals recommended for OJT and JSA were combined into a single service strategy group. Estimates were developed for three groups based on recommended service strategy—classroom training, OJT/JSA, and "other." The report included estimates for each service recommended strategy group, but it should be kept in mind that individuals in a particular group may have received no service or some service other than the recommended service or services. Impact estimates per person assigned were first estimated, and estimates per person who enrolled were developed using the procedure suggested by Bloom (1984).

JTPA Impact estimates for the 30 months following random assignment for adult women and men are shown in Table 9.5.[16] Estimates for both adult women and adult men were over $2,000 annually, but only the estimates for women were statistically significant. In comparison, classroom training had impacts of $630 and $1,287 for women and men, respectively. The impact for "other" services was higher than for OJT/JSA and statistically significant for women ($3,949) but smaller and not statistically significant for men ($941). It is important to stress that these estimates were for people where either OJT or JSA was recommended, and the actual service received need not have been OJT or JSA.

After reviewing the literature, we were surprised about how little is known about the effectiveness of OJT. The program is widely perceived to be a highly effective strategy, but the evidence is more anecdotal than statistical. The estimates from CETA were generally positive, but they were based on relatively weak statistical designs and are over 25 years old. The JTPA findings are based on randomized controlled trials, but the estimates are for OJT and JSA combined, so it is impossible to identify the effects of OJT alone. Unfortunately, the dearth of information on the effectiveness of OJT likely will not change anytime soon.

Table 9.5 The Impact of JTPA on Earnings of Adult Enrollees Assigned to On-the-Job Training or Job Search Assistance for the 30 Months Following Random Assignment

Group	Impact
Adult women	2,292**
Adult men	2,109

NOTE: **p < 0.05.

Although USDOL funded a randomized controlled trial impact evaluation of WIA, that evaluation will not include estimates of the impact of OJT.

WHY EMPLOYER-BASED TRAINING IS NOT COMMONLY USED

Although there is limited evidence from rigorous impact evaluations documenting the impact of employer-based training initiatives, there are many examples of the success of customized training and sectoral programs, indicating that when they can be implemented, all parties find them to be beneficial.[17] There are, however, a number of barriers that inhibit wider use of employer-based training in all its forms.[18]

- **High costs to recruit and engage employers combined with small number of trainees needed by individual employers**. Employer-based training requires up-front marketing to interest employers in OJT, customized training, or sectoral training. Moreover, for individual firms, the number of openings they may have is likely to be small. Finally, both WIA and WIOA require employers to pay a portion of the costs of customized and sectoral training, although under WIA waivers were granted to some states to reduce the employer contribution for employers with 250 or fewer employees. With limits on how much they can spend on marketing and an uncertain payoff, local programs are likely to be wary of such endeavors. Sectoral programs offer an important way around some of these issues. Although each hospital in a metropolitan area may require a small number of nursing assistants, if they can combine their efforts, the number may no longer be small.

- **Difficulty in financing curriculum development**. Although WIOA funds can be used to pay for the training itself, funding must also be obtained to develop the curriculum. In the case studies described in Isbell, Trutko, and Barnow (2000), community colleges often paid for the course development when they delivered the training. Recent competitive grants administrated by USDOL allow for resources to be used for curriculum development and other forms of capacity building.

- **Institutional barriers to being responsive to employer needs.** Workforce programs are often subject to state and local regulations, as well as the regulations set at the federal level. Community colleges may also have requirements on the development of new programs and curricular changes. Many businesses are accustomed to swiftly implementing strategies and can be put off by too much regulation. Some local workforce programs establish employer units that are tuned in to the needs and wants of employers. Sectoral programs often make use of specialized intermediaries that attempt to isolate business from the problems of dealing with government. Workforce intermediaries may be better positioned to respond quickly, but they are still subject to local regulations and contracting requirements of partners.

- **Training programs may not know how to communicate with employers.** Public sector organizations may not be able to speak the same language as employers because of their different views of the world. For example, employers view their workers as a means to producing their goods and services, but government agencies and other workforce organizations may see it as their mission to help the less fortunate escape from poverty. They may find it difficult to recognize employers as a primary customer. Approaches to dealing with this type of issue include specialized employer units within the workforce program and using workforce intermediaries.

- **Firms are often wary of working with the government.** Although workforce development agencies are rarely a threat to employers, firms may not readily distinguish levels and components of government and lump them all together. Overcoming these problems requires communication and a great deal of time. Once again, the use of specialized units in agencies and intermediaries can help assure that employers are dealing with people who "speak their language."

- **Firms are often wary of working with other firms.** Sectoral programs require cooperation of the participating industries so that a uniform training program can be developed and offered. Firms that compete with each other may believe that having their own training program enables them to bcat the competition, and they may be reluctant to share decisions about curricula with their rivals. Once again, sometimes a neutral intermediary may be needed to bring the parties together.

CONCLUSIONS AND LESSONS

Employer engagement in workforce development programs has been increasingly recognized as an important feature for the success of these programs. Although progress has been made in this area, there is still a long way to go in learning how best to get meaningful employer involvement on a wide scale. Key lessons from our review include the following:

- **Although WIA required that employers compose a majority of the local Workforce Investment Boards, two national evaluations of the implementation of WIA find that employer involvement in these boards was generally insufficient**. Both the D'Amico et al. (2004) and Barnow and King (2005) studies of WIA implementation find that although employers constituted a majority on local WIBs, they generally did not play a major role in directing the local programs. Studies of local boards that have been more successful in actively involving employers would be useful in shedding light on how to engage employers more effectively in workforce system oversight, particularly in the context of the passage of WIOA, which places new emphasis on employer engagement. Although efforts should continue to increase the role of employers on these boards, perhaps greater gains are likely to accrue from getting employers to participate more actively in the training programs themselves. Workforce organizations may seek employers to serve on boards as an initial step toward eliciting their deeper involvement in training programs.

- **Although the evaluations of employer-based training generally show it to be more effective than training focusing solely on the supply side of the market, there is a need for addi-**

tional rigorous evaluations of all forms of employer-based training, including OJT, customized training, and sectoral training. Both qualitative and quantitative evaluations show that approaches that include more employer involvement are effective in increasing employment and earnings. However, the evidence is not as strong as is needed to be in the top tier. For example, the major evidence on the effectiveness of OJT itself stems from studies over 30 years old before modern approaches such as propensity score matching were developed. The only major evaluation of sectoral programs making use of randomized controlled trials deliberately selected three strong programs, so it is not clear if the findings apply more broadly to sectoral programs. To remedy this situation, USDOL and other interested organizations should, to the extent possible, support demonstrations with rigorous evaluations to learn more about how effective employer-based strategies are and which aspects of such programs make the greatest contributions. Key to the usefulness of these evaluations will be the inclusion of strong implementation studies so that policymakers, funders, and practitioners can learn not only about the effectiveness of these approaches but also how they work.

- **Because of the barriers that limit the use of employer-based training, strategies should be explored to promote employer-based training, including the following:**
  - Financial incentives can encourage programs to make investments in setting up these programs. For example, financial incentives can be used by states to promote buy-in from employers on the expansion of certain types of employer-centered models, such as sectoral programs or registered apprenticeship. WIOA makes an important first step in reducing barriers to participation by eliminating the WIA requirement that employers contribute half of customized training costs and allowing reimbursement of up to 75 of wages for on-the-job training. However, depending on WIOA's regulations and how they are implemented, required employer contributions might still create a barrier to participation. Nonfinancial incen-

tives can be used to award higher scores in competitive demonstration programs to applicants who use employer-based training approaches. Applicants for publicly funded workforce development programs should be evaluated not only on whether they have a partner, but on the strength and purpose of that partnership. For example, the decision could be based in part on how long the partnership has been in existence prior to application and the level of engagement that is planned.

- ○ Some sectoral programs make use of intermediaries to connect employers who often do not trust government agencies or other employers. By supporting the use of intermediaries along with rigorous evaluation of such activities, more organizations can be encouraged to use sectoral training strategies, and we can learn more about the effectiveness of intermediaries.

- ○ Given the challenges of employer engagement, workforce organizations may also benefit from technical assistance on how to most effectively engage employers in programs. Practitioners need more information about the key components of effective employer-centered models and effective employer engagement strategies, which can be drawn, in part, from high-quality implementation studies. In addition, the staffs of workforce organizations need the skills and knowledge base to work effectively with employers.

In sum, involving employers more in training programs makes good sense from a theoretical perspective, and the evaluations to date indicate that a variety of approaches appear to provide substantial gains for participants and employers. But, clearly we need to learn more about the effectiveness of these programs, as well as the costs and benefits of various approaches relative to each other and more traditional training programs.

Notes

1. See http://www.astd.org/Publications/Blogs/ASTD-Blog/2013/12/ASTD-Releases
   -2013-State-of-the-Industry-Report (accessed June 21, 2014).
2. For research on the effectiveness of apprenticeship as an employer-centered strategy, see Hollenbeck and Huang (2013) and Reed et al. (2011). For research on
   state-funded customized training programs, see Duscha and Graves (2006).
3. For a description of the introduction of private industry councils (PICs) in the
   CETA program in 1978, see U.S. General Accounting Office (1983).
4. The local Employment Service business advisory groups are generally referred to
   as Job Service Employer Committees, or JSECs.
5. Roughly one-half of the states have received waivers under WIA to reduce the
   match requirement for small businesses.
6. Under WIA and WIOWA, working with groups of employers is considered a form
   of customized training, as long as other requirements are met, as defined under
   each law.
7. A number of foundations, through the National Fund for Workforce Solutions,
   have supported the key elements of sectoral and intermediary-driven strategies
   through what has been termed "workforce partnerships," which are defined as
   employer-driven strategies that organize multiple institutions and funding streams
   around the common goal of career advancement for low-wage, low-skilled workers in specific industry-sectors. See http://www.nfwsolutions.org/ (accessed June
   21, 2014).
8. Material in this section is based on Maguire et al. (2010).
9. Sample attrition is analyzed in Appendix B of Maguire et al. (2010). The analysis
   indicated that in the follow-up sample, treatment group members were more likely
   to be married and to be immigrants and less likely to have ever been incarcerated.
   Tests for attrition bias using a regression of treatment status on characteristics
   produced an F statistic that was not statistically significant. Similar tests were
   conducted at each site. The most notable difference in samples occurred at JVS-
   Boston, where 80 percent of the treatment group participated in the follow-up
   survey compared to 73 percent of the control group; the two groups differed little
   on baseline characteristics and the regression of treatment status on characteristics
   produced an insignificant F statistic. Thus, there is no evidence of serious attrition
   bias in the overall sample, and it does not appear to be a problem in the individual
   sites.
10. See http://www.capitalidea.org/about/# (accessed April 19, 2014).
11. It is not obvious how to interpret the variable capturing filing for a UI claim. A
    training program that is effective should reduce unemployment and thus the need
    to file a claim; on the other hand, among job losers, being qualified to file a claim
    is a positive outcome. We do not discuss results for this outcome.
12. Smith, King, and Schroeder (2011) note that applying calipers might have led to

some treatment group members being eliminated from the analysis.

13. In personal communication, Tara Smith, one of the Ray Marshall Center Capital IDEA evaluators, stated that Capital IDEA staff have told her that less than 14 percent of applicants to the program are accepted.

14. Some models of OJT focus on creating employment opportunities for certain disadvantaged populations, such as individuals with criminal records and welfare recipients. While not the focus of this chapter, there is some evidence that such interventions may have an impact on employment outcomes in the short term. (See Redcross et al. [2012] and Roder and Elliott [2013]).

15. The translation to today's dollars were made using the Bureau of Labor Statistics' inflation calculator, assuming that the impacts occurred in 1978. Http://www.bls .gov/data/inflation_calculator.htm (accessed June 21, 2014).

16. None of the reported impacts for out-of-school youth were statistically significant, and for males they varied a great deal depending on the source of data used for the estimation. OJT impacts were negative for women and for male youth who had not been arrested.

17. See, for example, Martinson (2010) and Woolsey and Groves (n.d.) for examples of current successful sectoral programs.

18. For a discussion of barriers to employer participation in customized and sectoral training programs, see Isbell, Trutko, and Barnow (2000).

References

Association for Talent Development. 2013. *State of the Industry Report.* Alexandria, VA: ASTD Press.

Bailey, T. R. 1988. "Market Forces and Private Sector Processes in Government Policy: The Job Training Partnership Act." *Journal of Policy Analysis and Management* 7(2): 300–315.

Barnow, Burt S. 1987. "The Impacts of CETA Programs on Earnings." *Journal of Human Resources.* 22(2): 157–193.

Barnow, Burt S., and Christopher T. King. 2005. "The Workforce Investment Act in Eight States." Occasional Paper 2005-01. Washington, DC: USDOL.

Bassi, Laurie J. 1983. "The Effect of CETA on the Postprogram Earnings of Participants." *Journal of Human Resources* 18(4): 539–556.

Bassi, Laurie J., Margaret C. Simms, Lynn C. Burbridge, and Charles L. Betsey. 1984. *Measuring the Effect of CETA on Youth and the Economically Disadvantaged.* Final report prepared for USDOL under Contract No. 20-11-82-19. Washington, DC: Urban Institute.

Bloom, Howard S. 1984. "Accounting for No-Shows in Experimental Evaluation Designs." *Evaluation Review* 8(2): 225–246.

Bloom, Howard S., and Maureen A. McLaughlin. 1982. "CETA Training Programs—Do They Work for Adults?" Joint Congressional Budget Office-National Commission for Employment Policy report. Washington, DC: National Commission for Employment Policy.

Bloom, Howard S., Larry L. Orr, Stephen H. Bell, George Cave, Fred Doolittle, Winston Lin, and Johannes M. Bos. 1997. "The Benefits and Costs of JTPA Title II-A Programs: Key Findings from the National JTPA Study." *Journal of Human Resources* 32(3): 549–576.

Clymer, Carol. 2003. "By Design: Engaging Employers in Workforce Development Organizations." Philadelphia: Public/Private Ventures.

Conway, Maureen, Amy Blair, Steven L. Dawson, and Linda Dworak-Muñoz. 2007. "Sectoral Strategies for Low-Income Workers: Lessons from the Field." Washington, DC: Aspen Institute.

D'Amico, Ronald, Kate Dunham, Jennifer Henderson-Frakes, Deborah Kogan, Vinz Koller, Melissa Mack, Michaene Magnotta, Jeffrey Salzman, Andrew Wiegand, Gardner Carrick, and Dan Weissbein. 2004. *The Workforce Investment Act after Five Years: Results from the National Evaluation of the Implementation of WIA.* Oakland, CA: Social Policy Research Associates.

Dickinson, Katherine P., Terry R. Johnson, and Richard W. West. 1984. *An Analysis of the Impact of CETA Programs on Participants' Earnings.* Final report prepared for USDOL under Contract No. 20-06–82-21. Menlo Park, CA: SRI International.

Dunham, Kate, Jeff Salzman, and Vinz Koller. 2004. *Business as Partner and Customer under WIA: A Study of Innovative Practices.* Oakland, CA: Social Policy Research Associates.

Duscha, Steve, and Wanda Lee Graves. 2006. "The Employer as the Client: State-Financed Customized Training." Washington, DC: USDOL, Employment and Training Administration.

Geraci, Vincent J. 1984. "Short-Term Indicators of Job Training Program Effects on Long-Term Participant Earnings." Report prepared for USDOL under Contract No. 20-48-92-16. Austin, TX: University of Texas at Austin.

Giloth, Robert P. 2004. "Introduction." In *Workforce Intermediaries for the Twenty-First Century*, Robert P. Giloth, ed. Philadelphia, PA: Temple University Press.

Gross, Julian. 2008. "Community Benefits Agreements: Definitions, Values, and Legal Enforceability." *Journal of Affordable Housing* 17(1-2): 35–58.

Gutman, Robert. 1983. "Job Training Partnership Act: New Help for the Unemployed." *Monthly Labor Review* 106(3): 3–10.

Hollenbeck, Kevin, and Wei-Jang Huang. 2013. *Net Impact and Benefit-Cost Estimates of the Workforce Development System in Washington State.* Upjohn Institute Technical Report 13-029. Kalamazoo, MI: W.E. Upjohn Institute for Employment Research.

Isbell, Kellie, John Trutko, and Burt S. Barnow. 2000. "Customized Training for Employers: Training People for Jobs That Exist and Employers Who Want to Hire Them." In *Improving the Odds: Increasing the Effectiveness of Publicly Funded Training*, Burt S. Barnow and Christopher T. King, eds. Washington, DC: Urban Institute Press.

Job Training Partnership Act, Pub.L. 97–300, 29 U.S.C. § 1501, et seq. (1982).

Lerman, Robert I., Signe-Mary McKernan, and Stephanie Riegg. 2004. "The Scope of Employer-Provided Training in the United States: Who, What, Where and How Much?" In *Job Training Policy in the United States*, Christopher J. O'Leary, Robert A. Straits, Stephen A. Wandner, eds. Kalamazoo, MI: W.E. Upjohn Institute for Employment Research, pp. 211–244.

Maguire, Sheila, Joshua Freely, Carol Clymer, Maureen Conway, and Deena Schwartz. 2010. *Tuning in to Local Labor Markets: Findings from the Sectoral Employment Impact Study*. Philadelphia: Public/Private Ventures.

Martinson, Karin. 2010. "Partnering with Employers to Promote Job Advancement for Low-Skill Individuals." Washington, DC: Urban Institute.

Mikelson, Kelly S., and Demetra Smith Nightingale. 2004. *Estimating Public and Private Expenditures on Occupational Training in the United States*. Washington, DC: USDOL.

Pindus, Nancy, and Kellie Isbell. 1996. "Involving Employers in Training: Literature Review." Washington, DC: USDOL, Employment and Training Administration.

Redcross, Cindy, Megan Millenky, Timothy Rudd, and Valerie Levshin. 2012. "More than a Job: Final Results from the Evaluation of the Center for Employment Opportunities (CEO) Transitional Jobs Program." New York: MDRC.

Reed, Debbie, Albert Yung-Hsu Liu, Rebecca Kleinman, Annalisa Mastri, Davin Reed, Samina Sattar, Jessica Ziegler. 2011. "An Effectiveness Assessment and Cost-Benefit Analysis of Registered Apprenticeship in 10 States." Oakland, CA: Mathematica Policy Research.

Roder, Anne, and Mark Elliott. 2013. "Stimulating Opportunity: An Evaluation of ARRA-Funded Subsidized Employment Programs." New York: Economic Mobility Corporation.

Smith, Tara C., and Christopher T. King. 2011. *Exploratory Return-on-Investment Analysis of Local Workforce Investments*. Austin, TX: Ray Marshall Center for the Study of Human Resources, LBJ School of Public Affairs, University of Texas at Austin.

Smith, Tara C., Christopher T. King, and Daniel G. Schroeder. 2011. *Local Investment in Workforce Development: 2011 Evaluation Update*. Austin, TX: Ray Marshall Center for the Study of Human Resources, LBJ School of Public Affairs, University of Texas at Austin.

U.S. General Accounting Office. 1983. *Federal Job Training: A Comparison of Public and Private Sector Performance.* Report GAO/IPE-83-5.Washington, DC: U.S. General Accounting Office.

Westat. 1981. *Continuous Longitudinal Manpower Survey Net Impact Report No. 1: Impact on 1977 Earnings of New FY 1976 CETA Enrollees in Selected Program Activities.* Report prepared for USDOL under Contract No. 23-24-75-07. Rockville, MD: Westat.

———. 1984. *Summary of Net Impact Results.* Report prepared for USDOL under Contract No. 23-24-75-07. Rockville, MD: Westat.

Woolsey, Lindsey, and Garrett Groves. n.d. "State Sector Strategies Coming of Age: Implications for State Workforce Policymakers." Washington, DC: National Governors Association.

10
A New Way of Doing Business

The Career Pathway Approach
in Minnesota and Beyond

Vickie Choitz
Aspen Institute and Center for Law and Social Policy

Thomas Norman
*Minnesota Department of Employment
and Economic Development*

Whitney Smith
Joyce Foundation

with Nola Speiser
Minnesota FastTRAC Adult Career Pathways Initiative

and Brian Paulson
Pohlad Family Foundation

THE NEED FOR CAREER PATHWAYS

The economy has gone through a dramatic transformation over the past 40 years, making postsecondary education and technical training the primary gateway out of low-wage work and into the middle class (Carnevale, Smith, and Strohl 2010). Yet, for numerous reasons, too many Americans cannot access such education and training. According to a recent international survey, *Program for the International Assessment of Adult Competencies 2012*, 18 percent of U.S. adults have low literacy skills and 30 percent have low numeracy skills (Goodman et al. 2013). Their skill levels are too low to succeed in postsecondary education, and many of these lower-skilled adults struggle to succeed in the workplace.[1] Additionally, tuition and fees at postsecondary institutions have increased nearly four times faster than median family income, and are far beyond what low-income and lower-skilled individuals can afford (Reimherr et al. 2013). Low-income students with children also struggle to afford basic necessities like child care and transportation to stay in school.

Compounding these challenges is that many workers and job seekers do not know where or how to get the education or training necessary to begin a career. They lack access to career guidance (Choitz, Soares, and Pleasants 2010) and face a confusing array of education and training options. Most attend multiple institutions, but the credits and credentials earned in one program often do not transfer to another. Navigating the maze of education and training offerings is not any easier for small and medium-sized employers, who often want to expand their capacity to offer learning options for their workforces or need help finding workers with the right skills and credentials. All of these dynamics mean both workers and employers waste tremendous economic opportunity because they are not getting what they need. It also means that public dollars supporting existing programs could be better leveraged if educational opportunities and services were better coordinated and aligned.

AN INNOVATIVE APPROACH TO WORKFORCE DEVELOPMENT IN THE TWENTY-FIRST CENTURY

The career pathway approach connects progressive levels of education, training, support services, and credentials for specific occupations in a way designed to optimize the progress and success of individuals with varying levels of abilities and needs (including those with limited education, skills, English, and/or employment experience). The goal is to help individuals earn marketable credentials, engage in further education and employment, and achieve economic success. Importantly, the career pathway approach deeply engages employers and helps meet their workforce needs; it also helps states and communities strengthen their workforces and economies. However, it is not simply a new model—it is a *systems transformation* strategy (Alliance for Quality Career Pathways [AQCP] 2014).

According to the AQCP, career pathways operationalize this approach and include three essential features and four functions as summarized in Box 10.1. Career pathways include secondary career and technical education programs of study, adult career pathways, and apprenticeships, among others. This approach can benefit low-income, lower-skilled adults, and youth in particular—who often must balance work, family, and school—by providing manageable segments of education and training that are tailored to learner needs, closely tied to regional industry and employer needs, infused with supportive services and career navigation assistance, and connected to marketable credentials that can be stacked throughout one's career. This case study on Minnesota and the AQCP focuses on career pathways for low-income, lower-skilled adults.

Box 10.1 Career Pathway and Program Features and Functions

Features:

1) Well-connected and transparent education, training, support service, and credential offerings (often delivered via multiple linked and aligned programs)

2) Multiple entry points that enable both well-prepared students and targeted populations with limited education, skills, English, and work experiences to successfully enter the career pathway

3) Multiple exit points at successively higher levels leading to self- or family-supporting employment and aligned with subsequent entry points

Functions:

1) Participant-focused education and training

2) Consistent and non-duplicative assessments of participants' education, skills, and assets/needs

3) Support services and career navigation assistance to facilitate transitions

4) Employment services and work experiences

Each career pathway includes a progressive set of competencies and credentials that often span across education and training partners, including adult education and English language instruction, high schools, workforce service providers, and/or postsecondary education institutions. Each career pathway also includes a range of support services provided by community-based organizations or human service agencies, depending on needs of the participants. Given the breadth and depth of a good career pathway, most often they are made up of individual linked and aligned programs, for example, an adult education "bridge" program that connects adult education students to a one-year technical certificate program in manufacturing production and operations, which is linked and aligned with a two-year associate of applied science degree in manufacturing production and operations.

The idea to align services and programs around the concept of a career pathway began to emerge in the 2000s (Fein 2012) and included Oregon's Career Pathways Initiative, Washington State's Integrated Basic Education Skills Training (I-BEST) program, and California's Career Ladders Project—all three unique efforts. Many other states quickly followed with their own variations on career pathways: in 2007 Minnesota launched its FastTRAC Adult Career Pathways initiative, and Wisconsin created the RISE (Regional Industry Skills Education) Initiative. Today, at least a dozen states have their own career pathway initiatives that are growing into more comprehensive career pathway systems supported by state policy and multiple funding streams, and more are coming online every year. This acceleration is in part due to federal guidance—issued jointly by the U.S. Departments of Labor, Education, and Health and Human Services in 2012—that cited evidence and encouraged states to consider career pathway adoption. Also, there have been multiple federal technical assistance initiatives and public and private funding for career pathways (see U.S. Department of Education 2010; U.S. Department of Labor 2010).[2]

A body of evidence to support career pathways is beginning to emerge. The career pathway approach truly is a new way of doing business; therefore, it has taken time for partners to come together and align services, programs, funding, and data—all of which must be well-established before rigorous evaluation is appropriate. The integrated, multi-intervention nature of career pathways also poses challenges for evaluation. However, program evaluations are beginning to provide evidence that the core functions or practices in career pathway programs are more effective than traditional education and training strategies. For example, studies of the Washington State I-BEST (Integrated Basic Education and Skills Training) program find that students achieved greater basic skills gains and were more likely to continue into credit-bearing course work, earn college credits, and attain occupational certificates than similar non-I-BEST students (Zeidenberg, Cho, and Jenkins 2010; Jenkins, Zeidenberg, and Kienzl 2009). I-BEST is a career pathway bridge program in which basic skills instruction occurs concurrently with college-level career training and is contextualized.[3] Another study from Stanford University provides support for contextualized math in particular (Wiseley 2011).

Evaluations of programs in Illinois and New York City have shown that support services and student success services—one of the categories of essential functions in career pathways—can play a key role in improving student persistence, credit accumulation, and graduation (Bragg et al. 2009; Linderman and Kolenovic 2009; Scrivener and Weiss 2009). Students in the New York City program overwhelmingly credited enhanced supportive services—financial aid, free access to textbooks, a transportation card, and comprehensive academic, social, and interpersonal support—as the reason they were able to complete their educational programs. Other research provides evidence of effectiveness for these and other core functions and practices often utilized in career pathways (Bailey, Smith Jaggars, and Jenkins 2001; Werner et al. 2013).[4] An analysis by CLASP reasoned that, "[w]hile the impact of any one of these strategies alone is often modest, the I-BEST experience lends weight to the idea that such strategies may have more impact when combined" (Strawn 2011).

Building from the body of evidence on common *practices* in career pathways, the federal government and foundations have recently invested in rigorous evaluation of career pathway *programs* that integrate several of these practices. The U.S. Department of Health and Human Services (HHS) has funded the Health Profession Opportunity Grants and a set of corresponding evaluations, including a randomized control study. HHS also has funded the Innovative Strategies for Increasing Self-Sufficiency, a rigorous evaluation that should have results available in 2017. A group of philanthropic funders is supporting the Accelerating Opportunity initiative, which includes a rigorous evaluation with results expected in 2015–2016.

THE ALLIANCE FOR QUALITY CAREER PATHWAYS

While the body of evidence grows, local practitioners, agency leaders, employers, and policymakers are forging ahead to adopt the career pathway approach in their states and communities. However, without definitive guidance on the strongest practices and processes to adopt and implement, it is difficult to know if they are on the right track. In 2012, CLASP recognized this challenge and invited 10 leading career pathway states and their local/regional partners—Arkansas, California, Illinois, Kentucky, Massachusetts, Minnesota, Oregon, Virginia, Washington, and Wisconsin—to form the AQCP supported by the Joyce Foundation, the James Irvine Foundation, and the Greater Twin Cities United Way. The purpose of the Alliance in the first two years was to develop a framework based on existing evidence and "wisdom from the field" that could provide a shared vision and definition of quality career pathways and *systems*.[5] CLASP and the AQCP purposefully called the first iteration of this framework "version 1.0" because it is expected to evolve as the field generates more evaluation evidence of what works and what makes for quality. Since the field is still at an early stage, career pathway partnerships are continually refining their efforts to improve education, training, and employment outcomes and to scale up and sustain their pathways work.

This comprehensive AQCP framework is a three-part package. The first is a refined set of definitions for the career pathway field; many have been included in the section above. These definitions are inclusive of a variety of career pathways, including those for youth and adults, for job seekers and incumbent workers, and for lower-skilled, nontraditional students as well as more traditional ones. The second part of the framework is a set of criteria and indicators for what constitutes quality career pathway systems (see Box 10.2). The third is the inaugural

---

Box 10.2 AQCP Criteria and Indicators for Quality Career Pathway Systems

A career pathway system is the cohesive combination of partnerships, resources and funding, policies, data, and shared performance measures that support the development, quality, scaling, and dynamic sustainability of career pathways and programs for youth and adults.

Commit to a shared vision and strategy for industry sector-based career pathways for youth and adults and for building, scaling, and dynamically sustaining career pathway systems.

Engage employers and integrate sector strategy principles to ensure multiple employers, business associations, and labor unions are partners in creating demand-driven career pathways.

Collaborate to make resources available by identifying, prioritizing, and leveraging resources for career pathway systems, partnerships, and programs.

Implement supportive policies for the career pathway systems, pathways, and programs.

Use data and shared measures to measure, demonstrate, and improve participant outcomes.

Implement and integrate evidence-based practices and processes (specifically for local/regional career pathway systems).

---

set of career pathway participant metrics to measure and manage participant progress and success in a joint, cross-system, and cross-partner approach (AQCP 2014). As of this writing, the AQCP is entering its second phase in which partners will implement the framework, using the criteria and indicators to self-assess their career pathway systems and evolving into using the participant metrics to inform continuous improvement and performance measurement.

MINNESOTA'S FastTRAC ADULT CAREER
PATHWAY PROGRAM AND EVOLVING STATE
CAREER PATHWAY SYSTEM

Minnesota FastTRAC (Training, Resources, and Credentialing) is an adult achievement initiative to help educationally underprepared adults achieve success in high-demand careers that pay family-sustaining wages—the strategy is to integrate basic skills and career and technical education along a continuum from foundational skills preparation to a postsecondary credential. It is a critical career pathway program in the state's emerging career pathway system that provides entry points to career pathways in a variety of in-demand fields—including health care, manufacturing, business, construction, transportation, and early childhood education/child development—for low-wage, lower-skilled workers and job seekers.[6]

Minnesota provides an example of a strong state-led career pathway initiative that is evolving into a wider and more comprehensive state career pathway system. Over the years, the state has built a suite of career pathway initiatives for different types of individuals. For example, like most states, Minnesota's career and technical education (CTE) programs provide entry points to postsecondary technical career pathways for many high school students. In 2007, Minnesota took its first steps toward providing career pathways for lower-skilled adults with a planning grant through the Joyce Foundation's Shifting Gears initiative to design FastTRAC. The original core group of partners included the Minnesota State Colleges and Universities System (MnSCU), Adult Basic Education (ABE) at the Department of Education, the Department of Employment and Economic Development (DEED), and the Greater Twin Cities United Way.

In addition to the economic imperative of needing more skilled and credentialed workers, a primary motivational factor was that each entity was serving the same lower-skilled population, but in a disjointed way that failed to fully utilize each other's resources effectively. They agreed that they could do better *together* and developed the Minnesota FastTRAC Adult Career Pathway partnership and initiative. This partnership—convened by DEED—has grown over the years to also include the state's Department of Human Services (DHS), Department of Corrections, Office of Higher Education, Department of Labor and Industry, Governor's Workforce Development Council, and employers, in addition to the original core partners. This partnership aligns resources to fund grantees, supports the importance of career pathways within each agency through an agreed-upon shared vision, and uses shared data made possible with data sharing agreements to support the evaluation and continuous improvement of career pathway programs and local systems.

One example of a FastTRAC career pathway program is the Rochester Medical Careers FastTRAC Pathway program in which participants are trained to become Advanced Hospital Certified Nursing Assistants. It provides participants with two courses of contextualized basic skills instruction linked to a for-credit Advanced Hospital Certified Nursing Assistant (CNA) course at Rochester Community and Technical College.[7] Partners include Workforce Development Inc., Rochester Adult and Family Literacy, Olmsted County United Way, and Mayo Clinic. Entry points into this program include the adult basic education program, the workforce service providers, as well as referrals from the college. The main exit point is an Advanced Hospital CNA credential; however, partners have created seamless transitions for participants into subsequent career pathway programs in health emergency medical technician, unit coordinator, human service technicians, practical nursing, coding specialist, surgical technology, and medical secretary. Credits earned in FastTRAC count toward these subsequent pathways. A staff person called a navigator provides guidance, makes referrals to the supports participants may need, and serves as a central point of contact throughout the pathway. Participant-focused education and training includes contextualized instruction as well as integrated ABE and Advanced Hospital CNA technical skills instruction.[8]

Partners have implemented consistent and nonduplicative assessment of participants' education, skills, and assets/needs by aligning their intake processes. If the participants pass the contextualized basic education bridge course, they can skip the college placement exam and continue taking courses in their health care career pathway of choice. Workforce Development Inc. provides supportive services and career navigation. The navigator supports students through recruitment, assessment, career counseling, individual plan development, job search, and entry into a job. Eligible participants are coenrolled in applicable support and career navigation programs offered through the workforce system.

The Rochester Medical Careers FastTRAC Pathway program has garnered enthusiastic support from its employer partner. According to Guy Finne, human resources manager at the Mayo Clinic, "[t]his new education model guides learners to GED/diploma attainment AND college/career readiness AND a higher level of employability with college education. The model's vision created an individualized job training/education experience connecting diverse populations to demanded career pathways in health care. The model's strategy utilizes an innovative support system (from assessment to job placement) that allows students to enter and exit job training, developmental education and support services at various points based on individual learner's academic/personal assessments."[9]

Another example of a career pathway is the new West Metro Pathway to Manufacturing Careers FastTRAC program in Hennepin County (Minneapolis and western suburbs).[10] This pathway offers ABE students, English Language Learners, and long-term unemployed individuals a fundamentals of manufacturing bridge course in which participants gain foundational knowledge and skills necessary to complete the integrated soldering class at Hennepin Technical College. They also earn an industry-recognized soldering certification. From there, participants can seamlessly continue on a manufacturing education and career pathway via the nationally recognized M–Powered precision manufacturing program, which is a partnership among Hennepin Technical College, HIRED (a community-based organization), employers, and the local workforce agency. Career navigators support and guide participants through the West Metro bridge program and into the linked college manufacturing program. Participants can access support services throughout the program as needed.

Results and Scale

Since 2009, the state partnership has funded six rounds of Fast-TRAC grants. The last two rounds in 2013 and 2014 have been supported with funds from the state workforce development fund as authorized by the state legislature and have funded 25 FastTRAC career pathways. During the previous four rounds (2009–2012), Minnesota

FastTRAC programs were supported through braided funds combining multiple federal, state, and philanthropic sources and served 3,385 individuals. Self-reported data through quarterly program reporting indicates that 88 percent of these individuals completed industry-recognized credentials and/or credits toward those credentials, and 69 percent attained employment and/or continued education in the career pathway (see Table 10.1). Recently, Minnesota has been able to access wage record data from the state Unemployment Insurance records for program exiters in calendar years 2010–2013. On average, almost 60 percent of all exiters entered employment, and 85 percent retained employment for at least 6 months.[11] Exiters who had wages in all four quarters after exit earned an average of $21,080 annually, which is 33 percent more on average than what they earned prior to FastTRAC enrollment ($15,856). This average percentage increase has risen steadily since 2010, suggesting that, as the programs mature, they may be better able to assist participants in finding better jobs.[12] This increase lifts a family of three out of poverty; however, the average participant is still among the "working poor," which is why it is critical that Minnesota FastTRAC programs link and align with subsequent programs along career pathways to provide participants with further education and credentials and higher-paying employment.[13]

Table 10.1 Minnesota FastTRAC Participant Outcomes

Quarterly self-reported program data; 2009–2012 (N = 3,385)	
Completed industry recognized credentials and/or credits toward those credentials (%)	88
Attained employment and/or continued education in the career pathway (%)	69
Administrative data (Unemployment Insurance wage records) 2010–2013 program exiters (N = 1,019)	
Entered employment (%)	57.2[a]
Retained employment (%)	84.8
Average wage one year after exit for those with wages in all four quarters ($)	21,080

[a] This percentage includes 2013 program exiters, whereas the other data points only include exiters in 2010–2012.

SOURCE: State of Minnesota Department of Employment and Economic Development Workforce One system and Unemployment Insurance wage records.

A 2013 study by MnSCU finds that FastTRAC participants were more likely to enroll in college courses than their traditional ABE peers and were more likely to be able to skip developmental education. Seventy percent of the FastTRAC participants flagged in the MnSCU data system in the 2011–2012 academic year were enrolled in college courses (credit and noncredit) during or within one year after participation in FastTRAC, compared to only 16 percent of ABE students who had not participated in FastTRAC (see Figure 10.1). Only 31 percent of FastTRAC participants registered for a developmental education course in the 2011–2012 academic year, compared to 61 percent of traditional ABE learners (see Figure 10.2; Minnesota State Colleges and Universities 2013). Incorporating remedial education into early course work such as career pathway bridge programs greatly increases students' chances of earning a credential and accelerates their progress. As data become available, state FastTRAC partners will work together to ana-

Figure 10.1 Percentages of FastTRAC and ABE Students Enrolled in College Courses during or within One Year of Program Participation (2011–2012 academic year data)

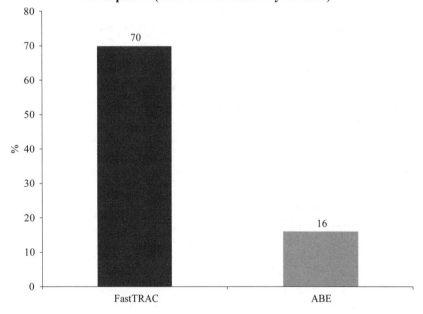

SOURCE: Minnesota State Colleges and Universities (2013).

Figure 10.2 Percentages of FastTRAC and ABE Students Enrolled in a Development Education Course (2011–2012 academic year data)

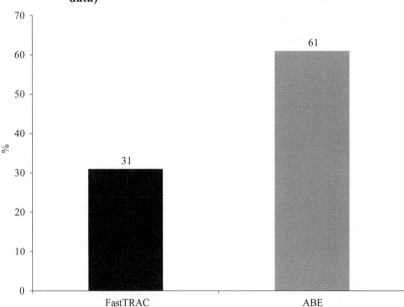

SOURCE: Minnesota State Colleges and Universities (2013).

lyze the employment and earnings outcomes of Minnesota FastTRAC Adult Career Pathway participants compared to students participating in traditional adult basic education courses required prior to entering occupational skills training programs.

Since 2010, 44 Minnesota FastTRAC programs have been started across all 16 Workforce Service Areas (workforce investment board regions in Minnesota) and on 29 of the 47 MnSCU campuses. Also, approximately 90 percent of Minnesota's ABE service delivery consortia have created career pathway programming.

Building a Minnesota Career Pathway System

This proliferation of Minnesota FastTRAC programs has been supported by a committed and persistent state partnership dedicated to continually refining the model and to building a state career pathway system

(AQCP 2014).[14] The FastTRAC partnership of state agencies (workforce, postsecondary, adult and secondary education, human services, corrections, and others); philanthropy; and employers has met consistently over the last seven years and provides a solid base for a system that supports a suite of different types of pathways. Partners have grown to know each other's systems and have a shared vision of the FastTRAC initiative and desired outcomes. They collaborate to make resources available, improve and/or implement new agency policies and practices to support FastTRAC, work to align data systems, and use a set of shared metrics to measure FastTRAC participant success. They contribute funds to support joint requests for proposals to the field and also coordinate resources that may be outside the joint grant-making process. For example, in 2012–2013, the state partnership "braided" several funding sources together to grant $1.5 million to 20 FastTRAC partnerships.[15] In 2013, the state legislature significantly increased FastTRAC sustainability by appropriating $1.5 million per year for FastTRAC from the state's Workforce Development Fund; partners continue to support FastTRAC programs with their own resources as well.

Each partnering agency has made policy changes supportive of career pathways. The state adult basic education office has revamped its State Strategic Plan to reflect the FastTRAC Adult Career Pathway framework and has hired regional transition coordinators to assist Fast-TRAC programs; it now leads joint professional development for local/ regional career pathway partnerships. MnSCU has adopted administrative guidelines for program referral and curriculum alignment between adult basic education and community/technical colleges. The state workforce office has revised state Workforce Investment Act Title I guidelines to require local workforce board plans to support FastTRAC Adult Career Pathway programs and provide staff support to coordinate the state partnership and manage the grants (Roberts and Price 2012). ABE, MnSCU, DEED, and DHS have engaged in the very difficult work of coordinating data across systems to longitudinally track participant progress and success.

Minnesota has been a key partner in the AQCP and is using its framework to strengthen its career pathway efforts. The state has used the framework at the local level, where FastTRAC career pathway programs employed an early version of the self-assessment tool to identify strengths and areas for improvement. Building from the state FastTRAC partnership and from the AQCP framework, the Governor's Workforce Development Board (the state workforce investment board) has issued recommendations for building a statewide, sector-based career pathway system inclusive of all career pathways, including but not limited to FastTRAC and career and technical education.

CONCLUSION

The career pathways approach has taken root in Minnesota and elsewhere out of an imperative to do better for workers and employers. Early evidence is mounting, rigorous evaluations are under way, and a national framework is emerging to more clearly understand this robust, multifaceted approach to aligning and integrating resources. Supported by a variety of public and private investments, the roots of this education and workforce movement are growing. However, to ensure that emerging career pathway systems at the state and local/regional levels do not topple with the next gubernatorial or presidential change or budgetary shift, systems need to establish deeper roots. We need policy changes across federal and state agencies that support the career pathways approach, such as allowing student financial aid for shorter-term programs that successfully produce graduates with marketable credentials. Also, "formula" funding—federal or state noncompetitive grant funding based on a predetermined formula—should be shaped to support this approach (in addition to discretionary grant funding deployed thus far). And data and performance measurement systems should facilitate career pathway partnerships working together to achieve shared outcomes rather than reinforcing the silos and disconnects in the status quo, for example, performance measured by participant success along the career pathway rather than simply by separate federal programs or funding streams.

The Workforce Innovation and Opportunity Act passed in July 2014 to reauthorize federal workforce and adult education programs is a significant step in that direction. The law supports the career pathway approach in its requirements for state and local workforce boards, unified plans, youth activities, and performance measurement. It also makes career pathways an allowable activity in state leadership activities and funding.

Additionally, a group of leading career pathway partnerships—including state and local partners in Minnesota—has joined together in the AQCP alliance to identify and hone a framework that can help them grow these deeper roots. This *system transformation* work is not easy, but the fruits of the partners' labor promises to improve the way they do business together; to help meet business demand for an educated workforce; to help individuals—with varying needs and abilities—access credentials, careers and economic security; and to strengthen our economies and communities.

Notes

1. For example, adults with low literacy skill levels cannot find the name of a particular congressperson within a summary information sheet that lists the congressional district, the name of the district's representative, and the representative's date and place of birth. Adults with low numeracy skills are unlikely to be able to calculate the total cost of a daily car rental when provided with miles driven that day, cost per day, and the cost per mile driven. (Examples drawn from the American Institutes for Research PIACC Gateway; see www.piaccgateway.com.)

2. Publicly funded examples include but are not limited to the Department of Labor's 2010–2011 Career Pathway Institute and the Trade Adjustment Assistance Community College and Career Training grants; the Department of Education's Advancing Career and Technical Education in Career Pathways initiative and the Moving Pathways Forward initiative; and Innovative Strategies to Improve Self-Sufficiency and Health Profession Opportunity Grants administered by the U.S. Department of Health and Human Services. Philanthropic examples include the Ford Foundation's Bridges to Opportunity initiative, the multifunder Accelerating Opportunity, and the Joyce Foundation's Shifting Gears initiative.

3. Contextualization is an instructional technique that integrates concepts from occupational areas, industries, or sectors with basic skills education.

4. Also see the summary of the research in Foster, Strawn, and Duke-Benfield (2011).

5. According to the AQCP, a career pathway system is the cohesive combination of partnerships, resources and funding, policies, data, and shared performance measures that support the development, quality, scaling, and dynamic sustainability of career pathways and programs for youth and adults.

6. A 2013 implementation study of the 2011 FastTRAC grantees showed that, on average, 57 percent of participants entered the program at or below the 6th–8th grade education level, 31 percent of participants had no wages prior to enrollment, and 53 percent had annual wages of $20,000 or less. (See Burns et al. [2013].)

7. Minnesota FastTRAC defines contextualized basic skills instruction as building foundational academic and technology skills within an occupational context to prepare for college level work.
8. The integrated course consists of an ABE instructor and a technical instructor teaching in the same classroom.
9. Personal communication with Nola Speiser, April 25, 2014.
10. This program is in its first year of operation; participant numbers will be forthcoming.
11. Employment retention is defined as the proportion of people employed during the first quarter after exit who are also employed during the second and third quarters after exit.
12. Fifty-three percent of all exiters during 2010–2012 had wages in all four quarters after exit. For the exiters who had wages in any of the four quarters after exit (but not all quarters), their average wage increase was 23 percent from an average of $13,136 to $16,101. As with the other group of exiters, the average wage increase has steadily increased over the reporting period.
13. Minnesota FastTRAC staff is tracking the number of FastTRAC completers who return to the educational pathway after having been in the workforce. Because many FastTRAC program graduates who left for work have been working for just a few years, this longitudinal data will emerge over time.
14. Dynamic sustainability means not only continuing career pathways, programs, and systems beyond initial development, but also supporting their adaptation and continuous improvement over time based on experience, new information, data, and outcomes. In some cases, it may mean discontinuing career pathways and programs that are not working or no longer in demand.
15. Funding sources included the federal Workforce Investment Act (WIA) Title II adult education discretionary funds ($300,000), WIA Incentive funds ($650,000), Greater Twin Cities United Way ($300,000), and Department of Human Services TANF (public assistance) Innovation Funds ($250,000).

References

Alliance for Quality Career Pathways. 2014. *Shared Vision, Strong Systems: The Alliance for Quality Career Pathways Framework Version 1.0.* 2014. Washington, DC: Center for Law and Social Policy.

Bailey, Thomas, Shanna Smith Jaggars, and Davis Jenkins. 2001. *Introduction to the CCRC Assessment of Evidence Series.* New York: Community College Research Center, Teachers College, Columbia University.

Bragg, Debra, Tim Harmon, Catherine L. Kirby, and Sujung Kim. 2009. *Initial Results of Illinois' Shifting Gears Pilot Demonstration Evaluation.* Champaign, IL: Office of Community College Research and Leadership, University of Illinois Urbana–Champaign.

Burns, Melanie, Susan Lindoo, Julie Dincau, Rachel Speck, and Dana

DeMaster. 2013. *Implementation Study of 2011 Adult Career Pathways*. St. Paul, MN: Minnesota FastTRAC Initiative, Department of Employment and Economic Development.

Carnevale, Anthony P., Nicole Smith, and Jeff Strohl. 2010. *Help Wanted: Projections of Jobs and Education Requirements through 2018*. Washington, DC: Georgetown University Center on Education and the Workforce.

Choitz, Vickie, Louis Soares, and Rachel Pleasants. 2010. *A New National Approach to Career Navigation for Working Learners*. Washington, DC: Center for American Progress.

Fein, David J. 2012. *Career Pathways as a Framework for Program Design and Evaluation: A Working Paper from the Innovative Strategies for Increasing Self-Sufficiency (ISIS) Project*. OPRE Report 2012-30. Bethesda, MD: Abt Associates.

Foster, Marcie, Julie Strawn, and Amy Ellen Duke-Benfield. 2011. *Beyond Basic Skills: State Strategies to Connect Low-Skilled Students to an Employer-Valued Postsecondary Education*. Washington, DC: Center for Law and Social Policy.

Goodman, Madeline, Robert Finnegan, Leyla Mohadjer, Tom Krenzke, and Jacquie Hogan. 2013. *Literacy, Numeracy, and Problem Solving in Technology-Rich Environments among U.S. Adults: Results from the Program for the International Assessment of Adult Competencies 2012: First Look*. NCES 2014-008. Washington, DC: National Center for Education Statistics, U.S. Department of Education.

Jenkins, Davis, Matthew Zeidenberg, and Gregory S. Kienzl. 2009. *Educational Outcomes of I-BEST, Washington State Community and Technical College System's Integrated Basic Education and Skills Training Program: Findings from a Multivariate Analysis*. New York: Community College Research Center, Teachers College, Columbia University.

Linderman, Donna, and Zineta Kolenovic. 2009. *Early Outcomes Report for City University of New York (CUNY) Accelerated Study in Associate Programs (ASAP)*. New York: City University of New York and the NYC Center for Economic Opportunity.

Minnesota State Colleges and Universities. 2013. *Enrollment, Persistence, Graduation, and Employment of Adult Basic Education and FastTRAC Participants at Minnesota State Colleges and Universities*. St. Paul, MN: MnSCU System Office Research, Planning and Policy.

Reimherr, Patrick, Tim Harmon, Julie Strawn, and Vickie Choitz. 2013. *Reforming Student Aid: How to Simplify Tax Aid and Use Performance Metrics to Improve College Choices and Completion*. Washington, DC: Center for Law and Social Policy.

Roberts, Brandon, and Derek Price. 2012. *Strengthening State Systems for*

Adult Learners: An Evaluation of the First Five Years of Shifting Gears. Chicago: The Joyce Foundation.

Scrivener, Susan, and Michael J. Weiss. 2009. *More Guidance, Better Results? Three Year Effects of an Enhanced Student Services Program at Two Community Colleges.* MDRC's Opening Doors Project. New York: MDRC.

Strawn, Julie. 2011. *Farther Faster: Six Promising Programs Show How Career Pathway Bridges Help Basic Skills Students Earn Credentials That Matter.* Washington, DC: CLASP.

U.S. Department of Education. 2010. "Use of Funds Provided under the Adult Education and Family Literacy Act (AEFLA) for Integrated Education and Training (IET)." Program Memorandum FY 2010-02. Washington, DC: U.S. Department of Education. http://www2.ed.gov/about/offices/list/ovae/pi/AdultEd/aefla-funds-for-iet.pdf (accessed September 10, 2014).

U.S. Department of Labor (USDOL). 2010. "Joint Letter on Career Pathways from the U.S. Department of Labor's Employment and Training Administration, the U.S. Department of Education's Office of Career, Technical, and Adult Education, and the U.S. Department of Health and Human Services' Administration for Children and Families." TEN 36-11, April 4. Washington, DC: USDOL. http://wdr.doleta.gov/directives/attach/TEN/ten2_36_11.pdf (accessed February 3, 2015).

Werner, Alan, Catherine Dun Rappaport, Jennifer Bagnell Stuart, and Jennifer Lewis. 2013. *Literature Review: Career Pathways Programs.* OPRE Report No. 2013-24. Cambridge, MA: Abt Associates.

Wiseley, W. Charles. 2011. "Effective Basic Skills Instruction: The Case for Contextualized Developmental Math." PACE Brief 11-1. Stanford, CA: Stanford University.

Zeidenberg, Matthew, Sung-Woo Cho, and Davis Jenkins. 2010. *Washington State's Integrated Basic Education and Skills Training Program (I-BEST): New Evidence of Effectiveness.* New York: Community College Research Center, Teachers College, Columbia University.

11
Capital IDEA and Austin Community College

A Case Study of a Nonprofit-Community College Partnership

Matt Helmer
Maureen Conway
Aspen Institute

Postsecondary credentials are increasingly important for workers in today's economy. Nearly two-thirds of the 30 fastest-growing jobs through 2022 typically require a postsecondary education, according to the Bureau of Labor and Statistics (2013). A postsecondary education is also linked to higher earnings. According to research conducted by the Center on Education and the Workforce at Georgetown University, workers with at least some college earn slightly more than $1.5 million on average over the course of their careers, which is $250,000 more than workers with only a high school diploma. Workers with an associate's degree earn a little over $1.7 million during their lifetimes (Carnevale, Rose, and Cheah 2011). These of course are averages, and the proportion of college graduates who find themselves employed in low-quality, noncollege jobs has increased over the past decade (Abel, Deitz, and Su 2014). Course of study matters, however, and at both the subbaccalaureate and baccalaureate levels, the quality of employment outcomes varies markedly according to type of certificate or degree (Fry and Parker 2012; Hanson, Carnevale, and Rose 2012). General recognition of the importance of postsecondary education to economic success has played a role in the increased college enrollment and college attainment we've seen over the past decade (Fry and Parker 2012). And, given the cost of postsecondary degrees, more and more students are turning to community colleges for postsecondary education.

According to the American Association of Community Colleges, nearly half of today's college students are enrolled at community colleges, many of whom represent a new type of student. They are more racially and ethnically diverse, and many of them are also working, older, low-income, and parents. The most recent data on community college enrollment showed nearly 13 million students enrolled in community college in fall 2009, including 8 million students who enrolled in for-credit courses, and approximately 5 million who enrolled in noncredit coursework. Nearly 60 percent of these students enrolled part time. The majority of community college students, 57 percent, were women, and over one-third were racial or ethnic minorities. The students' average age was 28, and 15 percent of students were over age 40. More than 40 percent of these students were first-generation college students, and most were employed full or part time while in school (American Association of Community Colleges 2012).

Many of these students face significant challenges in community college. Students unfamiliar or inexperienced with postsecondary education may struggle to navigate the college bureaucracy, such as financial aid and registration processes. Some students do not know what skills are in demand in their labor market or what occupations they should pursue. Many lack the basic skills they need to succeed in the classroom; others lack the professional networks and job search and interview skills they need to successfully transition to the labor market. Personal and family responsibilities can also be barriers. Seventy-five percent of today's community college students are juggling family responsibilities, work, and school (Complete College America 2011). These students often need a range of support services such as assistance with child care, transportation, or covering the costs of tuition and fees. As a result of these challenges, many community college students are finding success difficult to achieve.

Part-time students, as well as minority and low-income students, are much less likely than other community college students to earn a degree or certificate. Older students who attend part time also struggle to complete a degree or certificate (Complete College America 2011). The primary reason that students drop out of community college and university is the stress of combining work and school, according to a national survey of college students aged 22–30 (Public Agenda 2009).

Many community colleges are responding with new strategies to meet the needs of today's workforce. Funding challenges and institutional constraints, however, limit how much colleges can do alone. In many communities, nonprofit organizations are partnering with community colleges to help students overcome these challenges to succeed in the classroom and labor market. The Aspen Institute's Workforce Strategies Initiative (AspenWSI) identified and named these collaborations Courses to Employment (C2E) partnerships. This case study will discuss findings from AspenWSI's research into C2E partnerships and present a case study on a partnership between Capital IDEA, a nonprofit organization, and Austin Community College.

COMMUNITY COLLEGE-NONPROFIT PARTNERSHIPS: COURSES TO EMPLOYMENT STRATEGIES

Courses to Employment partnerships, as defined by AspenWSI, are collaborations between community colleges and workforce nonprofit organizations that use a range of strategies and combine the strengths of each institution to serve students more effectively than either could alone. Most of these partnerships target a specific industry or cluster of occupations, developing a deep understanding of the interrelationships between business competitiveness and the workforce needs of the targeted industry. These partnerships support students to improve their workplace skills and persist on an education pathway in pursuit of a higher-quality job. Along the way, partnerships provide motivational support and counseling, as well as access to needed social services and academic supports, including basic skills development. As workers transition to the workplace or aim to climb the career ladder, partnerships may provide labor market navigation services that help students find jobs and build the professional networks and communication skills they need to retain jobs and succeed within a local industry.

While many partnerships share similar goals, their work is often structured and organized in different ways. For example, some partnerships focus on short-term vocational skills training, and others have students pursue associate degrees. In some cases, the nonprofit provides most of the training, and in others the college assumes all the responsibility for curriculum design and instruction. However, most of these partnerships have three common elements: 1) a high-quality education program that has a clear link to in-demand employment opportunities and provides appropriate technical skills training and basic skills development, 2) a range of student academic and nonacademic support services, and 3) an industry strategy that focuses on meeting business needs and helping students enter and succeed in the local labor market.

Partnerships leverage each other's institutional competencies and resources in different ways to serve their students. The activities and services of partnerships often differ because they serve different worker populations and businesses, use and have access to different funding streams, have different institutional strengths and weaknesses, and operate in different policy and regulatory environments. Because each partnership is unique and customized based on these factors, the field of nonprofit-community college partnerships consists of a rich and diverse set of strategies and approaches.

In 2013, the AspenWSI conducted a national survey of nonprofit-community college partnerships that generated responses representing 177 partnerships that demonstrated a lot of diversity in approach. Nonprofits engaged in partnerships with colleges represent a mix of institutions, including community-based organizations, funder collaboratives, union-affiliated nonprofits, worker centers, and Workforce Investment Boards. Table 11.1 summarizes some of the survey findings (Aspen Institute Workforce Strategies Initiative forthcoming).

In the next section of this case study, we profile a partnership between Capital IDEA and Austin Community College to provide a better understanding of what a Courses to Employment collaboration does, and how nonprofit organizations and community colleges can work together to support the success of low-income students.

CASE STUDY: CAPITAL IDEA AND AUSTIN COMMUNITY COLLEGE

Partnership History

In the late 1990s, many hospitals, semiconductor companies, and businesses in Austin were finding it difficult to find skilled workers, and many families were struggling to make ends meet as the cost of living rose in the Austin area. Local policymakers had attracted semiconductor plants with tax incentives. In response, Austin Interfaith, a broad-based coalition of religious congregations, schools, unions, and other community institutions of the Industrial Areas Foundation, worked to hire disadvantaged workers and create a policy that links abatements to a fund for high-skill, long-term training (Bennett and Giloth 2008). When Samsung located a plant in Austin, it proposed to hire operators at low wages. Austin Interfaith organized the community to ensure a higher starting wage.

Around the same time, Austin Interfaith created Capital IDEA— based on Project Quest, an initiative of Austin Interfaith's sister organization in San Antonio—to help lift Central Texas working families out of poverty by providing supports, counseling, and connection to educational services that lead to lifelong financial independence. Using funding from the new long-term job training fund established by the Samsung tax abatement deal, this program began preparing disadvantaged workers to become semiconductor technicians, as well as other high-skill occupations. Through this early work, Capital IDEA established the organization's guiding framework for identifying living wage jobs in their labor market, and then creating education pathways to those jobs. Today, Capital IDEA works with students and employers in a variety of industries, including health care, technology, and the trades, as a sponsor of educational services for Austin's low-income workers. A central component of the program's strategy is to work with local community colleges and training providers to supply those educational services.

Capital IDEA's partnership with Austin Community College (ACC) began in 1999 in part through an introduction by leaders at Austin Interfaith. Capital IDEA and ACC jointly developed the College Preparatory

Table 11.1 Courses to Employment Partnerships: Summary Findings from a National Survey

Student populations served	Partnerships are designed to serve numerous populations. The highest percentages of partnerships identified low-income individuals, adults with limited or no work history, youth between the ages of 18 and 26, and ethnic, racial minorities as among populations they most commonly serve.
Industries targeted	Nearly 80 percent of partnerships reported that they are preparing students for employment in a particular industry or set of occupations. Partnerships responding to the survey commonly cited health care, manufacturing, construction, and information technology as industries within which they are preparing students for employment.
Training provided	Partnerships provide a variety of different types of training, including basic and technical skills education. Sixty-four percent of partnerships reported offering training in credit certificate programs, 60 percent reported offering noncredit vocational skills training, and 43 percent reported supporting students in associate degree programs.
Support services and job placement assistance provided	Partnerships provide a range of support services and job placement assistance. Over 80 percent of partnerships reported providing case management services, and nearly 90 percent of partnerships provide job search assistance. Many partnerships also reported providing assistance with transportation, monetary assistance to help cover the cost of tuition and living expenses, and assistance with obtaining uniforms, tools, or other work supplies.
Industry engagement activities	Over 80 percent of partnerships said businesses inform their curriculum design or career pathways development, and almost 60 percent of partnerships said businesses provide in-kind resources such as materials, equipment, or training space. Eighty percent of partnerships said partnering businesses hire students, and 60 percent said businesses provide internships. Almost 60 percent of partnerships reported that businesses provide in-kind resources. Fewer partnerships, however, said businesses provide monetary resources to support the partnerships' work.

291

Partners' roles and responsibilities	In C2E partnerships, community colleges typically assume responsibility for delivering training, nonprofits usually manage support services and job placement activities, and both institutions often play a strong role in engaging industry and business partners.
Partnership funding	Nonprofits and colleges use many different funding streams to finance their partnership work. Both nonprofits and colleges commonly identified the Workforce Investment Act, philanthropic foundations, and state government dollars as among the top funding sources their organization uses to support the partnerships' work.
Outcomes of students served by partnerships	Over 80 percent of nonprofits said a student served by their partnership typically obtains employment in a training-related field, obtains any kind of employment, and/or receives a wage increase or promotion. Nearly half of community colleges said students served by their partnership are more likely to complete their educational goals than students in similar training programs at the college, and 40 percent said students served by the partnership find training-related jobs more easily than other students in similar training programs.

SOURCE: Aspen Institute Workforce Strategies Initiative (forthcoming).

Academy as an alternative to the traditional developmental education model after recognizing that many adult learners in Austin could not pass the college entrance exam and were not prepared to enter college course work. The academy serves as an important bridge into the college's vocational and technical skills training for Capital IDEA–supported students. Nearly a year after beginning the partnership, the collaborative graduated its first students from the Licensed Practical Nursing program. Today, the partnership supports hundreds of students each year in various programs and continues to develop new innovations and supports in response to the needs of its students.

Between 2003 and 2008, Capital IDEA enrolled 991 students into its health care training pathways program with ACC. Eighty-eight percent of these students were female, 44 percent were Latino, and 26 percent were African American; the median age of students was 27. Over one-third of the students were single parents (Helmer and Blair 2011). As described in the rest of this case study, Capital IDEA provides an extensive amount of support and financial assistance, which includes covering the costs of tuition and fees to their students, with funding primarily coming from local government and foundations.

Education Strategy

ACC delivers all related academic education and training to Capital IDEA–supported students, including the College Prep Academy, which prepares Capital IDEA participants to pass the Texas Higher Education Assessment, a prerequisite to enter community college in Texas. Students receive over 300 hours of instruction from ACC faculty in reading, writing, mathematics, test taking, and study skills through the training that operates six hours a day, five days a week, for 12 weeks. Students who need additional math instruction can opt for another 12 weeks of instruction (half-time).

To help participants address the financial burdens of pursuing postsecondary education, Capital IDEA fully funds all education-related costs, including tuition, fees, books, supplies, uniforms, and vaccinations. Capital IDEA allows students who qualify for Pell Grants to keep those resources to help cover essential, ongoing living expenses.

ACC provides the training and instruction to Capital IDEA–supported students for the in-demand careers they are pursuing. Prior to entering an educational program, these students undergo a thorough assessment that includes Student Assessment of Growth and Excellence testing to assess the students' vocational interest, skills interests, learning styles, and aptitudes; a Test for Adult Basic Education testing for math and reading academic levels; an interview to evaluate the participant's motivation and commitment to the program; and assessments designed to determine what barriers students face that may prevent their success in the classroom and labor market.

Capital IDEA career navigators and the participant use the assessments to craft an agreed-upon customized education and career plan that may include attending the College Prep Academy or applying for and entering a vocational program at ACC. The plan is also developed based on availability of training slots at the college and labor market information gathered by the partnership about high-demand occupations. While Capital IDEA strives to ensure students are matched with a career opportunity that meets the students' interests, the organization is demand-driven and will only fund and support students in training that leads to employment.

Prior to acceptance by Capital IDEA, participants may be asked to do more career exploration, meet with an ACC recruiter, or attend an ACC information session, change their housing situation to reduce living expenses, or resolve outstanding financial debts. Some may be referred to other partnering organizations to improve their English language skills or earn their General Educational Development. Capital IDEA is also actively preparing participants for college advising and is in close communication with career counselors at the college about participants' needs and progress as they begin and continue their studies.

ACC provides a wide range of for-credit certificates and degrees in the allied health, technology, and trades fields, including training for dental hygienists, licensed vocational nurses, registered nurses, carpenters, and automotive technicians. Extra tutoring and study skills instruction are available to students, and Capital IDEA coordinates a comprehensive package of support services to support students in training, as described in the next section.

Support Service Strategy

Capital IDEA coordinates and manages a wide array of student support services, financial assistance, and career and college navigation. In addition to the individualized assessment, career counseling, and academic planning described earlier, the program helps students navigate the college experience. It provides individualized assistance with college enrollment, course sequencing, and financial aid processes. It also teaches participants how to navigate financial aid and registration processes at the college, and serves as a student advocate when needed. Capital IDEA may help participants address administrative obstacles to enrollment and registration, such as appealing poor academic records from previous study or paying past due parking or library fines.

In addition to covering students' academic expenses as noted earlier, Capital IDEA also provides direct financial assistance for nonacademic needs such as child care, transportation, and emergency-related living expenses. The program's wide network of community partners also helps provide assistance in these areas when needed. Though its students are generally encouraged not to work so they can focus on their studies, Capital IDEA recognizes that this is not possible for all students and helps those who need to work find interim employment opportunities while in training to help cover their living costs.

Capital IDEA continues to provide financial support and intensive case management services until graduation and placement, often two to five years. Career navigators meet with most participants regularly, in peer group sessions and one on one, while they are in training. ACC and Capital IDEA staff and faculty collaborate in a variety of ways in order to make this support system effective. The college developed a waiver system that allows faculty and staff to share information with career navigators about individual students' progress and challenges in real-time. Staff in numerous departments communicate with career navigators to keep them informed about advising, registration, and course requirements. ACC also regularly invites navigators to attend staff information sessions where information that is relevant to students is shared. Consistent communication among Capital IDEA staff, participants, and college staff allows the partnership to quickly identify students who are struggling and provide the necessary supports in response.

To keep students motivated, Capital IDEA organizes and facilitates regular peer support sessions that are held at locations and times that are convenient to students—usually where they attend classes. Sample topics include communications with instructors, self-esteem, budgeting, dealing with professors, attitude, accountability, and personality.

Industry Strategy

The partnership between Capital IDEA and ACC aims to prepare students for high-demand careers that provide self-sufficient wages. To meet this goal, the partnership must stay attuned to what jobs are in demand, who is hiring, and what skills and education students need to obtain those jobs. To gather that information, the partners work to develop and sustain close relationships with businesses in high-demand sectors in their region, such as allied health, and they engage business partners at several levels and points of contact. Both ACC and Capital IDEA are members of the Healthcare Workforce Alliance of Central Texas, an industry-led and community-sponsored group that exists to address collectively the workforce needs of the health care industry in Austin. Members include community colleges, universities, high school tech programs, major hospitals, and many other smaller health care providers. The partnership also relies on labor market intelligence and regional economic forecasts from local area chambers and Workforce Solutions, the local Workforce Investment Board, to inform the partnership's strategy.

ACC learns about businesses' needs to inform their curricula and educational strategies through other business relationships as well. For example, businesses, such as hospitals, contract with ACC to provide them employer-specific incumbent worker training. Some hospitals with long-standing relationships with ACC help to pay for lab equipment, fund faculty salaries, provide clinical slots for health care students, and provide other in-kind support. ACC often collaborates with businesses on grant proposals, and many business leaders serve on ACC's advisory committees.

Capital IDEA, which is primarily responsible for connecting students served by the partnership to jobs, maintains a consistent, real-time dialogue with businesses to stay informed about their employment projections and workforce needs. Program staff work to create close relationships and formal agreements with local businesses, some of which have representation on Capital IDEA's board of directors. By conducting ongoing information gathering about health care and other in-demand careers from the businesses directly, Capital IDEA is able to obtain real-time labor market information, including base employment projections and actual starting wages, which can be different from that of broader regional forecasts. Placement staff use this information to steer students toward businesses that are hiring as they approach graduation. On occasion, businesses have paid Capital IDEA a placement/ retention fee after hiring a graduate supported by Capital IDEA, as described further in the next section.

Partnership Costs and Funding

Per student costs for Capital IDEA–supported students can vary greatly. Some students need more intensive support services and/or a longer time frame to complete their educational goals. Capital IDEA's extensive use of referral organizations to provide additional support services and assistance are unaccounted costs that can also mask the full costs of supporting students. The organization also provides case management, counseling, and structured peer supports to students, which are costs that also cannot be attributed to an individual student.

To help one student obtain her certificate as a Licensed Vocational Nurse, Capital IDEA provided nearly $16,000 in direct support over a six-year period, with the majority of the support going to tuition (47 percent) and child care (29 percent), books (9 percent), and rental assistance (5 percent). For this particular student, Capital IDEA used nine different funding streams to support these costs (Conway 2011).

Capital IDEA spends a significant amount of resources paying for students' tuition, books, and other financial assistance, such as child care. It budgeted more than $1.2 million for tuition, books, and educational costs out of an overall budget of $3.4 million in 2014. Financial assistance for child care, transportation, housing, utilities, and other living expenses account for another nearly $300,000. In total, direct payments for tuition, books, and other supports account for approximately 45 percent of the program's budget for supporting students in training programs. Capital IDEA devoted the other 55 percent of the budget to covering staff salaries for the industry engagement, career navigation, and case management activities, as well as necessary operating expenses and administrative functions.

As noted earlier, students may spend anywhere from a few to several years with Capital IDEA pursuing their education. Some students may take breaks in their studies, and others may persist straight through to completion. Capital IDEA may be actively supporting upward of 800 students per year in its training programs in any given year. The organization estimated total per participant costs at $4,254 in 2014.

The partnership between Capital IDEA and ACC often draws on a mix of funding streams to support students. Capital IDEA has a very diverse funding base, including public and private sources, that allows it to provide and sustain over time a wide variety of critical nonacademic services to students. In fiscal year 2008, Capital IDEA obtained approximately $4.2 million in funding from 21 different sources to support students in training. The organization obtained funding from 3 national philanthropic sources, 11 regional or local philanthropy sources, 3 federal government sources, 3 local government sources, and 1 state government source. Local government was the organization's largest funding source, accounting for nearly 44 percent of its revenue. Another 40 percent of funding came from national, regional, and local philanthropic sources, 4 percent from federal government, 6 percent from business or corporate contributions, and 4 percent from individual donors (Conway 2011).

Capital IDEA is unusual in the nonprofit workforce development field in that it receives substantial amounts of funding from city and county general revenues. With the support of active advocacy organized by Austin Interfaith, Capital IDEA has been able to make the case for public investment in its strategies. The positive outcomes brought about by the partnership's work have helped convince the local public sector to make these investments. The general revenue funds provided by Austin and Travis County to Capital IDEA are used to pay for support services, as well as tuition at ACC. This allows students to keep Pell Grants and use those funds for income support while in training. Donations from foundations, corporations, and individuals are another critical source of funding the program obtains to support its efforts. It receives private sector support through formal agreements with several health care employers who pay a $5,000–$8,000 retention fee over eight quarters after hiring a registered nursing graduate who was supported by Capital IDEA.

In addition, the partnership benefits from active and long-term collaboration with WIA-funded WorkSource Career Centers. WorkSource coenrolls eligible Capital IDEA–supported students into WIA for the final 1.5 years of training. These students qualify for Individual Training

Accounts to pay for tuition, fees, books, gas cards worth $200/month, uniforms, required tools, crisis payments for things such as utilities or car repairs that would be a barrier to completing school, and sometimes child care.

ACC was also recently awarded a grant from the Department of Labor Trade Adjustment Assistance Community College and Career Training. The grant is being used in part to support some new strategies the partnership is pursuing, as discussed in the next section.

Innovations and Future Directions

Capital IDEA and ACC founded the College Prep Academy in the early stages of their collaboration, a critical innovation that provided an alternative to developmental education and provided a framework for the partnership to use to test new educational and support strategies. Capital IDEA students serve as one of the college's testing grounds for experimenting with different types of strategies, and the feedback Capital IDEA provides to the college about its services helps ACC continuously adapt and improve based on the changing needs of students.

After the partners discovered that many students were failing their allied health prerequisite courses, ACC, with the funding from the Department of Labor, founded the Health Professions Academy to develop and deliver individualized, computer-based education to improve the prerequisite completion rate for students pursuing a health care career. Capital IDEA provided key input and advice on the structure of the academy based on their students' experience. With assistance from Capital IDEA, ACC is also redesigning prerequisite courses to be more interactive and include more hands-on training. ACC redesigned a biology prerequisite and is in the process of redesigning anatomy and physiology courses.

The process for exchanging ideas and information among the partners has also led to other important changes in service delivery. Capital IDEA has also intensified its efforts to support students through prerequisites and is colocating eight of its career navigators on a new ACC campus so they can be more readily available to students who need support. The partnership is exploring other new approaches that will facilitate accelerated learning and competency-based training.

Student Outcomes

The partnership's work led to some impressive educational and employment outcomes for students, according to a study completed by the Aspen Institute (Conway, Blair, and Helmer 2012). Over 80 percent of the 358 students enrolled in the partnerships' College Preparatory Academy between 2003 and 2009 completed the academy and passed the Texas Higher Education Assessment, qualifying them for entry into community college coursework. Of students enrolled during this same time period, 193 had received a credit certificate or associate's degree in an allied health field by the time Aspen's study ended. In the year following completion, 96 percent of these students were employed and earning a median salary of over $44,000 per year, over three times more than their median salary of $13,545 they had earned in the year prior to enrolling with Capital IDEA.

Capital IDEA and ACC's partnership stands out as an example of what two very different institutions can do to leverage one another's strengths and support the success of low-income students. The increased capacity and ability to improve student outcomes is a top benefit of these partnerships, according to many nonprofit organizations and community colleges that participated in AspenWSI's survey.

BENEFITS OF NONPROFIT-COMMUNITY COLLEGE PARTNERSHIPS

The outcomes demonstrated by Capital IDEA and ACC, as well as other partnerships researched by the AspenWSI during the Courses to Employment demonstration project, show that these collaborations are a promising approach to helping students get the credentials and skills they need to connect to better employment and higher wage opportunities. These types of outcomes and the ability to reach and serve students with barriers are some of the most commonly cited benefits as to why partners engage in these collaborations, according to AspenWSI's survey of nonprofit-community college partnerships.

Nonprofit organizations participating in AspenWSI's survey of partnerships reported that one of the top benefits from their partnership is the access to quality training opportunities and college credentials with labor market value the college provides to their worker constituency. They also noted that a top benefit was the positive education and employment outcomes they saw students achieve as a result of the collaboration. Some nonprofits said the partnership improved their ability to meet industry needs and improved their relationships and networks with business partners. Many nonprofit organizations also reported that the ability to leverage different resources and expertise from the college was another top benefit.

Community colleges reported that their collaboration allowed them to better serve their communities and a wider population of students, many of whom the college may not typically reach. One respondent said, "The partnership helps the college reach a population that may not otherwise make it to the campus." Colleges also said the ability to provide support services and the network the partnership provided to community resources is beneficial. Similar to nonprofit responses, colleges also noted that the nonprofit's access to different types of funding is beneficial and that improved student outcomes are also an advantage of these collaborations. Despite all these benefits, creating, sustaining, and expanding partnerships can be challenging.

CHALLENGES OF NONPROFIT–COMMUNITY COLLEGE PARTNERSHIPS

Nonprofit and community colleges face numerous challenges in creating, sustaining, and expanding their partnerships. AspenWSI observed partnerships struggling to balance different institutional goals and missions, to collect and analyze data, and to find enough resources to serve students with multiple barriers. The survey of partnerships conducted by AspenWSI confirmed many of these observations.

According to AspenWSI's survey results, over 80 percent of colleges and nonprofits said that sustaining resources to maintain or grow the partnership is a challenge, and 72 percent of both colleges and nonprofits said recent government funding cuts are a challenge (Aspen Institute Workforce Strategies Initiative forthcoming). When asked open-ended questions about their top challenges, nonprofits and colleges again reported that funding is a big challenge.

Nonprofits also commonly reported that working across institutions with different goals, missions, and cultures can be difficult, and that working with the bureaucracy of the college system can pose challenges. According to one nonprofit respondent, "The college operates in silos, so when we want to work across departments it can be challenging." Colleges also noted that different institutional cultures create a number of challenges. According to one college respondent, "We operate in different spheres, with different reporting requirements and 'language.' Sometimes people do not adequately understand the challenges faced by the other members of the partnership."

Colleges also reported that data collection and sharing is challenging. Eighty percent of colleges and 60 percent of nonprofit organizations agreed that collecting, evaluating, and reporting employment outcomes is a challenge for their partnership. Many nonprofits and colleges also said sharing data about student outcomes between their institutions is an issue. Helping partnerships overcome these challenges so the field can learn and grow from its success and failures in helping students complete their education and find employment will be critical to this emerging field's success.

CONCLUSION AND RECOMMENDATIONS

Today, many workers seek to upgrade their skills in order to compete for better-wage jobs. Unfortunately, too many of them lack the supports, guidance, and resources they need to gain appropriate skills and connect to better opportunities. By addressing these needs, these partnerships provide opportunity to a variety of low-income workers seeking to obtain a better education and a better job. In an era of funding cuts, however, these partnerships are struggling to put together the resources they need to support these workers. Federal, state, and local policymakers all have a role to play in supporting these partnerships and ensuring adequate investments are maintained so that workers have the educational opportunities and labor market connections they need. In an era of shrinking public resources, investing in partnerships is the best way to reduce inefficiencies. In particular, organizations that provide support services (so working adults have the time to participate meaningfully in an education opportunity) and offer industry intelligence and networking services (to help workers pursue credentials that will likely lead to better jobs and connect with employers looking for their skills) need greater support. More action needs to be taken to ensure sufficient funding is directed to these nonprofits so that workers pursuing education can succeed in school and in work.

Along with the direct support these partnerships need to provide services, they also need resources to improve their strategies and work together. This field of collaborative practice between nonprofit organizations and community colleges is still emerging. Over 50 percent of partnerships surveyed by AspenWSI are less than four years old. Investing in and incentivizing the start-up and expansion of nonprofit–community college partnerships right now is critical, as millions of workers continue to struggle and many partnerships report challenges in obtaining the resources they need to maintain or expand their work.

As illustrated throughout this case study, these collaborations are complex undertakings and can take time and resources to build. Partners must build trust and relationships with one another, identify common goals, develop industry engagement strategies, and create communication and project management processes. The field of C2E partnerships needs opportunities to learn about the practices and strategies of other partnerships. Investors should create opportunities for convening and information sharing among the field. Helping colleges and nonprofits build the organizational capacities, cross-institutional knowledge, and relationships they need to engage in these partnerships will help this field of practice develop more quickly, which can only serve to meet the needs of a greater number of workers and businesses.

Finally, the collection and use of student outcomes data are critical to how partnerships design their services and training. Quite simply, many partnerships are experimenting with a variety of instructional approaches, support services, and industry engagement strategies, and they need to know if their actions are leading to positive education and employment outcomes for their students. Collecting, managing, and analyzing this type of data, however, is not easy and it also requires resources. The data often reside within different institutions or, in the case of employment data, within a government agency. Sometimes the partnerships have access to these data and sometimes they do not. Assuming they do have access, partnerships may still struggle to collect and merge the data from the college, nonprofit organization, and outside agencies. Policymakers and investors need to work to open up more data to these partnerships and provide them with the resources and assistance they need to make use of it. Turning this field into one that is driven by data on student outcomes will help ensure the resources are spent efficiently and effectively.

References

Abel, Jaison R., Richard Deitz, and Yaqin Su. 2014. "Are Recent College Graduates Finding Good Jobs?" *Current Issues in Economics and Finance* 20(1): 1–8.

American Association of Community Colleges. 2012. *Reclaiming the American Dream: A Report from the 21st-Century Commission on the Future of Community Colleges.* Washington, DC: American Association of Community Colleges. http://www.insidehighered.com/sites/default/server_files/files/21stCentReport.pdf (accessed September 12, 2014).

Aspen Institute Workforce Strategies Initiative. Forthcoming. Unpublished data from a report on a national survey of nonprofit–community college partnerships. Washington, DC: Aspen Institute.

Bennett, Michael I. J., and Robert P. Giloth. 2008. *Economic Development in American Cities: The Pursuit of an Equity Agenda.* Albany, NY: State University of New York Press.

Bureau of Labor and Statistics. 2013. *Employment Projections 2012–2022.* Washington, DC: Bureau of Labor and Statistics. http://bls.gov/news.release/ecopro.nr0.htm (accessed March 10, 2014).

Carnevale, Anthony P., Stephen J. Rose, and Ban Cheah. 2011. *The College Payoff: Education, Occupation, Lifetime Earnings.* Washington, DC: Georgetown University Center on Education and the Workforce. http://cew.georgetown.edu/collegepayoff (accessed March 30, 2014).

Complete College America. 2011. *Time Is the Enemy: The Surprising Truth about Why Today's College Students Aren't Graduating . . . And What Needs to Change.* Washington, DC: Complete College America. http://www.completecollege.org/docs/Time_Is_the_Enemy_Summary.pdf (accessed March 20, 2014).

Conway, Maureen. 2011. "The Price of Persistence: How Nonprofit-Commu-

nity College Partnerships Manage and Blend Diverse Funding Streams."
Courses to Employment 2: 120. Washington, DC: Aspen Institute http://
aspenwsi.org/wordpress/wp-content/uploads/11-005.pdf (accessed June 20,
2014).

Conway, Maureen, Amy Blair, and Matt Helmer. 2012. *Courses to Employment: Partnering to Create Paths to Education and Careers.* Washington, DC: Aspen Institute. http://www.aspenwsi.org/wordpress/wp-content/
uploads/C2E.pdf (accessed April 5, 2014).

Fry, Richard, and Kim Parker. 2012. *Record Shares of Young Adults Have Fin-
ished Both High School and College.* Washington, DC: Pew Research Center.
http://www.pewsocialtrends.org/2012/11/05/record-shares-of-young-adults
-have-finished-both-high-school-and-college/ (accessed June 20, 2014).

Hanson, Andrew R., Anthony P. Carnevale, and Stephen J. Rose. 2012. *Certificates: Gateway to Gainful Employment and College Degrees.* Washington,
DC: Georgetown University Center on Education and the Workforce. http://
masters-certificate.com/Certificates.FullReport.061812.pdf (accessed June
20, 2014).

Helmer, Matt, and Amy Blair. 2011. *Initial Education and Employment Outcomes Findings for Students Enrolled in Healthcare Career Training 2003–
2008: Capital IDEA and Austin Community College Partnership.* Washington, DC: Aspen Institute. http://www.aspenwsi.org/wordpress/wp-content/
uploads/10-015.pdf (accessed June 20, 2014).

Public Agenda. 2009. *With Their Whole Lives Ahead of Them.* New York: Bill
and Melinda Gates Foundation. http://www.publicagenda.org/theirwhole
livesaheadofthem (accessed December 28, 2012).

12

Promising Practices of Community Colleges in the New Age of Workforce Development

Jim Jacobs
Macomb Community College

The impact of the Great Recession significantly changed many institutions, including community colleges. This was especially true in the area of workforce development. As the economy slowly improves and companies begin hiring in larger numbers, successful community colleges are adjusting both the substance of their programs and their processes of delivery. This is resulting in the emergence of a different workforce development practice for community colleges, with implications for the overall workforce development system in the United States. In this brief chapter, I examine changes resulting from the Great Recession and their impact on the large community colleges located in many manufacturing centers in the United States.

There are more than 1,200 community colleges in the United States, most of which are governed through a combination of state laws and local elected or appointed trustee boards. Of these, 250 are comprehensive community colleges, whose enrollments exceed 20,000 students and are typically located in urban and suburban centers. This subgroup of community colleges plays a major role with the dominant sectors of the U.S. economy and serves as the center of major community college efforts in workforce development.

This case study focuses on the practical experiences of a group of 20 major community colleges who have worked together for the past four years as the Community College Workforce Consortium. While these represent only a small fraction of the country's community colleges, many of these institutions are considered leaders by their peers, so their initiatives are likely to impact the future of community colleges as a whole. To understand their significance, it is necessary to examine the delivery of workforce development before 2008.

FORMER SYSTEM

By 2000, most major community colleges had a bifurcated organizational structure related to workforce development. There were traditional vocational or career and technical programs primarily designed to prepare traditional-age students for direct entry into career fields. These programs frequently integrated work-based experience (such as the hospital practicum for nursing students), but also often included traditional liberal arts electives and resulted in an associate's degree. They existed alongside shorter certificate programs that strictly concentrated on subject matter courses. Program enrollments fluctuated in response to local labor market demand, but by 2000 enrollment shifted away from traditional manufacturing and construction programs to business, health career, and information technology programs (U.S. Department of Education 2011).

From the early 1980s, most major community colleges began to also develop units, typically in another part of the institution, focused on providing short-term customized training for local business. Programs were usually developed in response to specific demand for training for incumbent workers, new hires, or start-ups. Many of these efforts were connected to existing state programs that provided funding for job training. These were also the units that interacted with the local workforce board to provide short-term, focused training for their clients. As a result, some community colleges constructed stand-alone "advanced technology centers," and, for a brief time, some community college leaders believed that these activities would provide significant revenue streams for the colleges (Grubb et al. 1997).

The growth of customized training programs at community colleges also influenced their interactions with the formal funding mechanisms of the national Workforce Investment System. While the relationships between the community colleges and the workforce system were too often dominated by state policies on board membership, generally the college's customized training units and local workforce boards provided a good connection to short-term training that prepared people for available jobs. In many areas, close ties were formed between the workforce board and community college, creating a more robust local workforce system (Fischer 2009).

However, private sector trends were at work even prior to the Great Recession that would recast the landscape. First, companies stepped away from on-the-job training and began to demand candidates who possessed the specific skills sets necessary for the job. They conducted rigorous assessment and evaluation of candidates before hiring. They were suspicious of the formal workforce system and sought out employment service firms, arranging to "try out" workers on a temporary basis and assessing on-the-job performance before deciding who to hire on as a full-time employee (Berger 2013).

Second, by 2000, much of the state-supported funding for training programs began drying up as fiscal challenges rose. Instead of continuing to invest in programs to maintain and build their local workforces, which benefited both business attraction and established firms, many states held back training resources to support special, one-shot projects that they thought would attract new, large plants and create a lot of new jobs.

Third, as state training funds evaporated, the local training market for community colleges began to decline. Many colleges began to convert their technology centers to serve traditional, for-credit programs, losing their capacity for short-term training and education. The emphasis shifted from training incumbent workers to serving the growing numbers of younger college students preparing for entry-level jobs.

IMPACT OF THE GREAT RECESSION

The Great Recession amplified these trends. Customized training and incumbent workforce training completely dried up as companies downsized their workforces and hunkered down in survival mode. This had a dual impact. First, existing pipelines of training demand ended for the colleges. But, additionally, many companies did away with their training units, severing the ties and relationships that had been carefully constructed by the community colleges.

At the same time that corporate ties were evaporating, enrollment in some community college career preparation programs surged. Large numbers of adults, primarily those in manufacturing and construction industries who were feeling the brunt of the recession, were attracted to community college degree programs, in part due to their eligibility for student aid and other funding, looking to gain skills in fields with available jobs. Many of these adults wanted to work in "secure" sectors such as health care and information technology. However, they often lacked basic math and science proficiencies necessary for success in college in these fields. In addition, many of the career programs required two years of course work to qualify for licenses, but these individuals were often looking for immediate entry into the labor market. As a result, courses to obtain a commercial driver's license or become a certified nursing assistant or teacher's aide began to proliferate. Typically, these were structured as noncredit programs, and students were heavily dependent on the local workforce boards for funding.

In response to the Great Recession, the Obama administration unleashed resources for education and training programs through the Workforce Investment System. Funds from the Troubled Asset Relief Program (TARP) were channeled through the existing workforce system. Some funding was targeted to new programs in solar energy and "green" construction, while another portion provided the basis for creative state programs that brought community college training to thousands of displaced workers. For example, Michigan introduced No Worker Left Behind, which provided free tuition for up to two years for students pursuing programs in high-demand fields. Approximately 140,000 took part in the program between 2007 and 2010, resulting in significant increases in program completions and new jobs obtained (State of Michigan 2009).

During the Great Recession, community colleges formed a collective response to four major trends shaping modern labor markets. First, the labor market became "privatized," with large companies working through employment service firms versus publicly advertising positions or utilizing the public workforce boards. So, while community college students could prepare for work, they often lacked the ability to connect their students with those hiring. As a result, community colleges began to play a more active and aggressive role in advocating for students, developing direct relationships with private employment service firms.

Macomb Community College found that these service firms were able to place students more effectively and efficiently in many occupations because they were able to focus on the needs of the industry.

Second, with the shift away from traditional manufacturing jobs, obtaining employment in sustainable wage jobs was now predicated on having credentials, including degrees that required longer-term preparation. However, many displaced workers needed jobs immediately. This meant that the traditional division between noncredit short-term job training programs and credit long-term programs needed to be addressed. Community colleges worked to close the gap between their credit and noncredit programs for an integrated approach. For example, at Macomb Community College, a 16-week noncredit course that prepares students for a certified nursing assistant job was "internally articulated," so that students receive some college credit that is applicable to the completion of a degree in many of the college's allied health programs, which include nursing, respiratory therapy, and physical and occupational therapy assistant. The merger of the credit and noncredit course offerings became a new organizational benchmark for colleges that were paying close attention to the workforce needs of their communities.

Third, because not enough employment opportunities existed in most labor markets, community colleges became increasingly involved in direct economic development activities. This was especially true for the colleges in communities where major segments of manufacturing were eliminated. They deepened their entrepreneurial programs to provide direct technical assistance to start-ups through business incubators, applied technology laboratories, and innovation funds. In other cases, community colleges played a role in the development of "green job" industries both through training and support for start-up operations. The colleges also began supporting community partners in developing new industry sector opportunities, as well as finding markets for those new industries (Jacobs 2012).

Fourth, as the recovery began, many large companies were faced with the challenges of restoring their talent pipelines. However, their search for highly skilled workers, including those with four-year technical degrees, was not compatible with community college programs. The HR Policy Association (2011) called for a national effort to deal with the needs of large, multistate employers in the report *Blueprint for*

Jobs in the 21st Century, criticizing the nation's current uncoordinated approach to workforce training and education programs that requires formation of separate, independent, and different relationships in each region and state. The association is the lead public policy organization of chief human resources officers of more than 350 companies, representing the largest employers in business in the United States and globally.

Finally, the Obama administration, more than any other presidency, began building policies to promote community college involvement in the economy. In announcing his Community College Initiative in July 2009 at Macomb Community College, the president asserted, "Community colleges are an essential part of our recovery for the present and our prosperity in the future." Community colleges were integrated into many administrative initiatives, such as efforts to increase manufacturing competitiveness or the promotion of green jobs through TARP funding, and the first federal initiative to build community college capacity in workforce development was rolled out through $2 billion of Trade Adjustment Act dollars. From 2011 to 2014, four $500 million grant pools were awarded to community colleges through a competitive process that requires connection with local business and industry to fill unmet skill needs in their communities (McCarthy 2014). This year, the administration has proposed a number of new federal initiatives to utilize the capacity of community colleges in areas of demand-driven training and the development of new apprentices.

NEW SOLUTIONS

These changes spurred community colleges to further integrate credit and noncredit programs, often developing new forms of credentials that would satisfy business demands. Moreover, the colleges also began to look beyond the needs of individual firms to industry sectors, employing a long-term view and economic development objectives. One such initiative was the Auto Communities Consortium. Initiated by community colleges in Michigan, Indiana, Ohio, and Iowa, and joined by colleges in Illinois, Wisconsin, Kentucky, and Tennessee, this learning network was established to address challenges faced by manufacturing communities. The consortium has now expanded into a national effort, changing its name to the Community College Workforce Consortium (CCWC).

Initially funded by the Joyce and Lumina foundations, and now an organization supported by member dues, the consortium works together to develop activities that help create employment within and outside the auto industry. For most communities, focusing on the auto industry for future employment growth is not realistic. Instead, the imperative is to collaborate with local economic development organizations to design meaningful programs that prepare students for jobs in new industries in emerging sectors.

Two key features of the CCWC are peer learning, a structure based on sector activities versus state boundaries, active leadership by college presidents to support institutional transformation, and fostering linkages with public policy advocates to develop a genuine federal response that builds on community college efforts to help restore the vitality of manufacturing communities in the United States. The consortium is not simply a group of community college workforce trainers, but an organization created by presidents who wish to adapt their institutions to the new realities of the labor market. This means confronting internal institutional issues such as the relationship between credit and noncredit programs, determining how to implement industry-driven credentials into their programs, and committing college resources to promote community economic development.

The consortium format has enabled community colleges to engage with larger employers and their professional associations, leading to a relationship with the HR Policy Association. Together, they have formed a Workforce Development Roundtable, which includes member job postings and advice for students seeking work. In addition, the HR Policy Association members' companies provide "sector snapshots" of long-term workforce needs to CCWC members and work cooperatively toward mutually beneficial changes in federal workforce policies (HR Policy Association 2013).

CONCLUSION

These developments suggest that community college workforce programs will be stretched in two main directions. First, internally, there will be more integration and alignment of all the workforce programs, both credit and noncredit, under a coordinated institutional structure. Both forms of learning are necessary, given the varied needs of the students and, often, the skill needs of employers. While learning activities will operate under one umbrella, learning outcomes (degrees, certificates, industry certifications, apprenticeship) could be different. The challenge will be to organize these activities into coherent pathways that meet the diverse objectives of students. For those coming to the community college in search of marketable skills, the college will not only teach the skills but also will use their local reputation to promote students in the workplace. This requires closer coordination with employers and a much more sophisticated understanding of local labor markets, specifically, the use of current job postings for a real-time view of local demand, as well as in-depth discussions with corporate human relations executives who are attempting to forecast talent management trends three to five years out. Taking a sector approach to workforce programs translates into more time, energy, and institutional resources devoted to understanding the trends in an industry and responding to them with a variety of programs.

At the same time that community colleges integrate their workforce activities to focus on local labor markets, they will also collaborate with other community colleges to address the needs of large corporations or regional industrial clusters located beyond their service areas or even their states. The CCWC is an example of what will emerge as colleges partner to deal with the workforce needs of specific industrial sectors, with practices developed through the Trade Adjustment Act grants serving as the basis for many of these new collaborations. These grants could be an impetus to spur both the creativity and the capacity of community colleges to perform at new levels that will be able to sustain the programs after the grants vanish.

The experience of community college workforce programs provides the basis for new federal policy toward talent management. For example, the largest federal postsecondary grant program for low-income students, Pell Grants, is now being considered a part of the workforce development system as well as a means to complete a college degree (College Board 2013). In addition, federal policies to promote a sector strategy of technical innovation need to engage community colleges to provide the technical training programs to provide a workforce that can sustain and expand these innovations. Federal policies toward adult education need to take into account employment as an end goal, not just achievement of a high school General Educational Development.

Finally, it means the federal government will need to develop practical policies that deal with the development of industry certifications and nondegree credentials that are increasingly found in postsecondary learning institutions. How are they to be assessed? How are they linked to work-based learning systems such as apprenticeship? What sort of federal support will they obtain?

Paradoxically, one of the areas where community college involvement is most uncertain is within the traditional Workforce Investment System through the U.S. Department of Labor. For the most part, the current system emerged out of traditional labor market and training structures developed before community colleges became integral in the training of unemployed and incumbent workers. For many federal policymakers, the advantages of community colleges have not been fully appreciated. One important future issue will be the extent to which the community colleges are integrated within a comprehensive system, leveraged to complement the workforce system, or even replace the present system. But even with this question in limbo as the implications of the impending authorization of Workforce Innovation and Opportunity Act, there is no question that community colleges have been emerging since the Great Recession as a major player in the nation's future workforce development system.

314   Jacobs

References

Berger, Suzanne. 2013. *Making in America: From Innovation to Market*. Cambridge, MA: MIT Press.

College Board. 2013. *Rethinking Pell Grants*. New York: College Board.

Fischer, Karen. 2009. "As an Auto Industry Shrinks, a Community College Retools." *Chronicle of Higher Education* 55(35): A1.

Grubb, W. Norton, Norena Badway, Denise Bell, Debra Bragg, and Maxine Russman. 1997. *Workforce, Economic, and Community Development: The Changing Landscape of the Entrepreneurial Community College.* Berkeley, CA; Columbus, OH; Chandler, AZ: National Center for Research in Vocational Education, National Council for Occupational Education, and League for Innovation in the Community College.

HR Policy Association. 2011. *Blueprint for Jobs in the 21st Century: A Vision for a Competitive Human Resource Policy for the American Workforce.* Washington, DC: HR Policy Association. http://www.hrpolicy.org/downloads/blueprint/Blueprint%20for%20Jobs%20Report.pdf (accessed November 24, 2014).

Jacobs, James. 2012. "The Essential Role of Community Colleges in Rebuilding the Nation's Communities and Economies." In *Universities and Colleges as Economic Drivers*, Jason E. Lane and D. Bruce Johnstone, eds. Albany, NY: SUNY Press, pp. 191–204.

McCarthy, Mary Alice. 2014. *Beyond the Skills Gap*. Washington, DC: New America Ed Central.

State of Michigan. 2009. *No Worker Left Behind—Outcomes for the First 18 Months*. State of Michigan. http://www.michigan.gov/documents/nwlb/NWLB_Outcomes_Report_2009_10_23_298741_7.pdf (accessed April 9, 2015).

U.S. Department of Education. 2011. *The Condition of Education 2011*. Washington, DC: U.S. Department of Education http://nces.ed.gov/pubs2011/2011033.pdf (accessed November 24, 2014).

13
Wired65

Driving a Cross-State Regional
Manufacturing Strategy

Maria Flynn
Jobs for the Future

The emerging consensus vision of a twenty-first century workforce system elevates a number of strategic principles and practical design elements that have emerged and been tested in the past two decades. These involve strategies rooted in addressing the particular needs of specific industry sectors or occupational clusters, aligning workforce and regional economic development priorities more explicitly, organizing employers and providers by labor market regions rather than political jurisdictions, balancing the needs of high-growth and high-wage employers with the societal interest in helping low-skill adults advance in earnings and careers, and increasing the supply of workers with formal credentials recognized and valued by employers.

While not prevalent in all parts of the nation, these strategies have evolved over the past 20 years as a result of philanthropic and government investment. The new Workforce Innovation and Opportunity Act (WIOA), as signed into law by President Obama in 2014, specifically requires the use of such strategies, including career pathways, sector strategies, and strategic use of labor market information.

In the years leading up to the enactment of WIOA, a growing number of communities have developed regional partnerships that share these forward-looking characteristics. These efforts have provided entrepreneurial and creative local Workforce Investment Boards (WIBs) with an opportunity to forge new relationships with education and service providers, employer associations, and other stakeholders committed to a public-private human capital development strategy for their regional economy. It is this type of strong intermediary and convener role for WIBs that is envisioned in the new federal workforce legislation.

WIRED65

One particularly innovative and mature regional partnership is Wired65, a cross-state effort involving 26 counties along the I-65 corridor spanning Kentucky and Indiana.

Seven years ago, realizing that their labor markets were becoming increasingly interconnected and looking for ways to increase operational and strategic efficiency, workforce development, economic development, and education leaders in this bistate region came together to promote economic competitiveness through better connections between economic and workforce development across the regional labor market. The initial catalyst was the successful application for a $5 million U.S. Department of Labor (USDOL) Workforce Innovation in Regional Economic Development (WIRED) grant. Wired65 was one of 39 regions nationwide to receive one of these grants between 2006 and 2007, which rewarded strategies to transform economies through an emphasis on sectors and talent development. Wired65 invested in initiatives to connect students to careers, train individuals for higher-skilled jobs, and align regional institutions and resources toward the common goal of developing, retaining, and attracting individuals who can drive a twenty-first century economy (Wired65).

Wired65 is composed of four local WIBs: KentuckianaWorks, Lincoln Trail, and Cumberlands in Kentucky; and Workforce Development Association/Region 10 in Indiana. All too aware that their region's historically low skill and education levels have hampered economic growth since the decline of manufacturing began several decades ago, these publicly funded WIBs committed to work outside their traditional boxes to reorient the region's workforce development system, which was a traditional supply-side approach to a demand-driven, sector-based approach.

The regional partnership has grown and matured since the federal grant ended after 2010. Its evolution has been bolstered in recent years by participation in the National Fund for Workforce Solutions (National Fund), an initiative of national and local funders that partners with businesses and philanthropy to develop employer-driven workforce strategies to help low-wage workers and job seekers obtain career opportunities, while creating talent supply chains that close skills gaps and strengthen local economies. Wired65 is included as one of the National Fund's regional sites, through a Social Innovation Fund (SIF) grant to Jobs for the Future, the National Fund's implementation partner. The SIF is a program of the Corporation for National and Community Service, which combines public and private resources to grow the impact of innovative, community-based solutions that have compelling evidence of improving the lives of people in low-income communities throughout the United States.

This engagement with a national network of similar partnerships, coupled with an infusion of new federal and philanthropic investment, has helped Wired65 establish a public/private regional funding collaborative, invest in new employer-led workforce partnerships in key sectors, attract new private resources to augment the local workforce boards' public dollars, and drive critical system change efforts to promote expansion and sustainability. Since 2011, a total of $1,045,000 in leveraged and aligned resources has been committed to support the Wired65 effort, matching $466,000 awarded from the National Fund.[1] The combined $1.5 million that has been invested to date has been used to fund training programs and workforce partnerships in key sectors.

PROMOTING COMMON CREDENTIALS TO GET ON A MANUFACTURING CAREER LADDER

Since joining the National Fund in 2011, Wired65 has invested in employer-driven industry partnerships in sectors identified through labor market analysis: food and beverage, moving and storage, and automotive dealerships (National Fund 2010). Across the region's four local workforce investment areas, the greatest traction has been with manufacturing employers around better signaling of entry-level skills and credentials. This traction stems from growth led by major employers such as Ford and GE as well as their ecosystem of suppliers. In general, regional growth in manufacturing was strong compared to statewide and national data.

The partners decided to push for regional adoption of the entry-level certified production technician (CPT) certification offered by the

Manufacturing Skills Standards Council (MSSC). When they learned the certificate was not offered in Kentucky, they looked into programs in other states, including the Advancing Manufacturing initiative in Lafayette, Indiana, and laid the groundwork for regional implementation. Cumberlands WIB was the first regional entity to offer the MSSC course, followed by the KentuckianaWorks region at the newly formed Kentucky Manufacturing Career Center. With National Fund for Workforce Solutions funding, classes were then introduced at Work One, Southern Indiana's WIB, and in the Lincoln Trail region of south central Kentucky.

The strategy was to foster buy-in through incremental engagement steps. The first MSSC CPT classes were offered to incumbent employees of manufacturing companies in industry partnerships. This enabled employers to evaluate the training and certifications and provide clear feedback to the training provider. Their experience has led many employers to express a preference for the credential among new hires.

While each local WIB has its own manufacturing industry partnerships, the common credentials support regional commuting patterns. MSSC-credentialed candidates from southern Indiana or Elizabethtown, Kentucky, are invited to attend job fairs in Louisville, and credentialed Louisville job seekers have applied at companies in Lincoln Trail knowing that their MSSC credential will be recognized.

KENTUCKY MANUFACTURING CAREER CENTER

In Louisville, KentuckianaWorks has built on the stackable credentials approach to launch a sector-based career center for manufacturing. As defined by USDOL, stackable credentials are a sequence of credentials that can be accumulated over time to build up individuals' qualifications and help them move along a career pathway or up a career ladder to different and potentially higher-paying jobs.

After a year of planning driven by a 30-company Employer Advisory Group, the Kentucky Manufacturing Career Center (KMCC) opened in April 2013. Operated by Jefferson Community and Technical College in Louisville, the center strives to

- supply a ready workforce for growing manufacturing companies,
- provide the skills needed for job seekers and incumbent workers to move into and advance within this growing sector,
- serve as a resource for manufacturing companies to find trained employees or train existing workers,
- encourage a career pathway from manufacturing to engineering based on the National Association of Manufacturers' stackable credentials system (Manufacturing Institute 2014b), and
- encourage more people to consider and pursue a career in manufacturing.

Between May 2013 and July 2014, the center has served more than 674 job seekers and placed over 175 individuals into employment at an average starting wage of $12.33 an hour. The center has increased job placement success by having its career specialists work more directly and regularly with manufacturing employers. Initial data validate this employer-focused approach: KMCC's rate of placement per career specialist is higher than other One-Stop Career Centers in the region.

EMPLOYER SYSTEM CHANGE

To date, more than 20 companies throughout the Wired65 region have recognized the National Career Readiness Credential and MSSC CPT credentials in hiring decisions. Several members of the KMCC Employer Advisory Group already list the credentials in job postings and on their Web sites; 15 companies have hired MSSC-certified job seekers. Most recently, GE Appliance Park, one of the region's largest manufacturing employers, endorsed both the National Career Readiness Credential and MSSC CPT credentials and has begun giving preference to KMCC applicants in production position hiring.

KMCC Employer Advisory Group firms have formalized the organization by establishing a formal membership agreement that outlines requirements of membership. These requirements include agreeing to pay a $75 yearly fee; formally recognize the KMCC training programs on Web sites or job postings ("recognition" means that candidates will be guaranteed an interview if other requirements are met); and provide earnings and retention data on employees hired from the KMCC. Moving forward, they will examine the possibility of requiring employers to pay a fee to the center for placements after 90 days' retention that will fund training scholarships.

EDUCATION SYSTEM CHANGE

Wired65 worked closely with Jefferson Community and Technical College (JCTC) and Elizabethtown Community & Technical College to make the case for certifying an MSSC instructor and offering the CPT course. The Wired65 collaborative also lobbied the community colleges to provide nine credit hours for the four-week MSSC CPT course, thereby enabling the certification to seamlessly articulate into a comprehensive manufacturing program of study. In November 2013, Jefferson Community and Technical College began offering a new five-credit-hour multiskilled technician course at KMCC.

Recognizing the need to support entry-level workers in their ongoing pursuit of training and education, JCTC also employs a transition counselor to work with all KMCC students. With the Workforce Investment Boards' support for these kinds of changes, JCTC became one of fewer than 100 colleges in the United States named to the National Association of Manufacturers' "M-List" for teaching manufacturing students to industry standards (Manufacturing Institute 2014a).

POLICY CHANGE AND ADVOCACY

Commitment to a consistent regional sector-based approach by four WIBs has enabled job seekers and companies across 26 counties to rally around a common set of entry-level credentials. The KMCC is providing a new model of combining federally funded employment services with additional, sector-focused training tied more closely to employer needs. This is not the first sector-based One-Stop Career Center in the nation—it is predated by others such as the Workforce1 Industrial and Transportation Center in Queens, New York. However, its strong employer connections and focus on systems change in addition to traditional job training outcomes make it unique. The fundamental change has been having the employers take the lead role in driving the training agenda. Through this approach, employers started to realize that they cannot be passive and simply express concerns about the skill level of job candidates. Rather, they need to drive the conversation. As a result, the KMCC has emerged as an attractive model at a time when the workforce field and state and national policymakers are striving to identify and scale more effective job-driven training approaches.

KMCC and other Wired65 initiatives have emerged as promising workforce development practices. U.S. Secretary of Labor Thomas Perez visited the center in late 2013; he toured the facility, watched students in classes, and participated in a discussion with both students and representatives of local manufacturing companies and their training partners. Also in late 2013, KMCC was selected as the location for the Manufacturing Institute's National Manufacturing Day celebration, in recognition of its adoption of industry-recognized credentials and its promotion of manufacturing careers.

At the state level, at the request of the Kentucky Economic Development Cabinet, Wired65 has supported the recruitment of companies looking to relocate in Kentucky. Companies have visited the KMCC and attended Employer Advisory Group meetings, gaining a strong sense of the region's ability to produce a trained workforce response to employer needs.

The establishment and growth of KMCC and the expansion of manufacturing training in Lincoln Trail, Cumberlands, and Work One/ Southern Indiana come at a critical time for the region's manufacturing sector. The region has experienced recent growth in several manufacturing specialties, significantly outpacing the growth in other industries since the trough of the recession in 2009. Between June 2009 and June 2013, manufacturing employers added 12,890 jobs in the region—a growth rate of 21 percent, which is more than double the 10 percent rate for other jobs. Today, manufacturing accounts for 13 percent of the region's employment.

IMPLICATIONS FOR THE FIELD

Wired65's strategy for addressing both the supply and demand sides of the talent development equation provides three key lessons for the broader workforce field.

1) **Local WIBs can drive public-private systems change through their role as workforce intermediaries.** By joining together to tackle common regional labor market challenges, the four WIBs in Wired65 have successfully adopted common priorities and tactics, including focus sectors, common industry-recognized credentials, and employer engagement. Wired65 is an exemplar of a WIB taking on the role of workforce intermediary, highlighting the potential for WIBs to serve as effective regional conveners and brokers.

2) **Expand effective practices and discontinue those that do not yield positive results.** Wired65 has made a series of strategic data-driven decisions that have demonstrated their agility and capacity to meet the needs of both employers and job seekers. The region is a leading user of real-time labor market information, which enables leaders to make informed decisions about investments and program design. They also track performance outcomes to be sure that an investment is working. For example, when a transportation and logistics workforce partnership was performing unsatisfactorily, due to difficulty attracting participants, Wired65 staff stopped investing in the effort but also provided specific feedback and recommendations to the industry association partner on how program design changes could improve recruitment. Meanwhile, given KMCC's success to date, Wired65 is developing a request for a proposal for a Health Career One-Stop driven by the industry partnership, the Health Care Careers Collaborative of Greater Louisville.

3) **Strong alignment of public and private dollars enables a region to build and deploy demand-driven solutions.** The constraints of federal funding can at times be perceived as a deterrent to innovation, if only because WIBs are understandably cautious in their stewardship of federal funding. At times,

there are unclear interpretations of federal policies that result in fear of audit findings. With the additional flexibility of private dollars leveraged with public funding, the WIBs in the Wired65 Regional Workforce Partners felt more confident moving quickly to respond to employer demands, even when the response took the partnership outside its historical comfort zone of focusing more on supply side issues. In the past, just determining whether an employer-driven project was allowed under federal rules would significantly delay implementation. Surprisingly, as the partners have implemented new approaches with more flexible funding, they have discovered that WIA was perhaps less of an obstacle than long-standing local policies that could be changed by the board. In addition, the very process of going to the private philanthropic sector for investment has helped the WIBs reenvision themselves and their ambition. The region has also benefited from technical assistance from USDOL during the WIRED initiative and from National Fund coaches as part of the Social Innovation Fund investment. These activities have brought significant new energy, ideas, capacity, and partners to the regional workforce landscape.

Note

1. The Wired65 funders are JPMorgan Chase Foundation, Gheens Foundation, Community Foundation of Louisville, James Graham Brown Foundation, PNC Foundation, Network Center for Community Change, Louisville Redevelopment Authority, and Community Foundation of South Central Kentucky.

References

Corporation for National and Community Service (CNCS). "Social Innovation Fund/Funded Organizations." Washington, DC: CNCS. http://www.nationalservice.gov/programs/social-innovation-fund/previous-competitions/2010/jobs-future (accessed May 2, 2014).

Manufacturing Institute. 2014a. "The M-List." Washington, DC: National Association of Manufacturers. http://www.themanufacturinginstitute.org/Skills-Certification/M-List/M-List.aspx (accessed May 2, 2014).

———. 2014b. "NAM-Endorsed Certifications." Washington, DC: National Association of Manufacturers. http://www.themanufacturinginstitute .org/Skills-Certification/Certifications/NAM-Endorsed-Certifications.aspx (accessed July 8, 2014).

National Fund for Workforce Solutions. 2010. *Workforce Partnership Guidance Tool*. Boston: National Fund. http://nfwsolutions.org/sites/ nfwsolutions.org/files/publications/NFWS_workforce_guidance_tool _111110.pdf (accessed May 2, 2014).

Wired65. "Overview." Louisville, KY: Wired65. http://www.wired65.org (accessed April 30, 2014).

14
Workforce Innovation in Regional Economic Development (WIRED)

Nancy Hewat
Synthesis Evaluation & Research

Kevin Hollenbeck
W.E. Upjohn Institute for Employment Research

This case study highlights key lessons learned through an evaluation of the Workforce Innovation in Regional Economic Development WIRED Initiative (Generations II and III) that was conducted by the authors.[1] WIRED grantees were responsible for conceiving, designing, allocating, implementing, and managing their initiatives within some basic parameters established by the U.S. Department of Labor's Employment and Training Administration (ETA). WIRED regions were expected to identify regional boundaries and establish strategic priorities. The success of their efforts hinged on the ability of WIRED partners (a cross-section of public, private, and nonprofit interests) to collaborate, leverage partner resources, and encourage and support innovation. They were responsible for results in the sense that their efforts were expected to affect their communities and the region as a whole. The flexibility to define and shape a regional strategy in response to regional needs resulted in a diverse group of initiatives that served as the basis for the national WIRED evaluation.

The evaluation was responsive to ETA's interest that the evaluation focus on WIRED as a national strategy. It was primarily an implementation study to document the activities that regions were undertaking with WIRED funding and their effectiveness. However, the evaluation did include a net impact study to attempt to estimate the impact of the WIRED grants on regions' economies.

This case study highlights and discusses the implications of the lessons learned from WIRED and its evaluation, as appropriate, for current regional innovation cluster initiatives (including the multiagency-funded Initial Clusters; the Small Business Administration's Pilot Contract-Based Clusters; and the multiagency-funded Jobs Accelerator Collaboration Clusters, Advanced Manufacturing Jobs Accelerator Collaboration Clusters, and Rural Jobs Accelerator Collaboration Clusters) and future related initiatives that may be undertaken with the support of federal or state funding. This chapter provides an overview of the WIRED Initiative, a description of the evaluation of WIRED, a discussion of the findings from that evaluation, and a presentation of the implications that we derive from WIRED. The findings and implications will be useful for policymakers, agency leaders, and regional administrators to improve the effectiveness of future regional innovation clusters.

OVERVIEW OF WIRED

The WIRED Initiative was conceived and launched in late 2005 as the United States was slowly recovering from the 2000–2002 recession. The major economic concern at the time was international competitiveness. The intellectual precursor of WIRED is the work of Porter (1998, 2003), who recognized the power of clusters to advance regional economic growth.[2]

In its Solicitation for Grant Applications (SGA), ETA justified its investment as a way for regions "to implement ground-breaking strategies that will result in their workforce investment system becoming a key component of their region's economic development strategy. The ultimate goal of the WIRED Initiative is to expand employment and advancement opportunities for American workers and catalyze the creation of high-skill and high-wage opportunities." The notion of WIRED as a catalyst was used often by ETA in its documentation of the initiative, suggesting that the agency saw the role of federal support as being catalytic: necessary to get the reaction—that is, regional collaboration and the related leveraging of partner resources—under way, but not necessary for sustainability.

Ultimately, ETA funded 39 regions as a result of two SGAs. The first SGA was released in late 2005 and offered regions grants with terms of up to 36 months and awards of approximately $5 million annually (i.e., total awards of approximately $15 million). In February 2006, ETA selected 13 regions to be awarded grants. These regions became known as Generation I (Gen I). Interestingly, the first SGA did not require a sectoral or cluster approach—it indicated that ETA was looking for an innovative/transformational way to integrate workforce and economic development at the regional level to support the creation and expansion of high-skill, high-wage jobs. However, most of the regions proposed and implemented one. Presumably, the regions understood explicitly or implicitly the benefits of the agglomeration economies that arise from focusing on a sector or cluster.

An additional 13 regions that responded to the initial SGA were awarded planning grants of approximately $100,000 in 2006. In January 2007, these 13 regions were awarded 36-month grants that totaled approximately $5 million, that is, one-third the size of the Gen I awards. These 13 regions became known as Gen II.

In early 2007, ETA released a second SGA for WIRED. This solicitation was quite similar to the earlier one, except that in alignment with Gen II, the awards totaled approximately $5 million for the entire 36-month term of the grants. Other changes were made as well. For instance, the second SGA was explicit in describing the focus of WIRED: "Applicant(s) must describe the high-growth industries and economic sectors that will be the focus of the strategies."

In addition, grantees were required to include a "senior representative" of the workforce investment system of the region (i.e., chair or executive director of a local workforce investment board) as the lead or colead of the partnership.[3] In fall 2007, the final 13 regions of the WIRED Initiative were named, and dubbed Gen III.

With a total of $325 million invested in 39 regions, WIRED attracted considerable attention nationally as a large-scale effort by a federal agency to promote and support regional cluster development and growth. In Figure 14.1, the darkest shaded regions are Gen I, the next darkest are Gen II, and the lightest shaded regions are Gen III.

Figure 14.1 WIRED Regions in the United States and Puerto Rico

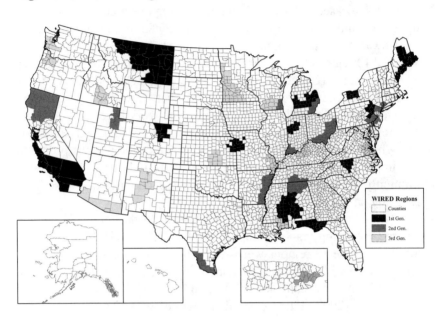

SELECTED FEATURES OF THE WIRED GRANT PROGRAM

Funding

The funding for WIRED came from fees paid by employers to obtain H-1B visas for their employees. These fees were intended to support the development of skills in U.S. citizens so that they could compete with the foreign workers for whom the visas were being obtained. Congress established allowable expenditures for these funds, generally permitting their use for job training and related curriculum development. ETA "captured" these funds and allocated them to the WIRED Initiative. The official grant applicants were states, and as fiscal agent, they were ultimately held accountable for unallowable costs. Due in part to the problems that Gen I grantees encountered about allowable uses of H-1B funds, the second SGA was far more explicit about how H-1B funds could be used.[4]

To achieve its goal of enhancing regional economic development, the WIRED solicitation expected, but did not require, applicants to align resources and leverage funds from federal, state, and regional/local partners; the private sector; investor community; and philanthropies.

The second SGA was quite explicit about this, offering applicants extra points for providing information about local matching resources.

Activities

Across the 39 regions, the WIRED Initiative supported a wide gamut of activities. Most regions offered some sort of customized training to incumbent workers. The training was often located at community colleges and conducted by their staff members. In many cases, the training activities involved curriculum development as well as the provision of the training. Many of the regions also funded small business technical assistance, entrepreneurship programs, and occasional seminars on special topics.

WIRED represented a change in how ETA approached grant making by asking grantees to define the geographic boundaries of their economic regions. They were not constrained by predetermined jurisdictional boundaries such as workforce investment areas or community college service areas. In fact, seven of the regions crossed state lines.

ETA required each region to complete a comprehensive implementation plan that had to be approved before any funds were released. This turned out to be problematic in many instances. For most regions, the ETA review took several months. There was some benefit to having grantees think through the implementation process, but the delays caused by multiple layers of review and a back and forth revision process compromised the momentum that had been established between public and private partners during the proposal and plan development process. The review process furthermore reinforced opinions among some employers of the inefficiency of the federal government.

Another ETA requirement was the development of an asset map for the region (Kempner and Levine 2008). All of the WIRED grantees met this requirement, but very few grantees said that the map was useful or had any lasting strategic or operational value. In general, the grantees felt that they were well aware of the regional assets and felt that it was inefficient to have to use resources to formalize a list of them.

States were the fiscal agent for the grants, but at the regional level the grants were administered by an intermediary organization: a community college, workforce investment board, regional chamber, or an arm of a university. The region had the authority to decide how they would allocate grant funds as long as federal rules and regulations were followed.

Grantees that predetermined how WIRED funds would be allocated had less flexibility in how to respond to changing conditions and needs over the three-year grant period. The lack of flexibility was particularly problematic in regions that were hardest hit as the economy began to spiral downward in early 2008 and continued to follow that trajectory over the course of the WIRED grant period.

Performance Measures

A variety of performance measures were referenced in the SGAs.

- Common performance measures were to be used to report outcomes for individuals who received training. In all three grant generations, regions were required to report this data.

- Process-oriented measures associated with activities mentioned in regional implementation plans (e.g., curricula developed, articulation agreements established). The specific mix of measures was unique to each WIRED grantee.

- System-based outcome measures focused on the longer-term effects that WIRED efforts would have on participating regions, including the elimination of barriers to innovation, increased interdisciplinary collaboration, the elimination of redundant programs, and increased efficiency. To our knowledge, none of these system-based measures were ever defined, nor were data on them collected. Whereas the fact that these metrics were not reported (and probably not produced), having them listed in the SGA may have served the purpose of getting regions to consider the longer-term outcomes of their activities.

According to the SGAs, these measures were to be monitored throughout the three-year implementation period.

Technical Assistance

ETA contracted with national vendors, including Mathematica Policy Research, to provide technical assistance to regions on a voluntary basis. Furthermore, ETA organized several annual national convenings for grantees from all three generations, which appeared to us as quite useful in terms of sharing best practices, discussing challenges, and informal networking. In addition to the national technical assistance and convenings, many of the regions set up informal affinity communities or hosted regional convenings.

EVALUATION DESIGN

ETA funded two evaluation contracts. One evaluator conducted an assessment of the Gen I regions (Berkeley Policy Associates), and the second evaluator (our team) examined the Gen II and III regions. Both evaluations were primarily implementation studies using mixed methods: documents were reviewed, all sites were visited at least twice, partner surveys were fielded, and social networking data were collected and analyzed.

Both evaluations also attempted to estimate the net impact of the WIRED grant on the regions' economies, although these facets were not central to the evaluations. The Gen I evaluation examined postgrant regional economic activity relative to the states in which the grants were located. Our evaluation used a matched region approach in which the regional economic activity in each WIRED region was compared to the overall economic activity in a region that was matched to it based on characteristics such as size, population, median income, education, and industrial mix.

In general, the evaluations relied on grantee self-reported data on the Common Performance Measures, and on other customized data such as training enrollments and completions, curricula developed, and technical assistance provided. There was no requirement for regions to employ their own evaluator, and that rarely occurred.

A key topic for ETA was the sustainability of the regional collaboratives. In theory, the WIRED funding was intended to be a catalyst that would result in an ongoing collaborative effort. We explored this topic during each of the site visits, and since the evaluation period of performance exceeded the implementation period of the grants, we were able to interview (by phone) a few partners in each of the regions after their grants had expired, and we visited a half dozen of the sites that seemed to have viable sustainability plans.

DISCUSSION

Funding

The overall funding level for the Initiative, approximately $325 million for grants plus additional funds for a national technical assistance effort, attracted a lot of national attention. The notoriety helped to build momentum, but it was not necessarily sufficient to replace the momentum that had been lost through the slow review and approval of implementation plans prior to releasing funds.

Leveraging

Because of its emphasis on providing catalytic support, ETA had each regional collaborative produce a resource mapping report that documented potential sources of resources in the area. The need for leveraging was more acute for Gen II/III. The SGA expectations for these grants were the same as those for Gen I, despite the fact that the WIRED grants had been cut by 66 percent.

In addition to asking grantees to furnish information about leveraged resources (direct and in-kind) in their original grant proposals, ETA used its regional offices to gather ongoing information about leveraged funds. The quality of this evidence was questionable, however. Regional administrators found it difficult to attribute recent federal and state grant awards to the fact that the region had received a WIRED grant and to determine how aligned other grant projects were with the region's WIRED goals.

Limitations of Single Funding Source

ETA was fortunate to have funds available through H-1B to implement the WIRED Initiative. However, as noted above, Gen I and Gen II regions' activities were constrained because of limitations on the uses of H-1B funding. Actually, the problems arose because ETA did not announce the limitations until after it had approved implementation plans. Our presumption is that the individuals in ETA who were responsible for the initial SGA and grantee selection did not learn about the constraints on the H-1B funds until late 2006 or early 2007. In many cases, the grantees were committed to the activities that were identified in their implementation plans, so they needed to search for additional funds to support activities that were not allowable under H-1B. They were quite often successful at finding the funding alternatives.

Grant Program Design and Implementation

Among the first activities undertaken in each region was the formation of a governing board that included public and private sector partners. Their primary role tended to be in the early phase of the initiatives: overseeing allocations and expenditure of grant funds.

In theory and in practice, allowing the grantees to define the boundaries of their regions and to identify industry clusters that were important to their regional economies increased the sense of ownership among regional partners and allowed them to target their efforts based on their knowledge of regional needs. Not only could the regions identify activities that met local needs, but regions could also establish meaningful economic areas and labor sheds. However, in regions that had more than one community college and/or local Workforce Investment Board (which was the vast majority of the regions), competitiveness among these institutions and agencies persisted. In our view, the most successful regions were able to overcome these divisive influences through effective leadership and timely and accurate communication.

Employer and Partner Engagement

Perhaps the most difficult challenge for WIRED regions to address was the engagement of private sector employers. The opportunity costs for employers to become involved were substantial, and so they rightfully wanted to see substantial value added for their organizations before they invested time, effort, and resources. As might be expected, individuals from smaller firms were particularly time- and resource-challenged. Some WIRED regions targeted activities on technical assistance or training for small businesses, and these were generally well attended and considered effective. Staff from larger businesses were somewhat more inclined to participate, although oftentimes these individuals were active in the regional activities from an altruistic or civic duty obligation, rather than as recipients of value added, such as having incumbent workers participate in customized training or having management receive technical assistance.

Activities

In almost all the regions, WIRED funds were used to purchase training equipment for educational institutions. The H-1B funding carried many constraints on the purchase of equipment, but basically, as long as the equipment was proposed to be used for training purposes and not for inventory acquisition or general business operations, it was okay. The potential for problems arose when grant partners used equipment acquisition procedures of their home institution that were inconsistent with H-1B requirements. Limited monitoring, poor communications, and delays in processing reimbursement invoices exacerbated this problem. This was an issue among regional partners and between the regions and ETA.

Outcomes

As noted, even though the first SGA enumerated specific outcomes for regions, data were reported sporadically, and to our knowledge, there was no effort to confirm their validity. Toward the end of the grant period, ETA required regions to enter training data into its automated data system, called Workforce Investment Act Single Record Data (WIASRD). Despite sporadic compliance with this requirement, the WIASRD database contained several thousand observations of training. Furthermore, in customized outcome reporting, regions noted that literally hundreds of curricula were developed.

Less quantitative, but perhaps more important, site visitors noted that an important outcome that had occurred in some regions was the adoption of "regionalism," defined as a general attitude that economic development that occurred anywhere in the region was to be applauded whether or not it directly benefited a particular locale in the region.

Also noted during site visits was the fact that partners used informal networks that were established as part of the regional collaboration. While the use of these networks oftentimes was unrelated to WIRED, they were useful for the productivity of the firms that were involved in networking activities. Through partnership meetings or through general communication means such as newsletters, the participants in the collaboration got to know each other and each other's workforce development needs and interests. These individuals became resources that were relied upon for general business purposes. That is, when participants were interviewed, they often noted that a major advantage of participating was developing a network of other individuals involved in the cluster.

Sustainability

The theory behind the WIRED Initiative was that the funding provided by ETA would be a catalyst for regions to develop effective collaborations that would become self-sustainable. Using sustainability as a criterion, the WIRED Initiative had very little success. Most of the regional collaborations disbanded.

There are many possible reasons for the lack of sustainability/catalytic momentum. The limited timeline of the grants (formally three years that usually stretched to four years with no-cost extensions) made it difficult to achieve sustainable momentum, especially given the delays caused by the implementation plan review and approval process. The few WIRED regions that were able to continue their regional efforts had already established a strong foundation for regional action before the WIRED grant was awarded. Another problem was that many of the grantees, especially those led by education and workforce development agencies, interpreted sustainability as the continuation of funding for specific projects or programs that were developed during the grant period.

Perhaps the most important reason that sustainability failed was the onset of the Great Recession in 2007–2009. Firms that survived the recession cut their training budgets severely, trimmed their employee rolls, cut costs, and did whatever they could to survive. As a result, incumbent training demand fell precipitously. Emerging worker training also was hard to justify since very little hiring was being done in the economy.

IMPLICATIONS FOR FEDERAL AND STATE AGENCIES

Providing seed funding for a region may be a useful catalyst for bringing together economic and workforce development entities. However, the funding should have reasonable expectations about achievable outcomes that can be accurately measured. Indicators used to measure the success of a grant program need to be aligned with the goals of the regional initiatives that receive funding.

Having a single source of funding, and in particular, having a source of funding that is constrained in many ways, makes it difficult to implement viable initiatives at the local level. Smaller grants funded by several different agencies would increase the sense of ownership and engagement in activities at the federal, state, and regional levels. Many of the regional partners were attracted to WIRED because of the potential it offered for short- and longer-term skill development benefits. However, the limitations on the use of the H-1B funds made it more difficult for grantees to address all the elements of their regional strategies. Furthermore, engaging federal partners other than ETA proved to be difficult, due at least in part to the fact that ETA's H-1B revenue stream was the only source of support.

Grant programs that provide multiyear funding and that are intended to have long-term impact need to have very general goals that are achievable under changing economic and political circumstances. WIRED started out with very clear expectations that grants were intended to catalyze the creation of high-skill, high-wage jobs. Local regions adopted implementation plans consistent with that goal. Several years into the effort, ETA altered the goal and requested that regions assist low-wage workers. Then the Great Recession hit and ETA communicated a goal of reducing layoffs. The regions felt whipsawed by the changing priorities.

Concomitant with the notion that the federal agency needs to have very general, flexible goals is the idea that local agencies also need to maintain flexibility. The ability of regions to respond to changing economic conditions was compromised when they preallocated all or most of the WIRED grant funds at the proposal stage, which was done because ETA announced that H-1B funds needed to be competitively bid unless partners and their respective projects were listed in the winning proposal.

Large federal grants gain the attention of stakeholders but also increase political pressure on the funding agency and grantees to perform. WIRED funds attracted national attention because of their large grant awards and ETA's national communications campaign promoting WIRED. This attention attracted the notice of policymakers, who were aware that the funds were allocated rather narrowly to a relative few rather than distributed broadly to workforce agencies across the nation. This development added pressure on ETA, and the grantees, to achieve measureable (job placement) results. The pressure began to grow midway through the grant period as the Great Recession began to deepen.

The high-profile nature of WIRED led to a lesson in grant management for ETA. Initially, ETA assigned fairly high-level staff to serve as intermediaries between the regions and the federal government, which helped to open lines of communication, making the federal agency more accessible and responsive to regional needs. ETA soon learned how important it was to use staff who had recent, field-based workforce system experience. The initial strategy of assigning high-level agency leaders as intermediaries proved to be problematic because the leaders were not well versed on the detailed implementation questions and issues that were raised by the regions.

It is not clear whether there was any value to having (the governor of) the state be the official applicant and fiscal agent for the regional grants. When regions involved multiple states, it caused conflicts between the state that was awarded the grant and other states that were involved. Furthermore, states were being held accountable for decision making at the substate regional level.

Giving local and regional stakeholders the flexibility to define their economic regions, set grant goals, and allocate grant funds maximizes the ability of grantees to be responsive to regional needs. Both the federal and regional entities need to be aware, however, of how limited the infusion of funding is compared to the size of the regional economy. The first SGA and the evaluation request for proposals incorporated a set of assumptions about what WIRED could achieve; these assumptions—that there would be measureable results on a wide range of business-expansion-related indicators—were not realistic. Not only were the expected outcomes unrealistic given the size of the grants, in many cases they were not measurable. And even when data were available, it was not possible to attribute those outcomes to the efforts undertaken by WIRED partners.

ETA initiated and administered WIRED with a belief that its support would be catalytic. Assessing the success of the catalytic power of federal support may be accomplished by examining the sustainability of the regional collaborations. Evidence of short-term sustainability may include the continuation of funding for a specific training program or the continued operation of a regional planning board that was formed as a grant-sponsored governance group. A longer time period is needed to assess the broader catalytic effects of a regional initiative. By extending the timeline for the evaluation beyond the grant period, it will be possible to assess the longer-term catalytic effects of the grant investment on the collaborative relationships, resource leveraging, and other follow-up activities.

Finally, public agencies need to consider whether innovation is a realistic goal for a taxpayer-funded (or otherwise publicly funded) initiative. Administrative issues and accountability are necessary in such situations, and these may constrain the "thinking outside the box" that is necessary for innovation to occur.

Notes

1. The authors have a unique perspective, having undertaken the evaluation of WIRED (Gen II and III) (see Hewat and Hollenbeck [2009, 2010]) and recently having become involved in an evaluation of the Jobs and Innovation Accelerator Challenge (JIAC and AM/JIAC) grants. The second round of JIAC grants were targeted on advanced manufacturing; hence the acronym AM/JIAC).
2. The work from Mills, Reynolds, and Reamer (2008) is an important contribution to the literature on regional innovation clusters.

3. In many private conversations with staff from ETA and with persons in leadership roles in the regions, we were told that ETA had received criticism about the lack of involvement of the local workforce investment system in Gen I and Gen II, and so it included this requirement in the Gen III SGA.

4. In developing their formal implementation plans, some of the Gen I regions had included summer science camps, many targeted for young girls, and some regions had included curriculum development in science, technology, engineering, and mathematics (STEM) areas for K–12 and postsecondary institutions. After these plans had been approved, ETA announced that H-1B funds could not be spent on youth under 16. Other problems that were encountered included a prohibition on the use of H-1B funds for marketing or for foreign travel.

References

Hewat, Nancy, and Kevin M. Hollenbeck. 2009. *Nurturing America's Growth in the Global Marketplace through Talent Development: An Interim Report on the Evaluation of Generations II and III of WIRED.* Report submitted to the U.S. Department of Labor, Employment and Training Administration. Washington, DC: U.S. Department of Labor, Employment and Training Administration.

———. 2010. "Evaluation of Regional Collaborations for Economic Development." Paper presented at the 32nd Annual Fall Research Conference of the Association for Public Policy Analysis and Management (APPAM), held in Boston, November 4–6.

Kempner, Randall, and Bruce Levine. 2008. *Asset Mapping Roadmap: A Guide to Assessing Regional Development Resources.* Report submitted to the U.S. Department of Labor Employment and Training Administration. Washington, DC: Council on Competitiveness. http://www.compete.org/images/uploads/File/PDF%20Files/CoC_Illuminate_2008.pdf (accessed September 26, 2014).

Mills, Karen G., Elizabeth B. Reynolds, and Andrew Reamer. 2008. *Clusters and Competitiveness: A New Federal Role for Stimulating Regional Economies.* Washington, DC: Brookings Institution. http://www.brookings.edu/~/media/research/files/reports/2008/4/competitiveness%20mills/clusters%20report.pdf (accessed September 26, 2014).

Porter, Michael E. 1998. "Clusters and the New Economics of Competition." *Harvard Business Review* November-December: 77–90.

———. 2003. "The Economic Performance of Regions." *Regional Studies* 37(6-7): 549–578.

15
Workforce Development in a Targeted, Multisector Economic Strategy

The Case of State University of New York's College of Nanoscale Science and Engineering

Laura I. Schultz
State University of New York Polytechnic Institute

Alan Wagner
Angela Gerace
University at Albany, State University of New York

Thomas Gais
Rockefeller Institute of Government

Jason E. Lane
Lisa Montiel
State University of New York

Cutting-edge strategies for regional economic development aim to harness and leverage the expertise and resources of universities, industry, and government to generate economic growth. Such strategies often follow the Triple Helix innovation model, building out innovation infrastructure to stimulate regional economic activity (Etzkowitz and Leydesdorff 1997). Economic growth emerges, in part, from a workforce with the skills needed to take up jobs within the R&D clusters and to attract new firms in associated sectors to the region (Schultz 2012; see also Bartik 2009 and Moretti 2012). This case study describes how the State University of New York's (SUNY) Colleges of Nanoscale Science and

Engineering (CNSE)—a state-supported, high tech/higher education, public-private partnership geared toward economic development—has led to transformation in the Capital Region's workforce. More specifically, the case demonstrates CNSE's roles in fostering the development of the nanotechnology workforce at different levels and types of education skills, in response to information about local employer demand. Initial results indicate the potential of CNSE's approach to workforce development to address growing and evolving nano-related skill and workforce needs in the region and beyond, though further research is required.

CNSE AND ECONOMIC DEVELOPMENT

Established in 2001, CNSE emerged as a key component of state policy development geared to reversing a long-term decline in New York's upstate economy, particularly the loss of high-tech manufacturing, which had fallen to less than 4 percent of New York State's economic output. At CNSE's founding, New York State and IBM jointly invested $150 million for the creation of a research center dedicated to nanoelectronics and nanotechnology, with CNSE also offering graduate degrees in nanoscale science and engineering. CNSE was selected to host the center based on its already extensive research portfolio in semiconductor fabrication and existing relationships with industrial partners such as IBM, SEMATECH, Texas Instruments, and General Electric (Schultz 2011). Following the Triple Helix framework, CNSE manifests a unique university-industry-government collaborative research center with a core mission of nanotechnology research and development, deployment, and economic development.

Since 2001, Tokyo Electron, Applied Materials, SEMATECH, and 300 other collaborators have joined IBM in colocating research operations at CNSE to take advantage of state of the art infrastructure for the development of next-generation technologies. To date, CNSE has attracted $20 billion in private and public investment in the physical infrastructure needed for the research, development, and manufacturing scale-up of advanced nanotechnologies in areas such as semiconductors, electronics, energy, and pharmaceuticals (Schultz 2011). Nanotechnology R&D carried out at CNSE has complemented substantial public and private investment in nanotechnology-related manufacturing in the Capital Region. In 2012, GlobalFoundries commenced production at its new $4.6 billion chip manufacturing facility, Fab8 (with $1.2 billion in New York State subsidies), in Malta, New York, which employs more than 2,200 workers. A $10 billion expansion is expected to increase employment to 3,200 (Rulison 2014). Other companies now located in the Capital Region include equipment manufacturers Vistec and clean-room construction contractors M+W Group. In 2014, the SUNY Board of Trustees approved the merger of CNSE and the SUNY Institute of Technology (Utica, New York). The merged institution is named SUNY Polytechnic Institute.

CNSE AND WORKFORCE DEVELOPMENT IN NEW YORK'S CAPITAL REGION

There is limited but growing information on labor market demand and needs for the Capital Region's nanotechnology economy. A particular difficulty with extant employment data from routine collections carried out by the U.S. Department of Labor is that existing classification schemes do not enable a good delineation of enterprises and employment in the nanotechnology economy. Specialized studies undertaken for nanotechnology-related industry nationally suggest that a wide range of education levels and skills is needed (Roco 2011; Yawson 2010). For the Capital Region, CNSE conducts its own quarterly census of nanotechnology employment. With the help of industrial partners, CNSE assembles information on the number of employees in nano-related manufacturing, by job description. As of 2013, CNSE and regional industrial partners accounted for over 7,000 employees in the Capital Region's nanotechnology economy.

Evidence on skills gaps and likely needs with respect to the regional nanotechnology economy is limited. The Siena Research Institute's (2014) annual survey of upstate business leaders elicits broad projections of hiring and broad assessments of the quality of the local workforce. These projections and assessments lack the detail necessary to guide the development and/or expansion of degree or training programs geared to nano-related industry. As employment in the sector has ramped up, the largest nanotechnology-based employer (Global Foundries) reported that the Capital Region's workforce supplied about half of those needed to fill its own job openings (Hagerty 2013). Many employers confront similar conditions, as reported in a Siena Research Institute survey, from a tabulation of responses to the question, ". . . is there an ample supply of local workers that are appropriately trained for your employment needs?" About half of upstate business leaders responded "yes," with somewhat lower shares for business leaders in the Albany region or for all upstate manufacturing. According to Global Foundries, the greatest difficulties appeared in recruitment of those with two-year degrees and specialized training in applied science, technology, engineering, and math (STEM) fields (Hagerty 2013). A 2008 report assessing upstate New York's potential for attracting nanoscale manufacturing, however, found that CNSE is a good source for well-trained engineering graduates (Semico Research Corporation 2008).

CNSE obtains information on likely employment needs, by education level and skill, partly through discussions with ongoing and new industrial partners. Within structured partnerships designed specifically to provide education and training, employers provide some indication of hiring needs. That input helps shape the size and design of the training provided. One very distinct example is the Center for Construction Trades Training, a partnership between primarily CNSE and M+W Group that provides specialized apprenticeship for union members needing to meet special demands of nanoscale construction. The partnership developed on the basis of skill needs of the industrial partner; it relies on CNSE for development and delivery of the curriculum and access to CNSE's industrial scale facilities for real-world experience.

CNSE also obtains information on likely employment needs from firms anticipating hiring. These firms seek the assistance of CNSE in recruitment of qualified workers in the near term through job fairs. From 2006 to 2013, CNSE-hosted job fairs have accounted for more than 1,500 job postings, covering the full span of education and training requirements as identified by the participating industrial partners. The volume and profile of posted job openings provide real-time measures of additional demand from employers. In addition, information on nano-related employment demand is fouond in publicly available agreements established between New York State and firms receiving incentives to relocate in the Capital Region. These firms are obliged to report the number of jobs created and retained.

Table 15.1 contains brief descriptions of new, expanded, or modified workforce development programs yielding the qualifications and skills needed for nano-related jobs. As shown there, workforce development for the Capital Region's nano-related economic development aligns with the profile of the skill demands noted above. An important finding of this study is that CNSE is engaged at all levels and in all types of workforce development, not just its own academic degrees in nanoscale science and engineering. In what follows, we elaborate on the brief descriptions to convey more fully the levels and types of education and training provided, how information on workforce needs shaped the provision, CNSE's role, and specific program outcomes insofar as they can be gauged.

Graduate and Undergraduate Degrees

CNSE's most direct role in workforce development is through the supply of graduates in nanoscale science and engineering at the bachelor's, master's, and PhD levels. The degree programs strongly complement CNSE's research and development work, as the most advanced students participate in that work and some graduates remain as postdocs. More broadly, expansion of the master's and bachelor's degree programs has followed growth in nanotechnology-related industry and associated employment demands. The college graduated its first PhD and master's degrees in 2004 and its first bachelor's degrees in 2013. Curricula are cross-disciplinary, with concentrations in materials engineering, nanobiology, nanoelectronics engineering, energy applications, and economic impacts. Graduates in nanobiology, for example, will have learned the physical, chemical, and engineering principles underlying the methods they are using.

CNSE's own data on graduates show that one-third have accepted positions in the nanotechnology economy in the Capital Region. At the graduate level, a little more than half (54 percent) take up jobs in New York State, almost all in nano-related industry. These data come from a regularly updated database of graduates, containing information on employment status, location of job, and salary. On selected metrics, CNSE's graduates are more likely to be employed in-field and in-state

Table 15.1 College of Nanoscale Science and Engineering (CNSE) Engagement in Workforce Development for the Capital Region's Nanotechnology Economy

Level and type of skill development	CNSE as provider.	CNSE as partner.
Higher education		
Degree and certificate studies	Bachelor's degrees in nanoscale science and engineering. Graduates: 49 since 2013; 16 in 2014.	Nanotechnology-related associate's degrees and certificates offered at six regional community and technical colleges. Coordinated through the Northeast Advanced Technological Education Center (NEATEC), a training and information center built on a community college/higher education/industry partnership. Funding: $3 million from the National Science Foundation to establish NEATEC. Graduates (Four New York community college sites only): 156 since 2008, 36 in 2013.
	Master's and PhDs in nanoscale science and engineering. Graduates: 159 since 2004; 18 in 2014.	
Internships	Summer research internships for undergraduates, open to students outside CNSE	Internship for community college students, consisting of 20 weeks at CNSE and GlobalFoundries.
Apprenticeship		Center for Construction Trades Training, with M+W Group, offering training in nano-related construction. Funding: $3.5 million, from state of New York, M+W Group, CNSE, and Arsenal Business and Technology Partnership. Completers: estimated 200 per year.

On-the-job training	CNSE technicians.	GlobalFoundries.
K–12 education		
Curriculum		Tech Valley High School, regional "school of choice," under governance of Capital Region and Questar III BOCES Funding: Boards of Cooperative Education Services (BOCES), New York State, school districts, and corporate and philanthropic sponsors. Graduates: 85 since 2011; 29 in 2013.
		NanoHigh, with Albany City School District Completers: 125 since 2007; 13 in 2014.
		Early College in High School, Ballston Spa Central School District, and Hudson Valley Community College. Funding: estimated $350,000 to date from New York State and agencies, plus additional public funds through regional BOCES. Completers: 65 since 2013, 43 in 2014 (next year from 17 area school districts).
		Field trips to CNSE and teacher development activities to enrich science, technology, and math classes.

SOURCE: Information assembled from program materials, agency reports, newsletters, press releases, and interviews.

than is the case nationally or for other SUNY programs. With respect to field of employment, the most recent national survey of doctorate recipients showed that 11 percent of science and 40 percent of engineering doctorates accepted positions in industry—both lower than the CNSE experience. With respect to employment, unpublished results from an analysis of matched wage records for all SUNY graduates show that slightly less than half of all graduates with postbachelor's engineering degrees were employed in New York State. The latter figure is not comparable to the CNSE estimate. The SUNY-matched wage record data pick up employment two quarters after graduation, while CNSE's data are updated as faculty and staff learn about graduate employment. Moreover, the SUNY-matched record data include any employment for which a wage record is generated (and so would include, for example, doctoral graduates on postdoctoral appointments at CNSE or elsewhere in New York State). On this SUNY-matched record metric, the comparable in-state employment rate for CNSE master's and doctoral graduates is about two-thirds.

Community Colleges

In 2005, Hudson Valley Community College, in partnership with CNSE and with input from local firms, established a new specialized semiconductor manufacturing technology associate degree program aimed at preparing graduates for jobs as clean-room technicians or workstation operators in the region's nano-related economy. By 2010, CNSE's engagement in such programs extended to six area community and technical colleges (four in New York, one in Vermont, and one in Massachusetts). The National Science Foundation–funded Northeast Advanced Technology Education Center provides the formal framework for the community colleges to engage with CNSE, other universities, and local employers to identify workforce training needs and develop and offer nanomanufacturing modules and specialized degrees. CNSE participates in curriculum development and offers hands-on instruction in its clean-room labs. Recently, CNSE and GlobalFoundries partnered with the programs to offer capstone internships that provide real-world experiences as students approach graduation.

The degree programs are relatively new, with limited information on the numbers of students enrolled, eventual graduates, and of graduates, those employed. With reference to unpublished analyses from matched wage records for all SUNY graduates, an estimated 53 percent of all SUNY associate's degree recipients in engineering fields were employed in New York State in the second quarter after graduation. The comparable figure for the community colleges in New York providing specialized technology degrees in partnership with CNSE was slightly higher, at 54 percent. However, the latter calculations include all associate's degrees in engineering, and so do not provide a good measure of in-state employment rates for graduates from the specialized technology degree programs alone.

On-the-Job and Advanced Vocational Training

Targeted nano-related workforce training needs are identified and programs developed in response to employer demand. At both the Center for Construction Trades Training, a partnership between CNSE and M+W Group to provide apprenticeship training related to nanoscale construction, and GlobalFoundries, which provides on-the-job training for workstation operators, employer-identified skill needs drive provision. CNSE's role resides in the development and delivery of the curriculum.

K–12 Education

Workforce development associated with the region's nano-related economic development extends to the high school level. The learning opportunities include innovative nano-related science and technology coursework offered at Tech Valley High School, a regional "school of choice" relocating to CNSE, Albany High School's NanoHigh, and Ballston Spa's Early College High School, among others. Initiated by the school districts or regional Boards of Cooperative Education Services (BOCES) with state funding as additional incentive, these programs are shaped in part through engagement with CNSE. Teachers participate in CNSE workshops and receive curriculum materials from CNSE. Students learn in class sessions led by CNSE staff or on field trips to the clean-room labs at CNSE.

While similar if less intensive support for teaching and learning is made available by CNSE to schools and teachers throughout the Capital

Region, the more structured programs identified here purposefully lead students to advanced studies and eventual jobs in the field. In Ballston Spa's Early College High School program, students dual-enroll at Hudson Valley Community College, attend project-based classes at Hudson Valley's site in Malta, New York (some classes delivered by community college faculty), in the mornings, and on completion earn up to 20 credits toward a specialized nano-related associate's degree at the community college.

Information supplied by school officials shows that more than half of graduates of Tech Valley High School and a similar share of completers of Ballston Spa's Early College High School program appear to continue studies in science, technology, engineering, and math fields, including nano specializations. This rate of continuation into these fields is about four times the rate for all college-going high school graduates. The comparison, however, does not take account of differences in interests or other characteristics between students in the structured programs and those following regular high school course work. Yet, according to information supplied by school officials, the innovative technology-based programs just described enroll a good mix of students, from both urban and rural schools and from a range of socioeconomic backgrounds (as many as one-third are on free or reduced lunch and almost 20 percent have special needs).

CONCLUSION

CNSE's engagement in workforce development follows the model of university-industry-government partnership adopted in the Capital Region's nanotechnology economic development strategy. As shown in Table 15.1, the school serves as a partner in most of the examples of education and training. In this way, it contributes to a much larger volume of nano-related workforce development than the number of its own degrees would suggest. Partnerships for CNSE take the form of collaboration with industry in identification of employment needs and the development of curricula, with other educational providers for delivery of instruction at all levels, and with local, state, and federal governments as well as industry partners for funding.

As the brief descriptions suggest, CNSE's engagement in work-force development varies by level and type and training. The school is fully responsible for the design and delivery of its own degree programs and internships and training for those working in clean labs on-site. For community college partnerships, CNSE works with industrial part-ners as well as other universities and the community colleges to discern the employment needs, design the curricula, and deliver the instruc-tion. For specialized training partnerships, it assumes responsibility for the development and delivery of the training, but it relies on industrial partners for information on skill needs and program volume as well as financial support. For the high school partnerships, CNSE's role is largely in the domain of curriculum development and delivery. The school provides consistency across these levels and types of education and training insofar as it ensures coverage and depth of nanotechnology content and associated skill development. This consistency is achieved through CNSE's participation in curriculum development, instruction, and hands-on learning experiences. Yet, CNSE assumes no responsibil-ity for the overall coordination of provision of the workforce develop-ment programs. It relies on partnership, and particularly on employer demand in terms of recruitment needs and skills requirement as mani-fested to CNSE or within existing partnerships, to initiate development of the programs.

Evidence on the effectiveness of such an approach remains lim-ited, if suggestive. Job postings, employer requests for training, and employer expectations of likely employment needs are anchored on the demand side, and thus are more closely tied to near-term economic activity. Data on employment outcomes of the programs remain incom-plete and dispersed. Information needed to assess the supply response to evolving employment needs is not (yet) available. The development of such information represents a useful target for further work.

Notwithstanding the limitations, such evidence as exists raises the possibility that workforce development programs organized through partnerships may facilitate a dynamic response to changing employ-ment needs in the nano-economy, allowing for expansion of provision where demand for skills warrant it and for elimination of provision when demand or requisite program requirements are not met. Moreover, for CNSE, engagement through partnerships makes sense when the levels and types of education and skills being developed extend beyond its own specialized bachelor's and advanced degrees in nanoscale science and engineering. Through CNSE and with financial incentives and other considerations, New York State now seeks to replicate the collaborative university-industry-government model for economic development in other upstate regions.

References

Bartik, Timothy. 2009. "What Works in State Economic Development?" In *Growing the State Economy: Evidence-Based Policy Options.* Wisconsin Family Impact Seminar Briefing Report FIS 27, Stephanie Eddy and Karen Bogenschneider, eds. Madison, WI: University of Wisconsin Co-operative Extension, pp. 15–29.

Etzkowitz, Henry, and Loet Leydesdorff, eds. 1997. *Universities in the Global Knowledge Economy: A Triple Helix of University-Industry-Government Relations.* London: Cassell Academics.

Hagerty, James R. 2013. "Math, Science Degrees? Apply Here." *Wall Street Journal,* October 21, B:4.

Moretti, Enrico. 2012. *The New Geography of Jobs.* New York: Houghton Mifflin Harcourt Publishing.

Roco, Mihail C. 2011. "The Long View of Nanotechnology Development: The National Nanotechnology Initiative at 10 Years." *Journal of Nanoparticle Research* 13(2): 427–445. doi:10.1007/s11051-010-0192-z (accessed September 27, 2014).

Rulison, Larry. 2014. "Major Bucks into Fab8." *Albany Times Union,* March 27, E:1.

Schultz, Laura I. 2011. "Nanotechnology's Triple Helix: A Case Study of the University at Albany's College of Nanoscale Science and Engineering." *Journal of Technology Transfer* 36(5): 546–564. doi:10.1007/s10961-010-9201-8 (accessed September 27, 2014).

———. 2012. "University Industry Government Collaboration for Economic Growth." In *Universities and Colleges as Economic Drivers,* Jason E. Lane and D. Bruce Johnstone, eds. Albany, NY: State University of New York Press, pp. 129–162.

Semico Research Corporation. 2008. *Upstate New York: Assessing the Economic Impact of Attracting Semiconductor Industry.* Phoenix, AZ: Semico Research Corporation.

Siena Research Institute. 2014. 7th Annual Upstate New York Business Leader Survey. NYCEO2013 Crosstabs. Loudonville, NY: Siena College.

Yawson, Robert M. 2010. "Skill Needs and Human Resources Development in the Emerging Field of Nanotechnology." *Journal of Vocational Education and Training* 62(3): 285–296.

16

Connecting Workers to Credentials

The Promise and Pitfalls of Awarding Academic Credit for Prior Learning

Heath J. Prince
University of Texas

THE RECESSION, THE WEB, AND THE WORKFORCE

The practice of awarding academic credit for learning gained outside the classroom is not new. For decades, postsecondary institutions have established credit equivalency for skills or experience students have gained elsewhere. Add to this the longstanding practice of awarding academic credit via the Defense Activities Non-traditional Education Support (DANTES) system, or the College Level Examination Program (CLEP), and it becomes clear that postsecondary institutions, to various degrees, have long been attempting to avoid penalizing students by requiring them to sit through courses that they may have already mastered.

What is new for postsecondary institutions, however, is the rapid growth of this practice. One indication has been the evolution in the terminology used to refer to the practice, reflecting the debates around competency-based assessment that have expanded commensurate with the growth in its use: *prior-learning assessment*, most frequently associated with the Council for Adult and Experiential Learning's Learning-Counts.org initiative, gave way to *competency-based education* as the term du jour among proponents. More recently still, *direct assessment* more closely reflects the current discussions, as well as the direction in which the practice appears to be heading.

Moreover, as the terminology has evolved, the focus of the practice has shifted more recently from nontraditional students (e.g., adults) looking for academic credit for workforce experience to any and all students able to demonstrate competency in a given postsecondary education subject. There is a difference in the distinction between assessment for the purposes of awarding traditional academic degrees and assessment related primarily to shorter-term educational certificates designed for nearer-term employment. This difference, I would suggest, is at the heart of tension between proponents and opponents of using assessment of competency to award credentials. I will return to this at the end of the chapter.

Growth in competency-based assessment is driven in large part by the confluence of four relatively contemporaneous forces: 1) the dramatic expansion of online learning, 2) the shift in the labor market to a demand for higher skills, 3) the most protracted economic downturn and slowest recovery in generations, and 4) a shift in responsibility for skills upgrading from one shared with their employers to one that workers are now largely expected to carry on their own. Each of these factors has led increasing numbers of students, many of whom are non-traditional students, back to postsecondary institutions. Increasingly required, as they are, to compete on the "spot-market" for labor, many of these nontraditional students are returning not for a traditional academic degree but for educational certificates that can be quickly translated into employment.

Much of the recent attention given to assessment can be traced back to the efforts of advocates in the mid-2000s to address the apparent need to improve the skill levels of the growing percentage of the labor force who found themselves beyond the typical college-going age, without a postsecondary credential, and with skills that were rapidly becoming obsolete as automation and globalization took the toll that many had predicted. For proponents, assessment was viewed as a way to both address the shortage in higher skills and provide workers with more employment security by way of marketable skills and a postsecondary credential.

The U.S. Census Bureau's Economics and Statistics Administration reports that just over 75 percent of the adult working population lack any sort of "alternative credential," defined as either a certification, a license, or an educational certificate (Ewert and Kominski 2014). Notably, the report finds that 86.5 percent of those not in the labor force, and 84.2 percent of the unemployed lack an alternative credential, compared to 68.8 percent of the employed. The authors report that, "[o]ver-all, people working full-time with alternative credentials earned more than those without any alternative credentials, and people working with professional certificates and licenses earned the most" (p. 7). And, in his State of the Union address in 2009, President Obama called for a commitment from every American to "at least one year or more of higher education," among a list of prescriptions for pulling the economy out of decline, shoring up the middle class, and providing upward mobility for all (Obama 2009). This request, along with the goal to see the United States first in the world in college graduates by 2020, formed the core of the president's "completion agenda." The perceived need for some sort of postsecondary credential to succeed in the labor market, coupled with the brake on economic growth presumed to result from the high percentage of working adults without any sort of postsecondary credential, has added momentum to the rapid expansion in recent years in competency-based credentials, as well as to calls for the creation of a framework to help define the approach.

The chapter is organized as follows. The next section briefly reviews the terminology and gives an overview of the shortcomings of the current noncredit system, as perceived by advocates for a competency-based approach, in meeting the education and skill needs of the workforce. The section following illustrates how three states and three organizations assess skills for credit using a competency-based approach, bridging the gap between noncredit and for-credit postsecondary education. The next section outlines how the arguments used in favor of a competency-based framework for awarding occupational credentials have been adopted by advocates for direct assessment of competency for academic degrees, and the implications of this for competency-based assessment of occupational credentials. A brief note on the evidence of effectiveness of this approach follows, which is then followed by suggestions for disentangling the competency-based framework for awarding occupational credentials from the broader movement toward direct assessment for academic degrees.

TERMINOLOGY

Regional accrediting bodies have begun to develop policies in response to new competency-based education approaches that potentially permit greater flexibility for students to learn at their own pace. This process has led to useful clarifications in terminology, such as that provided by the Southern Association of Colleges and Schools/Commission on Colleges (SACSCOC), the regional accrediting body for the 11 southern U.S. states. In 2013, SACSCOC adopted a policy statement on direct assessment and competency-based educational programs, becoming among the first of the regional accrediting bodies to do so. According to SACSCOC (2013), the policy is designed to provide guidance to institutions and evaluation committees on "the Commission's expectations regarding the establishment and review of direct assessment competency-based programs and its [*sic*] hybrids," in both career-technical and degree programs (p. 1).

SACSCOC identifies several defining characteristics (shown in Table 16.1) of direct assessment competency-based educational programs.

- Programs are distinct from conventional notions of the clock hour, seat time, term length, or the credit hour; rather, programs rely on the student's ability to demonstrate clearly defined and measurable competencies in a designated program.

- Programs are designed and delivered within the framework of the program's defined knowledge, skills, and competencies as demonstrated by students, rather than in terms of prescribed courses.

- A student may acquire the requisite competencies from multiple sources and at various times other than, or in addition to, the learning experiences provided by the institution. As such, the length of time it takes to demonstrate learning may be different for each student.

- Programs often allow for alternative approaches to teaching and learning.

- Programs may rely almost exclusively on students using direct assessment testing models to demonstrate their mastery of program and degree content.

Table 16.1 SACSCOC Definition of Terms

Terms	Definitions
Competency	A competency is a clearly defined and measurable statement of the knowledge, skill, and ability a student has acquired in a designated program.
Competency-based educational programs	A competency-based educational program is outcome-based and assesses a student's attainment of competencies as the sole means of determining whether the student earns a degree or a credential. Such programs may be organized around traditional course-based units (credit or clock hours) that students must earn to complete their educational program, or may depart from course-based units (credit or clock hours) to rely solely on the attainment of defined competencies.
Direct assessment	A competency-based educational program as an instructional program that, *in lieu of credit hours or clock hours as a measure of student learning,* uses direct assessment of student learning *relying solely on the attainment of defined competencies,* or recognizes the direct assessment of student learning by others (emphases added). The assessment must be consistent with the accreditation of the institution or program using the results of the assessment.
Hybrid competency-based educational programs	A hybrid competency-based educational program combines course-based competencies (clock and credit hours awarded) with non-course-based competencies (no clock or credit hours awarded).

Elements of SACSCOC's definition of direct assessment programs appear in many of the efforts undertaken by postsecondary institutions, and in a growing number of states, to award academic credit for education and skills earned outside a traditional postsecondary setting. In theory, this approach potentially benefits unemployed and underemployed workers who are faced with few options for advancing in the labor market other than earning a postsecondary credential that signals a marketable skill. These state and institutional efforts are taking hold, moreover, as a result of the current disconnection between the noncredit and credit-bearing sides of postsecondary education.

NONCREDIT VS. CREDIT-BEARING PROGRAMS

The perceived need for a competency-based approach for awarding academic credit is influenced, at least in part, by the significant percentage of the working population that typically enrolls in a wide variety of noncredit postsecondary courses, often for skills training directly tied to employment, and often outside higher education institutions. Advocates for a competency-based approach see this population as a source of potential candidates for credential-conferring programs if equivalence between noncredit and credit offerings can be determined. Academic credit for prior learning could, so the argument goes, be awarded as an enticement to matriculate into credit-bearing courses, and participants who may typically be reluctant to return to higher education (or enter for the first time) would then do so with the understanding that they would earn a certificate or credential at an accelerated rate. When this approach succeeds, as it appears to have in Ohio, Indiana, Wisconsin, and a few other states, it has the potential to address both the worker's need for higher-level skills and the "completion agenda" meant to benefit the broader economy.

However, this relatively straightforward rubric—identify credit-bearing equivalencies for noncredit prior learning, award credit to workers, enroll them in credit-bearing programs, and award them an industry-recognized credential with value in the labor market—is not without significant hurdles, as discussed below.

This rubric has evolved, fairly rapidly, into an approach far afield from its origins, with policy and pedagogical implications that threaten to undermine what has the potential to significantly increase the education and skill levels of the workforce. As it has morphed into an approach to higher education in general, competency-based assessment as a workforce development strategy has suffered from the backlash that has come primarily in response to the perception of direct assessment of competency as a threat to traditional notions of how higher education is best delivered (i.e., seat time).

Identifying the Need for a Competency-Based Framework

Advocates for a competency-based credentialing system cite several shortcomings in the current noncredit system that prevent it from meeting the demands of the labor market. Inadequate data reporting on noncredit programs, poor quality-assurance mechanisms, and a lack of transparency regarding the value of noncredit occupational credentials are just a few of the more significant barriers cited.

Data reporting

The vast bulk of noncredit postsecondary education operates outside the traditional discussions of postsecondary policy, and most federal and state data collection systems exclude these programs. The federal Integrated Postsecondary Education Data System (IPEDS), for example, collects data only on students enrolled in credit-bearing programs, and it even excludes students enrolled in for-credit but nondegree programs. State and institutional data systems use different metrics for counting credit and noncredit programs, and there is variation within states in the metrics used for counting noncredit education (e.g., hours of training, unduplicated enrollment, type of programs, outcomes). Neither the federal government nor the states collect data on certificates and certifications offered outside higher education (Bird, Ganzglass, and Prince 2011). In the absence of reliable data on enrollment and completion, the labor market impacts of noncredit postsecondary education are difficult, at best, to determine.

Quality assurance

Advocates for a competency-based approach also point to the absence of consistent measures or processes for assessing program effectiveness. Noncredit education is rarely subject to academic or faculty protocols associated with securing approval to offer courses for credit. Moreover, noncredit programs offered by community colleges, the primary source for these programs, use diverse measures of quality, reflecting their diverse purposes and customers. For example, the accountability measures for training low-income adults and dislocated workers funded through the Workforce Investment Act focus on students' employment and earnings outcomes, while the effectiveness of training customized to employers' specifications may be measured in terms of improved worker performance. Other training may be measured in terms of students' success in passing industry certifications or earning professional licenses (Bird, Ganzglass, and Prince 2011).

Further, there is a wide array of private sector certifying and accrediting bodies, each with its own protocols and quality-assurance mechanisms. And, while some employer-financed education leads to postsecondary credentials or degrees—for example, through tuition reimbursement programs—most employer-sponsored and employer-funded technical training is noncredit and is offered by either the employer directly, educational institutions, or private vendors (Bird, Ganzglass, and Prince 2011).

Transparency of credential value

For advocates of a competency-based approach, perhaps the highest hurdle between the current noncredit system and a system that can, with a high degree of fidelity, produce a workforce with the education and skills required by the labor market is the perception that the current credential landscape is "crowded, chaotic, and confusing" to individuals, institutions, and employers (Bird, Ganzglass, and Prince 2011, p. 9). Each of these stakeholders report difficulty in navigating the education and training system and making choices that will give them access to the appropriate programs and credentials. Credentials include credit and noncredit certificates, educational degrees (e.g., diploma, associate's degree, bachelor's degree), registered apprenticeship certificates, and other credit and noncredit certifications of skills attainment. In some cases, students receive industry-approved certifications based on standardized tests; in other cases, they earn industry-approved licenses; in many cases, individual institutions offer certificates for completion of courses or programs with or without third-party validation. Some certificates target general learning outcomes; others reflect specific occupational competencies. Furthermore, critics of the current state of affairs in the United States also note that credentials are not always transferable across programs and geographies.

The lack of common definitions and standards underlying the myriad noncredit occupational credentials is said to contribute to confusion about which ones represent value and how they relate to academic credentials. Moreover, the lack of industry-recognized credentials for lower-skilled jobs complicates efforts to build on-ramps to good jobs for low-skilled workers (Bird, Ganzglass, and Prince 2011).

Each of these factors has contributed to calls for a framework, based on an assessment of competency, for awarding industry certifications and postsecondary credentials. While early advocates for this sort of framework may have had in mind nontraditional postsecondary students who required a postsecondary credential to advance in the labor market, the use of assessment of competency as the primary metric for awarding academic credit toward a credential has expanded to include more advanced degrees and a wider cast of key players. As described below, Wisconsin provides one of the clearer examples of how a practice originally focused on relatively short-term occupation-oriented credentials has evolved, in short order, into an approach to higher education more generally.

THE REFORMATION: BRINGING COMPETENCY-BASED ASSESSMENT IN HIGHER EDUCATION OUT OF THE SHADOWS

State-Level Innovations

A competency-based framework would necessarily build on successful experiments in a handful of states over the past several years. Driven by local and regional economic development needs, as well as the need to increase the education and skills of the workforce, these states have effectively addressed the shortcomings of the noncredit system noted above, and have created noncredit-to-credit systems within their higher education institutions.

Much of this state- and institution-level innovation in matching noncredit learning to credit-bearing courses in the two systems falls into three broad categories:

1)   Evaluation of prior learning through assessments of life and work experiences to document learning that is equivalent to college-level courses or competencies

2) Preapproval of courses through an articulation process or agreement that permits crosswalks or the determination of equivalencies between credits and industry certifications and other noncollegiate learning

3) Integrating noncredit learning into credit-bearing courses of study

Ohio, Indiana, and Wisconsin are among the leading states in operationalizing a competency-based approach for awarding postsecondary credit for education and skills acquired in a variety of nonpostsecondary settings.

Ohio

The Career Technical Credit Transfer (CT^2) initiative, which began in 2005, evolved from the Ohio Board of Regents' efforts to increase completion rates and improve the ability of students to transfer across the state's postsecondary institutions. (CT^2) is a collaborative effort among the Ohio Board of Regents, the Ohio Department of Education's Office of Career-Technical Education, public secondary/adult career-technical education institutions, and state-supported colleges. The goal is to help ensure that workers can earn educational credit for technical instruction.

More recently, and with Governor Kasich's support, what began as an effort to ensure that postsecondary credits can transfer has led to a process for awarding academic credit for occupational and technical instruction provided through the state's Adult Career Centers (state-supported providers of career and technical education). (CT^2) establishes criteria, policies, and procedures whereby students receive college credit for agreed-upon technical knowledge and skills in equivalent courses or programs that are based on industry-recognized standards.

Critical to the early success of Ohio (CT^2)—16 different certifications awarded in 11 different occupations—is the process by which faculty and other stakeholders determine which types of occupational and technical instruction merit educational credit. The process involves several steps:

• Defining learning outcomes based on industry-recognized credentials

- Coming to agreement among members of faculty from Ohio public institutions of higher education and career-technical education institutions and content expert panels on these learning outcomes

- Matching course and learning materials based on the learning outcomes using the state's Course Equivalency Management System

- Submitting course and learning materials for approval

- Continuously reviewing course and learning materials for equivalency

Representatives from the state's Department of Education and postsecondary faculty collaborate on joint faculty/industry advisory panels that meet annually to align curricula with industry needs. And, while (CT^2) may have been originally motivated primarily by a desire to improve the education and skill levels of Ohio's workforce, the state's recently adopted performance-based funding for all of its public higher education institutions has been a key driver of the state's continuing focus on assessment.

Indiana

In addition to a portfolio review process to assess prior learning, as well as direct assessment through DANTES and the CLEP exams, Indiana's Ivy Tech Community College system uses a "certification crosswalk" to award academic credit for a wide range of industry certifications, including apprenticeships, provided through third-party certification organizations.

The certification crosswalk permits students seeking credit for prior learning to avoid the often lengthy portfolio review process, as well as the fees associated with it. Institutions potentially save time and money because they do not have to review each student's prior learning. The consistency achieved through the crosswalk also facilitates the transfer of credit across institutions. Ivy Tech's 23 campuses are in alignment on the approach as to how students and faculty develop and document their portfolio assessment for determining the awarding of credit for prior learning. In addition, each of the campuses agree on consistent cut scores for standardized tests that measure prior learning, such as the DANTES and CLEP exams.

Evolving role of faculty. A faculty-driven process in 2005 developed the crosswalk, and faculty continue to be involved in expanding and keeping it up to date as certifications and licenses change; each curricula committee meets at least once annually, and crosswalks are standing items on committee agenda. New academic advisors are trained in prior learning assessment (PLA) and in advising new students on how to take advantage of it.

This level of faculty support is a marked improvement from the early days of the crosswalk process, when the attitudes of all but a few of the more devoted faculty and advisors ranged from ambivalent to reluctant. Concerns among faculty centered on three main issues: 1) reputation of the institution, 2) the integrity of the degrees, and 3) standards regarding the institution's 15 credit hour residency policy. As the process has evolved, so have faculty concerns, with relatively few expressing dissatisfaction with the approach. As with traditional transfer, some faculty expressed a sentiment similar to, "If they didn't learn from me, they didn't learn it." Additionally, it is up to the receiving institutions whether credits earned via assessment are acceptable. However, articulation agreements between Ivy Tech and other Indiana higher education institutions have largely minimized this particular issue.

Employer engagement. Generally speaking, employers have played a smaller role in the certification crosswalk process than originally anticipated. However, administrators note that, for the most part, hiring employers are unaware of Ivy Tech's reliance on PLA, the certification crosswalk, or direct assessment, and seem to be largely unconcerned whether credits are earned though traditional seat time or via some type of competency-based assessment strategy.

Wisconsin

Wisconsin's technical colleges consider apprenticeship-related instruction as approved academic programming with full program status. Students can earn 39 credits through an apprenticeship program, which can be applied toward the 60-credit Journeyworker Applied Associate in Science degree. While initially focused on the construction trades, Wisconsin's Department of Workforce Development and the Wisconsin Technical College System have taken steps to expand this practice to include health care apprenticeships and skilled apprenticeship programs in green construction and energy-related occupations.

In addition, and with strong encouragement from the governor's office, the University of Wisconsin (UW) System has recently implemented its "UW Flexible Option" program, which, possibly more than any public university system to date, establishes a competency-based approach as the cornerstone to multiple degree and certificate programs. The UW System's approach provides self-paced, assessment-driven, competency-based certificates, as well as AA, BA, and BS degrees in a wide range of disciplines. The approach is promoted with television ads and online videos, and is targeted to nontraditional and adult learners as a way to earn a credential while working, maintaining a household, or being unemployed. All of the program offerings are accredited by the Higher Learning Commission of the North Central Association of Colleges and Schools, and, with a nod to what is understood to be their target population's motivation, are touted to be valued by employers just as highly as those earned through traditional routes.

A few other states, including Kentucky and Oregon, have attempted to create similar competency-based postsecondary programs with varying degrees of success. Each, however, has as a common denominator the perceived need to shift from an input-based metric ("seat time") to an output-based metric (demonstration of competency) as the primary metric for determining postsecondary education and training effectiveness.

THIRD-PARTY ASSESSMENT

Assessment of experiential or prior learning includes a variety of approaches, including portfolio assessments, standardized exams, and credit recommendations based on institutional or third-party evaluators of credit using nationally recognized criteria to recommend credit equivalencies for noncredit learning, and other types of learning that take place outside the traditional for-credit, postsecondary settings. The three examples below illustrate these approaches.

LearningCounts.org

The Council for Adult and Experiential Learning (CAEL) has built a business around establishing and disseminating standards for awarding credit through PLA. The CAEL promotes a range of PLA options—including standardized exams, challenge exams, and formal evaluation of noncredit instruction—but it places special emphasis on the portfolio method of assessment.

CAEL's focus on PLA is motivated, in part, by the findings from its study, *Fueling the Race to Postsecondary Success* (CAEL 2010). In it, CAEL examines data on 62,475 adult students at 48 colleges and universities across the country and finds that students with PLA credit completed degrees at much higher rates than students without it. PLA students also had higher persistence rates and a faster time to completion. According to the study, student advisors believe that earning PLA credit can motivate students to persist in their studies and complete their degrees. It is also assumed once students understand that they have already learned "college-level" material, they may be more motivated to enroll.

While the portfolio option is available to many students, faculty evaluators must be trained to do the assessments according to nationally accepted standards, like CAEL's. As a result, CAEL reports that institutions often find it difficult to offer the portfolio option to many students or across a range of disciplines.

The CAEL study also finds that PLA had limited use in community colleges and served few students. When asked about these low usage rates, respondents reported to CAEL that PLA offerings were often inconsistent across colleges and departments, not promoted or advocated by advisors or faculty, or too narrow in scope or availability to meet students' needs.

The American Council on Education's College Credit Recommendation Service (CREDIT)

ACE's CREDIT program, serving adults, educational institutions, and organizations, connects workplace learning with colleges by helping adults gain academic credit for formal courses and examinations taken outside traditional degree programs. CREDIT evaluates and validates credit recommendations from organizations providing noncollegiate-sponsored instruction, including job training, apprenticeship, and work-force-readiness programs provided by employers, unions, CBOs, and business or professional associations.

Since 1945, ACE's Military Evaluations Program has used subject-matter experts and academic faculty to review courses and conduct site visits to analyze course and program content, and it has relied on evaluator consensus in determining the learning outcomes and appropriate educational credit recommendations. CREDIT provides guidance to service members, civilians, military education centers, and colleges interpreting military transcripts and documents.

National College Credit Recommendation Service

Since 1973, the Board of Regents of the University of the State of New York has operated the National College Credit Recommendation Service (NCCRS). Similar to ACE's CREDIT program, the NCCRS reviews formal courses and educational programs in a wide variety of subjects sponsored by noncollegiate organizations, makes college-level credit recommendations for the courses and programs evaluated, and promotes academic recognition of these learning experiences to the nation's colleges. Over 1,500 institutions have said they are willing to consider awarding credit for learning experiences evaluated by the NCCRS, and additional institutions use these credit recommendations in conjunction with individualized portfolio assessments for adult learners.

FEDERAL SUPPORT

Seen by advocates as a federal-level endorsement of a competency-based approach to credentials, the U.S. Department of Education (2013) issued a "Dear Colleague" letter, in which it reiterated the leeway granted to postsecondary institutions for providing federal student aid for competency-based programs in the final rule for the Higher Education Reconciliation Act of 2005. The department also acknowledged the expansion of competency-based programs over the past several years and endorsed them for their potential for "assuring the quality and extent of learning, shortening the time to degree/certificate completion, developing stackable credentials that ease student transitions between school and work, and reducing the overall cost of education for both career-technical and degree programs." While the department recognized that the guidance may not fully address the need for Title IV support, particularly regarding financial aid for fees associated with assessments of prior learning, the letter served as a clear indication that the department would be unlikely to slow the trend toward assessment in competency-based programs over traditional seat-time programs.

THE LUMINA FOUNDATION'S TUNING USA PROJECT

As long as it remained limited to occupational skills and experience earned outside of higher education setting, the competency-based approach to awarding academic credit remained relatively uncontroversial. Indeed, in states like Indiana, faculty and higher education administrators have been integral in the approach's expansion within institutions. A turning point in this attitude, however, may be dated to approximately the time when a competency-based approach began to be applied to traditional academic degrees. The Lumina Foundation's Tuning USA project may mark the beginning of this shift.

The Lumina Foundation's Degree Qualifications Profile, a product of the foundation's Tuning USA initiative, builds on the work of similar and ongoing processes in the European Union to identify specific learning outcomes for associate's, bachelor's, and master's degrees. Tuning USA is the most comprehensive effort to date to create a national, competency-based qualifications framework for postsecondary education.

Since 2009, the Lumina Foundation has administered the Tuning USA pilot, with the aim to

- award comparable degrees based upon defined, criterion-referenced learning outcomes;
- promote college access and student mobility; and
- embrace the need for increased degree attainment (McKiernan and Birtwistle 2010).

In January 2011, the foundation issued *Degree Qualifications Profile for Associate's, Bachelor's and Master's Degrees* (the *Degree Profile*) (Adelman et al. 2011). The *Degree Profile*

> highlights specific student learning outcomes that should define associate's, bachelor's, and master's degrees in terms of what students should know, understand and be able to do upon earning these degrees. *As the Degree Profile defines competencies in ways meant to emphasize both the cumulative integration of learning from many sources and the application of learning in a variety of practical settings, it seeks to offer benchmarks for high quality learning.* . . . . It is meant also to provide a common vocabulary to encourage the sharing of good practice, to offer a foundation for better public understanding, and to establish reference points for accountability far stronger than those now in use (emphasis added). (Adelman et al. 2011)

The *Degree Profile* begins to define the overarching student outcomes, rather than subject-specific learning outcomes and competencies, that a student must demonstrate in order to be awarded a degree at the associate's, bachelor's, and master's levels in the United States. For each degree level, the profile identifies core competencies that collectively define the requirements for a specific degree. These cores grow progressively larger as students build on their knowledge, and the growth in learning is expected to be predictable and transparent to all involved.

> The *Degree Profile* describes student performance appropriate for each degree level through clear reference points that indicate the incremental and cumulative nature of learning. *Focusing on conceptual knowledge and essential competencies and their applications, the Degree Profile illustrates how students should be expected to perform at progressively more challenging levels.* Students' demonstrated achievement in performing at these ascending levels creates the grounds on which degrees are awarded (emphasis added). (Adelman et al. 2011)

As the competency-based approach has moved beyond identifying overarching student outcomes and competencies and, in fact, adopts *subject-specific* outcomes and competencies, it has begun to court controversy. Moreover, as it evolves from a workforce development strategy into a strategy that has implications for all of postsecondary education, the approach runs the risk of being undermined altogether by staunch supporters of more traditional higher education methods.

EVALUATIONS OF COMPETENCY-BASED APPROACHES TO AWARDING CREDENTIALS

Despite the proliferation of institutions employing the practice, a review of the evaluation literature finds that there have been no recent, rigorous evaluations of competency-based assessment outside the medical field. Left unaddressed are critical questions regarding the practice, not least of which is whether acceleration of awarding of credentials undermines learning. The vast bulk of the material produced on the practice is descriptive and normative, with some solid analysis of the political dynamics produced by postsecondary education industry journalists (e.g., see Fain [2012, 2013]).

Even anecdotal evidence, beyond the promotional spots in online and television advertisements, in favor of or opposed to competency-based assessment is difficult to come by. Its intuitive appeal—the potential to increase enrollment, speed up time to completion, minimize duplication of a student's effort, and more rapidly equip the national workforce with higher-order skills—rather than evidence has been the practice's primary selling point. However, the practice has been in place, in multiple variations, long enough that it would appear that this is a topic ripe for an impact evaluation.

A bill introduced in the 113th Congress, H.R. 3136, would create the "Advancing Competency-Based Education Demonstration Project Act of 2013," and would require that the demonstration be evaluated in terms of student progress toward retention and completion of recognized degree programs. The introduction of this bill follows the guidance provided by the U.S. Department of Education (described above), which outlines how institutions can have competency-based programs approved under current regulations relating to direct assessment programs. If passed, H.R. 3136 would potentially provide federal support for substantive evaluations of the practice.

THE COUNTER-REFORMATION: BACKLASH AGAINST COMPETENCY-BASED ASSESSMENT

While the Lumina Foundation's Degree Profile is focused primarily on competency assessment within general education degree programs rather than on programs oriented more toward occupational education and training, its emphasis on defining competency, assessing competency, and basing advancement on demonstration of competency clearly parallels similar efforts by postsecondary institutions with regard to shorter-term, occupationally oriented offerings. And while competency-based assessment may be able to credit its recent popularity to the completion agenda and that agenda's desire to equip the workforce with college credentials, concerns over the approach have grown as it has moved onto more traditional postsecondary turf.

As it has shifted from a means to improve the occupational skills of the workforce (i.e., a workforce development strategy) to a shortcut to a traditional academic degree (i.e., a postsecondary education strategy), assessment has engendered a backlash among academics who argue that earning an occupational certificate in a postsecondary institution is all well and good, but granting academic credit for work experience in order to speed students through college undermines the purpose of higher education. Worse still for critics is direct assessment, which requires even less interaction with professors, students, and all else that postsecondary education has to offer. Competency as the sole means for determining academic credit is, for critics, a minimalist concept, and the entire movement from PLA to competency-based education to direct assessment represents a "creeping minimalism" that will likely lead to a devaluing of postsecondary credentials in general. The entire approach threatens the creation of multiple "universities without intellectuals," as noted critic of competency-based assessment Johann N. Neem refers to Western Governors University and similar institutions (Neem 2012, p. 70).

Perhaps the clearest signs of the emerging backlash can be found in the American Association of Colleges and Universities' (AAC&U) 2014 conference, the vast majority of which was devoted to competency-based education and direct assessment. Framing the issue in terms of educational quality over technologically acquired efficiencies, and in terms of equipping postsecondary students with an education that can help them tackle the big questions and real-world challenges rather than simply provide them with skills required for their first job, AAC&U asks, "But in our fascination with the promise of technology, are we paying sufficient attention to the connection between innovation and educational quality . . . (and) can we instead judge the value of innovations by how well they create long-term opportunity, strengthen students' capacities, and reverse the most inequitable features of U.S. higher education?" (AAC&U 2014).

Descriptions of panel presentations at the conference alluded to the tension suggested by the conference title. Panels included those addressing how institutes of higher education might best continue to develop civic-minded students in an atmosphere characterized by an increasing focus on workforce development, or those that defend the long overdue technological revolution that can give employers assurances of student competencies in workforce skills. Other panels, which included for-profit and nonprofit participants, spoke to the issue of quality in direct assessment competency-based programs. Still other sessions asked whether the road to competency-based education leads to an educational utopia or dystopia. A common denominator among each of these discussions appeared to be the recognition that postsecondary credentials are increasingly required for success in the labor market, and that the increasing cost of postsecondary education was driving toward innovation in terms of delivery.

The online journal *Inside Higher Ed* has documented the rapid evolution of assessment from helpful tool for nontraditional students looking for postsecondary credit for prior learning to at least a "disruptive" force, or at worst part of the "creative destruction" of postsecondary education as we know it (*Economist* 2014). *Inside Higher Ed*'s coverage from approximately May 2012 forward has couched the growth of assessment of competency in terms of career advancement, and as an approach with particular appeal to workers looking to convert technical trade certificates and skills into credit for academic credentials. *Inside Higher Ed* also foreshadows the potential for online learning and massive open online courses (MOOCs) to drive demand for competency-based assessment in ways that are difficult to predict. Fain (2012) writes, "One reason many colleges are skittish about granting credits for prior learning is because to do so is to acknowledge that the academy doesn't have a lock on college-level learning. Some faculty members also view the process warily, arguing that it can be an academically suspect money grab and a weak substitute for college. Prior learning could also threaten professors' jobs."

By early 2013, *Inside Higher Ed* had documented the push for "alternative credit pathways" coming from "the college completion agenda, workforce development, and money worries (buffeting) colleges." In addition, the journal reported on ACE's endorsement of extending credit recommendations to courses delivered via MOOCs and other nonaccredited online providers. Despite ACE's endorsement, as well as deep-pocketed support from the Bill and Melinda Gates Foundation and the Lumina Foundation, IHE reported that the acceptance of ACE's credit recommendations for courses delivered by nonaccredited providers was perhaps most popular with open access institutions and least popular with more selective colleges (Fain 2013).

Perhaps the most illuminating component of IHE's coverage, at least for the purposes of this chapter, is its chronicling of the evolution of the competency-based approach from one focused primarily on sub-baccalaureate workforce credentials to one that has become so intertwined with online instruction and the "creative destruction" of higher education that critics and advocates alike have difficulty teasing the two ideas apart. This is detrimental to PLA as a potentially transformative workforce development strategy.

As long as the labor market requires credentials to signal skill attainment, there will be a need for occupational training by a credential-granting institution. However, this brings into question the need for postsecondary education to validate skill attainment. Early advocates for community and technical colleges in this role believed that these institutions were better equipped to provide education and training services because, crucially, they have the potential to provide participants with career pathways and a mix of academic education and occupational skills (see Grubb [2000]).

However, an alternative rationale may have to do with the shift from a paradigm in which skills training was provided through apprenticeships or training on the job, where proof of skill attainment was demonstrated on the job and observed by supervisors. As this paradigm has shifted away from training done at the job site, with sharp reductions in the amount of training invested in lower-level workers, employers are no less concerned about the skill levels of those they hire, only now the "proof" of skill attainment must come from elsewhere. Two-year postsecondary institutions have moved to fill this gap. If this alternative explanation better reflects reality, then the move by postsecondary institutions to conduct training has less to do with the type, rigor, or robustness of the training received, as suggested by early advocates, and more to do with the absence of traditional forms of skill validation, that is, demonstration of skill attainment on the job.

Occupational skills training programs are increasingly enrolling an older student population, often with significant work experience, who primarily want to earn a credential in order to advance in the labor market. For this population (as well as for the institutions), there is a premium placed on short-term, highly focused training. For employers, globalization has meant a push to reduce production costs, which results in investments in skills training, as well as pressure to hold wages down. This shifts the burden for the provision of needed skills to postsecondary institutions and, ultimately, to the workers themselves in the form of tuition and fees. In this environment, the evolving model—competency-based education, online instruction, direct assessment of skills, and learning for credit—makes some sense for occupational skills training, although it is probably not an ideal type.

This motivation does not apply to traditional postsecondary academic programs, in which students are believed to benefit from longer-term exposure to a wide range of subjects, unlike the short-term, highly focused instruction provided through programs that are primarily occupational-skills oriented. The exploratory aspect associated with academically oriented higher education is potentially undermined by directly assessing skills and knowledge in order to fast-track a student from enrollment to credential attainment. Yet, what might be seen as two distinct functions of postsecondary education—one driven primarily by the need to equip individuals with occupational skills, and one driven by an academic mission—becomes conflated beneath the push toward granting any type of credential based on a demonstration of competency. The backlash against competency-based credentials and direct assessment will then inevitably include occupational skills credentials.

PRIVATE SECTOR INTEREST

Proprietary institutions have moved quickly into the space opened up by the confluence of online learning, the demand for higher skills to advance in the labor market, and the need for a more highly educated (credentialed) and skilled workforce. However, concerns have begun to surface about the potential for for-profit schools to lower standards for determining competency (a more recent version of long-held suspicions that the practice was simply a cover for unscrupulous diploma mills), as well as the fact that the expansion of the practice has significantly outpaced the research on its effectiveness.

Nonetheless, private, for-profit schools are among the mix of schools, along with private nonprofits, public, and online schools recently invited to participate in the Lumina Foundation's "Competency-Based Education Network." Per the press release issued from the Competency-Based Network (C-BEN) in 2014, the network will address "shared challenges to designing and developing competency-based degree programs and related business models" (C-BEN 2014). C-BEN roots its raison d'etre in both social and economic necessity: "The movement toward competency-based academic delivery comes as the United States, to meet social and economic demands for more college graduates, must provide more education options for more students. Advocates believe academic programs that clearly define what students must know and be able to do to earn degrees in specific disciplines create significant potential to affordably help students from all backgrounds prepare for further education and employment."

UNHITCHING THE COMPETENCY-BASED WORKFORCE CREDENTIAL FROM THE DIRECT ASSESSMENT DEGREE WAGON

Recent work by advocates for competency-based credentials, especially the Corporation for a Skilled Workforce (CSW), may help to disentangle the practice of awarding "competency-based workforce credentials" from the more controversial "direct assessment" trend en vogue in higher education more generally. For CSW and allies, including the Center for Law and Social Policy (CLASP), the American National Standards Institute and the National Skills Coalition, a distinction can be, and needs to be, made between these two by emphasizing several key strategies in the implementation of competency-based workforce credentials, including

- ensuring quality through the use of external accreditors who are attuned to the current needs of industry;
- expanding the use of competency-based workforce credentials by employers, including demonstrating a return on the investment of their time engaging in the credentialing effort;
- expanding the use of competency-based assessment among workers and students;
- expanding the take-up rate of competency-based workforce credentials among postsecondary institutions; and
- creating an infrastructure that can promote a market for competency-based workforce credentials, including quality assurance mechanisms, federal, state, and institutional policy support, and better coordination across the various competency-based credentialing efforts (CSW 2013).

These strategies, it is assumed, will contribute to a competency-based framework in which individuals can readily earn competency-based credentials and apply them to the labor market, providing the quality assurance that CSW and allies find missing in today's market for subdegree certificates, licenses, and credentials.

However, even this corrective action taken on by CSW runs the risk of being undermined by efforts led by its allies to create a "competency-based credentialing ecosystem" (CLASP 2014), as long as that particular effort fails to clarify the distinction between a market for "subdegree" credentials and a market for competency-based credentials in general, in addition to its implied support for "deinstitutionalizing education" (see CLASP [2014]).

STRAW MAN OR WICKER MAN?

Critics of competency-based assessment typically question the motive behind the movement, and its shift into the higher ends of higher education has opened the practice up to questioning in a way that, while under the radar as a means to a relatively short-term occupational credential, it had not been. Now, the pedagogy appears to critics as market-driven, rather than education-driven, with metrics that include cost savings at the expense of instruction. However, some would argue that this is an inevitable outcome of the decades-old trend toward conflating vocational education with postsecondary education, or at least the liberal arts–oriented sort of postsecondary education that is designed to expand an individual's capabilities to choose multiple paths, rather than simply equip him with a skill that will enable him to better compete for work.

This trend is part and parcel of the broader tendency to shift to the individual the burden that was once more broadly shared with employers and society. Personal responsibility, instead of collective responsibility, has been a driving force in public policy in recent decades, so it follows that it falls to the individual to upgrade skills and maintain personal competitiveness. This shift toward personal responsibility for labor market success has opened the door to the current debate about how, rather than whether or to what extent, postsecondary education should meet the demand for skills required by employers. With the weakening of the labor movement has come the near-disappearance of apprenticeship programs and union contracts that performed many of the functions now expected of higher education.

The initial push that started the current assessment ball rolling was justified by claims that the existing credential landscape is too confusing to serve either employers or workers well, and that a simpler, more transparent method (i.e., awarding credentials based on an assessment of competency) is required if workers, employers, and the economy as a whole are to regain their competitive edge. However, while it is logical to assume that an undereducated workforce serves no one well, it is a leap to then assert that awarding postsecondary credentials based on a demonstration of competency will solve this problem. Given the absence of research pointing to the confusing credential landscape as the, or even a, culprit behind our dulled competitive edge, arguments pinning the blame on the status quo seem a bit too much like a straw man for advocates for the "creative destruction" of the postsecondary system.

Instead, the infrastructure being built up around the push for competency-based assessment can seem at times more like a wicker man, in which traditional higher education is meant to be offered up in the name of the "free market" and its demands for better, faster, cheaper.

A helpful exercise for advocates would be to return to the rubric outlined near the beginning of the chapter—identify credit-bearing equivalencies for noncredit, prior-learning; award credit to workers; enroll them in credit-bearing programs; and award them an industry-recognized, competency-based workforce credential with value in the labor market—and to keep the focus on this approach as a workforce development approach, rather than a means to "disrupt" postsecondary education in general. Advocates would benefit, too, from revisiting successful approaches to identifying credit equivalencies for noncredit learning, as is currently practiced in Ohio and Indiana, and building scalable approaches based on the years of experience put into these practices. The benefits of remaining tightly focused on meeting the demand for competency-based workforce credentials would likely outweigh the costs of wading about in the mire that is the debate around self-paced, online, direct assessment of competencies in pursuit of a postsecondary degree.

References

Adelman, Cliff, Peter Ewell, Paul Gaston, Carol Geary Schneider. 2011. *The Degree Qualifications Profile*. Indianapolis, IN: Lumina Foundation.

American Association of Colleges and Universities (AAC&U). 2014. "About the Annual Meeting." Presented at the AAC&U annual meeting, held in Washington, DC, January 22–25.

Bird, Keith, Evelyn Ganzglass, and Heath Prince. 2011. "Giving Credit Where Credit Is Due: Creating a Competency-Based Qualifications Framework for Postsecondary Education and Training." Washington, DC: Center for Law and Social Policy.

Center for Law and Social Policy (CLASP). 2014. "Call for a National Conversation on Creating a Competency-Based Credentialing Ecosystem." Washington, DC: CLASP.

Competency-Based Education Network. 2014. Press release, March 5. http:// cbennetwork.org (accessed December 17, 2014).

Corporation for a Skilled Workforce (CSW). 2013. *Making a Market for Competency-Based Credentials*. Ann Arbor, MI: Corporation for a Skilled Workforce.

Council on Adult and Experiential Learning (CAEL). 2010. *Fueling the Race to Postsecondary Economic Success*. Chicago: CAEL.

Economist. 2014. "Creative Destruction: A Cost Crisis, Changing Labour Markets and New Technology Will Turn an Old Institution on Its Head." June 28. http://www.economist.com/news/leaders/21605906-cost-crisis -changing-labour-markets-and-new-technology-will-turn-old-institution -its (accessed December 17, 2014).

Ewert, Stephanie, and Robert Kominski. 2014. "Measuring Alternative Educational Credentials 2012: Household Economic Studies." Washington, DC: U.S. Department of Commerce, Economics and Statistics Administration.

Fain, Paul. 2012. "Creditworthy in the Keystone State." *Insider Higher Ed*, August 23. https://www.insidehighered.com/news/2012/10/01/competency -based-education-may-get-boost (accessed November 20, 2014).

Fain, Paul. 2013. "Change from Within." *Insider Higher Ed*, March 4. https:// www.insidehighered.com/news/2013/03/04/ace-doubles-down-prior -learning-assessment (accessed November 20, 2014).

Grubb, W. Norton. 2000. "Second Chances in Changing Times: The Roles of Community Colleges in Advancing Low-Skilled Workers." In *Low-Wage Workers in the New Economy*. Richard Kazis and Marc S. Miller, eds. Washington, DC: Urban Institute, pp. 283–306.

McKiernan, Holiday Hart, and Tim Birtwistle. 2010. "Making the Implicit Explicit: Demonstrating the Value Added of Higher Education by a Qualifications Framework." *Journal of College and University Law* 36(2): 512– 560.

Neem, Johann N. 2012. "A University without Intellectuals: Western Governors University and the Academy's Future Thought and Action." *The NEA Higher Education Journal* (Fall): 63–79.

Obama, Barack. 2009. "Remarks of President Barack Obama—As Prepared for Delivery Address to Joint Session of Congress, February 24. Washington, DC. http://www.whitehouse.gov/the_press_office/Remarks-of-President -Barack-Obama-Address-to-Joint-Session-of-Congress/ (accessed December 17, 2014).

Southern Association of Colleges and Schools/Commission on Colleges. 2013. Direct Assessment Competency-Based Educational Programs: Policy Statement. Decatur, GA: Southern Association of Colleges and Schools/Commission on Colleges.

U.S. Department of Education. 2013. "Dear Colleague Letter." Gen-13-10, March 19. Washington, DC: U.S. Department of Education. http://ifap .ed.gov/dpcletters/GEN1310.html (accessed February 3, 2015).

Part 3

Building Evidence-Based
Policy and Practice

17
Toward a More Intelligent
Workforce Development System

Randall W. Eberts
W.E. Upjohn Institute for Employment Research

To meet the challenges of developing a high-quality workforce for the twenty-first century, the next generation of workforce development programs will need to be smarter in providing information to customers. Job matching is an information-intensive process. For the workforce development system to maintain and even improve its effectiveness in assisting job seekers to find work and businesses to find qualified workers, the system will need to transform itself into a more intelligent one. An intelligent system, as envisaged in this chapter, not only provides customers with data essential to make informed decisions but also places this information in the proper context, personalized to the characteristics and circumstances of specific customers and made easily accessible at the time decisions are being made.[1]

When the Workforce Investment Act (WIA)—the major national workforce development system in place at the writing of this chapter—was enacted in 1998, it called for more integrated service delivery through One-Stop Service Centers, and subsequently more integrated data systems. While making some progress toward that end, information provided by WIA remains fragmented, and the administrative data generated by the WIA program are used more for accountability than for informing customers.

In July 2014, Congress passed the Workforce Innovation and Opportunity Act (WIOA), which replaces WIA to become the first major workforce development system of the twenty-first century. In drafting WIOA, Congress recognized the need for a more intelligent system by directing local boards to "develop strategies for using technology to maximize the accessibility and effectiveness of the workforce development system for employers and workers and job seekers" (H.R.

803, sec. 107, subsec. d [7]). More specifically, the bill requires the development of "strategies for aligning technology and data systems across One-Stop partner programs to enhance service delivery . . . and to improve coordination" (H.R. 803, sec. 101, subsec. d[8]). The bill leaves considerable latitude for designing such a system. This chapter offers insight into what information is needed and describes a few pilots and demonstrations funded by the U.S. Department of Labor (USDOL) in recent years that could serve as a basis for a more integrated and comprehensive information system. While it is difficult to pinpoint a precise estimate of the benefits of such a system, several of the previous initiatives, which could serve as components of an integrated information system, have been rigorously evaluated and show positive and statistically significant net impacts for customers and society.

INFORMATION CUSTOMERS NEED

The purpose of the public workforce development system is two-fold: 1) to help people find jobs through job search assistance, counseling, and training; and 2) to help employers find qualified workers through referrals, training, and assessment. Both groups of customers face complex decisions in finding the right job match. Job seekers must choose from among different job prospects and career paths as well as reemployment services and training and education options, typically without sufficient information about the benefits and costs of the various options. Employers must identify the skill sets of job prospects and match them to their perceived workforce needs. Furthermore, both job seekers and businesses must deal with future uncertainties and incomplete information in making these decisions.

Job seekers and employers can benefit from an intelligent information system that provides them with access to personalized data at critical decision points as they navigate the labyrinth of complex decisions within the job search and talent search processes. Such a system requires more than simply placing information on the shelf in a One-Stop Service Center or on a Web site link, which customers must not only locate at the time they need the information but must also recognize its relevance for their specific circumstances. Instead, it requires the information to be readily accessible, personalized, and easily understood in the proper context at each key decision point.

In a recent article on the nexus of behavioral economics and labor market policy, Babcock et al. (2012) assert that "research has found that a large number of complex choices hinders decision-making and that interventions providing personalized and transparent information on the most 'relevant' choices can improve decision-making outcomes" (p. 12). The authors go on to say that not only is information essential in navigating the sequence of decisions involved in finding work but that behavioral economics suggests the context in which information is presented can matter in how individuals respond to choices. Furthermore, they suggest that "a successful workforce investment system is likely to be one that reduces complexity and the need for willpower from the perspective of workers, and relies less heavily on well-informed, patient participants for its smooth operation and success" (p. 10).

ELEMENTS OF AN INTELLIGENT WORKFORCE SYSTEM

Based on the needs of customers to make more informed decisions and to navigate the complex process of job matching and the lessons derived from behavioral economics, an intelligent workforce development system requires five basic elements. First, the system is data-driven. Longitudinal files are constructed for each workforce program participant in order to relate personal demographic information, educational and skill attainment, and past work history with postprogram employment outcomes. Second, information is customized for each participant so he or she can see the relevance of the information and can easily access the information at each critical decision point. Third, the system is evidence-based. The returns to training and the effectiveness of reemployment services are estimated for different groups of individuals facing different circumstances. Fourth, reemployment services and training are targeted to individuals with specific needs to ensure that provision of these services is cost-effective. Fifth, performance management of the workforce development system is based on measures that reflect the value-added of the system and not simply gross outcomes.

Many of these elements are either already embedded in the current workforce system or have been tried over the past years as pilots, demonstrations, or new initiatives. These elements must be closely intertwined to be effective. For instance, the construction of longitudinal data files is necessary in order to customize information for each participant and to compute the returns to training investment; in turn, the estimated effectiveness of services is needed to target resources to participants and to develop a value-added performance system.

However, these elements have yet to be brought together in an integrated and comprehensive fashion, which requires more than the integration of new technology; it requires, also, an inculcation of an evidence-based, data-driven culture. Fostering and sustaining such a culture requires more than simply presenting data; rather, it requires an analysis of the data and the capacity of the system to present the higher-level analytics to customers in meaningful formats on a timely basis.

CURRENT WORKFORCE DEVELOPMENT SYSTEM

Two workforce development programs—WIA and the Wagner-Peyser Employment Service (ES)—serve the vast majority of participants and set the guiding principles for the way reemployment and training services are delivered in the United States.[2] The three WIA programs—Adult, Dislocated Worker, and Youth—provide job search assistance, counseling, and training to the three groups targeted by these programs; the ES program provides job search assistance to job seekers, including dislocated workers receiving Unemployment Insurance (UI) benefits. Both programs provide recruitment services to businesses seeking to fill job openings. Local Workforce Investment Boards (LWIBs), which number nearly 600 across the nation, administer the WIA programs and contract with private providers to deliver most of the services. In many states, the reemployment assistance services provided by both WIA and ES are colocated within One-Stop Centers. Training services are typically provided at the facilities of the training provider, such as on the campus of a community college. The WIA and ES programs share similar employment assistance services, even to the extent that many states coenroll participants in both programs. Therefore, to simplify the discussion without limiting the generalizations that one can draw from the concepts presented in the chapter, much of the discussion will focus on the three WIA programs.

Several components of an intelligent workforce development system already exist within WIA, although they need to be improved in order to provide the information in the form and context necessary to better inform customers and program administrators. First, WIA has produced the elements of a data-driven system by compiling longitudinal data of its participants. Second, performance management is based on labor market and educational outcomes. Third, the basic elements of a resource-targeting system exist within ES programs under the Worker Profiling and Reemployment Services (WPRS) system. Although WPRS is not tied directly to WIA programs, it offers an example of the effectiveness of targeting resources within the workforce system. Current initiatives are under way or have been attempted through pilots that can help enhance and improve the existing components.

DATA-DRIVEN SYSTEM

The WIA legislation requires the construction of performance measures of employment and educational outcomes for each program at the national, state, and local levels. The measures are constructed by merging administrative records from the three programs with UI wage record data to form a longitudinal file for each program participant. The administrative records contain information about each participant's demographic characteristics, educational attainment, some skill-related certifications, barriers to entry, occupation and industry of the participant's most recent employment, and services received during enrollment in a program, among other data fields. Merging quarterly UI wage records with these files adds several quarters of employment history of each participant immediately prior to that participant's registering with a program and several quarters of employment outcomes immediately after his or her exiting from a program. The administrative data are obtained from state management information systems and are compiled in the Workforce Investment Act Standardized Record Data (WIASRD) database, which is updated quarterly. The availability of longitudinal data provides a data platform that can become the foundation for an intelligent workforce system.

In addition to administrative data generated by the workforce development programs and the UI system, customers typically have access to labor market information compiled by state labor market information agencies and the U.S. Bureau of Labor Statistics (BLS). One-Stop Service Centers also provide assessment tools (which are typically self-administered), forecasts of demand for occupations, and a partial listing of job openings in the local labor market. In most if not all cases, none of this information is customized to the personal needs, attributes, or circumstances of each customer. Furthermore, most occupation-demand forecasts look at long-run trends and are not tied to near-term business demand, and job postings cover only a portion of the actual jobs available.

Workforce Data Quality Initiative

States, with encouragement from the federal government, have started to develop data systems that augment the administrative data compiled in WIASRD by expanding the longitudinal files of each participant to include a person's K–16 education outcomes and linking that series to an expanded series of quarterly employment outcomes. The Workforce Data Quality Initiative (WDQI), a federally funded collaboration between the U.S. Departments of Education and Labor, is a competitively bid national program that provides funds for states to pull together educational records, workforce administrative data, and UI wage records in order to construct a longitudinal history of each worker's education and employment.

The information can be used in a variety of ways to inform the decisions of workforce program customers. For example, WDQI can track the educational and employment outcomes of each student by the individual training provider with which each is enrolled. This information on "success" rates is useful for prospective students in choosing training providers and educational institutions and for program administrators in holding service providers accountable for student outcomes. It also provides the basis for estimating the economic returns to education and employment services.[3] Furthermore, the WDQI expands the coverage of WIASRD to include all employees who are covered under the UI system, not only those who are enrolled in the WIA programs.

WDQI is still in the development stage, with 26 states participating in rounds one and two. Under contractual agreement, participating states are expected to use their data analysis to create materials on state workforce performance to share with workforce system stakeholders and the public. According to USDOL, high-quality and consistent data about services offered and the benefits received as they enter or reenter the labor market are integral to informed consumer choices (USDOL 2013). Colorado, for example, has merged K–12 longitudinal data with UI wage records of college graduates from all public colleges and universities and three private colleges in the state to provide prospective students with information about the earnings potential of various academic majors at each educational institution. This information helps students make informed decisions in choosing career paths and shows the value of various levels of educational attainment. The Workforce Data Quality Campaign tracks the progress of states in using longitudinal data for informing workforce- and education-related decisions.

Timely Labor Demand Information

The growing use of the Internet to post job openings offers another source of data that can be useful to customers, particularly with respect to the demand for skills by businesses. While not a statistically valid survey, the use of "spiders" to search and compile Web-based information on job postings has the advantage over surveys of being timely and including all jobs posted on the Internet and not simply a sample of postings. Several states and LWIBs have contracted with vendors to gain access to this information on job openings posted on the Internet. The more sophisticated approaches use algorithms to reduce duplication of job postings and to aggregate them by industry and occupation classifications.

Web-based information can be broken out into highly detailed occupational categories and even reported by individual businesses. These services can be customized for specific locations and can glean from the job postings requirements related to educational attainment, certifications, experience, and other qualifications. However, a current difficulty with relying on job postings found on the Internet, or from other sources, is that no more than half the job postings list education requirements or other skill requirements sought by the employer. Without such information, it is difficult for job seekers to determine what skills they may need to qualify for a job opening and what training they may need to qualify in the future. Perhaps as the use of Web-based data increases and employers recognize the value of this data source for projecting skill needs, employers will be more willing to include skill and education requirements in their postings.[4]

VALUE-ADDED PERFORMANCE MANAGEMENT

To hold program administrators accountable for the outcomes of WIA programs and to foster continuous improvement, USDOL has established a performance-management system based on the longitudinal files of individual participants, described in the previous section (USDOL 2010).[5] Accountability of the programs is established by setting targets at each level of government and monitoring whether or not local workforce investment areas (LWIAs) and states meet or exceed their targets. When performance measures exceed their targets, the program is considered effective; when performance measures fail to meet their targets, the program is considered ineffective. Financial incentives are tied to these performance targets.

However, there is no clear relationship between a program meeting or exceeding its targets and its effectiveness in helping someone find or keep a job. Therefore, under the current performance system, program administrators have little if any information generated on a regular basis about the effectiveness of their programs, and thus little guidance in how to improve the system. Furthermore, it is unclear whether these performance measures provide administrators with the proper incentives to operate programs effectively. This section describes the performance measures currently in use by WIA programs, states their shortcomings, describes research findings of their incentive effects, and outlines methods USDOL has adopted to adjust the measures for confounding factors.

Common Performance Measures

For the two WIA adult programs, the performance measures focus on employment outcomes—the entered employment rate, employment retention rate, and earnings levels.[6] For the Youth program, the measures relate to educational attainment—placement in employment or education, attainment of a degree or certificate, and literacy and numeracy gains. WIA is a partnership among federal, state, and local governments and their nongovernmental intermediaries, and these performance measures are common across all three levels. Each year, USDOL sets national targets for each program; it then negotiates targets with each state, and the states in turn set targets for each of their LWIBs. Performance measures may vary from year to year and across states and LWIBs, depending on local economic conditions and characteristics of program participants. WIA requires that negotiations take into account these factors when setting targets, but it is unclear to what extent these factors are actually embedded in the targets, since negotiations are subjective and not transparent. Even more rigorous methods of adjusting targets for these factors, such as regression analysis, cannot purge the performance measures of these factors completely, although such an approach is more objective and transparent than negotiations.

The problem with interpreting performance measures as a reflection of the effectiveness of the workforce programs is that the common measures are not designed to be used in that way. The common measures focus, as they should, on whether or not a participant finds and keeps a job, but the measures cannot distinguish the contribution of the workforce programs from other factors that affect a person's employment. Other factors include a person's innate abilities, signaled by his or her educational attainment and work experience, and local labor market conditions. Evidence shows that these two sets of factors generally influence employment more than the reemployment and training services offered by the workforce system (Eberts and Huang 2011). Therefore, a program administrator may conclude that the services provided are effectively contributing to the employment outcomes of participants when the performance of the administrator's program exceeds its predetermined target, whereas it could simply be the case that the participants are more capable than was expected when the targets were set, or that labor market conditions are more favorable. Unless the performance measures are adjusted for these factors in a rigorous way, they provide administrators with little information as to the effectiveness of their programs and what they may need to do to improve the delivery of services. Typically, rigorous evaluations, using comparison groups, are conducted to estimate the net effect of a program.[7] Because of the expense in conducting such an evaluation, they are done infrequently, and thus their relevance may diminish over time.

Possible Adverse Incentives

In addition to concerns that the performance system implemented under WIA provides little guidance to administrators to improve their services, policymakers and researchers have for some time been concerned about the possible adverse behavioral responses to performance measurement systems. Questions have arisen as to whether the performance system may lead local administrators to "game" the system by admitting more qualified individuals in order to improve the performance of their programs, without actually improving the effectiveness of the services provided. Concerns have also surfaced as to whether financial incentives were sufficient to influence positive behavior.

James Heckman and a group of his graduate students conducted a series of studies on how performance standards and incentives influence the behavior of program administrators and staff and contribute to program outcomes or unintended consequences (Heckman et al. 2011). While the studies focused on the Job Training Partnership Act (JTPA), the predecessor to WIA, sufficient similarities exist between the two programs for their findings to be relevant to the current system.

The body of research drew two key lessons: First, agencies respond to incentives, even seemingly small ones, and second, the concern about "cream-skimming" is overstated. With respect to incentives, the researchers found that "low-powered cash incentives may, in fact, be high-powered because of the value of the budgetary awards in establishing the reputation of bureaucrats and the recognition that comes with them" (Heckman et al. 2011, p. 306). However, they cautioned that bureaucrats may learn over time the weaknesses of the system and how the weaknesses can be exploited to their advantage. They recommended that the incentive system and performance measures be reviewed regularly and redesigned when deemed necessary to achieve the desired outcomes.

Researchers also found that the financial incentives incorporated into the performance measurement system were further enhanced by performance-based contracting. Under both JTPA and WIA, contracts with local service providers, such as community colleges and nonprofits, are based on the performance of the subcontractors. Heinrich (2000), in a detailed study of an Illinois Service Delivery Area under JTPA, found that the inclusion of performance incentives in service contracts has a very strong positive effect on participants' realized wages and employment at termination and for up to four quarters after they leave the program. Based on this result and that of others (Dickinson et al. 1988; Spaulding 2001), one can conclude that performance-based contracts yield higher performance on the rewarded dimension. However, as previously mentioned, one has to ensure that incentives are properly aligned with desired outcomes.

The second lesson from the studies is that the cream-skimming problem is overstated. There has been serious concern that local administrators of the workforce system game the system by enrolling program participants with high abilities to find employment at the expense of those who truly need assistance. Administrators were also suspected of gaming the system by exiting participants only when they had achieved a positive outcome, such as obtaining a job. However, the researchers found little evidence that this had occurred in the JTPA programs. Since WIA replaced JTPA, there has been a growing industry of consultants who purport to help LWIBs maximize their outcomes, and it is unclear whether this influence has led to more gaming under WIA than under JTPA. An assessment by Barnow and King (2005) of the first five years of WIA found that gaming or "strategic behavior" took place in the majority of states studied. However, they did not analyze, as Heinrich did, the actual impact of gaming behavior on performance outcomes.

Statistical Approaches to Adjusting Performance Measures

One possibility for the low incidence of cream-skimming could be related to the methodology used to adjust for factors that lead to such behavior. JTPA used a regression approach to adjust targets for factors that affect participants' ability to find employment. By adjusting targets upward when a local program has a higher percentage of participants with characteristics more favorable to achieving positive employment and educational outcomes, the performance standards are raised for those trying to game the system by enrolling those who are more likely to find employment because of their own higher capabilities.

WIA legislation replaced the statistical approach to adjusting targets adopted by JTPA with a more subjective approach based on negotiations between the different levels of government. The reliance of WIA on negotiations to adjust for outside factors rather than using the quantifiable and transparent system adopted by JTPA led Barnow and Smith (2004) to conclude that WIA took a step backward from JTPA in measuring the contribution of the workforce system to achieving outcomes. As the performance system is adjusted more accurately for such factors, the system moves closer toward an indicator of the value-added of the program.[8]

Beginning with program year 2009, USDOL adopted a regression-adjusted approach for setting national targets for the three WIA programs and other federal workforce development programs. The regression-adjusted methodology followed the JTPA methodology to a large extent by controlling for factors related to personal abilities and local labor market conditions. However, USDOL did not return completely to using the method of setting targets under JTPA. Instead, it used a hybrid approach for states and LWIAs. As with JTPA, targets were determined for states and LWIAs using the regression methodology. These regression-adjusted targets were offered only as a starting point for negotiations, and the final targets were determined by the negotiation process (USDOL 2011). Nonetheless, by offering states and LWIBs regression-adjusted performance targets, they have objective data describing the factors that affect their performance outcomes and a transparent, objective method of understanding how these factors actually affect their performance (Eberts and Huang 2011). Several states use these data in the negotiation process.

Value-Added Performance Improvement System

Recognizing the need to provide better and more timely information to program administrators, the state of Michigan, with support from

USDOL, developed the Value-Added Performance Improvement System (VAPIS). Michigan provided VAPIS to local workforce administrators for several years (Bartik, Eberts, and Kline 2009; Eberts, Bartik, and Huang 2011). The system was similar to the regression-adjusted targets described previously, except that instead of adjusting the targets, the methodology adjusted the common measures. In this way, the performance measures themselves reflected to a greater extent the value-added of the workforce system. Performance measures were adjusted downward for participants who had a greater ability to find employment, and upward for those with less ability. The same approach was used for local labor market conditions: Performance measures in areas with favorable conditions were adjusted downward, and such measures were adjusted upward for areas with less favorable conditions. By purging the performance measures of factors unrelated to the actual effectiveness of the program services, the adjusted measures were more reflective of the value-added of the system.

VAPIS also addressed the issue of the timeliness of performance measures. Performance measures, based on UI wage records, are not available for up to a year after participants exit the program. The long lag makes it difficult for administrators to base management decisions on these measures or to use them for continuous improvement. VAPIS forecast the possible outcomes of participants currently receiving services so that local administrators could get some idea of how their current decisions may affect future outcomes.

While regression-adjusted performance measures may theoretically reflect more closely the value-added of a program, they still may not closely approximate the findings from a rigorous evaluation of effectiveness. A recent evaluation of the use of regression-adjusted performance outcomes in the Job Corps program found little relationship between these "value-added" measures and the net impact results from a rigorous randomized evaluation (Schochet and Fortson 2014). The authors attribute much of this effect to the weak associations between the unadjusted performance measures and long-term outcomes, as well as to unobserved factors. While performance outcomes were never intended to substitute for rigorous evaluations, the question still remains of whether a regression-adjusted approach provides administrators with information that can inform their decisions better than no information at all.[9]

Including Business Satisfaction Indicators

Businesses look to the workforce development system to help identify, assess, and train workers to meet their specific skill requirements. In return, the workforce development system looks to businesses to communicate their talent needs in order to assist with proper job matches and to ensure that workers are trained to meet the future needs of employers. Despite the importance of engaging businesses as customers and partners, the common measures currently adopted by USDOL do not include any direct measure of how businesses use the system, how they may benefit from using the system, or their satisfaction with the system. Obviously, the mere act of hiring a workforce-program participant is beneficial to the employer. However, the current performance measurement system does not record whether an employer used the workforce development system to find specific workers, nor does it record the length of time that employer retained the worker hired through the workforce system.

The Commonwealth of Virginia and the state of Washington considered including indicators reflecting the business use and satisfaction of public workforce development programs. Of particular interest is a measure they constructed to record the use by employers of WIA services. It measures repeat employer customers and is calculated as the percentage of employers served by WIA who return to the same program for service within one year (Hollenbeck and Huang 2008). More specifically, an employer was categorized as "satisfied" if the business hired someone who had exited from a program in the first quarter of the fiscal year and then hired another individual from the program before the fiscal year was over. The denominator for this indicator is the number of employers who hired someone in the first quarter of the fiscal year. Hollenbeck and Huang (2008) calculated the measure for the two WIA adult programs in Virginia and found that 52 percent of employers who hired someone from one of the two programs hired at least one more worker from the same program within the year. Of course, this is contingent on the number of times an employer hires during the year, but it can be normalized by a state or industry average.

The measure adopted by Virginia assumes that employers are repeat customers because the programs have provided them with job applicants with the appropriate skills and other qualifications. However, the measure, while easy to calculate and inexpensive to administer, may be a poor substitute for more in-depth information obtained directly from employers. First, it does not offer any specific information about the level of satisfaction or exactly what services businesses found helpful in their recruiting efforts. Second, the measure may not reflect what it is intended to record. Rather, it may be the case that the same business did not return to the workforce programs in search of job applicants simply because it was not hiring during the period covered by the measure. Consequently, the lack of hiring needs may be confused with lower satisfaction with the workforce services. Third, the measure may be of little use to workforce administrators seeking better ways to help guide participants with sought-after skills to the appropriate employers, and of little use to training providers in determining the appropriate curriculum and the appropriate capacity in their training facilities to meet employers' demands.

CUSTOMIZED INFORMATION AND TARGETED SERVICES

The merit of providing information customized to the personal characteristics and circumstances of individual participants is supported by lessons from behavioral economics. According to Babcock et al. (2012), job search assistance and employment services should be simplified and streamlined by making tools available that gather information on an individual's background and interests, provide feedback on the education and employment opportunities pursued by others like the participant, list job openings that may interest the participant, and provide information on the projected growth in occupations (p. 8). The next logical step then is to use that information to find the services that best meet the needs of individual participants. Therefore, initiatives that combine customized information and targeting will be discussed in this section.

Frontline Decision Support System

The Frontline Decision Support System (FDSS) pursues an approach to customizing information and targeting resources that is consistent with the lessons drawn from behavioral economics. FDSS offers a set of decision tools that provides job seekers and frontline staff with customized information about employment prospects and the effectiveness of services. Of the various initiatives considered, FDSS comes the closest to combining all five elements of an intelligent workforce system, including evidence-based decision making, and offers the possibility that the results of rigorous evaluations can be incorporated into the FDSS framework. FDSS uses existing administrative data and statistical algorithms to help staff and customers make better decisions about job prospects and about appropriate services that meet the customer's needs in finding employment. The Web-based screens guide job seekers through key decision points and provide them with easily accessible and customized information. The pilot was implemented in Georgia in 2002 as a joint effort of USDOL's Employment and Training Administration, the Georgia Department of Labor, and the Upjohn Institute (Eberts, O'Leary, and DeRango 2002).

FDSS walks job seekers through a systematic sequence of steps and presents customized information at each critical decision point. Using the case of a dislocated worker as an example, FDSS moves that individual through the reemployment process, beginning with understanding his or her likelihood of returning to work in the same industry, proceeding to explore job prospects in occupations that require similar skills and aptitudes, then accessing information about the earnings and growth of jobs in particular occupations within the individual's local labor market, and ending with an understanding of which reemployment and training services might work best for that person, if none of the previous steps leads to a job. At each of these critical decision points, personalized information is made available to help inform the decisions.

The personalized information is based on statistical relationships between a customer's employment outcomes, personal characteristics, and other factors that may affect his or her outcomes, all of which are available from workforce administrative files already collected by the various agencies. The statistical algorithms provide an evidence-based approach to determining which services are most effective for specific individuals. The algorithms also personalize labor market information so that it presents information that is pertinent to the participant's abilities and circumstances, such as the probability of someone with the observed characteristics of the specific individual returning to his or her previous occupation and industry. By using administrative data that capture the experience of all customers who have recently participated in the state's workforce system, this evidence-based approach offers a more comprehensive and "collective" experience of what works and what doesn't than relying on the narrower experience of individual caseworkers.[10]

Barnow and Smith (2004), in a critique of the performance management system of the federal workforce system, recommend using FDSS as the centerpiece for a redesign of the performance system. In what they describe as an "ideal" performance system, "randomization would be directly incorporated in the normal operations of the WIA program . . . [through] a system similar in spirit to the Frontline Decision Support System" (p. 49). They contend that such randomization need not exclude persons from any intensive services, but only assign a modest fraction to low-intensity services—that is, the core services under WIA. The randomization would then be used, in conjunction with outcome data already collected, to produce experimental impact estimates that would serve as the performance measures. However, one of the drawbacks with randomization is sample size. A relatively large sample—typically larger than the inflow of participants into many local workforce programs—would be required. Because of the need for large samples, this approach would be most applicable for state-level performance incentives, which is not the level at which contracts are administered and services delivered. Furthermore, for purposes of informing management decisions, the effect of either individual services or bundles of services is more useful than the overall effect of the program. To use randomization to estimate service-specific effects would require even larger sample sizes.

Another approach to estimating the effects of programs and services is to use propensity scoring techniques to construct counterfactuals. While this is thought to be not as reliable in estimating net impacts as randomization, it is considered a viable alternative and has been used extensively in program evaluations, most recently in evaluating the net impact of WIA programs (Heinrich, Mueser, and Troske 2009; Hollenbeck et al. 2005). For the purpose of providing pertinent information to decision makers, it has several advantages over randomization. One is the need for a smaller sample size; a second is that one need not exclude participants from any services. With randomization, a control group is constructed by randomly excluding individuals from services. With propensity scoring, the control group is constructed by identifying observationally similar individuals who were not enrolled in any of the services being evaluated. One of the drawbacks of the latter approach is that individuals may not have enrolled for reasons that are not observed and thus could bias the net impact estimates. However, finding individuals who are similar in observed characteristics helps to control for these unobserved attributes, and the previously mentioned studies have used as comparison group members those who participate in the Wagner-Peyser Employment Service. A third advantage is that propensity score matching methodologies can be "built in" to a performance system and can be refreshed periodically as new data are entered into the system. While not completely automatic and self-functioning, it does require a minimal amount of intervention during the updating phases.

FDSS has never been rigorously evaluated to determine whether the information provided and the way in which it was presented improved the effectiveness of the WIA programs compared with the typical conveyance of information within One-Stop Service Centers. However, the development and implementation of FDSS was based in part on the success of two U.S. Department of Labor initiatives, both of which were rigorously evaluated and found to be effective. These two initiatives, Welfare-to-Work and WPRS, are discussed in the next two sections.

Targeting Services to Welfare-to-Work Participants

The Welfare-to-Work referral system used a statistical methodology, similar to that used in FDSS, to target services to program participants. The purpose of the pilot was to improve the employment outcomes of participants by referring them to services that best meet their needs. Funded by USDOL and developed by the Upjohn Institute, the pilot referred Welfare-to-Work participants to one of three service providers based on a statistical algorithm that used administrative data to determine which provider offered services that were shown to be most effective for customers possessing specific characteristics and employment backgrounds. Each provider offered different services and different approaches to delivering those services. Before the pilot was established, the LWIB where the pilot took place randomly referred participants to the three different providers. Therefore, the relationships between different types of services and employment outcomes for groups of participants with different characteristics were based on a randomized sample. Using this sample, the observed employment outcomes were regressed against personal characteristics of the participants, and these relationships were then used to refer new enrollees to providers based on the enrollees' personal characteristics.

The initiative demonstrated that customizing services based on participant characteristics could increase the effectiveness and efficiency of the intervention. A random assignment evaluation of the pilot showed that targeting services in this way significantly increased the 90-day employment retention rate of participants by 20 percentage points, yielding a benefit-cost ratio of greater than three (Eberts 2002).

Worker Profiling and Reemployment Services

WPRS is a national program signed into law in 1993, which requires each state to identify UI claimants who are most likely to exhaust their UI benefits before finding employment and then to refer them as quickly as possible to reemployment programs. The purpose of WPRS is to encourage a targeted subset of UI beneficiaries to use reemployment services intensively at the beginning of their unemployment spell rather than toward the end, when they face the prospect of exhausting their benefits. The identification procedure uses statistical methods similar to some of the algorithms used in FDSS. Independent evaluations show that WPRS reduces the use of UI benefits and the length of unemployment spells by statistically significant amounts compared with appropriate comparison groups (Dickinson, Decker, and Kruetzer 2002).

Value of Information and Guidance about Training Outcomes

The training programs delivered under WIA offer fertile ground for exploring ways to guide participants through the process of determining the type of training. WIA-funded training is offered primarily through Individual Training Accounts (ITAs), which provide job seekers with a fixed amount of money they can use to pay for training from providers of their choice. With this high degree of choice, individuals are faced with a series of complex choices involving the calculations of future returns to training and the selection of the type of training and, subsequently, choice of occupation, in addition to the psychological barriers of investing time and money in training with distant payoffs. Babcock et al. (2012) suggest that training programs through One-Stop Centers should "emphasize reducing complexity and providing guidance to participants as priorities" (p. 11).

To help job seekers make more informed decisions, WIA requires states to compile and post Eligible Training Provider Lists, which provide job seekers with information about past success rates of participants enrolled with specific training providers. To be eligible to receive WIA funding for postsecondary training, a training provider must meet the criteria for being included on the list. Most pertinent for this discussion is the requirement that training providers post information on specific student outcomes, such as the percentage graduating from the program and the percentage completing the training and finding employment. To construct the Eligible Training Provider List, student data from each provider was to be linked with UI wage records. However, for many providers, this linkage was never completed. The Workforce Data Quality Initiative has rekindled interest in completing the information for training providers and educational institutions in general.

In addition to providing information about the education and employment outcomes of training providers, USDOL considered the relative effectiveness of offering different levels of guidance to prospective training participants. USDOL commissioned an evaluation that considered three models, which varied along two dimensions: first, the freedom that trainees were given in selecting a training provider, and second, the gap between the cost of training and the funds provided by WIA to pay for training.

Findings from the randomized control trial evaluation suggest that customers and society would benefit markedly from intensive counseling and higher potential ITA awards, compared with less information and direction from counselors and fixed awards. Estimates from the benefit-cost analysis indicate that society would benefit by about $46,600 per ITA customer by participants' receiving more guidance from counselors compared to less oversight (Perez-Johnson, Moore, and Santillano 2011). Results also show that customers who were given more guidance were significantly more likely to be employed in the occupation for which they trained, offering additional support for the suggestion from behavioral economics of providing guidance to participants.

EVIDENCE-BASED DECISIONMAKING

Evidence-based decisionmaking permeates many of the initiatives described in this chapter, and various methodologies of estimating the effectiveness of programs have already been discussed. One of the trade-offs inherent in providing information on the effectiveness of programs and services is between the rigor of the evaluation and the timeliness of the information. Another trade-off is between the rigor of the evaluation and the granularity of the information, such as obtaining effectiveness estimates of specific services or bundles of services for subgroups of the population. The latter is important for customizing information to individual customers and for targeting resources to individuals. Some researchers, such as Barnow and Smith (2004), have suggested embedding a randomized trial evaluation in a system such as the FDSS. Researchers at the IAB in Germany have experimented with that approach.[11] Others have explored the possibility of incorporating an evaluation instrument based on propensity scoring within a similar framework. And still others have looked at refining a regression-adjusted approach. As previously mentioned, some research has already examined the trade-offs between the different approaches, and more needs to be done to find the right balance for the different applications of evidence-based information.

EXTERNAL PARTNERS

The workforce development system depends on close relationships with other entities in order to provide effective reemployment and training services. Many LWIBs act as facilitators to bring together various local organizations, such as economic development entities, businesses, social agencies, educational institutions, and labor groups, to help address workforce aspects in their local areas. According to a Government Accountability Office report (GAO-11-506T, p. 12), One-Stop Centers provide an opportunity to coordinate the services among a broad array of federal employment and training programs. The study also points out that colocation of services affords the potential for sharing resources, cross-training staff, and integrating management information systems.

Regional Sector Alliances

Several states have initiated programs that engage businesses and form partnerships with local educational institutions and economic development agencies through a sectoral approach. Two examples are the Michigan Regional Skills Alliance and the California Regional Workforce Preparation and Economic Development Act (Eberts and Hollenbeck 2009). Typically, local areas engage in a strategic planning process that includes an analysis that identifies the key growth sectors in the region. Partnerships are formed within these sectors by bringing together key businesses within these sectors with local entities that provide training and economic development initiatives.

Beginning in 2006, USDOL funded WIRED (Workforce Innovation in Regional Economic Development), which supported the development of a regional, integrated approach to bring together workforce development, economic development, and educational activities. The goal of WIRED was to expand employment and career advancement opportunities for workers and catalyze the creation of high-skill and high-wage opportunities. WIRED consisted of three generations of regional collaborations, totaling 39 regions (Hewat and Hollenbeck 2009). The WIRED initiative was a competitive program in which selected regions received from $5 million to $15 million over three years to support the formation of partnerships. The evaluation of WIRED, funded by USDOL, found that the WIA programs within the WIRED regions had statistically significantly higher entered employment rates and retention rates than WIA programs in the comparison group (Hewat, Hollenbeck, and others 2011, chapter 5).

The information requirements to foster effective partnerships across entities external to the workforce system are similar to the information needs within the system. Partnerships work best when organizations share a common vision and strive to meet common goals. The performance of one organization, therefore, affects the success of another organization within the partnership. Consequently, each organization needs to be able to understand its contribution to the common goal, which requires each to develop value-added performance measures.

Moreover, since it is likely that each organization will have a different management information system, a common platform is needed upon which relevant data from the various organizations can be shared. Such platforms are available, through which organizations can share data at various levels of disaggregation and thus disclosure. Probably the most challenging barrier to sharing information is to establish trust between partnering entities and leadership to identify a common vision and act collectively toward a common goal.

SUMMARY: AN INTELLIGENT, INTEGRATED INFORMATION SYSTEM

As outlined in this chapter, customers and managers of the workforce system require more relevant and current information to make informed decisions. Job seekers ask for information that will help them identify the occupations and skills demanded by businesses, find jobs, and move into more meaningful careers. Businesses seek information about the pool of qualified workers. Workforce program administrators seek information to help them make better management decisions. To meet these needs for relevant information, an intelligent workforce system, therefore, needs to incorporate five elements: 1) a data-driven system, 2) information customized to the specific needs and circumstances of each customer, 3) an evidence-based system, 4) targeted reemployment and training services, and 5) value-added performance management. The current workforce system embodies various aspects of these elements, but significant improvements must still be made.

The WIOA, which replaces the current workforce development system, encourages states to target services, integrate data-driven counseling and assessments into service strategies, more fully integrate programs, and provide easy and seamless access to all programs. It even requires states to periodically evaluate the workforce system using comparison-group methodologies. Something like the FDSS comes the closest to incorporating these functions: It integrates administrative workforce data with education and wage data, it develops statistical algorithms that provide personalized information to help customers understand what various trends and circumstances mean to them, and it brings this information back down to the customers and frontline staff who are making decisions. Such a system incorporates some of the lessons gleaned from behavioral economics that demonstrate the benefit of customized information, feedback on the possible returns to education and training choices, and personalized employment prospects and labor market information. As Barnow and Smith (2004) suggest, this framework can be combined with counterfactuals that provide a better sense of the value-added of programs and, more specifically, the services provided within those programs. Such a system is not perfect, of course. It does not substitute for rigorous evaluations of the effectiveness of programs, nor does it guarantee that incentives are properly aligned with desired outcomes. However, it does make significant advances in getting relevant information in an easily accessible format to the customers and decision makers of the workforce system.

Development of an intelligent workforce system will not happen all at once, even though much of the foundation has already been laid by past initiatives and within the current workforce system. To begin the process, one possible approach is for the federal government to provide innovation dollars to one or two interested states with the specific purpose of developing such a system. Once the system is up and running, other states can see how it works and begin to recognize the merits of such a system. To ensure that statistical algorithms and other key innovative aspects of the system are continually updated, regional data centers could be established to give researchers who are interested in creating, updating, and improving such a system access to administrative data. Involving researchers and practitioners in the ongoing development of the system will help to ensure that the system continues to evolve to meet the current and future needs of customers and administrators of the workforce development system.

Notes

1. This chapter draws from Eberts (2013).
2. WIA was enacted in 1998, and the Wagner-Peyser was established in the 1930s. WIOA is based on principles similar to WIA (and its predecessor, JTPA) of a federal-state-local partnership with authority given to local boards to administer the programs.

3. For an example of using similar data for computing rates of return for worker training programs, see Jacobson and LaLonde (2013).

4. Some analysis has been conducted to compare the accuracy of job openings data obtained from vendors with the survey-based Job Openings and Longitudinal Time Series (JOLTS) data compiled by the BLS. While the actual numbers of job openings differ between the two sources, they both seem to track similarly, with turning points occurring at roughly the same time. Brad Hershbein has conducted this research at the Upjohn Institute, and the results are available upon request.

5. Training and Employment Guidance Letter (TEGL) 17-05, issued February 17, 2006 (USDOL 2010). The Government Performance and Results Act (GPRA) of 1993 requires that all federal programs set performance targets and establish performance tracking systems. Even before GPRA was enacted, the ETA incorporated an outcomes-based performance system into many of its programs. Today, 15 federal workforce programs, serving nearly 20 million people annually, are subject to performance measures and targets. GPRA was updated in 2010 with the enactment of the Government Performance and Results Modernization Act.

6. Performance measures of the WIA adult programs include educational attainment outcomes in addition to employment outcomes.

7. The legislation to replace WIA requires that each state periodically evaluate its workforce programs using methodologies that include comparison groups.

8. Heckman's team of researchers also found that the short-term outcomes are not highly correlated with longer-term outcomes, which suggests that the regression-adjusted targets do not substitute for a rigorous evaluation of the program, no matter how well the adjustments may move the gross outcomes toward value-added outcomes.

9. Barnow and Smith (2004), in an assessment of performance management of the WIA system, expressed concern that short-term performance outcomes mandated by WIA do not correlate with long-term program impacts. They recommended that the performance system be suspended until research identifies such short-term measures.

10. While not indicting all caseworkers, Lechner and Smith (2007) provide evidence that caseworkers do not do a very good job in referring displaced workers (in Switzerland) to services that maximize their employment prospects.

11. The German public employment service, through its research arm, the Bundesagentur fur Arbeit (IAB), used randomized experiments to develop an evidence-based system that identifies services that have been shown to contribute the most to the improvement of employment outcomes of individual workforce participants. The approach grew out of the Hartz reform to improve the effectiveness and efficiency of German's active labor market programs. Dr. Susanne Rassler was the project director.

References

Babcock, Linda, William J. Congdon, Lawrence F. Katz, and Sendhil Mullain-athan. 2012. "Notes on Behavioral Economics and Labor Market Policy." *IZA Journal of Labor Policy* 1(1): 1–14.

Barnow, Burt S., and Christopher T. King. 2005. *The Workforce Investment Act in Eight States*. Washington, DC: U.S. Department of Labor, Employment and Training Administration.

Barnow, Burt S., and Jeffrey A. Smith. 2004. "Performance Management of U.S. Job Training Programs." In *Job Training Policy in the United States*, Christopher J. O'Leary, Robert A. Straits, and Stephen A. Wandner, eds. Kalamazoo, MI: W.E. Upjohn Institute for Employment Research, pp. 21–55.

Bartik, Timothy J., Randall W. Eberts, and Kenneth J. Kline. 2009. "Estimating a Performance Standards Adjustment Model for Workforce Programs That Provides Timely Feedback and Uses Data from Only One State." Upjohn Institute Working Paper No. 09-144. Kalamazoo, MI: W.E. Upjohn Institute for Employment Research.

Dickinson, Katherine P., Paul T. Decker, and Suzanne D. Kreutzer. 2002. "Evaluation of WPRS Systems." In *Targeting Employment Services*, Randall W. Eberts, Christopher J. O'Leary, and Stephen A. Wandner, eds. Kalamazoo, MI: W.E. Upjohn Institute for Employment Research, pp. 61–82.

Dickinson, Katherine P., Richard W. West, Deborah J. Kogan, David A. Drury, Marlene S. Franks, Laura Schlichtmann, and Mary Vencill. 1988. *Evaluation of the Effects of JTPA Performance Standards on Clients, Services, and Costs*. Research Report No. 88-16. Washington, DC: National Commission for Employment Policy.

Eberts, Randall W. 2002. "Using Statistical Assessment Tools to Target Services to Work First Participants." In *Targeting Employment Services*, Randall W. Eberts, Christopher J. O'Leary, and Stephen A. Wandner, eds. Kalamazoo, MI: W.E. Upjohn Institute for Employment Research, pp. 221–244.

———. 2013. *Improving the U.S. Workforce System by Transforming Its Performance Measurement System*. College Park, MD; Washington, DC: University of Maryland School of Public Policy and Atlantic Council.

Eberts, Randall W., Timothy J. Bartik, and Wei-Jang Huang. 2011. "Recent Advances in Performance Measurement of Federal Workforce Development Programs." In *The Workforce Investment Act: Implementation Experiences and Evaluation Findings*, Douglas J. Besharov and Phoebe H. Cottingham, eds. Kalamazoo, MI: W.E. Upjohn Institute for Employment Research, pp. 233–276.

Eberts, Randall W., and Kevin Hollenbeck. 2009. "Michigan Regional Skills Alliances: A Statewide Initiative to Address Local Workforce Needs." In *Designing Local Skills Strategies*, Francesca Froy, Sylvain Giguère, and Andrea-Rosalinde Hofer, eds. Paris: Organisation for Economic Co-operation and Development, pp. 129–153.

Eberts, Randall W., and Wei-Jang Huang. 2011. *Description of the Methodology for Setting State and WIB PY2011 WIA Performance Targets*. Final Report. Washington, DC: U.S. Department of Labor, Employment and Training Administration.

Eberts, Randall W., Christopher J. O'Leary, and Kelly J. DeRango. 2002. "A Frontline Decision Support System for One-Stop Centers." In *Targeting Employment Services*, Randall W. Eberts, Christopher J. O'Leary, and Stephen A. Wandner, eds. Kalamazoo, MI: W.E. Upjohn Institute for Employment Research, pp. 337–380.

Government Accountability Office. 2011. "Employment and Training Programs: Opportunities Exist for Improving Efficiency." Statement of Andrew Sherrill, Director of Education, Workforce, and Income Security Issues. GAO-11-506T. Testimony before the Subcommittee on Labor, Health and Human Services, Education and Related Agencies, Committee on Appropriations, House of Representatives.

Heckman, James J., Carolyn J. Heinrich, Pascal Courty, Gerald Marschke, and Jeffrey A. Smith, eds. 2011. *The Performance of Performance Standards*. Kalamazoo, MI: W.E. Upjohn Institute for Employment Research.

Heinrich, Carolyn J. 2000. "Organizational Form and Performance: An Empirical Investigation of Nonprofit and For-Profit Job-Training Service Providers." *Journal of Policy Analysis and Management* 19(2): 233–261.

Heinrich, Carolyn J., Peter R. Mueser, and Kenneth R. Troske. 2009. *Workforce Investment Act Non-Experimental Net Impact Evaluation*. Final report. ETAOP No. 2009-10. Washington, DC: U.S. Department of Labor, Employment and Training Administration.

Hewat, Nancy, and Kevin Hollenbeck. 2009. "Nurturing America's Growth in the Global Marketplace through Talent Development: An Interim Report on the Evaluation of Generations II and III of WIRED." USDOL ETA Occasional Paper No. 2009-19. Washington, DC: U.S. Department of Labor, Employment and Training Administration.

Hewat, Nancy, Kevin Hollenbeck, and others. 2011. *Transforming America's Talent and Economic Development*. Draft final report to the Employment and Training Administration of the U.S. Department of Labor, June. Washington, DC: U.S. Department of Labor, Employment and Training Administration.

Hollenbeck, Kevin, and Wei-Jang Huang. 2008. *Workforce Program Performance Indicators for the Commonwealth of Virginia.* Upjohn Institute Technical Report No. 08-024. Kalamazoo, MI: W.E. Upjohn Institute for Employment Research.

Hollenbeck, Kevin, Wei-Jang Huang, Christopher King, Daniel Schroeder, 2005. *Net Impact Estimates for Services Provided through the Workforce Investment Act.* USDOL ETA Occasional Paper No. 2005-06. Washington, DC: U.S. Department of Labor, Employment and Training Administration.

Jacobson, Louis S., and Robert J. LaLonde. 2013. "Using Data to Improve the Performance of Workforce Training." A Hamilton Project Discussion Paper. Washington, DC: Brookings Institution.

Lechner, Michael, and Jeffrey A. Smith. 2007. "What Is the Value Added by Caseworkers?" *Labour Economics* 14(2): 135–151.

Perez-Johnson, Irma, Quinn Moore, and Robert Santillano. 2011. *Improving the Effectiveness of Individual Training Accounts: Long-Term Findings from an Experimental Evaluation of Three Service Delivery Models.* Final Report. Princeton, NJ: Mathematica Policy Research.

Schochet, Peter Z., and Jane Fortson. 2014. "When Do Regression-Adjusted Performance Measures Track Longer-Term Program Impacts? A Case Study for Job Corps." *Journal of Policy Analysis and Management* 33(2): 495–525.

Spaulding, Shayne Lauren. 2001. "Performance-Based Contracting under the Job Training Partnership Act." Master's thesis, Johns Hopkins University, Baltimore, MD.

U.S. Department of Labor (USDOL). 2010. *Training and Employment Guidance Letter No. 17-05.* Washington, DC: U.S. Department of Labor, Employment and Training Administration. http://wdr.doleta.gov/directives/corr_doc.cfm?DOCN=2195 (accessed July 9, 2014).

———. 2011. *Training and Employment Guidance Letter No. 29-10.* Washington, DC: U.S. Department of Labor, Employment and Training Administration.

———. 2013. *Workforce Data Quality Initiative.* Washington, DC: U.S. Department of Labor, Employment and Training Administration. http://www.doleta.gov/performance/workforcedatagrant09.cfm (accessed July 9, 2014).

18

Improving the Effectiveness of Education and Training Programs for Low-Income Individuals

Building Knowledge from Three Decades of Rigorous Experiments

Richard Hendra
Gayle Hamilton
MDRC

While many low-income individuals have jobs—or eventually find them after periods of unemployment—many do not consistently earn wages that will foster upward mobility. To address this, a number of initiatives have aimed to help low-wage workers acquire "better" jobs, stay employed, and advance in the labor market. This chapter reviews a large body of rigorous evidence, accumulated over the past 30 years, on the effectiveness of dozens of different types of human capital development programs that had these goals and targeted public assistance recipients and other low-wage workers. It shows how knowledge gained from each set of multisite randomized control trials (RCTs) led to the development and testing of a subsequent results-based "next generation" of programs. The chapter explains how this progressive evidence-development process has led to a current focus on rigorously examining the effectiveness of programs emphasizing several approaches: the alignment of services with employer demand, longer-term advancement opportunities (rather than a focus on simply finding a job), and the provision of training that is tailored to the needs of particular industry sectors, in terms of both hard skills (such as how to operate certain machinery) and soft skills (such as how to adjust to the "culture" of employment in that sector).

The studies drawn upon in this chapter all used random assignment research designs (also called RCTs or experimental designs), which allow the effects of program strategies to be disentangled from the effects of other factors, such as participants' characteristics.[1] In this type of rigorous design, individuals who meet programs' eligibility requirements are randomly assigned to either a program group or a control group. Those in the program group are eligible for the new initiative, and those in the control group are not. Individuals in both groups are followed, and information is collected on their employment and other outcomes of interest. Random assignment eliminates systematic differences between the research groups in individuals' characteristics, measured or unmeasured (such as motivation). Thus, any statistically significant differences between the groups that emerge after random assignment—for example, in employment rates or average earnings—can be attributed to the initiatives under study.

Following an initial discussion of some broad economic trends, the next section of the chapter reviews a set of studies that first tested the effectiveness of requiring welfare recipients (recipients of Aid to Families with Dependent Children [AFDC] prior to 1996, and recipients of Temporary Assistance for Needy Families [TANF] post-1996) to engage in job search assistance, basic education, or training as a condition of receiving welfare benefits, and then tested the relative effectiveness of requiring participation in specific program components. The results of these early studies led to the testing of programs that would help people work more stably and advance in their jobs, and subsequently to examining the effects of programs that focused more on job training. The evaluation results are discussed in the next two sections. At the same time, important studies were conducted of programs using another approach—a "sectoral" strategy, the results of which are examined next. Findings from all of these rigorous studies have led to a current research focus on a hybrid program, described in detail in the following section. The final section of the chapter provides some concluding thoughts about the value of building research evidence in a systematic fashion and possible future directions.[2]

THE ECONOMIC PROBLEM

Broad economic trends have reduced the availability of high-paying jobs for people who do not have a college education. Wages at the bottom of the labor market have been stagnant and declining (in real terms) due to numerous factors, including the decline of unions, changes in labor norms, increased competition, and globalization (Howell 1997). Individuals with no more than a high school education have seen their wages remain flat in real terms for decades, and their employment is often unsteady (Mishel, Bernstein, and Shierholz 2009). These trends have implications for a broad swath of the U.S. labor market. Considering all workers today, one out of four earns less than $10 per hour (Bureau of Labor Statistics 2013; National Employment Law Project 2012). While some of these low-wage workers are teenagers, they are increasingly older workers with more education (Schmitt and Jones 2012). Moreover, the situation is particularly dire for low-wage, low-income workers with children: Only a third of them have more than a high school diploma and another third are high school dropouts (Acs and Nichols 2007).

The labor market has also restructured in fundamental ways. First, there is a proliferation of low-skill, low-wage service jobs that are often inadequate to help individuals escape poverty. Many of these jobs have little prospect for advancement, so the returns to experience can be low. Therefore, for many workers, the path to higher earnings is to work at jobs with higher skill requirements. However, middle-skill jobs that pay more are becoming harder to get. Due in part to automation, the growth rate has slowed in middle-skill job categories that employed large numbers of American workers in the early 1980s, such as "production, craft, and repair" and "operators, fabricators, and laborers." While there is substantial debate over whether middle-skill jobs are truly disappearing or instead are largely shifting to different industries and occupation types, there is a consensus that the skill requirements of jobs are increasing (Autor 2010). More and more jobs require specialized skills and the performance of nonroutine tasks (Holzer 2010). Because of these shifts, it is becoming more difficult for workers with only a high school diploma, and particularly for those who do not even have this credential, to access jobs that can help pull them out of poverty (Carnevale, Smith, and Strohl 2010).

In addition, there is evidence that employers in some industries are having trouble finding qualified applicants for some jobs (Morrison et al. 2011). Surveys show that employers feel the K–12 education system is not sufficiently equipping students with the range of skills needed in the workplace (Peter D. Hart Research Associates/Public Opinion Strategies 2005). Employers also appear less willing than in the past to absorb the training costs of providing workers with needed skills, particularly when they are considering hiring new employees (Hilliard 2013), possibly out of a concern that they may lose their investment when workers leave (Cappelli 2012). On the supply side, surveys reveal that, compared with employers, low-wage workers are less confident in the utility of training and education to help them advance in their careers, and many feel that their jobs have little potential for advancement. Workers also often lack awareness about training opportunities, and take-up rates of both employer- and government-sponsored training programs are low (Tompson et al. 2013). Finally, the availability of government funding for training through the Workforce Investment Act (WIA), as one example, has declined nearly 60 percent from 2000 to 2010, at a time when unemployment rates increased dramatically (Hilliard 2013). More recently, funding for the seven largest federal employment and training programs dropped 35 percent from fiscal year 2009 to 2013 (Center for Law and Social Policy 2014).

The result of these trends—increased skill requirements, employer reluctance to bear training costs, low levels of human capital, diminished government funding for training, and workers' doubts about the effectiveness of training—points toward a possible skills mismatch, in which the skills workers have do not match the skills needed by employers (Osterman and Weaver 2014). Whether or not this skills mismatch is as severe as is sometimes claimed, it is clear that workers who lack postsecondary education or training have more difficulty obtaining jobs that offer higher wages. As a result, programs that train individuals in areas that match the skills demanded by employers can be highly efficient, since they potentially benefit both workers and employers with minimal displacement.[3]

The lingering effects of the Great Recession are also noteworthy. In recent years, the labor market has been weak and slowly recovering, a situation in which even relatively experienced and skilled workers have struggled to find work (Kolesnikova and Liu 2011).[4] Recent studies indicate that employers have responded to this increased supply of unemployed workers by being more selective, particularly about recent work experience. Those who have been out of the labor market for six months or longer are much less likely to receive calls for job interviews—even when they have extensive relevant experience (Kroft, Lange, and Notewidige 2012). This situation presents a special challenge for training programs that seek to place such individuals into the labor market now.

THE EFFECTIVENESS OF ALTERNATIVE WELFARE-TO-WORK MODELS

Rigorous studies in the 1980s and 1990s provided the first seeds of evidence—and subsequent modification—that led to the next-generation demand-driven training model described later in this chapter. The studied programs were embedded in public benefits systems, rather than the unemployment system. Therefore, program participants were generally parents, often single parents, and usually female.

The programs studied during these two decades embodied efforts to assist applicants and recipients of AFDC into employment. The programs thus reflected the ebbs and flows in the welfare system's shifting emphases on education, training, and/or job placement alone as the best means for helping move individuals from welfare to work.

Multistate studies in the 1980s, conducted as part of the Demonstration of State Work/Welfare Initiatives, indicated that programs requiring individuals to look for jobs as a condition of receiving welfare benefits sped up the entry of individuals into the labor market, compared to imposing no requirement at all (Gueron and Pauly 1991).[5] These were low-cost interventions that also were found to provide a positive return on the government's investment. However, their positive effects were limited: Many people helped into work had difficulty staying employed, and the jobs they found were usually low paying. As a result, the programs did not improve welfare recipients' chances of escaping poverty.

Seeking to do better, policymakers and program operators in the late 1980s and early 1990s began to focus on the possible value of providing education and training in welfare-to-work programs. Two major multisite RCTs were subsequently launched to assess the effects of including these types of emphases in models. The first, launched in 1988, evaluated California's statewide Greater Avenues for Independence (GAIN) program, which required people to participate in a range of services, starting with education (provided in a regular classroom setting) for those who scored poorly on a literacy test, lacked a high school diploma or General Educational Development (GED), or were not proficient in English. Others received job search training and other services. The model designers hypothesized that this approach would produce better results than the lower-cost, job-search-focused approach of the earlier programs. GAIN's effects on employment and earnings were positive, in some respects more so than the earlier, more limited models, but impacts on increasing income over a five-year follow-up period were small (Freedman et al. 1996).

A second major multisite study—the National Evaluation of Welfare-to-Work Strategies (NEWWS)—set out to test, beginning in 1989, "What works best?" Most significantly, this study directly compared mandatory job-search-first and mandatory education-or-training-first programs in the same sites (using, as is the case for all studies cited in this chapter, RCTs). These "head to head" tests showed that both program approaches increased employment and earnings over a five-year follow-up period, compared with having no program at all. But the job-search-first approach (often called "work first" programs) got people into jobs sooner and, while people in the education-or-training-first programs eventually caught up by the fifth follow-up year, they were not more likely to get into "good" jobs as of the five-year follow-up point and, as many as 15 years later, they did not have higher earnings growth (Hamilton 2012). An indirect comparison, however, of the above two types of programs with a third type—one where some people were urged to get a job quickly and others were initially required to enroll in work-focused short-term education or training—showed that the third type (a mixed model) had the best five-year results. Nevertheless, while all of these strategies increased people's earnings within the first few years of follow-up, none produced increases in earnings that were long lasting (effects generally faded by the end of the fifth year of follow-up). And, while a number of these programs did allow people to participate in occupational skills training, *increases* in attendance in skills-building classes (comparing program group activity to control group activity) were primarily in the realm of basic education and not in the realm of occupational skills training, since participation rates in occupational skills training were often almost as high among control group members as among people in the program. As a result, the GAIN and NEWWS studies (along with others conducted at the time) pointed to a role that occupational skills training might be able to play. But it was also apparent that knowledge was lacking regarding the types of skills-building activities that might be best and the ways in which skills building could be most beneficially structured, targeted, and encouraged. Finally, additional insight into a broader range of skills-building activities came from the Job Training Partnership Act (JTPA) study described in Box 18.1.

Notably, while the studies described in this section yielded substantial knowledge about how to help low-income individuals prepare for and find jobs, many participants in the programs that successfully boosted employment over a five-year follow-up period still ended up in unstable, low-paying jobs. Thus, the research also suggested a need to focus on ways to effectively increase employment stability and wage progression.

APPROACHES TO EMPLOYMENT RETENTION AND ADVANCEMENT: THE PESD AND ERA PROJECTS

By the mid- to late 1990s, the federal government and states focused squarely on the problem of employment retention and advancement. An initial multisite RCT, the Postemployment Services Demonstration (PESD), operated in the mid-1990s. It examined the effectiveness of offering services such as counseling and support, frequent and flexible payments for work-related expenses, and other services to newly employed welfare recipients (Rangarajan and Novak 1999). The programs studied in the PESD, however, had little effect on employment or earnings.

Box 18.1 A Concurrent Evaluation: The National JTPA Study

Around the same time that the GAIN and NEWWS studies were examining the benefits of basic education and other types of services, another evaluation attempted to focus more squarely on the benefits of vocational training. The National JTPA Study measured the earnings and employment effects of several education and training services funded under Title II-A of the JTPA of 1982. The study attempted to learn which types of training and services were most effective by evaluating three individual service strategies: 1) classroom training in occupational skills, 2) on-the-job training, and 3) other services funded through JTPA. Study participants were randomly assigned after being recommended for one of these three strategies, allowing researchers to measure effects relative to a control group within each strategy. The study design, however, did not allow a direct comparison of one service strategy to another. Overall, the results indicated that adults in the evaluation experienced modest earnings gains throughout the 30-month follow-up period, with more pronounced effects seen for women than men, and substantial variability by site. For adult women, both "other" services and on-the-job training produced earnings impacts. For adult men, on-the-job training appeared to work best, but no statistically significant impacts by service strategy were found (Bloom et al. 1997). Despite these somewhat positive 30-month findings, effects on earnings had faded for both adult women and men by follow-up year five (U.S. General Accounting Office 1996). The JTPA results showed that training could work, in some places, using some strategies, and for some populations, but they also revealed that training programs were by no means a sure investment and had to be carefully designed, a theme that would reemerge several times in the years that followed (D'Amico 2006).

The next set of RCTs exploring this issue, operated in the late 1990s to mid-2000s, examined a wide variety of retention and advancement strategies, reflecting the paucity of positive results in the past. These studies, part of the Employment Retention and Advancement (ERA) project, examined programs different from the ones studied under the PESD: ERA programs, compared with the PESD ones, had greater customization of services, worked with individuals who were not employed, had more services and additional features, had greater diversity of primary service providers, and had more variation in service delivery methods (Hendra et al. 2010). ERA investigated programs that served populations at risk of needing to access welfare benefits as well as individuals already receiving them. The strategies studied under ERA, however, did not attempt to address labor market, or demand-side, issues. Rather, they all tried to address supply-side, or "worker-based," obstacles to economic success.

The results of the ERA trials highlighted the difficulty of achieving upward mobility through simple strategic placement of people into jobs and generic on-the-job coaching alone. Of the 12 programs studied in the ERA project (those that did not target "harder to employ" enrollees, such as individuals with substance abuse issues), only 3 were found to be effective at increasing earnings for participants. The 9 unsuccessful programs offered guidance and advice after people found jobs (i.e., post-employment), but little else. All 12 programs were built upon a variety of hypotheses about what might be advantageous, for example, maintaining small caseloads; offering services at individuals' workplaces; collaborating between welfare, WIA, and community college staff to offer services; and continuing counseling relationships from pre- to post job placement. None of these features produced sustained positive impacts on earnings, in and of themselves. (While the counseling and coaching produced a low yield on their own, researchers concluded that it was possible that these services could be very valuable when combined with other, more concrete services.) These findings suggested that more needed to be done than simply helping participants navigate the labor market better (Hendra et al. 2010).

Lessons from the three ERA tests that *did* produce positive effects also provided ideas for ways programs could move forward. A studied program in Texas, for example, provided former welfare recipients with wage supplements of $200 per month for working full time. The supplement provided a strong incentive to work and also gave participants some extra cash to better handle work-related financial issues, such as emergency car repairs. When combined with high-quality post-employment services (as was the case in one Texas site), the program produced long-term effects on earnings and employment that were sustained through the fourth year of follow-up, the last year when data were available. The Texas findings were consistent with those found for many other wage supplement programs (Martinson and Hamilton 2011). One implication of these results is that when effective take-home pay is higher, participants may work more stably. However, apart from using wage supplements, few job placement programs have been able to increase participants' wage rates.

An ERA test in Chicago also suggested ideas to pursue. In this studied program, a for-profit employer intermediary provided job matching services, which enabled participants to move from very low-paying informal jobs to jobs in the higher-paying security and health care sectors. The Chicago results suggested that organizations that have close relationships with local employers in high-growth sectors can foster positive effects, even for program participants already employed. These findings also provided experimental evidence that proactive job change—taking the initiative to move from one employer to another, prompted by a desire for higher wages and/or a more suitable work arrangement and not by a negative event—can increase earnings.

Finally, positive effects in an ERA test of a program in Riverside, California, suggested the worth of providing assistance to rapidly reemploy individuals who lose their jobs. These findings suggested that it might be more effective to focus on helping people to quickly replace lost employment, that is, assist people to retain overall employment, as opposed to concentrating on helping people retain particular jobs.[6]

The ERA project also provided important insight into employment dynamics. Analyses of the ERA data set revealed that employment spells for low-income populations are highly unstable. Importantly, there is negative duration dependence of spells, meaning that the probability of job loss is highest in the period soon after a job start. Intensive intervention during this critical period thus could be cost effective (Dorsett et al. 2013). While rapid intervention seems critical here, other analyses pointed to the need to provide long-run follow-up as well, as rates of job loss stay high well past the six-month period that most performance measures capture (Riccio et al. 2008). The ERA results also implied that strategies should focus on *employment* stability rather than *job* stability, that is, on developing multiple job placements over an extended time frame as opposed to solely on the initial job placement. Finally, the analyses showed that proactive job change was associated with advancement among low-wage workers, particularly among those who held jobs with smaller employers and had little prospect for advancement (Miller, Deitch, and Hill 2009).[7]

A REFOCUS ON VOCATIONAL TRAINING AND SKILLS: THE UK ERA AND WASC STUDIES

As results from the PESD and ERA evaluations unfolded, some programs moved to incorporate more job training, acknowledging that some kind of vocational skills building was needed in order to increase wages for low-wage workers. One initiative that attempted this was studied as part of the United Kingdom's Employment Retention and Advancement project (UK ERA). This UK program was similar in many ways to the Texas program studied within the United States' ERA project, but it added tuition assistance while individuals remain engaged in training and financial incentives for training completion.

The UK ERA results supported a long-standing lesson in the field of employment and training: training does not work if it is not aligned with employer demand.[8] The UK ERA program boosted training engagement, but labor market benefits attributable to training were not found, suggesting that there was a mismatch between the training undertaken and the labor market demand for individuals with that training (Hendra et al. 2011).[9] The leading explanation for this result related to the program staff's capacity. The UK ERA advisory staff functioned as employment "generalists"—they offered participants general advice and guidance on adapting to work, encouraged them to consider seeking full-time work, helped them address issues of balancing work and family life, advised them on seeking promotions and finding better jobs, and urged them to enroll in training courses in whatever areas interested them. However, UK ERA advisory staff did not have in-depth knowledge of particular occupations or industries or expertise on the career ladders and training requirements for jobs in those areas. Nor did they steer participants assertively toward particular occupations known to offer real advancement opportunities. They were also not positioned to connect participants who had trained in particular occupational areas with relevant employers who were hiring people with the new skills those participants had acquired. These limitations likely undermined the benefits of the extra participation in training that UK ERA caused. The findings point toward providing career advice that is sector-specific and more narrowly focused on opportunities available in the local labor market.

A subsequent test of an approach with a more deliberate demand-driven focus occurred in the late 2000s, in the Work Advancement and Support Center (WASC) Demonstration. The programs examined in WASC aimed to increase the incomes of low-wage workers by stabilizing employment, building skills, increasing earnings, and easing access to work supports. One of the central hypotheses of WASC was that providing training through WIA One-Stops would result in better alignment between training and work. Two of the WASC programs increased (relative to control groups) participation in education and training and also increased earnings in the third follow-up year (Miller et al. 2012). In one program, these effects faded somewhat in the subsequent follow-up year; in the other, longer-term follow-up was not available. In both programs, the level of staff capacity to provide employer-informed advice was lower than anticipated. Still, because funding for training was mainly through WIA, there were conditions in place to try to assure that training was in high-demand fields. In particular, in one of the programs, many of the training vouchers were used to pay for training in the rapidly growing health care field. These results suggested the promise of focusing training in high-demand areas, a central aspect of the sector-based programs discussed in the next section.[10]

PROMISING EVIDENCE FROM SECTOR INITIATIVES: THE SECTORAL EMPLOYMENT IMPACT STUDY

The idea that increases in skills lead to increases in earnings is one of the most established ideas in labor economics (Mincer 1974). But many programs for low-income individuals have been designed with an apparent optimism that any kinds of skill increases will reliably lead to earnings increases, a view that does not fully consider local labor market demand. In particular, the capacity of most social services programs to work effectively with employers and properly read the labor market is an open question.

"Sector strategies" approaches in workforce development programs, pioneered by community-based organizations across the United States beginning in the late 1980s, attempt to keep local labor markets in focus (Magnat 2007). Although programs employing sector strategies vary widely, the Aspen Workforce Strategies Institute defines a sector-based strategy for workforce development as one that

- targets a specific industry or cluster of organizations;
- intervenes through a credible organization, or set of organizations, crafting workforce solutions tailored to that industry and its region;
- supports workers in improving their range of employment-related skills;
- meets the needs of employers; and
- creates lasting change in the labor market system to the benefit of both workers and employers (Conway 2007).

Importantly, sector-based strategies go well beyond simply specializing in one area of training. By Aspen's widely accepted definition, a training provider that trains in a specific field, but does not have strong relationships with employers and/or industry associations in that field, would not be considered a sector-based provider. To qualify as a sector-based program, an initiative must bring together multiple employers in a given field to collaborate on developing a qualified workforce (Woolsey and Groves 2013).

While nonexperimental work by the Aspen Institute (Zandniapour and Conway 2002) and others (Henderson, MacAllum, and Karakus 2010) have produced some encouraging evidence on the benefits of the sector-based approach, the most powerful evidence to date comes from the Sectoral Employment Impact Study, an RCT of four sector-focused training programs conducted by Public/Private Ventures (P/PV) (Maguire et al. 2010). The study finds that the programs, targeted to low-income workers and job seekers, increased earnings, employment, job stability, and access to benefits for participants over the two-year period for which follow-up was available. Participants' earnings over two years were $4,500 (or 18 percent) higher than earnings for the control group. Earnings in the year after training were 29 percent higher than the control group average. In addition, there was evidence of increases in wage rates, which rarely had been found in prior RCTs. The effects of prior programs were generally much more modest than these, which led to enthusiasm about sector-based programs (National Network of Sector Partners 2010) and several attempts to promote the strategy in Congress.[11]

Key elements of the sector-based programs studied by P/PV included the maturity of the service providers, their strong relationships with local employers, the provision of job readiness training in addition to occupational skills training, a stringent screening and intake process, and the provision of individualized services. Although the programs aimed to place workers in "good" jobs—jobs that are higher paying and more stable, there was no "advancement" component. Some of these same elements, however, particularly the small size of the programs, the heavily screened participants, and the experienced and community-rooted nature of the program providers, caused some policymakers to view the results as having limited generalizability. Therefore, while the P/PV results are encouraging, it is critical to test sector-based programs with a more representative set of providers, larger and more disadvantaged samples, and in a broader range of sectors and economic conditions (and some of that testing is under way, as discussed below).

Thus, a "next stage" of research—one part of which is described below—is attempting to understand sector-based programs better, confirm whether they are effective, and determine how they perform at a larger scale and under different conditions, for example, when operated by a more typical range of providers, in weaker economic demand conditions, and for a different sample of workers. Longer-term follow-up is also investigating whether participants in sector-based programs stay in the sector in which they were trained and whether they are able to advance over time, beyond their initial placement. Finally, this next stage of research will consider whether it appears possible to embed sector-based approaches in national training systems and community colleges without losing the local/focal emphasis that is so critical to the strategy.

WORKADVANCE: A "CURRENT GENERATION" MODEL INFLUENCED BY PRIOR RESEARCH FINDINGS

One of the consequences of the above research findings and open questions has been the development of the WorkAdvance model, a sector-based training program. First and foremost, the model reflects a belief, informed by several studies mentioned above, that only through deep knowledge of and relationships with employers in a particular sector can staff in programs serving low-income individuals provide the required level of specialized guidance needed for participants to succeed in their jobs and advance in their careers while also meeting employers' demand for specific skills. The model also reflects a reading of the evidence that, while required job search and required attendance at classes in basic reading and math skills instruction can produce earnings gains, more is needed to truly produce long-term impacts on employment advancement. Finally, the model is an effort to address matching problems in the labor market, in which many individuals are having trouble meeting the skill and experience requirements of middle-skill jobs, and employers are having trouble filling those positions with qualified workers.

A fundamental focus on employer input and long-term career advancement is reflected in each of the five WorkAdvance program elements:

1) Intensive screening of program applicants prior to enrollment—a practice not common in training programs offered to low-income individuals—is intended to assure that program providers select participants who are appropriate for the sector and the particular training programs offered. From one perspective, the brokering and screening role played by sector-based programs might seem duplicative of what happens in a normal, well-functioning labor market. These are tasks typically performed by employers, but disadvantaged workers often have difficulty competing for jobs with advancement potential. Sector-based programs can help workers who would ordinarily not make it through employer screening to obtain the hard and soft skills needed to gain access to better positions (after they receive training at the provider). Providers seek to

identify low-income applicants who have the ability to complete the program services and be attractive to employers, but who are not so qualified that they will likely find high-quality jobs in the sector on their own. This was identified as one of the key elements of success in the P/PV sector study.

2) Sector-focused *preemployment and career readiness services* include an orientation to the sector, career readiness training, individualized career coaching, and wrap-around services that sustain engagement and assist participants to complete their training and find employment.

3) Sector-specific *occupational skills training* seeks to impart skills and lead to credentials that substantially enhance workers' employment opportunities. Providers offer training only in particular sectors and for occupations that the providers, in ongoing consultation with employers, have identified as being in high demand with the potential for career advancement.[12]

4) Sector-specific *job development and placement* facilitate entry into positions for which the participants have been trained and for which there are genuine opportunities for continued skills development and career advancement. To ensure that job development and placement are linked with the occupational skills training, the providers' job developers (or "account managers") maintain strong relationships with employers who hire individuals with the kinds of skills the program has imparted.

5) Postemployment *retention and advancement services* assist participants to advance in and retain their jobs. Providers maintain close contact with workers and employers to assess performance, offer coaching to address any "life issues" that might arise for workers, help identify next-step job opportunities and skills training that could help participants move up career ladders over time, and help with rapid reemployment if workers lose their jobs.

The WorkAdvance model is currently being implemented via four programs, operated in three cities by four local organizations that focus on a range of sectors and bring differing backgrounds to the project. Sectors of focus include transportation, information technology, environmental remediation and related occupations, health, and manufacturing.[13]

Reflecting a continuing need for clear evidence about the best ways to promote the upward mobility of low-income individuals, MDRC is evaluating the WorkAdvance model using an RCT. Through rigorous testing, the study will determine whether a strategy that integrates the most promising features of sector-based and retention/advancement strategies can produce larger and longer-lasting effects on employment, earnings, and career paths than either strategy might produce on its own. The RCT is following individuals who qualified for the WorkAdvance programs between mid-2011 and mid-2013. Program participants will receive program services for up to two years after enrollment.

The WorkAdvance demonstration seeks to assess whether providing sector-based training will lead to advancement by establishing a pipeline from training into work. Several pieces must fall into place for that to happen, however. First, the programs have to find the right participants, those who—*with the benefit of the training*—are within reach of the targeted jobs. Then, participants, many of whom are low-income and disadvantaged, have to finish training and earn a credential. At the same time, job developers have to build relationships with employers who will recognize the earned credentials and hire employees into jobs with future advancement opportunities. Once on the job, participants have to apply both their soft and hard skills training in order to excel in their jobs and pursue advancement opportunities. While the economic effects of the WorkAdvance programs will not be known until late 2015, the WorkAdvance implementation analysis is currently examining the extent to which all of these conditions for advancement are being put into place.

Finding the Right Participants

As was the case with the P/PV Sectoral Employment Impact Study, marketing and outreach to potential WorkAdvance enrollees has required a substantial investment of time and resources in all four of the WorkAdvance programs. This is not surprising, since one of the key contributions of sector-based programs (from the perspectives of businesses) is to reduce screening and acquisition costs by identifying job applicants who (with some training) are qualified for the positions that they are seeking to fill. On average, only one in five program applicants have been found to be eligible and qualified for WorkAdvance. Program providers are using both objective selection criteria (such as income guidelines and test scores) and subjective criteria (such as staff assessments of potential barriers to employment) to screen applicants.[14] Most commonly, however, individuals who do not eventually enroll in the program either withdraw on their own accord during the screening process or fail to achieve a required score on assessments of their academic level; the screening out of applicants as a result of staff discretion has been rare.

Reflecting the minimum level of education required in some of the targeted sectors, almost all applicants who have actually enrolled in WorkAdvance programs have at least a high school diploma or GED, and over half have at least some college education. Thus, the population being served in WorkAdvance, though still disadvantaged, is different from that served in many of the above-discussed studied programs. Among those training in the information technology sector, for example, less than 1 percent lack a high school diploma or GED. Almost all enrollees also have preenrollment work experience, although only one in five were working as of enrollment. At the same time, over a third of enrollees were unemployed for at least seven months prior to enrollment—a likely indication of the lingering (and damaging) effects of the Great Recession. Another possible barrier to finding work posttraining is enrollees' past involvement with the criminal justice system: One quarter of all enrollees have had a previous criminal conviction, and the rate is even higher (40 percent or above) among enrollees training in the transportation and manufacturing industries.

Implementation of Various Components of WorkAdvance

As mentioned above, past research has suggested that programs need to address several issues in order to convert training into advancement. One concern is whether individual programs can handle all of these components (versus a networked approach where several programs coordinate). Thus far, the findings from the implementation analysis suggest that WorkAdvance program providers have been able to implement all of the major elements of the WorkAdvance model, including preemployment and career readiness services, occupational skills training, job development and placement, and retention and advancement services, but the last-listed services have taken the most time to develop, particularly in a robust way, and are still being strengthened.

The preemployment coaching has sought to help enrollees set and follow through on career advancement goals, while the career readiness classes are teaching enrollees about their sector of focus and helping them acquire "soft skills." The structure and manner of delivering these services differ across program providers, but the content is similar: introductions to the sector, advice on resumes and cover letters, job interview preparation, and development of individualized career plans. These services are demand driven: two of the programs use employer advisory groups to help develop the curricula for these classes, another program receives help from existing business intermediary groups, and the fourth program relies on input from individual employers to serve this function. In many cases, these employer partners come to the program offices to conduct mock job interviews, and they also host worksite visits to give program enrollees firsthand exposure to the type of environment in which they can expect to work.

In WorkAdvance, occupational skills training varies across providers and sectors in terms of its duration, whether it is on-site at the provider or contracted with an off-site provider, and the breadth of training offerings. Examples of occupations for which trainings are being provided include help desk technician, environmental remediation technician, pest control technician, aviation manufacturing assistant, computer numerical control operator, diesel maintenance technician, and patient care assistant. Depending on the material and certification requirements, training course duration ranges from two weeks (for example, for patient care assistant training) to eight months (for example, for diesel mechanic training). All programs offer training in cohorts, but the programs differ in terms of whether WorkAdvance enrollees are in training with or without non-WorkAdvance students. Combined with the career readiness classes, the skills training classes usually require full-time involvement, and training takes place during regular business hours or, in two of the programs, optionally during evenings. In previous programs, getting occupational training aligned with ever-changing employer demands has been a struggle. Thus far, the implementation research suggests that WorkAdvance providers have been responsive to demand fluctuations and have adapted the training offerings as the local economy changes.

The Sectoral Employment Impact Study identified "brokering" on the part of job developers as a critical element of sectoral programs. For the most part, in WorkAdvance, job developers appear to have the understanding of local labor markets and of the specific needs of employers necessary in order to prepare enrollees for the best jobs in particular sectors that are available in the localities. The job developers have been able to maintain close relationships with employers and to provide program management with timely feedback on employer needs. Job developers use a mix of networking and cold calls to make initial contact with employers, pitching the value that WorkAdvance programs offer: prescreening of job applicants, career readiness training, and, in some cases, supplying job applicants who already have certifications that employers might otherwise have to arrange and pay for (such as Occupational Safety and Health Administration certification). This raises a potential concern that this type of intervention is simply subsidizing employers by enabling them to shed legitimate training costs. One possible justification for public or private investment in these services is that programs such as WorkAdvance provide disadvantaged workers with an opportunity to enter better-paying jobs than they typically have access to. By providing these individuals with assistance to obtain important certifications, the program makes them more marketable to employers. There are also benefits to employers and the local economy if these investments promote a better-trained workforce.

Most of the previous studies described above find that labor market programs often have short-term effects. The goal of postemployment services is to extend these effects into long-term career trajectories. This is currently the weakest link in the implementation of WorkAdvance. While postemployment services are being delivered, they are currently focused mostly on job retention (for example, addressing relationships with supervisors by coaching workers while they are encountering on-the-job conflicts or issues) and much less on advancement (for example, identifying each participant's next career goals and establishing the steps the worker needs to take to reach those goals). To strengthen this component, the programs are currently focusing on the following: establishing an intentional follow-up plan to contact and communicate with enrollees at strategic points after they start employment, updating career plans periodically to focus on advancement, and maintaining regular contact with enrollees' employers.

Early Training Participation and Completion Rates

In previous programs, getting participants to complete training and other services has been a struggle. Given all of the components of WorkAdvance, and the fact that participants are often in poverty and have little economic support, an open first-order question has been the extent to which participants will complete program services. Results at this point indicate that all of the WorkAdvance providers have been able to engage a substantial share of enrollees in program services, particularly in career readiness activities and occupational skills training: More than 93 percent of enrollees have participated in career readiness activities, and about 70 percent of enrollees have started occupational skills training—all within six months of enrolling. Dropout rates from the training programs have also been low: Only about one in eight of those who started training have dropped out within six months of program enrollment. These high rates may be attributable, at least in part, to the screening done at the beginning of the program.

Finally, and perhaps most critically, most enrollees who have completed training have obtained an industry-recognized credential. (Given the length of the training, statistics on six-month training completion rates are not reliable.) In three of the four programs, over 90 percent of individuals who completed the program have earned a license or certificate. In the fourth program, focused on the health and manufacturing sectors, about half of those who completed training have earned such credentials. Two of the programs have worked with local employers and/or training providers to abbreviate and adapt some formal certifications in the manufacturing sector that normally require years of training. These new credentials are unique to the local employers in the specified industries and have created a certified and viable way for program enrollees to enter that sector's workforce.

Variations in the WorkAdvance model have also suggested an early lesson, one that echoes some of the findings from earlier studies. Two of the WorkAdvance programs initially implemented the program model with two separate tracks: one track emphasized gaining skills first through training (similar to most other sector-based programs), and the other sought to place people into jobs first. The placement-first track was intended to be less expensive than the training-first track, but one that would still impart skills, albeit through work experience and on-the-job training. However, both of these programs eventually shifted mostly to the training-first approach, since the job-placement-first track often resulted in participants' entering low-wage jobs that in practice did not lead to on-the-job acquisition of skills. These shifts were made before a robust set of postemployment services was in place, and it is possible that the placement-first track could have been more effective with the underpinning of those types of services.

CONCLUSIONS AND FUTURE DIRECTIONS

As discussed in this chapter, evidence suggests that skills building can be a means of increasing earnings in the long run for disadvantaged workers, as long as it is well aligned with the needs of employers. Several generations of experiments have also made it clear, however, that there are limits as to what can be done on the worker side of the equation. Sector-based programs, in contrast to many programs from the past, are heavily demand-driven and bring workers and employers together in ways that solve local and regional economic challenges. The evidence suggests that future programs and evaluations thus should continue to include and examine this potentially promising demand-side focus.

WorkAdvance is not the only program under evaluation that is designed to use more of a demand-driven skills acquisition approach as a means toward advancement for low-income individuals. Several programs in the Innovative Strategies for Increasing Self-Sufficiency demonstration use a broadly similar strategy (Martinson and Gardiner 2014).[15] In addition, evaluations are under way of some programs funded through Health Programs Opportunities Grants that also use a demand-driven training approach to help TANF recipients advance in the health care sector (Lower-Basch and Ridley 2013). Finally, some programs undergoing evaluation in the U.S. Department of Labor's Social Innovation Fund portfolio use a similar strategy.[16] The fact that so many agencies and foundations are operating or supporting programs that have evolved in this direction suggests that the interpretation of the evidence presented in this chapter reflects a commonly held view. Therefore, in coming years there should be much more evidence available on the reliability and scalability of this demand-driven skills-building approach. These projects have a strong potential to inform workforce policy.

Even if the results of these studies are positive, however, the difficulty of implementing successful sector-based interventions, coupled with the small size and specific focus of some of the models, raises questions about scalability. WorkAdvance in particular is a difficult model because individual providers have to implement several components on their own. An alternative approach, which might aid scalability, would be to have different organizations coordinate to implement different components of the model. For example, a key way to scale the model may be to take advantage of the ability of the community college system to provide some program components, as some of the WorkAdvance providers have done.

Another challenge with scaling this strategy is that sector-based programs are inherently small and local, owing to the specialization that is necessary to truly understand the high-demand niches of the local labor market and to match appropriate individuals to job openings. While programs may need to stay small to maintain this specialization, it is possible to view them as being part of broader sectoral systems (or "career pathways" systems). In some cities and some labor markets, sector-based programs have been embedded in much broader initiatives (which also take advantage of feeder systems from "bridge" programs to enable a broad segment of disadvantaged workers to enter the initiative). Project Quest (Osterman and Lautsch 1996), or the initiatives implemented by the Instituto del Progreso Latino in Chicago (Martinson and Gardiner 2014), are some programs that apply some of the sector-based strategies on a larger scale and/or for a more disadvantaged set of workers. So, while these programs can seem "boutique," they can be parts of larger systems.

Future directions should explore incorporating the involvement of employers even more centrally into program operations and research. A recent study, for example, has shown the promise of paying employees more or providing better benefits (so-called high-road employment practices), not only for workers but also for the bottom lines of employers (Ton 2012). This is an example of work where employers are central to the intervention and the evaluation. While past experience has made it clear that it can be difficult to engage employers in programs and research (Schultz and Seith 2011), the results of recent studies have indicated that it is possible to work with employers quite directly to implement innovative advancement strategies and determine their effectiveness (SRDC 2013). One challenge of implementing advancement programs at employers, however, is that the goals of employers do not always align with the needs of employees. For example, in some settings an employer's goal may be retention, but the best way for employees to advance is to change employers (Miller, Martin, and Hamilton 2008). It can also be challenging to study programs within employers, particularly using random assignment designs, which might give one segment of employees an unfair advantage. Despite all of these challenges, it seems critical that future advancement programs work closely with employers, who ultimately have the resources and pathways in place to help provide for meaningful advancement in the labor market.

This chapter is an effort to demonstrate what has been learned from the rich, diverse, and many rigorous past studies that have tackled the long-standing problem of lack of upward mobility among disadvantaged workers. Though the context has changed, the studies provide several salient lessons that should inform future program designs and trials. This chapter has presented one reading of the body of evidence that has accumulated regarding the effectiveness of dozens of different types of human capital programs, and has tried to illustrate how the evidence and lessons have been used to develop a recent initiative, called WorkAdvance.

Therefore, to conclude, we would like to emphasize the need to systematically build evidence and draw upon it when designing new programs. The economic problems discussed in this chapter have evolved, but they are essentially old problems. Thus, the findings from well-designed evaluations, accumulated over time, can inform future policy designs. As an example, when one of the authors of this chapter was recently asked to help develop a new model that combines sector-based training with subsidized employment, it quickly became apparent that this was essentially the same model that had been rigorously researched (and found to be promising) in the 1980s Homemaker-Home Health Aide Demonstration (Bell, Burstein, and Orr 1987). Without closely considering what we have learned in the past, we risk relearning old lessons and not realizing the vision of policy *evolution* put forth by Donald Campbell (1973) and other pioneers of the "experimenting society" approach to policy making.

Notes

1. Many of the studies were also conducted by MDRC, the nonprofit, nonpartisan social policy research organization that employs the authors.
2. Some aspects of this chapter, particularly the description of the economic problem and the section on the WorkAdvance program, draw from an MDRC report on WorkAdvance (Tessler et al. 2014).
3. Displacement in employment programs occurs if programs have effects only by favoring some workers over others who would have gotten the job without the program. In a general equilibrium sense, there is no improvement. However, if programs help fill vacancies with better-trained employees, then there would be positive effects that go beyond simply switching workers in the employment queue.
4. It is also very important to recognize that the previous recovery was notable for the lack of job creation and earnings growth. The period up to 2007 was sometimes called the *jobless recovery*. Thus, low-wage workers have confronted an extended period of labor market stagnation.
5. See Gueron and Rolston (2013), which also discusses these early studies, but importantly, in addition, provides a comprehensive history of RCTs in the welfare reform field.
6. It also may be relevant that the program providers in this particular Riverside test were mostly well-rooted community-based organizations, whereas the program providers in several other tested ERA programs were local government offices.
7. This finding is also consistent with the earlier work of Holzer, Lane, and Vilhuber (2004).
8. For example, this was a central argument regarding the effectiveness of the Center for Employment and Training program in San Jose, California, which was evaluated as part of the JobStart evaluation (see Meléndez 1996).
9. The UK ERA program did have labor market effects, but the effects do not appear to be attributable to training. It is more likely that the effects were due to the combination of a wage supplement and retention and advancement services (similar to the ERA Texas program). For the long-term unemployed, the UK ERA program had long-term impacts on employment (similar to the effects found for the Corpus Christi, Texas, program).
10. Another finding from the WASC study was that increasing access to work supports (such as food stamps and child care subsidies) does not necessarily lead to advancement. Part of the theory of change in WASC was that by providing more access to work supports in the short- term, the program would give participants the

financial stability to help support longer-term labor market advancement. However, although the intervention increased work support take-up and earnings in some sites, no association was found between the two effects. Put differently, in some sites and for some subgroups, the intervention increased earnings, but these were not necessarily the same sites or subgroups in which work support take-up was increased.

11. The National Network of Sector Partners (2010) found that 47 percent of sector initiatives profiled were less than five years old. The Strengthening Employment Clusters to Organize Regional Success (SECTORS) Act, which proposed to amend WIA to include additional funding for sector initiatives, was introduced in Congress in 2008, 2009, 2011, and 2013 without ever moving out of committee (*SECTORS Act of 2013*). The Workforce Innovation and Opportunity Act was passed with bipartisan support in July 2014, reauthorizing WIA from 2015 to 2020. The bill promotes sector strategies, specifically requiring states to implement industry or sector partnerships and career pathways (*Workforce Innovation and Opportunity Act* 2014).

12. During the program design phase, providers were asked to provide career advancement "maps" that outlined the necessary steps for advancement in targeted occupations and to justify that targeted positions had a reasonable prospect for advancement. Providers were discouraged from placing participants in "dead-end" jobs. There was also a goal to place participants in "better" paying jobs (for this population, wages beyond $12–15/hour are a reasonable goal, depending on the local labor market) and jobs that provided benefits such as health insurance. Some targeted jobs initially offered low pay, but were deemed to have strong advancement potential.

13. Some of these sectors overlap with ones in the programs studied in P/PV's Sectoral Employment Impact Study. In the P/PV-studied programs, sectors included construction, manufacturing, health care, medical billing and accounting, and information technology.

14. For WorkAdvance, applicants needed to be adults who had a monthly family income below 200 percent of the federal poverty level and earned less than $15 per hour at the time they entered the study.

15. This evaluation has been renamed "Pathways to Advance Career Education."

16. See http://www.doleta.gov/workforce_innovation/ (accessed October 9, 2014).

References

Acs, Gregory, and Austin Nichols. 2007. *Low-Income Workers and Their Employers: Characteristics and Challenges.* Washington, DC: Urban Institute.

Autor, David. 2010. *The Polarization of Job Opportunities in the U.S. Labor Market: Implications for Employment and Earnings.* Washington, DC: Center for American Progress and The Hamilton Project.

Bell, Stephen H., Nancy R. Burstein, and Larry L. Orr. 1987. *Evaluation of the AFDC Homemaker–Home Health Aide Demonstrations: Overview of Evaluation Results.* Cambridge, MA: Abt Associates.

Bloom, Howard S., Larry L. Orr, Stephen H. Bell, George Cave, Fred Doolittle, Winston Lin, and Johannes M. Bos. 1997. "The Benefits and Costs of JTPA Title II-A Programs: Key Findings from the National Job Training Partnership Act Study." *Journal of Human Resources* 32(3): 549–576.

Bureau of Labor Statistics. 2013. "May 2013 National Occupational Employment and Wage Estimates." Washington, DC: Bureau of Labor Statistics. http://www.bls.gov/oes/current/oes_nat.htm (accessed October 9, 2014).

Campbell, Donald. 1973. "The Social Scientist as Methodological Servant of the Experimenting Society." *Policy Studies Journal* 2(1): 72–75.

Cappelli, Peter. 2012. *Why Good People Can't Get Jobs: The Skills Gap and What Companies Can Do About It.* Philadelphia: Wharton Digital Press.

Carnevale, Anthony, Nicole Smith, and Jeff Strohl. 2010. *Help Wanted: Projections of Jobs and Education Requirements through 2018.* Washington, DC: Georgetown University Center on Education and the Workforce.

Center for Law and Social Policy. 2014. *A New Look at the GAO Report on Workforce Funding.* Washington, DC: Center for Law and Social Policy.

Conway, Maureen. 2007. *Sector Strategies in Brief.* Workforce Strategies Initiative. Washington, DC: Aspen Institute.

D'Amico, Ronald. 2006. *What's Known about the Effects of Publicly-Funded Employment and Training Programs.* Final report. Oakland, CA: Social Policy Research.

Dorsett, Richard, Richard Hendra, Philip Robins, and Sonya Williams. 2013. "Can Post-Employment Services Combined with Financial Incentives Improve Employment Retention for Welfare Recipients? Evidence from the Texas Employment Retention and Advancement Evaluation." IRP Discussion Paper No. 1413-13. Madison, WI: Institute for Research on Poverty.

Freedman, Stephen, Daniel Friedlander, Winston Lin, and Amanda Schweder. 1996. *The GAIN Evaluation: Five-Year Impacts on Employment, Earnings, and AFDC Receipt.* Working Paper No. 96.1. New York: MDRC.

Gueron, Judith M., and Edward Pauly. 1991. *From Welfare to Work.* New York: Russell Sage.

Gueron, Judith M., and Howard Rolston. 2013. *Fighting for Reliable Evidence.* New York: Russell Sage.

Hamilton, Gayle. 2012. *Improving Employment and Earnings for TANF Recipients.* Washington, DC: Urban Institute.

Henderson, Kathryn, Crystal MacAllum, and Mustafa Karakus. 2010. *Workforce Innovations: Outcome Analysis of Outreach, Career Advancement and Sector-Focused Programs.* Rockville, MD: Westat; New York: Metis Associates.

Hendra, Richard, Keri-Nicole Dillman, Gayle Hamilton, Karin Martinson, and Melissa Wavelet. 2010. *How Effective Are Different Approaches Aiming to Increase Employment Retention and Advancement? Final Impacts for Twelve Models.* New York: MDRC.

Hendra, Richard, James A. Riccio, Richard Dorsett, David H. Greenberg, Genevieve Knight, Joan Phillips, Philip K. Robins, Sandra Vegeris, and Johanna Walter. 2011. *Breaking the Low-Pay, No-Pay Cycle: Final Evidence from the UK Employment Retention and Advancement (ERA) Demonstration.* New York: MDRC.

Hilliard, Thomas. 2013. *Building the American Workforce.* New York: Council on Foreign Relations.

Holzer, Harry J. 2010. *Is the Middle of the U.S. Labor Market Really Disappearing? A Comment on the "Polarization" Hypothesis.* Washington, DC: Center for American Progress.

Holzer, Harry J., Julia I. Lane, and Lars Vilhuber. 2004. "Escaping Low Earnings: The Role of Employer Characteristics and Changes." *Industrial and Labor Relations Review* 57(4): 560–578.

Howell, David. 1997. *Institutional Failure and the American Worker: The Collapse of Low-Skill Wages.* Annandale-on-Hudson, NY: Jerome Levy Economics Institute of Bard College.

Kolesnikova, Natalia A., and Yang Liu. 2011. "Jobless Recoveries: Causes and Consequences." *Regional Economist* April: 18–19. St. Louis, MO: Federal Reserve Bank of St. Louis.

Kroft, Kory, Fabian Lange, and Matthew Notewidige. 2012. "Duration Dependence and Labor Market Conditions: Theory and Evidence from a Field Experiment." NBER Working Paper No. 18387. Cambridge, MA: National Bureau of Economic Research.

Lower-Basch, Elizabeth, and Neil Ridley. 2013. *Navigating TANF and WIA to Build Health Profession Career Pathways—A Guide for HPOG Programs.* Washington, DC: Center for Law and Social Policy.

Magnat, Ravinder. 2007. *Sector Snapshots: A Profile of Sector Initiatives, 2007.* Oakland, CA: National Network of Sector Partners.

Maguire, Shelia, Joshua Freely, Carol Clymer, Maureen Conway, and Deena Schwartz. 2010. *Tuning in to Local Labor Markets: Findings from the Sectoral Employment Study.* Philadelphia: Public/Private Ventures.

Martinson, Karin, and Karen Gardiner. 2014. *Improving the Economic Prospects of Low-Income Individuals through Career Pathways Programs: The Innovative Strategies for Increasing Self-Sufficiency Evaluation.* OPRE Report No. 201417. Washington, DC: Office of Planning, Research and

Evaluation, Administration for Children and Families, U.S. Department of Health and Human Services.

Martinson, Karin, and Gayle Hamilton. 2011. *Providing Earnings Supplements to Encourage and Sustain Employment.* New York: MDRC.

Meléndez, Edwin. 1996. *Working on Jobs: The Center for Employment Training.* Boston: Mauricio Gastón Institute.

Miller, Cynthia, Victoria Deitch, and Aaron Hill. 2009. *The Employment Retention and Advancement Project: Paths to Advancement for Single Parents.* New York: MDRC.

Miller, Cynthia, Vanessa Martin, and Gayle Hamilton. 2008. *Findings for the Cleveland Achieve Model.* New York: MDRC.

Miller, Cynthia, Mark van Dok, Betsy L. Tessler, and Alexandra Pennington. 2012. *Strategies to Help Low-Wage Workers Advance: Implementation and Final Impacts of the Work Advancement and Support Center (WASC) Demonstration.* New York: MDRC.

Mincer, Jacob. 1974. *Schooling, Experience, and Earnings.* New York: National Bureau of Economic Research, Columbia University Press.

Mishel, Lawrence, Jared Bernstein, and Heidi Shierholz. 2009. *The State of Working America: 2008–2009.* Ithaca, NY: Cornell University Press.

Morrison, Tom, Bob Macieiewski, Craig Giffi, Emily Stover DeRocco, Jennifer McNelly, and Gardner Carrick. 2011. *Boiling Point? The Skills Gap in U.S. Manufacturing.* Washington, DC: Deloitte Development LLC and the Manufacturing Institute.

National Employment Law Project. 2012. *Big Business, Corporate Profits, and the Minimum Wage.* Data brief. New York: National Employment Law Project.

National Network of Sector Partners. 2010. *Sector Snapshot: A Profile of Sector Initiatives, 2010.* Oakland, CA: National Network of Sector Partners.

Osterman, Paul, and Paula Lautsch. 1996. *Project Quest: A Report to the Ford Foundation.* New York: Ford Foundation.

Osterman, Paul, and Andrew Weaver. 2014. *Why Claims of Skills Shortages in Manufacturing Are Overblown.* Issue Brief No. 376. Washington, DC: Economic Policy Institute.

Peter D. Hart Research Associates/Public Opinion Strategies. 2005. *Rising to the Challenge: Are High School Graduates Prepared for College and Work? A Study of Recent High School Graduates, College Instructors, and Employers.* Washington, DC: Peter D. Hart Research Associates/Public Opinion Strategies.

Rangarajan, Anu, and Tim Novak. 1999. *The Struggle to Sustain Employment: The Effectiveness of the Postemployment Services Demonstration.* Princeton, NJ: Mathematica Policy Research.

Riccio, James, Helen Bewley, Verity Campbell-Barr, Richard Dorsett, Gayle Hamilton, Lesley Hoggart, Alan Marsh, Cynthia Miller, Kathryn Ray, and Sandra Vegeris. 2008. *Implementation and Second-Year Impacts for Lone Parents in the UK Employment Retention and Advancement (ERA) Demonstration*. New York: MDRC.

Schmitt, John, and Janelle Jones. 2012. *Low-Wage Workers Are Older and Better Educated than Ever.* Washington, DC: Center for Economic and Policy Research.

Schultz, Caroline, and David Seith. 2011. *Fort Worth: Career Advancement and Work Support Services on the Job*. New York: MDRC.

SECTORS Act of 2013, S.1226, 113th Cong. (2013).

SRDC. 2013. *Outcomes Report for the Workplace Training Program, British Columbia*. Ottawa, Canada: SRDC.

Tessler, Betsy, Michael Bangser, Alexandra Pennington, Kelsey Schaberg, and Hannah Dalporto. 2014. *WorkAdvance: Implementing a Sector-Focused Advancement Model for Low-Skilled Adults*. New York: MDRC.

Tompson, Trevor, Jennifer Benz, Jennifer Agiesta, and Dennis Junius. 2013. *America's Lower-Wage Workforce: Employer and Worker Perspectives.* The Associated Press-NORC Center for Public Affairs Research.

Ton, Zeynep. 2014. *The Good Jobs Strategy: How the Smartest Companies Invest in Employees to Lower Costs and Boost Profits*. Seattle: Amazon Publishing.

U.S. General Accounting Office. 1996. *Job Training Partnership Act: Long-Term Employment and Earnings Outcomes*. GAO/HEHS-96-40. Washington, DC: U.S. General Accounting Office.

Woolsey, Lindsey, and Garrett Groves. 2013. *State Sector Strategies Coming of Age: Implications for State Workforce Policymakers*. Washington, DC: National Governors Association Center for Best Practices.

Workforce Innovation and Opportunity Act, H.R. 803, Pub. L. 113–128. 113th Cong. (2014).

Zandniapour, Lily, and Maureen Conway. 2002. *Gaining Ground: The Labor Market Progress of Participants of Sectoral Employment Development Programs*. Sectoral Employment Development Learning Project Research Report No. 3. Washington, DC: Aspen Institute.

19

Doing More with Less

Leveraging Advances in Data Science to Support an Intelligent Workforce System

William Mabe
Scott Powell
Alex Ruder
Rutgers University

In the aftermath of the Great Recession, shrinking budgets and high caseloads all but guarantee that the workforce system of the twenty-first century will have to serve more job seekers with fewer resources. Maximizing the system's efficiency and effectiveness will require the U.S. workforce system to evolve into an intelligent workforce system, where data drive the decisions of all stakeholders—from policymakers to workforce program staff, education and training providers, job seekers, and employers. For the system to be truly intelligent and data driven, state workforce agencies (SWAs) and local workforce areas must be able to extract meaning from multiple types of data, including numeric, location, and text data, stored across multiple state agencies; properly analyze these data to generate accurate insights and integrate them into stakeholder decision making; and foster an organizational culture that values data collection, quality, analysis, and dissemination.

Advances in data science, coupled with the ever-expanding capabilities of open-source and low-cost software, offer the workforce system a genuine opportunity to do more with less. Specifically, developments in two areas—mining information that states have collected for years but examined only infrequently (such as location data and textual data), and analyzing their data in such a way as to generate more accurate insights, especially in the field of prediction—can be harnessed to help states deliver services more effectively to workforce system customers. This chapter describes how SWAs can adopt tools to analyze nontraditional data sources such as geospatial and text data and to improve their predictive practices.

During the past several decades, SWAs have developed tools to analyze more traditional types of data, such as numbers (0, 1, −27.15) and categories (male and female). In addition to numeric and categorical data, however, SWAs also store important geospatial (location) and textual information. Examples of geospatial information include addresses of job seeker customers when they register for services, the addresses of employer customers and the establishments where they have job openings, and the Internet protocol addresses—which can be linked to physical locations—of job seekers who are using state online job boards to search for employment. At the same time, SWA data systems capture vast amounts of textual information. For example, every time a counselor enters a comment or note about a customer into an SWA database, the database records critical qualitative information about the job seeker, such as his skill deficits, the counselor's assessment of his job readiness, and possibly his attitude toward his job search. Although SWAs have made little use of either location or text data, open-source and low-cost software are available to help SWAs extract meaning from them. Incorporating location and textual data can support learning about how SWAs serve their customers, the effectiveness of their programs, and strategies for program improvement.

In an intelligent workforce system, data analysis adds value in many different ways, including performance metrics for tracking program implementation, scorecards for public accountability, rigorous evaluations to identify the programs that most benefit customers, and predictions of which customers are most in need of services and most likely to benefit from them. For SWAs, one of the most widely used data applications is prediction: learning from the data so that when a new customer enters the workforce system, the SWA knows what the experiences of thousands of customers like her have been and can therefore predict how she is likely to fare and what services might benefit her the most. To be more specific, an intelligent workforce system can use prediction to assist SWAs in better serving customers by identifying customers likely to experience an adverse event such as prolonged unemployment, matching customers to the job openings for which they are best suited, or identifying the set of reemployment and job training services that are likely to be the most effective at helping a customer achieve a positive labor market outcome. Of course, prediction cannot foresee the future perfectly. On the contrary, prediction is almost always prone to at least some error. But high-quality prediction can allow us to see the future more clearly than with no prediction at all, and this extra insight can significantly improve program outcomes.

While innovations in data science hold the promise of greatly improving the ability of SWAs to serve their customers, realizing this promise requires the effective use of their resources and capabilities. Fortunately, states already possess the resource that is the most costly and time consuming to develop—namely, detailed customer-level data that they have collected for decades. Effective use of individual-level data begins with high levels of data security to safeguard the privacy and confidentiality of the information the SWAs have collected from the public. Once data security is established, combining data from many different programs affords SWAs a fuller understanding of each customer they serve and allows for more detailed analyses than have generally been possible before. Through the Workforce Data Quality Initiative, the U.S. Department of Labor (USDOL) has funded 32 states to securely link data that have traditionally been housed in separate databases and maintained by multiple state agencies. We aim to introduce SWAs to a number of methods for leveraging this wealth of existing data.

The chapter is organized into two parts. In the first, we examine how location data and then textual data can be analyzed to yield value for SWAs. For each data type, we walk through an application to illustrate how SWAs and local areas can derive insights from these data. In the second part of the chapter, we describe the prediction process and the steps that these agencies need to follow in order to be able to generate accurate predictions and incorporate them into service delivery. We then illustrate how SWAs can improve their predictive practices by applying predictive modeling to identify job seekers who are most likely to experience long-term unemployment.

GEOSPATIAL AND TEXT DATA IN
WORKFORCE DEVELOPMENT

Modern analytics involves using a variety of different types of data. The more traditional types, such as numeric and categorical data, are now found alongside data types such as geospatial (Burrough and McDonnell 1998) and text data (Schutt and O'Neil 2014). Geospatial data, which refers to address and location information, and large collections of text—such as online job listings, job seeker profiles, and counselor notes on individual customers—are increasingly available to workforce development professionals. A challenge workforce counselors face is deciding how to make use of these valuable data collections.

Geospatial Data

Spatial data are features—roads, buildings, and addresses—whose locations can be mapped onto the earth's surface along with the feature's descriptive characteristics. Workforce data systems often store data elements on customers and employers that are spatial in nature, such as an employer's address, along with attributes such as current job openings and contact information. Data visualization through geographic information systems (GIS) can be a powerful tool for helping SWAs and workforce boards turn this geospatial data into innovative new service solutions. Specifically, SWAs and local areas can improve their targeting of workforce services to better meet job seekers where they are, including making decisions about where to locate satellite offices and where to concentrate outreach efforts.

While workforce professionals have been using maps to improve services for decades, the last few years have produced an exponential increase in mapping possibilities. As a result of innovations in both workforce data and mapping software, powerful maps need not be costly or time-intensive to create. Through programs such as the Workforce Data Quality Initiative, state and local governments are increasingly linking administrative data that are housed across multiple agencies. This allows governments to create powerful maps that display not only workforce information, such as wages and WIA participation, but also data related to education and human services programs.

Regarding innovations in mapping software, applications such as ArcGIS easily combine location-based information with workforce data. This software can be preloaded with local census-based labor market information and demographic characteristics, while local infrastructure information, such as roads and public transportation routes, is easily integrated. With so much data already assimilated into the software, workforce agencies need only provide a single piece of information: customer location. Finally, due to the proliferation of geospatial data use in the public sector, trained GIS professionals are often available at all levels of government, as well as in local colleges and universities. Thus, governments frequently already employ all the staff necessary to leverage geospatial data for making workforce policy decisions, making data visualization tools that use geospatial data accessible and affordable, even at the local level.

Application: customer outreach

We illustrate the value of geospatial data by mapping workforce information from Essex County, New Jersey, and the city of Newark. The map below (Figure 19.1) plots the location of occupational training participants, aggregating the information by census tract to protect customer privacy (U.S. Census Bureau 1994). The trainees are represented by circles, with larger circles signifying more trainees within a given census tract. The unemployment rate of each census tract is also represented, with darker-shaded tracts representing higher unemployment rates. Finally, American Job Center (AJC) offices are represented with triangles.

Created for the Newark Workforce Investment Board (WIB) to assist with recent exploration into strategies for customer outreach, these maps quickly convey a large amount of information that is critical to identifying the areas where the WIB can most efficiently target its efforts. For example, the areas with the most customers in need of services are concentrated in close proximity to the city of Newark, with the areas farther out in Essex County benefiting from relatively low levels of unemployment. So while there are currently no offices in the outer tracts of the county, there is also not necessarily a need to increase outreach efforts in this region. Within the city itself, there is substantial variation in unemployment, and many of these areas are underserved. Specifically, the tracts with high unemployment but few trainees could

Figure 19.1 Number of Trainees by Census Tract, Essex County, New Jersey, 2012

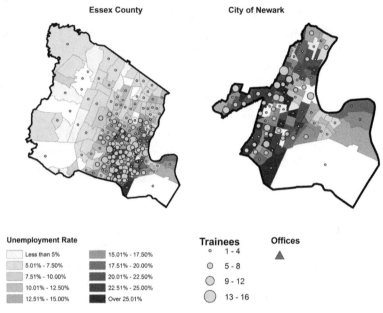

be prime candidates for outreach efforts. And, in determining where to place a new outreach center, GIS software can easily overlay roads and public transportation routes onto this map to find a location that would be accessible to the underserved customers in need of assistance.

Perhaps most importantly, the WIB needed to provide only a single piece of workforce information to create this map: the location of trainees. All other data were either publicly available or integrated into the GIS software application. Thus, the maps are not only powerful in their ability to quickly convey information that is critical to developing an outreach strategy but also relatively undemanding to create.

Text Data

Like geospatial data, text information holds a great deal of unlocked potential for improving SWA services. In a workforce system, text data can include titles of job openings, descriptive information on skill requirements and job duties from job postings, counselor comments on job seeker skills and aptitudes, and customer feedback on their satisfaction with the services they have received.

Although many states are moving to apply text analysis algorithms to match job seekers to the jobs with the skill requirements and job duties that most closely align with their experience, nearly all of them use commercial products to do so. A number of companies have developed proprietary algorithms that allow job seekers to use a search function that automatically reviews job postings and notifies them of jobs that match the skills listed in their resumes. Whether organizations analyze text data themselves or enlist the services of a private sector firm, an understanding of the basic tools of text mining aids the use and interpretation of these methods. In addition, advances in computer software have made text mining methods accessible to a wide range of practitioners, increasing opportunities for organizations to conduct "in-house" analyses of text.

Text mining is a collection of analytic methods used to extract useful information from large volumes of text (Sebastiani 2002; Witten 2005). These methods are particularly suited for large text collections whose size makes human reading and coding prohibitively costly. Computer algorithms automate the process of searching the texts for patterns and information. Text mining methods can be used for text summarization and document retrieval, for clustering texts into predefined or previously unknown categories, and for extracting structured information such as Web addresses from texts.

This section reviews several text mining methods that are well suited to workforce development applications.[1] Often, the first challenge is deciding how to summarize the text in a collection. We highlight several text mining methods that can help workforce professionals summarize large text collections and organize similar documents into a set of categories. Then, to give a sense of how these tools might be applied, we analyze open-ended survey responses from a survey of individuals who received services from AJCs in a state in the eastern half of the United States.

Summarization and classification of text

Faced with a large collection of text, an organization may first need a simple method for summarizing the content of the collection.[2] One of the simplest methods that an organization can use is count-based analysis. As the name implies, it involves calculating the most frequently used words in both a text collection and in individual documents. A count-based approach can reveal, for example, that the words *transportation* and *warehouse* are the two most frequently used words in a collection of job ads.

A next step toward summarizing a text collection is to calculate word associations. Word associations reveal which words are highly correlated with the use of a selected word. For example, an organization may calculate associations for both *transportation* and *warehouse*. Word association can reveal that *full-time* and *truck* are strongly associated with the words *transportation* and *warehouse*. In this example, these two simple methods have given the organization preliminary evidence that its collection of jobs ads features many ads for full-time, tractor-trailer truck drivers.[3]

Classification and clustering

Many text mining problems involve grouping documents into natural clusters of similar documents. Consider a scenario in which a workforce organization has a database of thousands of job postings and wants to group them by industry of employment. Human-based coding of these job ads is prohibitively expensive: the organization likely lacks the staff and the time to read and code thousands of job ads. Text mining classification methods offer an automated approach to accomplish this task.

One of the first steps in text classification is choosing the approach that is appropriate for the task. Generally, this choice is determined by the large variety of classification methods, which can be grouped into two general approaches: supervised and unsupervised (Grimmer and Stewart 2013).

Supervised methods

In the phrase "supervised learning methods," the term *supervised* is used to refer to methods where the categories are known in advance. The researcher supervises the automated classification process by providing the computer a training set of documents already labeled with the known categories. The supervised method estimates the words or phrases predictive of the label. The researcher then uses the estimates from the training set to infer the labels for documents in the test set. Popular supervised methods include k-nearest neighbor classification, support vector machines, string kernel clustering, and the Naïve Bayes classifier.[4]

Dictionary methods are a relatively simple and intuitive way to organize texts into known categories (Neuendorf 2002). To assign texts to a given category, dictionary methods use the rate at which certain predefined key words appear in the text. More specifically, a dictionary method takes a list of words (the dictionary) and counts the proportion of words in a text that are also in the dictionary. An organization may use a sample of existing job ads to create a dictionary of keywords that identify the likely industry of new job ads. Another common application of dictionary methods is sentiment analysis, where the goal is to assess degree of positive, neutral, or negative language in text.

When using dictionary methods, organizations must choose dictionaries appropriate for the application, such that the meaning of the words in the dictionary corresponds to the way words are used in the text (Loughran and McDonald 2011). The word *work*, for example, can be positive in many contexts, such as *the machine works*. In workforce context, work is more often a neutral term: *looking for work, I worked as a machinist*. Organizations can acquire free text analysis dictionaries on the Web, or construct their own dictionary tailored to the specific application.

Unsupervised methods

In some applications, the categories may not be known in advance, making the application of supervised methods infeasible. Unsupervised learning methods apply when no predefined categories are available and the researcher still seeks to group similar documents into clusters. Unsupervised methods can also help to explore a large collection of text documents by summarizing its thematic content.

Since the methods are fully automated, they can discover both expected categories (e.g., health care jobs) and unexpected categories. For example, the method can reveal that multiple categories define the broader health care industry; one category may feature the words *hospital*, *surgery*, and *nurse*, while another category features *home*, *health*, and *nurse*. In this example, the unsupervised model infers that two broad categories of jobs are prominent in the collection of job ads: hospital-based surgical nurses and nurses employed in home health care services. If the organization were to use a supervised method, it would have to know these two categories in advance. It is possible that the organization may be unaware of the extent of local demand for home health care nurses. If the organization were to rely solely on supervised methods, it would overlook an important piece of information about the local labor market.

Unsupervised methods range from fully automated clustering algorithms (Grimmer and King 2011) to computationally demanding topic models (see Blei [2012] for a review and discussion of topic models). With all unsupervised methods, the goals are generally the same: either explore the categories (or thematic topics) that constitute a text collection, or cluster similar documents together into previously unknown categories.

Application: analysis of open-ended survey responses

Organizations often employ surveys that ask respondents to rate a service along some preset scale, such as poor to excellent. However, these closed-ended responses, while useful, are often too coarse to answer questions such as why respondents selected the rating they did. In contrast, open-ended survey questions allow respondents to elaborate on previous answers, suggest improvements, or offer praise in their own words, rather than in the predefined language of the survey developer.

One challenge that responses to open-ended survey questions present to researchers is how to analyze large amounts of text data. Generally, organizations require a team of human coders to read the responses and code them in a manner consistent with the organization's goals. Human coding is a time-consuming task. An alternative strategy for systematically analyzing open-ended survey responses is to use simple, computationally based text mining tools.

In a recent survey of individuals who received workforce services in a state in the eastern half of the United States, we asked respondents a closed-ended question: *How valuable was this service to you—not at all valuable, somewhat valuable, or very valuable?* We followed this question with an open-ended question:

Is there anything else that you would like to add about your experience, either positive or negative, that could inform the improvement of aspects of the program that did not work as well, or ensure the retention of those things that did work well?

We sought to use the open-ended question to analyze why respondents gave the rating that they chose. In particular, we wanted to know which aspects of the program were prominent in more negative reviews compared to the aspects mentioned in more positive reviews.[5] Rather than human coding of all the responses, our first analysis involved the use of text mining tools provided in the "tm: Text Mining Package" in the open-source statistical software R (Feinerer, Hornik, and Meyer 2008). The tm: Text Mining Package includes tools to download and analyze the data, as well as to implement standard text preprocessing steps such as removing punctuation and numbers, and changing words to reflect their stems or roots.

Even this basic application of text mining revealed several differences across respondents who rated their overall experience negatively compared to those who rated it positively. Respondents who offered a negative rating were more likely to write longer responses and focus their comments on particular aspects of the program: the classes, courses, and the AJC counselors. In contrast, respondents who rated their experiences positively were less likely to identify any particular aspect of the program that they found helpful. Rather, the positive respondents were more likely to use the open-ended question as an opportunity to voice their general satisfaction with the services and the help they received finding a job.[6] The information gained from the open-ended survey responses can help organizational leadership strategically target improvement efforts to the aspects of service that contributed to customers' negative evaluations.

PREDICTIVE ANALYTICS

Although states have been using data to make predictions for over a decade, primarily to implement the Worker Profiling and Reemployment Services (WPRS) system, technological advances in predictive analytics, together with shrinking financial resources and demands for increased performance accountability, have precipitated wider interest in and adoption of predictive analytics for workforce development applications (the White House 2014). Many states and organizations, for example, have contracted with proprietary firms to leverage text data in resumes and job advertisements to make better predictions concerning which applicants are most likely to succeed in a given job.

Applications in predictive analytics generally share a common goal: to generate accurate predictions that contribute to improved organizational performance or service delivery. To meet this goal, SWAs must be able to measure the performance of their predictive analytic applications and design or modify them to improve prediction.

There are three ways in which SWAs could generate more accurate predictions. First, they could increase the accuracy of their predictions by comparing the performance of predictions based on multiple different predictive algorithms.[7] Second, SWAs could improve the predictive power of their models by regularly evaluating the accuracy of their predictions and adjusting their models over time.[8] Finally, they could improve predictive accuracy by including more diverse sets of predictors in their models.

The Prediction Process

When most people think about prediction in the context of workforce development, they probably think about something like the following example. John has worked for 10 years as an accountant at a retail store. He loses his job and files for UI. In filing the claim, he provides information about his occupation and industry, how long he worked for the company, and why he lost his job. John also lists his age, race and ethnicity, and level of education. The SWA might then use this information to estimate such items as how likely he is to suffer prolonged unemployment, the jobs for which he is the most qualified, and/or which services are likely to afford the most help in returning to work.[9] Although this example illustrates an important part of the prediction process—the assignment of a prediction to a current SWA customer—it is incomplete because it omits other parts of the process.

The prediction process actually begins with the identification of a substantive problem to which the application of predictive modeling might help the SWA overcome (Finlay 2014). In the case of workforce development, these problems largely revolve around identifying at-risk customers, matching customers to open jobs, and matching them to the most appropriate services.

After identifying a problem suitable for predictive modeling, the task of using prediction to improve service delivery involves a four-step process: 1) collecting, storing, and preparing for analysis data on the individuals whom the SWA serves; 2) testing many different predictive models on the data and selecting the one that generates the most accurate predictions;[10] 3) using the best model to generate predictions for each new customer and applying the predictions to serve customers better; and 4) assessing and improving the predictive model over time. Figure 19.2 depicts this process.

The more complete the data on workforce system customers, the more diverse the predictors that SWAs can include in their models and the more accurate their predictions are likely to be. Preparing data for analysis involves extracting data from diverse data systems, transforming the data so they can be analyzed using statistical software, and loading them into a database for analysis.

During model selection, researchers learn from the data by engaging in retrospective prediction (Siegel 2013). A SWA may want, as in the example we present below, to be able to predict which newly unemployed individuals are likely to remain unemployed for an extended period. SWA researchers would begin by examining a *subset* of the SWA's existing data, looking only at what was known about the unemployed individuals at the time they became unemployed, and use this information to "predict" who is likely to be unemployed a year later. The challenge is to find patterns that hold not just with the available data, but also in new data. So the researchers then test several predictive models for accuracy on a second subset of data, validate the results on a third subset of the data, and select for deployment in the field the predictive model that emerged from the validation phase with the highest accuracy. While this phase may provide the greatest challenge for

Figure 19.2 Predictive Modeling Process

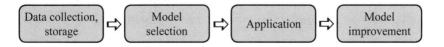

SWAs in terms of developing new expertise, we demonstrate below that these challenges are not as large as they appear. Additionally, this phase of the prediction process does not need to be repeated on a regular basis, providing SWAs with the opportunity to hire an outside party to perform model selection if they are not equipped to perform this task internally.

In the application phase, the organization uses the winning predictive model to predict which new customers are likely, in our example, to have long spells of unemployment and takes some action based on the predictions. This means that when a newly unemployed worker enters personal information on a UI claim application or an AJC intake form, a predictive model examines the worker's characteristics and predicts how likely the worker is to have a long spell of unemployment. The SWA could then target services to this customer based in part on the predictive score.

Finally, because economic conditions change over time, predictive models must be updated regularly to remain accurate. In addition, the effect of assigning services based on the predictions of the model needs to be rigorously evaluated to ensure that the predictive system not only makes accurate predictions but also positively affects the outcomes it was designed to improve.

Current SWA Uses of Prediction

In this section, we review the substantive problems to which SWAs currently apply prediction and examine how SWAs engage in prediction. To date, SWAs have used predictive models to assist in addressing two substantive problems. First, nearly all states apply predictive modeling to identify the newly unemployed workers who are most likely to remain unemployed for so long that they exhaust their UI benefits. Individuals are then assigned to various services, a process known as worker profiling (USDOL 2000). SWAs can also use predictive models to target services and place customers into programs that are most likely to assist them with labor market reintegration. As discussed in the first section, SWAs are also starting to mine text data and combine it with other data on job seekers in order to develop predictive job matching systems.

Worker profiling

In 1993, Congress passed the Unemployment Compensation Amendments, establishing a federal mandate for the WPRS initiative (Wandner 1997). The law requires SWAs to develop either characteristic screening processes or statistical models to identify the individuals who have been permanently laid off and who are most likely to exhaust their UI benefits, for the purpose of referring them to reemployment services. This process, known as worker profiling, produces a prediction of a UI claimant's probability of exhausting his or her UI benefits based on a set of personal and economic variables that differs from state to state, though five variables are recommended by USDOL—education, job tenure, industry, occupation, and unemployment rate (USDOL 2000).[11] The legislation, as well as subsequent guidance from USDOL, requires states to use data on the outcomes of individuals referred through WPRS to update their models over time. The WPRS Policy Workgroup called on states to "update and revise their profiling models regularly, as well as add new variables and revise model specifications, as appropriate" (WPRS Policy Workgroup 1999, p. 16).

Identifying optimal services

In 2001, with support from USDOL, the W.E. Upjohn Institute built and pilot-tested the Frontline Decision Support System (FDSS) in two Georgia workforce centers with the objective of improving customer and workforce staff decision making with respect to reemployment. The system consists of a series of tools to provide customers with better information on their employment prospects, their job search, and the services that would be the most effective at helping them to return to work. The system generates the probability of a worker being reemployed in the same industry, a list of occupations related to the job seeker's previous occupation, and the services that are likely to be the most effective at helping the job seeker return to work (Eberts and O'Leary 2002). Because FDSS was not implemented on a statewide basis, a rigorous evaluation of the program's effect on reemployment has not been conducted. The FDSS is discussed in more detail elsewhere in this volume.

How states conduct predictive modeling

Although SWAs have applied predictive modeling to various substantive issues, they most commonly use prediction in implementing WPRS. Through WPRS, nearly every SWA in the nation uses a predictive model on a daily or weekly basis to assign a probability of UI benefit exhaustion to newly unemployed UI claimants and to refer individuals to services based on their scores. Since WPRS is the biggest predictive modeling enterprise that the SWAs undertake, we sought to learn how states engage in predictive modeling by surveying them about their WPRS predictive modeling practices. Specifically, we were interested in learning about three aspects of how they engage in predictive modeling: 1) the variables they include in their predictive models, 2) the algorithms they use to calculate predictions, and 3) the frequency with which they update their predictive models.

In April 2014, we e-mailed the survey to the UI directors in the SWAs of all 50 states, the District of Columbia, Puerto Rico, and the U.S. Virgin Islands. We received 34 responses, which enabled us to draw three primary conclusions with respect to how SWAs engage in predictive modeling.

First, states primarily include in their models the variables recommended by USDOL (education, job tenure, industry, occupation, and unemployment rate). Of the 34 responding states, 27 use at least the variables recommended by USDOL. The majority of states, however, include few variables beyond this list. The results of our survey are consistent with what others have previously learned about how SWAs conduct predictive modeling. The U.S. Government Accountability Office (2007); Sullivan et al. (2007); and Black, Smith, Plesca et al. (2003) find that many states do not include in their models a number of variables, such as the number of previous employers, past wages, and previous UI receipt, that might improve the predictive power of their worker profiling models. In their reanalysis of Kentucky's UI claims data, Black, Smith, Plesca et al. (2003) conclude that states could improve the predictive power of their models by incorporating more variables, including whether the customer received welfare benefits, the office where the individual received services, and whether the customer was enrolled in postsecondary education at the time of filing a claim. They note, however, that most states' models do not include these variables, and neither did many of the respondents to our survey.

Second, states primarily use a logit model to predict benefit exhaustion. Of the 34 responding states that use predictive models to assign claimants to services, 23 of them use a logit model. While one state used a neural network model, two states did not use a statistical model at all, and instead assigned customers using a characteristic screen, which selects individuals for services based on a handful of individual attributes.

The third conclusion is that many states do not regularly update their models. Despite the requirements of the original legislation and the guidance issued by USDOL, states are not regularly updating their profiling models. In their survey of state profiling models, Sullivan et al. (2007) find that many states had not updated their models in years. In some cases, states were using models estimated possibly 10 years previously to predict worker employment outcomes in the present day. Our survey from this year finds that updating of profiling models remains infrequent, with 16 of the 34 responding states indicating that they have not updated their models since before 2008. In other words, despite the substantial changes in the U.S. labor market over the past six or more years, these states have used models based on the prerecession period to predict job seeker outcomes during the recession and for the postrecession period.

Many of the states that had not updated models since before the recession cited an inability to update due to a lack of resources. This was particularly the case for states that have no in-house statistical staff and those that had their existing models set up directly by USDOL. Nevertheless, when model coefficients are not updated, it increases the chances that the predictive model misallocates services away from those most in need. Indeed, the U.S. Government Accountability Office (2007) finds that not only were many states not updating their profiling models, but also that neither USDOL nor the states had conducted any recent study to evaluate whether assigning individuals to services based on the predictions of the profiling models was having any positive effects on UI claimants' outcomes. The studies that have been conducted (e.g., Black, Galdo, and Smith 2007; Black, Smith, Berger et al. 2003; and Black, Smith, Pleasca, et al. 2003), although they employ rigorous methodological designs, are using data from the 1990s. Without updated research, it is impossible to know whether the states' profiling models are having the desired effect of reducing the duration of unemployment.

Application

In this section, we present an application of predictive modeling to a substantive workforce problem, predicting which customers are likely to have difficulty finding employment and need more extensive services before falling into long-term unemployment. Although our application addresses a substantively important issue, we have selected this application to illustrate the predictive modeling *process*. In particular, we present three approaches that states can take to improve the accuracy of their predictions using three different predictive algorithms, use the results to show the importance of updating predictive models over time, and describe some steps for diagnosing problems with and improving a model's predictive accuracy.

In our application, we assess the predictive accuracy of three algorithms—logit, regularized regression, and neural network—encountered both in our survey of the states and in the statistical literature on predictive analytics.[12] These algorithms represent three different approaches that states can use to improve the accuracy of their predictive models. We present an example in which the predictive accuracy varies only slightly across the three models, in order to highlight a cautionary point for states acquiring data for predictive applications: big data and sophisticated statistical models are not enough to solve every problem. If the statistical model is a poor approximation of the real-life process (e.g., long-term unemployment) that is being modeled, then neither more data nor more complicated methods will greatly improve predictive accuracy. We discuss this issue in more detail below.

Data

We use two primary data sources from the state of New Jersey to construct the sample for this chapter: America's One-Stop Operating System (AOSOS) and UI Wage Record data. AOSOS records the enrollment of customers in the workforce system, their demographic characteristics, the services they receive, and their exit from the system. AOSOS also tracks the participation of workforce system customers in the three largest welfare programs that serve working-age adults: Temporary Assistance for Needy Families (TANF), Supplemental Nutrition Assistance Program (SNAP), and the General Assistance (GA) program, a state-funded program that serves adults without dependent children. The UI wage data system records the wages of all employees at employers that report wages every quarter in the course of paying their UI taxes.

Sample

The sample for this chapter consists of all individuals who interacted with a New Jersey AJC for the first time in 2012. However, we exclude certain groups of individuals from the sample when they differ significantly from other AJC customers both in how they enter and how they interact with the workforce system. Specifically, we remove individuals who had any interaction (in terms of application for benefits or receipt of benefits) with TANF, SNAP, or GA, as well as customers under the age of 25. For both welfare program recipients and youth customers, it is more appropriate to run a separate predictive model for these individuals. In order to highlight the usefulness of predictive models for smaller geographic units than the state-level, we limit the data to a single state workforce investment area. The results presented below are substantively similar when analyzing statewide data.

Predictors

The predictors for the model consisted of demographic characteristics that appeared in the AOSOS data and wage history variables constructed from the UI wage data. Although AOSOS has the capacity to accommodate the entry of hundreds of different job seeker attributes that could be significant predictors of labor market success, in practice a much more limited set of characteristics is available for most job seekers. These include sex, race/ethnicity, education level, and date of birth.

We create wage histories for each workforce system customer relative to their date of entry into the workforce system. The wage history consists of each customer's earnings in each of the 24 quarters prior to enrollment in the workforce system, except for the first 2 quarters prior to enrollment, as the six-month lag in the UI wage data means that these quantities would not be available for inclusion in a predictive model at the time a customer enrolled. We then created additional variables, including the total number of quarters worked in the past six years and the number of consecutive quarters the job seeker was employed before entering the workforce system.[13]

Comparison of predictive models

In the predictive models presented below, we operationalize long-term unemployment as collecting zero wages in the four quarters after a customer's initial AJC visit. We then compare the predictive accuracy of three competing models. When the outcome variable is dichotomous, one of the first classification methods that researchers apply is logistic regression, which often achieves high predictive accuracy. However, when the model includes few observations and many variables, some of which may be highly correlated with each other, a statistical problem called *overfitting* may reduce the model's accuracy on new data sets. When a model overfits, it is fitting the random noise in the data and not the underlying relationship between the variables, meaning that it is likely to perform poorly when called upon to make predictions on new data. Numerous and highly multicollinear variables are features of large administrative data sets in workforce development. Regularized regression models, such as the ridge and lasso, were developed to improve predictive accuracy in situations where models are overfitting the data. Thus, in addition to the logit model, we estimate a modified regression model called ridge regression (Hastie, Tibshirani, and Friedman 2009; Kuhn and Johnson 2013).

The third model we show is called a neural network, which at least one state uses for its worker profiling model. The chief advantage of the neural network is its ability to model complex relationships between the predictors and the outcome, which can lead to improved predictive accuracy when compared to competing models. States can implement a neural network, as well as the logit and the ridge regression, without a substantial investment in technical capacity. The models can be estimated using freely available and easy-to-use software such as R (discussed in the Predictive Analytics section on p. 452).

In estimating the models, we follow common practice in predictive analytics by splitting the customer data into three separate data sets: a training set, a test set, and a validation set. The reason we split the data involves choosing models that have high predictive accuracy on new observations. The danger of the overfitting phenomenon mentioned above is that the model estimates may have excellent predictive accuracy on the data set used in estimation while having poor predictive accuracy on any new data. A predictive model should not be assessed on how well it predicts outcomes on the data that were used to estimate the model, but rather on new data for which the outcomes are unavailable. For example, a model may perform well predicting outcomes on past One-Stop customers while poorly predicting outcomes on any new customers. Splitting the data set into a training, test, and validation set helps reduce the possibility that our models overfit the data and thus have poor predictive accuracy on new customers.

Specifically, we follow these four steps:

1) Estimate the logit, ridge, and neural network models on the training data

2) Assess the predictive accuracy of each model on the test data

3) Choose the logit, ridge, and neural network specification with the highest predictive accuracy on the test data[14]

4) Assess predictive accuracy of each model on the validation set to establish final benchmark model accuracy

In practice, a predictive model should produce at least higher predictive accuracy than an alternative strategy of using no model at all. For example, workforce agencies can simply classify all customers as likely to be unemployed. The predictive accuracy of this system will equal the average of the outcome variable for averages above 0.5 and 1 minus the average for values below 0.5. If 60 percent of customers in the data are unemployed, then this system would achieve a predictive accuracy of 60 percent, since it would classify all the 60 percent of unemployed individuals correctly and all of the 40 percent of employed individuals incorrectly. We call this system the *null model*. At a minimum, we want to choose predictive models that have higher predictive accuracy than the null model.

Note that we estimate and validate the model using 2012 customer data. The estimates thus reflect the most current data available for this application. However, as we found in our survey of the states' predictive modeling practices, some states are not updating their models with the most current data. For example, many states are using 2008 customer data to predict 2012 customer outcomes, despite the large differences in the labor market conditions and typical customer profiles across this period of time.

To illustrate the consequences of not updating predictive models, we follow the same steps as those listed above but train and test the models using data from 2008 only. With the estimates from the 2008 data, we measure predictive accuracy using the same 2012 validation set as that used above.

The results are shown in Figure 19.3. The black horizontal bars mark the predictive accuracy of the models that are fit to the 2012 data, with the bottom horizontal black bar representing the null model's predictive accuracy. The three models achieve similar predictive performance on the validation data. The logit, ridge, and neural network models correctly classify 60 percent of customers as experiencing a long spell of unemployment. Each model does significantly better than the null model, which features only 53 percent of customers correctly classified.

The grey horizontal bars in Figure 19.3 represent predictive accuracy for the models estimated using the 2008 data. Recall that the expectation is that the predictive accuracy of a model will decrease when the model's estimates are not updated with more current data. The results confirm our expectation. Across all three models, the predictive accuracy on the validation data is approximately equal to the accuracy of the null model. In other words, when we estimate models using older data, we achieve results no better than simply assuming every customer who enters an AJC will experience a long spell of unemployment.

A natural question to ask is why the performance of the three models is so similar. Why, in other words, do the more sophisticated ridge and neural network models provide little improvement over the logit model? The answer relates to the concepts of the bias and variance of a predictive model.

The variables included in the application we present are only weakly associated with the outcome variable of unemployment. These variables thus do a relatively poor job representing the complex process that leads individuals to experience long-term unemployment. This phenomenon—the failure of a model to be a good approximation of a real-life process—is called *bias*. Rather than overfitting the data, the logit model is underfitting, so the ridge regression offers little or no gain

Figure 19.3 Predictive Performance of Neural Network, Ridge, and Logit Models

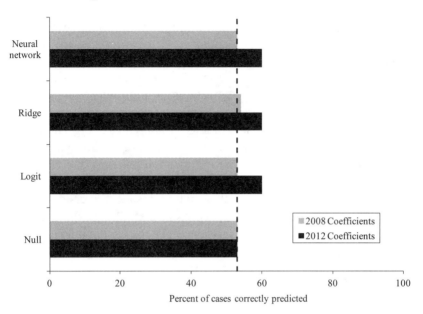

over the logit. In addition, even the complex neural network is unable to model the complexity in the data in a manner superior to the logit and the ridge regression. The result is three models that perform similarly and achieve prediction accuracy at only about 60 percent when, ideally, the model should achieve much higher accuracy. This suggests that additional work needs to be done collecting not more data but more high-quality variables that are associated with the outcome of interest.

A crucial point about a high-bias model is that more data will not substantially improve predictive accuracy. Even when we expand our data set to include hundreds of thousands of additional observations, the results change little. Big data will help primarily when the model has an opposite problem called *high variance.* A high variance model features poor predictive accuracy on data that were not used to estimate the model. Generally, more data can reduce the variance of the model by reducing overfitting, but more data will not reduce its bias.[15] Bias reduction requires the inclusion of additional predictors in the model.

CONCLUSIONS

Building an intelligent workforce system requires high-quality data and the ability to mine insights from all types of data, not just numeric and categorical data, and to analyze that data as accurately as possible. Data science and low-cost software offer SWAs and local workforce areas a series of valuable tools for improving the labor market outcomes of AJC customers. When described using terms such as geospatial analysis, text mining, predictive analytics, or big data analytics, these models can appear new and intimidating. However, despite states' limited experience examining location and text data, the tools for mining these data for insights are within the capabilities of SWA research staff—possibly in collaboration with state university partners or private sector firms. Moreover, many states are already quite familiar with predictive modeling, as nearly every state already implements predictive models through their UI programs. While it is true that the field of predictive modeling offers a wide range of algorithms for predicting workforce outcomes, SWA staff do not need to understand their mathematical intricacies any more than they do the basic logistic regression models currently in use for worker profiling because existing statistical software does most of the heavy lifting.

What SWAs *do* need to ensure is the proper expertise in the application of location and text analysis and in predictive modeling. For location and text data, this requires identifying staff capacity internal to the SWA or available in other agencies of state or local government, universities, or the private sector. In the case of prediction, this may require some training for staff members who currently oversee worker profiling models or hiring an outside party to develop and implement a new predictive model, as setting models up the first time requires careful design and evaluation. But once the models are established, they need to be updated with new data only on an annual basis, which is a much less costly process. In short, while states will need to find resources to develop new models, these resources need not be extensive.

Beyond resource constraints, the much larger and more crucial impediments to an intelligent workforce system are data limitations. If address information is not updated regularly or textual data are collected only sporadically, then these potentially useful sources of information may not be available in an accurate or complete enough form to provide the type of value they could potentially provide. The chapter has also demonstrated that having a large quantity of data is not enough to produce highly accurate predictive models. The *quality* of workforce data is just as important. In order to fully leverage the power of location-based analyses, text analysis, and predictive models, SWAs need not only a large number of observations but also a multitude of variables that are related to workforce outcomes. In the current state of the workforce data, these variables are often not available because state agencies silo their data into separate systems. Furthermore, states often only collect the bare minimum of variables necessary to meet federal reporting requirements.

Data quality is an area where the workforce system needs to strive for improvement, and to some extent this process has already begun. The need for high-quality data is becoming more apparent to public officials, and a limited number of projects are under way at all levels of government to foster improvements in data quality. For instance, the USDOL Workforce Data Quality Initiative has provided grants to 32 states to integrate administrative data systems, breaking down silos and providing the diversity and number of variables that make accurate predictive modeling possible. Other examples of data integration projects include the Workforce Innovation Fund projects in Chicago and Newark, as well as recent efforts to create a federal workforce data system.

In order to derive insights from location and textual data and develop accurate predictive models, the collection of high-quality workforce data must begin now, and an intelligent workforce system should look beyond data integration to further improve the quality of workforce data. For instance, a key component of data quality is data completeness, and in our experience performance metrics have had a significant effect on which fields of data are the most thoroughly recorded and least missing. Those that are required for SWAs to meet their federal reporting requirements are the fields that are the most complete. Data quality improvements may therefore depend on how the federal system holds states and local areas accountable. A system that genuinely incentivizes states, local areas, and workforce counselors to collect and record a greater variety of data elements may be the essential first step to building a truly intelligent workforce system. SWAs can also take other steps to improve data quality, such as designing new customer intake procedures that collect additional variables and provide training to ensure consistent data entry across AJCs. Location data, text data, and predictive models hold much promise for the future of workforce development, and states can capture the benefits that these models provide only by improving data collection in the workforce investment system.

Notes

1. More extensive reviews of the field can be found in Grimmer and Stewart (2013) and Witten (2005).
2. Generally, before any analysis begins, a researcher must preprocess the text for analysis. This step usually involves stemming words, removing punctuation and common stop words such as *the* and *than*, removing numbers, and converting words to lower case. Analysts often apply a weighting scheme to words, such as *tf-idf* weights.
3. For a detailed R example as the count-based method and word associations, see Feinerer, Hornik, and Meyer (2008).
4. Monroe, Colaresi, and Quinn (2008) and Taddy (2013) discuss methods for estimating words that are predictive of category or group labels.
5. At alternative strategy is to look at specific aspects and assess their overall positivity and negativity (Liu 2010). Our research question here is focused on understanding aspects that factor into respondents' overall evaluation of the program rather than understanding variation in ratings across different services.
6. For a discussion of more advanced analyses of open-ended survey items, see Roberts et al. (2014). The result presented here is consistent with the informational negativity effect in psychology whereby individuals are better able to identify more precise justifications to support a negative reaction than a positive one (Lewicka 1997; Peeters and Czapinski 1990).
7. An algorithm is a step-by-step process for making a calculation.
8. A model is a mathematical equation that expresses a formal relationship between variables. In the case of predictive modeling, the model expresses the mathematical relationship between the predictors and the outcome being predicted.
9. To prevent discrimination, federal laws and regulations may prohibit the inclusion of some personal characteristics, such as age, race, sex, and disability status, in models that automatically assign individuals to services.
10. There are many different criteria that a researcher may use to guide her choice of the "best" model. For classification problems where the dependent variable is not skewed, accuracy is a good model evaluation parameter, as is the area under the receiver operating characteristic (ROC) curve. With a skewed dependent variable, it may be necessary to use other metrics, such as precision, recall, the F-score, etc. For models that predict continuous outcomes, the researcher might compare models based on their root mean squared error. For a detailed analysis of model evaluation, see Japkowicz and Shah (2014).

11. USDOL prohibits states from including some personal characteristics, including age, race, sex, and disability status, from the worker profiling model.
12. We define predictive accuracy as the percent of customers that the model accurately predicts as remaining unemployed.
13. We have no data on individuals who earn wages outside New Jersey. In an effort to partly mitigate the out-of-state employment problem, we delete from our list customers without any recorded education or employment history in New Jersey. Of course, this also removes weaker job seekers who are living in New Jersey but have poor employment histories. The results presented here are substantively similar to the results we obtain when we include those individuals.
14. We choose the ridge regression regularization penalty and the neural network decay parameter and node size to optimize predictive accuracy on the test data.
15. For more information about diagnosing bias and variance, see the concept of learning curves in the statistics and machine learning literature.

References

Black, Dan A., Jose Galdo, and Jeffrey A. Smith. 2007. "Evaluating the Worker Profiling and Reemployment Services System Using a Regression Discontinuity Approach." *American Economic Review* 97(2): 104–107.

Black, Dan. A., Jeffrey A. Smith, Mark C. Berger, and Brett J. Noel. 2003. "Is the Threat of Reemployment Services More Effective than the Services Themselves? Evidence from Random Assignment in the UI System." *American Economic Review* 94(4): 1313–1327.

Black, Dan A., Jeffrey A. Smith, Miana Plesca, and Shannon Seitz. 2003. *Profiling UI Claimants to Allocate Reemployment Services: Evidence and Recommendations for States: Final Report*. Washington, DC: U.S. Department of Labor, Employment and Training Administration.

Blei, David M. 2012. "Probabalistic Topic Models." *Communications of the ACM* 55(4): 77–84.

Burrough, Peter A., and Rachael A. McDonnell. 1998. *Principles of Geographical Information Systems*. New York: Oxford University Press.

Eberts, Randall W., and Christopher J. O'Leary. 2002. "A Frontline Decision Support System for Georgia Career Centers." Upjohn Institute Staff Working Paper No. 02-84. Kalamazoo, MI: W.E. Upjohn Institute for Employment Research.

Feinerer, Ingo, Kurt Hornik, and David Meyer. 2008. "Text Mining Infrastructure in R." *Journal of Statistical Software* 25(5): 1–55.

Finlay, Steven. 2014. *Predictive Analytics, Data Mining, and Big Data: Myths, Misconceptions, and Methods*. New York: Palgrave Macmillan.

Government Accountability Office. 2007. *Unemployment Insurance: More Guidance and Evaluation of Worker-Profiling Initiative Could Help Improve State Efforts.* GAO-07-680. Washington, DC: GAO.

Grimmer, Justin, and Gary King. 2011. "General Purpose Computer-Assisted Clustering and Conceptualization." *Proceedings of the National Academy of Sciences* 108(7): 2643–2650. Washington, DC: The Academy.

Grimmer, Justin, and Brandon M. Stewart. 2013. "Text as Data: The Promise and Pitfalls of Automatic Content Analysis Methods for Political Texts." *Political Analysis* 21(3): 267–297.

Hastie, Trevor, Robert Tibshirani, and Jerome Friedman. 2009. *The Elements of Statistical Learning: Data Mining, Inference, and Prediction.* 2d ed. New York: Springer.

Japkowicz, N., and M. Shah. 2014. *Evaluating Learning Algorithms: A Classification Perspective.* New York: Cambridge University Press.

Kuhn, Max, and Kjell Johnson. 2013. *Applied Predictive Modeling.* New York: Springer.

Lewicka, Maria. 1997. "Is Hate Wiser than Love? Cognitive and Emotional Utilities in Decision Making." In *Decision Making: Cognitive Models and Explanations.* New York: Routledge, pp. 90–108.

Liu, Bing. 2010. "Sentiment Analysis and Subjectivity." In *Handbook of Natural Language Processing.* 2d ed. Nitin Indurkhya and Fred J. Damerau, eds. London: Chapman and Hall/CRC, pp. 627–666.

Loughran, Tim, and Bill McDonald. 2011. "When Is a Liability Not a Liability?" *Journal of Finance* 66(1): 35–65.

Monroe, Burt L., Michael P. Colaresi, and Kevin M. Quinn. 2008. "Fightin' Words: Lexical Feature Selection and Evaluation for Identifying the Content of Political Conflict." *Political Analysis* 16(4): 372–403.

Neuendorf, Kimberly A. 2002. *The Content Analysis Guidebook.* Thousand Oaks, CA: Sage Publications.

Peeters, Guido, and Janusz Czapinski. 1990. Positive-Negative Asymmetry in Evaluations: The Distinction between Affective and Informational Negativity Effects. In *European Review of Social Psychology.* Vol. 1. Chichester, UK: Wiley.

Roberts, Margaret E., Brandon M. Stewart, Dustin Tingley, Christopher Lucas, Jetson Leder-Luis, Shana K. Gadarian, Bethany Albertson, and David G. Rand. 2014. "Structural Topic Models for Open-Ended Survey Responses." *American Journal of Political Science* 58(4): 1064–1082.

Schutt, Rachel, and Cathy O'Neil. 2014. *Doing Data Science.* Sebastopol, CA: O'Reilly Media.

Sebastiani, Fabrizio. 2002. "Machine Learning in Automated Text Categorization." *ACM Computing Surveys* 34(1): 1–47.

Siegel, Eric. 2013. *Predictive Analytics: The Power to Predict Who Will Click, Buy, Lie or Die*. Hoboken, NJ: John Wiley and Sons.

Sullivan, William F., Lester Coffey, Lisa Kolovich, Charles W. McGlew, Douglas Sanford, and R. Sullivan. 2007. *Worker Profiling and Reemployment Services Evaluation of State Worker Profiling Models: Final Report*. Washington, DC: U.S. Department of Labor, Employment and Training Administration.

Taddy, Matt. 2013. "Multinomial Inverse Regression for Text Analysis." *Journal of the American Statistical Association* 108(503): 755–770.

U.S. Census Bureau. 1994. *Geographic Areas Reference Manual*. Washington, DC: U.S. Department of Commerce.

U.S. Department of Labor (USDOL). 2000. Worker Profiling and Reemployment Services. http://www.doleta.gov/programs/wprs.cfm (accessed September 4, 2014).

Wandner, Stephen A. 1997. "Early Reemployment for Dislocated Workers in the United States." *International Social Security Review* 50(4): 95–112.

The White House. 2014. *Ready to Work: Job-Driven Training and American Opportunity*. Washington, DC: The White House.

Witten, Ian H.. 2005. "Text Mining." In *Practical Handbook of Internet Computing*, Munindar P. Singh, ed. Boca Raton, FL: Chapman and Hall/CRC, pp. 14.1–14.22.

Worker Profiling and Reemployment Services Policy Workgroup. 1999. *Worker Profiling and Reemployment Services Policy Workgroup: Final Report and Recommendations*. Washington, DC: U.S. Department of Labor, Employment and Training Administration.

20
Chicago's Journey toward Better Data and Performance for the Workforce Development System

Elizabeth Weigensberg
University of Chicago

Amanda Cage
Chicago Cook Workforce Partnership

The recent economic downturn has led many job seekers and policymakers to ask questions about which workforce development programs are effective at helping people acquire skills and obtain employment. In Chicago, as in many other jurisdictions nationwide, the local workforce development system is a complex array of public and private organizations that provide services ranging from job search assistance to education and occupational training (Chapin Hall at the University of Chicago 2010). Information about program performance is inconsistent and difficult to obtain, given fragmented program funding silos coupled with various data and reporting requirements. Even when data to assess programs are available, they are often limited to participants within a particular service provider agency or public funding stream, providing only a partial understanding of program outcomes. Furthermore, data quality and access can be inconsistent, since organizations are often required to use multiple cumbersome data management systems with limited reporting capacity (Weigensberg et al. 2013).

The need for better data to understand program performance is not only shared among policymakers and job seekers but is also expressed by workforce program administrators and frontline practitioners seeking more information about their outcomes (Corporation for a Skilled Workforce and The Benchmarking Project 2013; Weigensberg et al. 2012). The demand for data to make informed decisions about workforce development programs created a culture of desired change in Chicago. Since 2009, numerous public and nonprofit agencies, local policymakers, foundations, and researchers have collaborated to engage in several strategic and innovative initiatives to improve organizational governance and the structure of the local workforce system as well as to access, create, and analyze data to assess programs and inform decision making.

CHICAGO WORKFORCE INVESTMENT COUNCIL AND CWIC*STATS*

In 2009, Chicago Workforce Investment Council (CWIC), a nonprofit, was created to help align programs and promote effectiveness of the local workforce development system. CWIC was chaired by Mayor Richard M. Daley and governed by a board of influential businesses and community partners to provide cross-systems oversight of key public agencies, including high schools, community colleges, and workforce development programs. CWIC's mission was to ensure that Chicago had a skilled and educated workforce to keep Chicago's businesses, economy, communities, and families thriving. It aimed to improve the skills and earning potential of residents, meet the labor needs of local businesses, and strengthen Chicago communities. The council focused on aligning the diverse public agencies and program funding streams within the workforce development system and was charged with ensuring that programs were effective for both residents seeking employment and businesses needing to hire a skilled workforce. It monitored over $350 million in annual workforce investments and coordinated resources across numerous city agencies to maximize the return on public investment.

To support the information needs of CWIC and other stakeholders, numerous workforce development policymakers, program administrators, and foundations partnered with Chapin Hall at the University of Chicago to establish a Chicago workforce data and research initiative called CWIC*stats*. The model for CWIC*stats* emerged from the need for a workforce data consortium that could provide reliable data from the diverse and fragmented local workforce development system. CWIC-

stats researchers worked with state and local public agencies to access and analyze administrative data on program participants and outcomes, including data on Workforce Investment Act program participants and secondary students in the Chicago Public Schools, and then to link that information to employment earnings. CWIC*stats* produced program performance measures, reports synthesizing local labor market indicators, and periodic research studies providing an in-depth understanding of targeted populations and programs. The CWIC*stats* initiative served as an innovative model of cross-system data integration and analysis to address data and research gaps, assisting policymakers with data-informed decision making (Weigensberg 2013).

CHICAGO-COOK WORKFORCE PARTNERSHIP AND IWIS

In 2012, building on recent political transitions, the local workforce development system evolved along with the approach to address the need for data on program performance. Mayor Rahm Emanuel and Cook County Board President Toni Preckwinkle established the Chicago Cook Workforce Partnership (the Partnership) to oversee the local workforce development system. The Partnership combined city and county resources to promote collaboration and efficiency for services supported by the federal Workforce Investment Act (WIA), which were previously administered by three separate local Workforce Investment Boards that covered Chicago and Cook County. Since its inception, the Partnership has reduced administrative and programmatic redundancy within the local system and helped to align local training opportunities with the needs of businesses. To achieve its goals of effective and streamlined workforce services, the Partnership also saw the need for improved data for workforce programs.

Although CWIC*stats* made great progress to link and analyze data across multiple programs and data sources to assess program performance and pursue research, the fragmented and incomplete nature of workforce development data remained a challenge, especially for program management purposes. With support and recommendations from research efforts conducted at Chapin Hall (Weigensberg et al. 2012) and Public/Private Ventures (Miles et al. 2010), a growing need for an improved data system for local workforce development programs emerged. Furthermore, the need for better data was being voiced from community-based service providers, not just public agency administrators. In 2013, the Partnership, in collaboration with public agency partners and service providers, embarked on a three-year project to develop and implement a comprehensive integrated workforce information system (IWIS) to capture and report data on all participants served by workforce development programs in Chicago and Cook County. This effort, which is funded by a U.S. Department of Labor Workforce Innovation Fund grant and several local foundations, is the first attempt to create a management information system to integrate administrative data across public and private agencies, as well as funding streams, to provide data on all individuals served by local workforce development programs. IWIS will reduce the need for frontline staff to enter data with numerous management information systems because it will serve as an interface among multiple data systems. IWIS will also promote the use of data through customizable reporting for agency staff and program administrators, as well as common reporting among private funders. In addition to the robust reporting features, IWIS will benefit frontline staff by creating a dashboard where they can easily navigate data entry, obtain information across numerous backend data systems, share referrals, and assess outcomes that were previously unavailable or labor-intensive to obtain. Once in operation, IWIS will allow for the comprehensive assessment of workforce development programs for the first time, while also streamlining data processes for improved program management. Although these technical advances with IWIS will assist policymakers, administrators, and frontline staff, the system will also ultimately benefit job seekers by providing enhanced information sharing, efficient referrals, and better data to improve services.

LESSONS LEARNED

The CWIC*stats* and IWIS initiatives to improve data and program performance in Chicago have provided several key lessons that could benefit others embarking on similar efforts to improve workforce data.

Shared Need and Vision for Improved Data

The CWIC*stats* and IWIS efforts emerged from a common need for better data on the workforce development system, which was shared among multiple stakeholders, including policymakers, public agencies, community-based service providers, private foundations, advocates, and researchers. CWIC*stats* was developed as an excellent strategy to link and analyze data to address the initial need to provide periodic performance measures and research on the overall effectiveness of the system. However, stakeholders wanted more comprehensive data, particularly on those individuals served by the workforce development system, yet not supported by public funds and not typically included in those corresponding data systems. Therefore, stakeholders, especially the frontline provider organizations, rallied around the need for IWIS as a comprehensive data system that could be used not only for analysis purposes but also for program management.

Strong Leadership and Partner Collaboration

To build on a shared vision of improved workforce development data, strong leadership and partner collaboration were essential to implement strategies to achieve this vision. For both CWIC*stats* and IWIS, political leadership and local public agency leaders helped to champion the work and engage partners. Also, with both efforts, an advisory council of key stakeholders was established to assist with oversight and to provide input. In addition to leadership, collaboration with public agencies and community provider partners was essential to implementing both data initiatives. Specifically, collaboration among public agency partners, such as the Illinois Department of Commerce and Economic Opportunity and the Illinois Department of Employment Security, was essential to establishing data sharing agreements to access and use their program data. Also, in regard to IWIS, extensive stakeholder engagement efforts were used to solicit input from public agencies and community providers to help define the system requirements and to ensure IWIS will meet the data collection and reporting needs of users (Weigensberg et al. 2013). Strong leadership and collaborations among partners were key to overcoming many challenges with both CWIC*stats* and IWIS, including obtaining buy-in, securing legal data permissions, data sharing and interface development, identifying common measures and reporting, and executing effective implementation plans.

Data and Research Expertise

Another important aspect of both data initiatives was the engagement of partners with data and research expertise in using administrative program data from the workforce development system. CWIC*stats* was housed at Chapin Hall at the University of Chicago, where experts could apply their many years of experience analyzing administrative program data, while serving as a third-party entity to provide unbiased research for partners. With the development of IWIS, data expertise was provided by Chapin Hall, the Chicago Jobs Council, and independent consultant Marty Miles, who helped to develop the system requirements plan with the input from public agencies and private providers. Leveraging expertise from experienced researchers and data partners was essential to promote innovation, ensure a high level of rigor, and lend authority for these data efforts.

Data Linkages across Multiple Programs

The innovation with both CWIC*stats* and IWIS was to link data across programs to look at the workforce system holistically rather than operating within fragmented program and funding silos. Data from workforce programs, educational institutions, and earnings were linked to assess program outcomes but also to pursue research about the experiences and trajectories of participants over time. These efforts highlighted the importance of focusing on a more systemwide and longer-term perspective to understand how programs can support the pathway and outcomes of individuals as they moved through the workforce development system and into employment.

Meaningful Analysis for Decision Making

Another important element of these data initiatives was to ensure data reports and analysis were useful and meaningful to policymakers and program administrators, who needed this information to make decisions. The analysis and research products from CWIC*stats* were often shared in a variety of formats, including presentations and policy briefs, to convey data in a user-friendly format to help make applied decisions. IWIS was also designed to ensure practical reports were included in the data system along with the ability for users to develop their own queries to analyze data, assisting users with obtaining what information they needed for management as well as service provision purposes.

Diverse Funding

Given the array of staff and resources needed to implement data initiatives, funding should be diversified among numerous sources. CWIC*stats* operations cost approximately $500,000 annually, which was supported by numerous grants from foundations as well as contracts with public agencies.[1] These funds supported the role of researchers at Chapin Hall at the University of Chicago to perform the data and analysis aspects of CWIC*stats*. However, the development of a new data system with IWIS cost significantly more, with the initial development costing approximately $3 million. The main financial support for the development of IWIS was provided by the U.S. Department of Labor and augmented by additional funds from private foundations.[2] Although developing a new data system is expensive, the investment is expected to lead to substantial savings with program management and service provision, owing to less redundancy, more efficiency with data entry, and anticipated improvements in program performance through an increased ability of providers to assess and improve services. Despite generous investments for development, obtaining funding to maintain and grow IWIS past the initial implementation will be a challenge. Future financial sustainability will likely come from a combination of funding from participating public agencies, private providers, and foundations. After the initial development, continued support costs for IWIS are estimated to be about $500,000 per year.

These lessons learned from Chicago's experience with CWIC*stats* to link data and conduct research, along with the current development of IWIS, can help other jurisdictions that are also struggling to obtain improved data to assess and manage their workforce development systems.

Notes

1. Numerous organizations provided funding for CWIC*stats* development and research efforts, including the Chicago Cook Workforce Partnership, Chicago Workforce Investment Council, the Chicago Community Trust, the Searle Funds at the Chicago Community Trust, the Boeing Company, the Ford Foundation, the Joyce Foundation, the Annie E. Casey Foundation, the Lloyd A. Fry Foundation, the Chicago Department of Family and Support Services, and the Steans Family Foundation.
2. In addition to the U.S. Department of Labor Workforce Innovation Fund grant, funding for IWIS was provided by the Chicagoland Workforce Funder Alliance.

References

Chapin Hall at the University of Chicago. 2010. *Chicago Workforce Development Programs: System Map and Inventory.* Chicago: Chapin Hall at the University of Chicago. http://www.chapinhall.org/research/report/chicago-workforce-development-programs-system-map-and-inventory (accessed October 9, 2014).

Corporation for a Skilled Workforce and the Benchmarking Project. 2013. *Apples to Apples: Making Data Work for Community-Based Workforce Development Programs.* Ann Arbor, MI: Corporation for a Skilled Workforce. http://benchmarking.skilledwork.org/wp-content/uploads/2011/06/Benchmarking_Mainreport_FINAL-2.pdf (accessed October 9, 2014).

Miles, Marty, Sheila Maguire, Stacy Woodruff-Bolte, and Carol Clymer. 2010. *Putting Data to Work: Interim Recommendations from the Benchmarking Project.* Philadelphia: Public/Private Ventures. http://benchmarking.skilledwork.org/?p=825 (accessed October 9, 2014).

Weigensberg, Elizabeth. 2013. "CWIC*stats*: A Collaborative Model to Address the Research and Data Needs of Local Workforce Development Policymakers." Paper presented at the Federal Reserve System Community Development Research Conference, held in Washington, DC, April 11–12.

Weigensberg, Elizabeth, Jeffrey Gawel, Robert Goerge, Jennifer Keeling, and Marty Miles. 2013. *Integrated Workforce Information System (IWIS) Systems Requirements Plan: Overview and Scope.* Report prepared for the Chicago Cook Workforce Partnership. Chicago: Chapin Hall at the University of Chicago. http://www.workforceboard.org/media/8899/iwis-system-requirements-plan-exec-summary.pdf (accessed October 9, 2014).

Weigensberg, Elizabeth, Colleen Schlecht, Faith Laken, Robert Goerge, Matthew Stagner, Peter Ballard, and Jan DeCoursey. 2012. *Inside the Black*

Box: What Makes Workforce Development Programs Successful? Chicago: Chapin Hall at the University of Chicago. http://www.chapinhall .org/research/report/inside-black-box-what-makes-workforce-development -programs-successful (accessed October 9, 2014).

21

Piloting and Replicating What Works in Workforce Development

Using Performance Management and Evaluation to Identify Effective Programs

David S. Berman

New York City Center for Economic Opportunity

What can cities do to identify and build evidence for effective strategies in workforce development, and how can they use these findings to drive funding decisions and improve workforce delivery systems? The New York City Center for Economic Opportunity (CEO) addresses poverty by developing, implementing, and evaluating innovative approaches to better understand what works and what does not.

Low-wage workers, and by extension workforce providers, face a tough job market. Unemployment remains high following the Great Recession, and the unemployment rate of 8.6 percent in New York City in late 2013 hides the great variation across the boroughs; for example, in the Bronx, unemployment climbs as high as 12 percent (Bureau of Labor Statistics 2014). According to CEO's research, 1.7 million New York City residents are in poverty. Many of the poor are engaged in the world of work yet still struggle to make ends meet. In New York City, there were nearly 685,000 residents in poverty who live in a household with at least one full-time year-round worker (CEO 2014).[1]

Nationally, a majority of the new jobs created in the aftermath of the recession are in low-wage occupations, while midwage industries have nearly a million fewer jobs than at the start of the recession (National Employment Law Project 2014). In addition, low-income workers face wage stagnation (Shierholz and Michel 2013).

This is the context in which New York City has worked to promote the economic well-being of low-wage workers, both through workforce development initiatives and through strategies that enhance low-wage workers' economic security, such as uptake of Food Stamps and creation of local tax credits and paid sick leave policies. New York City has a robust system of workforce services provided by multiple city agencies in partnership with service providers; CEO's goal has been to develop and assess new strategies, address gaps, and bring new resources and evidence-based approaches to improve systems and service delivery.[2]

HOW DOES CEO PILOT AND EVALUATE WORKFORCE PROGRAMS?

CEO works like a research and development lab within city government to try new strategies, determine which are effective, and scale up what works. CEO's work was shaped by a 2006 commission that was established by the mayor to comprehensively review poverty in the city and to recommend areas for investment and intervention. The commission—composed of leaders of government, business, nonprofits, academics, and philanthropy—prioritized workforce development efforts to help the working poor enter and advance in the labor market. Other focus areas included young adults (aged 16–24) who were out of school and out of the labor market ("disconnected youth"), people with a history of involvement with the justice system, and young children.

The center was quickly established to implement the commission's recommendations, and from 2007 through 2013, it piloted over 60 initiatives with a mix of public/private funding. Substantial investments focus on helping disconnected youth and the working poor to enter and advance in the workplace, and since its start, CEO has invested hundreds of million dollars in human capital development and workforce strategies. Programs represent new strategies, expansions of strong local programs, and replications of evidence-based models.

CEO is housed in the mayor's office, giving it a cross-agency vantage point, and its programs are implemented in partnership with city agencies. Most workforce programs are contracted out to local providers that deliver services to the community. All programs undergo rigorous results-focused performance monitoring, including monthly narrative reports and quarterly data reports that track progress toward targets.

Regular meetings with agency partners and site visits to providers complement the data. Performance data focus on outcomes rather than just process measures and are tracked against performance targets. Common measures, such as participant demographics, are aligned across programs to the extent possible. For CEO's workforce programs there is an emphasis on what is important: placements, wages, job quality (e.g., full-time/part-time, benefits), and promotions.

Data are periodically reviewed, with the recognition that context matters. Staff consider the range of information known about the program's performance (e.g., have there been recent staffing changes, are particular providers struggling compared to others), the labor market context, and changes in performance over time. CEO and agency partners, informed by the data, adjust and improve programs as needed. For example, a weak provider may receive a corrective action plan and assistance tailored to its shortfalls, or data showing weak job placements in particular occupations could cause a shift in focus to new areas. Meetings that convene providers often highlight the best practices of strong performers to promote peer-to-peer learning. Annual awards are given to high-performing providers that hit target outcomes and demonstrate ongoing use of data to strengthen their service delivery, as a positive strategy to encourage a data-driven culture.

Data are also shared externally. CEO shares aggregated data publicly via its Web site on an annual basis.[3] In recent years CEO began working with its partner agencies to share site-level data back to providers so that they can see how their program performance compares to fellow nonprofits operating the same model. This process also provides an opportunity for the city agencies to ensure that partners are defining and reporting variables consistently and accurately.

Once fully operational, promising program models are also evaluated to document outcomes and impacts on job placement rates and wages. Key factors in determining the shape of the evaluation include the length of program operations, the timing of expected outcomes, existing knowledge in the field, CEO's level of financial investment, and the quality of the data available. Evaluations range from qualitative assessments to quasi-experimental data analyses, up to random assignment studies that measure program impacts. CEO works with nine external evaluation partners to conduct independent evaluations, and these reports are made public.[4]

The center's overall approach is characterized by evidence-based policymaking, and accountability is built into the system. Data from performance monitoring and evaluation findings have been used to determine annual funding decisions. Successful programs are continued with the focus on bringing the program to scale and promoting system changes, while unsuccessful programs are discontinued.

WHAT SPECIFIC MODELS HAVE WORKED?

CEO's workforce development programs served more than 43,000 participants across nearly 25 programs in 2013. Its workforce strategies have spanned a range of approaches, targeting specific populations (e.g., probationers or young adults), industries (e.g., health care or transportation), or communities (e.g., particular public housing developments). Service delivery is adapted to reflect these different characteristics in recognition that there is no one-size-fits-all solution. For example, an initiative focused on a particular industry tailors its job readiness services and employer engagement strategies to that particular sector, and a program targeting people with a criminal history tailors services to address the particular needs and challenges faced by that group. CEO has documented a number of successful or promising strategies, which are discussed in the sections below.

Sector-Focused Career Centers

These centers deliver services to job seekers and employers tailored to specific industries and have demonstrated success in helping participants achieve higher wages and job placements relative to customers of the typical One-Stop Career Center. The centers are similar to One-Stops but they focus on a narrow range of occupations that help them build robust employer relationships and enable them to tailor all services to the particular industry. Starting in 2008, CEO has worked with the Department of Small Business Services (SBS) to create New York City's first sector-specific career center focusing on transportation. The results were powerful: placement rates and wages increased when compared to the traditional One-Stops that did not have an industry specific focus. Additional sector centers were added in manufacturing and health care, and a recent evaluation comparing the city's sector centers to the One-Stops found that the sector approach increases the likelihood of participants finding employment, and achieves substantially higher wages for those placed (an estimated $5,800 increase in earnings in the first year), and participants had a 39 percent increase in steady employment (working all four quarters in the year after exit from the program). Of those who received services at the sector centers, those that received hard-skills occupational training services had the greatest income gains (Gasper and Henderson 2014).

WorkAdvance

Building on its experience with sector-focused workforce programming, as well as earlier incumbent worker initiatives that had focused on career advancement, CEO worked with partners to create Work-Advance, a new sector-focused career advancement program for low-wage workers being replicated nationally through the Social Innovation Fund.[5] WorkAdvance addresses the need for quality workforce services that go beyond the initial placement to help workers keep their jobs and to continue to advance. Each WorkAdvance site focuses on a narrow range of occupations and provides robust participant screening, job readiness services, occupational training, job placements, and retention/advancement coaching beyond the initial placement. Each component of the program model is closely tailored to the target industry and informed by employer feedback. A randomized control trial is under way by MDRC to evaluate the impact of WorkAdvance, with results expected in late 2015. An early look at the program's implementation yielded important lessons about the challenges for providers in operating these programs, including the difficulty in keeping training offerings aligned with changes in the target industry, and in recruiting potential workers who meet the educational and other background screening criteria set by training providers and employers (Tessler 2013).

Jobs-Plus

This cross-agency initiative takes a geographically based approach to connect public housing residents at targeted developments to employment opportunities. The strategy delivers on-site workforce services, promotes neighbor-to-neighbor outreach, and offers rent-based financial incentives through the housing authority to "make work pay." A seven-year evaluation of the program by MDRC in the late 1990s finds that housing developments that had fully implemented the program experienced earnings growth of $1,141 on average for *all* residents, regardless of whether they participated in Jobs-Plus (Riccio 2010). The results endured even after the program had closed its doors. Specifically, residents in Jobs-Plus sites had increased their earnings 16 percent more than residents of non-Jobs-Plus sites (Riccio 2010). Based on MDRC's research and an initial pilot site that CEO launched in 2009, the city expanded the program to 10 sites through funding from the federal Social Innovation Fund and the city's Young Men's Initiative, a mayoral initiative to address disparities faced by young African American and Latino men.

Business Solutions Training Funds

This program engages directly with employers as a strategy to help incumbent low-wage workers advance in their current jobs, while also helping businesses stay competitive. It works by providing grants for customized training to businesses in exchange for their commitment to provide wage gains to their low-wage workers (with a particular focus on businesses that propose upgrading workers who earn less than $15 an hour). The current program grew out of SBS's existing Workforce Investment Act (WIA) customized training funds program. CEO funds and partnership brought a greater priority focus on low-wage workers and more flexibility in the program structure and training offerings. The program is now supported by a blend of CEO, WIA, and employer funds, and a recent independent evaluation of the program found that the model successfully led to increases in wages for the employees that received training. Program participants earning less than $15 an hour at the start of the program benefited from an 11 percent wage gain post-training and had greater wage gains than a group of similar workers at the standard career centers when compared six months after training (Hamilton and Chen 2014).

Subsidized Jobs for Young Adults

Although subsidized jobs programs for the general adult population have had mixed results in terms of their impact on helping workers enter the labor market, subsidized jobs and paid internships have been an important strategy for CEO's young adult programs. In particular, CEO has found that these programs are successful when the workforce focus of a subsidized job is added to educational programs that help young adults learn skills or advance toward their educational goals. Several recent evaluations have found promising results for disconnected youth. Sixty percent of participants in the Young Adult Internship Program complete the subsidized job program, and 50–60 percent remain in employment, education, or training after the program (Westat and Metis Associates 2009).[6] Participants in the Youth Adult Literacy Program who also held a paid internship while in pre–General Educational Development classes were more likely to graduate, attend class, and stay enrolled in the program longer than students at sites that did not offer internships (Meisch and Tunik 2011).[7]

Scholars at Work

A workforce program for students that connects the education and workforce systems, Scholars at Work draws on the employer engagement expertise of the sector-focused One-Stop to set up relevant paid internships for high school Career and Technical Education students. While the program has not yet been formally evaluated, performance monitoring suggests that the program has resulted in several participants' obtaining job offers from their internship. Interestingly, a large percentage of participants chose to go to college following the program, even though recruitment targeted students who were not considered college bound and had been planning to go directly into the workforce. Since 2010, Scholars at Work expanded the number of students placed in internships from 17 to more than 100 in 2013, grew to include community college students, and expanded its reach from 11 partner employers to 43 in 2013.

All of these programs are examples of models that have been shown to help low-wage workers enter and advance in the labor market. They are complemented by a range of other CEO initiatives that promote completion of high school (or its equivalent) and community college, as well as strategies to promote financial and asset development, and to lift the floor for low-wage workers.

LESSONS LEARNED FROM PERFORMANCE MANAGEMENT AND EVALUATION

Over the years, CEO has gleaned a wide range of lessons from doing this work. These lessons are cross-cutting and derive from multiple pilot initiatives.

Lesson 1: Programs Need to Be Labor Market Driven and Tailored to Employer Demand

While this lesson is now commonly accepted in the workforce world, it is less commonly well implemented. Program staff need to develop strong relationships with employers and use information from them to develop appropriate program screening criteria, tailor their hard- and soft-skills training offerings, and learn about career ladders within targeted occupations to provide appropriate retention and advancement services. Sector programs are a strong model for serving two constituencies: they help job seekers obtain quality employment while also meeting the human resource needs of local businesses. The approach has rigorous evidence behind it (Maguire et al. 2010) and has been increasingly embraced at the federal level.

Demand-driven hard-skill occupational training investments show particularly robust results in helping low-wage workers obtain good jobs. For example, CEO's recent sector program evaluation noted that participants in the program who received training were more likely to work the entire year after program exit, and they increased their annual earnings by $9,071 on average over those who used standard career centers. They also earned nearly $3,500 more on average than those who used sector-focused career centers but did not receive hard-skill training.

A cautionary note: programs that are too narrowly tailored can fail. Two of CEO's discontinued workforce programs were built around the needs of specific employers or a single occupation. An initiative to train young people in green jobs related to arboriculture and landscaping failed to place graduates when demand at the Parks Department and other local employers failed to materialize. A Licensed Practitioners Nursing training program built to meet the demand for nurses in the city's public hospital system was unable to place its graduates when the economy shifted and the demand for nurses (particularly those without significant relevant work experience) lessened as fewer nurses retired because of the recession. While these programs were well delivered and had high graduation rates, they did not move enough people into employment. Because they were built around a single occupation, they were not well designed to nimbly adapt to rapid changes in the labor market.

Lesson 2: Subsidized Jobs Are an Important Service Element for Young Adults

Several CEO young adult programs have found that incorporating subsidized jobs or paid internships into their educational interventions have been an effective tool to help young people get a foothold in the labor market while keeping them engaged in their classes.[8] By adding a subsidized job, programs help meet a young person's immediate need for income and also provide opportunities for exploring careers and learning valuable basic job-readiness skills. When programs are well designed, they incorporate youth development principles, match students to opportunities that meet their expectations, tailor strategies to the skills and level of job readiness of the young person, and provide both skill instruction and social/emotional support through mentoring and supervision.[9] These subsidized work opportunities often have a community service element and thereby contribute to local neighborhood improvements as well.

Lesson 3: Funders Must Invest in Building the Capacity of Workforce Providers

Operating quality workforce programs requires capacity in the field to implement. CEO programs utilize competitive requests for proposals (RFPs) to select providers that have experience with the target population or sector and demonstrate an experienced and well-qualified staff. Skilled providers are necessary to run a robust program, particularly when they are being asked to implement a specific program model that is new for their organization or represents a change in their historical way of operating. While some providers are able to continuously adapt and develop locally tailored strategies, many require the help of specialists to implement a well-delivered program. This often requires workforce funders to support technical assistance that builds needed skills to help nonprofits launch and operate new service strategies. CEO has supported the work of several experts in providing technical assistance to community groups.

Lesson 4: Performance Management and Evaluation Are Key from the Start

Low-wage workers deserve quality programs, and funders want to ensure they are getting robust outcomes for their investments. While a focus on outcomes and evaluation has grown tremendously in the workforce field broadly since CEO's creation in 2006, there is still a lack of clear and consistent focus on measuring results. While strong providers have systems in place to regularly collect data, measure progress against targets, and review data regularly to inform programmatic changes, many organizations need support in managing their data, learning from them, and using them to make programmatic changes effectively. Agencies need a functional management information system that can produce dashboards to help program staff see program data in real time, and all staff need training in data entry and metric definitions. The Benchmarking Project can provide a valuable resource for program managers in interpreting performance by showing how completion, placement, and retention measures stack up to similar workforce programs around the nation.[10] Federal agencies also provide valuable performance management resources online, such as the U.S. Department of Labor's Employment and Training Administration online training and tutorials for frontline staff, and the Department of Health and Human Services' Results Oriented Management and Accountability framework.[11]

Some additional key lessons in performance management of workforce programs include the following:

- Assessing program performance must factor in the job readiness and barriers of the target population, and how long the program has been operating. While funders are tempted to compare programs to each other, some populations need more assistance, time, and resources to move into self-sufficiency. In weighing program performance, CEO takes into consideration the context of the population served (e.g., low-literacy young adults and criminal justice system involvement), the types and intensity of services provided, how long the program has been operating, and the size of the budget. Evaluations often conduct regression analyses using individual-level data to further illustrate how work history, demographics, and other individual-level characteristics shape how a program impacts a given group of participants.

- Targets need to be revisited periodically with partners to ensure they are in line with the level of investment, the past performance of the program, the context of what is happening in the labor market, and other factors.

- Numbers alone do not tell the full story; performance monitoring and improvement requires both qualitative and quantitative information. CEO collects both narrative and data reports, conducts site visits, holds meetings with agency partners, and reviews budgets. Client profiles, case studies, and qualitative evaluations can provide valuable insights into how programs work and communicate impacts to the public in a way that resonates.

- Having evaluation partners with an expertise in particular methodologies and issue areas helps ensure the findings will be relevant. Not every program needs a random assignment study, and the size of the investment and the existing knowledge base in the field are key factors. In addition, the timing of evaluations is an important consideration, and programs should be mature before investing in evaluation. Rather than only conducting single evaluations, CEO often conducts multiple evaluations of a program, each building on the previous study's learnings. For example, the Young Adult Literacy program's first evaluation tested the impact of adding paid internships to the program model that delivered literacy, numeracy, and support services. Based on findings showing increased attendance and retention at literacy sites that provided internships, paid internships were added to the model at all sites. A second evaluation of the program looked at longer-term reading and math gains of participants, and most recently, a third evaluation provided a qualitative study of high-performing sites to identify best practices.[12]

- Program participants need information about available training options and their value, and more work needs to be done in this arena. CEO is committed to sharing data about programs, and its Web site shows high-level aggregate outcomes annually. One of the center's early initiatives in partnership with SBS was to create the New York City Training Guide to help consumers find the best local training program.[13] CEO also supported an interagency public information campaign to educate consumers about for-profit job training schools/colleges. The effort highlighted the cautions needed with proprietary and for-profit institutions and encouraged consumers to research programs, to use free or low-cost educational options, to be cautious about taking on excessive debt, and to report negative experiences. Components included online resources, connections to free financial counseling, free review of loan applications by volunteers, and intake of complaints.[14]

Lesson 5: Innovation Requires Flexible Funding

Flexible City and private funds have enabled CEO to quickly pilot innovative approaches and allowed city agencies to try new strategies without threatening their ability to meet their outcomes for WIA or other existing funding streams. Once programs demonstrate success, agency partners have been able to dedicate federal grants funds to support them, as with the sector-focused career centers and the Customized Training program. Given ongoing threats to federal funding streams, this can be a challenging path to sustainability without continued local and philanthropic support.

Although the strategies above contribute to a robust system to help low-wage workers advance, workforce development alone cannot address the needs of all low-wage workers. CEO has funded strategies such as expanding and promoting uptake of the EITC and supporting a local child care tax credit as ways to lift the floor and enhance the incomes of low-wage workers. As an example, the center worked with the city's Department of Finance to mail prepopulated amended tax returns to New Yorkers who potentially qualified for the EITC but had not filed for it (a strategy that has since been replicated in other states). In tax year 2009, this initiative helped over 6,239 households receive the EITC that would not have otherwise, cumulatively receiving $6.09 million. Recently, New York City passed expansions of paid sick leave policies and launched a universal prekindergarten expansion. Furthering policies such as these is a vital part of the strategy to support the working poor and address long-term mobility.

There is significant work still to be done. With limited public funding, even programs that demonstrate positive impacts can be challenging to maintain and expand. As a promising development, the Obama administration increased its emphasis on encouraging federal agencies to direct funding toward evidence-based programs (Executive Office of the President 2013). At the local level there is also a need to continue working to bring successful pilot programs to scale by integrating them (wholly or in part) into the larger workforce delivery system that is shaped by federal, state, and city funds, as well as private philanthropy. Some CEO pilot programs have achieved this; for example, a program that connected the One-Stops to low-income clients at community nonprofits was successful, and SBS subsequently integrated it fully into the standard operating practices of all of New York City's WIA-funded career centers (see Henderson, MacAllum, and Karakus [2010]).

With so many workforce initiatives supported through diverse funding streams, it remains a challenge to create a system where unemployed and underemployed can easily access the program that best meets their particular needs. Building stronger connections between education and workforce systems can also further the goal of longer-term engagements that help people advance along their career pathway over time.

CONCLUSION

Government is increasingly outcome driven and focused on investing in evidence-based strategies. CEO's leadership in these realms was recognized in 2011 with Harvard's Innovation in Government award (see Ash Center for Democratic Governance and Innovation [2012]). While workforce development initiatives are an important component of a strategy to help low-wage workers, they are a piece of a larger strategy to promote economic opportunity. CEO has had success, for example, in increasing graduation from community college through its Accelerated Study in Associates Program (ASAP) program, which more than doubled the graduation rate while saving the system much needed funds (Levin and Garcia 2013). Recognizing the fact that many people work full time but still remain in poverty, CEO is testing an expansion of the EITC for single tax filers without children in an effort to see if a more generous benefit will help increase incomes and draw more men into the labor market.

Incorporating lessons from successful pilots can improve workforce systems and reach scale to achieve greater impact. By sharing what has worked and what has not, local government has the potential to affect public policy and help increase economic opportunity.

Notes

The views expressed in this case study solely reflect the opinions of the author and do not represent any other person or entity. The author extends his gratitude to his colleagues from the Center for Economic Opportunity who provided feedback on this chapter, and especially Courtney Jones for her outstanding research assistance.

1. Based on 2012 data. CEO developed a more accurate measure that takes into account the local cost of living as well as the impact of government benefits for low-income populations. See nyc.gov/ceo for more information.
2. For an overview of New York City's workforce system, see City of New York (2011).
3. See http://www.nyc.gov/ceo (accessed January 20, 2015).
4. Evaluation reports are available at http://www.nyc.gov/html/ceo/html/data/reports.shtml (accessed January 20, 2015).
5. The Social Innovation Fund is a public/private funding initiative of the federal Corporation for National and Community Service to identify and expand promising programs.
6. The Young Adult Internship Program helps out-of-school and out-of-work young adults obtain needed skills through a combination of educational workshops, counseling, short-term paid internships, and postinternship support to obtain further education, advanced training, or employment.
7. The Young Adult Literacy Program provides literacy and numeracy services,

social support, and paid internship opportunities to 16–24-year-olds who read below the 8th grade level.

8. CEO programs that have provided subsidized job opportunities for young adults include Project Rise, Scholars at Work, Young Adult Internship Program, Young Adult Literacy Program, Work Progress Program, and NYC Justice Corps. See nyc.gov/ceo for more details.

9. A youth development approach is one that incorporates youth leadership into programming, sets a culture of high expectations, ensures young people are matched with caring adults who provide individualized attention, focuses on young adults' assets rather than deficits, provides support to young people to overcome barriers and develop positive coping skills, emphasizes key academic and/or occupational skills, and supports community connections to additional programs and services.

10. See http://www.skilledwork.org/benchmarking-project-workforce-benchmarking -network for more information the Benchmarking Project (accessed November 18, 2014).

11. See the USDOL ETA Web site: http://www.doleta.gov/performance/training tutorials/PEP.cfm; see also the HHS ROMA training and technical resources Web site: http://www.roma1.org/557/interior.html (accessed November 18, 2014).

12. All evaluation reports are available on CEO's Web site at www.nyc.gov/ceo (accessed November 18, 2014).

13. See www.nyc.gov/trainingguide (accessed November 18, 2014).

14. See http://www.nyc.gov/html/ohcd/html/policy/know_before_you_enroll.shtml for more information (accessed November 18, 2014).

References

Ash Center for Democratic Governance and Innovation. 2012. "Center for Economic Opportunity Wins Harvard Innovations in American Government Award." Press release. Cambridge, MA: Ash Center, John F. Kennedy School of Government, Harvard University.

Bureau of Labor Statistics. 2014. "Monthly Borough Labor Force Data." Labor Statistics for the New York City Region. Washington, DC: U.S. Department of Labor.

Center for Economic Opportunity (CEO). 2014. *The CEO Poverty Measure, 2005–2012: An Annual Report from the Office of the Mayor*. New York: Center for Economic Opportunity.

City of New York. 2011. *One System for One City: State of the New York City Workforce System, Fiscal Year 2010*. http://www.nycedc.com/sites/default/ files/filemanager/Resources/Studies/SWFSReport_FINAL_2011_05_24 .pdf (accessed November 18, 2014).

Executive Office of the President. 2013. "Memorandum to the Heads of Departments and Agencies." July 26. http://www.whitehouse.gov/sites/

default/files/omb/memoranda/2013/m-13-17.pdf (accessed November 18, 2014).

Gasper, Joseph, and Kathryn Henderson. 2014. "Sector-Focused Career Centers Evaluation: Effects on Employment and Earnings after One Year." Rockville, MD: Westat.

Hamilton, Jennifer, and Eva Chen. 2014. "Assessment of the NYC Business Solutions Customized Training Program." Rockville, MD: Westat.

Henderson, Kathryn, Crystal MacAllum, and Mustafa Karakus. 2010. "Workforce Innovations: Outcome Analysis of Outreach, Career Advancement and Sector-Focused Programs." Rockville, MD, and New York: Westat and Metis Associates.

Levin, Henry M., and Emma Garcia. 2013. "Benefit-Cost Analysis of Accelerated Study in Associate Programs (ASAP) of the City University of New York (CUNY)." New York: Teachers College, Columbia University.

Maguire, Sheila, Joshua Freely, Carol Clymer, Maureen Conway, and Deena Schwartz. 2010. "Tuning In to Local Labor Markets: Findings from the Sectoral Employment Impact Study," Executive Summary. Philadelphia: Public/Private Ventures.

Meisch, Allison D., and Jonathan Tunik. 2011. "CEO Young Adult Literacy Program and the Impact of Adding Paid Internships." Rockville, MD, and New York: Westat and Metis Associates.

National Employment Law Project. 2014. "The Low-Wage Recovery: Industry Employment and Wages Four Years into the Recovery." Data brief. New York: National Employment Law Project.

Riccio, James A. 2010. "Sustained Earnings Gains for Residents in a Public Housing Jobs Program: Seven-Year Findings from the Jobs-Plus Demonstration." New York: MDRC.

Shierholz, Heidi, and Lawrence Michel. 2013. "A Decade of Flat Wages: The Key Barrier to Shared Prosperity and a Rising Middle Class." Washington, DC: Economic Policy Institute.

Tessler, Betsy. 2013. "WorkAdvance: Testing a New Approach to Increase Employment Advancement for Low Skilled Adults." New York: MDRC.

Westat and Metis Associates. 2009. "Evaluation of the Young Adult Internship Program (YAIP): Analysis of Existing Participant Data." Rockville, MD, and New York: Westat and Metis Associates.

22
Scorecards for Postsecondary Education and Training Programs

Tiffany L. Smith
Aaron R. Fichtner
New Jersey Department of Labor and Workforce Development

Individuals, government, and businesses make significant investments in postsecondary training programs that are designed to prepare adults for employment or careers. Despite the magnitude of these investments, there is often limited information on the effectiveness of these programs, leaving most students to choose a training program and a training provider based on anecdotal information, word of mouth recommendations, and marketing materials from training providers. As a result, the market for postsecondary training functions inefficiently.

While the Workforce Investment Act of 1998 (WIA) attempted to address this inefficiency by requiring states to develop a consumer report card for training programs and an eligible training provider list (ETPL) based on performance data, a significant majority of states failed to implement these requirements for a wide variety of reasons (Van Horn and Fichtner 2011). However, a small number of states, most notably New Jersey, Washington, and Texas, have more than a decade of experience of successfully implementing these systems. This case study profiles New Jersey's online consumer report card for training programs. The experience and lessons learned from New Jersey and other successful states can provide a roadmap for other states to follow.

DESCRIPTION AND IMPORTANCE OF POLICY PROBLEM

Almost four out of five jobs in the United States (78 percent) require some form of postsecondary education. Middle-skill jobs are those that require education and training beyond a high school diploma but less than a bachelor's degree. Educational attainment can serve as a proxy to define middle-skill occupations; however, analysis that takes into account education plus formal postsecondary training as well as significant on-the-job training estimates that half of the jobs in today's economy are middle-skill jobs (Achieve 2012). Middle-skill jobs are projected to increase at a rate faster than other types of jobs in the United States. According to the Bureau of Labor Statistics, jobs requiring more than a high school diploma but less than a bachelor's degree will increase 15.8 percent between 2012 and 2022, compared to just 10.8 percent for all occupations. Occupations requiring a bachelor's degree are expected to increase 12.2 percent, while those needing a high school diploma or less will increase just 9.1 percent.

Government programs, individuals, and businesses spend significant amounts each year to prepare individuals for these middle-skill jobs. The federal government spends over $18 billion on the administration of close to 50 employment and training programs (U.S. Government Accountability Office 2011). Much of these investments are spent on short- to mid-term, postsecondary occupational training. In addition, a recent survey estimated that U.S. companies spend more than $164 billion annually on training and development, including both internal expenses and tuition reimbursement programs (American Society for Training and Development 2013). These investments estimate the expenditure by government and private businesses; however, additional significant monies are spent by individuals to improve their preparation for employment.

A wide variety of entities, from for-profit proprietary schools to nonprofit organizations and public institutions of higher education (including community colleges), provide this training, marketing their services to individuals, managers of government programs, and businesses. In addition, there are many different types of training programs offered. These programs vary by length, by cost, by whether they offer a credential, or by whether they offer college credit. Within this context, individuals must first choose which program is the right one for them to pursue, and then they must choose which provider is best able to provide that training.

NATIONAL CONTEXT

WIA required states to create consumer report cards (CRCs) in order to foster informed consumer choice in the public workforce system. It also required that states use performance data from all students in a program, regardless of the funding source, to certify those training providers and programs that would be eligible to receive funding. In addition, WIA required states to maintain an ETPL of these providers and programs. Many states expressed concerns that the CRC and ETPL requirements were too onerous to training providers and would thus limit the number of programs and providers available to WIA customers. As a result of these and other concerns, 39 states received waivers from the U.S. Department of Labor to ease implementation by extending the period of initial eligibility of providers on their lists.

In recent years there has been increasing attention to data on outcomes for education and training programs. In early 2013, the Obama administration introduced a College Scorecard, which includes data on college costs, student loans, default rates, and graduation rates. There are plans for the site to also include employment outcomes of graduates. At the state level, a limited number currently provide information online.

The federal government has increasingly recognized the importance of scorecards by funding states to develop data systems to support them. Since 2006, the U.S. Department of Education's State Longitudinal Data System Grant Program has supported state efforts to develop K–12 and P–20W (early childhood through the workforce) data systems. The U.S. Department of Labor's Workforce Data Quality Initiative provides support to states to integrate workforce development and employment data with K–12 and postsecondary education data. Both efforts are designed, in part, to help states develop employment outcomes for education and training programs.

New Jersey Solution

This case study reviews the CRC used by the New Jersey Department of Labor and Workforce Development (NJLWD). The CRC, which has been provided as an online tool to job seekers and workforce development professionals for over 15 years, is a strategy that can increase the efficiency of the training provider market by providing consumers with information on program quality. The experience of New Jersey and of other states such as Washington and Texas can provide important lessons for states as they implement WIOA and postsecondary training scorecards.

New Jersey's CRC for training providers (www.NJTopps.org) is an online searchable directory of more than 1,000 training providers offering over 9,000 programs. The site is an important tool included on the state's workforce services portal, known as Jobs4Jersey.com. The site is also promoted through NJLWD's Web site and through the New Jersey Career Assistance Navigator (NJCAN.org) Web site, a career awareness resource for high school students. During the 12 months from June 2013 through July 2014, the NJTopps site received over 63,000 hits.

NJTopps.org allows individuals to search for training programs using a variety of search terms, including program of study, occupation, and location. The result of the search is a list of the training programs that meet the user's needs. For each training program, users can view information on the provider, including a description, costs, and information on program performance. The provider and program descriptive information is developed by the providers themselves and is reviewed by state staff before it is posted online.

Program performance information includes the employment rate, retention rate, and average earnings of training programs. Labor market outcomes are shown at the program level, the cluster level (grouping together similar programs offered by the same provider), and the provider level. Data are reported for the first, fourth, and eighth quarters after program completion.

While most states found it difficult to implement these systems, New Jersey was able to create a successful system by reducing the burden on training providers while increasing the incentives for their participation. That approach has ensured that students have a broad array of choices of training programs and providers through the ETPL. Additionally, the approach has shown that the CRC is a valuable resource to a wide range of individuals and companies as they choose a training provider and program.

Broad Scope of the System

Unlike many other states, the New Jersey ETPL is not solely used by WIA programs. State legislation passed in 2006 requires all training providers who receive federal *or* state training funds to be listed on the state ETPL. By applying the ETPL requirements to more than 50 separate workforce development programs, the law creates a stronger incentive for training providers to participate in the system.

The state law also requires NJLWD to develop a CRC to disseminate information on the labor market outcomes of all students who participated in the training program, and not just of those students who received government assistance. As a result, any individual or company interested in selecting a training program or provider, even those who plan to use their own resources to pay for that training, can find value in the NJTopps Web site. This broader audience of potential users of the CRC further increases the incentive for providers to be listed on the ETPL.

Reliance on Existing Student Record Data

The New Jersey system relies heavily on existing data sets to calculate employment outcomes for participants. This has two benefits: it reduces the data collection burden on training providers, and it helps to ensure greater data quality.

Instead of conducting expensive surveys of their program participants, training providers report student records to NJLWD, using NJTopps.org to securely upload data files on a quarterly basis. Those providers who report their student records to other government agencies are not required to report their student records to NJLWD. The department, through data sharing agreements with other state agencies, is able to obtain data on students who attend institutions of higher education or on adults who attend programs funded by the Carl D. Perkins Act.

New Jersey, through a partnership with Rutgers University's Heldrich Center for Workforce Development, combines all three sources of student records with administrative data from the state's workforce development programs to create a comprehensive file of a significant percentage of all the students who have attended postsecondary education and training programs in the state.

To obtain employment outcomes for the programs on the ETPL, Rutgers University matches the student records with New Jersey Unemployment Insurance (UI) wage records and with wage records from other states through the Wage Record Interchange System. These UI wage records are collected by all states during the collection of UI payroll taxes and include wages earned in a particular quarter for individuals and information on their employers. As a result, UI wage records provide a significant record of the employment and wage experiences of the vast majority of individuals working in the state.

By combining these data sets, New Jersey can efficiently calculate employment and earnings outcomes for large numbers of programs in a standardized manner. New Jersey continues to expand and refine the use of these various data sets to calculate employment outcomes for training providers. In 2012, NJLWD was awarded a three-year grant from the U.S. Department of Labor as part of the Workforce Data Quality Initiative program. The scope of work builds on the partially developed longitudinal data system (the ETPL) by incorporating data from additional LWD administrative data systems, including UI, vocational rehabilitation, and more comprehensive adult basic education data. Links are also made to postsecondary programs and are planned for pre-K–12 public education. Three additional years of funding were awarded in 2014, which supports the addition of more data from partner agencies and expands research efforts in order to help job seekers make better training choices, program staff apply more effective workforce strategies, and policymakers support the most effective programs.

Reducing the Burden on Training Providers

To further lessen the burden on training providers, providers can use the NJTopps Web site to apply to be on the ETPL. Department staff review all applications online and can approve the applications online as well. They compare the information submitted online with information provided to the state through the licensing process for training providers, allowing for an important cross-check of the data.

Use of the System

New Jersey workforce development partners, specifically, staff at local Workforce Investment Boards and American Job Centers, use

NJTopps.org to manage and monitor training programs and use the site to help job seekers make more informed decisions on training providers. Some local Workforce Investment Boards have, at different points during the system's history, required funded providers to meet specific performance thresholds. For example, one area currently uses a 65 percent placement rate requirement, and when clients want to use providers with a lower rate, the request is given additional review by staff.

Finally, the inclusion of the NJTopps Web site on the Jobs4Jersey portal helps to expand the use of the CRC beyond those students served by the American Job Centers. In turn, the Jobs4Jersey Web site is promoted through marketing and public information efforts that have included advertising on transit buses, partnerships with community colleges and libraries, and partnerships with the state's talent networks.

FUTURE DIRECTIONS

New Jersey continues to implement improvements to the NJTopps .org system to ensure better data quality and to expand the use of the Web site. New Jersey is preparing to implement a state law that requires all private and nonprofit career schools to be included on the CRC as a condition of licensing. In addition, in early 2014, legislation was signed that expands the required data to be displayed on the CRC, including licensing and examination information, which will include information on the number of students who obtain industry recognized credentials.

CONCLUSIONS AND NATIONAL IMPLICATIONS

The Workforce Innovation and Opportunity Act (WIOA), signed into law in July 2014, continues many of the CRC and ETPL provisions of WIA, thus signaling to states that they must find new solutions to the challenges they faced in implementing WIA.

The successful efforts in New Jersey, Texas, Washington, and a handful of other states have shown that states can effectively implement CRC systems to provide individuals and employers with valuable information that can be used to choose a training program and a training provider. Such systems have the potential to create a more efficient market for postsecondary training by helping consumers to make more informed training decisions and to take into account the labor market experiences of former students when they make those decisions. Given the significant investment in money and time that students make in training, this information can be particularly valuable to students.

References

Achieve. 2012. *The Future of the U.S. Workforce: Middle Skills Jobs and the Growing Importance of Postsecondary Education.* Washington, DC: Achieve. http://www.achieve.org/files/MiddleSkillsJobs.pdf (accessed June 16, 2014).

American Society for Training and Development. 2013. "$164.2 Billion Spent on Training and Development by U.S. Companies" (blog). Alexandria, VA: American Society for Training and Development. http://www.astd.org/Publications/Blogs/ASTD-Blog/2013/12/ASTD-Releases-2013-State-of-the-Industry-Report (accessed June 16, 2014).

U.S. Government Accountability Office. 2011. *Multiple Employment and Training Programs: Providing Information on Co-locating and Consolidating Administrative Structures Could Promote Efficiencies.* GAO-11-92. www.gao.gov/new.items/d1192.pdf (accessed June 16, 2014).

Van Horn, Carl E., and Aaron Fichtner. 2011. "Eligible Training Provider Lists and Consumer Report Cards." In *The Workforce Investment Act: Implementation Experiences and Evaluation Findings*, Douglas J. Besharov and Phoebe H. Cottingham, eds. Kalamazoo, MI: W.E. Upjohn Institute for Employment Research, pp. 153–173.

Part 4

Targeted Strategies

23
Pink to Green

Promising Workforce Development Practices for Women in Nontraditional Occupations

Mary Gatta
Lauren Sugerman
Matt Unrath
Katie Onachila Spiker
Wider Opportunities for Women

Geri Scott
Deborah Kobes
Alexandra Waugh
Jobs for the Future

The majority of women in the United States do not work in jobs where they have an opportunity to get by, let alone get ahead. Fifty percent of women work in just 26 occupational categories, or only 5 percent of the 504 occupations tracked by the Bureau of Labor Statistics, and over two-thirds of women are concentrated in just 51 occupations. Today, as was true 60 years ago, "secretary" ranks as the top occupational category for women. Other leading occupations include cashiers, retail salespersons, home health aides, and jobs in the hospitality sectors, such as waitresses and housekeepers at hotels. Many of these jobs are among our economy's lowest paying. With average hourly wages of between $8 and $12, these jobs do not enable women to afford the basics, let alone care for their families. Men, on the other hand, with similar levels of education are much more likely than women to access training in the trades or science, technology, engineering, and math fields, which generally offer higher pay and better career prospects.

However, women represent a small portion of the workers in the building trades, science, technology, advanced manufacturing, and other traditionally male occupations. The small numbers of women who are in these nontraditional occupations typically earn 20–30 percent more than women in traditional occupations (such as those in health care, retail, and hospitality). An increase in women's participation in nontraditional occupations results in increased economic security for women, which means more economically secure children, families, and communities.[1]

Gender stereotypes and women's lack of knowledge about these jobs and their entry paths are significant obstacles to increasing their representation in nontraditional occupations. Women may also lack the preparatory skills to be competitive in the selection process, and selection requirements and procedures still have a disparate and unfair effect on women's acceptance into apprenticeship programs. Worse, women who overcome these barriers and enter these fields often find discriminatory practices such as minimal support, inequitable training, hostile work conditions, and job opportunities limited by employer hiring bias.[2]

Overcoming the historical and cultural obstacles that prevent women from accessing these higher-wage nontraditional careers is challenging and requires direct interventions. Targeted, effective workforce programs that are developed and implemented with a gender lens are critical to the success of individuals and communities facing these significant barriers to employment (Lufkin et al. 2007). Wider Opportunities and Women (WOW) and Jobs for the Future (JFF) partnered on an innovative Green Jobs Innovations Fund project that provided the needed specialized technical assistance to address these gender barriers. This three-year project, called GreenWays, spanned seven cities and supported eight workforce partnerships, including two preapprenticeships to registered apprenticeships. GreenWays also included several sectors and occupations, including advanced manufacturing (quality assurance inspectors, computer numeric controlled machine operators), construction and building trades (weatherization technician, residential energy auditor, hazardous-waste remediation), landscaping and urban forestry (landscape technician), renewable electric power (solar photovoltaic panel installer, solar thermal installer, solar sales, electric line worker), and transportation (alternative fuels maintenance technician, hybrid electric auto technician).

Through targeted technical assistance and resources, WOW and JFF were able to expand their site partner's capacity to increase the numbers of women served and placed into training programs and jobs that are nontraditional for women. Specifically, the GreenWays project served 283 women—roughly 25 percent of the total participants. Further, 80 percent of women completed the training programs, 77 percent obtained an industry-recognized credential, 64 women were placed in apprenticeships (out of 176 total placed in apprenticeships), 42 percent were placed in jobs, and the average starting wage of women in the program was $15.71.[3]

CASE STUDY: TECHNICAL ASSISTANCE PROGRAM DESIGN

In order to successfully recruit, train, and place women in nontraditional jobs, WOW and JFF provided comprehensive and customized technical assistance to each site. In this chapter, we will provide a snapshot of the technical assistance provided to ensure that a gender lens would be incorporated into the project.[4]

By identifying barriers within the workforce development that limit women's participation in training programs for these jobs, WOW helped each site develop program practices and address the unique barriers that women face moving into nontraditional jobs. Based on thorough assessments, the organization drew on our best practices and materials to assist each site with phone and online services and a minimum of one visit annually. The visits enabled them to offer feedback and suggestions to improve outreach, intake, and assessment material and practices, as well as observe how well gender-inclusive job readiness, curriculum, and instruction styles are integrated into classroom and workshop training.[5] WOW assisted each site in strategic planning to guide the expansion of programming or for the greater integration of women into training, including the following six strategies:

1) Establish goals for women's participation in job training and placement into nontraditional occupations

2) Establish strategic work plans to meet goals for women's participation in job training and placement into nontraditional occupations with partners' leadership and staff

3) Identify how to best work with industry partners, workforce systems, educational institutions, and other strategic partners to ensure that women are able to enter and succeed in high-paying, blue-collar jobs

4) Gain employer commitment and investment for gender equity from recruitment to career advancement through a variety of strategies, including professional development training, establishing partnership agreements, memorandum of understanding, and in-kind and tangible support

5) Share research about successful strategies and trends in curriculum development, credentialing, and labor market analyses

6) Create sustainability plans to maintain program strategies and practices, ensure ongoing integration of a gender lens, and maintain goals and outcomes that reflect incremental increases in women's participation in programming and nontraditional employment

Although strategic planning with a gender lens provided the critical overview and goals of the project, that was only part of the intervention. In order to help the organizations build capacity, WOW worked with partners to develop orientations and outreach to women, online and classroom setting survey courses to introduce women to nontraditional occupation training programs, and feeder courses that build women's prevocational skills. The organization helped the sites establish role model and mentor banks, job shadowing opportunities, support groups, career clubs, and links to professional associations. Technical support also offered a review of job readiness and wraparound case management services to ensure adequate support for women's successful participation and completion in training programs and their transition to employment.

WOW provided the following customized site-based technical assistance to each of the sites:

1) Identify site-specific strategies for attracting/recruiting women and engaging strategic partners in reaching out to their female clients, including creating orientation programs, survey classes, and preparatory courses. For example, at the annual Peer Learning Conference, WOW led hands-on learning labs to

craft outreach and recruitment flyers that included images of women performing the work.

2) Customize intake and assessment practices, gender-inclusive curriculum, and teaching practices. Across programs, WOW created a standardized assessment of the sites' assessment materials by evaluating each program's assessment requirements. For example, one site was able to transition from using a lifting requirement as a flat weight (i.e., participants must lift x pounds) to using a percentage of the participant's body weight. This seemingly small change allowed the site to continue assessing physical fitness, but also to respect that smaller participants—both men and women—may still be able to complete tasks properly without the ability to lift as much weight.

3) Develop programs on how to use gender-targeted and inclusive policies, practices, and materials. For example, in Milwaukee, WOW was able to add curriculum modules to the training program that were based on gender issues women often encounter in the workplace. In addition to sexual harassment, modules included health and safety issues and gender differences in learning and communication styles. For example, women are more likely to end their statements with an inflection. This can lead instructors to interpret women as less confident in their knowledge, despite this not being true.

4) Provide professional development and technical assistance on how to add a gender lens to the core elements of programs.

- Recruitment. In Milwaukee, WOW analyzed current recruitment and retention practices for the site's job training. Key takeaways from this analysis included the site's relationship building with other external workforce development agencies as outside recruitment sources, as well as the staff committing to follow up with applicants.

- Intake. Perhaps most often misunderstood by providers, the intake process is a key step in ensuring women's participation in nontraditional jobs. Best practices involve a theme of being inclusive of women as opposed to exclusive. For example, one site performs intake and assessment, including literacy and mathematical testing, on the same day. By combining these two steps, the site was losing qualified applicants who were anxious about the testing required before allowing time for preparation.

- Case management. In Philadelphia, WOW worked with frontline staff on case management techniques. While all staff were exposed to the benefits of adding a gender lens to their management techniques, site leaders noted that many of the women working as case managers had more preconceived notions about what their female participants needed than did the male frontline staff. By ensuring that both men and women working with female participants are able to overcome stereotypes and work with the individual, the site's procedures have added a sharper gender lens.

- Core competencies for job readiness. Successful job readiness training varied throughout the sites, but each included the core requirement that all participants regularly and in a timely fashion attend their trainings. Job readiness trainings also included exercises to raise and discuss self-esteem, rights in the workplace, and skills to develop support systems. The training also targeted interviewing and application skills, maintaining healthy habits, balancing work/family, and surviving and thriving in a male-dominated environment. By mirroring the workplace requirements and realities, each training program ensured graduates had exhibited the skills necessary to be successful once graduated.

- Instruction and classroom practices. In Philadelphia, WOW observed classroom instruction for the site's solar installation trainees. The organization then offered feedback on instructional practices that prevented women's full participation, productivity, and comfort in the classroom. Key lessons include explaining differences in the way women and men respond to competition in the classroom, and coaching instructors to use gender-neutral pronouns when sharing anecdotal lessons.

- Job development. WOW presented daylong training to partners in Detroit, focusing on building a diverse workforce, confronting employer perceptions of women in nontraditional jobs and subsequent reluctance to hire women, compliance with Equal Employment Opportunity/Affirmative Action agency requirements at the local level, and leveraging public investments as employment opportunities.

- Retention and career advancement. In Detroit, WOW was able to work with staff to design a mentorship program for future intervention. Successful elements of mentorship programs often involve working with a group of mentees assigned to a group of mentors, instead of a one-on-one relationship. This group approach removes much of the pressure that individualized mentorship relationships put on the participants and allow both mentors and mentees to grow a more organic relationship with a wider variety of more senior or junior women.

5) Facilitate partnerships with organizations that serve women trainees, American Jobs Centers, women in nontraditional career networks, professional associations to develop applicant pools, support services, and mentorship programs. One site was able to create a new preapprenticeship program, Access for All. Through this planning process, WOW spearheaded the evaluation of partner participation in the program, which included identifying partner agencies and community-based organizations, defining partners' roles and responsibilities, creating an internal organizational chart, identifying the individuals responsible for fostering each external relationship, and identifying resources necessary to make the relationships work for the agencies, employers, and the site.

REPLICATION

The GreenWays project demonstrates that if a program is developed and implanted with a gender lens, it can make a significant impact on the numbers of women entering into nontraditional occupations. WOW and JFF have compiled the best practices and resources into an online curriculum, "Pink to Green Toolkit," that programs can use to aid in replication, and is freely available online.[6] The toolkit contains

- tools to help workforce development providers assess their capacity for recruiting, assessing, placing, and retaining women in nontraditional occupations;
- ways to assist training providers in developing relevant plans, processes, and curricula for recruiting and retaining women in nontraditional occupations;
- guidelines for case management of women and matters related to the unique wraparound and support services required for women to advance on a career path in nontraditional occupations; and
- tools to assist training programs in understanding and linking to organized labor, apprenticeships, and major employers to ensure women have access to jobs posttraining.

Notes

1. For a larger discussion of nontraditional occupations for women, see U.S. Department of Labor (2008).
2. For an additional discussion of the discrimination women face in nontraditional occupations, see Bergmann (2011).
3. Wage data are self-reported by each of the sites.
4. A gender lens involves approaching or examining an issue, paying particular attention to the potentially different ways that men and women are or might be impacted. For a fuller discussion see Neimanis (2005).
5. Gender-inclusive job readiness includes targeted training to identify interviewing and communication styles typical for women. For example, women often respond to interview questions with answers that end with inflections or words such as "right?". This communication style can convey that the interviewee is unprepared or uncertain of her answers, despite this not being the case.
6. The toolkit can be found at http://www.jff.org/pinktogreen (accessed October 17, 2014).

References

Bergmann, Barbara. 2011. "Sex Segregation in the Blue-Collar Occupations: Women's Choices or Unremedied Discrimination?" *Gender and Society* 25(1): 88–93.

Lufkin, Mary, Mary M. Wiberg, Courtney Reed Jenkins, Stefanie L. Lee Berardi, Terri Boyer, Ellen Eardley, and Janet Huss. 2007. "Gender Equity in Career and Technical Education." In *Handbook for Achieving Gender Equity through Education.* 2d ed. S. Klein, B. Richardson, D. Grayson, L. Fox, C. Kramarae, D. Pollard, and C. Dwyer, eds. Mahwah, NJ: Lawrence Erlbaum Associates, pp. 420–442.

Neimanis, Astrida. 2005. *Gender Mainstreaming in Practice: A Handbook.* 2d ed. Regional Bratislava, Slovak Republic: Centre for Europe and the CIS (UNDP RBEC).

U.S. Department of Labor. 2008. "Quick Facts on Nontraditional Occupations for Women." http://www.dol.gov/wb/factsheets/nontra2008.htm (accessed October 17, 2014). Washington, DC: U.S. Department of Labor.

24
Signaling Success

A Case Study in Using Labor Market Information to Retool Workforce Development Strategies and Programs

Paul Harrington
Drexel University

Nancy Snyder
Commonwealth Corporation

The share of employed teens in Massachusetts plummeted from 53 percent in 1999 to 27 percent by 2012, reflecting a broader national trend in declining teen employment rates over the last decade. The decline in employment among young people is worrisome because a growing body of evidence suggests that work experience during the teen years exerts strong positive influences on the future educational, employment, and earnings prospects of young people (Steinberg 2013). Declining employment among teens means that increasing shares of young people are losing access to an important avenue to develop productive abilities. This is especially true for teens from low-income households (Sum et al. 2013). Teens who work have substantially higher earnings a decade after leaving high school and are more likely to enroll in college. Furthermore, early work experience is thought to contribute to the focus and direction young people need to make decisions about their future life paths (Harrington and Snyder 2013; Mortimer 2003).

Commonwealth Corporation and the Drexel University Center for Labor Markets and Policy launched a study in 2012 to improve our understanding of the underlying causes of this dramatic decline in teen employment rates. We sought to identify employer perceptions of teens in the workplace compared to other sources of entry-level workers and, using what we learned, to develop pragmatic strategies to reverse the

12-year decline in teen job access. In the spring and summer of 2012, we conducted a survey, interviews, and focus group discussions with nearly 200 businesses in Massachusetts and Philadelphia. The research questions in this effort focused on five areas: 1) perceptions of teens' hard skills (reading, writing, math, technology), 2) perceptions of teens' work behaviors, 3) the effect of teen employment laws on hiring decisions, 4) factors affecting hiring decisions, and 5) hiring preferences.

A major purpose of this study is to understand why the job market fortunes of teens have declined and to attempt to develop a set of remedies that have the potential for improving the ability of teens—both in school and out of school—to find unsubsidized private sector jobs that help improve their long-term employment and earnings experiences. We find that many of the barriers to hiring teens that are identified in the study can be addressed through training, coaching, and supports that develop job seeking and retention skills of teens and address the perceived risk of hiring teens on the part of employers. In addition, organizations and institutions that serve teens, including high schools, can play a role in preparing and supporting teens and vouching for them with businesses in their local labor market. The findings of this study can inform the ways that schools, community-based organizations, workforce boards, career centers, and businesses can intervene to help increase youth employment.

KEY FINDINGS OF THE RESEARCH

Our research finds that employers do not view entry-level workers as a readily substitutable, homogeneous source of labor supply, even though by definition entry-level jobs require very low levels of ability, knowledge, or skill (Fogg, Harrington, and Knoll 2014; Fogg, Harrington, and Petrovich 2013). Rather, employers take considerable care in their hiring decisions and engage in a variety of activities to find prospective workers whom they believe will contribute to output and profitability. Almost all employers that we contacted had utilized a variety of formal screening tools to hire workers for positions with essentially no education, training, or prior work experience requirements in occupations such as retail sales clerks, food service workers, cashiers, and a host of other entry-level positions that require essentially no occupational preparation at all. However, employers did work very hard to distinguish entry-level applicants on the basis of their behavioral characteristics and ethical norms.

The following were among the most important screening criteria employers used for entry-level positions:

- Educational attainment served as a readily available and powerful screening tool for employers, even when the job did not require much in the way of formal schooling. Employers preferred college students and graduates over other teens. Many considered the behavioral traits of college students and graduates to be superior to those of high school students and graduates with no college. The one exception was students and graduates of career and technical education (CTE) high schools, whom the employers found to possess superior behavioral traits such as dependability, self-control, ethics, and initiative that make entry-level workers productive.

- Employers often require third-party references, but they value references from a source that they know and trust, sometimes a current high-performing employee (Rosenbaum 2004). References from CTE instructors who often had long-term connections with local employers were highly valued. Non-CTE high school teachers rarely recommended a teen for a job, although employers said that they would trust references for prospective hires from local high schools that built relationships with their companies.

- Surprisingly, the majority of employers in our study discounted prior work experience for an entry-level position. Although some employers thought prior work experience, particularly in the fast-food industry, would be advantageous for teens seeking entry-level jobs, most employers were much more interested in directly determining the ethical and behavioral traits of job applicants.

- Formal and informal testing of job applicants was found to be a very common practice and has become a basic screening tool for most entry-level occupations. Large firms most often use Web-based tests that are embedded in the online application process.

We find that quite often smaller firms that do not opt to use online tests administer informal tests of various types, such as asking the applicant to prepare a brief biographical essay or solve some basic math problems.

- Despite some very convincing evidence that interviewing is not a good predictor of worker productivity, it remains a centerpiece of entry-level hiring—after the applicant has successfully completed the testing phase. To find a successful applicant, employers look for eye contact, a good handshake, a candidate who asks questions, has an acceptable appearance, and is available for a sufficient number of hours. All too often teens fail one of these interview standards and are quickly screened out of the hiring process.

- A large number of employers told us that the simple act of stopping by a business to pick up an application frequently sends a strong signal to employers about the suitability of the potential applicant for employment at the firm. Signals such as sloppy dress, bringing several friends along, or cell phone and text usage while interacting with an employer often exclude the job seeker from consideration for a position—before the teen has even submitted an application.

- Employers of entry-level workers view the reading and math skills of teens as comparable to those of adults and view their technology skills as better than those of adult entry-level workers. However, employers found behavioral attributes of teens, such as attendance, punctuality, and the chance of quitting the job quickly after being hired, to be inferior compared to adults, college students, and young college graduates.

- Many employers indicated that they were interested in working with comprehensive high schools and local job training organizations but that they found high schools and job training organizations to be largely disconnected from the labor market. Referrals based, in part, on daily attendance performance of students as well as other screening criteria would likely exert an important influence on a firm's decision to hire, especially if the school or jobs program were able to establish a record of good quality referrals to local employers. One key concern about working with local schools and jobs programs related to the lack of long-term relationships between employers and local schools and programs, especially in youth summer jobs programs.

RESPONSE TO THE CHANGING ENTRY-LEVEL LABOR MARKET

These findings about employer screening for entry-level jobs and the signals that teens send during the hiring process have led to the following efforts to retool, refocus, and reorient teen and young adult employment strategies and program models.

Retool Subsidized Programs as Springboards into Employer-Paid Positions

Massachusetts is one of the few states in the nation that has made a long-term commitment of public funds to support teen employment. Through the YouthWorks program, the Commonwealth has committed $53 million over six years to put nearly 32,000 young people to work in summer and year-round subsidized jobs. The Signaling Success research led Commonwealth Corporation to rethink the state's YouthWorks effort to better address what employers consider to be the primary limitations of teens seeking entry-level jobs.

Youth programs for too long have been focused on short-term subsidized summer jobs designed to keep teens busy and put some income into their pockets. As a result, summer jobs and related programs have become pretty distant from the realities of the job market. For example, teen participants often do not engage in a summer job search but are assigned to subsidized slots. Indeed, employers are frequently not involved in the summer jobs hiring decision, and the contribution of these youth employed through the summer jobs programs to the success of their organization remains a mystery to them.

Based on the Signaling Success findings, the Massachusetts workforce system is retooling its YouthWorks programs to include a mix of experiences and training with a clear focus on subsidized work experience leading to unsubsidized employment. By the end of a subsidized work placement, young people will come away with job readiness skills, an adult who can serve as a reference and vouch for the teen's work behaviors, a clear statement about what they learned in their work experience, and how their talents and experience would apply to a new unsubsidized job opportunity. Critical work behaviors such as dependability, initiative, communication, and collaboration will be taught through standardized work readiness training and reinforced through supervision and reflection in the development of their portfolio. Formal assessments will be used to determine the effectiveness of work readiness training.

Piloting YouthWorks Plus

Commonwealth Corporation is piloting a work readiness curriculum that combines 120 hours of work readiness training and intensive coaching for staff and students, with progressive subsidized work experiences over an 18-month period, leading to unsubsidized employment. The pilot, known as YouthWorks Plus, is being tested in an alternative competency-based high school and a community-based General Educational Development program. Piloting with three comprehensive high schools began in the fall of 2014. The curriculum development and coaching are supported by philanthropic funds that leverage state YouthWorks resources to support subsidized employment.

Every YouthWorks Plus student participates in work readiness training, and a smaller number participate in subsidized employment, but only if they "earn" this opportunity by high levels of participation and demonstration of good work readiness behaviors in the classroom. The work readiness curriculum focuses on dependability, initiative, communication, and collaboration skills.

Commonwealth Corporation plans to bring this model to scale through partnerships with comprehensive high schools and nonprofit organizations serving disadvantaged teens. In the current pilots, the curriculum is taught by a teacher during the school day as an elective or during an advisory period. Behaviors such as attendance and punctuality are reinforced during the training and are used as an incentive to attain a subsidized job. Commonwealth Corporation supports the teacher through an initial training and ongoing coaching. High schools indicate an interest in delivering the curriculum in the freshman year to develop and reinforce the behaviors that will not only prepare the teen for work but also prepare the teen to succeed in his or her educational pursuits. The pilots to date have been through classroom instruction. We are exploring technology add-ons to reinforce behaviors in job seeking and job retention.

Employer Engagement Activity

Given the fast-paced changes in the labor market, we recognize the need to continue to engage with businesses to provide guidance on the design of workforce development programs for teens and young adults. Engagement with employers will also provide ongoing intelligence about changes in their staffing structure, skills requirements, and hiring process in order to ensure that the workforce development strategies and programs adapt with the labor market. Commonwealth Corporation is organizing a formal employer advisory committee on teen and young adult employment to seek advice and keep abreast of developments in entry-level hiring practices and skill requirements in key industries. The advisory committee represents sectors that hire teens and young adults, including retail trade, hospitality and food services, manufacturing, and health care.

As part of the employer outreach, Commonwealth Corporation is seeking opportunities to work with individual employers to serve as a lab to experiment with practices that can bolster teen hiring in an environment of a formalized entry-level hiring process. For example, we are currently working with a national retailing chain to provide entry-level internships for teens and young adults. Part of the internship experience requires participants to complete the company's formal online screening tool called a "virtual job try-out," which is the methodology that this employer uses to tailor the online screening to one of a number of specific entry-level jobs, each of which may require different personality and behavioral traits. The online screening takes 90 minutes to complete and focuses on the consistency of answers. The screening ranks the applicant into three tiers, with the top tier receiving an interview. Participants are also encouraged to gain current employee references that will provide extra points in the online scoring process when the intern applies for a permanent job at any of the retailer's locations across the nation. The goal of this pilot is to position teens to succeed within this very formalized hiring process by familiarizing them with a sophisticated entry-level screening process and by building workplace relationships that can aid them in gaining an unsubsidized job.

Teen Staffing Agencies

A recurrent theme in the employer feedback was the need for help with short-term projects throughout the year. Placement in temporary projects through teen staffing agencies could improve a teen's likelihood of entering the labor market by providing him or her with on-the-job training, work readiness skills, a professional network, and, most importantly, a series of paid work experiences.

Teen staffing agencies also provide workforce development organizations with a real-world employer engagement strategy—one that can help match the demand of local businesses with the supply of youth prepared for a range of seasonal, part-time, temporary, and full-time entry-level positions. Additionally, the staffing agency model would enhance youth employment service providers' ability to offer relevant business services to the participating local employers. These business services could include prescreening and training of youth and young adults in specified entry-level jobs; they could also include short-term subsidized job "tryouts" or sampling to promote successful job placements. This concept is one that Commonwealth Corporation is studying and assessing for future implementation as part of the YouthWorks or YouthWorks Plus programs.

CONCLUDING THOUGHTS

Developing productive programs to improve the employment and earnings prospects of teens and young adults must go well beyond a summer jobs effort. We utilized several key pieces of labor market information to gain better insight about the magnitude and nature of teen joblessness and to rally support for the teen employment efforts. We used the public use microdata files from the Current Population Survey and the American Community Survey to understand where teens worked and the crowding out that was occurring in teen labor markets over the last decade. The occupational proficiency requirement data from the O*NET data system were crucial in aiding our efforts to understand the relative ability, knowledge, skill, and behavioral requirements of entry-level occupations. These findings were invaluable in framing our discussions with both employers and working-age teens.

Using the insights we developed from the LMI databases to organize our discussion with employers and test the findings of those discussions against objective job market data was immensely helpful. Gathering labor market intelligence from employers helped us better interpret our empirical findings and develop curricular strategies rooted in an understanding of the hiring actions of employers. Despite the rise of the Internet and new technologies to engage in job market matching, the labor market very much remains a social institution. Using both labor market information and labor market intelligence, we gained some key insights into how a segment of that institution makes hiring decisions and helped us develop a program based on that understanding.

References

Fogg, Neeta, Paul Harrington, and Laura Knoll. 2014. *Estimating the Size of the Low Skill Labor Market in Greater Philadelphia.* Philadelphia: Job Opportunities Investment Network.

Fogg, Neeta, Paul Harrington, and Anja Petrovich. 2013. *Building Blocks of Labor Market Success: Evidence from O*NET Job Analysis Surveys.* Boston, MA: Commonwealth Corporation.

Harrington, Paul, and Nancy Snyder. 2013. *Signaling Success: Boosting Teen Employment Prospects.* Boston: Commonwealth Corporation.

Mortimer, Jeylan T. 2003. *Working and Growing Up in America.* Cambridge, MA: Harvard University Press.

Rosenbaum, James. 2004. *Beyond College for All: Career Paths for the Forgotten Half.* New York: Russell Sage.

Steinberg, Sarah Ayres. 2013. "The High Cost of Youth Unemployment." Washington, DC: Center for American Progress.

Sum, Andrew, Ishwar Khatiwada, Walter McHugh, and Sheila Palma. 2013. *The Dismal State of the Nation's Teen Summer Job Market, 2008–2012 and the Employment Outlook for the Summer of 2013.* Boston: Center for Labor Market Studies, Northeastern University.

25

Basic Food Employment and Training

How Washington State Brought to Scale
Skills Training for Its Food Stamp Population

David Kaz
Seattle Jobs Initiative

Washington's Basic Food Employment and Training (BFET) program, the state's federal Supplemental Nutrition Assistance Program Employment and Training (SNAP E&T), is a remarkable success story. In a time of diminished public resources for workforce development programs—particularly those targeting low-income/low-skilled individuals with multiple barriers to employment—BFET demonstrates how, with careful planning and a spirit of innovation and collaboration, SNAP E&T can be a vehicle for states to scale effective workforce programs for the sizable, underserved, and largely unskilled SNAP (Food Stamp) population.[1] BFET has provided training leading to economic advancement for thousands of participants, while driving closer collaboration between community colleges and community-based organizations to serve participants more effectively.

SNAP E&T, administered by the Food and Nutrition Service (FNS) of the U.S. Department of Agriculture, is intended to support states in their efforts to help their SNAP populations become economically self-sufficient through a variety of employment and training services. All states must operate SNAP E&T programs but are afforded significant flexibility in their design and scope.[2] SNAP E&T is composed of five distinct funding streams. Two are fully funded by the federal government (100 percent funds), and three are 50-50 matching funds, meaning that the federal government will reimburse states for 50 percent of their expenditures for SNAP E&T activities covered by these funds. As of this writing, 100 percent funds are capped at $90 million disbursed among states on a formulaic basis, while 50-50 funds are theoretically uncapped.[3] Any work-ready SNAP participant not receiving Temporary Assistance for Needy Families (TANF) is eligible for SNAP E&T. States have the discretion to determine who may be served in their SNAP E&T programs, including whether participation is mandatory or voluntary.

To date, most states have made scant use of the SNAP E&T program, operating programs limited in both scope and resources. This was true in Washington State until 2005, when a small group of state government, community college, and community-based organization (CBO) leaders came together in Seattle to imagine how to utilize the SNAP E&T program to better meet the needs of low-income/low-skilled residents for skills leading to better-paying jobs. Little did the group know that the SNAP E&T model they were developing—BFET—was something that had never before been attempted. Nor did they foresee that in just eight years from its October 2005 launch, BFET would grow from a $150,000 program to a more than $29 million program; from serving the Seattle area exclusively to serving the entire state; and from serving just a few hundred individuals each year to nearly 30,000.

A NEW MODEL OF SNAP E&T: THE THIRD-PARTY MATCH

Washington's BFET program is a unique example of a SNAP E&T "third-party" match model. This simply means that rather than the state expending its own funds to serve as match for federal SNAP E&T 50-50 funds, the match is being provided by third parties: community colleges and CBOs. The state contracts these agencies to provide SNAP E&T services using their own nonfederal funding sources as match. The state utilizes its 100 percent and 50 percent reimbursement SNAP E&T funds to pay for partner services (with 100 percent funding also paying for the state's administrative costs). In this way, the state is able to tap into the expertise of colleges and CBOs in providing employment, training, and support services, vastly expand services available to SNAP participants, and limit/leverage its own investment. BFET is a decentralized model in which contractors not only provide E&T services but are also primarily responsible for recruitment, assessment, referral, and tracking of participants. The state remains responsible for setting the overall strategy and procedures for the program, developing the annual SNAP

E&T plan, securing reimbursement from and reporting to FNS, working with contractors to "eligibilize" individuals for BFET services, and managing the fiscal and other key administrative aspects of the program (e.g., outreach, contracting, monitoring, processing invoices for reimbursement, and collecting data).

The administrative burden on third-party partners to participate in BFET is not minimal. Not only must a provider offer appropriate services for BFET clients; it must also have the capacity to assess participants, verify their eligibility for BFET, and track their progress. Moreover, because BFET is a reimbursement program, agencies must have ample eligible (nonfederal) sources of matching funds, as well as the liquidity to front the funds for services pending reimbursement (often a protracted process). Agencies also must be able to track costs spent on BFET clients, which can require sophisticated cost allocation systems to distinguish eligible costs spent on BFET clients versus non-BFET clients.

BFET: FROM IDEA TO PILOT TO STATEWIDE PROGRAM

The potential for an expanded SNAP E&T program, specifically one utilizing a third-party match model, first came to the attention of the state's Department of Social and Health Services (DSHS, the agency charged with administering SNAP and SNAP E&T) in 2004 from the Seattle area's White Center Community Development Association and its primary funder, the Annie E. Casey Foundation. A Planning Group, led by DSHS Region 4 (Seattle/King County), was formed to explore SNAP E&T's potential. Washington was already operating a small SNAP E&T program with an annual budget of just $150,000 focused exclusively on serving mandatory Basic Food populations. This program was funded with 100 percent SNAP E&T funds and met the minimum federal requirements of providing workfare, contracted job services, and very limited support services. The structure of SNAP and SNAP E&T in Washington prior to BFET, as in most states, did little to provide participants with a real opportunity to gain the skills they needed to become self-sufficient.

In October 2005, after nearly a year of planning and building political support, the BFET pilot was launched. It focused on serving Seattle's White Center residents and included one college and four CBO contractors. DSHS initially staffed the pilot without any new dedicated funding, which was necessary for the pilot to win approval. The early success of BFET, coupled with outreach efforts by DSHS, spurred ongoing interest among other colleges and CBOs in joining the program. DSHS ensured that BFET grew at a measured clip to avoid outpacing available staffing to manage the program and to provide FNS sound justification for expansion each year within the state's SNAP E&T plan. Still, BFET was brought rapidly to scale in terms of number of contractors, budget, and individuals served by the program (see Figure 25.1). Today, all 34 of Washington's community and technical colleges, as well as more than 31 CBOs, are BFET providers.

KEY PRINCIPLES OF BFET

The DSHS-led Planning Group set out key principles and facets of the new BFET program, which has guided its success both as a small pilot and as a statewide program today. These principles include the following:

- BFET's goal is to move underserved, low-income populations to economic self-sufficiency and eventually off public benefits; it does this by helping individuals attain the job skills and postsecondary credentials to compete in local labor markets for living-wage jobs.

- The program seeks to provide a more robust and effective set of services for the target population than offered by traditional workforce (and related) funding streams. It seeks to complement and integrate into the state's workforce system, such as by providing employment and training options for individuals leaving TANF (as well serving as a diversion from TANF) and for those with multiple barriers who aren't well served by the Workforce Investment Act.

- It recognizes the value of coupling services provided by community colleges with those provided by CBOs (e.g., wrap-around

Figure 25.1 The Growth of the Basic Food Employment and Training Program, 2006–2014

Individuals served			2,990	5,251	5,603	7,175	9,105	26,108	28,000
CBOs	4	7	7	7	6	8	13	28	29
Community colleges	1	7	7	10	11	13	14	34	34

Total budget ($ millions)	1.41	2.87	6.23	11.2	18.1	14.2	17.1	29.9	29.6
	2006	2007	2008	2009	2010	2011	2012	2013	2014

SOURCE: Washington State Department of Social and Health Services, 2014.

supports, career/college navigation, and coaching) to offer participants the best chance of completing education and training programs and transitioning successfully to employment.

- It is structured as a true collaboration between the state (DSHS) and contractors; from the outset, DSHS has viewed contractors as equal partners in developing and continuously improving the program to meet shared goals for participants.

- It incorporates a "no wrong door" (honest broker) approach of cross referral to ensure participants are assessed and matched to the most appropriate services.

- It commits to demonstrating impact, with outcome measures and data collection incorporated into DSHS's contracts for BFET services.

- Over time, BFET has become an all-voluntary program. This model reduces the administrative burden on the state and contractors relating to enforcement and ensures more effective programs by serving individuals most prepared and motivated to improve their job skills.

BFET PROGRAM SERVICES

Eligible BFET services provided by community colleges and CBOs include a wide array of employment and training services as well as supports. Employment and training services offered are categorized by DSHS into various components, with participants assigned to one or more of the following components (DSHS 2013):

Job search. Job search workshops, computer basics workshops, labor market information, job-seeking skills instruction, resume writing, job skills assessment, counseling, life skills and work ethic training, and job placement services.

Job training. Includes training (outside vocational education) that enhances a person's employability by providing specific marketable job skills. This may include hands-on training and employment and training-related case management.

Basic education. Includes basic math, literacy, General Educational Development preparation, and/or vocational English as a Second Language instruction from either a community college or CBO.

Vocational education. Includes vocational education (typically provided by colleges) to enhance employability or as part of a job placement program requiring industry-specific training.

Job retention services. Services provided for up to 90 days post-employment to individuals who participated in a job search or job training component. Services must help participants achieve satisfactory job performance, keep employment, and/or increase earnings.

In addition to the employment and training services described, BFET participants are also eligible for support services that are reasonable and necessary for helping participants succeed in completing employment and training components. The primary support services provided through BFET include child care (through the state's Working Connections program or otherwise arranged by providers); transportation and clothing needed to participate in a BFET component (both are subject to cost limits); housing directly related to helping BFET participants prepare for self-sufficiency through training or other approved activity; work/training permits and fees; work/training tools, supplies, and books; and tuition/fees.

PROGRAM OUTCOMES

BFET collects a robust set of outcomes data on participants in order to facilitate continuous improvement as well as to provide evidence of impact. DSHS included Washington's Employment Security Department as well as the state's community college system to institute a cross-match process for both the Unemployment Insurance wage files and student achievement milestone reporting at the colleges. The availability of data to demonstrate the effectiveness of BFET has been vital in efforts to sustain and grow the program and preserve SNAP E&T funding at the federal level.

In August 2013, an independent report was published on the outcomes of the BFET program, which at that time had served 57,000 participants (Watrus 2013). The analysis focused on longer-term employment and wage outcomes of BFET participants, in particular, a cohort of 21,400 participants, served from 2007 to 2011, for which robust data were available. This cohort had a one-year entered employment rate of 58 percent (median wage range $10.15 to $10.66/hour overall and $10.50 to $11.44 for those receiving vocational education). The two-year entered employment rate was 69 percent (median wage range $10.42 to $11.08/hour).

The report noted that employment and wage rates of BFET participants were negatively affected by the Great Recession, while also finding that BFET participants were much more apt—34 percent more likely in 2009 and 42 percent in 2010—to have remained employed during the recession than a similar demographic of individuals on Basic Food but not enrolled in BFET (Watrus 2013). Finally, the report found that many BFET participants had begun hitting student achievement milestones (college credit and credential attainment) at the community colleges, and that more than 950 BFET participants had obtained postsecondary certificates and degrees or completed apprenticeship training in the 2011–2012 academic year alone. Moving forward, a quasi-experimental evaluation of the effect of BFET services on participants would be beneficial for program improvement and sustainability.

Notes

1. According to recent data, about 47 million people in the United States are enrolled in SNAP (http://www.fns.usda.gov/pd/34SNAPmonthly.htm, accessed April 21, 2014). In federal fiscal year 2010, about 80 percent of SNAP households did not include anyone with education beyond high school, while approximately one-third of these households did not include a high school graduate (National Skills Coalition 2012).
2. For a comprehensive overview of the SNAP E&T program, see U.S. Department of Agriculture, Food and Nutrition Service (2011).
3. Though 50-50 funding is uncapped, it is subject to overall federal budgetary restrictions.

References

National Skills Coalition. 2012. *Training Policy in Brief: SNAP Employment and Training Program.* Washington, DC: National Skills Coalition.

U.S. Department of Agriculture, Food and Nutrition Service. 2011. "Supplemental Nutrition Assistance Program, Employment and Training Toolkit." Washington, DC: U.S. Department of Agriculture, Food and Nutrition Service. http://www.fns.usda.gov/employment-and-training-et-resources-states (accessed October 21, 2014).

Washington State Department of Social and Health Services (DSHS). 2013. *Basic Food Employment and Training (BFET) Program Partner Manual/ Contractor Handbook.* Olympia, WA: DSHS.

Watrus, Bob. 2013. *The State of Washington's Basic Food Employment and Training (BFET) Program and Its Results: 2013 Update.* Report for the Annie E. Casey Foundation. Seattle, WA: White Center Community Development Association.

26
Social Enterprise

An Innovative Strategy to Create Real Jobs for People with Disabilities

Elaine E. Katz
Kessler Foundation

With the increasing prevalence of social enterprise (SE) businesses established by nonprofit organizations, it is clear that this promising trend is advancing employment opportunities for individuals with disabilities (Katz 2014a; Katz and Kauder 2011; National Social Enterprise Field Study 2008). These ventures are defined as being socially minded businesses run by nonprofit organizations, which generate new revenue, provide jobs, and benefit local communities. Social enterprises can be a viable alternative to traditional job generation, especially for underserved populations such as people with disabilities.

Kessler Foundation's "Transition to Work" grants program has invested $30 million over the past eight years toward the goal of creating jobs for people with disabilities, including support for several SE businesses in New Jersey and nationally. Social enterprises are particularly promising in creating new opportunities for individuals with disabilities in emerging industries. These businesses are easily customized to meet a diversity of skill levels for participant employees, and the right stakeholders, planning, and business leadership can provide a new source of jobs and revenue.

SOCIAL ENTERPRISE AS A MODEL EMPLOYER

While there is no common or legal definition of an SE business (Katz and Kauder 2011; Social Enterprise Canada 2010), most agree that an SE business is socially minded and revenue generating. Sometimes this is referred to as the *double bottom line*, that is, providing both financial and social returns (REDF 1999, formerly Roberts Enterprise Development Fund), or *triple bottom line* (Lamb 2010), when a green component is added. Commonly, a nonprofit organization initiates or launches the SE and may be referred to as the parent organization. Typically, it is responsible for SE operations and capacity (Alter 2000).

However, the main difference between an SE and other earned-income activities is that the main goal of the SE is to achieve sustainability by being planned and operated as a business by individuals with industry expertise (Katz and Kauder 2011; MaRS Discovery District 2014). It sometimes can be thought of as the "missing middle" straddling the intersection of business, government, and nonprofit entities to address social concerns (Social Enterprise Alliance 2014).

Social values and innovation coexist with a bottom line focus. Furthermore, the SE business has distinct resources devoted to its operations and is governed by a nonprofit board of directors. Any excess revenue or profits are reinvested in the organization's work, reducing the need for external donor dollars to cover program costs or as a means to cross-subsidize other social programs (Alter 2000).

Increasingly, SE businesses are established to improve employment opportunities for groups that are underrepresented in the labor market, such as low-income women, ex-offenders, or people with disabilities, as direct employers of the target populations they aim to serve (Katz 2014a; REDF 1999). The possibility of job creation and income for the parent organization are motivating factors that cannot be ignored. Starting and operating a business is not an easy endeavor, especially for a nonprofit organization. Startups require a substantial investment of time, resources, and expertise. These endeavors frequently require organizations that traditionally have embraced values of social good to shift their focus to marketing, return-on-investment, revenue generation, and other business principles. Because of its mission, Kessler Foundation has chosen to support nonprofit organizations that are well positioned to adopt this strategy for people with disabilities. The two case studies below illustrate how inclusive SE ventures create jobs at living wages and provide opportunities for advancement.

Hudson Community Enterprises, Jersey City, New Jersey

Enterprise Content Management

Hudson Community Enterprises (HCE) began in 1957 as a community rehabilitation program, which throughout the years offered traditional job placement services, along with job preparation, training, and job coaching for individuals with disabilities.

Changing demographics, reduced government funding, and a decrease in local job openings led HCE in 2004 to explore the option of SE businesses and to develop a new operating model that would create employment opportunities for its target populations. Enterprise Content Management (ECM), a company with a suite of document management suite services, was the outcome. ECM met all the right criteria for an SE business opportunity, that is, marketplace potential and employment for people with disabilities in large numbers. Subsequently, Metro Shredding, a mobile shredding business, was launched in 2004.

Metro Scanning, a document imaging and digital archiving business, was launched in 2005, with $100,000 in seed funding from Kessler Foundation. Job applicants completed a nine-week document imaging specialist-training course before employment. HCE rapidly acquired new contracts, which soon necessitated being a full-service shop for its customers. Subsequently, Metro Digital Mail Management, a service bureau using high-speed scanners to open envelopes, capture images, and classify and distribute data via a secure Internet portal, was created in 2008 with $387,700 in start-up funding from Kessler Foundation, supplemented by loans and other private and public monies. In 2012, HCE further expanded its business line using a $250,000 grant and a $250,000 no-interest loan from Kessler Foundation to build a microfiche laboratory to fulfill government contracts (Katz 2014a).

As HCE expanded employment opportunities, success stories became more commonplace. Hired in 2011, Phillip was initially referred by the New Jersey Commission for the Blind and Visually Impaired because of the inability to maintain employment due to depression, substance abuse, and vision loss. Phillip's potential as a self-starter and talented employee soon became clear, and within one year, he was leading a key scanning project at the Jersey City Surrogates Office. He became the go-to person for this project, overseeing production and tracking employee hours with minimal supervision. Gradually, Phillip became a valued employee, setting a strong example for others, and was promoted to his current position as team leader, which entails assisting other workers and overseeing general production.

Today, HCE operates a continually expanding family of SE businesses that saves clients money and contributes to a sustainable environment. By the end of 2013, ECM employed 139 people, approximately 85 percent with disabilities, scanned more than 12 million images per year, and processed more than 23,000 containers of records. Entry-level pay is $8.50–$10.50 per hour, with employees eligible for productivity incentives that can increase earnings up to $14.00 per hour. All employees—full and part time, with and without disabilities—receive a full fringe benefit package. Business revenue was almost $3.4 million in 2013 and accounts for close to 32 percent of overall agency income. Net revenue is projected to be $369,000, meaning that the enterprise is financially self-sustaining.

Success for HCE has meant careful planning and attention to the bottom line by staff experienced in business, specifically, the content enterprise field. Operating a green business in a growth sector was the result of market research, business planning, and a blending of a social mission focus with revenue generation. Regular assessment and opportunities for advancement or movement to outside employment are available to all employees.

The Center for Head Injury Services, St. Louis, Missouri

Destination Desserts

Since 2006, the Center for Head Injury Services (CHIS) has been providing vocational placement for persons with brain injury and other neurological impairments in the greater St. Louis region. Job development and placement has become increasingly more difficult for vocational staff over the past few years, owing to the poor economy. Social enterprise ventures were explored as a way to provide training opportunities and new jobs. Since many of CHIS's clients had previous job success in the hospitality industry, food service was targeted as an area to explore. The key was to identify an SE business that relied on assembly-style steps and a diversity of job skills to accommodate different skill levels. With a $50,000 planning grant from the Kessler Foundation in

2012, CHIS explored a business concept centered on a door-to-door cookie bakery service, which delivered sweets to college students as a nightly snack option, similar to a pizza delivery business. Through market research, CHIS identified potential difficulties with product delivery and thus eliminated the idea. In addition, the costs of renting space and outfitting a commercial bakery/kitchen were considered too high. Although the bakery concept was scrapped, the diversity of job skills needed, such as mixing, baking, ordering, shipping, and cashiering, could accommodate individuals with memory or learning impairments and facilitate learning new tasks and strategies at all levels of ability.

With the help of a small-business consultant who pointed out the importance of an expanded customer base and target markets, Destination Desserts, a new, staged business concept was developed. Desserts and beverages would be sold from a food truck at events and office parks throughout the St. Louis metropolitan area. Telephone and Internet sales would supplement truck sales. The mobile unit would itself serve as a key marketing tool, taking product to customers while operating as an additional training and employment site. CHIS secured a local grant to build a commercial kitchen at its offices and hired an experienced bakery manager to begin recipe development. CHIS began selling cookies, cupcakes, and brownies to local corporations and the community, while simultaneously finalizing recipes, developing training protocols, and testing sales. During a four-month test phase, CHIS sold 6,000 cookies and cupcakes and grossed approximately $30,000 in revenue.

Based on successful pilot data, Kessler Foundation awarded CHIS a $500,000 grant in 2012 to fully launch Destination Desserts. In April 2013, CHIS purchased a 14-foot box truck, which a local conversion company renovated to CHIS's specifications, featuring a customized pink exterior wrap with bold graphics. Truck renovations and equipment cost approximately $90,000. In May 2013, the truck officially hit the streets, selling fruit smoothies, coffee, lattes, cupcakes, breakfast pastries, cookies, and brownies.

All program participants train in food handling and safety, basic recipe production, and product finishing. Individuals have the opportunity to work hands-on in each of the workstations including measuring, mixing, baking, glazing, decorating, packaging, and cleanup and sanitation, or they can work directly with the public as trainees on the food truck. Soft-skills training, such as getting to work on time, following directions, and problem solving are also taught (Katz 2014b).

Although Destination Desserts is still in its start-up phase, total gross revenue record for 2013 was $187,687. Net revenue for calendar year 2013 was $110,314, which reflects $85,360 in sales, approximately 81 percent, from its food truck. Of the 17 individuals currently employed, 70.6 percent are persons with disabilities. Entry-level pay is $7.35 per hour. Staffing is expected to increase by four people later this year, with the introduction of a new food line of cookies with edible logos.

With almost 900 followers on social networks such as Facebook, Twitter, Instagram, and Yelp, the Destination Desserts team desperately needed support in managing its social media. Posting on these sites is critical to attract customers—it is the most common way food trucks publicize their locations around town. Daily posts highlight specials, answer questions, and list truck stops. Postings must occur frequently throughout the day and evening in order to be effective with followers.

Kara, a responsible 22-year-old, came to the attention of Destination Desserts. Though physical disabilities limited her job choices, she was a perfect fit for the position of social media associate for Destination Desserts. She trained with social media professionals and, using her newly acquired skills to market this SE business through various media outlets, helped launch the company's social media presence and branding.

CONCLUSION

Social enterprise businesses can be a viable strategy for nonprofit, community-based organizations to increase employment for individuals with disabilities. Although Kessler Foundation, the Roberts Enterprise Development Fund, and other organizations have invested in such businesses with promising results, it is important to understand the inherent risks taken by the parent organization looking to undertake these types of ventures. Business planning for social enterprises commonly projects break-even at one to two years after start-up, similar to a for-profit business. Excess revenue over expenses (profit) may take longer to develop before a business may be considered self-sustaining.

Therefore, trustees and senior management must commit to long-term support of a social venture to successfully capture a market opportunity.

Often, finding sufficient capital to launch a social venture can be problematic for a nonprofit organization. In the United States, start-ups such as those described in this case study have integrated public and private funding as seed capital. Funds may come from individual or corporate donors, foundations such as REDF and Kessler, or organizations may be eligible for public monies, such as community revitalization or development funds.

Social return on investment is also a benchmark of success. Greenwald and Associates (2012) conducted a study on behalf of Hudson Community Enterprises, which showed that New Jersey gains $4,745 through reduced entitlements and taxes paid for each person with a disability who is employed in one of HCE's businesses. Furthermore, a job paying $11,000 a year in salary produces an annual economic benefit of $6,750, including $1,650 in combined income and sales tax, and $5,100 in reduced assistance.

Destination Desserts is still too new a venture for CHIS to evaluate its return on investment. The organization is on target for break-even status at the end of this fiscal year and is currently moving to larger office space to accommodate the growth of its social enterprise. A second business, baking and selling organic dog biscuits, is about to be launched.

Both organizations in these case studies have seen individuals gain real work experience and valuable skills by working in social enterprise businesses. Some individuals have left to accept private sector employment with a work history and references.

Social enterprise businesses that have sufficient capitalization, business expertise, and a commitment to sound business practices can be an alternate model for providing meaningful jobs with living wages for individuals with disabilities. Additional revenue over expenses produced by the venture spun can further reduce the need for other public or private funding for the parent organization.

References

Alter, Sutia Kim. 2000. "Managing the Double Bottom Line: A Business Planning Reference Guide for Social Enterprises." http://www.virtueventures.com/files/mdbl-preface.pdf (accessed April 14, 2014).

Greenwald and Associates. 2012. Private study commissioned by the State Use Programs Association. Greenwald and Associates, Washington, DC.

National Social Enterprise Field Study. 2008. Durham, NC; Washington, DC: Center for the Advancement of Social Entrepreneurship, Community Wealth Ventures, and Social Enterprise Alliance.

Katz, Elaine E. 2014a. "Social Enterprise Businesses: A Strategy for Creating Good Jobs for People with Disabilities." *Journal of Vocational Rehabilitation* 40(2): 137–142.

———. 2014b. "Social Enterprise Businesses: A Strategy for Creating Good Jobs for People with Disabilities." *Journal of Vocational Rehabilitation* 40(2): 137–142.

Katz, Elaine E., and Ronnie. Kauder. 2011. *Social Enterprise Businesses: A Strategy for Creating Good Jobs for People with Disabilities.* New Brunswick, NJ: Disability and Work Research Report. A Joint Publication from the John J. Heldrich Center for Workforce Development and Kessler Foundation. http://kesslerfoundation.org/news/Social_Enterprises_Report.pdf (accessed April 18, 2014).

Lamb, Paul. 2010. "The Business of Hope." Huffington Post. http://www.huffingtonpost.com/paul-lamb/the-business-of-hope_b_788236.html (accessed April 18, 2014).

MaRS Discovery District. 2014. "Social Enterprise Business Models." http://www.marsdd.com/articles/social-enterprise-business-models/ (accessed April 18, 2014).

REDF. 1999. *A Double "Bottom Line": Lessons on Social-Purpose Enterprise from Venture Fund Initiative.* Los Angeles, CA: REDF.

Social Enterprise Alliance. 2014. "What's a Social Enterprise?" Minnetonka, MN: Social Enterprise Alliance. https://se-alliance.org/why#whatsasocial enterprise (accessed April 18, 2014).

Social Enterprise Canada. 2010. *The Canadian Social Enterprise Guide.* 2d ed. Vancouver, BC: Social Enterprise Canada.

27

Selling Work Sharing in Virginia

Lessons from the Campaign to Enact Short-Time Compensation, 2011–2014

David E. Balducchi
Research and Policy Consultant

Democratic laws generally tend to promote the welfare of the greatest possible number; for they emanate from the majority of the citizens, who are subject to error, but who cannot have an interest opposed to their own advantage.

—Alexis de Tocqueville (1964, p. 78)

Work sharing is a layoff aversion strategy designed to help preserve jobs during weak economic periods. Probably no program under public administration in the United States is as important to the unemployed as unemployment insurance (UI), a federal-state cooperative program of temporary income support for workers who lose their jobs through no fault of their own. Under federal UI law, compensated work sharing (also known as shared work) is called the short-time compensation (STC) program. Unemployment insurance laws in over half the states provide employers with the opportunity to use STC, a type of partial unemployment benefits for workers who experience a reduction in hours on their existing jobs. States at federal option may enact STC laws.

Rather than terminate employees during production or sales slumps, employers that participate in a state STC program reduce work hours and pay employees prorated wages; employees also receive STC to help compensate for their reduced work hours. Implementation of STC requires a change in state UI law. Because states are not required to adopt STC, support for amending the UI law must be mobilized one state at a time. Although work-hour reductions rather than layoffs might be assumed to generate widespread support, lawmaking can be one of the most arduous and intricate tasks in U.S. federalism. This case study focuses on efforts in the Commonwealth of Virginia to build support for an STC bill. The study first summarizes STC policy in the United States and then examines the legislative process both inside and outside the Virginia statehouse, highlighting seven lessons learned from the three-year campaign.

A LOOK AT SHORT-TIME COMPENSATION

The practice of work sharing to avoid layoffs is not new. Before the advent of the UI program, Presidents Hoover and Roosevelt during the Great Depression tested work sharing, urging employers to reduce employees' hours instead of terminating them. During a brief period in 1933, over 2.4 million workers kept their jobs as a result of reduced weekly work hours. Bolder temporary and permanent actions by the federal government (including establishing the UI program in 1935) were required to avert an economic collapse and prevent future depressions. It was not until the recession cum inflation period of 1973–1975 that states considered adopting STC bills as a means to utilize partial unemployment benefits to offset part of the earnings lost by reduced work hours (Nemirow 1984, pp. 35, 39).

Short-time compensation was first adopted in California in 1978 to ease expected government layoffs that ultimately did not occur from tax reductions under Proposition 13 that limited state and local spending. A temporary federal law in effect for three years between 1982 and 1985 enabled states to enact STC laws, and a permanent federal law was adopted in 1992. Since the 1980s, states have enacted STC laws at a snail's pace, generally through bipartisan lawmaking during and after each recession; nonetheless, the allure to adopt STC as a means to cushion future economic downturns quickly dissipated soon after recoveries—until the Great Recession of 2007–2009.[1] For technical and ideological reasons between 1992 and 2012, the U.S. Department of Labor (USDOL) made little effort to advocate for STC, nor during this period did Congress promote or amend the federal law.[2] As a result, no state law was adopted between 1994 and 2010 (see Table 27.1).

Table 27.1 Short-Time Compensation State Laws, 1978–2014

State	Year enacted	State	Year enacted
Arizona	1981	Missouri	1987
Arkansas	1985	*Nebraska*	2014
California	1978	*New Hampshire*	2010
Colorado[a]	2010	*New Jersey*	2012
Connecticut	1991	New York	1985
District of Columbia	2010	**North Dakota**	2006
Florida	1983	*Ohio*	2013
Illinois	2014	***Oklahoma***	2010
Iowa	1991	Oregon	1982
Kansas	1988	*Pennsylvania*	2011
Louisiana	1985	Rhode Island	1991
Maine	2011	Texas	1985
Maryland	1984	Vermont	1985
Massachusetts	1988	*Virginia*	2014
Michigan	2012	Washington	1983
Minnesota	1994	Wisconsin	2013

[a] States in italics enacted laws after the Great Recession. States in bold abolished STC laws: Illinois (1983–1988), Louisiana (1985–August 1, 2014), North Dakota (2006–2007), and Oklahoma (2010–November 1, 2014).
SOURCE: Author's compilation, February 2015.

Short-time compensation is funded by the same state employer tax that supports regular unemployment benefits, and STC is paid out of the same state accounts in the Unemployment Trust Fund (UTF). Employers are charged for STC in the same manner as regular unemployment benefits. There has been no rigorous experiment conducted to evaluate STC; policymakers have relied on administrative studies. According to the most recent national study, STC appeared to be as well funded as regular unemployment benefits and did not threaten the solvency of state accounts in the UTF (Walsh et al. 1997). A later study of the Washington program found the same result (Rix 2010, p. 10). These studies also show that UI taxes for individual employers using STC increased somewhat, but it appears that these increases can be exceeded by savings through reduced hiring and training costs and other measures. Employers are not mandated to participate. They use the program willingly, and repeat use has been high. There has been no evidence that STC has impeded the mobility of labor or that it disproportionately favors age, gender, or racial groups. Short-time compensation has been used as a temporary policy solution to mitigate job loss, but it is not suitable for all employers or circumstances. As in other states, a California study (MaCurdy, Pearce, and Kihlthau 2004, p. 5) found that manufacturing firms were more likely than other employers to use STC.

At the onset of the Great Recession, 17 states administered STC programs (see Table 27.1).[3] In those states during 2008 and 2009, employers increased STC claims activity tenfold. It is estimated that since 2008 STC has saved over half a million jobs nationally (National Employment Law Project 2014). Despite the program's improved use, STC beneficiaries constituted less than 3 percent of all regular beneficiaries (see Table 27.2). The program will likely always remain small compared to UI, but it can help relieve some disruptions for the businesses and workers who use it.

High unemployment rates during and after the Great Recession prompted reexamination of STC policy and its potential to reduce job loss on a wide scale. Numerous economists from across the political spectrum supported STC expansion. It was estimated that every dollar spent on STC resulted in a $1.69 increase in the gross national product (Zandi 2010, pp. 5, 7). Bills were introduced in Congress starting in 2009 to spur STC use. Congress and the Obama Administration acted belatedly; the Middle Class Tax Relief and Job Creation Act of 2012 revised federal STC requirements and provided $100 million for states to expand program use.[4] Each state could receive a one-time grant to implement or improve STC programs. Virginia's grant share was capped at $2,739,420, provided it enacted an STC law consistent with federal requirements and applied for the grant before December 31, 2014. As

Table 27.2 STC and UI Beneficiaries in States with Laws, 2008–2011

Year	STC beneficiaries	Regular UI beneficiaries	STC beneficiaries as a percentage of regular UI beneficiaries (%)
2008	96,388	10,059,554	0.96
2009	288,618	14,172,822	2.04
2010	314,102	10,738,550	2.92
2011	236,379	9,474,445	2.49

SOURCE: Shelton (2012, p. 5).

a condition for receipt of one-time grants, states were also prohibited from including a sunset—i.e., repeal—provision in STC law.[5] An added incentive in the federal law enabled states to be reimbursed from federal funds for the costs of state STC benefits through August 22, 2015 (USDOL 2012).

Campaigns to enact the program in some states became a probusiness and proworker undertaking that at times broke the political gridlock that stalled other UI reforms. Throughout the lawmaking debate in Virginia, its principal backer, Democrat Senator George Barker, often said STC "is not a red state or blue state issue" (Ross 2013). Senator Barker's political shorthand was correct. During the postrecession period 2010–2013, nine states and the District of Columbia enacted STC laws, and six of those states were led by Republican governors.[6] Virginia became the first state in the Old South since the 1980s to enact an STC law in 2014 (see Table 27.1). The study now examines the lessons learned during the Virginia lawmaking campaign.

Lessons Learned: 1) Respect the state's heritage and ideology

Lawmaking in Virginia. Since colonial times, Virginia has maintained a citizen legislature.[7] Legislative sessions are short (alternating 45-day and 60-day assemblies), and legislators commonly have jobs besides their legislative duties. The Virginia General Assembly is made up of two chambers, the House of Delegates and the Senate. Republicans controlled the Senate and House during the sessions of 2012 and 2013. Democrats regained narrow control of the Senate in January 2014 through special elections, but Republicans retained control of the House of Delegates. A legislator who introduces a bill in Virginia is called the bill's patron. A bill must pass with the same wording in the House of Delegates and the Senate before it can go to the governor. Under constitutional authority, the governor may send a bill back to the assembly with amendments, which must be approved by a majority vote in both houses. Veto of a bill by the governor may be overridden by two-thirds vote in both houses.

Virginia advocacy groups. Advocacy groups are indispensable to the functioning of the U.S. political system. They provide a means for individuals to share their views with lawmakers and other public officials. Citizen groups concerned with social justice and poverty in Virginia sometimes operate as a political counterbalance to other more organized segments.[8] Throughout the legislative campaign, Social Action Linking Together (SALT), Virginia Interfaith Center for Public Policy, Virginia Poverty Law Center, Commonwealth Institute for Fiscal Analysis, and Legal Aid Justice Center collaborated irregularly to push for the adoption of STC. The primary advocate was SALT. Boasting 1,200 members, SALT is an unaffiliated faith-based group concerned with social justice and economic security. SALT's credibility within the advocacy community and among legislators, promotional machinery including door-to-door marketing in the statehouse and among other groups, electronic mail alerts, and statements at public forums were crucial to the STC bill's enactment.

2) Find committed and knowledgable advocates and sponsors

Campaign origins. At a social justice conference at Catholic University in May 2011, I met John Horejsi, coordinator for SALT. I told Horejsi about STC and that the Virginia law did not authorize the program. Horejsi said STC sounded like a program SALT might support and asked to be sent material. After reviewing it, Horejsi sought and received approval from the SALT executive board to seek patrons to introduce an STC bill in the Virginia legislature.

Armed with a one-page explanation of how STC worked and a copy of an STC bill, the SALT team members, Horejsi, and I met with several Virginia Democrats—Delegate Patrick Hope and Senators Charles Colgan, Barbara Favola, and Barker—to explain STC and to ask if they would "carry the bill."[9] The advocacy campaign received a psychological lift in September when an editorial endorsing STC was published by the influential *Richmond Times-Dispatch* (2011)[10]: "It is time for Gov. Bob McDonnell and the General Assembly to modernize the commonwealth's unemployment insurance program by adding shared work as a job-saving business option. Work sharing is a way to keep more Virginians working, supporting their families, paying taxes and preserving their dignities and sense of contribution."

Delegate Hope was first to agree to patron a House bill. Senator Barker reviewed STC material and in late December met for two hours with the SALT team.[11] Barker asked about the pros and cons of the STC program, business and labor groups' support in other states, particularly New Jersey (whose legislature had sent a bill to Republican governor Chris Christie for signature), and tax implications for employers. He appeared to like what he heard and pledged to check with the business community and the Virginia Employment Commission, the agency responsible for UI program administration, among others. Before year's end Barker informed SALT that he and Republican Senator William Stanley would introduce a bipartisan Senate bill. Like Barker, Stanley was eager to alleviate joblessness in his district and throughout the commonwealth.

3) STC is harder to explain than to fund, the opposite of most workforce development programs

Explaining the program and financing. Unemployment insurance is a complicated program with wide-ranging benefit payment and tax consequences. As reporter Victoria Ross (2013) phrased it, STC is "unemployment insurance in reverse . . . (keeping employees) in their jobs instead of supporting them after they are laid off." How STC worked and the nature of its relationship with UI were sometimes harder to explain than figuring out how to pay for the mostly self-financing STC program.

Discussions at committee and floor meetings were time-constrained but, as might be expected, concerns about the program's effect on employer taxes arose routinely. Fiscal impact statements on the anticipated costs of the program were required. With each legislative session, a new forecast was prepared estimating the additional taxes STC employers would pay per employee. Forecasts in 2012 indicated that the UI tax per employee was likely to increase by an average of $1.18 over eight years (Virginia Legislative Information Service 2012), but as a result of better data by 2014, the probable estimated tax increase declined to an average of $0.19 over eight years (Virginia Legislative Information Service 2014).

The costs of STC would be borne mostly by the employers who choose to participate. When these costs were raised in debates, it was stressed that STC was a voluntary program, and individual employers would make participation decisions based on their business self-interest and circumstances. The prospect of STC potentially increasing Virginia employer UI taxes in 2014 prompted House Tea Party Republicans to instigate an eleventh-hour revision. The final bill included a provision eliminating any potential costs to non-STC employers.[12]

4) Use the same example over and over, and recognize that when STC is challenged, it is not necessarily opposition

Packaging the program. To surmount the challenge of explaining how STC would operate within UI requirements, Barker and an expanding SALT team consistently used a straightforward example, similar to this one:

An employer with five employees facing a 20 percent reduction in production normally would lay off 20 percent of his workforce—one employee. Instead, under STC the employer places all five employees on a four-day workweek and everyone keeps working. A reduction from 40 hours to 32 hours cuts production by the same 20 percent. Employees receive 80 percent of their wages and 20 percent of their weekly unemployment benefits. They also retain their health care and retirement if those benefits are currently provided by the employer. Thus, STC reduces work hours rather than employees, and combines a paycheck with unemployment benefits. Employers with STC plans can resume full production rapidly once demand increases and save on the costly hiring and training of new workers.

Other times the SALT team would refer to states that had adopted STC, particularly Washington, a state similar to Virginia in population, number of employers, and UI benefit-ratio tax structure. By happenstance in 2010, Washington had approved a hefty 2,539 STC employer plans (McDonald 2011).[13] The SALT team would often follow up with an employer testimonial endorsing the program.[14]

Early on, Senator Favola sharpened SALT's presentations by challenging the need for a law "when employers could reduce hours without legislation." The SALT team agreed but said the employees of those employers could not receive unemployment benefits under current law for their reduced hours of work. After more discussion, Favola agreed to co-patron the bill in 2012, and continued to back succeeding bills (Balducchi 2011).

Meetings of the Commission on Unemployment Compensation. While many states have UI advisory councils administered by the executive branch, a decade ago Virginia instead established a Commission on Unemployment Compensation (CUC) in the legislative branch. The purpose of the CUC is to assess and recommend action on proposed UI bills and monitor trust fund solvency; the assembly has generally concurred with CUC recommendations. Membership of the CUC in 2012–2013 consisted of eight Senate and House members, five Republicans, and three Democrats (Virginia General Assembly 2014).

The powerful CUC met three times prior to General Assembly sessions to discuss the STC bills, twice in 2012 and once in 2013. Republican Senator John Watkins, a moderate with a textbook knowledge of UI, chaired the CUC (and the Senate Commerce and Labor Committee); throughout the campaign Watkins ensured that STC received fair consideration. When told of the opportunity for federal incentives, the CUC members expressed no reaction, possibly in deference to a states-rights tradition that eschews federal involvement. However, Republican Delegate Kathy Byron, a staunch conservative, voiced reservations about STC, indicating the program sounded too good to be true; she appealed to members for additional time to study the bill. Apparently sensing a split among Republican members, Watkins deferred voting on whether to endorse STC at the August and December 2012 meetings; instead he requested that the VEC provide additional information (Balducchi 2012a). After the House referred the STC bill back to committee in 2013 because the CUC had not considered the program, Watkins took up STC a third time at the CUC meeting in December. With Tea Party Republicans absent from the meeting, Watkins probably felt he could gain approval and did so by a vote of 4-0-1; the STC bill was recommended to the General Assembly (Virginia CUC 2013).

5) Success requires groundwork, strategic adjustment, and compromise

Two-chamber strategy—2012. Throughout the campaign, the SALT team prepared STC briefing papers and responses to questions from inside and outside the statehouse. Opponents in the House tagged Delegate Hope's House bill (HB 837), a liberal program with no chance of passage; the likelihood for STC to gain any traction was in the Senate

(SB 376), where the program might draw support from Democrats and moderate Republicans.

Statehouse canvassing by the SALT team began first with members of the Senate and House Commerce and Labor committees, explaining to each what STC was and why it was needed.[15] Delegate Hope and the SALT team met with John Broadway, Commissioner of the Virginia Employment Commission, and others to seek advice and support. The administration of Republican Governor Bob McDonnell did not take a position on the bill. Virginia is a right-to-work state, and throughout the campaign, organized labor offered tacit support but did not testify on behalf of the program. Initially, the Virginia AFL-CIO expressed reservations about several provisions that were resolved without difficulty; one was an antiquated provision from the 1980s adopted in a few states that required employers to develop reemployment assistance plans for employees.

The Senate and House Commerce and Labor committees in February 2012 voted to continue the STC bills to the next session, pending a review by the CUC. The federal policy ground shifted when, on February 22, President Obama signed the Middle Class Tax Relief and Job Creation Act, which included revisions to federal STC requirements. The federal law set in motion additional consultation with the VEC as patrons drafted bill language to comply with new federal requirements.

6) "Legislative branch tilts rightward structurally, no matter who holds power; measures can be foiled even with bipartisan support" (Dionne 2014)

One-chamber first strategy—2013. Between sessions, Senator Barker conceived and, with Senator Stanley, initiated a new legislative strategy where a single bipartisan Senate bill might be approved and then sent to the House. If the bill enjoyed broad Senate support, the patrons speculated it would be docketed on the House uncontested calendar and approved along with other bipartisan measures. Delegate Hope agreed with the approach and remarked that "he would do whatever it took to get STC enacted, including not reintroducing a House bill" (Balducchi 2013b). The Senate in 2013 passed the STC bill (SB 1230) unanimously. Residue, however, from the unresolved CUC meetings led to a Republican split in the House Commerce and Labor Committee; yet the bill was approved. On the House floor, Delegate Byron asserted that the CUC had failed to take up the question of whether to endorse STC; the full House agreed to her fatal motion to refer the bill back to the House committee.

One-chamber first strategy with low visibility of liberal groups—2014. Mounting evidence of business backing of STC in New Jersey, Michigan, and Wisconsin aided receptivity by the Virginia Associated Builders and Contractors and the Chamber of Commerce, and perhaps avoided opposition by the Federation of Independent Businesses. There were three phases of business support during the legislative struggle: business did not contest STC in 2012; some business groups backed STC but did not testify in 2013; and a key business group, the Chamber of Commerce, testified in behalf of the bill in 2014.

One national policy issue, health care, crept into the legislative debate with the likely intent of derailing the bill. On various occasions legislators asked what effect the STC program would have on the Patient Protection and Affordable Care Act of 2010. Some legislators appeared worried that STC might somehow result in the conversion of full-time employees to permanent part-time, resulting in the loss of employer-provided health insurance. In each instance, proponents held that the Patient Protection and Affordable Care Act had nothing to do with the STC program, and conversion to permanent part-time status of employees was not part of federal or state STC laws. The bill's proponents emphasized that the purpose of STC is to avert layoffs. Moreover, federal UI law requires employers who participate in STC to continue health insurance (if currently provided) to employees who are part of the program (Balducchi 2013a, 2014).

In previous sessions, Senator Barker played the lead role in championing the bills. In 2014 the patrons engineered a switch in control of the bill to Senator Stanley to boost Republican support. Republican Stanley made entreaties on behalf of STC to business groups and opponents. Stanley's name appeared alone for the first time on the CUC meeting agenda held in December 2013, first on the new bipartisan bill, SB 110, introduced on January 8, and first on committee dockets. Stanley and Barker took active roles in testifying before committees. After Senate approval (36-2), Stanley conducted a radio interview telling listeners that STC allowed employers time "to get back on their feet" (Stanley 2014).

The Chamber of Commerce testified on behalf of the bill at committee meetings and took other actions (Virginia Chamber of Commerce 2014). As the presence of business interests increased, Senator Barker sought and received assurances from liberal advocacy groups, including SALT, to lower their visibility. This tactic, new to some groups, was designed to diminish the capacity of opponents to label STC as a liberal initiative. Liberal advocacy would make it easier for Tea Party Republicans to unravel the proponents' coalition of Democrats and moderate Republicans. A legislative aide plainly explained the new tactic, saying, "[P]olicy advocacy is over, it is now politics" (Balducchi 2014). The SALT team did not testify on the bill's behalf in 2014 except to provide technical advice, and it counseled other liberal advocates to do the same. State and national liberal groups muted their public advocacy.

7) Don't let the perfect be the enemy of the good

House Republicans in 2014 outnumbered Democrats as Democrat Governor Terry McAuliffe took control of state government. In the House Commerce and Labor committee, STC was contested. To safeguard the support of moderate Republicans, a hasty motion was offered to sunset the STC program in five years; by a voice vote, the motion carried. The committee then approved the bill by a vote of 15-5, with Tea Party Republicans still in opposition. The impulse to find a compromise prevailed, but with an unintended casualty, the loss of a one-time federal grant. Under the federal law, to qualify for a grant, a state's STC law could not be subject to discontinuation. It is probable that had committee Democrats insisted on a "no sunset" provision the bill would have been shelved, resulting in another dead end.

In a well-timed editorial, the *Roanoke Times* (2014) urged the House to "at least let the state give (STC) a try." Two days later on the House floor, conservative Republicans offered a substitute bill.[16] The substitute, among other things, precluded increasing taxes as a result of the STC program for non-STC employers, barred STC employees from receiving job training, required employees to search for new work even though they were employed, and retained the five-year sunset provision adding a new twist: if a federal grant for implementation and promotion was not received by July 1, 2016, the STC program would expire. Some provisions conflicted with federal STC requirements, and the sunset provision separately challenged federal authority because the USDOL was prohibited by federal law from approving a grant under such condition.[17] To avoid defeat, the Democrats acceded to the substitute, thus for the first time the House with its Tea Party wing approved an STC bill. Days before adjournment, the Senate approved the House substitute to SB 110 rather than force a conference committee. The fate of the engrossed STC bill was in uncharted territory, requiring gubernatorial action to avert a potential federal clash over the bill's language. The governor on April 8 submitted to the assembly six corrective amendments. In a reconvened session on April 23, both chambers agreed to all but one of the amendments: the House failed to strike the sunset provision. The reengrossed bill was sent forward, and the governor signed it on May 23, 2014.

CONCLUSION

No matter how worthy advocates or legislators may think the policy is, enactment of a bill often requires education and compromise (or the perception of compromise). Such was the case in Virginia, where the lawmaking process moved at lightning speed in short legislative sessions, with little time for deliberations. The merits of STC motivated legislators, and the prospect of federal incentives was rarely emphasized. Enactment in 2014 resulted from advocacy groundwork and a legislative strategy of adjustment and compromise to gain support across the political spectrum. The legislative process allowed conservatives, moderates, and liberals to talk across the political divide. The one-chamber first strategy with muting of liberal advocacy groups prevented House opposition to use a liberal club to beat the bill. Business support and adaptive leadership were crucial to the three-year lawmaking campaign. Senator Barker (2014) said that four traits were essential to achieve legislative success: "[P]atience, persistence, compromise, and creativity." These traits made the difference in bridging opposing viewpoints, and they likely would in other states as well. What's more, the lessons learned in Virginia might help states that have not enacted STC or other UI improvements better understand the mechanics of mobilizing legislative support. However, the federal law prohibiting states from enacting sunset provisions in STC laws as a condition for one-time federal grants may have curbed the ability of some non-STC states to seek legislative compromises.

The Virginia STC law requires that the Virginia Employment Commission make periodic performance reports to the General Assembly, but the fate of STC beyond July 2016 is unknown. Implementation of the program in Virginia may give some employers an extra means to withstand future economic shocks, strengthen their ability to compete for skilled workers, and help working families. If STC is still in place in Virginia during a next recession, the program should help preserve the jobs of some workers.

Notes

The author thanks Sara Rix for steadfast support and valuable edits and comments throughout the development of this study. Neil Ridley and Stephen Wandner also provided helpful observations. The views expressed in this study or errors in the text are solely the responsibility of the author.

1. The exception was the 2001 recession, when no state enacted an STC law. North Dakota enacted a one-year STC demonstration in 2006 but did not implement it.
2. For analysis of the stalemate in federal STC policy during this period, see Balducchi and Wandner (2008).
3. Louisiana had an STC law but suspended operations.
4. Specifically, Subtitle D of Title II, known as the Layoff Prevention Act.
5. Failure to conform to federal UI law could result in the state's loss of the administrative grant under the Social Security Act and employer UI tax off-set credit under the Federal Unemployment Tax Act. These uber-penalties in the federal-state UI program commonly tilt the balance of power to national authority.
6. States that enacted STC under Republican governors were Maine, Michigan, New Jersey, Ohio, Pennsylvania, and Wisconsin. Colorado, New Hampshire, and Oklahoma enacted STC under Democratic governors.
7. Data were drawn from the Virginia General Assembly Web site (http:// virginiageneralassembly.gov/). Unless otherwise noted, assembly composition and committee and floor votes may be found at this reference.
8. As Virginian James Madison foresaw, factions in a democratic republic were "sown in the nature of man," (Madison 1787) and government acts to sort out the policy differences between them.
9. Retiring Senator Mary Margaret Whipple in 2011 introduced an STC bill (SB 1474), and it received no consideration. In 2012, the House and Senate bills were based on the Whipple bill, which was modeled on language drafted by USDOL in 1983 and the Maryland STC law.

10. Written mostly by the SALT team, the editorial was attributed to the paper's staff, thereby enabling it to be cited as opinion of one of Virginia's leading newspapers.

11. Advocacy often requires adaptability to accommodate lawmakers' schedules. For example, the SALT team met with Barker and aide Carter Batey at the Corner Bakery in Arlington.

12. To avoid some cost sharing by all employers, the bill excluded participation in STC of maximum-rated employers, those with ineffectively charged rates.

13. E-mail to David Balducchi from Bill McDonald, Washington Employment Security Department, September 23.

14. For example, this testimonial used at a CUC meeting: "Vermeer (Manufacturing of Pella, Iowa) Vice President Vince Newendorp says that work sharing enables the company to keep its skilled workforce in place so that when orders start up it can take advantage of the rebound and beat the competition" (Balducchi 2012b).

15. The SALT team attempted to drum up support for STC in each session and in 2014 met with a record 11 legislators in one day (Ross 2014).

16. They likely were aided by the Virginia Manufacturers Association.

17. Barring employees from job training and requiring them to search for work while employed with the STC employer raised conformity issues with federal UI law. The sunset provision was a matter of federal compliance related solely to the one-time grant for implementation and promotion.

References

Balducchi, David E. 2011. "Notes from Meetings with Senator-Elect Barbara Favola." Photocopy, December 16.

———. 2012a. "Notes from Commission of Unemployment Compensation Meetings of August 20 and December 4." Photocopy, December 4.

———. 2012b. *Shared Work Gives Employers Options to Keep Competitive and Save Jobs.* Social Action Linking Together, Senate Bill 376. Virginia Commission on Unemployment Compensation, August 20. http://services.dlas.virginia.gov/User_db/frmView.aspx?ViewId=3108&s=11 (accessed March 27, 2014).

———. 2013a. "Memorandum to Files, Subject: SALT Advocacy and Actions at House Commerce and Labor Committee, February 12." Photocopy, February 13.

———. 2013b. "Notes from General Assembly Public Hearing, January 4." Photocopy, January 4.

———. 2014. "Notes from the Senate Commerce and Labor Committee, January 13." Photocopy, January 13.

Balducchi, David E., and Stephen A. Wandner. 2008. "Work Sharing Policy: Power Sharing and Stalemate in American Federalism." *Publius: The Journal of Federalism* 38(1): 111–136.

Barker, George. 2014. *The Barker Bulletin (One Week to Go)*, Newsletter (via e-mail), February 28.

De Tocqueville, Alexis. 1964. *Democracy in America*. New York: Washington Square Press.

Dionne, E. J. Jr. 2014. "A More Modest Agenda." *Washington Post*, January 30, A:19.

Madison, James. 1787. "The Federalist No. 10. The Utility of the Union as a Safeguard against Domestic Faction and Insurrection (continued)." *Daily Advertiser*, November 22. http://www.constitution.org/fed/federa10.htm (accessed February 27, 2014).

MaCurdy, Thomas, James Pearce, and Richard Kihlthau. 2004. "An Alternative to Layoffs: Work Sharing Unemployment Insurance." *California Policy Review* August: 1–11.

National Employment Law Project. 2014. "Virginia Becomes 28th State to Enact Work-Sharing Program to Help Employers Avoid Layoffs." Press release. New York: National Employment Law Project. http://www.nelp.org/page/-/Press%20Releases/2014/PR-Virginia-Nebraska-Work-Sharing.pdf?nocdn=1 (accessed June 18, 2014).

Nemirow, Martin. 1984. "Work-Sharing Approaches: Past and Present." *Monthly Labor Review* 107(9): 34–39. Washington, DC: U.S. Department of Labor, Bureau of Labor Statistics.

Richmond Times Dispatch. 2011. "Obama: American Jobs Act." September 10. http://www.timesdispatch.com/news/obama-american-jobs-act/article_f60a549a-d806-5423-9b52-dc7646fe5ad7.html (accessed February 24, 2014).

Rix, Sara E. 2010. "Saving Jobs through Work Sharing." *Insight on the Issues* 45: 1–21. http://assets.aarp.org/rgcenter/ppi/econ-sec/insight45_worksharing.pdf (accessed June 18, 2014).

Roanoke Times. 2014. "Our View: Work-Share Could Be a Win-Win." March 2. http://www.roanoke.com/opinion/editorials/our-view-work-share-could-be-a-win-win/article_d78210b6-a0c7-11e3-bc15-0017a43b2370.html (accessed April 12, 2014).

Ross, Victoria. 2013. "Saving Jobs in Hard Times." *Burke (Virginia) Connection*, September 5. http://www.burkeconnection.com/news/2013/sep/05/saving-jobs-hard-times/ (accessed September 5, 2013).

———. 2014. "Mr. Horejsi Goes to Richmond." *Virginia Connection Newspaper*, March 12. http://www.connectionnewspapers.com/news/2014/mar/12/mr-horejsi-goes-richmond/ (accessed March 14, 2014).

Shelton, Alison M. 2012. *Compensated Work Sharing Arrangements (Short-Time Compensation) as an Alternative to Layoffs*. Congressional Research Service Report. Washington, DC: Congressional Research Service. April 23.

http://greenbook.waysandmeans.house.gov/sites/greenbook.waysandmeans
.house.gov/files/2012/documents/R40689_gb.pdf (accessed June 24, 2014).

Stanley, William. 2014. "Senate Approves Shared Work Bill." Virginia Public Radio Interview with Tommie McNeil, January 17. http://virginiapublic radio.org/2014/01/17/senate-approves-shared-work-program/ (accessed January 20, 2014).

U.S. Department of Labor. 2012. "Short-Time Compensation Provisions in the Middle Class Tax Relief and Job Creation Act of 2012." Unemployment Insurance Program Letter No. 22.12. Washington, DC: U.S. Department of Labor, Employment and Training Administration, June 18.

Virginia Chamber of Commerce. 2014. "Bills We're Watching." Richmond, VA: Virginia Chamber of Commerce, February 17. http://www.vachamber .com/wp-content/uploads/2014/02/BWW-week-of-2-17-14.pdf (accessed March 31, 2014).

Virginia Commission on Unemployment Compensation. 2013. Meeting summary. Richmond, VA: Division of Legislative Services, December 17. http://services.dlas.virginia.gov/User_db/frmView.aspx?ViewId=3935 (accessed March 31, 2014).

Virginia General Assembly. 2014. "Interim Studies and Commissions Listings." Richmond, VA: Virginia General Assembly. http://studies.virginia generalassembly.gov/studies/157 (accessed February 6, 2014).

Virginia Legislative Information Service. 2012. "Fiscal Impact Statement SB 376." January 16. Richmond, VA: Virginia Legislative Information Service, Department of Planning and Budget. http://lis.virginia.gov/cgi-bin/ legp604.exe?ses=121&typ=bil&val=sb376 (accessed February 28, 2014).

———. 2014. "Department of Planning and Budget. 2014. Fiscal Impact Statement SB 110." January 27. Richmond, VA: Virginia Legislative Information Service, Department of Planning and Budget. http://lis.virginia .gov/cgi-bin/legp604.exe?ses=141&typ=bil&val=sb110 (accessed January 28, 2014).

Walsh, Stephen, Rebecca London, Deanna McCanne, Karen Needels, Walter Nicholson, and Stuart Kerachsky. 1997. *Evaluation of Short-Time Compensation Programs, Final Report.* Oakland, CA; Princeton, NJ: Berkeley Planning Associates and Mathematica Policy Research.

Zandi, Mark. 2010. "Using Unemployment Insurance to Help Americans Get Back to Work: Creating Opportunities and Overcoming Challenges." Testimony of Mark Zandi, Chief Economist, Moody's Analytics. U.S. Congress, Senate Finance Committee. http://www.economy.com/mark-zandi/ documents/Senate-Finance-Committee-Unemployment%20Insurance -041410.pdf.\ (accessed June 18, 2014).

28
The Plus 50 Initiative

Nancy Latham
Learning for Action

Mary Sue Vickers
American Association of Community Colleges

The Plus 50 Initiative is a project of the American Association of Community Colleges that supports the development, refinement, and replication of a workforce development program model for community college students 50 and older. When the initiative launched in 2008 by making its first grants to 15 colleges, it actually focused on two additional "tracks" beyond workforce development: volunteering and lifelong learning/enrichment. Each grantee was required to build its program on *any* two of the three tracks. But the initiative soon shifted direction, homing in specifically on workforce development as it responded to historical events (the Great Recession), and to a programming gap discovered through its research.

THE GREAT RECESSION

The recession hit older workers especially hard. When older people are laid off they tend to stay unemployed for much longer periods of time than younger workers (Bureau of Labor Statistics 2010). In addition, the financial crash devastated retirement accounts, and older workers have fewer years than younger workers to rebuild their savings. For these reasons, people 50 and older had a more urgent need for workforce development programs. Grantee colleges learned about these needs as their program participants shared with program staff stories of layoffs, of the need to unexpectedly return to the workforce, or of their desire to learn new skills to stay competitive in the job market. Responding to local needs, many colleges shifted a greater share of program resources to the workforce track (LFA Group 2012).

A PROGRAMMING GAP

In 2008, the Plus 50 Initiative commissioned a national survey of community colleges to learn about the programs and services that colleges were offering to students 50 and older (LFA Group 2009). The findings from this study highlighted what was missing from workforce development programming for plus 50 students. Almost half of the colleges reported that they did not offer workforce development programs geared to students in this age cohort. And of the colleges that did, "offering programs" usually meant that they simply marketed their standard programs to this age group; thcy did not develop programs to address the particular needs and challenges that plus 50 students face.

Community college enrollment for plus 50 students had been on a slow but steady rise through 2009 (Mullin 2012), and, given the recession's impact, at least some were likely to be coming to campus looking for career support. Judging from the survey results, however, community colleges were not prepared to meet these students' needs for workforce programming. Beginning in 2009, Plus 50 got down to the business of developing a Plus 50 workforce development program model that could help community colleges across the United States fill this gap. This case study first shares the key program components, and then describes Plus 50's unique approach to scaling the model.

THE PLUS 50 PROGRAM MODEL

The model does not have strict requirements; each college customizes their Plus 50 program to its local context. However, over the years its colleges have accumulated knowledge about what effective implementation looks like for each of the program components.

Workforce Training

At the core of every Plus 50 program is a workforce training program (or a set of programs) that the college offers. As program directors identify particular training programs for Plus 50 participants to enroll in, they leverage the work that the Workforce Development Departments have already done to develop programs that lead to credentials with "workforce value": credentials that can function as on-ramps to jobs with local employers or in growth industries. To tailor the set of workforce programs offered as part of the Plus 50 program, program directors also

- conduct a needs assessment among plus 50 students at the college to learn which training programs will align well with students' career interests and skill-building needs;
- focus on accelerated programs or short-term certificates because older students typically seek to move through the program quickly and efficiently; and
- offer professional development workshops designed to build faculty skills and knowledge about the appropriate pedagogical strategies to address the needs, interests, challenges, and learning styles of plus 50 students. Some examples of these strategies are in lectures, including real-life examples beyond those aimed at the 18–34 demographic; setting up a meet-and-greet with older students before the first class meets so that students feel comfortable with instructors; encouraging older students to share from their life experience—without referring to them condescendingly as "old-timers teaching the young-uns"; using 14-point font on handouts; putting together cross-generational working groups (without explicitly pointing to age diversity); and going out of one's way to encourage plus 50 students in casual conversations after class, because although plus 50 students are often highly motivated and excellent students, they can be nervous about returning to the classroom.

Credit for Prior Learning

Because plus 50 students often want to complete as quickly as possible, Plus 50 colleges offer a range of services that help students capture credits either for prior learning gained through work or life experience, or from earlier educational experiences. Methods of awarding credits for prior learning include standardized testing and evaluation of past work using published guides (such as the American Council on Education's guide for industrial and corporate training programs).

Math and English Refresher Courses and Supports

For students entering a program that includes math and English requirements, these subject areas often become a threat to completion. Students unprepared for college-level math and English are routed to remedial courses—and research shows that remedial education is associated with taking longer to complete and with lack of completion (for students of all ages) (Rath, Rock, and Laferriere 2013). Plus 50 programs can offer refresher courses or other supports that can help students reacquaint with topics they may not have studied for many years. Examples of tailored math or English refresher courses include short courses or workshops that help students to place out of the developmental or remedial courses, supplemental courses in math or English that are taken along with the primary workforce course, and courses designed for students to take concurrently with a developmental or remedial course to ensure they don't get stuck at the remedial level.

Computer Skills Building

Plus 50 colleges have found that many of their program participants need supports to build computer skills. They may have previously had jobs that did not require working with programs such as Excel or PowerPoint, and they need to learn these applications to advance their careers or switch fields. Colleges sometimes offer basic and intermediate computer courses tailored to plus 50 students, and also they steer plus 50 students to courses designed for those (of all ages) who have little or no familiarity with computers. They also offer computer tutoring or other individualized help. Individualized support can be especially helpful because older students can feel stigmatized by a lack of knowledge in our tech-savvy culture.

Advising

Advising is another core component of the program. "High-touch" guidance and counseling is typically a critical element of programs that support students who are at risk of noncompletion (College Board 2012). When students feel that they do not fit in, they are likely to interpret challenges as signs of "nonbelongingness" and thus lose the motivation to persevere (Yeager and Walton 2011). Since plus 50 students are a nontypical age group for college, they can often feel out of place. Personalized guidance, then, is an important part of helping these students rise to the challenges of postsecondary education. But if the advisor treats a plus 50 student just like any other student, this treatment can actually reinforce feelings of alienation and lack of belonging. It is therefore important that the advisor provide empathetic guidance, with an understanding of the challenges an older student could face, and also with knowledge of additional resources available to plus 50 students. Plus 50 programs may hire advisors to work only with plus 50 students, but they often partner with the advising and counseling departments to leverage the time of existing advising staff. Plus 50 programs either identify staff that have the knowledge and skills to work with their program participants or they provide professional development to counselors.

Career Services

These services support plus 50 students in finding work and advancing their careers. Services are sometimes individualized, and in this case the career counselor needs the same types of specialized skills that the Plus 50 advisor has. In addition, colleges hold group workshops tailored to plus 50 students looking to advance their careers. Workshop topics are typical (e.g., career assessment and planning, job search, resume writing, interviewing skills, and networking). However, when it has been many years since people have conducted a job search, they often need additional orientation to current job search and networking approaches (e.g., LinkedIn). Some colleges have a physical space dedicated to the career needs of plus 50 students.

THE PLUS 50 INITIATIVE'S APPROACH TO SCALING

Ever since the Plus 50 Initiative's shift to the focus on workforce development, it has worked to continually develop and refine the Plus 50 program model by learning from the experiences of its grantees. As colleges have experimented, learned by doing, and shared their learnings with one another and Plus 50 staff, the Plus 50 Initiative has created and curated an extensive knowledge base stored online. From the beginning, the vision for the Web site has been to provide the field with a knowledge base of research, tools, templates, presentations, promising practice examples, and other resources that colleges can use to implement Plus 50 programming on their own campuses.

While the site is a rich resource for colleges seeking to implement a Plus 50 program, colleges also benefit from the high-touch involvement of experienced colleges that act as "mentor colleges."[1] The mentoring approach was used for the first Plus 50 grantees, and the mentor colleges worked closely with their mentee colleges, meeting often by phone and conducting site visits. While mentee colleges found this personalized, high-engagement approach very helpful, this model places a natural limit on the rate at which Plus 50 programs can replicate across the nation, because a mentor college can work with only a few colleges at a time.

In 2012, the Plus 50 Initiative opened a new chapter in scaling the model. Supported by funding from Deerbrook Charitable Trust, the initiative set the goal of replicating the Plus 50 program at 100 new colleges.[2] To achieve this goal, Plus 50 has built an online, interactive program development platform called C-PAD (College Progress Assessment Database), which guides colleges through the five phases of program development and continuous improvement.[3] There are five phases in the Program Implementation Map (with associated tasks for each phase):

1) Readiness: Identify resources and mobilize support
   - Convene the Plus 50 team and begin planning
   - Secure internal support
   - Establish advisory committee
   - Identify internal resources
   - Identify external resources

2) Needs assessment: Data collection and diagnosis

- Prepare for needs assessment
- Conduct needs assessment
- Share results with key stakeholders

3) Program development: Design Plus 50 programming

- Prepare for program development
- Establish Plus 50 Program vision and mission
- Establish Plus 50 Program goals
- Design Plus 50 Program

4) Implementation planning: Develop detailed action plan

- Develop marketing strategy
- Develop or update action plan
- Develop the Plus 50 program budget
- Establish mechanisms for continuous improvement

5) Continuous improvement: Assess and improve program design

- Collect process and outcome data
- Gather feedback from program participants and partners
- Share results with key stakeholders
- Plan for program improvement

On C-PAD, the steps to complete each phase are articulated, and tools and resources for completing each step are provided. It does not, however, function simply as a self-guided tour through an online map; in fact, C-PAD couples its high-tech platform with a high-touch coaching model. Plus 50 central office staff assign "mentor colleges" to the new "replication colleges." The replication colleges can work with their mentors *through* the map, by submitting deliverables associated with each phase and getting feedback. C-PAD also provides a quality rubric that outlines what counts as a high-quality deliverable. Once the replication college has incorporated the mentor's feedback and completed a deliverable, the mentor signs off and the replication college continues on through the phases of program implementation. This way, an experienced Plus 50 college provides guidance, encouragement, and accountability throughout the program-building process.

The conundrum of scaling for Plus 50 has been that colleges have had great success with an intensive, high-engagement approach, but the time demands that come with high engagement limit the rate of replication. C-PAD creates scale economies, opening up the possibility of "high-touch at scale." Currently, the database allows mentor colleges to work closely with up to nine replication colleges at a time.

C-PAD—and how mentor colleges can maximize its ability to create efficiencies—is still a work in progress. Mentors have found that not all colleges are using it as much as they had hoped. However, mentor colleges have identified strategies that may boost usage of the database: Mentor colleges sending out e-mails to all their colleges at once to encourage them to use C-PAD, periodically pointing the replication colleges to the online C-PAD training, and hosting a screen-sharing session showing how to use it. Mentors agree that for the colleges that are using C-PAD, they progress very fast in getting the program up and running, and the time that it takes mentors to support replication colleges is reduced. The future will no doubt continue to bring additional improvements in facilitating the use of C-PAD, and continue to support the scaling of high-quality Plus 50 programming.

Notes

1. Colleges must apply to be mentors, and the Plus 50 Initiative director reviews applications to determine if they have sufficient experience to coach other colleges. Currently, many of the mentor colleges are colleges that were Plus 50 grantees in the past.
2. Deerbrook Charitable Trust is the third funder of the Plus 50 Initiative; the first two were the Atlantic Philanthropies and Lumina Foundation. Without the generous support of the first two funders, Plus 50 would not currently be in a position to pursue its scaling efforts.
3. Plus 50 worked with the Center for the Advancement of Social Entrepreneurship at Duke University's Fuqua School of Business to create the Program and Implementation Map.

References

Bureau of Labor Statistics. 2010. "Record Unemployment among Older Workers Does Not Keep Them Out of the Job Market." *Issues in Labor Statistics* Summary 10-04: 1–3.

College Board. 2012. *Securing the Future: Retention Models in Community Colleges.* New York: College Board Advocacy and Policy Center.

LFA Group. 2009. *Educating Plus 50 Learners: Opportunities for Commu-

nity Colleges: State of Community College Plus 50 Programs Nationwide. Washington, DC: American Association of Community Colleges.

————. 2012. *The Plus 50 Initiative Evaluation: Initiative Impact.* Washington, DC: American Association of Community Colleges.

Mullin, Christopher M. 2012. *Why Access Matters: The Community College Student Body.* Policy Brief 2012-01PBL. Washington, DC: American Association of Community Colleges.

Rath, Bob, Kathryn Rock, and Ashley Laferriere. 2013. *Pathways through College: Strategies for Improving Community College Student Success.* Hartford, CT: Our Piece of the Pie, Inc.

Yeager, David S., and Gregory M. Walton. 2011. "Social-Psychological Interventions in Education: They're Not Magic." *Review of Educational Research* 81(2): 267–301.

29

Platform to Employment

Putting Long-Term Unemployed Back to Work

Joseph Carbone
The WorkPlace

Our experience operating an American Job Center through the recent recession has taught us that long-term unemployment militates against one's chances of finding new employment. It is a barrier preventing workers from competing on an even playing field for open positions. When hiring in today's labor market, employers are in a position to select from a bounty of highly skilled, well-educated, and cost-effective applicants. Those currently employed or those with short periods of unemployment have an advantage in a competitive marketplace.

Bringing the long-term unemployed (LTU) to a platform of readiness, emotionally and professionally, is critical as the job market recovers. As society becomes more comfortable with a slowly improving economy, which demands a smaller workforce, the LTU could be forgotten. With a national unemployment rate of 6.7 percent—10.5 million out of work and 7.4 million employed part time for economic reasons (Bureau of Labor Statistics 2014)—it is clear that businesses are being more circumspect in their decisions to hire. Since 2008 we have seen unprecedented economic loss, record-high unemployment, and millions of people exhausting unemployment benefits without finding employment (U.S. Department of Labor 2014). Based on our work, life for the LTU has become increasingly difficult: they often feel disconnected from their careers, they watch their skills become less relevant, and many choose to isolate themselves, which often leads to feelings of hopelessness and despair.

Regional Workforce Investment Boards (WIBs) and the American Job Center Network are the nation's support system for unemployed workers, and until recently the system has not addressed this group or their unique needs. Conventional workforce development programs are designed to respond to traditional, short-term unemployment in a steadily growing economy.

The Great Recession degraded the value of common workforce system tools, and established incentives for business to hire new workers will not work on their own. However, financial incentive programs, accompanied by wraparound supports that address a job candidate's ability to compete, can make a difference.

THE PLATFORM TO EMPLOYMENT PROGRAM

Platform to Employment (P2E) begins with a preparatory program designed to address the social, emotional, and skill deficiencies caused by long-term employment. P2E incorporates a program of self-assessment, change management, effective communication, and current job search strategies. Multimedia tools reinforce instructor-led programs and cohort learning.

The first part of P2E is a preparatory program where participants take action to realize their personal and professional potential. They develop new strategies for solving problems and create positive change in themselves. Counseling and behavioral health services are provided to manage stress and build confidence. P2E subsidizes a work experience program and pays for the participant's first eight weeks in a new job. This provides employers a risk-free opportunity to evaluate job candidates and see if a good match exists. The average cost per participant in P2E, including the preparatory program and wage subsidy, is $6,000.

Intensive Five-Week Preparatory Program

Participants receive 100 hours of training in job readiness and skills building over five weeks. The WorkPlace partnered with a for-profit training provider, Career TEAM, to customize and incorporate their Career Edge program into P2E. Participants learn how to identify their transferable talents, build effective networking and communication skills, and develop goals and a career action plan. Career Edge training also helps rebuild confidence and sense of self-worth, which plummets during long periods of unemployment. During the preparatory program, participants also receive a behavioral health assessment and have access to counseling from behavioral health consultants. These services help participants recover from damaging psychological issues and repair relationships strained by unemployment. Consultations are made available to P2E participants and members of their households. P2E participants also receive financial counseling and guidance on rebuilding their credit so that they and their families are better equipped to face the significant financial challenges that arise during extended periods of unemployment. This training is essential at a time when many are financially overextended and have endured a reduction in regular income, or have no income at all.

Work Experience Program

P2E helps participants who have completed the preparatory program find positions with local employers that are hiring. Employers are offered the opportunity to have a P2E participant work on a trial basis for up to eight weeks prior to making a final decision on whether to hire. During this work experience, participants can be placed on the payroll of The WorkPlace, and employers can opt to have up to 100 percent of the employee's wages subsidized by the P2E program. This arrangement enables employers to test a P2E participant without risk for eight weeks and helps overcome any prejudice employers might hold.

Since P2E seeks to leverage the job seekers' existing knowledge, skills, and abilities, employment is supported in a variety of industries, with work experience wage subsidies ranging between $19,000 and $73,000 annual equivalents. Position titles for participants that found employment through P2E include accountants, benefit advisors, paralegals, drivers, shipping clerks, tech support, and marketing managers.

Private funding plays an instrumental role in P2E and provides an advantage over publicly funded programs, which require employers to make a hire on the first day. Employers receive an immediate financial benefit, and The WorkPlace assumes liability for the program participant during the work experience by taking responsibility for unemployment insurance and workers' compensation.

Funding Sources

For the initial Connecticut pilot project, more than three dozen companies, nonprofits, foundations, and individuals donated $600,000 to fund P2E. In addition, Citi Community Development provided a substantial grant to support those experiencing long-term unemployment with financial counseling and credit rebuilding assistance. Subsequently, the AARP Foundation funded two additional Connecticut cohorts to assist jobless individuals over age 50. In 2013 and 2014, with additional support from the AARP Foundation, Citi Community Development, and the Walmart Foundation, P2E is being replicated in 10 cities across the nation.

Connecticut Pilot Program Results

Our pilot program began in 2011. Between August 2011 and summer 2013, we conducted eight cohorts of approximately 20 participants in each cohort. Participants were selected from a diverse pool of candidates. Initially, letters informing job seekers of the opportunity to apply to P2E were sent from the Connecticut Department of Labor to 1,400 unemployed workers who had exhausted unemployment benefits. Through The WorkPlace Web site, we received 392 applications in response to this letter. Subsequent outreach generated another 390 online applications. After conducting interviews with candidates, 164 Connecticut residents enrolled in P2E and began the five-week preparatory program. As shown in Table 29.1, 81 percent of the graduates of the preparatory program entered an eight-week work experience. Of this population, 88 percent were hired by employers. The remaining individuals continued to work with program managers and the local American Job Center on their search for employment.

REPLICATION ACTIVITY

In 2010, The WorkPlace began having roundtable discussions with LTU workers. Participants included leaders from business, government, and nonprofit agencies. The goal was to create a force in our community

Table 29.1 Results of Connecticut P2E Pilot

Connecticut cohorts 2011–2013	Enrolled in P2E	Preparatory program graduates	Number placed in work experience	Percent placed in work experience	Number hired after work experience	Percent hired after work experience
Totals	164	150	122	81	108	88

SOURCE: The WorkPlace, Platform to Employment program.

that will expand support and services for the LTU and gain widespread recognition about their specific challenges.

Together we realized that we needed to move beyond traditional remedies for the unemployed, not just in Connecticut but nationwide. In 2012, *60 Minutes* recognized P2E as a catalyst for change for the LTU. The show exposed the magnitude of being trapped in long-term unemployment and documented P2E's efforts to put the LTU back to work.

The *60 Minutes* episode generated significant interest in the program. Subsequently, The WorkPlace hosted 195 different organizations for a webinar, where P2E was explained and the requirements for replication were outlined. Several communities asked to continue the conversation and discuss how the program could be tailored to meet their specific needs. From this group of organizations we began to lay the foundation for 10 replication sites: Chicago, Cincinnati, Dallas, Denver, Detroit, Minneapolis, Newark, San Diego, San Francisco, and Tampa.

These sites were selected for geographical diversity, high rates of long-term unemployment, and institutional capacity. The objective was to enable each location to independently offer P2E and deliver services in a manner that best meet the needs of the local community. Funding for these 10 national replication sites was made possible by grants from the AARP Foundation, Citi Community Development, and the Walmart Foundation. The approximate cost to implement P2E in each community is $120,000–$130,000.

The WorkPlace gained the support of the local WIB in each of the identified locations. These WIBs oversee the operations of the local American Job Centers in their regions. The common experience and expertise of WIBs and the American Job Center network make P2E and the principles it is based on easily transferable to other locations. American Job Centers currently support special populations such as veterans and people with disabilities. These centers are ideally suited to examine regional workforce dynamics, engage partners in crafting innovative solutions, and provide supports to the LTU. P2E can be a vehicle to help LTU Americans become job ready. Providing a more comprehensive array of programming through the nationwide job center infrastructure will create a streamlined, comprehensive, and effective approach to serving these workers.

Leveraging the affiliations that exist within this network of partners is essential because they are committed to similar goals, and minimal operational restrictions are required. Management of program content is centralized and coordinated by The WorkPlace but delivered through local vendors. Including local vendors to deliver common services improves receptivity of the program and enhances transferability of P2E.

In January 2014, Connecticut Governor Dan Malloy announced his support of a statewide Platform to Employment program to help Connecticut's unemployed get back to work. The project will target 500 of Connecticut's LTU and dedicates $3.6 million for the effort. Program partners will include all five of Connecticut's WIBs and the Connecticut Department of Labor. Connecticut had the first statewide P2E program in the nation and became the first state to introduce public dollars in the program.

In January 2014, during his State of the Union address, President Obama discussed the alarmingly high number of LTU who remain ready and able to work but have been unsuccessful in finding employment. Days after his address, the president invited business leaders to the White House, where they pledged, "We are committed to inclusive hiring practices and pledge to remove barriers that may prevent qualified LTU job seekers from applying or being fully considered for jobs" (Executive Office of the President 2014). During this event, The WorkPlace's Platform to Employment program was cited by President Obama for our achievements and showing success in helping the LTU (National Cable Satellite Corporation 2014). Results from the replication sites closely mirror the Connecticut experience as indicated in Table 29.2.

Looking forward, The WorkPlace plans to revisit and expand the projects in these cities. Additionally, we are exploring options to expand the number of pilot projects during 2015.

Table 29.2 Results of P2E National Replication Sites

National replication	Enrolled in P2E	Preparatory program graduates	Number placed in work experience	Percent placed in work experience	Number hired after work experience	Percent hired after work experience
Totals	218	176	134	76	120	90

NOTE: Results are for seven locations that completed the program: Dallas, Denver, Chicago, Cincinnati, Minneapolis, Newark, and San Diego. Detroit, San Francisco, and Tampa are still in progress.

SOURCE: The WorkPlace, Platform to Employment program.

SOCIAL VALUE PROPOSITION

Through roundtable discussions at The WorkPlace we have witnessed that long-term unemployment has the ability to erode self-confidence and self-esteem. It separates people from their professions and their education, and it creates tremendous stress on the fabric of families. The future for the American Job Center Network is making our workforce smarter and ensuring that fundamentals are in place to empower people with basic values and skills to enhance personal effectiveness.

Beyond fundamental work readiness skills, the system needs to address the emotional and behavioral consequences associated with long-term unemployment. The workforce system has an obligation to provide the supports that enable the unemployed to ready themselves for work and convince employers they are worth keeping. In addition to creating a community resource center, the American Job Centers in southwest Connecticut have expanded services to offer financial and digital literacy and professional development seminars.

For the LTU we need to deal with the whole person by creating a systematic approach to overcoming their unique challenges. Confidence must be instilled and rebuilt. Emotional supports and stress management for the affected individual and immediate family members are essential elements of a responsive workforce system. Additionally, employer programs should incorporate options that are free of risk. Tax credits are not enough to incentivize employers when compared to the long-term risks associated with a hiring decision.

There are millions of Americans on involuntary, part-time work, and over two million more who are marginally attached to the labor force (Bureau of Labor Statistics 2014). This places the American workforce system at a crossroads, and we must accept this irreversible force and transform it into an opportunity through ingenuity and innovation. Transformations to the workforce system such as P2E can provide a valuable resource for employers and create a steady flow of LTU people back into the workforce with the knowledge that they are prepared to compete. P2E is generating community engagement and debate regarding systemic changes to help the LTU return to work and address the employer need to recruit skilled workers. P2E is an example of a working remedy that is fostering a discussion about the culture of workforce development.

References

Bureau of Labor Statistics. 2014. "The Employment Situation—March 2014." News release. Washington, DC: U.S. Department of Labor, Bureau of Labor Statistics.

Executive Office of the President. 2014. "Best Practices for Recruiting and Hiring the Long-Term Unemployed." Washington, DC: The White House. http://www.whitehouse.gov/sites/default/files/docs/best_practices_recruiting _longterm_unemployed.pdf (accessed February 14, 2014).

National Cable Satellite Corporation. 2014. "President Obama on Long-Term Unemployed." Washington, DC: C-SPAN. http://www.c-span.org/video/ ?317535-1/pres-obama-longterm-unemployed (accessed January 31, 2014).

U.S. Department of Labor, Office of Unemployment Insurance. 2014. *UI Data Summary for United States*. Quarterly reports, 2008–2014. Washington, DC: U.S. Department of Labor.

30
Supporting Experienced LTU Professionals

Preliminary Lessons from a Boston-Area Case Study

Ofer Sharone
Massachusetts Institute of Technology

Rand Ghayad
Brattle Group

Gokce Basbug
Massachusetts Institute of Technology

Alex Vasquez
Brandeis University

Michelle Rosin
Massachusetts Institute of Technology

The United States is in the midst of a crisis of long-term unemployment, with the percentage of unemployed workers jobless 27 or more weeks at levels unseen in decades. A broad literature associates long-term unemployment with a variety of social ills, including poverty, the loss of homes and retirement savings, and deteriorating physical and mental health (e.g., Van Horn 2013). The devastating emotional toll of prolonged unemployment can often lead to deep discouragement and self-blame, which make it difficult to continue job searching (Sharone 2013).

This case study focuses on long-term unemployment among experienced college-educated professionals. Contrary to popular perceptions, college degrees and industry experience offer no protection to the unemployed. Although college-educated workers do have lower levels of unemployment, once unemployed, they are just as likely to become long-term unemployed (LTU) as their non-college-educated counterparts (Mishel, Bernstein, and Allegretto 2007). And, upon becoming LTU, the most significant barrier to reemployment is not a lack of education, relevant skills, or experience, but simply the duration of their unemployment (Ghayad 2013).

To look more closely at long-term unemployment among college-educated professionals, and to explore possible interventions supporting this group in reentering the workforce, the authors invited LTU professionals to participate in research that would either offer them free career coaching/counseling or pay them to complete surveys. While we began by recruiting LTU job seekers at One-Stop Centers, networking groups, and libraries, the majority of participating LTU job seekers learned of our research from a prominent newspaper story in the Boston area (Woolhouse 2013). We asked LTU professionals interested in participating in our research to fill out a short sign-up survey to determine if they meet the following criteria: unemployed six months or longer, between the ages of 40 and 65, college-educated professionals, and, in order to control for labor market conditions, looking for work in the Boston area.

While over 800 unemployed job seekers signed up, many of them could not be invited to further participate in the research because they were unemployed for *less* than six months. Nevertheless, the information provided in the sign-up process gave us a chance to compare some of the basic characteristics of short-term and long-term college-educated professionals. Studies cited above show that college degrees do not offer protection from long-term unemployment for the unemployed, but are those with advanced degrees less likely to be LTU? Contrary to theories about long-term unemployment being driven by lack of sufficient educational credentials, our data show that the LTU are in fact more likely to have advanced degrees than the short-term unemployed. Specifically, from among the respondents to our initial sign-up survey, 6.3 percent of the LTU have doctoral degrees compared to 3.4 percent of the short-term unemployed; 12.5 percent of the LTU hold professional degrees compared to only 7.7 percent of the short-term unemployed; and 32 percent of the LTU hold a master's degree compared to 31 percent of the short-term unemployed (see Figure 30.1). This finding is consistent with other recent studies, including Krueger, Cramer, and

Figure 30.1 Highest Level of Education Completed

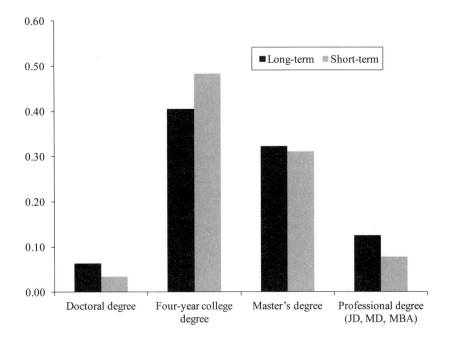

SOURCE: Data compiled from authors' survey results.

Cho (2014), which draws on Current Population Survey data, and an Executive Office of the President (2014) report, which, using Bureau of Labor Statistics data, shows that the LTU are equally or slightly more educated than short-term unemployed workers.

A CLOSER LOOK AT COLLEGE-EDUCATED 40+ LTU

LTU professionals invited to participate in our research completed an initial survey with detailed questions about their career histories and job search experiences. Given the high educational attainment of our LTU sample, we wondered if perhaps obstacles arose because of their job histories and past employment transitions. Bills (1990) reports a number of job screening criteria used by employers when assessing job candidates and identified "job hopping,"or staying at a job for less than a year, as a factor employers consider even before looking at educational credentials. Our data show that job hopping is unlikely to be an important factor underlying long-term unemployment among professionals. More than 70 percent of workers in our survey held three or fewer full-time jobs over the preceding 10 years (and over 50 percent held two or fewer jobs over these years), suggesting that the number of past job transitions is not the cause of their being out of work (see Figure 30.2).

Our data about LTU professionals also allow us to dispel some stereotypical notions about such job seekers being inflexible with high reservation wages or unreasonable expectations (for a critical review of these arguments, see Howell and Azizoglu [2011]). Our survey asked LTU professionals to compare the type of work looked for when they first started their job search with the type of work that they are currently looking for. Figure 30.3 shows considerable increase in job seekers'

Figure 30.2 Number of Full-Time Jobs Held over the Past 10 Years

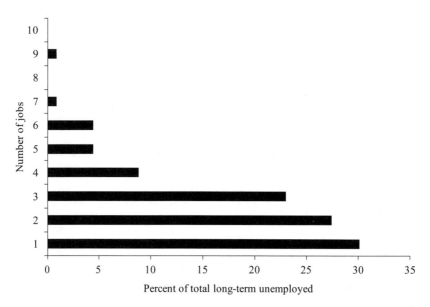

SOURCE: Data compiled from authors' survey results.

Figure 30.3 What Type of Work Are You Currently Looking For?

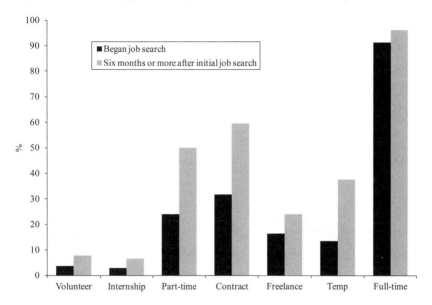

SOURCE: Data compiled from authors' survey results.

flexibility over time. For instance, while the percentage of individuals looking for part-time work at the beginning of their search was 24 percent, in their current situation as LTU job seekers, 50 percent are looking for part-time work. Similarly, the percentage of job seekers looking for contract work and temporary work shows a significant increase with long-term unemployment, rising from 32 percent to 60 percent, and 14 percent to 38 percent, respectively.

Our findings also show that over time, LTU professionals change the scope of their search in terms of industry, job level, and targeted salary. Compared to when they first began searching, 75 percent of our LTU respondents indicated that they have broadened their search to include more industries (see Figure 30.4), 82 percent are now looking for jobs in a wider range of levels (see Figure 30.5), and 77 percent are now open to a lower salary (see Figure 30.6). Our survey also shows that LTU professionals are willing to take much lower-level jobs than their recent full-time jobs. As reported by our respondents, in their most recent full-time jobs, nearly half were earning between $50,000 and

Figure 30.4 During the Past Month, Have You Changed the Industries in Which You Are Looking for Work?

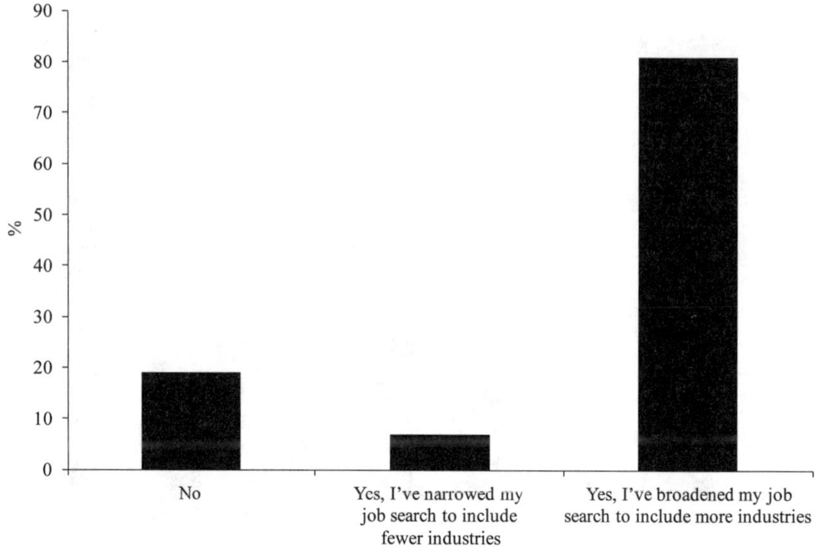

SOURCE: Data compiled from authors' survey results.

$99,000, and 42 percent were earning more than $100,000 a year. The mean work experience of our sample is 27 years. Only two individuals in our sample reported that they were working in an entry-level position in their last job, and 45 percent of our sample was working in a managerial position. Despite this employment history, 33 percent of our respondents reported that they are ready to take an entry-level position.

PILOT INTERVENTION TO SUPPORT EXPERIENCED LTU PROFESSIONALS

Given our findings that LTU professionals are facing obstacles in the labor market such as discrimination against the LTU (Ghayad 2013) and severe emotional distress (Sharone 2013), not lack of education, inconsistent job histories, or inflexibility, we hypothesized that job

Figure 30.5   During the Span of Your Current Job Search, Have You Changed the "Job Levels" in Which You Are Looking for Work?

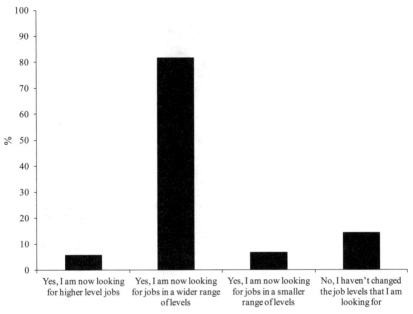

SOURCE: Data compiled from authors' survey results.

search support interventions may be helpful. While studies of interventions abound, to our knowledge no existing studies focus on support for 40+ LTU professionals. To explore this question, from among the over 800 job seekers who applied to participate in our study and who met the previously discussed criteria, we randomly selected 102 LTU professionals and randomly matched them with 42 career professionals who provided them with regular and free job search support for at least three months.[1] Prior to receiving any support, job seekers completed surveys about their search experiences as well as their emotional well-being, which were followed up with surveys to examine change over time. A subset also participated in in-depth interviews. From the same pool of 800 job seekers, we also randomly selected 22 LTU professionals to form a control group that would not receive support but be paid for completing our surveys.

**Figure 30.6   During the Past Month, Have You Changed the Salary
Brackets in Which You Are Looking for Work?**

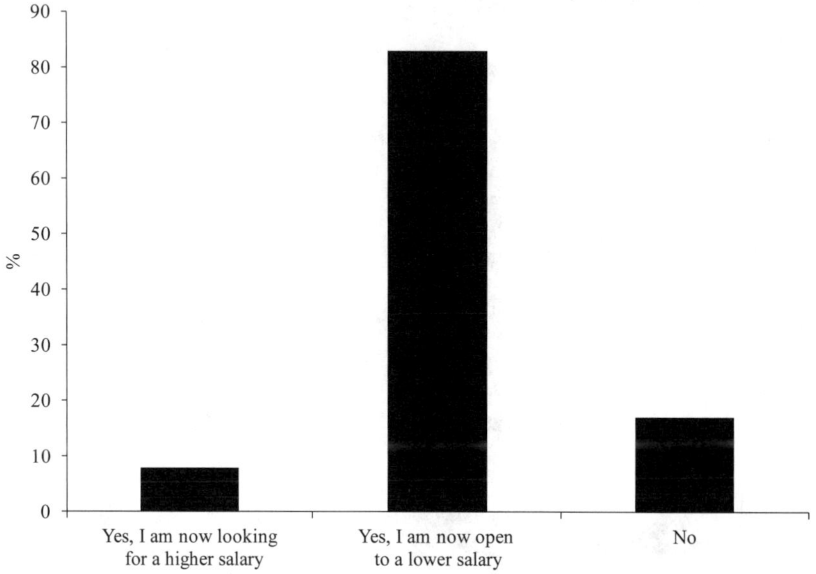

SOURCE: Data compiled from authors' survey results.

During a four-month period of data collection, 30 percent of the LTU professionals who were matched with support (31 out of 102) reported finding a full-time open-term job or a fixed-term contract position for at least three months. During the same period in our small control group, 18 percent reported finding such jobs (4 out of 22). These preliminary results suggest that while formidable institutionalized obstacles cannot be fully overcome by intensive support—with 70 percent of supported LTU professionals *not* finding work in a four-month period—the substantial improvement in the rate of finding jobs for the supported group compared to the control group also shows that support makes a significant and meaningful difference.

At this preliminary stage of data analysis, in examining how career support is helpful, we find most striking the reduction in job seekers' degree of self-blame, which likely increases job search effectiveness. Prior studies have found that although LTU professionals can develop a fear that "something is wrong with me," which results in a loss of confidence and discouragement, such self-blame and anxiety are not an inevitable result of LTU (Sharone 2013). Job seekers looking for work in similarly difficult labor market conditions can come to have very different subjective understandings, depending on the lens through which they interpret their difficulties (Sharone 2013). Our preliminary findings show that support can make an important difference to how LTU is experienced. Prior to receiving support, 61 percent of LTU professionals in our study either agreed or strongly agreed with the statement, "I fear there is something wrong with me." In a follow-up survey 10 weeks later, this fear had increased among our control group to 84 percent but decreased to 41 percent among job seekers receiving support. While the sample is not large enough for these numbers to be statistically significant, the direction of the results is consistent with our qualitative findings.

How does support help diminish self-blame? We find most illuminating the qualitative data from in-depth interviews with job seekers before and during the period of support that point to three key elements of support that produce this outcome, often as an unintended consequence. First, supporting job seekers to effectively present themselves to potential employers involves identifying the strengths and skills that underlie their past career successes. Job seekers report that this support is not only helpful to better present themselves externally, but it also helps create an internal "counternarrative" to the belief that "something is wrong with me." Second, in small facilitated groups, job seekers are typically encouraged to share their experiences so that they can learn useful strategies from each other. Job seekers report that in this context, the emotional hardships of unemployment are often shared, leading many to describe the relief that comes from recognizing that they are not alone in their experiences. Through group discussions, structural factors become more apparent, and job seekers receive a powerful, if indirect, message that negative outcomes in the labor market are not, as one job seeker put it, "just something about me." This form of support alters the lens through which job seekers interpret negative market outcomes and reduces self-blame by not overstating individual-level factors in determining search outcomes.

Finally, our preliminary data suggest that perhaps the way the intermediation of support can change the job search experience is more effective than anything that can be said to an LTU job seeker. The unmediated LTU job search experience can lead to unrelenting negative outcomes, which cause many job seekers to fear that "something is wrong" with them and to become discouraged. Support structures disrupt this dynamic and create an intermediary set of outcomes and institutionalized feedback that can show progress and success in achieving goals that are tied to skill, effort, and risk taking, but they use metrics that are independent of direct market responses. Rather than telling job seekers to avoid negative thoughts (as is done in many self-help books), these support structures create positive experiences similar to what workplaces often do for workers through evaluative structures, providing feedback and internal recognition for achievements that are otherwise invisible in the market.

While meaningfully addressing the crisis of long-term unemployment will require a broad array of policy responses, the findings in this case study suggest that such responses should include increased funding for job search support targeted at older LTU professionals, and that such support would not require as much funding as might be assumed. Specifically, our findings suggest that only some dimensions of support are best provided by expert counselors/coaches, while others can be provided by peer groups. LTU job seekers benefit from individualized advice from experienced career counselors for understanding available labor market information, opportunities for workers with their skills and interests, and getting on the right track in terms of search strategies. However, other crucial elements of support can come from being part of a peer group, which reduces isolation and self-blame and creates structure and accountability for executing one's strategy. While effective groups require some skilled facilitation, it is likely that such facilitation training can be provided by webinars and other cost-effective online education platforms. A promising hybrid approach to effective and relatively inexpensive support would combine weekly in-person peer-support with less frequent (perhaps monthly) virtual one-on-one strategic advice sessions with experienced counselors. In any such effort it would be important for counselors, just like the peer facilitators, to receive some training to help this particular group of LTU job seekers. The authors would welcome the opportunity to collaborate with any interested partners in creating such trainings.

Notes

We would like to thank the AARP Foundation for funding that made this research possible. We would also like to acknowledge the vital contribution to this research by the career professionals and experts in the field who volunteered their time to support our participating job seekers, advise our project, help us collect data, and write case studies: Amy Mazur, Deborah Burkholder, Fred M. Studley (Transition Solutions), Susan P. Joyce, Rachelle Lappinen, Cath Amory, Mark Biddle, Matt Casey, Arnold Clickstein, Tess Dedman, Joanne Dennison, Robert Dolan, Nancy Dube, Maggie French, Allyn Gardner, Tammy Gooler Loeb, Calre Harlow, Kit Hayes, Cindy Key, Pam Lassiter, Ed Lawrence, Debbie Lipton, Tom McDonough, Shannon O'Brien, Sara Pacelle, Bonnie Petrovich, Martha Plotkin, Ilene Rudman, Lisa Shapiro, Robin Slavin, Jan Stewart, Jennifer Straton, and Suzanne Greenwald.

1. Thirty-five were career coaches or counselors who have a private practice or work for other organizations and who agreed to provide their service pro bono, and seven were career consultants who work for an outplacement company, which volunteered to provide its consultants' time for the research.

References

Bills, David. B. 1990. "Employers' Use of Job History Data for Making Hiring Decisions: A Fuller Specification of Job Assignment and Status Attainment." *The Sociological Quarterly* 31(1): 23–35.

Executive Office of the President. 2014. "Addressing the Negative Cycle of Long-Term Unemployment." Washington, DC: The White House. http://www.whitehouse.gov/sites/default/files/docs/wh_report_addressing_the_negative_cycle_of_long-term_unemployment_1-31-14_-_final3.pdf (accessed October 21, 2014).

Ghayad, Rand. 2013. "The Jobless Trap." Working paper. Boston: Center for Labor Market Studies, Northeastern University.

Howell, David, and Bert Azizoglu. 2011. "Unemployment Benefits and Work Incentives: The US Labour Market in the Great Recession." *Oxford Review of Economic Policy* 27(2): 221–240.

Krueger, Alan, Judd Cramer, and David Cho. 2014. "Are the Long-Term Unemployed on the Margins of the Labor Market?" Paper presented at Brookings Panel on Economic Activity, held in Washington, DC, March 20.

Mishel, Lawrence, Jared Bernstein, and Sylvia Allegretto. 2007. *The State of Working America 2006/2007.* Ithaca, NY: Cornell University Press.

Sharone, Ofer. 2013. *Flawed System/Flawed Self: Job Searching and Unemployment Experiences.* Chicago: University of Chicago Press.

Van Horn, E. Carl. 2013. *Working Scared (Or Not at All): The Lost Decade, Great Recession, and Restoring the Shattered American Dream*. Lanham, MD: Rowman and Littlefield Publishing Group.

Woolhouse, Megan. 2013. "Project Aims to Assist Long-Term Unemployed." *Boston Globe*, November 17. http://www.bostonglobe.com/business/2013/11/17/the-science-rejection-helping-long-term-unemployed/sZRfIqC77cyYQ2ZZNcgv7L/story.html (accessed October 21, 2014).

31
Two-Generation Strategies for Expanding the Middle Class

Tara Smith
Rheagan Coffey
University of Texas

The lingering impacts of the Great Recession continue to adversely affect employment and family incomes worldwide. The recessionary period began in late 2007 (Ireland was one of the first countries to enter the recession) and continued through 2009; the number of months of official national recession varied by country from a few months to three years. Many countries, particularly in Europe, experienced a second national recession between 2010 and 2013. Despite investments and policy measures aimed at improving economic conditions, persistent unemployment and decreased opportunity continue to characterize economies around the world and the daily reality of many families.

EDUCATIONAL ATTAINMENT AND UNEMPLOYMENT

The Organisation for Economic Co-operation and Development's (OECD) *Education at a Glance 2013* "offers a snapshot of how education—and the people who participate in and benefit from it—fared during the first years of the worst economic crisis in decades" (Lalancette 2013, p. 1). While the share of younger workers (aged 25–34) with a tertiary degree is substantial across OECD, in most countries the majority of adults have lower levels of educational attainment. The share of 25- to 64-year-olds with less than a secondary education ranged from 11 percent in Canada and the United States to an average of 25 percent in the European Union and 27 percent in Ireland (Lalancette 2013). A closer look at the unemployment numbers shows that those with the least education experienced much higher unemployment than those with a tertiary degree (see Figure 31.1).

During the recession and sluggish recovery, unemployment for those without a high school credential in the United States reached 16.2 percent compared to 4.9 percent for those with a college degree. Across the European Union (EU21), the unemployment rate for those with the least education climbed to an average of 15.6 percent compared to an average of 5.2 percent for those with a tertiary degree (Heckmann 2013). In Ireland, unemployment reached 21.7 percent for those without an upper secondary education compared with 7.1 percent for those with a tertiary education. Ireland is one of five countries where the average earnings of those with tertiary degrees are more than double the earnings of those with a secondary or subbaccalaureate credential (Castaneda Valle and Heckmann 2013).

Young Adults Not Employed and Not in Education or Training

Of particular concern to policymakers worldwide is the growing share of young adults (aged 15–29) who are neither employed nor participating in education or training (often referred to as NEETs, or disconnected youth). "During recessionary periods, high general unemployment makes the transition from school to work substantially more difficult for young people, as those with more work experience are favored over new entrants into the labor market" (Lalancette 2013, p. 1). Between 2008 and 2011, the share of youth aged 15–29 who were classified as NEETs grew in most OECD countries. In 2011, more than one-fifth (22 percent) of 15- to 29-year-olds in Ireland were classified as NEETs compared with 13.3 percent in Canada, 15.3 percent in the EU21, 15.8 percent across OECD, and 15.9 percent in the United States (OECD 2013). "On average, young people in Ireland will spend more than three years either unemployed or out of the labor force altogether" (Castaneda Valle and Heckmann, pp. 1–2). Given that a significant portion of the NEET population group around the world is also parenting, this lack of connection with education or the labor market is particularly troubling.

Figure 31.1 Share of 25–64-Year-Olds Unemployed in 2011, by Educational Attainment

Panel A

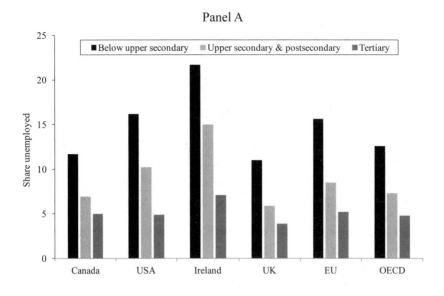

Panel B

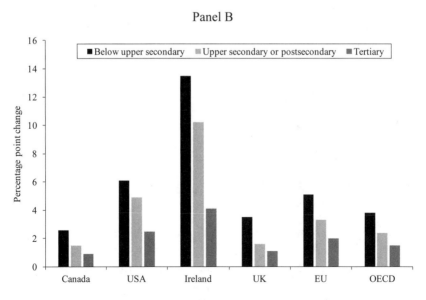

SOURCE: OECD (2013, Table 45.4A).

Consequences of Economic Insecurity

The economic challenges documented above underscore the need for action. Research has shown that economic insecurity can have long-term negative impacts on human development. In a study to identify lessons for antipoverty policy development, Stevens (2014) examines the consequences of prior recessions on family outcomes. She finds that income is a critical determinant of outcomes: "The evidence that job loss affects the income, health, and achievement of current and future generations speaks to the key role of income in helping or hurting poor families. The simple conclusion here: the loss of income and material resources does cause harm and suggests that income support and stability can play a role in reducing the long-term consequences of poverty" (p. 22).

Given the lingering effects on families of the Great Recession, there is an opportunity to rethink traditional investments in adult-only or child-only programs and develop two-generation approaches that recognize that families face challenges, grow, and prosper together. This chapter is intended to promote discussion of opportunities for developing two-generation strategies that help families around the world contribute to their own financial stability and their country's economic well-being. The section below describes the evidence base for two-generation strategies and related components and highlights model programs and innovative initiatives in the United States and Ireland. We conclude with a set of recommendations for developing opportunities to build and test two-generation strategies across a range of economic, political, and cultural contexts.

THE CASE FOR TWO-GENERATION STRATEGIES

Policy and program approaches that treat multiple generations of a family as the unit of service, also known as two-generation strategies, are a growing interest in the United States and other countries around the world. These efforts are intended to move whole families ahead on the path to middle-class economic security. By serving children and parents in the same family, two-generation programs are able to reinforce and expand on the value of individual educational achievements as a pathway for obtaining family economic security and stability over time.

Historically, education, workforce development, and social welfare policies have been established for a specific population (such as low-income children, low-skilled adults, or disconnected youth). There is often no expectation, support, or encouragement for programs to provide services to, or consider the needs of, other family members who may be affected by a family member's participation. In contrast, two-generation strategies share an explicit focus on families, bridging the needs of children and their parents with a combination of supports and an emphasis on human capital development to improve family economic security.

Two-generation approaches encompass a wide range of coordinated education, human, health, and other services. The conceptual framework for the type of two-generation model presented here was developed by Chase-Lansdale and Lindsay (2011) and further supported in a paper for the 2011 Association for Public Policy Analysis and Management (APPAM) conference (King, Smith, and Glover 2011). As shown in Figure 31.2, the conceptual framework for two-generation approaches posits that the thoughtful combination of services for multiple generations within a family leads to improved, even synergistic, outcomes over time.

Core Components of Two-Generation Approaches

The research literature at the foundation of each of the framework's inputs—high-quality early childhood education, family and wraparound support services, and adult/postsecondary (or tertiary) education/second-language literacy services—is reasonably well established (Chase-Lansdale and Brooks-Gunn 2014; Haskins, Garfinkel, and McLanahan 2014; King 2014; King et al. 2009; Smith and King 2011). As researchers and policymakers have explored ways to improve long-term outcomes and impacts, interest has grown in understanding the way these components interact and what works for families. The following section highlights current research on what works for parents and children and details why this matters for two-generation approaches.

Figure 31.2 Conceptual Framework for Two-Generation Strategies

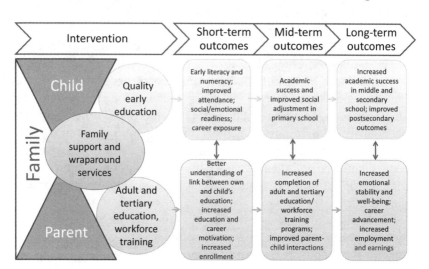

Adult postsecondary education and workforce training components

Many parents in two-generation programs lack the educational and/ or language requirements to succeed in the modern economy. Educational attainment has been demonstrated to have a strong association with family economic status and family outcomes over time. For parents, the goal of two-generation programs is to help them build credentials for the high-demand, middle-skill labor market, which provides family-supporting wages and benefits (in the United States, health insurance and paid sick leave are particularly important benefits provided by some employers).

The educational attainment of mothers in particular is highly correlated to child outcomes. In a recent study published by the Foundation for Child Development, Hernandez and Napierala (2014) examine 13 economic, education, and health indicators for children in the United States based on their mother's level of educational attainment. In the United States, 12 percent of children have mothers who have not earned a high school credential, while one-third of children have mothers who earned a bachelor's degree or higher. Hernandez and Napierala find that, compared to children whose mothers have a bachelor's degree, children whose mothers have not completed high school are much more likely to live in poverty and are significantly less likely to perform at grade level in reading or mathematics, to be enrolled in preschool education, to graduate from high school on time, or to be covered by health insurance.

Given the importance of adult education, U.S. Vice President Joe Biden recently led a governmentwide review of federally funded workforce development and training programs to identify what works for adults and youth and to develop recommendations for further investments and research. *What Works in Job Training* (U.S. Department of Labor et al. 2014) presents a synthesis of findings across the Departments of Labor, Commerce, Education, and Health and Human Services, along with other input. The review identifies six key features of effective adult programs:

1) Postsecondary education leading to industry-recognized credentials

2) Flexible and innovative skill building strategies

3) Work-based training and educational opportunities

4) Active employer and industry engagement

5) Guidance based on current, local labor market information

6) Cross-system coordination and integrated support services

The review outlines a plan for building additional evidence for what works in job training by expanding labor market information and research investments, investing in pilot and demonstration programs, and improving dissemination strategies.

Sectoral workforce development and workforce intermediaries

One approach to workforce development that has grown over the last decade is sector-based workforce development programs, often facilitated by workforce intermediaries. These programs seek to address the workforce needs of employers in identified industries important to the regional economy while helping low-income and disadvantaged populations build the skills they need to succeed in the labor market. King (2014) synthesizes recent research on sectoral programs and finds that sectoral education and training programs exhibit higher rates of participation, completion, and credential attainment than other types of programs. Further, programs based on a sectoral approach were estimated to lead to higher rates of employment and earnings.

Finally, review of the literature by Coffey and Smith (2011) finds that programs with coordinated and team-teaching approaches and those that invest in staff professional development show better outcomes for adult learners. Higher program intensity (more hours per day and/or more days per week) is also shown to be associated with better outcomes for adult and English-language learners. Finally, programs that are contextualized to a target industry or that align with subsequent education/training requirements are more likely to prepare participants for success.

Early childhood education components

Abbie Lieberman with the New America Foundation recently wrote, "Increased access to child care is an especially promising anti-poverty policy because it is intergenerational: it gives parents the time to work, and kids the educational opportunities they need to succeed. . . . For parents to take advantage of other anti-poverty programs, like apprenticeship schools and vocational programs, and eventually lift themselves out of poverty by participating in the labor market, they first need access to childcare" (Lieberman 2014, pp. 2–3).

The 2013 *Education at a Glance* finds that approximately two-thirds of three-year-olds in OECD countries were enrolled in an early education program in 2011. By comparison, approximately half of three-year-olds in the United States and Ireland were enrolled. The share enrolled in early education rises with age: by age four, 78 percent of American children, an average of 85 percent of children across OECD, and 95 percent of Irish children participate in an early education program (Lalancette 2013, p. 5). Figure 31.3 summarizes enrollment rates in early education programs.

Research shows that parents are more engaged and committed to training and employment when they are not worried about the quality of their child care arrangement, leading to stronger outcomes for both generations. For children, the benefits of high-quality early childhood education are well established in the research literature. A 2013 report

Figure 31.3 Enrollment Rates in Early Childhood, Preschool, or Primary Education

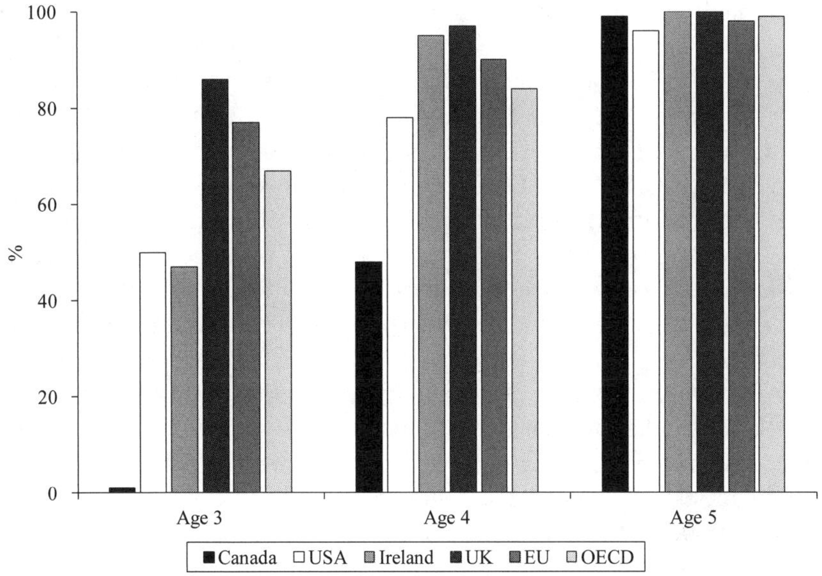

NOTE: Rates for Canada based on 2010 data; all others based on 2011 data.
SOURCE: OECD (2013).

released by the Society for Research in Child Development and the Foundation for Child Development synthesizes current research and finds that "higher-quality preschool programs have larger impacts in children's development while children are enrolled in the program and are more likely to create gains that are sustained after the child leaves preschool" (Yoshikawa et al. 2013, p. 6). Among these benefits, a recent study finds that children who participated in quality early education programs went on to have better adult health outcomes (Campbell et al. 2014). A meta-analysis by Camilli et al. (2010) finds significant long-term benefits from participation in early childhood education programs for the development of children's socioemotional and noncognitive skills. These interpersonal and life skills are important assets that help individuals at all ages reach their academic, career, and personal goals.

Family and wraparound support services

Two-generation models share a common operating principle as identified in a survey of current U.S. frameworks by Gruendel (2014): "Support and services are delivered simultaneously to the child *and* parent (as well as individually when needed) and are integrated across service domains and sectors to decrease cognitive load on the consumer, increase service effectiveness, and maximize resource efficiency and effectiveness" (p. 25). Wraparound support services are the benefits that remove barriers to participation and completion and provide important resources for family stability. These benefits include transportation assistance, out-of-school care, housing, schedule coordination, counseling, case management, financial supports, and performance-based incentives.

Job search assistance and developing the skills necessary to navigate the labor market are especially important for improving employment outcomes. Wendi Copeland, a vice president with Goodwill Industries International, has stated the following about these support services: "It's multigenerational. Once someone in that household knows how to navigate a career, how to access resources, how to make connections, everybody in that household learns, and then you start hearing from the neighbors and the people down the street and the people in their faith community. [The information] is viral when someone learns the secret rules of how to get a job and how to move up" (Ascend 2012, p. 29).

Other support services in two-generation models might include financial incentives, subsidized employment, individual development accounts, and other strategies aimed at encouraging and helping families afford to participate in education and training opportunities. Research has shown that improving family incomes by as little as $3,000 (U.S. dollars) per year can make an important difference for child outcomes (Chase-Lansdale and Brooks-Gunn 2014; Duncan, Magnuson, and Votruba-Drzal 2014; Kaushal 2014). Financial incentives can also smooth the transition from benefit income (i.e., unemployment) to earned income, thus helping families avoid the "benefit trap," where they are financially penalized for returning to work (Richardson and Bradshaw 2014).

Two-generation strategies may have other important benefits as well. From a provider or funder's perspective, colocating family services can reduce the service delivery cost and "facilitate the best possible outcomes for families" (Richardson and Bradshaw 2014, p. 33). Given the need for services documented in the next section, such effective efficiencies should be an important consideration.

Shifting Focus from Adults or Children to Families

The conceptual framework presented in Figure 31.2 shares its emphasis on the combination and coordination of services for families with other two-generation models. As identified by Gruendel (2014), a second common operating principle in two-generation models is that "[c]ommunity supports and services are wrapped around the family as a whole. They encourage and are supportive of family decision-making, and are committed to family engagement over a period that may extend for one or two years, or longer" (p. 24).

Despite differences in goals for education, financial security, health, or other outcomes, two-generation models are firmly focused on helping families prosper and thrive. The continuum presented in Figure 31.4 demonstrates how adult-only or child-only programs can move toward more family-focused strategies to improve both services and outcomes.

The spring 2014 issue of *The Future of Children Helping Parents, Helping Children: Two-Generation Mechanisms* features analyses by leading researchers on the current state of two-generation programs by examining key developmental influences in families, such as stress, education, health, income, employment, and assets. In one article, Kaushal

Figure 31.4 The Two-Generation Continuum

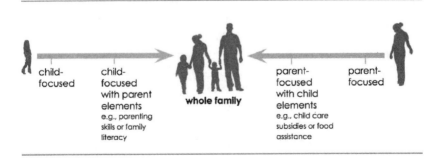

SOURCE: Ascend (n.d.).

(2014) finds that "education influences not only economic and noneconomic opportunities, but also lifestyle choices, for example, decisions about marriage, sex, and fertility" (p. 62). Parents with higher levels of education are more likely to invest in their child's development across a range of health, wellness, enrichment, and tutoring activities.

In another article, Heinrich (2014) cautions that the conditions around a parent's employment can greatly alter the impact on children. While income from employment can have a significantly positive impact on a child's basic well-being, there can be a downside to parental employment. Parents in employment arrangements with access to benefits, such as paid time off and flexible schedules, may face less stress than parents who work in inflexible positions with no access to paid time off or nonstandard hours.

The impact of stress on child development is further documented in the article by Duncan, Magnuson, and Votruba-Drzal (2014). The authors find that "environmental conditions create physiological and emotional stress in the lives of low-income children that may impair their socio-emotional, physical, cognitive, and academic development" (p. 103). Similarly, Chase-Lansdale and Brooks-Gunn (2014) highlight the risk and resilience theory that "posits that children can bounce back and even thrive in the face of short-term adversity, but their development is likely to be seriously hampered by chronic and cumulative stress" (p. 17).

The third core operating principle identified by Gruendel (2014) addresses the importance of building resilience in families: "In two-generation models, supports and services quickly focus on individual and family strengths and assets, including within the extended family, and seek to build on family and community protective factors with the goal of helping children and families become resilient, that is, strong in the face of adversity and chronic challenges" (p. 25).

Essentially, two-generation approaches are antipoverty strategies with investments in multiple members of the family unit. It is the multiple, coordinated investments that offer families the best opportunity for gaining and holding on to middle-class economic security. The next section highlights innovative and promising two-generation/family practices in the United States and Ireland.

INNOVATIVE PROGRAMS AND PROMISING
TWO-GENERATION STRATEGIES

Two-generation strategies provide an opportunity for policymakers and program developers to address current economic challenges and the potential for negative long-term consequences for families. By building onto existing policies and programs that are family-oriented and that support high-quality, evidence-based components for parents and children, with wraparound services, communities around the world are making the shift toward a two-generation perspective. A review of recent reports from the United Nations, OECD, the Ascend Program at the Aspen Institute, and others confirms that policies and programs targeting a range of human and social capital development needs have been implemented worldwide in the last decade to address growing inequality, often framed as antipoverty initiatives.

The following examples are intended to spur conversation about similar efforts and opportunities for collaboration and extension that may lead to additional evidence on the effectiveness of two-generation approaches. While the evidence base on most of these efforts is still emerging, connections to the two-generation conceptual framework and early findings suggest that these approaches may make a positive difference in persistence or completion of workforce development programs. The focus in this section is on two-generation approaches in the United States and Ireland, the countries with which we are most familiar.

Two-Generation Strategies in the United States

In the *Two-Generation Playbook*, Ascend (n.d.) identifies several basic factors favoring a two-generation approach for addressing societal and economic conditions in the United States. The core components of Ascend's framework for two-generation programs include social capital, early childhood education, postsecondary and employment pathways, economic supports, and supports for health and well-being.

In *Making Economic Security a Family Tradition*, Ascend (2012) summarizes the 2012 Aspen ThinkXChange, which brought together leaders from multiple domains "to discuss and debate opportunities and solutions for moving children and their parents toward economic mobility and opportunity" (p. 1). The ThinkXChange highlighted a number of programs and policies across the United States that exemplify the core tenets of its "Two-Generations, One Future" vision and demonstrate the variety of approaches that have been developed to meet the needs of specific political and economic contexts.

Colorado's two-generation perspective

The state of Colorado has made a deliberate shift toward coordinated two-generation approaches to address poverty and build family economic security. Lieutenant Governor Joseph Garcia describes how Colorado policymakers first expanded their unit of focus from individual adults or children to families: "In Colorado, we started by asking how we could improve third grade literacy. Teachers told us that it's . . . about those critical first three years. We can't talk about early literacy without talking about adult and family literacy. . . . It's a shared issue at the local, state, and national level" (Ascend 2012, p. 5).

Reggie Bicha, executive director of the Colorado Department of Human Services and an Ascend (Two-Generation) Fellow, describes an important distinction in the state's new approach. "At the state level, we already were doing the two-generation work, but we weren't thinking of it from a two-generation lens. We weren't connecting state agencies with different levels of support to help families be more independent. So now we're asking, how can we better realign and connect supports and services and eliminate the silo approach?" (Ascend 2012, p. 13). Key policy changes in Colorado have helped to emphasize the two-generation perspective, as indicated by Bicha: "Low-income parents need help finding not only a job, but a job that pays well, provides advancement, and provides stability for families. Changing the focus from work participation rates to outcomes has been critical, as has delving into untraditional areas of support like assisting, rather than penalizing, noncustodial parents" (p. 41). One change has been an increased collaboration across state and local agencies to improve kindergarten readiness, partly through a new emphasis on quality early childhood education programs over child care as simply a work support. Other changes in Colorado include "streamlined services through better technology, simplified application processes, and the elimination of over 800 rules that hamper the process of aiding families" (p. 41).

At the local level, Jefferson County, Colorado, has embraced the new two-generation policy approach, emphasizing wraparound family support services for families in the Head Start program and building accountability for children's educational attainment from early childhood on through to a high school diploma.

Tulsa, Oklahoma's Career*Advance*® Program

Career*Advance*® is a sectoral workforce development program targeting jobs in the health care industry with a ladder of education, training, and certifications in selected occupations offering opportunities for advancement and family-supporting earnings with fringe benefits.[1] Training is structured through a career pathways approach and provided at Tulsa Community College and the Tulsa Technology Center. The program began in mid-2009 as a pilot for the parents of children in Head Start/Early Head Start programs operated by the Community Action Project of Tulsa County (CAP-Tulsa). The program design initially featured a stackable series of training courses in nursing, from certified nurse aide through registered nurse. In 2011, a career path in health information technology was added, and later stand-alone programs for medical assistant and pharmacy technician training were added. Participants may "stop-out" (either temporarily or permanently) at each level with an industry-recognized credential that provides participants with opportunities for higher wages and advancement opportunities.

Career*Advance*® is designed to support and motivate participation through several key elements: a cohort training model; peer mentoring and support through regular (initially weekly) meetings of participants; tuition payments and other education/training expenses; incentive bonuses for good performance; adult basic education and tutoring services; and wraparound services such as before- and aftercare for children, and transportation assistance.

Career*Advance*® is currently the subject of a multimodal evaluation, including implementation, outcomes, and impact studies. The implementation study conducted by the Ray Marshall Center at the University of Texas at Austin has documented the project at multiple phases from design and testing to implementation and expansion (Glover et al. 2010; King et al. 2009; Smith et al. 2013). Throughout this process, focus groups of CAP-Tulsa parents and Career*Advance*® participants have provided critical perspective and context to the administrative data collected by the program for measuring outcomes and informing continuous improvement efforts. Challenges and opportunities identified by parents have been incorporated into successive program modifications targeted at helping more parents reach their career and family goals (Smith 2014). Recent analysis on program persistence led by researchers at Northwestern University found that three-fourths of participants earned a credential within one year, and approximately two-thirds of participants were still enrolled at the one-year mark. Of those who had exited the program within 12 months of enrollment, almost half had earned a credential (Sabol et al. 2014). Of those participants who did not advance in year one, most indicated that psychological distress rather than financial difficulty was a primary reason for not persisting. Participants who completed certification, despite worrying about their potential to succeed at subsequent stages, often described plans for the anticipated financial impact of the program. These results indicate that those participants who are thinking about the future (whether positively or negatively) are the ones more likely to persist in the program.

The ASPIRE Program with Communities in Schools–Central Texas

ASPIRE (Achieving Success through Parental Involvement, Reading, and Education) is an intensive family literacy program that has been operated by Communities in Schools in Austin, Texas, for two decades. The program is built around evidence-based practices in family development and adult and early childhood education. ASPIRE parents participate in adult education, early childhood education, parenting education, and their children's classrooms. The preschool children attend literacy-rich, developmentally appropriate early childhood education classes, and parent educators visit with the families in their homes once a month (Third Coast 2007, p. 1).

Using a matched comparison group evaluation, researchers found that ASPIRE students passed school-administered assessments and exams at higher rates than comparison students in each year examined from kindergarten through 4th grade. Importantly, evaluators found that for ASPIRE students, "any amount of home improvement, any parent involvement in children's classrooms, and any participation in adult education resulted in school performance higher than that of comparison children" (Third Coast 2007, p. 10).

The Jeremiah Program

Launched in the Twin Cities area of Minnesota and currently expanding to sites across the country, including Massachusetts, North Dakota, and Texas, the Jeremiah Program is a place-based "approach to transform families from poverty to prosperity two generations at a time" (Jeremiah 2014).[2] The program provides single-parent families with stable, subsidized housing and other on-site services, including a high-quality child development center; access to a library, computer labs, classrooms, and life coaches; and job placement assistance. Participants attend personal empowerment training to develop important personal characteristics that contribute to their success in workplace settings as well as participating in life skills education classes during their time as residents. The average family spends approximately 2.5 years with the Jeremiah Program.

A recent return on investment (ROI) study (Diaz and Piñá 2013) calculated both first- and second-generation outcomes in estimating benefits and costs for the mothers and children who participate in the Jeremiah Program. Second-generation benefits include projected increased lifetime earnings and tax revenues for child participants, as well as societal savings realized through reduced spending on special education services and future savings from crime reduction. With total costs at $112,057, the ROI for the Jeremiah Program was estimated at $2.47 per dollar invested for society as a whole, $1.66 per dollar invested by taxpayers, and $34.16 per dollar invested by participants. Because the contributions of private funders are critical to supporting the Jeremiah Program, costs to funders are included in the total cost calculations for society as a whole, but funder benefits are not included in societal ROI calculations. Diaz and Piñá calculated philanthropic (nonmaterial) benefits for private funders separately and estimated an ROI of $3.93 per private dollar invested (p. 15).

The MOMS Partnership in New Haven, Connecticut

This program was designed in 2010 to serve the needs of mothers with young children living in poor urban neighborhoods. After identifying multiple factors related with poor family outcomes, including poverty, unstable housing, social isolation, and maternal stress (including depression, addiction, and anxiety disorders), a collaboration of Yale

University, New Haven community partners, and other stakeholders developed the partnership. The program model includes neighborhood hub locations where mothers and their children obtain services and participate in a variety of interventions. Another component of the MOMS Partnership trains mothers in the community to serve as Community Mental Health Ambassadors at the neighborhood hub, providing "brief mental health intervention and intergenerational health promotion" (Gruendel 2014, p. 20).

The mental health intervention is intended to help mothers develop executive functioning skills and is further supported by an individualized smart phone application that allows mothers to earn rewards in a token economy to reinforce targeted behaviors. The program helps mothers prepare for the workforce by linking executive functioning skills with tiered skill development. Researchers gather data from the smart-phone application and track outcomes over time for both mothers and children. Early findings show that participating families have demonstrated increased executive functioning skills and reduced stress on the part of parents and children, improved parenting quality, and improved health, academic, and developmental outcomes for children (Gruendel 2014).

Family and Related Programs in Ireland

Workforce development and social welfare programs in Ireland traditionally have operated quite separately, with different funding streams, personnel, and chains of command. The tremendous economic challenges that Ireland has faced since 2007 have prompted a review and subsequent reform of the employment, vocational education, and training services. Ireland is moving to a system of "One Stop" centers to coordinate delivery of services, and to align needs of the labor market with the training programs being offered (OECD 2014, pp. 51–52). Although these reforms do not address the needs of the entire family unit, they are a step in the right direction, toward more coordinated, employment-focused workforce development.

Ireland is beginning to recognize the need for antipoverty strategies that encompass more than just the unemployed. The report *Work and Poverty in Ireland* states, "Addressing household joblessness through labor market activation [workforce development] policies is likely to be more complex and require a broader range of responses than addressing unemployment [alone]. . . . Training and assistance in job search, child-care and services or supports specific to people with a disability will need to be included" (Watson, Maitre, and Whelan 2012, p. v).

The examples listed below incorporate several of the ideals embodied in two-generation programs, such as a focus on supporting the family unit, or providing programs targeted to one area or need.

Ballymun Whitehall Area Partnership, Dublin, Ireland

The Ballymun Whitehall Area Partnership was established to support children and families and address social exclusion in Ballymun, an economically distressed area in Dublin. Funded primarily by the Irish government, the partnership was established in 1991 as a local community development program that addresses education, employment, child care, and enterprise and community development within the Ballymun area.

The partnership runs both the North West Dublin Childcare Resource Centre and the Local Employment Services, and provides a variety of wraparound services. Owing to the reorganization of the workforce development and training department, the partnership is currently in a state of flux. It is actively involved with the Innovate Ballymun organization, and with the Dublin City University Social Enterprise organization. Together, these programs are designed to facilitate jobs growth and economic stability within the Ballymun area.

youngballymun, Dublin

youngballymun is a 10-year strategy targeting prevention and early intervention services for children, young people, and families in the Ballymun area. The program started in 2007 with an aim to reduce child poverty and promote better outcomes for those from disadvantaged backgrounds. *youngballymun* is jointly funded through the Department of Children and Youth Affairs and the Atlantic Philanthropies. At the core of *youngballymun*'s mission is the desire for systems change around how services for disadvantaged children and families are organized and delivered. As stated on the program's Web site,

> [f]or too long the development of services to children and families
> in Ireland's most disadvantaged communities has relied on avail-

able funding lines, together with local knowledge, and available energy, interests and skills to develop services. They have often been developed in response to crises such as early school leaving, anti-social behaviour and child risk and protection and most frequently without access or reference to the national and international evidence of what works. They are usually developed piecemeal without the cohesion of an overarching vision and an integrated cross-sectoral community service strategy.[3]

youngballymun is designed to be evidence based, focusing on what works rather than what has been done in the past, with a focus on what can be translated into success at the national policy level. *youngballymun* follows a life cycle strategy, including the following:

- Ready Steady Grow: Encompasses zero- to three-year-olds, their parents, and services associated with this age group;

- 3>4>5 Learning Years: Aimed at children aged three to five, their parents, and early childhood education providers;

- The Incredible Years: Primary-school children, their parents, and teachers; and

- Write Minded: Literacy program for all parents, students, and community workers

Through these programs, *youngballymun* delivers coordinated services to parents and children. Services are provided through the Health Service Executive (similar to the U.S. Department of Health and Human Services), schools, and community workers. The program has served over 1,300 infants, 400 preschoolers, and over 400 primary school students, in addition to parents, teachers, and other individuals working with children and families in the Ballymun area. In the 2012 report, *An Economic Appraisal of youngballymun*, the return on investment was calculated to be €4.5 of savings for every euro invested in *youngballymun* (Lawlor and Gilloway 2012, p. 8).

Solas Project, Dublin

Solas is a nonprofit organization that helps young people overcome social and educational disadvantages. Solas works in an area of Dublin that is affected by high crime, high rates of intergenerational poverty, and low educational attainment. It has several different programs aimed at supporting children from primary school through university.

School-based programs:

- Y Not? College Awareness for 6th class children (12- to 13-year-olds)
- Dragon's Den—Business development/entrepreneurship program for 5th class children (11- to 12-year-olds). This is modeled after a very popular Irish television program by the same name.
- School sports program

Targeted programs:

- Primary after-school program—provides a safe, homelike environment after school for children living in "challenging circumstances"
- Step Up—Teen mentoring program for young people in secondary school
- Compass—Prison program aimed at reducing recidivism/reoffending. Inmates are mentored and participate in group activities to build motivation, self-worth, and self-discipline.
- The Yard—Skills-development program with the ultimate goal of increasing opportunity for employment for young people. The program is currently in the pilot stage, with three different activities: bike repair, woodworking, and car valeting (cleaning).

Although Solas is not specifically designed as a two-generation program, their targeted programs have many of the same attributes. The after-school program for primary school children aims to replicate a "home away from home" environment, where children are supported and cared for. The Yard is a pilot program to help young people develop the skills they need for employment. By providing a safe, reliable place for young people to go after school, their parents can focus on employment or furthering their education.

St. Andrews Resource Centre, Dublin

The St. Andrews Resource Centre provides support services and development activities to both individuals and families, with a particular focus on serving the residents of the surrounding neighborhoods. St. Andrews is unique in that it provides resources and wraparound services for the entire life-cycle needs of its clients, specifically,

- child care;
- youth programs—academic/homework programs, after school clubs, and outreach programs;
- adult education—basic English course, Irish language course, individual literacy training, and arts and crafts courses;
- employment preparation and placement services;
- training opportunities for the long-term unemployed;
- elderly services—home help, day center, meals on wheels; and
- welfare rights and advice services.

The center encompasses the needs of a full age range, from infants to elderly, thus strengthening the family unit. In addition to traditional employment assistance, St. Andrews Resource Centre provides direct employment assistance in the form of the Community Employment program. The program is designed for the long-term unemployed (in other words, those out of the labor market for one year or longer) and provides both basic adult education and job training for specific positions, including catering, bus driving, and receptionist, among others. The center currently has a capacity for 95 participants in this program.

CONCLUSION AND RECOMMENDATIONS

Economically secure families are the foundation of a strong middle class. By helping parents build the educational and occupational credentials they need to obtain employment with family-sustaining wages and benefits, two-generation strategies help to increase family economic stability. This chapter has defined a two-generation framework based on high-quality educational opportunities for parents and children, coordinated with wraparound and family support services that remove barriers to participation and completion.

Examining the economic environment and existing initiatives in the United States and Ireland, the authors identified ongoing needs as well as opportunities for helping families escape poverty. Existing initiatives highlight the breadth of two-generation interventions and underscore the common issues facing families all over the world. As two-generation strategies gain traction, more research is needed to under-stand the long-term effectiveness of the programs. Evidence is needed to establish that two-generation strategies do, in fact, lead to multipli-cative, lasting impacts for families. By definition, it will take years to build the database needed for that assessment. In the meantime, there is much work to be done.

Summary Recommendations

Policymakers at all levels should identify opportunities to improve services and supports to families, particularly through improved coor-dination and collaboration across systems.

- Invest in programs that provide career ladders with modular-ized programs and support services for adult participants. The European Union is studying several pilot programs in its Sector Skills Alliances (SSA). The goals of the SSA are to align the vocational education system with the needs of the labor mar-ket, and to increase portability of labor qualifications throughout the EU (SSA 2014). Similarly, in the United States, the Trade Adjustment Assistance Community College and Career Train-ing (TAACCCT) grants are a $2 billion investment over four years through the U.S. Department of Labor's Employment and Training Administration to improve coordination between growth sectors in the economy and workforce training programs (U.S. Department of Labor 2014). The recently passed Work-force Innovation and Opportunity Act of 2014 (WIOA) provides new encouragement for states and localities to develop sector-based and career pathway training programs, as well as bridge programs to help low-skilled adults. Importantly, the law pro-vides state governors with a reserve of 15 percent of the state's allocation to test new and innovative strategies, such as more explicit two-generation approaches.

- Two-generation initiatives can begin as small pilot programs or large-scale statewide programs, or at any point in between. Colo-rado began with a whole-scale shift in priority from serving indi-viduals to serving families throughout its human services system at the state and local level. This new priority has resonated at the local level and helped to spread two-generation approaches across the state. Another option is to begin with a pilot project before launching a full-scale change. Many successful two-generation programs began as small pilot projects before expanding. The Career*Advance*® program in Tulsa is one example of a small program that has grown over time. Greater flexibility should be granted for employment, education, and family services to adapt programs to changing social, economic, and labor market conditions. This recommendation was also highlighted in the OECD report, *Employment and Skills Strategies in Ireland* (2014), which recommended utilizing pilot programs to test new organizational models, similar to *youngballymun*, before implementing systems change throughout a large organization.

- Even in countries with the strongest social welfare policies, programs tend to serve one population (young children, adults, or the unemployed) without considering the larger family unit. Effective two-generation programs shift the focus from individuals to families in order to address barriers and maximize the benefits of participation. While programs like the SSA and TAACCCT provide an opportunity to help unemployed parents reconnect with the labor market, this connection could be counterproductive if the labor market opportunities or work schedule do not coincide with a child's early childhood care or school schedule. Both matter.

- Establish a tapered or "step-down" policy for social welfare programs to help families avoid the "benefits trap," where individuals and families incur an economic cost of returning to training and employment, rather than remaining on social welfare subsidies. Income supports should be offered during training, to encourage families to seek out sustainable forms of employment (Richardson and Bradshaw 2014, p. 33). As earnings increase and families become stronger financially, benefits can slowly be tapered off. Given the growing share of women in the workforce around the world, efforts to close the gender pay gap are also important to helping families build middle-class economic security.

- Communities, policymakers, and other stakeholders interested in testing a two-generation strategy need to bring a broad lens to their development efforts and consider how families are affected by a combination of investments, including economic and workforce development, education across the lifespan, health and social services, and public benefits (King, Coffey, and Smith 2013). Gathering data along the way from idea through implementation and from family enrollment through completion and beyond is essential to understanding how two-generation strategies work. As Shonkoff and Fisher (2013) state, "[there] is a critical need to expand the definition of evidence to include broadly accepted scientific principles from the biological and social sciences rather than restrict the definition to results of experimental evaluations and benefit-cost studies. . . . The most important question is not whether randomized control trials are important, but rather how can we strengthen the evidence base for policy and practice by including other sources of knowledge" (pp. 1646–1647). For example, periodic focus groups with participants and program staff, as well as interviews with partner organizations, local employers, and other stakeholders, provide key data for the ongoing implementation evaluation of the Career*Advance*® program. These early indicators are essential for understanding how it works in order to inform program development and sustainability over time. This early evidence is particularly important for assessing short- and midterm outcomes, given that it will take years to measure the real long-term outcomes and impacts of a two-generation approach.

Around the world, families face a similar economic challenge: security. Two-generation strategies expand the middle class by helping families earn economic and related benefits from investments in education and training. Through coordinated schedules, wraparound support services, and a new perspective on the family as the unit of service, two-generation approaches currently in use are showing promise in the United States, Ireland, and other countries. These efforts should inform the next wave of pilot and demonstration projects and policy initiatives needed to understand issues with scaling, replicability, and expansion of two-generation strategies across a range of economic, political, social, and cultural contexts. Based on current evidence, it will be worth the effort.

Notes

This chapter was prepared with generous support from the Foundation for Child Development through a grant to the LBJ School of Public Affairs' Ray Marshall Center at the University of Texas at Austin. The views expressed here are those of the authors and do not represent those of the Foundation for Child Development or the University of Texas at Austin. The authors are particularly grateful for the review and comments by Donald J. Hernandez and Christopher T. King in shaping the current draft.

1. The authors, along with Dr. Christopher King, a senior researcher at the Ray Marshall Center and an Ascend Fellow, worked with CAP-Tulsa to design the program and have been carrying out the implementation and outcomes analysis of it.
2. Jeremiah's executive director, Gloria Perez, is also an Ascend Fellow.
3. "Real Needs, Clear Evidence." www.youngballymun.org/our_model/our_prevention _and_early_intervention_model/real_needs_clear_evidence (accessed February 18, 2015).

References

Ascend. n.d. *Two-Generation Playbook.* Washington, DC: Ascend at the Aspen Institute.

———. 2012. *Making Economic Security a Family Tradition: Two-Generation Solutions from the Aspen ThinkXChange.* Washington, DC: Ascend at the Aspen Institute.

Camilli, Gregory, Sadako Vargas, Sharon Ryan, and W. Steven Barnett. 2010. "Meta-Analysis of the Effects of Early Education Interventions on Cognitive and Social Development." *Teachers College Record* 112(3): 579–620.

Campbell, Frances, Gabriella Conti, James J. Heckman, Seong Hyeok Moon, Rodrigo Pinto, Elizabeth Pungello, and Yi Pan. 2014. "Early Childhood Investments Substantially Boost Adult Health." *Science* 343(6178): 1478–1485.

Castaneda Valle, Rodrigo, and Corinne Heckmann. 2013. "Ireland Country Note." *Education at a Glance 2013.* Paris: Organisation for Economic Co-operation and Development.

Chase-Lansdale, P. Lindsay. 2011. "Escape from Poverty: Dual-Generation Education and Training Interventions for Low-Income Families." Presentation at the ASCEND Dual-Generation Roundtable, held in Washington, DC, March 29.

Chase-Lansdale, P. Lindsay, and Jeanne Brooks-Gunn. 2014. "Two-Generation Programs in the Twenty-First Century." *Future of Children* 24(1): 13–40.

Coffey, Rheagan D., and Tara C. Smith. 2011. *Challenges, Promising Programs, and Effective Practices in Adult and Developmental Education.*

Austin, TX: Ray Marshall Center for the Study of Human Resources, Lyndon B. Johnson School of Public Affairs, University of Texas.

Diaz, Jose Y., and Gabriel Piñá. 2013. *Return on Investment in the Jeremiah Program.* Saint Paul, MN: Wilder Research.

Duncan, Greg J., Katherine Magnuson, and E. Votruba-Drzal. 2014. "Boosting Family Income to Promote Child Development." *Future of Children* 24(1): 99–120.

Glover, Robert W., Tara C. Smith, Christopher T. King, and Rheagan Coffey. 2010. *Career*Advance®: *A Dual-Generation Antipoverty Strategy.* Austin, TX: Ray Marshall Center for the Study of Human Resources, Lyndon B. Johnson School of Public Affairs, University of Texas.

Gruendel, Janice M. 2014. *Two (or More) Generation Frameworks: A Look Across and Within.* Washington, DC: Center for the Study of Social Policy.

Haskins, Ron, Irwin Garfinkel, and Sara McLanahan. 2014. "Introduction: Two-Generation Mechanisms of Child Development." *Future of Children* 24(1): 3–12.

Heckmann, Corinne. 2013. "European Union Country Note." *Education at a Glance 2013.* Paris: Organisation for Economic Co-operation and Development.

Heinrich, Carolyn J. 2014. "Parents' Employment and Children's Wellbeing." *Future of Children* 24(1): 121–146.

Hernandez, Donald J., and Jeffrey S. Napierala. 2014. *Mother's Education and Children's Outcomes: How Dual-Generation Programs Offer Increased Opportunities for America's Families.* New York: Foundation for Child Development.

Jeremiah Program. 2014. Jeremiah Program Web site. http://www.jeremiaprogram.org/ (accessed August 30, 2014).

Kaushal, Neeraj. 2014. "Intergenerational Payoffs of Education." *Future of Children* 24(1): 61–78.

King, Christopher T. 2014. "Sectoral Workforce and Related Strategies: What We Know . . . and What We Need to Know." In *Connecting People to Work: Workforce Intermediaries and Sector Strategies*, Maureen Conway and Robert P. Giloth, eds. Washington, DC: Aspen Institute, pp. 209–238.

King, Christopher T., Rheagan Coffey, and Tara C. Smith. 2013. *Promoting Two-Generation Strategies: A Getting-Started Guide for State and Local Policy Makers.* New York: Foundation for Child Development and Austin, TX: Ray Marshall Center for the Study of Human Resources, University of Texas.

King, Christopher T., Robert W. Glover, Tara C. Smith, Rheagan Coffey, Brian Levy, Hirokazu Yoshikawa, William Beardslee, and Micah Kordsmeier. 2009. *The Career*Advance® *Pilot Project: Recommended Jobs Strategy for Families Served by the Community Action Project of Tulsa County.* Austin,

TX: Ray Marshall Center for the Study of Human Resources, Lyndon B. Johnson School of Public Affairs, University of Texas.

King, Christopher T., Tara C. Smith, and Robert W. Glover. 2011. "Investing in Children and Parents: Fostering Dual-Generation Strategies in the United States." Presented to the Annual Research Conference of the Association for Public Policy Analysis and Management, held in Washington, DC, November 5–7.

King, Christopher T., Tara C. Smith, and Daniel G. Schroeder. 2009. "Evaluating Local Workforce Investments: Results for Short- and Long-Term Training in Austin." Paper presented at the Association for Public Policy Analysis and Management's 31st Annual Research Conference, held in Washington, DC, November 3–5.

Lalancette, Diane. 2013. "United States Country Note." *Education at a Glance 2013.* Paris: Organisation for Economic Co-operation and Development.

Lawlor, Eilis, and Sinead Gilloway. 2012. *An Economic Appraisal of the young-ballymun Initiative; Summary Report.* Dublin, Ireland: *youngballymun.*

Lieberman, Abbie. 2014. "Child Care as an Intergenerational Solution to Poverty" (blog), June 24. http://www.edcentral.org/child-care-intergenerational -solution-poverty (accessed April 20, 2015).

Organisation for Economic Co-operation and Development (OECD). 2013. *Education at a Glance 2013: OECD Indicators.* Paris: Organisation for Economic Co-operation and Development.

———. 2014. *Employment and Skills Strategies in Ireland, OECD Reviews on Local Job Creation.* Paris: Organisation for Economic Co-operation and Development.

Richardson, Dominic, and Jonathan Bradshaw. 2014. "Family-Oriented Anti-poverty Policies in Developed Countries." Background paper for the United Nation's celebration of the twentieth anniversary of the International Year of the Family. New York: Division for Social Policy and Development, United Nations Department of Economic and Social Affairs.

Sabol, Terri, Terese Eckrich Sommer, P. Lindsay Chase-Lansdale, and Christopher King. 2014. "What Predicts Parents' Educational Success in a Two-Generation Human Capital Program? A Mixed-Methods Study." Presentation for the Health Profession Opportunity Grants—University Partnership Monthly Grantees Call. Washington, DC: Administration for Children and Families, U.S. Department of Health and Human Services.

Sector Skills Alliances. 2014. "Sector Skills Alliances—Selected Pilot Projects." Brussels and Luxembourg: European Commission. http://ec.europa .eu/education/policy/vocational-policy/sector-skills_en.htm (accessed September 7, 2014).

Shonkoff, Jack P., and Philip A. Fisher. 2013. "Rethinking Evidence-Based

Practice and Two-Generation Programs to Create the Future of Early Childhood Policy." *Development and Psychopathology* 25(4, part 2): 1635–1653.

Smith, Tara. 2014. "Evaluating Tulsa's Two-Generation Career*Advance*® Program: Focus Group Findings." Presentation at the National Governors Association Center for Best Practices and Alliance for Early Success meeting, "Bridging Policies for Young Children and Families," held in Washington, DC, June 2.

Smith, Tara, Kristin Christensen, Xueshu Chen, and Christopher King. 2013. *Career*Advance® *Implementation Study Findings through July 2013.* Austin, TX: Ray Marshall Center for the Study of Human Resources, Lyndon B. Johnson School of Public Affairs, University of Texas.

Smith, Tara, and Christopher King. 2011. *Exploratory Return-on-Investment Analysis of Local Workforce Investments.* Austin, TX: Ray Marshall Center for the Study of Human Resources, Lyndon B. Johnson School of Public Affairs, University of Texas.

Stevens, Ann Huff. 2014. "Labor Market Shocks: Are There Lessons for Antipoverty Policy?" *Pathways* (Summer): 19–22.

Third Coast Research and Development. 2007. *Evaluation Report: Communities in Schools ASPIRE Family Literacy.* Austin, TX: Third Coast Research and Development.

U.S. Department of Labor. 2014. *Trade Adjustment Assistance Community College and Career Training Program Summary.* Washington, DC: U.S. Department of Labor. http://www.doleta.gov/TAACCCT/eta_default.cfm (accessed September 9, 2014).

U.S. Department of Labor, U.S. Department of Commerce, U.S. Department of Education, and U.S. Department of Health and Human Services. 2014. *What Works in Job Training: A Synthesis of the Evidence.* Washington, DC: Departments of Labor, Commerce, Education, and Health and Human Services.

Watson, Dorothy, Bertrand Maitre, and Christopher T. Whelan. 2012. *Work and Poverty in Ireland: An Analysis of the CSO Survey on Income and Living Conditions 2004–2010.* Social Inclusion Report No. 3. Dublin: Department of Social Protection.

Yoshikawa, Hirokazu, Christina Weiland, Jeanne Brooks-Gunn, Margaret R. Burchinal, Linda M. Espinosa, William T. Gormley, Jens Ludwig, Katherine A. Magnuson, Deborah Phillips, and Martha J. Zaslow. 2013. *Investing in Our Future: The Evidence Base on Preschool Education.* New York: Society for Research in Child Development and the Foundation for Child Development.

youngballymun. youngballymun Web site. http://youngballymun.org/ (accessed September 7, 2014).

Authors

David E. Balducchi is a research and policy consultant specializing in unemployment insurance and employment programs. He is also principal investigator for IMPAQ International, Inc.

Burt Barnow is Amsterdam Professor of Public Service and Economics at the Trachtenberg School of Public Policy and Public Administration, George Washington University.

Gokce Basbug is a PhD student in the Institute for Work and Employment Research at the Massachusetts Institute of Technology Sloan School of Management.

David S. Berman is the director of program management and policy at the NYC Center for Economic Opportunity.

Amanda Cage is the director of strategic initiatives and policy at the Chicago Cook Workforce Partnership.

Joseph Carbone is president and chief executive officer of The WorkPlace.

Anthony P. Carnevale is research professor and director of the Georgetown University Center on Education and the Workforce, a position he has held since the Center was created in 2008.

Yvette Chocolaad is employment and training director at the National Association of State Workforce Agencies.

Vickie Choitz is a senior policy analyst on the workforce development team at the Center for Law and Social Policy and director of the Alliance for Quality Career Pathways.

Rheagan Coffey is a consultant with the Ray Marshall Center for the Study of Human Resources, part of the Lyndon B. Johnson School of Public Affairs at the University of Texas at Austin.

Maureen Conway is a vice president of the Aspen Institute and executive director of the Institute's Economic Opportunities Program.

Stephen Crawford is a research professor at the George Washington Institute of Public Policy at George Washington University.

Randall W. Eberts is president of the W.E. Upjohn Institute for Employment Research.

Tammy Edwards is vice president of public affairs and community development at the Federal Reserve Bank of Kansas City.

Aaron R. Fichtner is the deputy commissioner at the New Jersey Department of Labor and Workforce Development. He is currently chairing the Labor Market Information Committee of the National Association of State Workforce Agencies.

Maria Flynn is senior vice president of Jobs for the Future.

Thomas Gais is director of the Rockefeller Institute of Government.

Mary Gatta is a senior scholar at Wider Opportunities for Women.

Esther L. George is president and chief executive officer of the Federal Reserve Bank of Kansas City and a member of the Federal Open Market Committee.

Angela Gerace is senior assistant to the provost at the University at Albany. She is also a doctoral student in educational administration and policy studies at the University at Albany.

Rand Ghayad is an associate at the Brattle Group.

Larry Good is chair, cofounder, and senior policy fellow at the Corporation for a Skilled Workforce.

Todd Greene is vice president of community and economic development in the research department at the Federal Reserve Bank of Atlanta.

Gayle Hamilton is a senior fellow at MDRC.

Andrew R. Hanson is a research analyst at the Georgetown University Center on Education and the Workforce at the McCourt School of Public Policy, where he conducts economic research on issues related to education and the workforce at the state and national level.

Paul Harrington is professor and director of the Center for Labor Markets and Policy at Drexel University in Philadelphia.

Matt Helmer is senior research associate for the Aspen Institute Workforce Strategies Initiative.

Richard Hendra is a senior associate at MDRC.

Nancy Hewat is a nationally recognized researcher and evaluator with over 20 years of experience conducting multi-site, mixed-method research, and evaluation projects. She recently founded Synthesis Evaluation & Research LLC.

Richard Hobbie worked for NASWA for 16 years and was executive director for 11 years until he retired in 2014. He was recently appointed a visiting scholar at the Heldrich Center for Workforce Development at Rutgers University.

Kevin Hollenbeck is vice president, senior economist, and director of publications at the W.E. Upjohn Institute for Employment Research.

Harry J. Holzer is a professor of public policy at Georgetown University and an Institute Fellow at the American Institute for Research in Washington, DC.

Jim Jacobs is president of Macomb Community College.

Elaine E. Katz is senior vice president of programs and communications at the Kessler Foundation.

David Kaz is director of policy at Seattle Jobs Initiative.

Christopher King is a lecturer at the University of Texas's Lyndon B. Johnson School of Public Affairs and a senior research scientist at the Ray Marshall Center, which he directed from 1991 to 2014.

Deborah Kobes is a senior project manager with Jobs for the Future's Building Economic Opportunity Group.

Jason E. Lane is senior associate vice chancellor for and vice provost for academic affairs for the State University of New York. He is also an associate professor in the department of educational administration and policy studies at the University at Albany and deputy director for research at the Nelson A. Rockefeller Institute of Government.

Nancy Latham is chief learning officer at Learning for Action. She is also the lead evaluator for the American Association of Community Colleges' Plus 50 Initiative.

Dennis P. Lockhart is president and chief executive officer of the Federal Reserve Bank of Atlanta and is a member of the Federal Open Market Committee.

William Mabe is a faculty fellow in the Edward J. Bloustein School of Planning and Public Policy at Rutgers University. He is also the director of research and evaluation at the John J. Heldrich Center for Workforce Development.

Lisa Montiel is assistant provost for strategic enrollment management at State University of New York System Administration.

Thomas Norman is the director of workforce development for the state of Minnesota's Department of Employment and Economic Development.

Brian Paulson is program officer at the Pohlad Family Foundation.

Scott Powell is a researcher at the Heldrich Center for Workforce Development at Rutgers University.

Heath J. Prince is a research scientist and the director of the Ray Marshall Center at the University of Texas's Lyndon B. Johnson School of Public Affairs in Austin.

Michelle Rosin is a research consultant at the Institute for Work and Employment Research at the Massachusetts Institute of Technology Sloan School of Management and cofounder of the Institute for Career Transitions.

Alex Ruder is a researcher at the Heldrich Center for Workforce Development at Rutgers University.

Laura Schultz is an assistant professor of nanoeconomics at SUNY College of Nanoscale Science and Engineering.

Geri Scott manages Jobs for the Future's Pathways out of Poverty and GreenWays.

Ofer Sharone is an assistant professor of work and organization studies at MIT's Sloan School of Management.

Robert Sheets is a research professor at the George Washington Institute of Public Policy at George Washington University.

Tara Smith is a research sssociate at the Ray Marshall Center for the Study of Human Resources, part of the Lyndon B. Johnson School of Public Affairs at the University of Texas at Austin.

Tiffany Smith is the principal managing analyst for workforce research and analytics at the New Jersey Department of Labor and Workforce Development.

Whitney Smith is director of the Employment Program at the Joyce Foundation in 2005.

Nancy Snyder is president and chief executive officer of the Commonwealth Corporation.

Shayne Spaulding is a senior research associate at the Urban Institute, where she focuses on the evaluation of workforce development and postsecondary education programs.

Nola Speiser is a state program administrator for the Minnesota FastTRAC Adult Career Pathways Initiative.

Katie Onachila Spiker manages Wider Opportunities for Women's Women and Work projects, including the Opportunities for Women in Nontraditional Employment initiative.

Ed Strong is a senior fellow at the Corporation for a Skilled Workforce.

Lauren Sugerman directs Wider Opportunities for Women's nontraditional occupations programs and contributes to the organization's workforce advocacy initiatives.

Matt Unrath oversees Wider Opportunities for Women's national projects and serves as the principal contact for the organization's state and local partners across the country.

Carl Van Horn is a distinguished professor of public policy at the Edward J. Bloustein School of Planning and Public Policy and director of the John J. Heldrich Center for Workforce Development.

Alex Vasquez is a PhD student of sociology at Brandeis University and a researcher with the Institute for Career Transitions. She is also the cofounder of Lilipod.

Mary Sue Vickers is director of the Plus 50 Initiative for the American Association of Community Colleges, where she is responsible for developing and implementing the degree and certificate completion strategy for adults over age 50 at community colleges.

Alan Wagner is a professor in the department of educational administration and policy studies at the University at Albany.

Stephen A. Wandner is a visiting fellow at the Urban Institute and a visiting scholar at the W.E. Upjohn Institute for Employment Research. Until 2010 he was senior policy analyst, research director, and office director at U.S. Department of Labor, Employment and Training Administration.

Alexandra Waugh comanages Jobs for the Future projects focused on helping low-income adults train for and succeed in jobs with career advancement potential.

Elizabeth Weigensberg is a senior researcher at Chapin Hall at the University of Chicago.

Index

Note: The italic letters *b, f, n,* or *t* following a page number indicate a box, figure, note, or table on that page, respectively. Double letters mean more than one such item on a single page.